Sibelius 6

Reference

minim

cratchet

quaver

semi - quaver

demi - semi - quavers

hemi - demi - semi - quavers

Edition 6
April 2009

Reference written by Daniel Spreadbury and Ben & Jonathan Finn.

See the **About Sibelius** dialog for a full list of the software development team and other credits.

We would like to thank all those (too numerous to list) who have provided helpful comments and suggestions for Sibelius and its documentation.

Please email any suggestions for improvements to this Reference to **docs@sibelius.com** (but please do not use this address for suggestions or queries about the Sibelius program itself – see the separate **Latest information & technical help** sheet for the correct address for your country).

Contents

Contents

About this Reference

This Reference is a comprehensive guide to all of Sibelius's features. For explanations of Sibelius's more basic features, and when familiarizing yourself with the program, you will probably find it easier to refer to your Handbook, or your Upgrading to Sibelius 6 booklet if you have upgraded from a previous version of Sibelius.

The Reference comes both on-screen, and as an optional printed book, which you can buy from Sibelius or your country's distributor (**www.sibelius.com/buy**). Both forms of the Reference are identical.

Chapters and topics

Sibelius's Reference is divided into nine chapters containing smaller topics. You will find a list of all these topics in the **Contents**, though you will probably find the **Index** even more useful for finding information on specific areas of the program. Check the **Visual index** if you know how you want something to look, but you don't know what it's called. The **Glossary** explains musical and technical terms.

On-screen reference

To start the on-screen Reference, click the toolbar button shown on the right, or choose Help ▸ Documentation ▸ Sibelius Reference (shortcut F1 *or* ⌘?).

Whichever application your computer uses to view PDF files will open – on Windows this is normally Adobe Reader, and on Mac it is normally Preview – and the on-screen Reference will appear. To navigate the on-screen Reference, you can use the bookmarks and Edit ▸ Find features built in to Adobe Reader and Preview.

Bookmarks are like a table of contents that you can have open beside the document you're reading, allowing you to jump to any chapter, topic, or even sub-heading in the Reference. To show bookmarks:

* In Adobe Reader, choose View ▸ Navigation Panels ▸ Bookmarks; a panel like that shown below left will appear at the left of your screen
* In Preview on Mac, choose View ▸ Drawer; a panel like that shown below right will slide out of the right-hand side of the window.

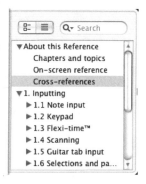

To search within the on-screen Reference, use the **Edit ▸ Find** feature, or alternatively:

- In Adobe Reader, you can simply type into the Find box on the toolbar shown below left, then use the next and previous result buttons to skip forwards and backwards

- In Preview on Mac, you can type into the Search box in the drawer, shown below right, then click in the list of results to skip forwards and backwards.

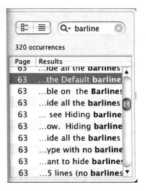

Cross-references

📖 **4.3 Mixer** means "see the **Mixer** topic within chapter 4 of Reference."

Refer to the separate Handbook for details of other typography and terminology used.

1. Inputting

1.1 Note input

 📖 **1.3 Keyboard window**, **1.4 Flexi-time™**, **1.7 Guitar tab input**, **1.8 Fretboard window**, **2.1 Accidentals**, **2.3 Articulations**, **2.6 Beam groups**, **2.14 Grace notes**, **2.25 Noteheads**, **2.30 Stems and leger lines**, **2.34 Tremolos**, **2.35 Triplets and other tuplets**, **2.36 Voices**, **8.9 Note spacing**.

There are six ways of creating and editing notes, chords and rests:

- Mouse input – see below
- Alphabetic and step-time input – see below
- Flexi-time input – 📖 **1.4 Flexi-time™**
- Importing files from other music programs (e.g. MIDI files and MusicXML files) – 📖 **9.5 Opening MIDI files**, **9.6 Opening MusicXML files**
- Scanning printed music – 📖 **1.5 Scanning**.
- Singing or playing into a microphone – 📖 **1.6 Audio input**.

Most of these are introduced in the Handbook. This topic is a detailed summary of mouse, step-time and alphabetic input.

Alphabetic and step-time input

Alphabetic (computer keyboard) and step-time (MIDI keyboard) input are perhaps the most efficient ways of writing your music in Sibelius, because you can create other objects (such as time signatures, key changes and text) as you go along.

To start off alphabetic or step-time input:

- Select a rest (you can also select anything else, such as a text object or a line, which will start writing notes at that point)
- Choose **Notes ▸ Input Notes** (shortcut N). This makes the caret (a vertical line, colored according to the voice in which you're inputting) appear.
- Choose a note value from the Keypad (unless the note value you want is already selected)
- If you like, choose other markings on the Keypad:
  - Accidentals from the first/sixth layout (not required for step-time input)
  - Articulations from the first/fourth layout
  - Ties and rhythm dots from the first/second layout (double dots are on the second layout)
  - Grace notes and cue notes from the second layout
  - Tremolos and beaming from the third layout
  - Jazz symbols and arpeggio lines from the fifth layout
- All of these buttons stay pressed down for successive notes until you re-choose them, with the exception of the accidentals on the first and sixth Keypad layouts. This means you can (say) input several notes with the same articulation.

1. Inputting

- You can choose buttons from more than one layout at once – they'll all be applied to the note/ chord when you input it. (Cycle through the different Keypad layouts using the **+** key; **F7** on Windows and **–** on Mac returns you to the first layout.)
- Then input the note by:
  - typing **A–G** or **R** (which repeats the previous note/chord, with any alterations made on the Keypad); or
  - playing a note/chord on your MIDI keyboard
- To input a rest of the selected note value, simply hit **0** on the **F7** Keypad layout. (To continue creating rests of the same note value, keep hitting **0**.)
- To input a complete bar rest, hit **0** on the **F8** Keypad layout.
- Go back to the first step to input the next note/chord.

There are some things you can do to the note you have just input and before you create the next, which are:

- To correct a mistake, you can adjust the pitch of a note you have input afterwards with ↑ or ↓; hold down **Ctrl** *or* ⌘ to change the pitch by an octave
- To build up a chord using alphabetic input, input one note of the chord, then add further note-heads using one of these methods:
  - hold down **Shift** and type the letter-name of the pitch you want to add above, so to add a G♯, first type **8** on the first Keypad layout to select the sharp, then type **Shift-G** to add the note; or
  - type a number **1–9** (from the main keyboard, *not* the keypad) to add a note of that interval above the current note, so to add a note a sixth above, type **6**; **Shift-1–9** adds notes *below* the current note, so **Shift-4** adds a note a fourth below the current note. (Usefully, this also works for selected passages, e.g. to create octaves); or
  - choose the appropriate option from the **Notes ▸ Add Pitch** or **Notes ▸ Add Interval** submenus, although it's much quicker to use the keyboard shortcuts described above
- To add a tie, hit **Enter** on the numeric keypad after inputting the note
- To create a tuplet, type **Ctrl+2–9** *or* ⌘**2–9** (or choose **Create ▸ Tuplet**) after inputting the first note of the tuplet
- To respell a note enharmonically (e.g. from a MIDI keyboard), choose **Notes ▸ Respell Accidental** (shortcut **Return** on the main keyboard) after inputting it.

Useful keys

A number of other useful keypresses are at your fingertips when creating notes:

- If you make a mistake, hit **Delete** or **Backspace**, which deletes the note and selects the preceding one.

  (What exactly happens when you delete a note is subtly different depending on the context of your music: if you delete a note, it is converted to a rest of identical duration; if you delete a rest or a bar rest, the caret moves past it, leaving it unchanged; if you delete all the notes of a tuplet, the tuplet bracket/number is selected – delete that, and it is replaced with a rest of the duration of the entire tuplet.)

- You can also use ←/→ to move between notes and rests

- You can swap the selected note(s) into another voice by typing Alt+1/2/3/4 *or* ⌥1/2/3/4; so you could select one note of a chord in voice 1 and, say, type Alt+2 *or* ⌥2 to move it into voice 2, merging it with any notes that may already be in that voice

- To add a time signature in the course of creating notes, type T and choose it from the dialog, then hit Return or click OK to create it at the beginning of the next bar

- To add a key change, type K and choose the required key signature from the dialog, then hit Return or click OK to create it in your score directly after the current note

- To add text, type the usual shortcut (e.g. Ctrl+E *or* ⌘E for Expression text), then type the required text; type Esc to go back to creating notes. Text is created at its default position above or below the staff, at the same horizontal position as the note that was selected before creating it.

- You can also add any other object from the **Create** menu during note input. Symbols and chord diagrams, for example, all appear at their default position above or below the staff at the same horizontal position as the selected note.

  For lines (especially slurs and hairpins), it's only practical to input ones lasting for two notes without stopping note input temporarily; this is because the right-hand end of the line needs a note to attach to, and you typically won't have entered that note yet. Hence it's usually easiest to go back and add lines after inputting a phrase or so of notes.

- Esc terminates note input (the caret disappears).

Mouse input

Mouse input is essentially the same as step-time and alphabetic input, except that there should be nothing selected before you start (hit Esc to deselect):

- Choose **Notes ▸ Input Notes** (shortcut N); the mouse pointer changes color (typically it goes dark blue, to denote voice 1)

- Choose a note value from the first Keypad layout; you can also choose accidentals, articulations etc. from other Keypad layouts (see above). To create a rest, choose the rest button from the first layout.

- As you move the pointer over the score, a gray *shadow note* appears, to show where the note will be created when you click. As you move the pointer vertically over the staff, leger lines are drawn as necessary; as you move horizontally through the bar, the shadow note snaps to the different beats of the bar (this behavior is configurable – see **Note input options** below). Usefully, the shadow note also shows the notehead type of the note you're about to create.

- To input the note, simply click where you want to create it

- A caret (a vertical line) appears in the score to the right of the note you just created – if you like, you could now start creating notes in step-time or using alphabetic input, but to continue adding notes with the mouse, simply continue clicking in the score to create more notes, changing the note value and other properties of the note on the Keypad when necessary. To build up a chord, simply click above or below the note you just created. If you create a note elsewhere in the bar, then go back and click above or below an existing note to try and make a chord, Sibelius will delete whatever was there before and create a new note at that position.

- If you input a long note at the start of a bar, and then add a note later in the bar, before the end of the long note at the start of the bar, Sibelius will replace the first note with rests by default, but can alternatively create the new note in voice 2 if you prefer – switch on **Use voice 2 when rhythms conflict** on the **Mouse** page of **File ▸ Preferences** (in the **Sibelius** menu on Mac)

- To input a rest, click the rest button (or type 0) on the first Keypad layout, then click in the score
- You don't have to input strictly from left to right with mouse input – you can hop about the score and click to input notes anywhere.

You can also use the mouse to input notes using the on-screen Keyboard and Fretboard windows – 📖 **1.3 Keyboard window** and 📖 **1.8 Fretboard window**.

Re-inputting pitches

It's often very useful to be able to change the pitches of a sequence of notes/chords without re-creating their rhythm. The main use of this is where you're writing for several instruments that have the same rhythm but different pitches – you can just copy one instrument's music across, and then re-input the pitches. You can change the pitch of individual notes using the mouse or the ↑/↓ keys, or letters A-G, or by playing a note on your MIDI keyboard, but if you want to re-input a whole passage:

- Select a note from which you want to start re-inputting pitches (either with the mouse, or by reaching it with the arrow keys)
- Choose **Notes ▸ Re-input Pitches** (shortcut **Ctrl+Shift+I** *or* ⇧⌘I)
- A dotted caret appears (rather than the normal solid line), which tells you that Sibelius will overwrite the existing pitches, but not their rhythms
- Type **A–G**, or play the new note (or chord) on your MIDI keyboard
- Sibelius changes the pitch of the first note, then selects the next note (skipping over any rests and grace notes that may precede it) so you can change its pitch right away
- If you need to change the enharmonic spelling of a note after you have changed its pitch, just choose **Notes ▸ Respell Accidental** (shortcut **Return** on the main keyboard) to respell it
- When re-inputting pitches using the computer keyboard you must type any accidentals and articulations *after* the note-name, not before (unlike when inputting notes or editing individual notes)
- If you don't want to change a particular note, hit 0 on the keypad to move onto the next one
- To turn an existing note into a rest, hit → to select it without changing its pitch, then hit 0 on the first Keypad layout (shortcut **F7**)
- To turn an existing rest into a note, use ←/→ to move onto the rest, then input the pitch you want
- When you have finished, choose **Notes ▸ Re-input Pitches** again, or hit **Esc** to return to editing your music, or type **N** to start inputting more notes.

While re-inputting pitches you can also build chords from existing notes in just the same way as when inputting notes: select a note and either type **Shift-A–G**, or type **1–9** or **Shift-1–9** on the main keyboard – see **Alphabetic and step-time input** above.

Editing note values, accidentals, articulations, etc.

- Select a note, chord or rest (either with the mouse, or by reaching it with the arrow keys)
- To change the note value, just choose the new note value on the first or second Keypad layout.

If the new note value is longer than the old one, subsequent notes will be replaced by appropriate rests; if the new note value is shorter than the old one, rests are created to pad out the original note value.

* To change other note properties, such as accidentals or articulations, just choose the appropriate Keypad button, and it will instantly edit the note (e.g. click **#** or type **8** to make a note sharp).

Notes ▸ Respell Accidental (shortcut **Return** on the main keyboard) respells an accidental – only normally required after step-time/Flexi-time input or when editing a MIDI file you've imported.

Note input options

The **Note Input** page of the **File ▸ Preferences** dialog (in the **Sibelius** menu on Mac) has various note input options:

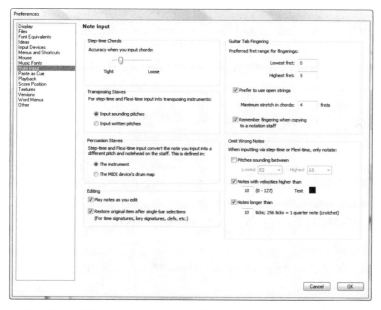

* **Step-time Chords**: this setting is for step-time input, especially via MIDI guitar, and determines how quickly or slowly you have to strum in order for Sibelius to interpret the notes you play as a chord rather than a series of individual notes. By default the slider is set quite a long way towards **Tight**, which is an appropriate setting for inputting via MIDI keyboard (where typically chords are not particularly spread), so if you use a MIDI guitar, you should try setting the slider further towards **Loose** to find the optimal position for your playing style.

* **Transposing Staves**: when using MIDI to play in music written at transposed pitch, it's useful to set this option to **Input written pitches** so you won't have to transpose at sight; the default is **Input sounding pitches** – see **Transposing instruments** on page 135

* **Percussion Staves**: you can input notes onto drum staves with your MIDI keyboard using either the actual keys on your keyboard that produce the correct sound, or using the pitches defined in the instrument definition of the chosen staff – 📖 **2.26 Percussion**

* The two **Editing** options allow you to choose whether or not Sibelius should **Play notes as you edit** (e.g. when you input, select or edit notes), and whether or not Sibelius should **Restore original item after single-bar selections**. If this option is switched off, Sibelius will only

restore the original time signature, key signature or clef at the end of a selection if it is longer than one bar.

- For details of the guitar tab fingering options, 📖 **1.7 Guitar tab input**.
- **Omit Wrong Notes**: these options allow you to prevent Sibelius from notating very short, or very high or low, or very quiet notes when inputting from a MIDI keyboard or MIDI guitar:
  - **Pitches between** *x* **and** *y*: this option is switched off by default (because it would be an inappropriate setting for other MIDI input devices, such as keyboards), but if you are inputting using a MIDI guitar, you may want to switch this option on and adjust the lower and upper notes you actually intend to be notated. Notes outside this range are ignored.
  - **Notes with velocities higher than** *x*: to avoid any very quiet notes being notated unintentionally, adjust the minimum velocity. Try playing notes as softly as you can on your guitar; when the note has a high enough velocity to pass the threshold, the little black indicator in the dialog will light up. Set this number such that the softest note you are likely to play will be notated.
  - **Notes longer than** *x* **ticks**: to avoid very short notes being notated unintentionally, adjust the minimum length. 256 ticks = 1 quarter note (crotchet), so the default value of 10 ticks is a little shorter than a 64th note (hemidemisemiquaver). If this seems to you like the kind of note value you never think you'd write, set this value to be higher.

Hiding notes

You may want to hide notes that nonetheless play back, e.g. a realization of an ornament. Select the note(s) you want to hide and choose Edit ▸ Hide or Show ▸ Hide (shortcut **Ctrl+Shift+H** *or* ⇧⌘H). Any accidental, articulation, stem or beam associated with that note is also automatically hidden. For more information on hiding notes, 📖 **5.9 Hiding objects**.

Turning into rests

To turn a note, chord or passage into rests, simply hit **Delete**, or choose the rest button (shortcut 0) on the first Keypad layout.

The subtle difference between **Delete** and 0 is that when turning a passage into rests, **Delete** consolidates the rests (i.e. groups them into conveniently-sized larger rests or bar rests), whereas 0 just turns each note into an individual rest (which is less useful). For more information on bar rests, 📖 **2.5 Bars and bar rests**.

If you end up with one or more bars that contain only rests of various denominations, you can turn them back into a bar rest by selecting the bar or passage (so it is enclosed in a light blue box) and hitting **Delete**.

Moving rests

You can move rests up/down with the mouse or arrow keys, just like notes.

For music in one voice you shouldn't have to adjust the vertical position of rests, as the position Sibelius uses is absolutely standard. However, in multiple voices you should adjust the vertical position as necessary to allow room for the other voice(s). Sibelius automatically displaces rests up or down a bit when in multiple voices, but feel free to adjust this.

Hidden rests

If you hit **Delete** when a rest is selected, it becomes hidden; the gap it occupied remains, and the music in other staves in the system is aligned as if the rest is still there. If **View ▸ Hidden Objects** is switched on (shortcut **Ctrl+Alt+H** *or* ⌥⌘H), the rest will be visible on the screen in light gray.

You can actually delete a rest altogether, by selecting a hidden rest and hitting **Delete** again, but there is usually no good reason to do this.

You shouldn't hide rests without a good reason, because it makes the length of the bar look incorrect, which can be confusing if you are careless. However, two good reasons for hiding a rest are:

• To make a voice disappear before the end of a bar or appear after the start. If you hide unwanted rests in (say) voice 2, the music will revert to being in one voice (with stems both up and down) – 📖 **2.36 Voices**.

• In order to replace it with a symbol or a line representing some effect that can't be indicated with notes. For instance, you could notate taped sound-effects in a modern score by hiding a rest of the required length and putting a wiggly line in its place.

1.2 Keypad

📖 **1.1 Note input, 2.36 Voices, 5.17 Properties**.

The Keypad mirrors on the screen the arrangement of keys on your computer's numeric keypad. It shows and lets you edit the characteristics of the selected note(s), chord(s) or rest(s), or of the note you are about to create if you are using alphabetic or step-time input.

To hide or show the Keypad, choose **Window ▸ Keypad** (shortcut **Ctrl+Alt+K** *or* ⌥⌘K).

Keypad layouts

The Keypad has six layouts (see below), which you can switch between as follows:

- click on the tabs at the top of the Keypad; or

- click ▶ on the Keypad to cycle through the layouts in order (shortcut **+**), and click ◀ to return to the first Keypad layout (shortcut **F7**, also **Shift-+** on Windows *or* **–** on Mac); or

- type **F7–F12** to view the six Keypad layouts.

You'll spend most of your time working with the first Keypad layout, which contains the common note values and accidentals, but here are all six layouts, for reference:

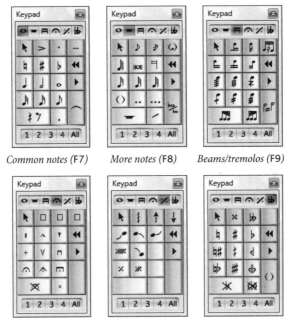

Common notes (F7)   More notes (F8)   Beams/tremolos (F9)

Articulation (F10)   Jazz articulations (F11)   Accidentals (F12)

- The first two Keypad layouts are concerned with inputting and editing notes; ties (not slurs) are created using the **Enter** key on the F7 layout; cue notes are created using the **Enter** key on the F8 layout. Note that the dot on the * key (**/** on Mac) is a staccato articulation, and the dot on the . (decimal point) key is a rhythm dot.

- Very short and very long note values, and double and triple rhythm dots, are created on the F9 layout – 📖 **1.1 Note input**
- The third Keypad layout (shortcut F9) concerns itself with editing beam groups (📖 **2.6 Beam groups**) and creating tremolos and buzz rolls (📖 **2.34 Tremolos**)
- The fourth Keypad layout (shortcut F10) is for adding articulations; three blank spaces at the top of the layout can be assigned to custom articulations – 📖 **2.3 Articulations**
- The fifth Keypad layout (shortcut F11) is for jazz articulations (📖 **2.19 Jazz articulations**), arpeggio lines for keyboard and harp music, and repeat bars (📖 **2.27 Repeat bars**).
- The sixth Keypad layout (shortcut F12) contains unusual accidentals – 📖 **2.1 Accidentals**.

The 0 key is appropriately used for "non-things" – either rests or for removing all articulations/accidentals.

Viewing and editing note characteristics

When you select a note, the Keypad shows you the characteristics of the selection. E.g. when you select a quarter note (crotchet) in your score, the quarter note button on the first Keypad layout lights up. Likewise, selecting a dotted quarter note rest will make the quarter note, rest and rhythm dot buttons on the Keypad light up.

To switch a particular Keypad characteristic on or off for the selected object, you can either:

- click the icon with the mouse; or
- hit the corresponding key on your numeric keypad.

If you are, say, looking at the first Keypad layout, and want to change the selected note into a half note (minim), you could simply type 5 on the numeric keypad. To add a tie, you could hit **Enter** on the numeric keypad, and so on. Similarly, to remove a tie, select the note on which the tie begins and hit **Enter**. You can add and remove characteristics from any of the Keypad layouts in this way – so if you wanted to add a fermata (pause) to your half note (minim), you could simply hit F10 (to reach the fourth Keypad layout), then hit 1 on the numeric keypad to add the fermata.

If a note has characteristics that are not on the currently selected Keypad layout, the tabs for the relevant Keypad layouts will also be illuminated in blue to show you. For example, if you are looking at the first Keypad layout and select a quarter note that has a quarter-flat and a fermata (pause), the fourth and sixth Keypad layout tabs will also be illuminated.

Voices

The row of buttons at the bottom of the Keypad is for specifying the voice of notes and staff-attached text and lines – 📖 **2.36 Voices**.

Extra shortcuts for Keypad functions

Though there is a simple and obvious correlation between the items on the on-screen Keypad and the numeric keypad on your computer keyboard, you can also assign additional keyboard shortcuts to specific items on the Keypad. For example, if you wanted to assign a specific shortcut to the fermata (pause) on the fourth Keypad layout – so that you do not have to hit F10 (to switch to the appropriate layout) followed by 1 on the numeric keypad (to add the fermata), but can instead type a single shortcut regardless of the current Keypad layout – you can do so, as follows:

- Choose File ▸ Preferences (in the Sibelius menu on Mac) and go to Menus and Shortcuts
- Having chosen your own feature set in which to create your new shortcut, choose Keypad (F11 articulations) from the Menu or Category list
- In the Feature list, choose Fermata (pause), then click Add to add your own keyboard shortcut.

For further help with defining your own keyboard shortcuts, 📖 **5.12 Menus and shortcuts**.

Accessing numeric keypad functions on a notebook (laptop)

Most notebook (laptop) computers do not have separate numeric keypads. Although Keypad functions can be accessed on some notebooks (except for recent Apple MacBook models) by holding down a key marked Fn together with other keys on the keyboard, Sibelius also has some alternative shortcuts built in that are more convenient.

Go to the Menus and Shortcuts page of File ▸ Preferences (in the Sibelius menu on Mac), and choose the Notebook (laptop) features feature set. Instead of using the numbers on the keypad, you can use the standard numbers on the main keyboard which will correspond to the same numbers on the keypad. When this feature set is in use, use Shift-1 to Shift-9 to enter intervals above a note – 📖 **5.12 Menus and shortcuts**.

Using the Keypad on Mac OS X

By default, Mac OS X assigns the keys F9, F10 and F11 to the Exposé feature, and F12 to the Dashboard feature, which means that you may get unexpected results when using these shortcuts to change between different Keypad layouts in Sibelius.

Use the Dashboard and Exposé pane in System Preferences to reassign the Exposé and Dashboard shortcuts to other function keys (e.g. F2, F3, F4 and F5).

1.3 Keyboard window

Sibelius's on-screen Keyboard window is a handy way to input notes using a familiar piano keyboard interface, using either the mouse or your computer's keyboard, and it also doubles as a useful playback read-out.

Showing and hiding the Keyboard window

To show or hide the Keyboard window, click the toolbar button shown on the right, or choose **Window** ▸ **Keyboard** (shortcut **Ctrl+Alt+B** *or* ⌥⌘B). The Keyboard window looks like this:

The Keyboard window has three sizes (the middle of which is shown above), and it is resized by grabbing its bottom edge (or its top edge, on Windows) and dragging. You can also change the width of the Keyboard window by dragging its left or right edge (Windows) *or* bottom right-hand corner (Mac).

Mouse input using the Keyboard window

To input notes using the mouse by clicking on the Keyboard window, simply select the point in the score where you want to start inputting notes, and then click the note on the Keyboard window you want to input. If you click on a black note and you want to change the enharmonic spelling, simply hit **Return** (on the main keyboard) immediately after inputting the note.

The note input caret advances automatically after you input each note, so if you want to input a chord, click the chord mode button on the Keyboard window's toolbar, shown on the right. Now each note you click is added to the current chord, and to advance the caret you must click the right arrow button to the right of the chord mode button.

Computer keyboard input using the Keyboard window

You can also input notes via the Keyboard window using your computer's keyboard. Normally when inputting notes using your computer's keyboard, you would type the name of the note you want to input (e.g. **C** for C, **G** for G, and so on). When using the Keyboard window, by contrast, you use a different set of keys, arranged roughly in the shape of an octave of keys on a piano keyboard. This is called *QWERTY mode*, so named for the top row of keys on an English keyboard.

Because most of the keys on your computer's keyboard are already set to do something (e.g. **T** for **Create** ▸ **Time Signature**, **Y** for **Create** ▸ **Clef** and so on), you must tell Sibelius that you want to override these regular shortcuts in order to use QWERTY mode, which you do by clicking the button on the Keyboard window's toolbar, shown above right, or type the shortcut **Shift+Alt+Q** *or* ⇧⌥Q.

1. Inputting

When QWERTY mode is on, notice that all but one of the octaves on the Keyboard window are grayed out:

The lit up octave shows the pitch of notes you will input when you type the keys on your computer keyboard. The keys to use are shown in gray in the picture below:

A corresponds to C, W to C♯ or D♭, S to D, E to D♯ or E♭, and so on, right up to K, which corresponds to C an octave above. Z hops down an octave, and X hops up an octave. It may help to remember that G inputs a G, F inputs an F, and E inputs an E♭.

To input a chord in QWERTY mode, simply press two or three keys together. Depending on your computer keyboard, you may not be able to input chords of four or more notes simultaneously.

QWERTY mode only works as long as the Keyboard window is shown: as soon as you hide the Keyboard window, QWERTY mode is disabled.

Following the score during playback

Aside from inputting notes, the other thing the Keyboard window can do is show you which notes are played during playback. You can choose which instruments to follow using the menu at the left-hand side of the Keyboard window's toolbar.

By default, it's set to **Auto**, which means that it will follow all staves (except for unpitched percussion staves), unless you have selected one or more staves before starting playback, in which case it will follow only those staves. If you always want to follow a particular staff during playback, choose the name of the staff from the menu on the Keyboard window's toolbar.

Notice that the keys on the Keyboard window light up in the same color as the voice colors used elsewhere in Sibelius.

Showing the selected note or chord

The Keyboard window also shows the currently selected note or chord when you're editing notes, which can be useful to check the voicing of a chord. The Keyboard window always shows notes in sounding pitch, even when **Notes ▸ Transposing Score** is switched on.

1.4 Flexi-time™

📖 **1.1 Note input**.

Flexi-time is Sibelius's unique intelligent real-time MIDI input system.

Real-time input

Real-time input on other computer programs is when the program tries to work out both the pitch and the rhythm of music played on a MIDI keyboard, and turn it into clean notation.

The big problem is rhythm: people never play rhythms quite as notated because of unconscious rubato (variation in speed), so real-time input can easily end up with notes tied to extra 64th-notes (hemidemisemiquavers) and other ridiculous things.

A standard improvement is produced by quantization: this is where you tell a program to round all note values to the nearest sixteenth-note (semiquaver), or whatever unit you specify. The trouble is that this only improves the situation for relatively simple music – and if you speed up or slow down as you play, the computer will get out of time with you in any case and produce garbage.

With Flexi-time, however, Sibelius detects if you're doing rubato and compensates accordingly. It quantizes automatically – there's no need to specify a quantization unit – and uses a smart algorithm that varies the quantization according to context. For instance, when you play short notes, Sibelius will quantize with a shorter unit than when you play long notes.

Even more usefully, thanks to its Live Playback feature, Sibelius separates the printed notation from the nuances of your recorded performance. This means that playback of music you have entered in Flexi-time can precisely match what you played – right down to the tiny variations in the length and dynamic of each note – while the notation will be clear and uncluttered.

Recording with Flexi-time

- Although you can change the time signature after inputting music, we recommend that you put the correct time signature in first, so that the metronome click indicates beats correctly
- Click a bar, note or rest from which to start recording, or:
  - If you want to record into two adjacent staves (e.g. a piano), select both staves: first, click the top staff, then **Shift**-click the lower staff
  - If you're just recording from the start of a score for one instrument, you don't need to select anything first as it's obvious where you're recording from
- Click the red record button on the Playback window, or choose **Notes ▸ Flexi-time** (shortcut **Ctrl+Shift+F** *or* ⇧⌘F)
- Sibelius will start ticking a metronome to count you in. It gives you one full bar of clicks (by default) – wait for this before you start playing!
- You can adjust the recording speed by dragging the tempo slider; the tempo readout on the tool-bar changes as you drag the slider. (If you want to record more slowly, start recording, adjust the

tempo slider to the desired point, then hit **Space** to stop, and start recording again – Sibelius will remember the tempo you set.)

- Start playing at the keyboard, following the click (at least approximately). As you play, the music you're playing will appear in notation on the screen.

  If you speed up or slow down, the metronome speeds up or slows down to follow you, as long as you're not too violent with the tempo.

- When you've finished recording, hit **Space** to stop.

If you add more music with Flexi-time on a different staff or staves, Sibelius plays back the existing music as you record.

If you want to add another melody to the same staff, you can record into one of the other voices – see **Voices** below.

Click settings

The settings for the metronome click you hear during Flexi-time recording are controlled via the **Window ▸ Mixer** window (shortcut **Ctrl+Alt+M** *or* **M** on Mac), or you can access some of them from the **Click** button on the **Notes ▸ Flexi-time Options** dialog (shortcut **Ctrl+Shift+O** *or* ⇧⌘O).

By default, the click marks the first beat of the bar with a high woodblock sound, and then subsequent beats with a low woodblock. In compound time signatures such as 6/8, it also subdivides the beat into eighth notes (quavers). For complex time signatures such as 7/8, the default behavior is to emphasize the beginning of each beat group.

For more information on these settings, 📖 **4.3 Mixer**.

Hints

- Listen to Sibelius's countdown beats, and start in time with them! If you start too soon, or at a different tempo from the countdown, Sibelius will not understand what you're up to.
- If you have difficulty recording two staves of music at once, try recording them one at a time.
- Play legato (smoothly).
- If you want music to be notated with staccatos, make sure the **Staccato** option is switched on in **Notes ▸ Flexi-Time Options**. If this option is switched off then playing staccato will produce short note values with rests.
- People are often sloppy about placing notes simultaneously when playing a chord. If you spread chords significantly, Sibelius will write out what you played literally rather than (say) adding a vertical wiggly line.
- Sibelius can pick up changes of tempo extremely quickly – one beat faster than a human can, in fact! However, if you make too violent a change of tempo Sibelius won't understand what you mean. So avoid making sudden tempo changes during recording.

  If Sibelius's beat gets out with you as you're playing, stop and go back to the point where it got out. If you just blunder on regardless, Sibelius may well get back in time again, but correcting the rhythm will take far longer than just playing it in again.

- If you find that Flexi-time produces complicated notation and you want to simplify it, try the plug-ins in the **Plug-ins ▶ Simplify Notation** folder, especially **Renotate Performance** – 🕮 **6.1 Working with plug-ins**.

Inputting into two instruments

You can input into two staves of different instruments if you like – such as Flute and Bassoon – so long as they're adjacent (and there are no staves in between that have merely been hidden from the system in question). Just like inputting into a piano, click the upper staff, then **Shift**-click the lower staff so both are selected, and start recording as normal.

Recording other MIDI data

When recording via Flexi-time, Sibelius records MIDI controller data along with the notes. For example, if you use a sustain pedal when inputting via Flexi-time, Sibelius will notate the appropriate MIDI messages and automatically hide them in the score. Other MIDI controller data that can be recorded include pitch bend, modulation, volume, etc.

If you would prefer these MIDI messages not to be recorded when using Flexi-time input, switch off the appropriate options on the **Notation** page of the **Notes ▶ Flexi-time Options** dialog – see **Flexi-time options** below.

Live Playback

By default, Sibelius plays back music you have inputted using Flexi-time using Live Playback, which retains the nuances of your recording (specifically, the precise dynamic and timing of each note). You can also edit this performance in complete detail. If you want to hear the music exactly as it is notated instead, switch off **Play ▶ Live Playback** (shortcut **Shift-L**).

For more information, 🕮 **4.8 Live Playback**.

Flexi-time options

To change the various Flexi-time options, choose **Notes ▶ Flexi-time Options** (shortcut **Ctrl+Shift+O** *or* ⇧⌘O):

On the **Flexi-time** tab are the following options:

- **Flexibility of tempo**: controls how Sibelius follows your speed. If you're used to playing to a click, set this to **None (non rubato)**, and Sibelius will keep a fixed tempo. The higher you set the flexibility, the more Sibelius is inclined to follow your tempo. If you find Sibelius seems to be changing tempo oddly, it's finding you hard to follow, so reduce the flexibility or set it to **None (non rubato)**.

- **Introduction ... bars**: determines how many bars introduction will be played when you start recording
- **Record up to ... bars**: if there aren't many bars left in the score for you to record into, this automatically adds enough bars when you start recording
- The **Click** button takes you directly to the dialog that determines the behavior of the metronome click during recording – 📖 **4.3 Mixer**.
- **Voices** options:
  - **Record into one voice** allows you to specify a single voice to use for your Flexi-time recording
  - **Record into multiple voices** is an alternative to specifying a single voice: when switched on, Sibelius will automatically split the music into two voices where appropriate; see **Voices** below.
- **Replace** and **Overdub** control what Sibelius does if you record over a passage that already contains music: if set to **Replace**, Sibelius will clear the existing music before notating the new music you play; if set to **Overdub**, Sibelius will add the new music you record to the existing music to make chords.
- **Internal MIDI time stamps**: if you have a computer with dual processors or a hyper-threading processor, you may find that the rhythm of the notated music becomes increasingly inaccurate as recording continues. If you encounter this problem, switch on this option (Windows only).

On the **Notation** tab are these options:

- **Note Values** options:
  - **Adjust rhythms** makes Sibelius clean up what you're playing. Leave this on!
  - **Minimum note value**: this sets the shortest note value Sibelius will write. This is not a quantization unit – Sibelius quantizes using a complex algorithm that varies with context. As a consequence, this value isn't enforced rigidly; it acts as a guide. If you set this to (say) quarter note (crotchet) but then play 16th notes (semiquavers), Sibelius has to notate notes shorter than quarter notes, or you'll end up with junk.
  - **Notate**: these are options to notate staccato and tenuto; if you are confident of playing the articulation exactly as you want it to be notated, switch these on. If you find lots of spurious staccato or tenuto articulations in your score after inputting with Flexi-time, switch them off, or adjust the **When shorter/longer than** thresholds (representing the percentage of the notated note value) beyond which these articulations are notated.
  - **Remove rests between notes on drum staves**: switched on by default. this option "joins up" shorter notes to remove superfluous rests in drum parts.
- **Keyboard Staves**: when inputting onto two staves, the split point determines which notes go into each staff (notes on or above the split point go into the top staff, and notes below go into the bottom staff). If you choose **Automatic**, Sibelius will guess where your hands are on the keyboard at any time and assign notes to staves accordingly. Alternatively, you can specify your own

Fixed split point. (Note that in Sibelius, middle C is called **C4** – which may be different from how it is described in other music programs.)

• **Tuplets**: for each of the tuplets listed, you can set Sibelius to detect **None/Simple/Moderate/Complex** ones. A "simple" triplet (say) means one with three equal notes. For tuplets such as a quarter note (crotchet) followed by an eighth note (quaver), use **Moderate**, and for tuplets with rests or dotted rhythms, use **Complex**.

• **MIDI Messages** options:

  ◦ **Keep program/bank messages** adds any program and bank changes to the score using Sibelius's MIDI message text format. These messages are automatically hidden.

  ◦ **Keep controller messages** similarly adds all controller messages (such as pitch bend, sustain pedal, channel volume, etc.) and hides them in the score.

  ◦ **Keep other messages** similarly adds any other MIDI messages to the score.

Our recommended Flexi-time options are the default values, as follows: **Adjust rhythms** on, **Minimum note value** sixteenth-note (semiquaver), **Flexibility of tempo** set to **Low**, **Staccato** and **Tenuto** on with thresholds of **35%** and **110%** respectively. For tuplets, set **3** to **Simple** or **Moderate**, maybe **6** as well, and the others to **None** unless you're into playing things like septuplets.

Recording transposing pitch

In the **Note Input** page of **File ▸ Preferences** (in the **Sibelius** menu on Mac), switch on the **Input written pitches** option if you're recording by playing the written notes from a transposing score; otherwise, Sibelius assumes you're playing notes at sounding pitch.

Spelling of accidentals

As with step-time input, Sibelius guesses how you want to "spell" black notes (e.g. as F♯ or G♭), but you can alter the spelling of any note or selection of notes afterwards just by hitting **Return** (on the main keyboard), or by using one of the accidental plug-ins (📖 **6.1 Working with plug-ins**).

Voices

As you record, by default Sibelius splits the notes into two voices if necessary (e.g. if you play polyphonic music such as a fugue). In most cases this is desirable, but if you are inputting onto a single staff or monophonic instrument you may prefer to force Sibelius to notate the music in a single voice or a specified voice. You can change this setting in the **Notes ▸ Flexi-time Options** dialog (see above).

Although Sibelius generally makes good decisions about how to split the music you play into separate voices, you may need to go back and edit certain passages to make the notation more closely fit your intentions. You could, for example, filter out the bottom note in voice 1 chords (📖 **5.7 Filters and Find**) and then, say, swap them into voice 2 by typing **Alt+2** *or* ⌥**2** – see **Splitting voices** in 📖 **2.36 Voices** for more details.

1.5 Scanning

INTRODUCTION

PhotoScore Lite from Neuratron is a music scanning program designed to work with Sibelius – the musical equivalent of a text OCR (optical character recognition) program.

It is a sophisticated program with many advanced features. If you intend to scan relatively complex scores such as orchestral/band music, or scores of many pages, we strongly recommend that you start with more simple music until you are proficient with PhotoScore Lite, and then familiarize yourself with the **ADVANCED FEATURES** section.

On-screen help

In addition to this topic, PhotoScore Lite has its own on-screen help: to access it, choose **Help ▸ Neuratron PhotoScore Help** (shortcut **F1**) from PhotoScore Lite's menus.

PhotoScore Ultimate

An advanced version of PhotoScore Lite, called PhotoScore Ultimate, is available to buy separately, with extra features and enhancements. PhotoScore Ultimate reads many more musical markings (including tuplets, slurs, grace notes, cross-staff beaming, guitar tab, chord diagrams, repeat barlines etc.) and reads scores with more than 12 staves.

For details of PhotoScore Ultimate, choose **Help ▸ PhotoScore Ultimate**, or contact your local dealer or Sibelius.

Scanning

Scanning text is difficult for computers to do, and has only achieved reasonable accuracy in the last few years. Music scanning is much harder because of the more complicated range of symbols involved, and because of the complex two-dimensional "grammar" of music.

The difficulty with scanning music or text is that by scanning a page, a computer does not "understand" it. As far as the computer is concerned, scanning a page merely presents it with a grid of millions of black and white dots, which could be music, text, a photograph or anything else.

The process of actually reading or interpreting music, text or pictures from this grid of dots is extremely complex and poorly understood. A large part of the human brain, containing many millions of connections, is devoted solely to solving this "pattern recognition" problem.

Installing and uninstalling PhotoScore Lite

Refer to the separate Handbook for help with installing and uninstalling PhotoScore Lite.

Suitable originals

PhotoScore Lite is designed to read originals that:

- Are printed rather than handwritten (and use notes with an "engraved" appearance rather than a "handwritten" appearance, e.g. from a fake book)
- Fit on your scanner (i.e. the music itself is typically no larger than Letter/A4 size, though the paper may be slightly larger)

- Have a staff-size of at least 0.12"/3mm

- Use no more than 12 staves per page, and 2 voices per staff. (Additional staves or voices will be omitted.)

- Are reasonably clear – for example, staff lines should be continuous and not broken or blotchy, half note (minim) and whole note (semibreve) noteheads and flats should have a continuous circumference and not be broken or filled in, beams on sixteenth notes (semiquavers) and shorter notes should have a significant white gap in between, and objects that are meant to be separate (e.g. noteheads and their preceding accidentals) should not overlap or be blotched together.

Music that does not match the above will probably work, but with considerably reduced accuracy.

Scanning from photocopies is not particularly recommended unless the photocopier is a particularly good one, as photocopying tends to degrade the quality of an original significantly. You may be obliged to scan from a reduced photocopy if your original is bigger than your scanner, but you should expect lower accuracy.

Using PhotoScore Lite without a scanner

In addition to reading music that you scan yourself using a scanner, it is possible to "read" music without using a scanner, either by opening individual pages that you have saved as graphics files, or by opening PDF files.

To work with graphics files, you will need each page of music stored as a separate graphics file on your computer in **.bmp** (bitmap) format on Windows, or **TIFF** and **PICT** (Picture file) format on Mac. (PhotoScore Ultimate can also open PDF files.)

PhotoScore Lite can also read PDF files. Reading a PDF file may be useful if the music you want to scan is available in PDF format from a web site, or if you want to convert a file from another music program by producing a PDF file and then opening it in PhotoScore Lite.

Before you decide upon using PDF files as the way of converting files from another music program, check that the program doesn't export a file format that Sibelius can read directly, e.g. MusicXML, as this would be preferable to using PDF files.

On Windows, PhotoScore Lite requires that you have Ghostscript installed in order to open PDF files. If you didn't install Ghostscript when you initially installed PhotoScore Lite, you can download it free from www.ghostscript.com.

Copyright music

You should be aware that if you scan someone else's music without permission you are likely to infringe copyright. Copyright infringement by scanning is illegal, and in any case is forbidden by the Sibelius license agreement.

Most music states if it is copyright and who the copyright owner is. If you have a piece of music that you want to scan and you are not sure about its copyright status, please contact the music's publisher, composer or arranger.

GETTING GOING

Like Sibelius, PhotoScore Lite functions in exactly the same way on Windows and Mac. You can start PhotoScore Lite either by choosing **File ▸ Scan with PhotoScore** in Sibelius's menus, clicking the **Scan with PhotoScore** icon on the Sibelius toolbar, or by running it from the Start menu (Windows) or double-clicking its icon (Mac). Sibelius doesn't need to be running when you use PhotoScore Lite.

The four stages

There are four stages when using PhotoScore Lite:

- *Scanning the pages or opening a PDF file.* When you scan a page, PhotoScore Lite takes a "photo-graph" of your original. Similarly, when you open a PDF file, PhotoScore Lite takes a "photo-graph" of it, so that it can read it in the next step.
- *Reading the pages.* This is the clever bit, where PhotoScore Lite "reads" the scanned pages to work out what the notes and other markings are.
- *Editing the resulting music.* Here you correct any mistakes that PhotoScore Lite has made. Edit-ing within PhotoScore Lite works in much the same way as editing music in Sibelius. Almost any marking can be corrected or input in PhotoScore Lite, but it is only essential at this stage to cor-rect rhythmic mistakes – other corrections can be made after sending the score to Sibelius if you prefer.
- *Sending the music to Sibelius.* This is done simply by clicking on a button. After a moment the music pops up as a Sibelius score just as if you'd inputted it all yourself.

You can then play the music back, re-arrange it, transpose it, create parts, or print it out.

Quick start

Before we examine how to use PhotoScore Lite in detail, let's run through the process quickly to introduce the four stages.

The first step is either to scan some music, or to open a page you have already scanned, or to open a PDF file:

- To scan a page, choose **File ▸ Scan pages** (shortcut **Ctrl+W** *or* ⌘**W**); your scanner interface will load. Scan a page and it is added to PhotoScore's list of scanned pages.
- To open a graphics file, choose **File ▸ Open**; when prompted for the resolution the image was scanned at, choose the appropriate setting and click **OK**. The graphics file is then added to the list of scanned pages.
- To open a PDF file, choose **File ▸ Open PDFs**. You will be prompted to choose the resolution; normally you can leave this at the default of **300 dpi** and click **OK**. If the PDF is password pro-tected, you will then be prompted to provide the password.

As soon as you scan a page or open a PDF or graphics file, each page appears in the Pages pane, which is at the left hand of the main PhotoScore Lite window. Each page first appears under **Pend-ing Pages,** and PhotoScore Lite immediately proceeds to read the pages you have added, Reading each page will take a little while (depending on the speed of your computer) and a green progress bar fills up behind the name of the page in the **Pending Pages** list. As PhotoScore Lite completes reading each page, it moves to the list below, **Read Pages.**

When PhotoScore Lite has finished reading the pages, the main editing window will appear:

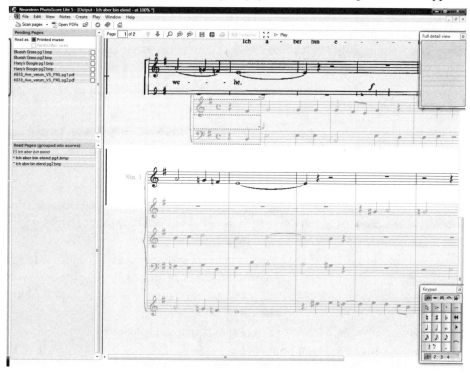

From this window you can edit any errors in the music.

When you are satisfied with the corrections you have made, choose **File ▸ Send to ▸ Sibelius** (shortcut **Ctrl+D** *or* **⌘D**) to send the music to Sibelius.

If Sibelius is not already running, it will start up, and the **Open PhotoScore File** dialog will appear, which allows you to choose various options concerning which instruments will be used in the Sibelius score. Don't worry about these now – just click **OK**. Moments later, the Sibelius score will appear, ready for editing, just as if you had inputted it yourself.

1. SCANNING OR OPENING A PDF

Before you scan, choose **File ▸ Scanner Setup** to choose whether you want to use PhotoScore's own scanning interface – in which case choose **PhotoScore** – or your scanner's own interface – in which case choose **TWAIN (scanner default)** – and click **OK**. By default, PhotoScore Lite will use your scanner's own interface, which is fine, since you are presumably familiar with the way your scanner's software works.

Next, measure the size (height) of staves in the page you want to scan and choose a resolution using the following table, and scan in black & white or gray – not color:

Staff size	Resolution
0.25"/6mm or more	200 dpi
0.15-0.25"/4–6mm	300 dpi
0.12-0.15"/3–4mm	400 dpi

1. Inputting

Reading accuracy and speed will be considerably reduced if you scan at too low or too high a resolution. So, for example, do not scan at 400 dpi unless the staves really are small.

Usually, you can choose whether to scan in black & white or grayscale (shades of gray). Scanning in gray produce significantly more accurate results – if the option is not available in your scanning dialog, consult your scanner's documentation.

Now you can scan your first page – try a page or two of simple keyboard music or something similar:

- Put the page of music (the "original") into your scanner, face-down and with the top of the page pointing away from you.

  Put one edge of the original flush against the raised edge of the glass.

  You can put the page on its side if it fits better. PhotoScore Lite will automatically rotate the page by 90 degrees if necessary. However you should normally align the top of the page with the left edge of the scanner to ensure it does not turn out upside down. Don't worry though if it is scanned upside down, as it is easy to correct later on.

  If you are scanning in gray, then the page does not need to be completely straight, providing that it is not more than 8 degrees off – PhotoScore Lite will automatically make the page level (to within 0.1 degrees) without loss of detail. It will still be rotated if scanning in black & white, but there will be loss of detail, and thus less accurate results.

- Choose **File ▸ Scan Pages**, or click the **Scan Pages** button on PhotoScore Lite's toolbar.

- After a moment, the scanner will whir into life and transfer the page to your computer. (If this doesn't happen, see **POSSIBLE PROBLEMS** below.)

- If you are scanning from a fairly thick book, *gently* press down the lid (or the book if easier) during scanning to keep the page flat on the glass.

- A window will appear for you to enter a name for the page, which will be something like **Score 1, Page 1** by default. You can change this to any name you like (although to avoid any unexpected results it should end with a number) – something like **Piano p1** would do – then click **OK**. Subsequent pages you scan will be automatically numbered e.g. **Piano p2**, and a dialog will not appear.

- Wait a few seconds while PhotoScore Lite makes the image level, chooses the best brightness, and locates the staves.

- PhotoScore will now be ready to scan the next page, so put the page of music in the scanner, then click the button that tells your scanner to start scanning again, and proceed as for the first page. If the scanning interface does not reappear, simply click the **Scan Pages** button again.

- Continue until you have scanned all the pages that you want to scan.

- A scan of the first page will then appear. The buff paper color indicates that you are looking at a scanned image (a "scan") of the original page.

  Check that all the staves are highlighted in blue – this shows that PhotoScore Lite has detected where they are.

  If the page has systems of two or more staves, check also that the staves within each system are joined at the left-hand end by a thick vertical (or near-vertical) red line.

If not all staves are blue, or not all staves within systems are joined with a red line, you can manually tell PhotoScore Lite where they are (see **ADVANCED FEATURES** below).

(Ignore the other buttons at the top of this window, which are also explained in **ADVANCED FEATURES** below.)

Scanning summarized

Once you've scanned a few pages you'll rapidly get into the routine of it. The procedure can be summarized as follows:

- Place page in scanner
- Click the scanner button or choose File ▸ Scan Pages
- Choose the resolution, and whether to scan in black & white or gray
- Click Scan
- If it's the first page, enter a name for the page (or leave the default name)
- Go on to next page.

Catalog of scanned pages

It's important for you to understand that whenever you scan a page, PhotoScore Lite adds it to a single list or "catalog" of scanned pages to be read later. You do not need to save scanned pages or the catalog – it is stored on your hard disk automatically.

This means that whenever you start using PhotoScore, it still remembers any pages you scanned previously. (You can delete pages that you no longer need to keep.)

We'll tell you more about the catalog later.

Hints on scanning

- If you want to read a page of music smaller than the size of your scanner, you should make sure that only that portion is scanned.

  Most scanner interfaces allow you to scan part of a page, usually by clicking a **Preview** button to produce a thumbnail image, which may seem a little "blocky." You can then adjust the required area by dragging from the edges of the thumbnail.

  Then click Scan to scan the selected area at high resolution. Every time you click Scan after this, only the selected area will be scanned, until you change it.

- Ensure that all of the music on the page you are scanning is on the glass of the scanner.

  It doesn't matter if your original is larger than Letter/A4, so long as the music itself will fit onto Letter/A4.

- If you are scanning a page that is smaller than Letter/A4 size, it doesn't matter where on the glass you position the original. However, it helps if you put the edge of the page flush against the edge of the glass, to ensure that it's straight.

- If you are scanning a small music book then you may be able to fit a double-page spread (two facing pages side-by-side) on the scanner glass, but don't try this – PhotoScore Lite can only read one page at a time. Scan each page separately.

- For simplicity, we recommend that you scan all the pages in a piece of music before reading them all. You are allowed to scan a page, then read it, then scan another and so on (see

ADVANCED FEATURES below), but we don't suggest you try anything like this until you are proficient with PhotoScore Lite.

2. READING

As mentioned earlier, just scanning a page simply presents the computer with a grid of millions of black and white dots, which as far as it's concerned could be anything from text to a photograph.

"Reading" the music is the clever bit, where PhotoScore Lite works out from the scan where and what the notes and other markings on the page are.

Pages Pane

On the left-hand side of the PhotoScore Lite window you should see the pages pane, as shown here. If you can't see this, choose View▸ Toggle Pages Pane.

Pages that have not yet been read appear in the upper half of the pages pane, under the heading Pending Pages. Notice how PhotoScore Lite helpfully shows you a thumbnail of the scanned page as you hover your mouse pointer over its name.

When you want to read a page you have scanned, click the little checkbox at the right-hand side, which expands to say Read when you hover your mouse pointer over it. PhotoScore Lite will start to think, and the blue bar behind the name of the page will turn green as PhotoScore reads the page.

If you accidentally scanned the pages in the wrong order, you can correct the order in the list of Pending Pages simply by clicking and dragging the pages into the correct order.

If you just scanned in some pages or opened a PDF, however, your pages have probably already been read by PhotoScore Lite, and so will be found in the lower half of the pages pane, under the heading Read Pages. The pages are automatically grouped into scores; you can show and hide the individual pages in each score by clicking the + or − button at the left-hand side. To view a page in order to edit it, click on its name under Read Pages.

What PhotoScore Lite reads

PhotoScore Lite reads the following musical markings:

- Notes & chords (including tail direction, beams & flags), rests
- Flats, sharps and naturals
- Treble and bass clefs, key signatures, time signatures
- 5-line staves (normal and small), standard barlines, 6-line guitar tab
- The format of the page, including the page size, staff-size, margins, and where systems end.

PhotoScore Ultimate, available separately, also reads text (including lyrics, dynamics, instrument names, fingering, etc.), a wider variety of clefs and accidentals, tuplets, guitar chord diagrams, and various other markings such as codas, segnos, ornaments, pedal markings and repeat endings. PhotoScore Ultimate can even read neat handwritten music!

Hints on reading

- You should not need to interrupt reading, but you can normally do so if necessary by hitting **Esc** or ⌘**.**, or by clicking **Cancel** on the progress window. PhotoScore Lite will show the part of the page it has already read. You should delete this page by choosing **Edit ▸ Delete page** before re-scanning or re-reading the page.

- If the computer gives a warning message while reading a page, or if a page seems to be taking a very long time to read, see **POSSIBLE PROBLEMS** below.

- If you like, you can ask PhotoScore Lite to read just a single scan or a choice of scans instead of the whole score; see **ADVANCED FEATURES** below.

3. EDITING

When PhotoScore Lite has finished reading the music, its interpretation of the first page pops up in a window called the output window. Here you can edit mistakes PhotoScore Lite has made.

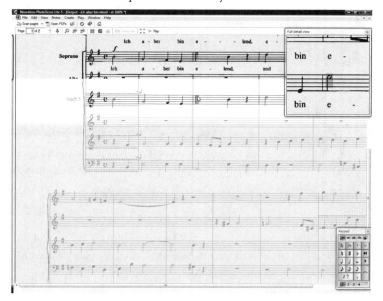

Notice how the pages pane doesn't appear in the picture above: in order to give yourself more room to edit the music, it's a good idea to hide it while you edit, by choosing **View ▸ Toggle Pages Pane** (shortcut **Ctrl+E** *or* ⌘**E**).

The top part of the window (with a buff-colored background) shows you the original page. The **Full detail view** window at the top right-hand corner shows a zoomed-in portion of the original page, according to where you point your mouse.

The large bottom part of the window (with a light gray background) shows PhotoScore Lite's interpretation of the first scan – that is, what PhotoScore Lite thinks the first page of the original says. Hence this part of the window is where PhotoScore Lite's mistakes can occur.

At the top left of the window it says (e.g.) **Page 1 of 2**, and by clicking on the arrows you can move through all of the pages that have been read (the output score). It makes sense to edit the first page completely, then advance to the second page and so on until the whole output score has been edited.

To the bottom right of the window is the Keypad, similar in function to Sibelius's Keypad. This can be repositioned by clicking its title bar, and dragging.

There is a **Create** menu at the top of the window, which is also similar in function to Sibelius's **Create** menu, though features not appropriate for PhotoScore Lite have been omitted.

What to correct

The minimum level of correction recommended before sending the output score to Sibelius is to correct key signatures and time signatures. Other mistakes such as pitch can be corrected in Sibelius, but correcting key signatures and time signatures is much easier in PhotoScore Lite, so we recommend you do that.

In particular, if the score you are scanning is a transposing score, you will need to correct the key signatures of the transposed instruments – to delete a single key signature, select it and type **Ctrl+Delete** *or* ⌘-**Delete**. Then add the correct key signature to that staff alone: choose **Create ▸ Key Signature** (shortcut K), and **Ctrl+click** *or* ⌘-click the staff to which you want to add the key signature.

To correct rhythmic mistakes, add the appropriate time signature if it's not already present: choose **Create ▸ Time Signature** (shortcut T) and click in one of the staves to add the time signature. Once PhotoScore Lite knows the time signature, any rhythmic inaccuracies are indicated by small red notes over the barline, showing the number of missing or extra beats. As you correct the mistakes, these red notes disappear – and once your score is free of red notes, you can send it to Sibelius.

Once you are more proficient with PhotoScore Lite, you can correct the music completely in PhotoScore Lite before sending it to Sibelius. The advantage of this is that you can spot errors by looking at the scanned original on the screen instead of having to refer to it on paper.

Checking for mistakes

Check for mistakes by comparing the bottom part of the window with the original scan at the top. The top and bottom parts move about to show the region of the page the mouse is pointing at.

Avoid the temptation to compare the output page with the original music on paper – it is almost always quicker to compare with the scan on the screen.

At the top right of the output window is the full detail view window, which shows in close-up the part of the original that the pointer is over. **Ctrl+clicking** *or* ⌘-clicking on this window makes the view larger or smaller. This window can be repositioned by clicking its title bar and dragging.

MIDI playback

Another way to check for mistakes is to have the output played back to you. Your computer will need a MIDI device attached to make use of this feature (if you have more than one attached, the default one will be used).

To play the whole page from the start, ensure that nothing is selected by clicking on an area of the page with no notation. Then choose **Play ▸ Play/Stop** (shortcut **space**), or click the **Play** button on the toolbar. Do the same to stop the music. To play from a particular point on the page, select an object in each of the staves you want playback from. It will commence from the start of the bar with the earliest selection.

By default, all the staves will play back with a piano sound, but you can change this: right-click (Windows) *or* **Control**-click (Mac) the names at the start of the first system (e.g. **Staff 1**), choose **Instruments** from the context menu, then click **Rename**. You will see a dialog that looks a little like Sibelius's **Create ▸ Instruments** dialog, from which you can choose the correct name (and therefore the sound) used by that staff.

While the music is playing, the currently played bars will be highlighted in gray.

4. SENDING TO SIBELIUS

Once you have edited all the pages in the score, you should send them to Sibelius. Choose **File ▸ Send to ▸ Sibelius** (shortcut **Ctrl+D** *or* ⌘**D**), or simply click the little 🖫 icon next to the **Save** button at the top of the output window.

If Sibelius isn't already running, it will start, and the **Open Photo-Score or AudioScore File** dialog will appear:

- **This is a transposing score**: switch on this option if your score contains transposing instruments, and you will be prompted to choose the correct instruments when you click **OK**

- **Use default instruments**: opens the file without trying to work out which instruments are used in the score

- **Choose instruments**: allows the user to choose an instrument for each staff in the score from a dialog similar to the usual **Instruments** dialog; choose the staff in the scanned music that you want to replace with a Sibelius instrument, then click **Add** as normal. If you add an instrument that normally uses two staves (such as a piano), this will 'use up' two of the staves in the left-most list on the dialog.

- **Let Sibelius choose instruments**: with this option switched on, Sibelius will attempt to work out which instruments are used in the score; it does this by checking the names of the staves that are set in PhotoScore – if a staff's name doesn't match an instrument Sibelius knows, it opens the file with the default piano sound

- **Use scanned page dimensions**: this option tells Sibelius to format the score according to the page size suggested by PhotoScore. By default, the page size of the selected manuscript paper used for importing will be used instead, but you can switch this on if you like.

- The **Page size**, **House style** and orientation (**Portrait** or **Landscape**) options determine the document setup of the resulting score.

Once your music has been opened in Sibelius you can do anything you like to it, just as if you had inputted it yourself – but see **Multi-staff instruments** below for some clarification.

Editing rhythmic mistakes

If you send a score from PhotoScore Lite to Sibelius which has bars that don't "add up," Sibelius will lengthen bars that are too short, and shorten bars that are too long.

To do this, Sibelius compares the length of the bars with the prevailing time signature. If a bar is too short, Sibelius simply inserts rests at the end. If a bar is too long, Sibelius shortens it by omitting one or more notes/rests at the end of the bar.

Although Sibelius adjusts the lengths of bars like this, you are strongly advised to correct faulty rhythms in PhotoScore Lite in the first place rather than trying to fix them in Sibelius afterwards, as it will save you extra work.

Format

Sibelius uses **Make Into System** and **Make Into Page** to ensure that the format of the music is the same as the original. However, if the notes seem uncomfortably close together or far apart in the end result, try changing the staff size in the **Layout ▸ Document Setup** dialog (shortcut **Ctrl+D** *or* **⌘D**). Alternatively, if you don't need the format of the music to match the original, select the whole score (**Ctrl+A** *or* **⌘A**) and unlock the format (**Ctrl+Shift+U** *or* **⇧⌘U**).

Multi-staff instruments

For instruments that use two staves by default, such as a piano, you may find that it isn't possible to use cross-staff beaming in music you have scanned. This is because PhotoScore Lite treats all staves as separate instruments, which means that, by default, multi-staff instruments such as keyboards will be sent to Sibelius as two separately-named staves without a brace.

When you send a PhotoScore file to Sibelius, you can use the **Open PhotoScore File** dialog to tell Sibelius that, say, staves 1 and 2 are actually the right- and left-hand staves of a piano – either choose the instruments yourself, or click **Let Sibelius choose instruments**.

For multi-staff instruments such as Flutes 1+2, if you want them to be written as two sub-bracketed staves with a single name, you could either import each staff as a flute and then change the name and add a brace in Sibelius, or import both staves as a piano, and then change the name and the sound (📖 **4.3 Mixer**).

If your original contains instruments that have a different number of staves on different systems – e.g. strings that are sometimes divisi – see **ADVANCED FEATURES** below.

Closing the output score

Once you have finished scanning a score and have sent it to Sibelius, and are satisfied with the result, you should close the score in PhotoScore Lite before you start scanning a new one. To do this, simply choose **File ▸ Close Score**; if the score has unsaved changes, you will be prompted to save.

Deleting unwanted scans

PhotoScore Lite automatically saves each page you scan as a scanned image. This occupies a not insignificant amount of hard disk space, so you should regularly delete scans that have been read. You do not, however, have to delete the scans before scanning the next piece of music.

To delete unwanted scans:

- If the pages pane is not currently shown, choose View ▸ Toggle Pages Pane (shortcut Ctrl+E *or* ⌘E)
- Click on the name of the page you want to delete; you can select more than one page at the same time by holding down Shift and clicking elsewhere in the list. When a page is selected, the word Remove appears to the right of its name: click Remove to delete the pages.
- PhotoScore will warn you that you are about to delete these pages: click Yes to confirm their deletion.

POSSIBLE PROBLEMS

Scanning takes a long time

If there are no signs of scanning happening – i.e. if after clicking on the Scan or Preview button the scanner remains silent with no lights moving or flashing – communication between the computer and the scanner has probably been interrupted.

Check that the scanner is switched on and that the cable between it and the computer is firmly connected at both ends. If this doesn't help, try reinstalling your TWAIN scanner driver software.

Beware that some scanners need to be switched on before the computer is turned on, otherwise they are not detected.

Not all staves/systems are detected

If after scanning a page you find that not all staves are highlighted in blue, or the staves are not correctly joined into systems by a thick red vertical line, this may be because:

- The original has 13 or more staves on a page: only PhotoScore Ultimate can scan scores with more than 12 staves.
- The original was not flat on the scanner glass: always close the lid when scanning, unless scanning a thick book. It may also help if you *gently* press down on the scanner lid during scanning.
- The page was scanned at too low a resolution (i.e. the staves are smaller than you think): check the staff size, alter the scanner setting accordingly, and re-scan.
- You tried scanning a double-page spread: PhotoScore Lite cannot read both pages of a double-page spread (e.g. from a miniature score) at once. Re-scan each of the pages separately. Ensure that the music on the facing page is completely off the glass, or not scanned – if any of it impinges on the scan, PhotoScore Lite will not read the music correctly.
- The staves are not clear enough in the original to be detected: in this case, you can tell Photo-Score Lite where any missing staves are located on the page – see **ADVANCED FEATURES** below.

Reading takes a long time

- If the page was scanned without being flat on the glass or with the lid open: you will get a black border around the page that may spread across and obliterate some of the music. This can make PhotoScore Lite take an extremely long time to read the page. If this happens, interrupt reading (see below), then re-scan the page.

- If not all staves were detected after scanning (i.e. some were not highlighted in blue): this can slow reading down, see **Not all staves/systems are detected** above.

Music reads inaccurately

If you find music seems to be reading very inaccurately, this may be because:

- the original is of poor quality, e.g. a photocopy or an old edition;
- the original is handwritten (or uses a music font that looks handwritten): PhotoScore Lite is not designed to read handwritten music;
- the music uses more than two voices;
- the music was scanned in black & white and was not straight enough: it is recommended that you scan in shades of gray;
- the music was not straight enough when scanned and **Make scans level** was not selected in the preferences (see **ADVANCED FEATURES** below);
- the music symbol designs used in the original are of a non-standard shape or size.

ADVANCED FEATURES

PhotoScore Lite has many features and options for more advanced use.

You are strongly recommended to familiarize yourself with this whole section before embarking on any intensive scanning, such as orchestral/band scores or scores with many pages.

Choosing between scanners

In the unlikely event that you have more than one scanner connected to your computer, you can choose between multiple scanner drivers by choosing File ▸ Select Scanner.

Adjusting detected staves/systems

When you scan a page, PhotoScore Lite highlights staves it detects in blue, and joins them into systems with vertical red lines.

However, if the original is of poor quality, PhotoScore Lite may not detect some of the staves/systems, and you should tell PhotoScore Lite where they are.

The easiest method is to select the nearest blue staff (by clicking on it) and copy it by Alt+clicking *or* ⌥-clicking over the center line of the missing staff (the horizontal position is not important).

You can create a blue staff from scratch by clicking and dragging it out with the left mouse button.

After creating the staff, ensure that it is joined to any other staves in the same system (see below).

PhotoScore Lite will automatically "clip" the staff in place, by adjusting the position and size of it, if it finds an appropriate staff underneath. If it fails to position/size the staff correctly, scale the image to full size (by clicking on the button at the top marked 100) and adjust it using the blue "handles."

- You can drag any blue staff up and down with the left mouse button. This also causes the staff to automatically clip in place.
- You can drag the ends of blue staves around, and can even put blue staves at an angle.

- You can alter the size of any blue staff – pull the "handles" in the middle of the staff up or down. PhotoScore Lite can read pages that have a mixture of staff-sizes, and each blue staff can have a different size. The top circular handle allows you to change the curvature of the staff. This is useful when scanning pages from thick books, where it is not possible to prevent the page from being curved at the edges.

- If any scanned staff is left with no blue staff on top of it, the scanned staff and any music on it will be ignored when the page is read. This can slow reading down, but is otherwise harmless.

- To join two adjacent staves together into the same system, click one staff so it goes red, then Alt+click *or* ⌥-click the other staff. They will be joined near the left-hand end by a thick vertical (or near-vertical) red line.

- To separate two joined staves into two separate systems, do exactly the same as for joining two staves.

- PhotoScore Lite automatically guesses whether staves should be joined together or not when you create new ones, or move existing ones.

- If you've messed up the blue staves and want to start again, Ctrl+double-click *or* ⌘-double-click the scan, and PhotoScore Lite will reset the blue staves to their original positions.

- When you have finished editing the staves/systems, check carefully that the staves are all joined into systems correctly, as you cannot alter this once the page has been read.

Scan window options

If you have chosen to use PhotoScore's scanning interface in File ▸ Scanner Setup, there are various further options and buttons available on the scan window:

- The Read this page button reads just this scan. Clicking the arrowed part of the button opens a menu that lets you choose where in the output score to insert this page once it has been read.

- Scale produces a dialog that lets you zoom in and out of the scan. The button to the right of Scale zooms the image to fit the main window; 50 zooms to 50%; 100 zooms to 100%.

- Upside down quickly rotates the image by 180 degrees, in case it was scanned the wrong way up.

- Re-scan re-scans the page.

- On side quickly rotates the image by 90 degrees, in case it was scanned on its side.

Omitted staves

In scores for many instruments, particularly orchestral scores, unused staves are often omitted.

If you replace the default instrument names (e.g. "Staff 1") at the start with proper names, then on subsequent systems PhotoScore Lite will allocate instruments to staves in order from the top down. Hence, if the original page omits an instrument from one system, then in the output window some of the staves will have the wrong names. To correct a name in this situation, Right-click *or* Control-click over the existing instrument name against the staff in question, and choose the correct instrument from the list of current instruments.

On any system that has staves omitted you will probably have to correct several instrument names like this. Do it with care, otherwise confusion will arise.

Multi-staff instruments

For multi-staff instruments such as keyboards and divided wind and strings, PhotoScore Lite treats each staff as a separately-named instrument.

If the number of staves for a multi-staff instrument varies at all in the original, e.g. where strings are divisi, then to avoid any confusion between the staves it's best to give them slightly different names, e.g. Viola a and Viola b. You can change the names back once the score has been sent to Sibelius.

Wherever any of the instrument's staves are omitted, follow **Omitted staves** (above).

N.B. If the number of staves for the instrument increases (say from 1 to 2) during the score, and the second staff has not occurred before, treat it by following **Instruments/staves introduced after the start** (below).

Instruments/staves introduced after the start

Some scores include instruments or staves that are not shown on the first system.

When this happens, on the system where the instrument/staff is first introduced you should do the following:

- First, correct the names of each of the other staves:
  Right-click (Windows) *or* Control-click (Mac) each name, and choose the correct name from the list of current instruments
- Then tell PhotoScore Lite the name of the newly-introduced instrument/staff
- Point over whatever name it has filled in (which may say e.g. Staff 5, or the name of an omitted instrument). Right-click (Windows) *or* Control-click (Mac), click New, and click a name from the list of instruments displayed (similar to Sibelius's Instruments dialog.) If you want a non-standard name, you can edit the name at the bottom.

You must do this with care – or else a lot of confusion can arise.

Small staves

In the output window, small staves are displayed at full size to make them legible, but they are indicated by the following symbol at the end of the staff:

Other preferences

The File ▸ Preferences dialog contains various other options, as follows.

On the Scanning page:

- Automatic scanning and Scan more quickly are only available in PhotoScore Ultimate
- PhotoScore: with this selected, PhotoScore uses its own simple scanning interface
- TWAIN (scanner default): when chosen, the standard TWAIN interface (that works with all scanning programs) will be used when you choose File ▸ Scan pages
- Select TWAIN scanner allows you to choose which scanning device PhotoScore should use

- ○ **Make scans level:** with this switched on, PhotoScore Lite will work out how rotated a scan is, and then rotate it so that the staves are level. It is recommended that this is left selected.

- ○ **Read pages after scanning/opening** is only available in PhotoScore Ultimate.

- On the **Reading** page, most options are disabled (since they are only available in PhotoScore Ultimate). The only option you can switch on or off is **Ties, Slurs and Hairpins**, which is partly enabled, because PhotoScore Lite can only read ties.

- On the **Editing** page:

  - ○ **Automatic page margins:** creates suitable page margins on each page

  - ○ **Attach scanned staff panel to current staff:** on the output window, this puts the original scan just above the highlighted staff instead of at the top of the window. This means you have to move your eyes less when comparing the output with the original, but the effect can be confusing.

  - ○ **Drag paper by:** allows you to choose whether you drag the paper either by clicking and dragging, or **Holding Shift and dragging** (in a similar way to the options in the **Mouse** page of Sibelius's **File ▸ Preferences** dialog).

- On the **Advanced** page:

  - ○ **MIDI playback device** allows you to choose which of your computer's playback devices PhotoScore should use for playback

  - ○ **System playback properties** launches your operating system's sound and audio device properties dialog, allowing you to choose your playback and recording devices for audio, and your preferred playback device for MIDI

  - ○ **Display splash screen at start-up:** allows you to switch off the PhotoScore Lite splash screen when you run the program

  - ○ **Auto-save to backup file every** *n* **minutes:** automatically backs up your score regularly at the time interval specified.

If you change any of these options, they will remain as the new default settings each time use you PhotoScore until you change them again.

1.6 Audio input

AudioScore Lite from Neuratron is a transcription program designed to work with Sibelius. You can use it to input music into Sibelius by playing a monophonic acoustic instrument (such as a flute, clarinet or trumpet) or singing into a microphone – or you can import an existing audio file in .wav or .aiff format. AudioScore listens to your performance, transcribes the notes, and allows you to edit them before sending them to Sibelius for further editing.

On-screen help

In addition to this topic, AudioScore Lite has its own on-screen help: to access it, choose Help ▸ Neuratron AudioScore Help from AudioScore Lite's menus.

AudioScore Ultimate

An advanced version of AudioScore Lite, called AudioScore Ultimate, is available to buy separately. AudioScore Ultimate can recognise up to 16 instruments or notes simultaneously, can import MP3 audio files, read music directly from audio CD, and supports more advanced note editing. The Windows version of AudioScore Ultimate can also be used to input notes into Sibelius directly, via step-time or Flexi-time input.

For details of AudioScore Ultimate, contact your local dealer or Sibelius.

Installing and uninstalling AudioScore Lite

Refer to the separate Handbook for help with installing and uninstalling AudioScore Lite.

Suitable microphones

AudioScore Lite will work with any microphone connected to your computer via the USB, microphone input or line input ports. However, cheap microphones – which typically produce large amounts of background noise – may not produce the best results. One indication that your microphone may not be of sufficient quality is that AudioScore Lite's level meter when recording shows a high level even when you are not playing or singing.

AudioScore Lite will attempt to recognise the performance regardless, but the result will be less accurate, particularly at extremes of pitch. Playing or singing more loudly or closer to the microphone (taking care not to touch or blow on it) may help, but if you want to use AudioScore most successfully, a good quality microphone will improve the quality of results you can obtain.

Suitable performances

For best results, try to perform as clearly and as cleanly as possible, at a steady tempo; for example, if you are playing violin, move your fingers between strings as silently as possible, and avoid tapping on the instrument's body with the bow or your fingers. Try to perform in quiet surroundings with as little background noise as possible (including electrical interference, which you will often hear as a low "hum" if your cabling is poorly shielded).

Copyright music

You should be aware that if you record someone else's music without permission you are likely to infringe copyright. Copyright infringement is forbidden by the Sibelius license agreement.

Starting AudioScore Lite

The simplest way to begin is to choose **File ▸ Transcribe with AudioScore** from Sibelius's menus. AudioScore Lite (or AudioScore Ultimate, if it is installed) will run.

In AudioScore Lite, choose **File ▸ Select Devices** to check that appropriate audio input and MIDI output devices are selected. You must make sure that you choose the input device that corresponds to the input to which your microphone is connected; unless your microphone is connected via USB, it may well be called something cryptic.

The three stages

There are three stages when using AudioScore Lite:

* *Creating tracks.* AudioScore records your performance, works out what notes and pitches are played, and determines the rhythm of your performance. AudioScore Lite allows you to create up to four tracks (i.e. four instruments, or four staves in Sibelius) in a single project.
* *Editing tracks.* Edit the performance to create a basic score containing the intended rhythm and pitches.
* *Sending to Sibelius.* This is done simply by clicking a button. After a moment, the music appears in Sibelius, as if you'd inputted it using any other input method.

You can then play the music back, re-arrange it, transpose it, create parts, or print it out.

1. CREATING TRACKS

The first stage is to create one or more tracks, either by recording using a microphone, or opening an existing audio file (in **.wav** or **.aiff** format).

Recording a new track using a microphone

Click **Record new track** on the toolbar (shortcut * on the numeric keypad). Before recording begins, this dialog appears:

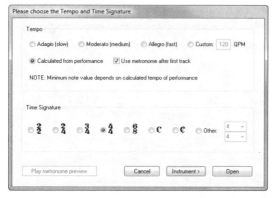

* If you want to record to a metronome click, you can choose between one of the predefined tempos (e.g. **Adagio (slow)** or **Allegro (fast)**), or enter a tempo of your own choosing in quarter note (crotchet) beats per minute.

1. Inputting

- If you want to record in your own time without a metronome click, choose **Calculated from performance**. AudioScore will do its best to work out the note durations automatically, and it's easy to adjust them if it makes any errors.
- Whether or not you are recording to a click, you should set the time signature before you begin: only simple time signatures are available in AudioScore Lite, so if you need compound time signatures (like 6/8) you will need to upgrade to AudioScore Ultimate.

Now you can simply click **Record** or **Open**, in which case AudioScore will automatically work out what instrument to use, or click **Instrument** to choose the instrument you are going to record with:

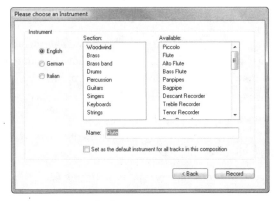

- First, choose whether to name your instruments in **English**, **German** or **Italian**.
- Next, choose the appropriate instrument family from the **Section** list.
- Finally, choose the instrument itself from the **Available** list, and set a custom **Name** if you want.

You can switch on **Set as the default instrument for all tracks in this composition** if you don't want to have to choose the instrument again for any other tracks you subsequently add.

Click **Record**, and if you chose to play to a metronome click, AudioScore will play one bar of clicks; otherwise, it will start recording right away. Sing or play into your microphone, and as you do so, you will see the music appear in the top half of the window, known as the *performance area*:

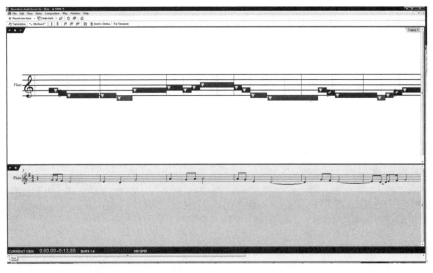

The performance area shows AudioScore's interpretation of the current track in terms of pitch and time, and is also where you edit the pitch, position and duration of notes.

Below the performance area is the *score preview area*, which shows AudioScore's interpretation of all tracks in notation: the current track shown in the performance area is highlighted in light blue in the score preview area.

You can resize the performance area and the score preview area by clicking and dragging the divider between the two areas.

You will also see a small *input level window*, which shows the current input level from your microphone. You can resize this window by clicking and dragging its edges.

When you have finished recording, click **Stop recording** on the toolbar, hit **Space** (Windows only), or hit * on the numeric keypad. Depending on the speed of your computer, AudioScore may need to finish recognizing the notes in your performance before you can proceed: the black *information bar* at the bottom of AudioScore's window shows you the progress.

Recording another track

To record another track, simply click **Record new track** again. The new track is inserted directly below the track selected in the score preview area. To select a track, click the instrument name in the score preview area; you can select multiple adjacent tracks by **Shift**-clicking, or multiple non-adjacent tracks by **Ctrl**+clicking *or* ⌘-clicking.

As you record your new track, AudioScore will play back all of the existing tracks (if no track was selected before you started recording), or just the tracks you selected before starting recording. AudioScore will use the same tempo and metronome settings as used for the previous track. If your first track was recorded freely without a metronome, AudioScore will use the tempo it worked out from your first performance as the basis of the metronome click for subsequent tracks.

Inserting music into an existing track

To insert or append more music to an existing track, select the track in the score preview area by clicking its name, then click in the performance area at the point at which you want to insert more music. Choose **File ▸ Record to Current Track**, or click the small red record button ◼ at the top left-hand corner of the performance area (not the main **Record new track** button on the toolbar).

Creating a new track from an audio file

To create a new track from an audio file, choose **File ▸ Open**, and choose the .wav or .aiff file you want to open. Just as when you record a track using a microphone, AudioScore prompts you to choose the tempo, time signature and instrument, so see **Recording a new track using a microphone** above for help with those settings. Unless you already know the tempo of your audio file, you should choose **Calculated from performance** instead of one of the preset tempos.

2. EDITING TRACKS

Having recorded one or more tracks, the next stage is to edit them.

Playing back the performance

To play back your performance, click in the performance area to set the starting position, then choose **Play ▸ Play/Pause Original** (shortcut **O**) or click the small green playback button  at the top left-hand corner of the performance area. The notes in the performance area are highlighted during playback.

Playing back an individual note

To play back an individual note, simply click it in the performance area. If the note is part of a chord, double-click the note to play the whole chord.

Deleting tracks

To delete the current track (i.e. the one displayed in the performance area, and highlighted in the score preview area), choose **Edit ▸ Delete Current Track**.

To delete multiple tracks, select them in the score preview area with **Shift**-click or **Ctrl**+click *or ⌘-click*, then choose **Edit ▸ Delete Selected Tracks**.

Beware: deleting a track cannot be undone, so be careful!

Editing notes

You can only edit notes in the performance area, not in the score preview area. As you move the mouse pointer over the performance area, the mouse pointer changes to help you understand what kinds of edits you can make. Notice also that the black information bar at the bottom of the screen updates to show you useful information about whatever your mouse pointer is hovering over:

Type of object	*Time position*	*Pitch*	*Frequency*	*Tuning meter*	*Tempo*

To select a single note, simply click on it. To select a range of notes, click and drag on a blank bit of the performance area. You can also select a continuous range of notes using **Shift**-click, or add individual notes to the selection using **Ctrl**+click *or ⌘-click*.

The edits you can make to notes are as follows:

- Drag a note up and down to change its pitch. Hold **Alt** or ⌥ to change the pitch by half-steps (semitones).
- Drag the left- or right-hand end of a note to change its duration. Rests are automatically created in the score preview area if notes don't adjoin. Where notes do adjoin, dragging the boundary between the notes lengthens one and shortens the other.
- Drag a note left or right to change its position in the bar.
- Delete a note by selecting it and hitting **Delete**.
- To split a note (e.g. because AudioScore did not correctly detect two or more notes of the same pitch one after another), select it, then choose **Notes ▸ Split Into Two/Three/Four**; you can also right-click (Windows) *or* **Control**-click (Mac) a note to see these options.

- To join two or more notes into a single note (which will end up with the pitch of the first note), select the notes you want to join, and choose **Notes ▸ Join Notes into One**. This option is also available when you right-click (Windows) *or* **Control**-click (Mac) a note.

Moving barlines

The vertical lines in the performance area denote beats and barlines: beats are shown in light gray, and barlines are shown in black. You can move barlines simply by clicking and dragging them. As you do so, the score preview area updates to show the resulting notation.

If your original performance was recorded to a click, you can adjust the barlines in any order, but if your original performance was recorded freely, you should adjust the barlines from left to right.

Inserting a bar

If you need to insert a bar, click in the performance area at the point at which you want to insert a bar, then choose one of the options from the **Notes ▸ Insert Bar** submenu:

- **In Current Track** adds a single empty bar to the current track
- **In All Tracks** adds a single empty bar to all tracks
- **Other** allows you to add more than one bar to the current track, the selected track(s), or all tracks. In the dialog that appears, you can also switch on **Fill with notes** to fill the newly-created bars with notes.

Changing the key signature

AudioScore attempts to set the appropriate key signature automatically, but in the event that you want to change it, choose **Composition ▸ Key Signature**, then choose the desired key signature from the **Major Key** or **Minor Key** submenu.

Changing the time signature

If you want to change the time signature after making your initial choice when recording your first track, choose **Composition ▸ Time Signature**, choose the desired time signature, and click **OK**.

Changing the instrument

If you want to change the instrument used by the current track, choose **Composition ▸ Set Instrument for Current Track**, choose the desired instrument, and click **OK**.

Staff display and piano roll display

AudioScore has two modes for displaying the notes in the performance area. By default, it displays the pitches on a regular 5-line staff. When you drag a note up and down in diatonic mode, it snaps to the next diatonic pitch, unless you hold down **Alt** *or* ⌥ to move the note by half-steps (semitones).

You can switch to a piano roll display by clicking the ⊟ button at the top of the performance area. A piano keyboard appears at the left-hand side of the performance area, and the selected note is highlighted on the keyboard. Switch back to staff display by clicking 𝄞 .

3. SENDING TO SIBELIUS

Once you are satisfied with the appearance of the tracks in the score preview area, it's time to send your music to Sibelius.

Create Score

You can choose File ▸ Create Score to format the music from the score preview area as a page of music, which you can edit in a similar way to editing scanned music in PhotoScore (📖 **1.5 Scanning**). However, since AudioScore Lite can't print, and since you have Sibelius, you can normally proceed directly to sending a score to Sibelius.

Send to Sibelius

To send your score to Sibelius, simply click the Send to Sibelius button on the toolbar, or choose File ▸ Send to ▸ Sibelius (shortcut Ctrl+D *or* ⌘D). If Sibelius isn't already running, it will launch, and a dialog will appear asking you to choose instruments and set the page size. This dialog is the same as the one that appears when you send music from PhotoScore to Sibelius – for more details, see **4. SENDING TO SIBELIUS** on page 35.

Saving an .opt file

If, for some reason, clicking the Send to Sibelius button doesn't work, you can use File ▸ Save As to save your current AudioScore project as a **PhotoScore (.opt)** file. Once you have saved your AudioScore project as an .opt file, you can open the .opt file directly in Sibelius using File ▸ Open.

1.7 Guitar tab input

📖 **2.10 Chord symbols, 2.15 Guitar notation and tab, 2.22 Lute tablature**.

This topic explains how to input tab directly using your computer's keyboard, a MIDI guitar, or by converting existing notation into tab. If you want to input tab in another way, by:

- using the on-screen Fretboard window, 📖 **1.8 Fretboard window**;
- importing a MIDI file, 📖 **9.5 Opening MIDI files**;
- scanning printed music, 📖 **1.5 Scanning**.

Sibelius automatically writes music as notation or as tab in any tuning. It doesn't have to "do" anything to convert between them – it treats tab just as a different way of displaying the underlying music. This means that with Sibelius you can do pretty much anything with tab that you can do with notation – you can play it back, transpose it, copy it (onto tab or notation staves) and so on.

This also means you can input music in tab and turn it into notation, or input it into notation and turn it into tab, or even change standard guitar tab to a different string tuning, or to bass guitar, mandolin, banjo or dobro. Or sitar. Or bass theorbo.

Creating a tab instrument

Guitar and other fret instruments are available from the **Create ▸ Instruments** dialog (shortcut I) with a tab staff created automatically. On the dialog they are called e.g. **Guitar [tab]**.

Alternatively, you can turn a notation staff into a tab staff using an instrument change: choose **Create ▸ Other ▸ Instrument Change**, choose the tab instrument you want to use, and then click at the very start of the score.

Turning notation into tab or tab into notation

Often you will want to have two staves – a notation staff and a tab staff, both showing the same music – or you may want to turn notation into tab or vice versa. This is done simply by copying the music between the staves.

- Create two guitars, one with notation and one with tab, or just use the **Guitar + Tab** manuscript paper
- Input all of the music onto (say) the notation staff
- Select all of this music as a passage by triple-clicking the notation staff
- Copy it onto the tab staff by **Alt**+clicking *or* ⌥-clicking onto the first bar. It will all turn magically into tab:

- You can then edit the tab staff to, for example, move some of the notes onto different strings.

You can also do this the other way around – input the tab, then copy it to the notation staff. Then if you don't need both staves (and just wanted to convert between notation and tab) you can delete the original one.

On a notation staff, a guitar is written one octave higher than it sounds; this means that if you copy music from another staff (e.g. for a non-transposing instrument like a piano), it will appear an octave higher on the guitar staff, but it will play back at the same pitch.

Inputting tab

Inputting tab using your computer's keyboard is very simple, and the basics can be summed up in just a few points:

* Select the bar in which you want to start inputting, then choose **Notes ▶ Input Notes** (shortcut N)
* The caret (a small vertical line) appears, showing you which string you're on
* Choose the length of the note you want to input using the Keypad window, or by typing the corresponding key on your keyboard's numeric keypad
* Use the ↑ and ↓ keys to move up and down the strings, and ← and → to move back and forth in the bar
* To input a note, type the fret number using the number keys on the main keyboard (not the numeric keypad).
* To create quarter-tones on a tab staff, create the note as normal and then (with the note selected) type =. A quarter-tone appears on a tab staff as a fret number followed by .5. To create quarter-tones on a notation staff, use the appropriate accidental from the sixth Keypad layout.

You can change the default note value used when moving around the bar using the ← and → keys in the **Mouse** page of the **File ▶ Preferences** dialog (in the **Sibelius** menu on Mac); change **Rhythmic positions to snap to** to whatever note value you prefer. Switch off the **Snap in guitar tab input** option if you'd rather the ← and → keys simply move you the same distance as the currently selected note value on the Keypad, unless there's an existing note between the current caret position and the next, in which case that note will be selected.

Notes out of range

When copying music between staves – e.g. from a 6-string guitar tab staff to a 4-string bass guitar tab staff, or from a notation staff to a guitar tab staff – some notes may be unplayable. In this case a red question mark (?) will appear on the tab staff, to show you that you'll need to correct this chord yourself.

Guitar tab fingering options

When Sibelius creates tab for you – when you copy from a notation staff to a tab staff, copy from one tab staff to another with a different tuning, input from a MIDI keyboard or guitar, or import a MIDI file – it automatically tries to produce the most playable fingering.

The **Guitar Tab Fingering** section of the **Note Input** page on **File ▶ Preferences** (in the **Sibelius** menu on Mac) allows you to specify the preferred range of frets that you would like Sibelius to use when it works out fingerings. You can specify the lowest and highest frets that Sibelius should attempt to use, whether or not it should try and use open strings where possible, and the number of frets you can stretch when playing chords.

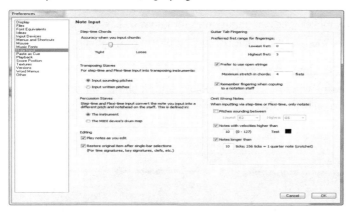

These options are not obeyed in all cases; they are merely recommendations. For example, if you switch off the **Prefer to use open strings** option but then Sibelius needs to create a note that can only be played using an open string, Sibelius will finger that note as an open string rather than not write it at all.

Sibelius will not rewrite all the *existing* tab in your score if you make a change in this dialog. But if you do want to apply new settings to existing tab, simply use **Notes ▸ Reset Guitar Tab Fingering** (see below).

Resetting tab fingering

You can reset the fingering of a tab staff to your preferred ranges at any time. Simply select the passage in which you want the fingering reset and choose **Notes ▸ Reset Tab Fingering**.

For example, if you decide that a particular passage would be more comfortably played around the fifth fret rather than at the nut, you could set new preferences in the **Note Input** page of **File ▸ Preferences** (in the **Sibelius** menu on Mac, see above), then apply those preferences to that passage by choosing **Notes ▸ Reset Guitar Tab Fingering**.

When does Sibelius automatically reset tab fingering?

Generally speaking, fingering is retained if you are copying within the same staff, or to another staff with the same tuning. If you copy music to a notation staff or to a tab staff with a different tuning, Sibelius will recalculate the fingering for you based on the settings in the **Note Input** page of **File ▸ Preferences** (in the **Sibelius** menu on Mac).

However, in the specific case of scores that consist of a notation and tab staff only (i.e. different representations of the same music), it is useful to retain the fingering information when copying between these staves as you may be copying back and forth between them repeatedly. In this case, you should switch on the **Remember fingering when copying to a notation staff** option in the **Note Input** page of the **File ▸ Preferences** dialog (in the **Sibelius** menu on Mac).

Using a MIDI guitar

Sibelius allows you to input from a MIDI guitar that supports multiple MIDI channels –
📖 **1.10 Input Devices**.

1.8 Fretboard window

Sibelius's Fretboard window makes it easy to input notes for guitar or bass using the mouse, and can also prove useful to show you how particular riffs or chords can be fingered.

Showing and hiding the Fretboard window

To show or hide the Fretboard window, click the toolbar button shown on the right, or choose Window ▸ Fretboard (shortcut Ctrl+Alt+E *or* ⌥⌘E). The Fretboard window looks like this:

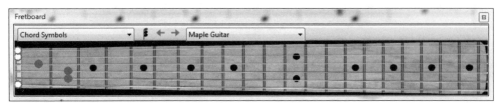

Using the menu at the right-hand end of the Fretboard's toolbar, you can choose between maple, rosewood and acoustic 6-string guitar fretboards, or maple and rosewood 4-string bass guitar fretboards, or a rosewood 5-string bass guitar fretboard.

The Fretboard window has three sizes (the middle of which is shown above), and it is resized by grabbing its bottom edge (or its top edge, on Windows) and dragging.

Mouse input using the Fretboard window

Although it is perhaps most natural to use the Fretboard window to input notes onto guitar tab instruments, you can use the Fretboard to input onto any kind of instrument in your score.

To input notes using the Fretboard window, simply select the bar or rest from which you want to start inputting. Sibelius will automatically choose the most appropriate kind of Fretboard based on the kind of instrument you have selected. Now click at the fret position on the appropriate string for the note you want to input.

The note input caret advances automatically after you input each note, so if you want to input a chord, click the chord mode button on the Fretboard window's toolbar, shown on the right. Now each fret position you click is added to the current chord, and to advance the caret you must click the right arrow button to the right of the chord mode button.

Following the score during playback

Aside from inputting notes, the other thing the Fretboard window can do is show you which notes are played during playback. You can choose which instrument to follow using the menu at the left-hand side of the Fretboard window's toolbar.

By default, it's set to Auto, which means that it will follow the topmost guitar or bass staff in the score, or failing that the topmost staff in the score, unless you have selected one or more staves before starting playback, in which case it will follow only the topmost of those staves. If you always want to follow a particular staff during playback, choose the name of the staff from the menu at the left-hand side of the Fretboard window's toolbar.

Notice that the Fretboard window can only follow notes in voice 1 during playback; other voices are simply omitted. If a note is too high to be displayed on the current fretboard, it is shown by an arrow pointing rightwards at the top of the highest string; similarly, if a note is too low to be displayed on the current fretboard, it is shown as an arrow pointing leftwards at the bottom of the lowest string.

The Fretboard window can also follow the chord symbols in the score, showing how they can be fingered on guitar; simply choose **Chord symbols** from the menu on the Fretboard's toolbar.

Showing the selected note or chord

The Fretboard window also shows the currently selected note, chord or chord symbol when you're editing notes, which can be useful to check the voicing of a chord. The Fretboard window always shows notes in sounding pitch, even when **Notes ▸ Transposing Score** is switched on.

1.9 Selections and passages

📖 **5.7 Filters and Find**.

When objects in the score are selected, they go colored, which shows that you can do things to them using the mouse and keyboard. Most operations in Sibelius involve selections.

There are three main kinds of selection:

- a single selection, where just one object is selected
- a multiple selection, where several separate objects are selected
- a selected passage, where a continuous stretch of music is selected, shown with a light blue box ("staff passage") or purple double-box ("system passage") round it.

You can do pretty much the same things to all three kinds of selection. The main difference is how you select the objects in the first place.

Additionally, you can select a rectangle of music in order to export it as graphics – 📖 **9.8 Exporting graphics**.

Selection colors

When an object is selected, it changes color to show that it's selected:

- Notes and staff-attached text and lines are colored according to the voice(s) to which they belong (voice 1 is dark blue, voice 2 is green, voice 3 is orange, and voice 4 is pink). If an object belongs to more than one voice, or all voices, it is colored light blue.
- Various other staff objects, e.g. symbols, clefs, instrument changes, etc., apply to all voices and so are also colored light blue.
- System objects (e.g. system text, lines and symbols, time signatures, key signatures, etc.) are colored purple when selected.

Single selections

To make a single selection, click an object – it's as simple as that. You can drag the object around to move it, which will cause the object to attach to new rhythmic positions along the staff, or even another staff, if you drag it far enough (📖 **8.7 Attachment**). You can also hold down specific keys when dragging an object around: first click the object, and keep the mouse button held down, then add the modifier key:

- Shift-drag: constrains the movement of the item in the direction in which you first move it.
- Alt+drag: moves the item without moving its attachment point.
- Ctrl+drag (⌘-drag on Mac): temporarily disables Magnetic Layout for that item so that it can move wherever you drag it, then pops back into its avoided position when you release Ctrl *or* ⌘.

These modifiers can also be used in combination (e.g. holding Shift and Alt to constrain an item's movement in a particular direction and move it without re-attaching it at any point).

You can also select and move an object without using the mouse: with nothing selected, hit **Tab** to select the first object on the top staff on the page. Then:

* You can select the next object on the staff using the arrow keys or **Tab** (to select the previous item, type **Shift-Tab**)
* If you want to select a particular notehead in a chord, use **Alt+↑/↓** *or* ⌥↑/↓ to select the next notehead above or below the currently selected one
* If there are no chords, **Alt+↑/↓** *or* ⌥↑/↓ selects the note at the nearest rhythmic position on the staff above or below
* You can also move between the different parts of lines using **Alt+←/→** *or* ⌥←/→ – 🕮 **2.21 Lines** and 🕮 **2.28 Slurs**.

If you have trouble selecting an object with the mouse, because there's another object very close that you keep selecting instead: first, hit **Tab** (or **Shift-Tab**) to move the selection to the object you want to select, or zoom in very close and try selecting it again; if this fails, move the other object out of the way temporarily.

Another way of making a single selection is to use the **Edit ▸ Find** (shortcut **Ctrl+F** *or* ⌘F) feature – 🕮 **5.7 Filters and Find**.

Multiple selections

* Click an object, then **Ctrl+click** *or* ⌘-click one or more other objects to add them to the selection. **Ctrl+click** *or* ⌘-click an object again if you want to remove it from the selection.
* Alternatively, **Shift-click** *or* ⌘-click on the paper and drag the light gray box around the objects you want to select (sometimes called a "marquee" or "lasso" selection). If you drag across a whole staff, you'll get a selected passage instead. You can then add/remove objects from the selection using **Ctrl+click** *or* ⌘-click. If you use this function a lot, changing the **Drag Paper** setting in the **File ▸ Preferences ▸ General** dialog (in the **Sibelius** menu on Mac OS X) allows you to select a passage simply by clicking and dragging (without holding down **Shift** or ⌘).
* With multiple text selections, you can also extend a single selection by choosing **Edit ▸ Select ▸ Select More** (type **Ctrl+Shift+A** *or* ⇧⌘A), which selects all similar text objects (i.e. in the same style) attached to the same staff within that system. This is a quick way of selecting a whole row of, say, chord symbols, lyrics, fingerings or expression marks.
* If you have a single note of a chord selected, **Edit ▸ Select ▸ Select More** selects all the notes in that chord; similarly, if you have a single note, rest or a whole chord selected, **Edit ▸ Select ▸ Select More** will select the whole bar.
* You can also use filters to make a multiple selection – 🕮 **5.7 Filters and Find**.

Multiple selections are mainly useful for objects other than notes, chords and rests – e.g. to delete several articulations or bits of text.

Selected passages

A "passage" is a continuous stretch of music – of any length from a couple of notes to the whole score, and for any number of staves from one to a complete orchestra. You can think of it as a "rectangle" of music – though this rectangle can run between systems and pages, and you can even include non-adjacent staves in a passage.

In contrast to multiple selections, selected passages are mainly useful for doing things to several notes, chords and rests.

There are two kinds of passages: normally, passages are surrounded by a single light blue box and can include any combination of staves in your score; *system passages*, by contrast, are surrounded by a purple double-box and include all the staves in your score.

To select a passage by clicking:

- Click the note/chord/rest at one corner (e.g. the top left-hand corner) of the "rectangle" you want to select. If you're selecting from the start of a bar, it's quicker just to click an empty part of the bar.
- **Shift**-click the note/chord/rest at the opposite (e.g. bottom right-hand corner) of the "rectangle." Again, if you're selecting to the end of a bar, just click an empty part of the bar.
- All selected objects will go colored and a light blue box will appear around the selection. The selection will also appear on the Navigator, which is useful for viewing passages that span multiple pages.
- To add further staves to the selection, hold down **Ctrl** *or* ⌘ and click further staves; this can be used to add non-adjacent staves to the selection
- You can also exclude certain staves from a passage selection by holding down **Ctrl** *or* ⌘ and clicking in turn on the staves you want to remove from the selection.

You can also make a passage selection using the **Edit▸ Select▸ Select Bars** dialog (shortcut **Ctrl+Alt+A** *or* ⌥⌘A). This is useful if you know you want to select, say, the first 16 bars of a score, or want to select from the current position to the end of the score. The **Make system selection** option will make the resulting passage selection into a system passage.

To select a system passage, do the same but start by **Ctrl**+clicking *or* ⌘-clicking a blank part of a bar, then hold **Ctrl** *or* ⌘ as you click on other notes/chords/rests in other staves to extend the passage.

Naturally, you can also select a passage using just the keyboard:

- With a note selected, type **Shift-←/→** to extend the selection horizontally a note at a time, or **Ctrl+Shift+←/→** *or* ⇧⌘←/→ to extend it a bar at a time. This is similar to word processors (as are various other uses of the arrow keys).
- To select multiple staves, type **Shift-↑/↓** to include another staff in the passage
- To turn the current selection into a system passage, choose **Edit▸ Select▸ Select System Passage** (shortcut **Shift+Alt+A** *or* ⇧⌥A).

To select a passage by dragging the mouse: hold down **Shift** *or* ⌘ and drag out a rectangle starting from above the top staff at the start of the desired passage and finishing below the bottom staff at the end. This is only practical for short passages.

Clearing a selection

Whether you have a single, multiple or passage selection, you can always clear the selection by hitting **Esc**. If you prefer to work with the mouse, you can clear a selection by clicking onto the page outside your current selection (e.g. in the margin, or between two staves). You can also click on the mouse pointer button (⬆) at the top left-hand corner of the Keypad (▯ **1.2 Keypad**), which is handy if you are working with an interactive whiteboard or tablet PC.

Usefully, you can also use Edit ▸ Undo and Edit ▸ Redo to undo and redo changes of selection.

Quick cases

There are various ways to select certain types of passage quickly:

- Clicking an empty part of a bar selects that bar on one staff (e.g. to copy a bar)
- Double-clicking an empty part of a bar selects that staff for the duration of the system (e.g. to copy those bars)
- Triple-clicking an empty part of a bar selects that staff throughout the score (e.g. to delete a whole instrument)
- After single-, double- or triple-clicking, you can Shift-click another staff to add all staves in between to the selection, or (as before) add or remove individual staves using Ctrl+click *or* ⌘-click
- If you hold Ctrl *or* ⌘ while single-, double- or triple-clicking initially, a system passage is selected (enclosed in a purple double-box)
- You can even select the entire score at once by choosing Edit ▸ Select ▸ Select All (shortcut Ctrl+A *or* ⌘A). This is particularly useful for transposing the whole score, altering the format of the whole score, or for selecting particular types of object throughout the score (see below).

  (If you think hard about it, Edit ▸ Select ▸ Select All does the same thing as Ctrl+triple-click *or* ⌘-triple-click. See?)

What can you do with multiple selections and selected passages?

You can do virtually anything to a multiple selection or selected passage that you can do to a single note, and more; for example:

- Copy it elsewhere with Alt+click *or* ⌥-click – very, very handy for arranging or orchestrating. (Copying overwrites unless you select a passage of bars with Ctrl *or* ⌘, in which case it inserts)
- Delete it – just hit Delete. If the passage was selected with Ctrl *or* ⌘ (and so had a double-box round it), the bars themselves will be deleted too.
- Repeat it with R – see **Repeating selections** below
- Transpose it, either using the Transpose dialog (⌑ **5.20 Transposing**) to transpose by a specific interval, or diatonically by step using the ↑/↓ keys. Ctrl+↑/↓ *or* ⌘↑/↓ shift by an octave.
- Produce chords by adding notes above or below – type 1–9 to add an interval above, or Shift-1–9 to add an interval below (but not the latter if you're using the Notebook (laptop) feature set – ⌑ **5.12 Menus and shortcuts**)
- Play it back by choosing Play ▸ Move Playback Line to Selection or hitting Y, then click on the play button in the Playback window or hit Space
- Arrange the music for a different combination of instruments, "explode" the passage onto a larger number of staves, or "reduce" it onto a smaller number – ⌑ **5.1 Arrange™**
- Run a plug-in to check, edit or add things to the selection – ⌑ **6.1 Working with plug-ins**
- Add articulations to all notes/chords using the first or fourth Keypad layout
- Reset the note spacing to default by choosing Layout ▸ Reset Note Spacing (shortcut Ctrl+Shift+N *or* ⇧⌘N).

Multicopying

Multicopying allows you to copy a single selection, multiple selection or passage several times either horizontally (along the same staff), vertically (onto more than one staff), or both at once.

Multicopying a single object

You can copy a single object, e.g. a note or some text, vertically across any number of staves. This is perhaps most useful for copying dynamic markings (e.g. ***mf***) across multiple staves at once:

* Select a single object and choose **Edit ▸ Copy** (shortcut **Ctrl+C** *or* **⌘C**) to copy it to the clipboard
* Select a passage in one or more staves and choose **Edit ▸ Paste** (shortcut **Ctrl+V** *or* **⌘V**) to copy the item *to the start* of the passage only, one copy on each staff.

Multicopying a multiple selection

As an extension of the above, you can select more than one object and copy them vertically across any number of staves. This is particularly useful for copying a row of dynamics:

* Make a multiple selection – **Ctrl+click** *or* **⌘-click** the objects you want to copy or select them with a filter (e.g. **Edit ▸ Filter ▸ Dynamics**), then choose **Edit ▸ Copy** (shortcut **Ctrl+C** *or* **⌘C**) to copy them to the clipboard
* Select a passage in one or more staves and choose **Edit ▸ Paste** (shortcut **Ctrl+V** *or* **⌘V**) to copy the selection *to the start* of the passage only, one copy for every staff, with relative distances between the original objects retained in the new copies. If hidden staves are included in the destination passage, multicopy will copy onto the hidden staves too.

Multicopying a passage

* Select a passage in one or more staves and choose **Edit ▸ Copy** (shortcut **Ctrl+C** *or* **⌘C**) to copy it to the clipboard
* Select another passage and choose **Edit ▸ Paste** (shortcut **Ctrl+V** *or* **⌘V**) to fill the new passage with multiple copies of the original passage. The new passage is filled in the following way:
  * *Horizontally*: if the destination passage is longer than the original, a *whole* number of copies is pasted into the new passage (with any leftover bars at the end left unchanged). If the destination passage is shorter than the original, only one copy is made.
  * *Vertically*: if the destination passage contains more staves than the original, a *whole* number of copies is made from the top downwards (with any leftover staves at the bottom left unchanged). If the destination passage has fewer staves than the original, only one copy is made.

Beware that multicopying overwrites the original contents of the destination passage, and copies onto any hidden staves that are included in the destination passage.

Repeating selections

You can also use **Edit ▸ Repeat** (shortcut **R**) to make multiple copies of any selection, as follows:

* Select a note, chord, passage, multiple selection, line, text object, symbol, chord diagram, imported graphic, instrument change, clef, key signature or barline and type **R**.
* The selected object(s) are repeated once to the right; to repeat again, keep hitting **R**.

1.10 Input Devices

📖 **1.1 Note input**, **1.4 Flexi-time™**.

If you have a MIDI keyboard or other external input device connected to your computer, you can use step-time and Flexi-time input. For information about setting up your computer for MIDI input, 📖 **MIDI setup for Windows** and **MIDI setup for Mac** in the Handbook.

Choosing input devices

The **Input Devices** page of **File ▸ Preferences** (in the **Sibelius** menu on Mac) has options affecting MIDI input:

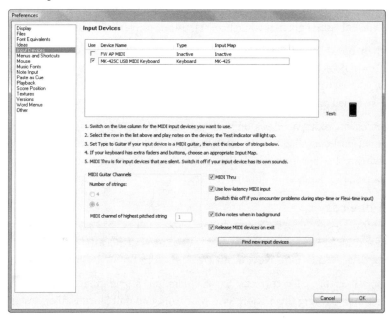

The table at the top lists any MIDI input devices you have. The options are as follows:

- **Use**: if the checkbox in this column is switched on, Sibelius will accept input from this device; if switched off, Sibelius will ignore any input from this device. By default, the **Use** checkbox is switched on for all input devices.

- **Device Name**: this column tells you the input device's name. If your MIDI port is provided by a soundcard or external MIDI interface, you will normally see the name of the MIDI port itself (e.g. **MIDISport USB 2x2 A** or **SB Live! MIDI Out**) rather than the name of any device connected to the MIDI port or interface. If your MIDI device connects to your computer directly (e.g. via USB), you will probably see the actual name of the MIDI device (e.g. **M-Audio Oxygen 8**) instead.

- **Type**: this shows what type of device this is. When clicked, a drop-down menu appears, allowing you to choose either **Keyboard** (the default) or **Guitar**. If you choose **Guitar**, then the MIDI **Guitar Channels** controls below the table are enabled – see **MIDI guitars** below.

- **Input Map**: this allows you to specify exactly what kind of keyboard a particular device is. This is useful because many keyboards have additional knobs, faders and buttons on them that can be used in Sibelius – see **Input maps** below.

Try playing notes on your keyboard (or other MIDI input device) while the dialog is open. If everything is working as it should, the little black indicator marked **Test** should light up green as you play. If the indicator doesn't light up, check your MIDI connections and ensure that you have the correct input device selected (if more than one is present).

You should switch on the **MIDI Thru** checkbox if and only if your keyboard has no built-in sounds – this option makes Sibelius reproduce notes played on your keyboard using your soundcard or other playback device.

Use low-latency MIDI input allows Sibelius to take advantage of the advanced capabilities of your input device's drivers in order to provide low-latency input. This option should be left switched on unless you encounter glitches while using step-time or Flexi-time input.

Echo notes when in background determines whether Sibelius should continue to play back notes played on your MIDI keyboard when the application is not in focus (e.g. when you are using another program on your computer). This option is switched on by default, and only has any effect if **MIDI thru** is also switched on.

Release MIDI devices on exit (Windows only) determines whether Sibelius should explicitly release the MIDI input ports on all active devices when you quit the application. Normally you should leave this switched on, but for some devices it may be necessary to switch this off, if you find that you cannot restart Sibelius after quitting (unless you restart your computer).

Finding new input devices

If you connect an external MIDI input device, such as a keyboard or control surface, to your computer while Sibelius is running, it may not automatically become available for input. To refresh the list of available input devices, click **Find New Input Devices** on the **Input Devices** page.

Not all devices report their presence correctly to your computer's operating system, so if your device doesn't appear after clicking this button, save your work and quit Sibelius, then restart the program, making sure your MIDI input device is switched on before you run Sibelius.

Problems with MIDI input

If MIDI input doesn't seem to work, check that MIDI OUT on the keyboard is connected to MIDI IN on your computer, and (if your keyboard has built-in sounds) MIDI IN on your keyboard is connected to MIDI OUT on your computer – not MIDI OUT to MIDI OUT and MIDI IN to MIDI IN. If your computer has two MIDI IN sockets, also try connecting the keyboard to the other MIDI IN socket instead.

Input maps

If your MIDI keyboard has a plethora of buttons, knobs and faders in addition to the usual piano-style keys, you can use them with Sibelius, e.g. to control the faders in the Mixer, to control playback, and so on.

Simply choose the most appropriate item listed under **Input Map** in the box at the top of the **Input Devices** page. By default, try **MIDI keyboard**, which will work with many MIDI keyboards, or if you have one of the specific keyboards listed there, choose the input map for that keyboard instead.

Input maps for many of the most popular M-Audio keyboards are included, as follows:

Axiom 25:

Set your Axiom 25 to its default Program. The eight knobs above the keyboard are mapped to the faders in the Mixer for the first eight staves in your score, and the transport buttons below the LCD display are mapped to the corresponding functions of the Playback window.

Axiom 49 + 61:

Set your Axiom 49 or Axiom 61 to its default program. By default, the first eight faders above the keyboard are mapped to the faders in the Mixer for the first eight staves, but you can switch them to control the virtual instrument output faders by issuing a program change to program 2. The ninth fader is always mapped to the master volume control. The buttons below the faders solo the corresponding staff or virtual instrument. The rotary controls to the right of the faders control pan for the first eight staves in the Mixer. The transport buttons below the LCD display are mapped to the corresponding functions of the Playback window.

Axiom Pro 49 + 61:

1. Inputting

Sibelius does not currently support the full HyperControl functionality of the Axiom Pro keyboard controller, but the transport buttons and faders are all mapped to useful functions in Sibelius. Set your Axiom Pro 49 or Axiom Pro 61 to program 1. By default, the first eight faders above the keyboard are mapped to the faders in the Mixer for the first eight staves, but you can switch them to control the virtual instrument output faders by issuing a program change to program 2. The ninth fader is always mapped to the master volume control. The transport buttons are mapped to the corresponding functions of the Playback window.

KeyStudio 49i (also known as the ProKeys Sono 49)

The **Piano volume** knob adjusts the master volume fader in the Mixer.

Keystation Pro 88:

Set your Keystation Pro 88 to use Preset 7. The transport buttons above the modulation and pitch bend wheels to the left of the keyboard are mapped to the corresponding functions of the Playback window. Button 9 on the keyboard to the right of the LCD display hides and shows the Mixer window. By default, the first eight faders above the keyboard are mapped to the faders in the Mixer for the first eight staves, but you can switch them to control the virtual instrument output faders by issuing a program change to program 2. The ninth fader is always mapped to the master volume control. The buttons below the faders solo the corresponding staff or virtual instrument. The bottom row of rotary controls to the left of the faders control the pan settings for the first eight staves; the middle row controls pan for staves 9–16.

MK-425c:

Set your MK-425c to its default program. The eight rotary controls above the keyboard adjust the volume of the first eight staves in the Mixer, and the buttons numbered 1–8 to the left of the keyboard solo the corresponding staff.

MK-449 + 461:

Set your MK-449 or MK-461 to its default program. By default, the first eight faders above the keyboard are mapped to the faders in the Mixer for the first eight staves, but you can switch them to control the virtual instrument output faders by issuing a program change to program 11 (send a program change to program 10 to switch back to controlling staff volume). The ninth fader is always mapped to the master volume control. The buttons to the left of the faders solo the corresponding staff or virtual instrument. The rotary controls to the right of the faders control the pan settings for the first eight staves.

Oxygen 8:

Set your Oxygen 8 to its default program. The rotary controls above the keyboard are mapped to the faders in the Mixer for the first eight staves. The transport buttons below the rotary controls are mapped to the corresponding functions of the Playback window.

Oxygen 49 + 61:

Set your Oxygen 49 or Oxygen 61 to its default program. By default, the first eight faders above the keyboard are mapped to the faders in the Mixer for the first eight staves, but you can switch them to control the virtual instrument output faders by issuing a program change to program 2 (send a program change to program 1 to switch back to controlling staff volume). The ninth fader is always mapped to the master volume control. The buttons below the faders solo the corresponding staff or virtual instrument. The rotary controls to the right of the faders control the pan settings for the first eight staves. The transport buttons below the rotary controls are mapped to the corresponding functions of the Playback window.

UC-33:

Set your UC-33 to its default program. By default, the first eight faders are mapped to the faders in the Mixer for the first eight staves, but you can switch them to control the virtual instrument output faders by issuing a program change to program 2 (send a program change to program 1 to switch back to controlling staff volume). The ninth fader is always mapped to the master volume control. The buttons labeled 1–8 to the right of the faders solo the corresponding staff or virtual instrument. The rotary controls in the bottom row above the faders control the pan settings for the first eight staves. The middle row controls the volume settings for staves 9–16, and the top row controls the pan settings for staves 9–16. The transport buttons at the bottom right-hand corner of the surface are mapped to the corresponding functions of the Playback window.

Additional input maps are available from the support section of the Sibelius web site, which you can visit by choosing **Help ▸ Online Support**.

Inputting

MIDI guitars

If you are using a MIDI guitar, Sibelius allows you to assign each MIDI channel to a string so that fingerings will automatically appear on the correct string of a tab staff. You can also set up various filters to eliminate "noise" being treated as notes.

If you have a guitar with a hexaphonic pick-up (such as the Roland GK-2A or GK-3) and a guitar MIDI interface (such as the Axon AX100, Roland GR-33 or GI-20, etc.), Sibelius can write notes played on a particular string on the correct string in tab, whether you play in using Flexi-time or step-time input.

To tell Sibelius that you are using a MIDI guitar that outputs each string on a separate channel, set Type to Guitar for the appropriate item in the list of input devices. If your MIDI guitar outputs everything you play on a single channel, leave Type set to Keyboard. *Note:* when Type is set to Guitar, the options under Guitar Tab Fingering on the Note Input page of File ▸ Preferences (in the Sibelius menu on Mac) have no effect during input (though they are still used when you e.g. copy music from one staff to another).

Then:

- Set the Number of strings as appropriate
- Set the MIDI channel of highest pitched string, if necessary. Sibelius assumes that the strings of your MIDI guitar are numbered sequentially; if they are not, consult the documentation for your guitar MIDI interface, and set its options appropriately.

You may also wish to set some of the options under Omit Wrong Notes, described in detail in **Note input options** on page 13. One of the traditional problems of inputting using a MIDI guitar is that the software accurately renders every note detected by the MIDI pick-up: even if you are able to play cleanly, it's common for very short or quiet notes that you had not intended to play to appear in the score; similarly, MIDI pick-ups occasionally detect high or low harmonics and notate these as very high or very low notes. Sibelius lets you tailor the sensitivity of its notation to your playing style. (You may also find these options useful for input devices other than a MIDI guitar.)

For more details on MIDI input (from a keyboard or guitar), see the **Handbook** or 📖 **1.1 Note input** and 📖 **1.4 Flexi-time™**.

Tips for successful MIDI guitar input

Sibelius accurately transcribes anything you play, exactly as you play it. However, a few factors can contribute to imprecise transcription. While Sibelius itself can filter out notes with a low velocity (see **Note input options** on page 13), it's also a good idea to ensure that your MIDI converter sensitivity settings are set fairly low when using a MIDI guitar; incidental string scrapes, ghost notes and other anomalies appear when the sensitivity settings are too high.

String buzz against tall frets or a poorly adjusted setup will confuse the MIDI converter and produce errant notes, so make sure to have your guitar adjusted by an experienced technician if your guitar exhibits symptoms of bad fret buzz.

On your MIDI guitar interface, experiment with the different picking modes. Both Roland and Axon support the option for pick-style (plectrum) and finger-style input via an internal setting.

1. Inputting

Make sure to experiment with these settings, as some players find that finger-style input is more accurate even when using a pick, and vice-versa.

Sibelius does not notate pitch bend information, slides or string bends on input. You can create them in your score later, but when you enter notes, play cleanly, without vibrato, slides or bends, to ensure accurate notation.

One last note: flatwound strings consistently produce the cleanest notation into Sibelius.

2. Notations

2.1 Accidentals

📖 **1.1 Note input**.

Creating an accidental with a note

When you create a note using mouse or keystrokes, you can give it an accidental at the same time by choosing one from the first or sixth Keypad layout (shortcuts **F7/F12**) before putting the note into the score. (You can also add articulations, rhythm dots, tremolos and non-standard beaming from the Keypad at the same time.)

Accidentals are automatically created when you input from a MIDI keyboard.

Adding accidentals to existing notes

Select the note(s) in question, then choose an accidental from the first or sixth Keypad layout.

To add accidentals to all the notes in a chord at once, double-click one of the notes in the chord and then choose an accidental.

Removing particular accidentals

- Select the note(s) in question, then choose the accidental from the Keypad again, to switch it off.
- Alternatively, the slow and fiddly way is to select the accidental(s) with the mouse (taking care not to select the associated note(s) at the same time), then hit **Delete**.

Removing lots of accidentals

Select the notes in question, then, from the sixth Keypad layout (shortcut **F12**), choose the **0** key on the numeric keypad or the corresponding button shown on the right.

Hiding accidentals

In some situations (such as in passages that use cross-staff beaming – see **Cross-staff beams** on page 95) you may want to hide an accidental rather than delete it (i.e. you want it to sound as if it has an accidental, but the accidental should not appear on the page).

To do this, select the accidental itself (not the notehead), and choose **Edit ▸ Hide or Show ▸ Hide** (shortcut **Ctrl+Shift+H** *or* ⇧⌘H). For more details, 📖 **5.9 Hiding objects**.

Automatic cautionary accidentals

A cautionary (or courtesy) accidental is used to show that a note had an accidental in the previous bar, as a way to remind the player that the note should now be played according to the key signature. Sibelius automatically shows cautionary accidentals under the following conditions:

- At the start of a bar where the previous note had a different accidental
- Where any note in the previous bar had an accidental
- Where a non-initial note in the subsequent bar has an accidental
- Where any note in the previous bar and a non-initial note in the subsequent bar have a different accidental

- Where a note with an accidental is tied over a barline, any note at the same pitch in the following bar has a cautionary "cancelling" the accidental
- Where a previous note in a different octave had a different accidental (e.g. if you write C♯5 C4, Sibelius will show a cautionary natural on the C4)
- Where a previous note in a different voice had a different accidental, either within the same bar or in the preceding bar.

Another common convention for cautionary accidentals is to show the cautionary only on the first note of the bar, i.e. if the first note of the next bar is at the same pitch as a note that has an accidental in the previous bar. To make Sibelius use this convention, choose **House Style▸ Engraving Rules**, go to the **Accidentals and Dots** page, and switch on **Apply auto cautionaries only up to first note of next bar**.

If you would prefer Sibelius not to show a cautionary accidental when a different accidental occurs in another voice, you can switch off **Restate accidental when seen in a new voice** on the **Accidentals and Dots** page of **House Style ▸ Engraving Rules**. If you are writing music in which two players or singers share the same staff, you are recommended to leave this option switched on; if, however, you are writing music where all the voices on a staff are to be read by the same performer, you can switch it off.

Changes of key signature cancel out cautionary accidentals by default: if you are in C major and have an F# in one bar, then have an explicit key change to, say, A major in the following bar, an F# in that following bar will not show a cautionary accidental, because the key signature renders it redundant. If you nonetheless want Sibelius to show cautionary accidentals under such circumstances, switch off **Reset cautionary accidentals** on the **Clefs and Key Signatures** page of **House Style ▸ Engraving Rules**.

Cautionary accidentals in parentheses

By default, Sibelius does not put cautionary accidentals in parentheses (round brackets), and you can change this setting by switching on **Show cautionary accidentals in parentheses** (and **Show restated accidentals in a new voice in parentheses**, if desired) on the **Accidentals and Dots** page of **House Style ▸ Engraving Rules**.

You can manually add parentheses to any accidental if you like – see **Editorial accidentals** below.

Suppressing cautionary accidentals

You can hide an automatic cautionary accidental by selecting the note on which the cautionary accidental appears, and choosing the **Suppress cautionary accidental** button (shortcut .) on the sixth Keypad layout (shortcut **F12**), as shown on the right.

Accidentals on tied notes

When a tied note has an accidental, and happens to be split by a system or page break, Sibelius restates the accidental automatically, in parentheses (round brackets), at the start of the new system.

If you would prefer Sibelius not to show the restated accidental in parentheses, switch off **Show restated accidentals on ties in parentheses**, on the **Accidentals and Dots** page of **House Style ▸ Engraving Rules**. If you would prefer Sibelius not to restate the accidental at all, switch off **Restate accidental when note is tied across a system break**.

Editorial accidentals

Editorial accidentals are sometimes written in parentheses (round brackets), and sometimes in square brackets.

To manually add parentheses to an accidental on a selected note (or group of notes), choose the parentheses button from the sixth Keypad layout (shortcut **F12**).

To manually add square brackets to an accidental, type the brackets as Technique text. (*Advanced users:* if you need to use square-bracketed accidentals frequently, you can easily create new symbols for common accidentals in brackets, or modify the parenthesized accidentals, which are already available as symbols.)

Small accidentals

Accidentals automatically go small on cue notes and grace notes. But if you want a small accidental on a normal-sized note, create the accidental from the **Create ▸ Symbol** dialog and choose **Cue size** or **Grace note size** before clicking **OK**. Beware that accidental symbols will not automatically play back or transpose.

Double accidentals and quarter-tones

Obtain these from the sixth Keypad layout just like normal accidentals.

Quarter-tones transpose automatically – try transposing E quarter-flat up a major 7th in your head; the answer's at the end of this topic. (Then write out the scale of E quarter-flat melodic minor.) What's more, Sibelius will respell quarter-tones (see below).

A plug-in to make quarter-tones play back called **Quarter-tone Playback** is included with Sibelius – see **Playback of microtonal accidentals** below.

Double accidentals

Double accidentals are used in obscure keys such as G♯ minor in order to avoid using too many naturals. For instance, the sixth note of D♭ minor is B♭♭, which means the same as A.

The symbols ♭♭ and ♮♯ are occasionally used instead of ♭ and ♯ when canceling a double-flat or sharp earlier in the bar.

Other microtones

You can obtain and design further microtones using symbols, but these will not automatically play back or transpose. You can change the design of the symbols by editing them – for instance, if you prefer your quarter-tone flats to be filled in in black, replace the backwards-flat in the fourth column in the **House Style ▸ Edit Symbols** dialog with a filled-in backwards-flat character – see **Changing existing symbols** on page 634 for more details.

"Spelling" of accidentals

When inputting from MIDI (Flexi-time, step-time or MIDI file), Sibelius guesses whether to spell black notes as a sharp or flat, based on the key signature and context.

To "respell" notes enharmonically (e.g. from F♯ to G♭), select the note(s) and choose **Notes ▸ Respell Accidental** (shortcut **Return** on the main keyboard).

This feature respells a double accidental (e.g. B♭♭) as a natural (A) but not vice versa, as you're much more likely to want to eliminate double accidentals than to introduce them. Obscurely, it even respells quarter-tones. (Most quarter-tones can be written in three ways, e.g. C quarter-sharp is the same as D three-quarters flat and B three-quarters sharp.)

Sibelius also includes two plug-ins for respelling accidentals called **Respell Flats as Sharps** and Respell Sharps as Flats – ⊞ **6.2 Accidentals plug-ins**.

Simplifying accidentals

If you transpose your music or add a new key signature to existing music, you may end up with lots of unwanted accidentals. Use the **Plug-ins ▸ Accidentals ▸ Simplify Accidentals** plug-in to fix this for you – see **Simplify Accidentals** on page 484.

In the none-too-likely eventuality that your score contains double accidentals that you want to eliminate, simply select the whole score (choose **Edit ▸ Select ▸ Select All**, shortcut **Ctrl+A** *or* ⌘A), then from the **Notes ▸ Transpose** dialog (shortcut **Shift**-T) transpose it up by a **Major/Perfect Unison** with **Double sharps/flats** switched off. All double accidentals will then be replaced with simpler equivalents.

Adding accidentals to notes

Sibelius comes with two plug-ins that allow you to quickly add accidentals to all the notes in a selection. To add accidentals to every note that doesn't "fit" in the current key signature, choose **Plug-ins ▸ Accidentals ▸ Add Accidentals to All Sharp and Flat notes**. This would, for example, add an accidental to every B♭ in C major and to every C natural in E major. You can also add accidentals to, literally, every note in a selection by choosing **Plug-ins ▸ Accidentals ▸ Add Accidentals to All Notes**.

Altered unisons

"Altered unisons" are two noteheads in a chord with the same pitch but different accidentals, e.g. G♭ and G♯.

Some composers such as Messiaen notate this as two noteheads side-by-side preceded by two accidentals, rather like the interval of a second (see left-hand picture). Create this notation in the obvious way: create a chord with two noteheads of the same pitch, then add an accidental to each as normal.

Other composers add the second notehead on a diagonal stem called a "stalk" (see right-hand picture). To write this, add the stalked notehead using one of the stalk symbols provided on the **Create ▸ Symbol** dialog (shortcut **Z**). (However, the disadvantage of this notation is that the extra notehead will not transpose or play back, as it is a symbol.)

Typing accidentals in text

You might want to add accidentals into text objects in your score – for example, if you wanted the title to include the key of the piece.

To type accidentals in text, type **Ctrl** *or* ⌘ and the numeric keypad key that corresponds to the accidental on the first Keypad layout (shortcut **F7**), e.g. **Ctrl+8** *or* ⌘8 produces a sharp sign, and **Ctrl+9** *or* ⌘9 a flat sign. Note that **Num Lock** must be switched on in order for this to work. Alternatively, just right-click (Windows) *or* **Control**-click (Mac) and choose the accidental from the word menu.

Moving accidentals

Accidentals are automatically positioned. For instance, if you add an accidental to a chord that already has some, the accidentals will shift positions if necessary to avoid colliding.

In the unlikely event that you want to move an accidental, just drag it horizontally with the mouse, or nudge it by typing Shift+Alt+←/→ *or* ⇧⌥←/→. To move in large steps, use Ctrl+Shift+Alt+←/→ *or* ⇧⌥⌘←/→.

If you need accidentals above the staff (e.g. for ficta) then you can use a symbol from the Create ▸ Symbol dialog, or if you want the ficta to play back, use the Add Ficta Above Note plug-in – see **Add Ficta Above Note** on page 484.

Playback of microtonal accidentals

Most playback devices provide a pitch bend function that can alter a note according to 32 equal divisions of a half-step (semitone), most easily accessed via Plug-ins ▸ Playback ▸ Quarter-tone Playback.

To alter the tuning of a note, first add a quarter-tone accidental. Repeat as necessary, then select the passage you want to retune (make sure to include the next note in normal tuning, so that the MIDI pitch bend will return to zero). Choose Plug-ins ▸ Playback ▸ Quarter-tone Playback, and click OK twice.

Now the notes you want to retune have an invisible MIDI pitch bend command attached to them (these invisible commands appear in gray if you switch on View ▸ Hidden Objects) that raises the pitch by a quarter-tone: ~B0,80. ~B0,64 returns the affected staff to normal tuning. You can edit this pitch bend command to apply values other than a quarter-tone by double-clicking it, and changing it as follows:

* ~B0,64 = normal tuning
* ~B0,80 = quarter-tone sharp
* ~B0,96 = half-step (semitone) sharp
* ~B0,48 = quarter-tone flat, etc.

Each increment is approximately 3 cents, a cent being 1/100th of a half-step (semitone). Therefore, if you want a pitch, say, 15 cents flat, you can edit the pitch bend command to be 5 less (15/3) than 64: ~B0,59. (Lowering the third of a major triad by this amount will create a more harmonious chord.) If you're not using quarter-tones as such and don't want the quarter-tone accidental, you may now delete it and the pitch bend MIDI message will remain.

Note that, due to the nature of MIDI channels, only one pitch bend command is possible at a time per instrument, so that different notes in a chord cannot be retuned by different amounts. If you attempt to attach different pitch bends to two different notes in a chord, the plug-in will mark the chord with an X to alert you to the failure to achieve your desired pitch bend.

For more details about the plug-in, see **Quarter-tone Playback** on page 512. For more information about MIDI pitch bend messages, see **Pitch bend** on page 357.

Engraving Rules options

In the even more unlikely event that you want to change the spacing between or around accidentals throughout a score, there are excitingly obscure options for this available on the Accidentals and Dots and Clefs and Key Signatures pages of the House Style ▸ Engraving Rules dialog (shortcut Ctrl+Shift+E *or* ⇧⌘E).

(Answer to transposing question: D quarter-sharp. We'll leave the scale for you to work out.)

2.2 Arpeggios

📖 **1.2 Keypad**, **2.21 Lines**, **4.9 Playback dictionary**.

In keyboard, harp and guitar music, it's common to see a vertical wiggly line denoting that the notes of the adjacent chord should be "spread" from bottom to top, or in the direction implied by an arrowhead on the line.

Creating an arpeggio

To create an arpeggio, select a note or chord, then choose the fifth Keypad layout (shortcut **F11**), where you will find three variants: a regular arpeggio line (shortcut **/** on Windows, **=** on Mac); an arpeggio line with an upwards-pointing arrowhead at the top (shortcut ***** on Windows, **/** on Mac); and an arpeggio line with a downwards-pointing arrowhead at the bottom (shortcut **−** on Windows, ***** on Mac).

Sibelius automatically creates the arpeggio to an appropriate length, and as you add or remove notes from the chord, or change their pitches, the length is updated automatically. You can also adjust the length of an individual arpeggio line by dragging either end (or selecting the end of the arpeggio and using the ↑/↓ keys). To restore the default length, choose **Layout ▸ Reset Position**.

You can also move arpeggios left and right with **Shift+Alt+←/→** *or* ⇧⌥←/→, if need be.

Engraving Rules options

The Lines page of House Style ▸ Engraving Rules contains a number of subtle options for determining the default length and positioning of arpeggios.

Space before arpeggios

You can change the minimum distance Sibelius tries to maintain before arpeggio lines in House Style ▸ Note Spacing Rule – 📖 **8.9 Note spacing**.

Changing arpeggio design

If you want, you can change the thickness of the wiggles used by arpeggios – 📖 **8.15 Edit Lines**.

Interpretation during playback

You can define how quickly the three types of arpeggio should play back by choosing **Arpeggio**, **Arpeggio Down** or **Arpeggio Up** on the **Staff Lines** page of Play ▸ Dictionary – 📖 **4.9 Playback dictionary**.

Printing problems

Some printer drivers have a bug that makes wiggly lines print in the wrong place; if you find this happens, 📖 **5.16 Printing**.

2.3 Articulations

📖 **1.1 Note input**.

Articulations are symbols above or below a note, chord or rest that indicate a playing technique, such as staccato, accent and down-bow. You can create and delete articulations in much the same way as accidentals.

Unusual articulation marks

You may not be familiar with the following articulation marks:

ᐟ *Staccatissimo (very short)*

ᐱ *Marcato*

⊓ *Medium pause*

ᐱ *Short pause*

V *Up-bow (for stringed instruments)*

⊓ *Down-bow*

○ *Harmonic, open hi-hat*

+ *Closed hi-hat (percussion), muted or hand-stopped (brass), left-hand pizzicato (strings), trill (some Baroque music)*

Creating articulations with a note

When you create a note, you can create articulations with it at the same time by choosing one or more articulations from the first or fourth Keypad layout before putting the note into the score. (You can also add accidentals, ties, rhythm dots, special noteheads, tremolos and non-standard beaming from the Keypad at the same time.)

Adding articulations to existing notes

To add articulations to a selected note or notes, simply choose the articulation(s) from the first or fourth Keypad layout.

When adding articulations to a chord, it doesn't matter which of the noteheads is selected, as articulations apply to all notes in a chord.

Removing particular articulations

- Select the note(s) in question, then choose the articulation(s) from the Keypad, to switch them off.
- Alternatively, the slow and fiddly way is to select the articulation(s) with the mouse (taking care not to select the associated note(s) at the same time), then hit **Delete**.
- To remove all articulations at once, choose the note(s) in question, then choose the fourth Keypad layout (shortcut **F10**) and hit **0** or click the corresponding button shown on the right.

Moving articulations

Articulations are automatically positioned. For instance, if you add an articulation to a note that already has one, they will shift positions to remain in the correct order and allow room for the new one. Sibelius also follows the most common conventions for the placement of articulations relative to the end points of slurs and tuplet brackets.

Occasionally, though, you might want to move an articulation. For example, an articulation is sometimes put at the "wrong" end if all articulations in the vicinity are at that end; so if there are six notes with staccatos, five of which have the staccato above the note, you can move the remaining staccato above the note to follow the pattern even if it should otherwise go below.

To flip an articulation, select it and choose Edit ▸ Flip (shortcut X) to flip it to the other side of the note. When you flip an articulation, the operation applies to *all* articulations attached to a note, except for any articulations which are only allowed to appear above the note, which will stay where they are. In the unlikely event that you do need to place some articulations above the note and others below in a manner that is not automatically accommodated by Sibelius, you can use symbols from Create ▸ Symbol instead of "real" articulations.

To move an articulation, use the arrow keys (or drag with the mouse) to move the articulation vertically. (As usual, Ctrl+↑/↓ *or* ⌘↑/↓ moves in larger steps.) If multiple articulations are stacked above or below a note, moving the articulation nearest the note will move the other articulations by the same amount; if you want to increase the distance between two individual articulations, select the one furthest from the notehead and move that one.

To undo all changes in position produced by flipping or moving articulations, select the affected note and choose Layout ▸ Reset Position. To move an individual articulation back to its original position, select only that articulation and choose Layout ▸ Reset Position.

To reposition articulations throughout the score, see **Engraving Rules options** below.

Copying articulations

When you copy a note or chord with Alt+click *or* ⌥-click or Edit ▸ Repeat (shortcut R), the articulations are copied too, which saves time. You can also use Plug-ins ▸ Notes and Rests ▸ Copy Articulations and Slurs to copy patterns of articulations from one passage to another without affecting the notes themselves – see **Copy Articulations and Slurs** on page 502.

Interpretation during playback

Sibelius plays back articulations as realistically as your playback devices will allow – 📖 **4.2 Interpretation of your score** and 📖 **4.9 Playback dictionary**.

Articulations on rests

The three types of fermata (pause) are the only articulations you can add to a rest, because the others don't make a lot of sense.

In the unlikely event that you should want some other articulation on a rest, obtain it using a symbol. (For instance, in scores by Stockhausen and other contemporary composers, accents on rests have occasionally been sighted, which apparently represent the sharp intake of breath induced by unexpected syncopation.)

When you add a fermata to a bar rest, it applies to all staves, and as a result is copied to all staves (and any instrumental parts).

Fermatas (pauses) on barlines

You might want to place a fermata (pause) above or below a barline; to do this, simply create it from the Create ▸ Symbol dialog (shortcut Z), setting it to attach to System. This creates a system symbol that will appear in all parts.

Keyboard shortcuts

Though all of the articulations can be accessed via the standard keyboard shortcuts for the Keypad, it is also possible to assign extra shortcuts to individual articulations – 📖 **1.2 Keypad**.

Custom articulations

If you want to change the appearance of articulations, edit them in House Style ▸ Edit Symbols –
📖 **8.17 Edit Symbols**.

There are three unused spaces on the fourth Keypad layout to which you can assign further
articulations if desired, corresponding to three spaces in the **Articulations** rows of House Style ▸
Edit Symbols:

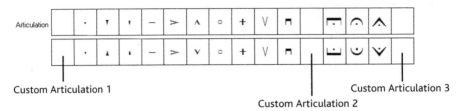

Which empty slot you use affects the order in which your new articulation will stack when
combined with other articulations; articulation 1 will go nearest the notehead, and 3 goes furthest
from the notehead. As you can see from the image above, you must define an "above" and "below"
symbol for every articulation, though in most cases these are actually the same symbol instead of
inverted versions.

Having defined your three custom articulations, be aware that the buttons on the fourth Keypad
layout won't update to show your new symbols, and that custom articulations are only available in
the score in which you redefined them; to make them available in other scores, export the house
style (📖 **8.8 House Style™**).

Articulations above the staff

In music for some instruments – for instance, percussion and singers – it is preferable to have
articulations always above the staff. Sibelius does this automatically for some instruments.

If you need to force articulations to appear above the staff for another instrument, switch on the
option **Always position articulations above the staff** on the **Notes and Rests** tab of the **Staff
Type** dialog (accessible from the **Edit Instrument** dialog – 📖 **8.14 Edit Instruments**).

Engraving Rules options

The Articulations page of the House Style ▸ Engraving Rules dialog (shortcut Ctrl+Shift+E *or* ⇧⌘E) has various fascinating options:

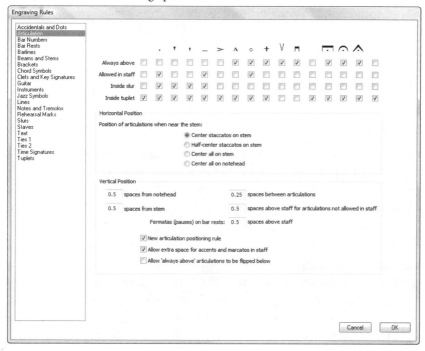

The four rows of checkboxes determine the positioning behaviour of all 16 types of articulations:

- **Always above:** most articulations go below most notes which have stems up, but some (including bowing marks) go above notes regardless of their stem direction. In some kinds of scores (e.g. jazz or commercial music) it may be preferable to show all articulations above the staff – see **Articulations above the staff** above.

- **Allowed in staff:** most publishers draw staccatos and tenutos in the staff, some draw harmonics, a few draw accents. We wouldn't recommend putting other articulations in the staff as, depending on the music font used, they wouldn't fit between two staff lines and so would be illegible.

- **...inside slur:** there are different conventions for whether the end point of a slur or certain articulations should appear closer to the notehead. Sibelius follows the most common convention by default, which is that staccato and tenuto articulations should go inside the slur, and other articulations should go outside the slur.

- **...inside tuplet:** as with slurs, there are different conventions for whether the tuplet bracket or certain articulations should appear closer to the notehead. By default, Sibelius only positions bowing marks outside tuplet brackets.

The **Position of articulation when near the stem** options are:

- **Center staccatos on stem:** this, the default choice, positions any articulations that are at the stem end of the note automatically: it centers the articulations on the stem if the nearest articulation is a staccato, staccatissimo or wedge. If the articulations are at the notehead end, they are positioned as normal.

- **Half-center staccatos on stem**: this option is identical to **Center staccatos on stem**, except that it centers the articulations halfway between the stem and the middle of the notehead, if the nearest articulation to the stem is a staccato, staccatissimo or wedge
- **Center all on stem**: fairly obviously makes articulations center on the stem rather than the notehead when at the stem end
- **Center all on notehead**: makes articulations at the stem end centered on the notehead, to one side of the stem.

The **Vertical position** options are:

- *n* **spaces from notehead**: when articulations go at the notehead end of a note/chord, this is the distance of the nearest articulation. If the articulation is forced outside the staff it will be further away than this.
- *n* **spaces from stem**: the corresponding distance when articulations go at the stem end
- *n* **spaces between articulations**: the distance between articulations when more than one is attached to a note
- *n* **spaces above staff for articulations not allowed in staff**: the distance between the top or bottom staff line and the innermost articulation that is not permitted to be drawn in the staff
- **Fermatas (pauses) on bar rests** *n* **spaces above staff** controls the distance above the staff of fermatas on bar rests. Normally this should be set to the same value as *n* **spaces above staff for articulations not allowed in staff**.
- **New articulation positioning rule** should normally be switched on, as it improves the positioning of articulations in various subtle ways
- **Allow extra space for accents, marcatos, wedges and staccatissimos in staff**: when switched on, this option will ensure that accents, marcatos, wedges and staccatissimos do not appear in the space adjacent to a note in the middle two spaces in the staff; instead, the closest articulation will appear one space removed from the notehead. This option only has any effect if accents, marcatos, wedges or staccatissimos are set to be **Allowed in staff**.
- **Allow "always above" articulations to be flipped below** should normally be switched off. In earlier versions of Sibelius it was possible to flip articulations that have **Always above** switched on below the staff; this option only exists to ensure that scores created in those earlier versions can appear the same when opened in the current version of Sibelius.

2.4 Barlines

Sibelius supports a wide variety of barlines, suitable for various kinds of music, which you can put at the end or in the middle of a bar.:

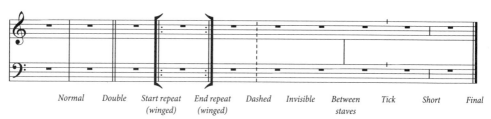

| Normal | Double | Start repeat (winged) | End repeat (winged) | Dashed | Invisible | Between staves | Tick | Short | Final |

Barlines at the end of bars

You don't need to put normal barlines at the end of bars into the score: just add bars, and barlines appear after every bar.

You can move barlines by dragging them left and right, or using the ←/→ keys (with **Ctrl** *or* ⌘ for larger steps). This changes the gap after the last note/rest.

You can't delete a barline in order to join two bars together; instead, you should normally double the length of the time signature (or create an irregular bar) to fit the music into one bar. Similarly, to split a bar into two, you should normally shorten the time signature instead of trying to draw a new barline.

Double barlines

Double barlines are used to denote new sections.

A double barline usually appears at a key signature change, but not at a time signature change or to coincide with rehearsal marks (unless these occur at the beginning of a new section).

Other barlines

These include double barlines, dotted barlines, repeat barlines, early music barlines, and so on. To create one, select the note after which you want the barline to appear, then choose the type of barline you want from **Create ▸ Barline**. Alternatively, you can place the barline with the mouse if you hit **Esc** to deselect everything before you create the barline you want.

When putting a barline in the middle of a bar, input the music in the bar first; then add the barline between two specific notes or rests. (If you inputted the barline first, it wouldn't be clear exactly where in the bar it was meant to go.) The barline may attach to the bar too close to the following note; if this happens, select the barline and change the **X** parameter on the **General** panel of the Properties window to change its offset.

If a barline occurs in the middle of a bar that has a bar rest in it, then in the interests of good notation you should split the bar rest into separate rests on either side of the barline.

It's common to split a bar between systems at a double barline or repeat barlines (e.g. at the end of a line of a hymn). To do this in Sibelius, create two shorter (irregular) bars and use a system break to split them between systems – 📖 **2.5 Bars and bar rests** and **8.5 Breaks**.

You can copy, drag and delete barlines; deleting any of these other barlines at the end of a bar (even an invisible barline) turns it back into a normal barline.

Final double barline

When you start a new score you are given a final double barline at the end, but you can delete it if you don't want it.

You're entirely permitted to put more than one final double barline into a score, for instance if it consists of more than one movement, song or piece.

Repeat barlines

Create start and end repeat barlines in the same way as other special barlines. To create 1st and 2nd endings (1st-/2nd-time bars), 📖 **2.21 Lines**.

If you want to create winged repeat barlines, common in handwritten and jazz music, switch on **Wings on repeat barlines** on the **Barlines** page of the **House Style ▸ Engraving Rules** dialog.

To create a double-repeat barline, which goes between two repeated sections,

put an **End repeat** barline at the end of the first bar and a **Start repeat** at the start of the second bar. You can drag the two repeat barlines further apart or closer together if you really want to.

Early music barlines

Sibelius includes barlines suitable for preparing editions of early music. In vocal music predating the convention of time signatures, one method used by editors to help present-day performers understand the metrical divisions of the music is to add barlines between the staves (sometimes called *mensurstriche*).

To use these barlines in your score, set the **Default barline type** to **Between Staves** on the **Barlines** page of the **House Style ▸ Engraving Rules** dialog (shortcut **Ctrl+Shift+E** or **⇧⌘E**).

Some editors prefer the convention that the music should behave as if the barlines are present, with notes over barlines being tied (as shown below on the left), and others prefer the opposite convention, with the music written as if there are no barlines at all (as shown below on the right):

Sibelius automatically ties notes across barlines, so your music will, by default, look like the left-hand example above. If you prefer the other convention, use irregular bars where appropriate to create a single bar of twice the normal length (📖 **2.5 Bars and bar rests**), then add the barline in the correct place yourself.

You can also create **Tick** and **Short** barlines, which are useful for notating plainsong:

These barlines are most useful in passages of music for a single instrument (or voice), but you can use them in music for multiple instruments if you want.

Designing your own barlines

While it is not possible to design new kinds of barlines that will appear in the Create ▸ Barline menu, it is possible to modify the appearance of normal barlines on an instrument by instrument basis, using the House Style ▸ Edit Instruments dialog – ⌨ **8.14 Edit Instruments**.

Barline joins

*For clarity, staves are normally joined by barlines to group similar instruments together. These groups often, but by no means always, reflect the way staves are grouped with brackets (⌨ **2.9 Brackets and braces**).*

In orchestral scores, staves with the woodwind, brass, percussion and string sections are normally joined by barlines but separated from adjacent sections.

Vocal staves are never joined to each other, nor to other instruments. Staves for the same keyboard instrument are joined together but separated from adjacent instruments.

When a score uses just a few instruments (such as a wind quintet), an unbroken barline is used to avoid looking fussy.

Barline joins

Sibelius automatically joins staves into groups of similar instruments with barlines (see box). However, you may want to change this, as follows:

• Preferably find a point in the score where there are no hidden staves, so you can check all barline joins at once

• Click carefully at the top or bottom of a normal barline (you can't use special barlines to change barline joins) in the score; a purple square "handle" will appear

• Drag the handle up or down the system to extend or contract the barline. This affects every system in the score simultaneously.

• You'll find that by extending or contracting the barlines down the system you can reorganize the way staves are joined by barlines any way you like.

Invisible barlines

You can hide a barline at the end of a bar by replacing it with an "invisible" barline from the Create ▸ Barline menu. The invisible barline appears light gray when View ▸ Hidden Objects is switched on (shortcut Ctrl+Alt+H *or* ⌥⌘H), but disappears when this option is switched off.

The main use of an invisible barline is to notate a bar split between two systems (see **Split bars** below). Because the bars on either side are still really separate, there are three inevitable side-effects: some rhythms can't run over the invisible barline (you may have to use tied notes); bar numbering will apparently get a bar out after the barline (but you can correct this with a bar number change – ⌨ **3.5 Bar numbers**); and bar rests will appear as two bar rests, one on either side. So use invisible barlines with care.

If you want to hide all the barlines in your score, change the Default barline type to Invisible on the Barlines page of the House Style ▸ Engraving Rules dialog (shortcut Ctrl+Shift+E *or* ⇧⌘E).

If you want to hide all the barlines in, say, a single staff, or all the staves belonging to an instrumental family, see **Hiding barlines on some staves only** below.

Hiding barlines on some staves only

To hide all the barlines in an instrumental family (where the staves are all joined by a continuous barline), click the top or bottom of the barline so that the purple handle appears, then hit **Delete**.

To restore barlines to those staves, click the top or bottom of the barline on an adjacent staff, and drag it across the staves with no barlines.

To hide all the barlines in a particular staff, define a new instrument with no barlines (📖 **8.14 Edit Instruments**):

- Select a bar in the staff in which you want to hide the barlines
- Choose **House Style ▸ Edit Instruments**
- You should see that the instrument in question is selected in the dialog; click **New Instrument**, and click **Yes** when prompted if you're sure you want to proceed
- In the **New Instrument** dialog that appears, change the **Name in dialogs** to something that you'll remember, then click **Edit Staff Type**
- On the **General** tab, switch off the **Barlines** option, then click **OK**
- Click **OK** in the **New Instrument** dialog and make sure that your new instrument is in a suitable ensemble so that you can find it.
- If you want no barlines in a particular staff throughout the whole score, make sure nothing is selected, then choose **Create ▸ Other ▸ Instrument Change**, choose your new instrument, click **OK**, then click at the start of the staff on the first page, to the left of the initial barline.
- If you want no barlines to appear for a particular passage, select the bar at which you want the change to occur, then **Create ▸ Other ▸ Instrument Change**, choose your new instrument, and click **OK**.

Initial barlines on single-staff systems

In lead sheets, it's customary for initial barlines to be drawn at the start of each system, even though normally initial barlines only appear where there are two or more staves in the system. To make an initial barline appear on single-staff systems, switch on **Barline at start of single staves** on the **Barlines** page of the **House Style ▸ Engraving Rules** dialog.

Split bars

It is sometimes desirable to split a bar into two halves, the first half at the end of one system and the second at the start of the next system. To do this, use **Plug-ins ▸ Other ▸ Split Bar** – 📖 **6.1 Working with plug-ins**.

Because split bars are still really two bars separated by an invisible barline, they have the same three drawbacks as invisible barlines (see above).

Engraving Rules options

The options on the **Barlines** page of the **House Style ▸ Engraving Rules** dialog (shortcut **Ctrl+Shift+E** *or* ⇧⌘E) allow you to change the default barline in your score to any of the other designs, which is useful for scores where you want most or all barlines to be invisible, or dashed, or in between the staves, etc.

You can also choose whether or not to use winged repeat barlines and adjust the thickness of barlines and the separation of double barlines, should you be struck by an irrepressible urge to do this.

2.5 Bars and bar rests

📖 **1.1 Note input**, **2.24 Multirests**.

Adding bars to the end of the score

Choose **Create ▸ Bar ▸ At End** (shortcut **Ctrl+B** *or* ⌘**B**) to add a single bar to the end of the score.

To add lots of bars, hold **Ctrl+B** *or* ⌘**B** down and, after a short delay, it will "auto-repeat."

Adding bars in the middle of a score

Choose **Create ▸ Bar ▸ Single** (shortcut **Ctrl+Shift+B** *or* ⇧⌘**B**), then click in the score where you want to create the bar.

Create ▸ Bar ▸ Single with a note, rest, or other object selected adds a bar after the one containing the selected object.

Alternatively, select the point in your score where you want to add more bars, choose **Create ▸ Bar ▸ Other** (shortcut **Alt+B** *or* ⌥**B**); type in the **Number of bars** you want, click **OK**, and Sibelius creates the bars. If you had nothing selected when you chose **Create ▸ Bar ▸ Other**, the mouse pointer will change color to show it is "loaded" with the empty bars, and you can click in your score to place them.

Deleting a bar entirely

To delete a bar, simply select it, then choose **Edit ▸ Delete Bars** (shortcut **Ctrl+Delete** *or* ⌘-**Delete**). This deletes everything in the bar and removes the bar itself. You can delete several bars at once by selecting them as a passage first – see **Selected passages** on page 55.

Deleting a bar in one staff

* Click an empty part of the bar, which ends up with a light blue box around it
* Hit **Delete** to turn it into a bar rest. This also deletes other objects in the bar attached to that staff (e.g. text).

You can delete the contents of several bars at once, or a bar in several staves, by selecting the bars and hitting **Delete** – see **Selected passages** on page 55.

Creating irregular bars

An irregular bar is one that is not the length specified by the previous time signature. Pick-up (upbeat) bars are a common example. To create an irregular bar:

* Choose **Create ▸ Bar ▸ Other** (shortcut **Alt+B** *or* ⌥**B**)
* In the dialog that appears, click **Irregular**
* From the drop-down menu, choose one or more note values adding up to the length you want, or type them on the numeric keypad (with **Num Lock** on)
* You can also specify a **Number of bars** if you want several irregular bars of the same length
* Click **OK**
* Click in the score where you want to create the bar(s).

Pick-up (upbeat) bars

Scores often start with a short bar, known as a *pick-up bar* (*upbeat bar*) or *anacrusis*. These are most easily created at the same time as creating the time signature (📖 **2.33 Time signatures**). Sibelius will automatically show the correct number of beats within the pick-up bar as rests, and will divide the rests it creates according to the time signature's Beam and Rest Groups. If you need to add a pick-up (upbeat) bar after creating the time signature:

- First make sure nothing is selected by hitting **Esc**.
- Choose **Create ▸ Bar ▸ Other**
- Create a bar of the suitable length and click at the start of the score to put it before the first full bar.
- Select the time signature in the first full bar and hit **Delete**, answering **No** when asked if you want to rewrite the following bars.
- Create the time signature again at the start of the new pick-up bar, making sure to switch off **Rewrite bars up to next time signature** (📖 **2.33 Time signatures**).
- Finally, use **Create ▸ Other ▸ Bar Number Change** to create a bar number change to bar 0 at the start of your pick-up bar (📖 **3.5 Bar numbers**).

Changing the length of bars

To change the length of bars because you are changing the time signature they are in 📖 **2.33 Time signatures**.

To change the length of an individual bar (i.e. create/delete notes from it) while retaining the music:

- Create an irregular bar of the desired length (see below), just before or after the bar in question
- Copy across the music you want to keep, as a passage (📖 **1.9 Selections and passages**)
- Delete the original bar.

Creating a bar rest in one voice

- Select a note or rest in the bar
- Hit **N** to make the note input caret appear
- Go to the second Keypad layout (shortcut **F8**)
- Choose the voice you want the bar rest to go in, using the buttons at the bottom of the keypad (shortcut **Alt+1-4** *or* ⌥**1-4**)
- Choose the bar rest button (shortcut **0**).

This can be used either to create a bar rest in a voice that didn't previously exist, or to turn notes back into a bar rest in one voice only. However, this only deletes notes or rests and leaves other objects alone. If you want to delete text, lines and other objects too, select the bar and hit **Delete**.

Beware that a bar rest is not the same as a whole note (semibreve) rest. Bar rests are centered, while whole note rests go at the left of the bar, in the same place a whole note itself would go, as shown on the right.

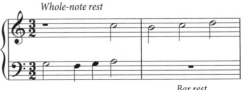

Whole-note rest

Bar rest

Deleting a bar rest symbol

Blank bars are useful if you want to put something else in the bar, such as a funny symbol. Select the bar rest symbol and choose Edit ▸ Hide or Show ▸ Hide (shortcut Ctrl+Shift+H *or* ⇧⌘H); the bar rest will then appear in gray if View ▸ Hidden Objects is switched on, but otherwise be invisible. If the music is in two voices, hit Delete first to clear the bar and restore the bar rest.

If you want blank bars throughout a score, as in some contemporary music, switch off Show bar rests on the Bar rests page of House Style ▸ Engraving Rules.

Changing a bar rest's width

Simply move the barline at the end.

Double whole note (breve) bar rests

In 4/2 and other time signatures where the bar length is equal to eight quarter notes (crotchets), Sibelius shows a double whole note (breve) bar rest, rather than a regular bar rest. If you would prefer Sibelius to show regular bar rests in all time signatures, switch off Use double whole note (breve) bar rests in 4/2 on the Bar rests page of House Style ▸ Engraving Rules (shortcut Ctrl+Shift+E *or* ⇧⌘E).

Moving a bar rest symbol

(Only really required when using two or more voices.)

Simply select the bar rest symbol and type ↑ or ↓. Sibelius won't let you move a bar rest left or right because – let's face it – it's not all that useful.

If you type Ctrl+↑/↓ *or* ⌘↑/↓ the bar rest moves by one and a half spaces, which is the right distance for the slightly larger guitar tab staves.

Split bars

It is sometimes desirable to split a bar into two halves, the first half at the end of one system and the second at the start of the next system. To do this, use Plug-ins ▸ Other ▸ Split Bar – see **Split Bar** on page 508.

General pause

A general pause is a rest in all instruments, normally lasting for at least one bar. For clarity, consider writing **G.P.** above the general pause bar using a system text style such as Tempo.

Notations

2.6 Beam groups

📖 **2.7 Beam positions**, **2.8 Beamed rests and stemlets**.

Beams are the thick lines used to join short notes into groups. Sibelius beams notes together into groups for you automatically, though you may sometimes want to adjust beaming yourself.

You can adjust beaming in many bars at once, or change it on a note-by-note basis if you want, including special notations such as cross-staff beaming.

Changing beam groups

Sibelius chooses sensible default beam groups for each time signature you create in your score, but depending on musical context you may prefer different groups. You can change the beam groups both for new time signatures you create, and for existing passages of music.

- To change the beam groups for a new time signature, choose **Create ▸ Time Signature** (shortcut T), select the time signature you want to create, and click **Beam and Rest Groups**.
- To change the beam groups for existing music, see **Resetting beam groups** below.

In either case, you will see a dialog with the following options:

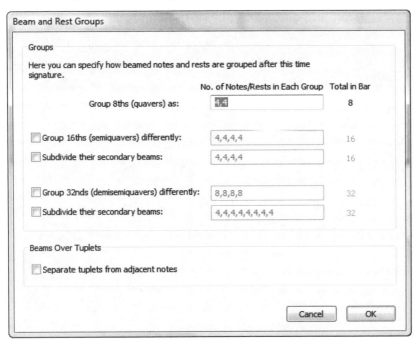

You can edit the beam groups for different note values independently. Beam groups are represented by the number of notes in each group, separated by commas, and they must add up to the number listed alongside the box in the **Total in Bar** column.

For example, in the time signature 4/4 you could set the **Group 8ths (quavers) as** option as follows:

As you edit the beam groups for one note value, shorter note values often inherit the same beam groups (except in 4/4 when eighth notes are set to beam in two groups of four, which is a special case – see below). This means that eighth note beam groups of (say) **5,2,1** would produce sixteenth note beam groups of **10,4,2**.

If you wish, you can override this behavior by setting the other options on the dialog, namely **Group 16ths (semiquavers) differently** and **Group 32nds (demisemiquavers) differently**. Again, you must ensure that the beam groups add up to the **Total in Bar** number alongside. Using our 4/4 example again, here are a few of the possibilities:

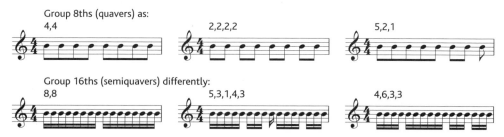

For any given time signature with a denominator larger than 8 (e.g. 9/16, 15/32, etc.) the longest note value you can adjust is the note value represented by the denominator (e.g. in 9/16 you cannot adjust eighth note (quaver) beam groups – they will always be beamed in pairs by default; in 15/32 you cannot adjust 16th note (semiquaver) groups either; these will always follow the eighth note beam groups).

Primary and secondary beams

The primary beam is the one furthest from the noteheads; secondary beams are any other beams, e.g.

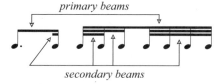

Notes grouped by secondary beams (which we'll call "sub-groups") should always indicate the rhythm as clearly as possible; this is achieved by splitting the sub-groups according to the smaller units of the beat. In simple time signatures, sub-groups typically occur every two eighth notes (quavers), and in compound time signatures, sub-groups often occur every three eighth notes. Sibelius handles all of this complexity for you, but allows you to define sub-groups in the **Beam and Rest Groups** and **Reset Beam Groups** dialogs if necessary.

Notations

To define sub-groups, switch on **Subdivide their secondary beams** for 16th notes (semiquavers) and/or 32nd notes (demisemiquavers), and type the sub-groups separated by commas, making sure that they add up to the number under **Total in Bar**. For example, in 6/8 you could subdivide 16th note secondary beam groups as follows:

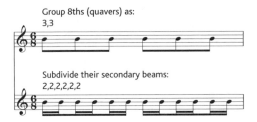

Sibelius only allows primary beams to be an eighth note (quaver) beam, i.e. a single beam. In some situations you may want 16th note (semiquaver) primary beams; in this case, add the extra beam using the line provided in the **Create ▸ Line** dialog (🕮 **2.21 Lines**).

Resetting beam groups

To regroup notes with beams, simply select the notes as a passage, then choose **Notes ▸ Reset Beam Groups**; a dialog will appear. If you want to reset the beam groups to Sibelius's defaults for the prevailing time signature, simply click **OK** without making any changes. If you want to regroup the notes according to your own preferences, change the settings in the dialog (see **Changing beam groups** above for details), and click **OK**.

The settings you choose in the **Notes ▸ Reset Beam Groups** dialog do not persist in the score after you apply them; if you edit the note values of the notes in bars you have reset, the beam groups will be reset to the groups specified in the prevailing time signature. If necessary, you can create a new time signature with the desired beam groups, click **Yes** when asked if you want the following bars rewritten, and then delete it after you finish inputting and editing (this time answering **No** when asked if you want the following bars rewritten).

Reusing beam groups

If you set up the beam groups for a time signature (e.g. 7/8) when creating it, those groupings will persist for all subsequent bars up to the next time signature change. But other 7/8 time signatures elsewhere in the same score will not necessarily have the same beam groups – setting up beam groups only affects that one time signature. However, if you want other 7/8 time signatures elsewhere in the same score to use the same beam groups, just copy the time signature.

If you want some 7/8 bars to use one beam grouping (e.g. 2+2+3) and others to use another (e.g. 3+2+2), create two 7/8 time signatures with the different groupings, then copy them to the relevant bars or passages, input the music, and then delete any superfluous time signatures (choosing **No** when asked if you want to the music to be rewritten).

Editing beam groups

To adjust beam groups in individual places, rather than setting them throughout the score or in a passage, you can use the buttons on the third Keypad layout (shortcut **F9**). Simply select the note(s), grace note(s) or rest(s) you want to adjust, then choose the appropriate button.

 Breaks the beam from the previous note

 Joins to the previous and next notes

 Ends the current beam (i.e. breaks the beam from the next note)

 Separates the note from those on either side

 Joins to the previous note with just a single (primary) beam.

Beams across barlines, system and page breaks

To make a note beam to the note before the previous barline, select the note at the start of the bar, choose the third Keypad layout (shortcut **F9**) and hit **8** on the numeric keypad.

If a beam over a barline happens to fall at a system or page break, Sibelius allows the beam to continue across the break, as in this example below from the bass clarinet part of Stravinsky's *Petrouchka*:

To make a beam continue across a barline, including a system or page break, use the **F10** Keypad layout to set the last note at the end of the system or page to **Start of beam** (shortcut **7** on the keypad) or **Middle of beam** (shortcut **8** on the keypad), and the first note of the note on the following system to **Middle of beam** (shortcut **8** on the keypad) or **End of beam** (shortcut **9** on the keypad).

If you need to adjust the angle of the beam, move the handle of the rightmost note's stem in the beam group *before* the break, and the stem's handle of the note at the rightmost end of the beam *after* the break. When you are not using Optical beam positions (see **Engraving Rules options** on page 96), adjusting the stem length of notes at the beginning of the beam will also have an effect on the slant of the beam. If a cross-staff beam is grouped to only one note after the break, its beam will be horizontal.

Beaming tuplets

If a tuplet falls within a beam group, it is typically joined to the other notes in the group (unless the notes in the tuplet are of the same duration as the notes on either side). However, you may prefer to always separate tuplets from notes on either side, to make the rhythm as clear as possible.

The option **Separate tuplets from adjacent notes** in the **Beam and Rest Groups** dialog, switched off by default, controls this behavior. You can see its effect in this example:

Switched off   *Switched on*
(default)

Beaming eighth notes (quavers) in 4s

By default, Sibelius beams eighth notes (quavers) in fours in simple duple (e.g. 2/4, 4/4, 2/2) time signatures. Four consecutive eighth notes that fall within beat divisions will be beamed together, but Sibelius will automatically break the beam groups if the rhythm within the group changes, e.g.

If you want to change this behavior, define new beam groups (e.g. set the **Group 8ths (quavers) as** option to **2,2,2,2** etc.) when creating the time signature, or when you choose **Notes▸ Reset Beam Groups** to reset the beaming of an existing passage. In addition, Sibelius does not apply this rule when **Beam over rests** (on the **Beams and Stems** page of **House Style▸ Engraving Rules**) is switched on (📖 **2.8 Beamed rests and stemlets**).

Feathered beams

In contemporary music, extra beams sometimes "splay out" from a single beam to indicate an accelerando or ritenuto, like this:

To create a feathered beam, select the first note of a beamed group or sub-group, switch to the third Keypad layout (shortcut F9), and then choose the desired type of feathered beam: click ▦ (shortcut 0) for an accelerando beam, or ▦ (shortcut .) for a ritenuto beam.

Feathered beams don't play back as an accelerando or ritenuto: if you want to produce an approximation for playback purposes, try using nested tuplets with hidden brackets – see **Nested tuplets** on page 193.

Hiding beams, flags and tails

To hide any beam, select it (not the note) and choose **Edit▸ Hide or Show▸ Hide** (shortcut Ctrl+Shift+H *or* ⇧⌘H). As with other objects, hidden beams are displayed in light gray if **View▸ Hidden Objects** is switched on (shortcut Ctrl+Alt+H *or* ⌥⌘H), and invisible if it is switched off.

You can also hide flags and tails, e.g. on single eighth notes (quavers), in the same way: select the flag or tail and choose **Edit ▸ Hide or Show ▸ Hide**. If you have beamed notes with flags (say, a dotted eighth note (quaver) followed by a sixteenth note (semiquaver)), you can even hide the flag independently of the main beam.

Hiding, say, the beam on a pair of eighth notes (quavers) doesn't actually turn them into quarter notes (crotchets) – it just makes them look like quarter notes!

Engraving Rules options

The **Beams and Stems** page of **House Style ▸ Engraving Rules** contains all the options concerning the appearance and position of beams. The **Beam Positions** options are explained on page 96, and the **Beamed Rests** options are explained on page 99.

Meanwhile, the options under **Beam Appearance** are self-explanatory, controlling the thickness and separation of the beam lines, and whether groups of beamed notes should be allowed to begin with a rest.

Perhaps most notable is the **French beams** option, where the stems of the notes in the beamed group only touch the innermost beam, as shown on the right. This convention is used particularly in music published in France (hence the name).

Notations

2.7 Beam positions

📖 **2.6 Beam groups**, **2.8 Beamed rests and stemlets**.

Beams are positioned vertically in and above or below the staff according to a complex set of conventions designed to ensure maximum legibility: a beam is, generally speaking, angled according to the contour of the notes in the beamed group, and the angle of the beam is determined by the position of each end, which must either sit on, straddle (i.e. be centered upon) or hang from a staff line.

Sibelius follows these principles through a set of rules we call Optical beam positions, so fortunately you don't need to worry about beam positions unless you really want to. Should you want to adjust beam positions, however, either on a case-by-case basis or for your entire score, Sibelius offers you complete control.

Beam angles

Occasionally you may want to adjust a beam's angle or position, either to prevent it hitting a grace note or other obstacle, or because you are a music engraver and have your own views on where beams should go. If you want to adjust many beams, it's better to adjust the **Engraving Rules** for beams (see **Engraving Rules options** below) so you can control beam angles en masse.

To move a beam, zoom in close on it so you can see what you're doing, and simply drag either end up or down with the mouse. When you drag the left-hand end, you alter the height of both ends of the beam, and when you drag the right-hand end, you alter the angle. Instead of dragging with the mouse, you can type ↑ or ↓. **Ctrl+↑/↓** *or* **⌘↑/↓** moves the beam by 0.25 spaces. You can also make quick adjustments to the angle of a beam by selecting the beam itself and dragging up and down; this does the same as dragging the left-hand end of the beam.

To set a beam back to its normal position, choose **Notes ▸ Reset Stems and Beam Positions**, which you can also do to a selected passage or multiple selection.

Adjusting a beam's angle is exactly the same thing as adjusting the lengths of the stems the beam is attached to.

Level beams

In some music (e.g. for percussion) it is customary for beams always to be flat, and never drawn at an angle. Sibelius always produces level beams on percussion staves by default, but if you want to use this convention on other instruments, edit the instrument in question using **House Style ▸ Edit Instruments**. In the **Edit Instrument** dialog, click **Edit Staff Type** and switch on **Beams always horizontal** on the **Notes and Rests** page – 📖 **8.14 Edit Instruments**.

Reversing beams

To move a beam from above a group of notes to below it – that is, to flip the stem-directions of all the notes along the beam – select any note in the group (just one note will do) and flip it by choosing **Edit ▸ Flip** (shortcut **X**); 📖 **2.30 Stems and leger lines** if you're not clear how. To restore the stem direction, flip the *same* note back, or select the group of notes and choose **Notes ▸ Reset Stems and Beam Positions**.

If **Edit ▸ Flip** doesn't seem to work on a beamed note, select all the notes along the beam and choose **Notes ▸ Reset Stems and Beam Positions**. Then flip just the first note.

Flipping fractional beams

Occasionally a fractional beam (also called a "flag") in a beamed group of notes will end up pointing leftwards when you want it to point right, or vice versa. To flip it the other way, select the note, and on the **Notes** panel of the Properties window switch on **Flip fractional beam**.

Cross-staff beams

Music for keyboard instruments often contains beamed notes flowing between the hands, like this:

To obtain this result:

- Input all of the music onto the staff that uses most of the music that crosses between the hands – in this case, the top staff:

- Select the notes that should cross over to the bottom staff (preferably as a multiple selection) – in this case, the B and Gs with leger lines
- Cross them to the staff below by choosing **Notes ▸ Cross-Staff Notes ▸ Move Down a Staff** (shortcut **Ctrl+Shift+↓** *or* ⇧⌘↓).

  Unsurprisingly, **Notes ▸ Cross-Staff Notes ▸ Move Up a Staff** (shortcut **Ctrl+Shift+↑** *or* ⇧⌘↑) crosses notes to the staff above.

  If you get into a muddle, you can also use **Notes ▸ Cross-Staff Notes ▸ Move to Original Staff**.

- You can put beams above both staves (as in the first beamed group in the first picture above) or between the staves (as in the last beamed group) simply by flipping the directions of the stems as appropriate by choosing **Edit ▸ Flip** (shortcut **X**).

  Don't do this by dragging the stems to the other side of the notes – this won't have the effect you intended!

- In the first picture above, the stems of the last three low notes in the left hand were also flipped to avoid colliding with the notes crossing from the right hand.

Note also that:

- Notes do not have to have beams to be crossed to an adjacent staff. You can even cross rests over.

- Notes can only cross over to another staff in the same instrument.
- You can beam across *three* staves by inputting the notes onto the middle staff, then crossing notes to the staves above and below. (It is not necessary for any notes to remain on the middle staff!)
- Notes crossing onto another staff do not affect that staff's voices at all. A staff can even have four voices plus further notes crossing onto it from adjacent staves!
- Notes are in many respects treated as being on the original staff – for example, if you transpose a passage on the original staff, then any notes that were crossed from that staff will also transpose.
- In some circumstances you may encounter redundant accidentals when you cross notes to another staff. Simply select the accidentals and hide them to solve this problem – 📖 **2.1 Accidentals**.

Beams between notes on the same staff

In older scores, particularly for violin music, if a group of notes is very low, then very high (or vice versa), you will sometimes see the beam running through the middle of the notes, with some stems pointing up and some pointing down, as shown above left.

To achieve this in Sibelius, input the notes as usual, then select the beam, which will either be above or below the beamed group, and drag it (or use the arrow keys) to move the whole beam up or down so that it is between the notes. To adjust the angle of the beam, select the right-hand end of the beam and drag it with the mouse or nudge it with ↑/↓.

Chords split between staves

It is common in keyboard music to split the notes of some chords between the two staves:

To achieve this, write each note of the split chord onto the staff it appears on, using a suitable voice; for example, in the case illustrated, put the treble notes of the split chords into voice 2 on the upper staff, and the bass notes in voice 1 on the lower staff. Then use Edit ▸ Flip (shortcut X) to point the stems of the notes on the lower staff downward. Finally, drag the end of each stem in the right hand downwards so that it meets the stem of the left-hand note.

In the case of chords using notes shorter than a quarter note (crotchet), hide the flags or beams by selecting them and typing Ctrl+Shift+H or ⇧⌘H, then extend their stems, flipping them if necessary using Edit ▸ Flip, to meet the rest of the chord.

Engraving Rules options

The Beams and Stems page of House Style ▸ Engraving Rules allows you to control the positions of beams and also their appearance (see page 93).

Most of the Beam Positions options only apply if Optical beam positions is switched on. (Switching off Optical beam positions will position beams according to the rules used in Sibelius 3 and earlier, which are generally not as good.)

Where the interval between the first and last notes of a beam is no more than an octave, you can specify an "ideal" angle for each interval under Default slant per interval. For some beams this angle has to be adjusted because beams are not allowed to appear in certain positions, such as in between two staff lines. Also when two notes are very close together, producing a steep beam, the angle may have to be reduced to the value specified in **Maximum beam gradient: Up to an 8ve, 1 in** *n*.

Maximum beam gradient: 1 in *n* controls the angle for intervals greater than an octave. The beam follows the angle between the first and last noteheads, as long as it is no steeper than this value.

If notes in the middle of a beam curve towards the beam, producing a concave shape, it is normal for the beam to be horizontal. You can control this using **Horizontal if middle notes intrude by** *n* **spaces** (which specifies the distance a note must protrude through an imaginary line between the first and last notes to make the beam horizontal). By default, this same rule also applies to beamed groups that include rests in the middle of the group (switch off **Also for middle rests** if you want to exclude beamed rests when considering whether the beam should be horizontal).

Avoid simple wedges prevents some cases of "wedges" in groups of eighth notes (quavers). These are white triangles whose three sides are a beam, a stem and a staff line, and are believed to look irritating by some music engravers. Other engravers are very unconcerned about them: to avoid wedges, the stems have to be lengthened, which to some eyes is worse than the wedges themselves. Therefore this option is truly optional.

The stem lengths specified in **Default beamed stem length** are typically less than for normal notes (and will be shortened further for very high or low notes). However, this is offset by the fact that stems are lengthened again if necessary to move the beam to a good position. You can further control stem lengths using **Minimum length** *n* **spaces** at the bottom of the page, which affects both beamed and unbeamed notes.

Cross-staff beams are always horizontal by default (assuming **Optical beam positions** is on), and go in between two staves. If you want cross-staff beams to go at an angle you should drag them on a case-by-case basis.

Notations

2.8 Beamed rests and stemlets

📖 **2.6 Beam groups**, **2.7 Beam positions**.

Beaming across rests can make rhythms easier to read. In some modern scores, beamed rests sometimes have "stemlets" (sometimes called "half-stems"), which are short stems extending from the beam to the rest (or stopping just short of the rest). Sibelius can automatically beam across rests, both within a beam group and at either end, using stemlets, if required.

Beams across rests

You can determine whether Sibelius should beam across rests with the following options on the Beams and Stems page of House Style ▸ Engraving Rules:

- **Beam from and to rests** allows a beamed group to start and/or end with a rest
- **Beam over rests** means that rests won't break a beam group if they fall within the defined grouping.

Some examples of these options in action:

<table>
<tr><td>Beam from and to rests</td><td>Beam over rests</td></tr>
</table>

You will notice that beams are always horizontal in beamed groups that start or end with a rest, regardless of the pitches of the notes under the beam. Where rests occur in the middle of a beamed group but not at the start or the end, the beam angle will follow the contour of the notes as usual.

Where notes occur on many leger lines above or below the staff in single-voice passages, Sibelius positions the rests in the middle of the staff, as normal, and ensures that the beam does not collide with the rests, with the result that the stems are longer than normal, as shown in the image below left. If you move the rest (by selecting it and typing ↑/↓), the beam will automatically move until the stems are at their ideal length, as shown in the image below right.

If you do not want Sibelius to behave this way, switch off **Adjust stem lengths to avoid beamed rests** on the **Beams and Stems** page of House Style ▸ Engraving Rules, but beware that with this option switched off, beams may well collide with rests in the middle of beamed groups.

When rests of the same duration as the surrounding notes occur in a beamed group, some publishers prefer to break the secondary beam above or below the rest:

Break secondary beams *off*   Break secondary beams *on*

By default, Sibelius produces the result shown above left, but you can obtain the result shown above right by switching on **Break secondary beams** on the **Beams and Stems** page of **House Style ▸ Engraving Rules**.

Editing beams across rests

You can edit whether or not rests should be beamed on a per-rest basis using the buttons on the third Keypad layout (shortcut **F9**), regardless of whether or not **Beam over rests** or **Beam to and from rests** are switched on. The operation of these Keypad buttons is discussed on page 91.

To restore a beamed rest to its default state, select it and choose **Layout ▸ Reset Design**.

Stemlets

To use stemlets in your score, switch on **Use stemlets on beamed notes** on the **Beams and Stems** page of **House Style ▸ Engraving Rules**. The other options relating to stemlets are:

Make beams horizontal for groups with stemlets   Extend stemlets into staff

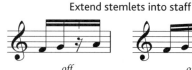

off   *on*   *off*   *on*

- **Make beams horizontal for groups with stemlets** tells Sibelius that the beam should always be horizontal if a stemlet is used in the group.
- When **Extend stemlets into staff** is switched on, stemlets can be drawn into the staff to extend towards the rests to which they belong. Sibelius will not allow a stemlet to be longer than the shortest stem on any of the notes in the beamed group by default; the stemlet will always end in the middle of the space outside the top or bottom of the rest.

  When **Extend stemlets into staff** is switched off, stemlets are drawn outside the staff, and end half a space above or below the top or bottom staff line (depending on whether the beam is above or below the staff). Sibelius enforces the **Minimum stemlet length** value in this case, and the result is that beamed groups including stemlets will always be horizontal when **Extend stemlets into staff** is switched off.
- **Minimum stemlet length** *n* **spaces** determines how far the stemlet should extend from the innermost beam. This is a minimum length rather than an absolute length, since stem length can vary depending on beam angle and the other settings that apply to stemlets.

Beamed groups that start or end with a rest will always draw with horizontal beams, but other beamed groups will have normal beam angles (unless **Extend stemlets into staff** is switched off). If you would prefer stemlets always to have horizontal beams, switch on **Make beams horizontal for groups with stemlets**.

Adjusting the length of a stemlet

To adjust the length of an individual stemlet, click on the end of the stemlet inside the beam: a small handle will appear. Click and drag with the mouse or use ↑/↓ (with **Ctrl** *or* ⌘ for larger steps) to adjust them. You can also use the **Y** parameter in the **General** panel of Properties to adjust the stemlet's length numerically. To reset a stemlet to its default length, select it and choose **Layout ▸ Reset Position**.

Notations

Manually editing stemlets

Stemlets can be added or removed for individual beamed rests using the new stemlet button on the third Keypad layout (shortcut – on Windows, * on Mac), shown on the left. In this way, you can create stemlets on specific beamed rests even if **Use stemlets on beamed rests** is turned off, or remove stemlets from specific beamed rests if they are shown everywhere else in the score.

To restore a beamed rest to its default state, select it and choose **Layout ▸ Reset Design**.

2.9 Brackets and braces

Brackets and braces are used at the left-hand side of systems to group similar instruments together. Sibelius chooses where they go by default, but you can change it if you like.

Notations

> **Brackets and braces**
>
> *Normally, instruments of the same family (e.g. woodwind, brass, percussion) are bracketed together. Percussion instruments and solo instruments are not normally bracketed.*
>
> *Instruments divided onto two or more staves, such as divisi strings, are joined by a sub-bracket (a thin bracket to the left of the normal one). Sub-brackets are also sometimes used to group similar instruments, e.g. Flute and Piccolo, Violin I and II. In older orchestral scores, curly braces are sometimes used instead of sub-brackets, particularly to group horns.*
>
> *Keyboard staves are joined with a brace, but an organ pedal staff is not braced to the organ manuals.*
>
> *Small groups of instruments are usually not bracketed at all.*
>
> *Instruments bracketed, sub-bracketed or braced together normally also have their staves joined by barlines.*

Moving brackets and braces

You can adjust which staves in a score are bracketed or braced together:

• Preferably find a point in the score where there are no hidden staves, so you can see all brackets and braces at once

• Click on the end of an existing bracket, sub-bracket or brace, so it turns purple

• Drag it up or down to extend or contract it

• To remove a selected bracket, sub-bracket or brace, simply hit **Delete**.

Adding a bracket, sub-bracket or brace

• From the **Create ▸ Other ▸ Bracket or Brace** menu, click **Bracket, Sub-bracket** or **Brace**

• Click to the left of a staff to put the bracket, sub-bracket or brace there

• Click and drag the top or bottom of it to extend it onto other staves.

Hiding a bracket or brace

Sibelius automatically hides brackets and braces if there is no barline at the left-hand side of the system. For example, if you hide one staff of a piano part, so that only one staff is visible, Sibelius hides the brace; similarly, if you hide all but one of a bracketed group of staves in one or more systems, Sibelius hides the bracket.

If you need to hide a bracket or brace in another situation (e.g. perhaps in a cut-away score), select the bar after the brace you want to hide, then open the **Bars** panel of the Properties window and switch off **Brackets**. For more information on properties of objects, □ **5.17 Properties**.

Placing braces mid-system

Occasionally in keyboard music (particularly organ music) it is necessary to show a brace in the middle of a system. This may also be necessary in "cut-away" scores (see **Staves with gaps in** on page 175), where a braced instrument is introduced halfway across a page.

If you need a brace to appear mid-system:

• Select the bar after whose initial barline you want the brace to appear

- Open the **Bars** panel of Properties, and increase **Gap before bar** very slightly with the arrows (e.g. to **0.03** or **0.06**) until a brace appears. (This effectively creates a divided system, like a coda, but with a minuscule gap.)
- Then in the same Properties panel switch off **Initial barline** and **Clefs**.

You will probably need to move the first note of the bar following the brace left to close the gap where the clefs would have gone: move it as far left as it will go, then with the note still selected decrease **X** in the **General** panel of Properties until it is correctly positioned (similarly for any note/rest at the start of the bar in the left hand). Then drag the second note leftwards until the gap between the first two notes is normal.

Note, however, that this method also causes brackets and braces to be restated for any other staves that appear at this point, which may not be desirable in a cut-away score. You can change this by defining a new instrument with the **Bracket** option (on the **General** page of the **Edit Staff Type** dialog, accessed from **Edit Instrument**) switched off; then apply an instrument change to the other staves that appear at this point. For further details, ⮡ **8.14 Edit Instruments**.

Style of brackets and braces

Various reassuringly obscure options can be found on the **Brackets** page of the **House Style ▸ Engraving Rules** dialog (shortcut **Ctrl+Shift+E** *or* ⇧⌘E), which allow you to adjust the thickness and position of brackets, sub-brackets and braces. These options are self-explanatory, except that the **Draw as brace** option for sub-brackets is for the old-fashioned style in which (for example) Violin I and II are joined by a brace rather than a sub-bracket.

If you are using Sibelius's Helsinki font, you will notice its brace is slightly thicker and more curvaceous than Opus's.

To create a bracket without hooks, used occasionally by composers such as Penderecki, modify a suitable bracket in the **House Style ▸ Edit Lines** dialog; simply set the **Cap** to **None**. You'll have to create this manually in your score – it won't automatically appear at the start of every system.

Braces are drawn by scaling a { symbol, found in the **General** row of the **Create ▸ Symbol** dialog. To change the brace design, substitute a brace character from a different music or text font (⮡ **2.31 Symbols**). Some printers can't print the brace as a stretched symbol; if you find that you can only print braces with the **Substitute Braces** option in the **File ▸ Print** dialog switched on, then your printer suffers from this limitation and you will not be able to change the design of braces in Sibelius.

2.10 Chord symbols

Chord symbols are objects that describe the harmony at that point in the music, and are commonly found in jazz, commercial and pop music compositions. Although many different chord symbol conventions are in use, depending mainly on the style of music, the most common convention uses the note name as the basis of the chord symbol.

 In Sibelius, a chord symbol consists of two parts, each of which may be displayed independently of the other if you like: chord text, and a chord diagram. Chord diagrams are sometimes known as *chord boxes*, *fretboard grids*, *guitar frames* and so on, and show graphically which fingers need to be on which fret on each string.

Regardless of whether you want either or both the chord text and the chord diagram to appear, any chord symbol can be input in one of two ways: by typing it into the score, or by playing it on a MIDI keyboard (or MIDI guitar).

Overview of creating chord symbols

* Select the note or rest on the staff above which you want to add chord symbols, and choose Create ▸ Chord Symbol (shortcut **Ctrl+K** *or* ⌘K, for "kord").
* A flashing cursor appears above the staff. Now either:
  ○ type the desired chord symbol, e.g. "Cmaj7" – see **Creating chord symbols by typing** below; or
  ○ play the chord on your MIDI keyboard in any voicing – see **Creating chord symbols by playing** below.
* Hit **Space** to advance the cursor to the next note or beat position (if you input a chord symbol via your MIDI keyboard, the cursor advances automatically); hit **Tab** to advance the cursor to the start of the next bar.
* If you make a mistake, hit **Backspace** to edit the previous chord symbol, or type **Shift-Tab** to jump back to the beginning of the previous bar.

Overview of editing chord symbols

You can edit chord symbols both globally and on an individual basis. Global edits include things like choosing how you want all chords with major 7ths in to appear, or whether you want guitar chord diagrams to appear on all staves or only on guitar notation staves, and so on. These settings are changed on the Chord Symbols page of House Style ▸ Engraving Rules, and in House Style ▸ Edit Chord Symbols, and are discussed in detail in 📖 **8.13 Edit Chord Symbols**.

Individual edits affect only the selected chord symbol:

* To edit an existing chord symbol, select it and hit **Return** (on the main keyboard) or double-click it.
* To enharmonically respell a chord symbol entered from the MIDI keyboard, e.g. a chord symbol based on F♯ that should be based on G♭, select the chord symbol, and choose Edit ▸ Chord Symbol ▸ Respell Chord Symbol, which is also available in the context menu when you right-click (Windows) *or* **Control**-click (Mac) with a chord symbol selected.

- To make a chord diagram appear or disappear for a single chord symbol, select it and choose **Edit ▸ Chord Symbol ▸ Add/Remove Chord Diagram**.
- To make chord text appear or disappear for a single chord symbol, select it and choose **Edit ▸ Chord Symbol ▸ Add/Remove Chord Text**.
- To cycle between equivalent text chord symbol types (e.g. Cm$^{7(b5)}$ and C^{ø7}), select the chord symbol and choose **Edit ▸ Chord Symbol ▸ Equivalent Chord Symbol**.
- To cycle between alternative voicings for the guitar chord diagram, select the chord symbol and choose **Edit ▸ Chord Symbol ▸ Revoice Chord Diagram**.

Creating chord symbols by typing

To type in chord symbols using the computer keyboard, you don't need to know how to type any special symbols, such as ø for half-diminished, or ∆ for major (or major 7th): simply start by using the keyboard shortcut **Ctrl+K** *or* **⌘K**, then type in a plain English version of the chord you want, and Sibelius will create any special symbols automatically as required, and following the preferences you have set on the **Chord Symbols** page of **House Style ▸ Engraving Rules** and in **House Style ▸ Edit Chord Symbols**.

To type a root note, simply type its name, e.g. "C#" or "Bb." If you want to type an altered bass note, type a slash followed by the note name, e.g. "/E."

The different elements following the root note that make up more complex chord symbols are called *suffix elements*, and Sibelius understands a specific list of suffix elements that you can type from your keyboard, as follows:

halfdim	add9	6/9	b5
add6/9	maj7	aug	#4
sus2/4	dim9	alt	nc
omit5	dim7	b13	9
omit3	sus9	#11	7
maj13	sus4	13	6
add13	add4	11	5
maj11	sus2	#9	m
dim13	add2	b9	/
dim11	maj	b6	
maj9	dim	#5	

The list above is largely self-explanatory, except perhaps for "nc," which means "no chord" and produces the chord symbol N.C., and for "/", which is normally used to precede an altered bass note, but when typed on its own produces a rhythm slash (╱).

Using the above suffix elements, you can quickly type very complex chord symbols just as you would expect (try typing "Cmaj7b13b9b5"). You don't need to include any parentheses or other separators in your text, or type the suffix elements in any particular order (though note that the order you type them in is disregarded when it comes to displaying the actual chord symbol: Sibelius always displays alterations in descending order by default).

If you should happen to type an unrecognised chord suffix (e.g. something unexpected like "banana") or produce a combination of chord suffixes that Sibelius doesn't understand (e.g. a nonsense chord symbol like "Dmaj9b11"), Sibelius will color your input red and advance the caret. You should go back and fix up this erroneous chord symbol later on!

If you want to define your own text input string for a particular chord type, e.g. to make it quicker to type in a particularly complex chord type, you can do so in House Style ▸ Edit Chord Symbols – 🕮 **8.13 Edit Chord Symbols**.

To navigate around while inputting chord symbols, Space moves on to the next note or beat (whichever comes first), Tab moves to the start of the next bar, Backspace moves to the previous chord symbol, and Shift-Tab moves to the start of the previous bar.

Creating chord symbols by playing

Before you attempt to input chord symbols from your MIDI keyboard or MIDI guitar, first check that it is correctly connected and that you are able to input notes from your MIDI device – 🕮 **1.10 Input Devices**.

To input chord symbols by playing them in, start chord symbol input with the keyboard shortcut Ctrl+K *or* ⌘K, and when you see the flashing text cursor, simply play the chord you want to input; the flashing cursor automatically advances to the next note or beat.

By default, Sibelius uses the voicing of the chord that you play to determine not only the chord type, but also the specific way in which the chord is notated, e.g. if you play the chord in one of its inversions, Sibelius will produce a chord symbol with an altered bass note, e.g. D/F♯.

Sibelius will normally produce the desired enharmonic spelling for the root note (and altered bass note, if present) based on the current key signature, but should you decide that you want to respell the chord symbol after input, this is simple – see **Respell Chord Symbol** below.

If you should happen to play a chord that Sibelius doesn't recognise, Sibelius will write the names of the notes you played in red and advance the caret. You should go back and fix up this erroneous chord symbol later on!

If you want to define your own specific MIDI input voicing for a particular chord type, e.g. to make it quicker to input a common chord type, you can do so in House Style ▸ Edit Chord Symbols – 🕮 **8.13 Edit Chord Symbols**.

Navigating around while inputting chord symbols via MIDI keyboard is the same as while inputting them using the computer keyboard – see **Creating chord symbols by typing** above.

Editing an existing chord symbol

To edit a chord symbol, simply double-click it, or select it and hit Return (on the main keyboard). You can then either delete the existing text in order to type a new chord symbol, or simply play a new chord on your MIDI keyboard to replace it.

Other kinds of edits to chord symbols can be done simply by selecting one or more chord symbols, then choosing the desired operation from the Edit ▸ Chord Symbol submenu, which is also available when you right-click (Windows) *or* Control-click (Mac) a chord symbol.

Equivalent Chord Text

There are often several different ways to represent the same pattern of intervals in a chord symbol. Sibelius makes it easy to cycle between the different possibilities, which is useful if you have played in a chord symbol and found that Sibelius has not automatically chosen the type that you prefer.

Simply select the chord symbol (or chord symbols) whose chord text you want to change, then choose **Edit ▸ Chord Symbol ▸ Equivalent Chord Text** (shortcut **Ctrl+Shift+K** *or* ⇧⌘K); each time you choose it, Sibelius chooses the next equivalent chord text, eventually cycling back around to the original chord appearance.

If you want to determine which chord type Sibelius should produce by default when you play a particular chord on your MIDI keyboard, ensure that you define a custom MIDI input voicing for your preferred chord type (even if it already has a default voicing that is the same as your preferred voicing, since that default voicing will be shared by other chord types, and the presence of a user-defined voicing tells Sibelius to prefer that chord type) – 📖 **8.13 Edit Chord Symbols**.

Revoice Chord Diagram

There are always many alternative ways to play a given chord type on a guitar. Each chord type has a preferred chord diagram associated with it (which you can edit in **House Style ▸ Edit Chord Symbols**), which is the chord diagram that is shown by default for that chord type.

To choose another guitar chord diagram, select the chord symbol (or chord symbols), then choose **Edit ▸ Chord Symbol ▸ Revoice Chord Diagram** (shortcut **Ctrl+Shift+Alt+K** *or* ⇧⌥⌘K); each time you choose it, Sibelius chooses the next voicing it can find.

Respell Chord Symbol

After having input a chord symbol via your MIDI keyboard, you may want to change the enharmonic spelling of its root note, altered bass note, or both. To do this, select the chord symbol (or chord symbols), then choose **Edit ▸ Chord Symbol ▸ Respell Chord Symbol**; each time you choose it, Sibelius respells the chord.

All valid spellings for a root note are considered, so C will change to B♯ and D♭♭ before arriving back at C. Altered bass notes will never be spelled using double accidentals unless the chord's root note is also spelled using a double accidental.

Choosing when chord diagrams should appear

Sibelius intelligently chooses whether to display both chord text and chord diagram components of chord symbols based on the type of instrument to which the chord symbol is attached. By default, Sibelius will show only chord text on all instruments except for notation staves (as opposed to tab staves) belonging to guitars and other fretted instruments.

When a chord symbol is attached to a notation staff, Sibelius determines the appearance of the chord diagram according to the implied tuning of that guitar or other fretted instrument; if the instrument is neither a guitar nor another kind of fretted instrument, when Sibelius shows a guitar chord diagram, it is for a 6-string guitar set to the standard tuning.

To change whether Sibelius should show either or both chord text and chord diagram components of chord symbols in your score, choose **House Style ▸ Engraving Rules** and go to the **Chord Symbols** page, then select the appropriate radio button in the **Appearance** group.

To change the type of instrument or tuning Sibelius should use for the chord diagrams on a given staff, select a bar in that staff, then choose **House Style ▸ Edit Instruments**. The instrument type used by the staff is selected for you in the dialog, so click **Edit Instrument**, then **Yes** when asked if you're sure you want to continue. In the **Edit Instrument** dialog, choose the desired tuning or instrument from the **Tab instrument to use for string tunings** menu at the bottom right-hand corner of the dialog, then click OK and **Close** to confirm your choice (📖 **8.14 Edit Instruments**).

If you want to change whether the chord text or chord diagram component of an individual chord symbol should appear, select the chord symbol, and choose **Edit ▸ Chord Symbol ▸ Add/Remove Chord Text** or **Add/Remove Chord Diagram** as appropriate.

To undo any changes you have made to an individual chord symbol and return it to its default appearance, select it and choose **Layout ▸ Reset Design**.

Transposing chord symbols

Chord symbols are automatically transposed when you transpose music or switch a score between concert and transposing pitch. (They don't transpose if you just change the pitch of the note under the chord symbol.)

Chord symbols on transposing instruments

When you use your MIDI keyboard to input chord symbols for a transposing instrument (such as alto saxophone), Sibelius will interpret your input according to the **Input sounding pitches** or **Input written pitches** setting on the **Note Input** page of File ▸ **Preferences** (in the **Sibelius** menu on Mac). For example, when **Input sounding pitches** is chosen and **Notes ▸ Transposing Score** is switched on, playing an E♭maj7 chord on an alto saxophone staff will produce a chord symbol of Cmaj7.

Although chord symbols transpose automatically on transposing instruments, be aware that the chord diagram component does not transpose (because guitars are not transposing instruments, and the chord that a guitarist would play would be the same regardless of how the chord text is displayed).

Playing back chord symbols

Chord symbols don't play back automatically, but Sibelius includes a plug-in that can generate simple accompaniments from the chord symbols and chord diagrams in your score; see **Realize Chord Symbols** on page 492 for more details.

Changing the size of chord symbols

- To change the size of the chord text component of all chord symbols in your score, change the point size defined for the Chord symbols text style – see **Changing the font used for chord symbols** below.
- To change the size of the chord text of a single chord symbol, select the chord symbol, open the Text panel of Properties, and adjust the Size there (📖 **5.17 Properties**).
- To change the size of the chord diagram component of all chord symbols in your score, adjust the Default size slider on the Guitar page of House Style ▸ Engraving Rules. (This also affects the default size of any guitar scale diagrams in your score – 📖 **2.16 Guitar scale diagrams**).
- To change the size of a single chord diagram, select the chord symbol, open the General panel of Properties, and adjust the Scale there (📖 **5.17 Properties**).

To reset the appearance of a chord symbol, undoing any changes made in the Properties window, simply choose **Layout ▸ Reset Design** (shortcut **Ctrl+Shift+D** *or* ⇧⌘D).

Changing the font used for chord symbols

Sibelius only supports its own set of chord symbol fonts, which are the following six:

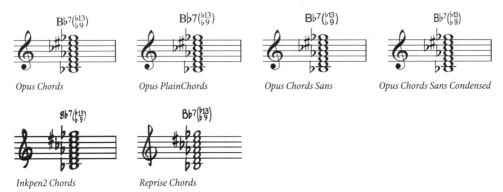

| *Opus Chords* | *Opus PlainChords* | *Opus Chords Sans* | *Opus Chords Sans Condensed* |

Inkpen2 Chords   *Reprise Chords*

- Opus Chords is the standard chord symbol font.
- Opus PlainChords uses non-superscript accidentals and numbers.
- Opus Chords Sans is a sans serif font and is the default in house styles that use Arial as the main text font.
- Opus Chords Sans Condensed is a condensed font and is useful in scores with many complex chords, as it takes up less horizontal space.
- Inkpen2 Chords matches the Inkpen2 music font and is the default in Inkpen2 house styles.
- Reprise Chords matches the Reprise music font and is the default in Reprise house styles.

Normally the most appropriate font will already be chosen based on your original choice of house style when you first created your score, but you can use any of these chord symbol fonts in any score. To do this:

- Choose **House Style ▸ Edit Text Styles** (shortcut **Ctrl+Shift+Alt+T** *or* ⇧⌥⌘T)
- Double-click the **Chord symbols** text style to edit it
- On the **General** tab, change to whichever of the fonts you want to use.
- You can also adjust the default point size of chord symbols here, if you like.
- Click **OK**.

Don't, however, change the font to a standard text font, or to a third-party chord symbol font (e.g. the Jazz font). If you want to use a font other than the six supplied chord symbol fonts, you will have to use legacy chord symbols instead of Sibelius's intelligent chord symbols – see **Legacy chord symbol input** below.

Default vertical position

The default vertical position of chord symbols can be changed from the **House Style ▸ Default Positions** dialog. Choose the **Other objects** radio button at the top left of the dialog, then choose **Chord Symbol** from the list of objects at the left-hand side – 📖 **8.12 Default Positions**.

Aligning a row of chord symbols

If you've input chord symbols along a staff and Sibelius has had to move some to avoid collisions with notes, it will attempt to keep them all neatly aligned in a row, but sometimes you may have to line them all up again.

To do this, select any chord symbol, choose **Edit ▸ Select ▸ Select More** (shortcut **Ctrl+Shift+A** *or* ⇧⌘A), which selects all chord symbols along that staff. Then you can:

- Align them in a row by choosing **Layout ▸ Align in a Row** (shortcut **Ctrl+Shift+R** *or* ⇧⌘R), after which you can move them all up or down with the arrow keys; or

- Choose **Layout ▸ Reset Position** (shortcut **Ctrl+Shift+P** *or* ⇧⌘P) to snap the chord symbols to their default vertical position.

Engraving Rules options

The **Chord Symbols** page of **House Style ▸ Engraving Rules** contains a dizzying array of options, allowing you to control many aspects of the default appearance of the chord symbols in your score:

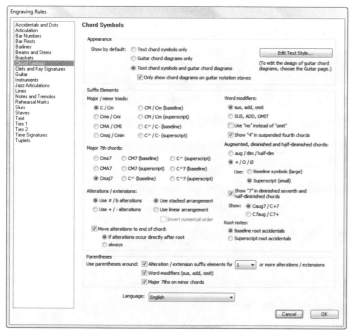

The options in the **Appearance** group allow you to determine whether either or both the chord text and chord diagram components of chord symbols should appear – see **Choosing when chord diagrams should appear** above.

Click **Edit Text Style** to edit the **Chord symbols** text style – see **Changing the font used for chord symbols** above.

The options in the **Suffix Elements** group allow you to choose between a number of alternative appearances for common suffix elements:

Major/minor triads:	
C / Cm	C / Cm
Cma / Cmi	C^{ma} / C^{mi}
CMA / CMI	C^{MA} / C^{MI}
Cmaj / Cmin	C^{maj} / C^{min}
CM / Cm (baseline)	CM / Cm
CM / Cm (superscript)	C^{M} / C^{m}
C^ / C- (baseline)	$C\triangle / C$-
C^ / C- (superscript)	$C^{\triangle} / C$-
Major 7th chords:	
Cma7	C^{ma7}
CMA7	C^{MA7}
Cmaj7	C^{maj7}
CM7 (baseline)	CM^{7}
CM7 (superscript)	C^{M7}
C^ (baseline)	$C\triangle$
C^ (superscript)	$C^{\triangle}$
C^7 (baseline)	$C\triangle^{7}$
C^7 (superscript)	$C^{\triangle7}$
Alterations/extensions:	
Use # / b alterations	$Cm^{7(\flat5)} / C^{7(\sharp5)}$
Use + / - alterations	$Cm^{7(-5)} / C^{7(+5)}$
Use stacked arrangement	$C^{ma7\binom{\flat13}{\flat5}}$
Use linear arrangement	$C^{ma7(\flat13\flat5)}$
Invert numerical order	$C^{ma7(\flat5\flat13)}$
Move alterations to end of chord: Always on	$C^{7(sus4\flat9)}$, otherwise $C^{7(\flat9sus4)}$
...If alterations occur directly after root on	$C^{(sus4\sharp11)}$, otherwise $C^{\sharp11(sus4)}$
Word modifiers:	
sus, add, omit	$C^{(sus4)} / C^{(add4)} / C^{(omit3)}$
SUS, ADD, OMIT	$C^{(SUS4)} / C^{(ADD4)} / C^{(OMIT3)}$
Use 'no' instead of 'omit'	On: $C^{(no3)}$ / Off: $C^{(OMIT3)}$
Show '4' in suspended fourth chords	On: $C^{(sus4)}$ / Off: $C^{(sus)}$
Augmented, diminished and half-diminished chords:	
aug / dim / half-dim	$Caug / Cdim / Chalf\text{-}dim^{7}$
+ / O / Ø	$C+ / Co / C\varnothing$
Baseline symbols (large)	$C+ / Co / C\varnothing$
Superscript (small)	$C^{+} / C^{o} / C^{\varnothing}$
Show '7' in diminished seventh and half-dim. chords	On: $C^{\varnothing7}$ / Off: $C^{\varnothing}$
Caug7 / C+7	$Caug^{7} / C+^{7}$
C7aug / C7+	$C^{7}aug / C^{7+}$
Root notes	
Baseline root accidentals	$F\sharp / B\flat$
Superscript root accidentals	$F^{\sharp} / B^{\flat}$

The options in the **Parentheses** group determine when Sibelius should use parentheses around various suffix elements:

- **Alteration / extension suffix elements for** *n* **or more alterations / extensions** determines whether Sibelius should use parentheses only when there are a certain number of alterations or extensions in the chord symbol; by default, this is set to **1**, but you may find parentheses unnecessary for chords with two or fewer extensions, in which case you could set this to **3**.
- **Word-modifiers (sus, add, omit)** determines whether Sibelius should place word modifiers such as "sus" inside parentheses. By default, this option is switched on.
- **Major 7ths on minor chords** determines whether Sibelius should write e.g. $Cm^{(ma7)}$ or Cm^{ma7}. By default, this option is switched on.

Finally, the **Language** menu allows you to choose how the root notes should be written:

- **English**: the default choice, this writes note names as A–G, with B and B♭.
- **German**: writes note names as A-G, with (e.g.) Fis for F♯, Ees for E♭, H for B and B for B♭.
- **Scandinavian**: writes note names as A-G, with H for B, but B♭ for B♭.
- **Solfege (do, re, mi, etc.)**: writes note names as Do, Re, Mi, etc.
- **Solfege (do, ré, mi, etc.)**: writes note names as Do, Ré, Mi, etc.

The **Language** setting only affects the display of chord symbols: for text input of chord symbols, you should always use the regular English note names.

You can override the global choices made on the **Chord Symbols** page of **House Style ▶ Engraving Rules** for individual chord types using **House Style ▶ Edit Chord Symbols** – 📖 **8.13 Edit Chord Symbols**.

Legacy chord symbol input

In earlier versions of Sibelius, chord symbols were a kind of text, and had to be typed in using special keyboard shortcuts or bits of chord symbol chosen from a word menu. For the purposes of backwards compatibility, it is possible to enable so-called *legacy chord symbol input*, which makes chord symbols behave the same way as in earlier versions, by switching on the **Use legacy chord symbol** input checkbox on the **Other** page of **File ▶ Preferences** (in the **Sibelius** menu on Mac).

Be aware that legacy chord symbols do not respond to the edits possible from the **Edit ▶ Chord Symbols** submenu, and do not change appearance when you change the options on the **Chord Symbols** page of **House Style ▶ Engraving Rules**. As a consequence, you are strongly recommended to use real chord symbols.

If you find yourself occasionally needing a legacy chord symbol, you can choose **Create ▶ Text ▶ Special Text ▶ Chord symbol** to type a single legacy chord symbol into the score. If you want, you can also assign a keyboard shortcut to the **Chord symbols** text style, and use that shortcut on the occasions when you require a legacy chord symbols – 📖 **5.12 Menus and shortcuts**.

2.11 Clefs

The clefs at the start of every system are drawn automatically by Sibelius. It puts in the standard clefs for you when you create instruments. You only need to think about clefs if you want to change them.

Creating clef changes

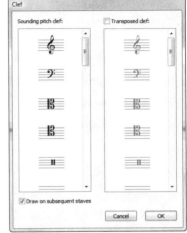

- If you want the clef to change mid-bar, input the music for the bar where the clef change is to go, so you can create it between the right notes

- Select the note or rest before the place where you want the clef to go, choose **Create ▸ Clef** (shortcut **Q** for "qlef"), and click the clef you want from the bewildering list provided. (The most common clefs are at the top.)

- You can tell Sibelius to use a different clef when **Notes ▸ Transposing Score** is switched on, which is useful for some transposing instruments (e.g. low brass and wind instruments); to do this, switch on the **Transposed clef** option and choose the clef to use

- The **Draw on subsequent staves** option, as its name suggests, draws the new clef on all subsequent systems; switching this off is useful for special kinds of music such as lead sheets, but normally you should leave it switched on

- Click **OK** and the clef is created in your score. All the music after the clef will shift up or down to ensure that it sounds the same as before.

You can also input a clef change with the mouse. Make sure that nothing is selected in your score (hit **Esc**), choose the clef you want from the **Create ▸ Clef** dialog, then point where you want the clef to go and click. For instance, to change the clef of an entire instrument, put the clef you've chosen on top of the existing clef at the very start of the score.

You can copy clef changes (e.g. with **Alt+click** *or* ⌥-click), though you can't copy the full-size clefs at the start of staves.

Moving clefs

If you drag a clef change around, you'll see that Sibelius automatically shifts the music up or down as the clef passes over it to keep the notes sounding the same.

Try this out – create a clef change somewhere, then drag it left and right along the staff, or up and down onto other staves, and watch the music instantly leap around. When you have nothing better to do, this can provide hours of harmless (if rather limited) enjoyment.

Deleting clefs

Clef changes can be removed with **Delete**. If the clef you want to delete changes at the start of a system, delete the clef change that appears at the end of the previous system. (That's because – if you think about it – the small clef on the end of the previous system is the actual change point; the big clef on the next system is really no more than the standard indication of what the current clef is.)

For unpitched percussion instruments you may want to use the "blank clef" (the one that consists of a bit of empty staff). Although this just makes the staff start with a gap instead of a clef, you position the blank clef just like any other clef instead of trying to delete the clef that's already there.

Once you have put a blank clef change somewhere, you can't select it and delete it – there's nothing there to select. Instead, put a different clef on top and hit **Delete**.

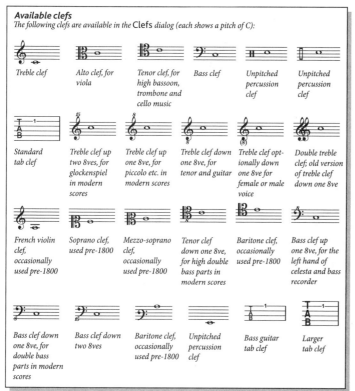

Available clefs
The following clefs are available in the Clefs *dialog (each shows a pitch of C):*

Treble clef	Alto clef, for viola	Tenor clef, for high bassoon, trombone and cello music	Bass clef	Unpitched percussion clef	Unpitched percussion clef
Standard tab clef	Treble clef up two 8ves, for glockenspiel in modern scores	Treble clef up one 8ve, for piccolo etc. in modern scores	Treble clef down one 8ve, for tenor and guitar	Treble clef optionally down one 8ve for female or male voice	Double treble clef; old version of treble clef down one 8ve
French violin clef, occasionally used pre-1800	Soprano clef, used pre-1800	Mezzo-soprano clef, occasionally used pre-1800	Tenor clef down one 8ve, for high double bass parts in modern scores	Baritone clef, occasionally used pre-1800	Bass clef up one 8ve, for the left hand of celesta and bass recorder
Bass clef down one 8ve, for double bass parts in modern scores	Bass clef down two 8ves	Baritone clef, occasionally used pre-1800	Unpitched percussion clef	Bass guitar tab clef	Larger tab clef

Hiding clefs at the start of a system

If you want a clef to appear on the first system but not on subsequent systems – for example, if you're working on a lead sheet – simply switch off **Draw on subsequent systems** when you create the clef; don't try and delete the clef at the beginning of each system!

If you don't want clefs to appear *at all* on a particular staff, select all the bars in that staff, then switch off the **Clefs** checkbox on the **Bars** panel of the Properties window (⌸ **5.17 Properties**).

Hiding cautionary clef changes

If a score contains several movements or songs, you may want to change clef at the start of one section without a cautionary clef appearing at the end of the previous section. To do this, select the cautionary clef, and choose **Edit ▸ Hide or Show ▸ Hide** (shortcut **Ctrl+Shift+H** *or* ⇧⌘H).

For more information about hiding objects, ⌸ **5.9 Hiding objects**.

Octave clefs

Some people write (say) piccolo with a normal treble clef, some with an "8" above (particularly in avant garde scores) – this is a matter of taste. A real-life piccolo playing music with a "treble 8" clef would not sound an octave higher than a piccolo playing the same music with a plain treble clef – they sound at exactly the same pitch. In other words, the "8" is just a hint or reminder to the reader that this is a transposing instrument.

Therefore in Sibelius clefs with or without "8s" (or "15s") on them are all precisely equivalent. The fact that a piccolo sounds an octave higher than a flute playing the same notes is an attribute of the *instrument*, not of the clef (after all, they could both be playing from a plain treble clef). This is indicated in Sibelius by the fact that a piccolo has a transposition change by default, namely it transposes up an octave both in a non-transposing score and in a transposing score. You can create a transposing instrument like this yourself using House Style ▸ Edit Instruments (🕮 **8.14 Edit Instruments**).

A tenor voice "instrument" in Sibelius is similar – it has a transposition change to make it transpose down an octave both in a non-transposing score and in a transposing score. The "treble 8" clef for a tenor is again just a hint to the reader – it's an alternative to a plain treble clef and has no direct effect on the sounding pitch of the notes.

Engraving Rules options

The Clefs and Key Signatures page of the House Style ▸ Engraving Rules dialog (shortcut Ctrl+Shift+E *or* ⇧⌘E) allows you to change the Gap before initial clef and the Initial clef width, should you be so inclined.

The Cue note size option on the Notes and Tremolos page of the dialog also determines the size of clef changes (compared with full size clefs).

2.12 Cues

📖 **2.14 Grace notes**, 📖 **7.1 Working with parts**.

Notations

Cue notes are small notes commonly used for one of two purposes. In instrumental parts, cue passages are included to help the player keep track of where they are, and are not meant to be played. Cue passages can also indicate optional music, for example a harmonica solo might be cued in a clarinet part with an indication to "play if no harmonica is available."

Don't confuse cue notes with grace notes (📖 **2.14 Grace notes**): cue notes occupy rhythmic space in the bar, and play back like normal notes. Because a cue can contain grace notes or special noteheads, any note – whether it's a normal note, special notehead or even a grace note – can be made cue-size. Rests, bar rests and other objects such as text, lines and symbols can also be cue-size.

The other chief uses for small notes are for writing optional keyboard accompaniments in choral and instrumental music, and the solo part on a keyboard accompaniment, but in these cases you should not use cue notes. Instead it looks better if you make the relevant staves small, which will make all the notes and other objects on it small too – 📖 **2.29 Staves**.

The size of cue notes is proportional to the staff size – normally cue notes go on a normal-size staff, but if you put cue notes on a small staff they will go even smaller. You can even put cue grace notes on a small staff, to get really, really tiny notes.

Paste as Cue

It only takes a moment to create a cue passage using Edit ▸ Paste as Cue:

* Make sure you are looking at the full score rather than one of the dynamic parts. Although you can use Edit ▸ Paste as Cue in a dynamic part, it's much more convenient to use it in the full score, so that you can see the staff you are taking material from, and paste the cue into multiple instruments at the same time

* Copy the music you want to use as a cue to the clipboard by selecting it, then choosing Edit ▸ Copy (shortcut Ctrl+C *or* ⌘C)

* Select the bar rest or rest in the staff or staves on which you want the cue to appear, then choose Edit ▸ Paste as Cue (shortcut Ctrl+Shift+Alt+V *or* ⇧⌥⌘V). If you select more than one staff, Sibelius will paste the cue onto all the selected staves using multicopy (📖 **1.9 Selections and passages**).

That's all there is to it! A number of useful things are done for you when pasting a cue passage:

* The copied music is pasted into the first unused voice, with all the notes and other markings made cue-size

* The cue is hidden in the full score but is shown in the parts (though if you want to, you can tell Sibelius to show the cue in the full score as well – see **Paste as Cue preferences** below)

- Any awkward transpositions (e.g. cueing a clarinet in A on a horn in F staff) are taken care of, and either if necessary a suitable clef or an octave line is added to ensure the cue is easily readable, according to your preferences – see **Paste as Cue preferences** below

- The name of the cued instrument is written above the cue, using the Instrument name (cues) staff text style (which you can edit if you want to change its appearance or default position – 📖 **3.9 Edit Text Styles**)

- If the staff type (e.g. number of lines) of the cued instrument and the destination staff don't match, appropriate instrument changes are created at the start and end of the cue

- Particular markings (such as lyrics, dynamics, slurs and hairpins) are automatically included or excluded, according to your preferences – see **Paste as Cue preferences** below

- Any instrument changes in the source passage are automatically excluded

- The cue notes are set not to play back (by automatically switching off the Play on pass checkboxes in the Playback panel of Properties – see **When to play back notes** on page 291)

- Suitable bar rests are added in an unused voice in both the full score and the parts, so that they look correct (though if you want to, you can tell Sibelius not to add bar rests in the parts – see **Paste as Cue preferences** below).

About the only thing Sibelius doesn't do is decide which instrument you should use for the cue, although it can even suggest where cues should be added – read on.

Suggest Cue Locations plug-in

When preparing parts for performance, one of the more time-consuming aspects is determining where cues would be most useful to the performers. You may want to add cues after a certain number of bars' rest, or after a certain length of time. Plug-ins ▸ Other ▸ Suggest Cue Locations can do this for you – see **Suggest Cue Locations** on page 508.

Check Cues plug-in

Any edits you make to the music in your score after cueing the parts may potentially lead to errors in the cues, because Sibelius doesn't automatically update the cue passages if the source staves from which they take their material are subsequently edited. However, a handy plug-in is included that can check cues against the music from which they are taken and warn you if it finds any disparities; simply select the passage in question and choose Plug-ins ▸ Proof-reading ▸ Check Cues – see **Check Cues** on page 514 for more details.

Paste as Cue preferences

Various options for determining exactly what happens when you do Edit ▸ Paste as Cue are found on the Paste as Cue page of File ▸ Preferences (in the Sibelius menu on Mac), as shown below.

The Pitch of Cue options provide three alternatives for how Sibelius should resolve differences in range between the source and destination staves:

- **Change clef if necessary** adds a clef at the start of the pasted cue, if the clefs used by the source and destination staves don't match. So if you paste a cue from, say, a cello staff onto a flute staff, Sibelius will create a bass clef at the start of the cue and restore the treble clef at the end. Note that these clef changes are only visible in the part.

- **Add octave line if necessary** adds an octave line (up to two octaves up or down, i.e. *8va, 15ma, 8vb* or *15mb*) over the pasted cue if Sibelius has to transpose the cue by one or more octaves to ensure that it fits comfortably on the staff.
- **Neither** will simply paste the cue into the clef of the destination staff without transposing the music by octaves.

The **Copy into Cue** options allow you to choose whether or not Sibelius should include **Slurs**, **Articulations**, **Dynamics**, **Lyrics** and **Technique text** in the pasted cue.

It's conventional for cue passages in parts to show bar rests in addition to the cue notes, as an extra visual indicator to the player that the notes are for informational purposes only, and not to be played. However, in some kinds of music, including jazz, it's common for cues simply to be written in smaller notes without adding bar rests. **Show bar rests with cue (in parts)** allows you to choose which of these conventions to follow: when switched on (the default), the part's original bar rests are shown in addition to the cue notes; when switched off, only the cue notes themselves are shown.

Again, in some kinds of music, commonly jazz, you sometimes see the word "Play" written after the cue, to remind the performer that she should now start playing again. **Write 'Play' after cue**, switched off by default, does this. It is most useful if you switch off **Show bar rests with cue (in parts)**.

In most kinds of music it's conventional for cues to be shown only in the parts, so **Hide cues in full score** is switched on by default. However, scores in some fields of music, such as musical theater, usually show cues in the full score, so switching this option off is useful in those situations.

Be aware that changing the options here will not affect cues you have already pasted; they only affect cues you subsequently create using **Edit ▸ Paste as Cue**.

Creating cue notes, rests and other objects

If you need to make a note, rest, line, symbol or staff text object cue-size yourself, select it and then choose the cue-size button shown on the right (shortcut **Enter**) from the second Keypad layout (shortcut **Enter**). When creating notes with mouse and keystrokes or step-time, notes continue to be cue notes until you switch the button off again.

If you want to make a passage of music cue-sized, simply select the passage and choose the same keypad button from the second Keypad layout. You can make cue notes and cue-size rests normal size again by re-choosing the cue note button in the same way.

You cannot make system text, system symbols or system lines cue-size, as these are never included in cue passages (since they already occur in all parts).

The **General** panel of Properties also includes a **Cue-sized** checkbox, which works the same way as the cue-size button.

Engraving Rules options

The **Notes and Tremolos** page of the **House Style ▸ Engraving Rules** dialog (shortcut Ctrl+Shift+E *or* ⇧⌘E) lets you modify the size of grace and cue notes relative to normal notes. Grace notes are normally a bit smaller than cue notes (60% of full size instead of 75%).

Big notes

In the unlikely event that you want extra-large notes on normal staves (a notation used occasionally by Stockhausen to denote loud notes) and don't also need cue-sized notes, set **Cue note size** on the **Notes and Tremolos** page of the **House Style ▸ Engraving Rules** dialog to, say, 130%, and input the big notes as cue notes.

2.13 Free rhythm

Music in free rhythm means that there are no time signatures (as in recitative, some avant garde music, or plainchant), or else the current time signature is ignored (as in a cadenza). Sometimes several instruments can play free rhythms at different speeds so that the notes don't even line up, as in aleatory music.

Normal free rhythm

For free rhythm in just one instrument, or in several where the rhythms align, create irregular bars of appropriate lengths (choose **Create ▶ Bar ▶ Other**, shortcut Alt+B *or* ⌥B) into which to put the music.

Depending on the type of music, you can input the music in one long bar or in several shorter bars with invisible barlines. The latter has the advantage that the music can split at any of the invisible barlines, which will be required for a long cadenza that wouldn't fit on one system. The downside is that the extra bars will upset the bar numbering, though you can correct this by putting an appropriate bar number change at the end (□ **3.5 Bar numbers**).

Independent free rhythms

Sometimes instruments play completely independent rhythms at the same time, like this:

Notate this in the same way as described above, but choose one of the staves as the "fundamental" rhythm and input it first. Then add the other rhythms, but change their apparent speed using tuplets with a suitable ratio – i.e. choose **None** and switch off the **Bracket** in the **Create ▶ Tuplet** dialog (or change it retrospectively from the **Notes** panel of the Properties window). For example, in the music above the first three notes on the lower staff are in a hidden triplet, so as to fit against the first two notes on the upper staff.

Sibelius will even play back the rhythms correctly, as if it were reading the spatial notation.

Music with multiple simultaneous time signatures

...or with barlines in different places on different staves: □ **2.33 Time signatures**.

Plainchant

To write plainchant, use irregular bars (choose **Create ▶ Bar ▶ Other**) of appropriate lengths (□ **2.5 Bars and bar rests**), and use stemless notes (□ **2.25 Noteheads**).

Recitative

Use irregular bars (choose **Create ▶ Bar ▶ Other**) of appropriate lengths. For help on lyrics in recitative, □ **3.3 Lyrics**.

Cadenzas

Here are a couple of approaches to creating cadenzas in Sibelius. It is helpful if you calculate the length of your cadenza (in terms of note values) before you start to input it:

- Create an irregular bar, or a series of them, using **Create ▸ Bar ▸ Other** (shortcut **Alt+B** *or* **⌥B**). Remember that each bar you create can be no longer than one system, so you may need to create multiple bars with invisible barlines in between. You can specify the exact duration of the bar(s), as complex as you like, and fill them with music as normal. You should avoid deleting (hiding) any unwanted rests if possible, as they will have an effect on note spacing even if they are hidden.
- If you need to have regular (measured) bars of music and free rhythm simultaneously, see **Independent free rhythms** above.

2.14 Grace notes

📖 **2.12 Cues**.

Grace notes are smaller than normal notes, and are drawn in between them. Unlike cue notes, grace notes don't count towards the total duration of the bar. This is because the performer is meant to fit them in between the main notes himself. Grace notes with a diagonal line through the stem are *acciaccaturas*, and ones without are *appoggiaturas* (this is the terminology Sibelius uses, anyway).

Grace notes

Grace notes are normally drawn with stems up, regardless of their pitch. They are only drawn with stems down to avoid colliding with other objects, e.g. in the second of two voices, and in bagpipe music.

Acciaccaturas (with a line through the stem) are normally used only for single grace notes. Single grace notes, particularly acciaccaturas, are almost always written as an eighth note (quaver) regardless of how long they actually last. Pairs of grace notes are usually written as sixteenth notes (semiquavers), with 32nd-notes (demisemiquavers) being used for groups of about four or more grace notes.

Grace notes are usually slurred from the first grace note to the following main note. The slur normally goes above if the main note is higher than the grace note, or if the grace note or main note has leger lines above the staff; otherwise the slur is below.

Creating grace notes...

Grace notes are always attached to the following normal note in a bar (so you cannot automatically create grace notes at the very end of a bar – see below). You can create grace notes in two ways, detailed below.

The quick way is to input the grace notes as you go along during step-time or alphabetic input; the slow way is to input the normal notes first, then add the grace notes afterwards.

...the quick way

To input grace notes as you go along:

• Start creating notes (📖 **1.1 Note input**)

• When you want to create a grace note, switch to the second Keypad layout (shortcut **F8**) and switch on the appropriate Keypad button:

      Acciaccatura   *Appoggiatura*

• Then create notes as normal, choosing note values from the first Keypad layout (shortcut **F7**)

• To stop creating grace notes, switch off the grace note button on the second Keypad layout.

...the slow way

To add grace notes to an existing passage of music:

• With nothing selected (hit **Esc**), choose the note value and the kind of grace note from the first and second Keypad layouts

• The mouse arrow changes color to show which voice you're going to create the grace note into; click where the grace note is to go

• If you didn't specify a note value before creating it, the grace note will appear as an eighth note (quaver). You can modify the note value afterwards in the same way as normal notes.

Notations

- Type A–G or use your MIDI keyboard to produce more grace notes after it.
- Type 1–9 (or Shift-1–9 for notes below) to produce grace note chords, or play the chords on your MIDI keyboard.

Editing grace notes

Most editing operations work for grace notes in exactly the same way as normal notes, including dragging, copying, deleting, adding/removing accidentals and articulations, beaming, and changing their note value or notehead.

Grace notes at the end of bars

Because grace notes attach to the note or rest following them, if you try to create a grace note at the very end of the bar (e.g. after a trill or other ornament), it has nothing to attach to. So to create a grace note at the end of a bar, enter a note in the next bar and create the grace note(s) before this note, then alter its position to before the barline using the X parameter in the General panel of the Properties window (📖 **5.17 Properties**). The main note after grace notes can then be deleted if necessary. (To move the grace note thereafter, only use the Properties window – not the mouse or arrow keys – or the grace note may reattach to a different note.)

Grace notes in unpitched percussion

Grace notes are used in unpitched percussion writing to represent flams, drags and ruffs. To write these drum rudiments, simply add a grace note (two for a drag) before a main note, and add a slur from the grace note(s) to the following main note.

Spacing grace notes

In the House Style ▸ Note Spacing Rule dialog, you can specify the Space around grace notes (i.e. the separation between each grace note) and the Extra space after last grace note (i.e. after the last grace note and before the next normal note).

Engraving Rules options

The Notes and Tremolos page of the House Style ▸ Engraving Rules dialog (shortcut Ctrl+Shift+E *or* ⇧⌘E) lets you modify the size of grace and cue notes relative to normal notes. Grace notes are normally a bit smaller than cue notes (60% of full size instead of 75%).

2.15 Guitar notation and tab

📖 **1.7 Guitar tab input, 2.10 Chord symbols, 2.22 Lute tablature**.

Guitar music features a wide array of special markings – including bends, pre-bends, slides, hammer-ons and pull-offs, and so on – all of which can be produced easily in Sibelius. The most common ones are listed below.

You can create these in either tab or notation staves, and they change design automatically when copied between tab and notation staves (with a few minor exceptions stated below).

Some of the tab markings involve hidden notes on the tab staff, which can be viewed and edited when **View ▸ Hidden Objects** (shortcut **Ctrl+Alt+H** *or* ⌥⌘H) is switched on.

Bend

Bends are produced by fretting a string and then pushing the string sideways to bend the note after playing it. Bends are normally either a half-step (semitone) or a whole step (tone) up or down, but it's possible to bend microtonal intervals too if you want.

On notation staves, a bend is drawn as an angled line between two notes, a bit like a crooked slur. On tab staves, it is drawn as an arrow that curves upwards if the second note is higher than the first, or downwards if the second note is lower than the first; additionally, for upward bends the second note is not notated on the tab staff, the interval for the bend instead being given above the curved arrow, in half-steps. A whole step bend is usually written as "full" rather than "1" (although you can change this in Sibelius from the **Guitar** page of the **House Style ▸ Engraving Rules** dialog by switching off the **Use full on tab bends** option).

To create a bend, select the first note and type **J** (which looks a little like a bend on a tab staff); the bend line will automatically be positioned between it and the next note (or will snap to the next note when you create it). You can also create a bend with the mouse: first ensure that nothing is selected in your score, choose **Create ▸ Line** (shortcut **L**) and select the bend line (shown as if on a notation staff) from the **Staff lines** panel. The mouse pointer changes color and you can click in the score to place the line.

Bend lines behave similarly to slurs: type **space** to extend the bend to the next note, or **Shift-space** to retract it; on notation staves, you can choose **Edit ▸ Flip** (shortcut **X**) to move the bend to the other side of the note. You can also adjust the position of either end of the bend line using the mouse or arrow keys. Like slurs, bends are magnetic, and position themselves automatically.

Bend intervals

To change the bend interval on a notation staff, simply change the pitch of the second note. On a tab staff, make sure **View ▸ Hidden Objects** (shortcut **Ctrl+Alt+H** *or* ⌥⌘H) is switched on, then select the hidden second note and change its pitch (either by playing a note on your MIDI keyboard, or by typing the fret number on the main keyboard).

To create a slight or microtonal bend, create a bend on a note and type **Shift-space** to retract the right-hand end so that it attaches to the same note as the left-hand end. A slight bend is drawn as a curved line on a notation staff, and as a quarter-tone bend on a tab staff.

Should you need to change the font or point size used by the numbers above bends on a tab staff, simply edit the **Chord diagram fret** text style – 📖 **3.9 Edit Text Styles**.

If you prefer bends on a tab staff to be written without an arrowhead, switch off **Use arrows in guitar bends** on the **Guitar** page of the **House Style ▸ Engraving Rules** dialog.

Bend and release

A bend and release is a bend upwards followed by a release back to the original note. To notate this, simply create an upward bend followed by a downward one.

When written on a tab staff, the final note is usually in parentheses (because it isn't actually played); to add parentheses to the note, select it and choose the round bracket button (🔘, shortcut **1**) on the second Keypad layout (shortcut **F8**).

Grace note bends and pre-bends

Both these kinds of bends are notated in the same way: first, from the second Keypad layout (shortcut **F8**), create the grace note (🔘, shortcut * on Windows, = on Mac) or pre-bend note (🔘, shortcut – on Windows, * on Mac); hit J to create a bend; then create the second note.

On a tab staff, a pre-bend is represented by a vertical arrow.

Pre-bend and release

A pre-bend and release is created in much the same way as grace-note bends and pre-bends, as above; as you would expect, create a pre-bend note followed by a grace note, create a bend, then create a full-size note, and create another bend between the grace note and the full-size note. Remember to add parentheses to the final note on the tab staff (see **Bend and release** above).

Unison bend

A unison bend is when you strike the two notes simultaneously, and bend the lower note up to the pitch of the higher. On a notation staff, the unison bend is written in a similar way to a pre-bend (see above), with two noteheads for the upper note.

On the tab staff, you will need to add the higher of the two initial notes as text; choose **Create ▸ Text ▸ Special Text ▸ Tablature numbers** and type the number.

Slide

A slide is achieved by striking the first note then sliding the same finger up or down to the second note, which is struck if the slide is a *shift slide*, and not struck if the slide is a *legato slide*.

On both notation staves and tab staves, shift slides are notated as a straight line (as shown on the left). Legato slides are notated as a line together with a slur. If the second note of the slide is higher, the line points upwards; if the second note is lower, the line points downwards. On tab staves, the line is at a fixed angle, but on notation staves, the line is angled according to the position of the notes to which it is attached.

To create a slide, input the first note of the slide and click the slide button (⬚, shortcut .) on the second Keypad layout (shortcut F8), then input the second note. You can also input the slide after creating both notes – just select the first of the two notes and click the slide button. To make a legato slide, just add a slur in the normal way (📖 **2.28 Slurs**).

Slides are magnetic and position themselves automatically. You can adjust their position by selecting either end and moving the handle with the mouse or the arrow keys.

Where there are several notes in a chord with slides, it is assumed that they are all sliding in the same direction. Should this not be the case, you should use straight lines from the **Create ▸ Line** dialog (shortcut L) to create the slides going in the opposite direction.

Vibrato (whammy) bar dive and return

The pitch of the note or chord is dropped a specified number of whole-steps (tones), then returned to the original pitch.

On a notation staff, a bar dive and return is written with two bend lines (see **Bend** above) and the "w/bar" line from the **Create ▸ Line** dialog (shortcut L).

On a tab staff, delete the middle note and add parentheses to the last note. Use two separate straight lines from the **Create ▸ Line** dialog for the V (because bends would appear as arrows). Type the number below the tab staff at the point of the V using **Create ▸ Text ▸ Special Text ▸ Tablature numbers**.

Vibrato bar scoop

A vibrato bar scoop is played by depressing the bar just before striking the note, then quickly releasing it.

To write this, use the symbol from the **Guitar** row of the **Create ▸ Symbol** dialog (shortcut Z). On a notation staff, you should also add a "w/bar" line from the **Create ▸ Line** dialog (shortcut L); to extend the line rightwards, hit space.

Vibrato bar dip

A vibrato bar dip is played by striking the note, then dropping a specified number of steps, then releasing back to the original pitch.

To notate this, use the V symbol from the **Guitar** row of the **Create ▸ Symbol** dialog, typing the numbers above using **Create ▸ Text ▸ Other staff text ▸ Small text**, then, on a notation staff, add a "w/bar" line from the **Create ▸ Line** dialog.

Other techniques

Other guitar markings are easily created as follows:

- *Hammer-on and pull-off*: use a slur – 📖 **2.28 Slurs**

- *Tapping:* use a slur, with a + articulation on the first note if appropriate (🕮 **2.3 Articulations**); for left-hand tapping, use the ○ symbol on the **Techniques** row of the **Create ▸ Symbol** dialog (🕮 **2.31 Symbols**)

- *Vibrato and wide vibrato:* suitable lines are provided near the bottom of the list in the **Create ▸ Line** dialog – 🕮 **2.21 Lines**

- *Trill:* use a trill line – 🕮 **2.21 Lines**

- *Arpeggiate:* use an arpeggio line – 🕮 **2.2 Arpeggios**

- *Tremolo picking:* use a tremolo – 🕮 **2.34 Tremolos**

- *Shake:* use a shake symbol – 🕮 **2.31 Symbols**

- *Harmonics:* on notation staves, use a diamond notehead (🕮 **2.25 Noteheads**), and on tab staves, write "Harm.", "H.H." (for a harp harmonic), or "P.H." (for a pinched harmonic) above the note in Small text

- *Slap:* write "T" above the note in Small text

- *Pop:* write "P" above the note in Small text

- *X notehead:* select a note and choose the X notehead from the **Notes** panel of the Properties window

- *Pick scrape:* use an angled wiggly gliss. line from the **Create ▸ Line** dialog and write "P.S." above the tab staff with Small text; on a notation staff, use a cross notehead

- *Muffled strings:* use cross noteheads – 🕮 **2.25 Noteheads**

- *Rake:* on a notation staff, create grace notes with cross noteheads; on a tab staff, either copy the music from a notation staff (in which case the noteheads are automatically copied as crosses) or change the noteheads after creating the notes, and then add a suitable "Rake" line from the **Create ▸ Line** dialog.

- *Fingering:* use **Create ▸ Text ▸ Other Staff Text ▸ Guitar fingering (p i m a)** and write the fingering above each note or chord

The **Create ▸ Line** dialog (shortcut L) contains lines for most of the common guitar techniques, such as "w/bar," "P.M." (for palm muting), and so on. Should you need to create additional lines for guitar techniques, 🕮 **8.15 Edit Lines**.

Showing tunings on tab staves

When using non-standard guitar tunings, it is helpful to show the pitch of each string directly on the tab staff, as shown on the left (depicting Open C tuning).

Sibelius shows these pitches by default for non-standard tunings. If you don't want them, select a bar in the staff, choose **House Style ▸ Edit Instruments**, click **Edit Instrument**, click **Yes**, then click **Edit Staff Type**, and finally switch off the **Key signatures / Tuning** option on the General page (🕮 **8.14 Edit Instruments**).

Customizing tab, tunings and fret instruments

Sibelius has more than 30 alternative guitar tunings built-in (not to mention half a dozen banjo tunings, 11 dobro tunings, two sitar tunings and several lute tunings!), but despite this comprehensive collection, you can also create your own, as follows.

Changing the tuning of an instrument

To change the tuning used by a staff in your score, simply change it to a different instrument. With nothing in the score selected, choose Create ▶ Other ▶ Instrument Change, select the instrument with the desired tuning, click OK, and then click in the score to the left of the initial barline at the very start of the score.

But if the tuning you're looking for available in a built-in instrument, you can easily modify one of the existing tunings or create one from scratch using House Style ▶ Edit Instruments – 📖 **8.14 Edit Instruments**.

White out around tab notes

Different publishers have different conventions for whether numbers in tab staves sit directly on the staff lines or whether they are cushioned by a little white space (so that the staff line does not go through the number). Naturally, Sibelius allows you to specify this yourself by editing the settings for individual instruments in the House Style ▶ Edit Instruments dialog. Choose the instrument in the dialog, then click Edit Instrument; if the instrument already exists in your score, you'll be asked if you're sure you want to continue, so click Yes, then in the Edit Instrument dialog click Edit Staff Type. The relevant option is White out around notes on the Tab page.

Sibelius's default settings are as follows:

- For tab staff types that show rhythms where stems are drawn in the staff, the White out around notes option is switched on; this makes the stems clearer.
- For tab staff types that show rhythms where stems are drawn entirely outside the staff, and for tab staff types that don't show rhythms, the White out around notes option is switched off.

Tab can be fun

Oh yes, it can!

In Sibelius, guitar tab is treated as a special type of staff (rather like a percussion staff), and just as Sibelius lets you change the number of staff lines mid-score, you can change from notation to tab mid-score, or even mid-staff – or for that matter, change the string tunings mid-score.

Try this out: from Create ▶ Other ▶ Instrument Change, choose a guitar tab instrument, then click in the middle of a notation staff that has music on it. From there onwards, the notation will turn into tab, and you'll find that the changeover point is in fact an "object" (a bit like a clef), which shows as a purple rectangle when selected. Now try dragging this rectangle left and right, or up and down from staff to staff, and you'll see that Sibelius instantly converts all the following notation to tab. Most excellent!

Engraving Rules options

The Guitar page of the House Style ▶ Engraving Rules dialog (shortcut Ctrl+Shift+E or ⇧⌘E) is mostly concerned with the esoterica of chord diagrams (explained on page 617), but there are a few tab-specific options, namely:

- **Use 'full' on tab bends:** with this option switched on, guitar bends of a whole step will be marked with the text "full"; switching the option off will make whole step (tone) bends use the number "1" instead

Notations

- **Use arrows on tab bends:** switch off this option if you prefer bend lines on tab staves to be drawn without arrowheads
- **Draw grace notes with 'tablature letters' text style:** this option allows you to adjust the size of grace notes on tab staves independently from the size of cue notes on notation staves. When this option is switched on, grace notes on tab staves take their size from the **Tablature letters** text style. The option is switched off by default.

You can also edit the text style used for tablature numbers by clicking the **Edit Text Style** button.

2.16 Guitar scale diagrams

Guitar scale diagrams are commonly found in guitar tuition and method books. They show all or part of a guitar's fretboard, either horizontally or vertically orientated, with dots to show each of the finger positions required to play a particular scale.

Sibelius comes with a library of hundreds of ready-made guitar scale diagrams for over 25 different types of scales, and you can easily edit these or create further diagrams to suit your own purposes.

Adding a guitar scale diagram to the score

To add a guitar scale diagram to your score, simply choose **Create ▸ Other ▸ Guitar Scale Diagram**. The following dialog appears:

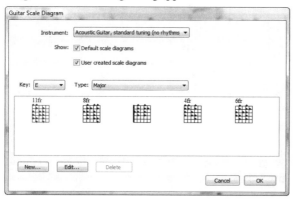

• The **Instrument** menu allows you to choose which instrument your scale diagram is for: the ready-made scale diagrams are all set up for a 6-string guitar using the standard tuning, so depending on the choice you make here, you may not have any pre-defined scales to choose from.

• **Default scale diagrams** and **User-created scale diagrams** allow you to choose whether the ready-made scale diagrams should appear, or your own user-defined scale diagrams, or both.

• Choose the **Key** and **Type** using the drop-down menus to determine which scale diagrams appear in the preview below.

To choose a scale diagram, simply select it in the preview area, then click **OK**. If there was no selection in your score before you invoked the dialog, your mouse pointer will now turn blue, and the scale diagram will be created where you click; if, on the other hand, there was a selection in your score, the scale diagram is created at the beginning of that selection.

Changing the size of scale diagrams

To make all guitar scale diagrams in your score larger or smaller by the same amount, choose **House Style ▸ Engraving Rules** and go to the **Guitar** page, where you will find the **Default size** slider. Drag this to the right to make all scale diagrams larger, and to the left to make them smaller. Be aware that adjusting the **Default size** slider also adjusts the size of any guitar chord diagrams displayed above chord symbols in your score.

To adjust the size of a single chord diagram, select it in the score, then open the **General** panel of Properties and increase or decrease the **Scale n%** value.

Editing or creating a new guitar scale diagram

To edit an existing guitar scale diagram, double-click the scale diagram in the score you want to edit, or select it in the preview area of the Guitar Scale Diagram dialog, then click Edit. To create a new guitar scale diagram, select the closest existing diagram in the Guitar Scale Diagram dialog, then click New. In both cases, you will see the following dialog:

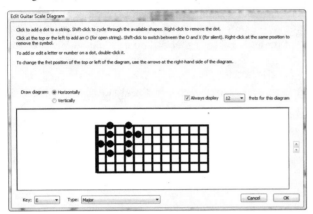

In this dialog you can choose whether the diagram should be drawn Horizontally (as shown above, with the nut at the left-hand side) or Vertically (with the nut at the top). You can override the default number of frets shown in the diagram (as specified on the Guitar page of House Style ▸ Engraving Rules) by switching on the Always display *n* frets per diagram option, and choosing the number of frets (between 3 and 15).

To add a dot to a string, simply click at the desired position; Shift-click will cycle through the available dot shapes (black circle, white circle, black square, white square, black diamond, white diamond). To remove a dot, right-click the dot you want to remove. To add an open string marker at the nut, simply click at the left or the top, as appropriate; Shift-click to turn that into an X (denoting that the string should not be played). To remove an O or an X, simply right-click it.

You can also add a fingering number or note name to a dot by double-clicking it: a flashing cursor will appear. Type the number or letter you want to appear in the dot, and right-click (Windows) *or* Control-click (Mac) to see a word menu, from which you can choose accidentals.

To change the scale type or root note, choose the desired values from the Key and Type menus at the bottom of the dialog, and click OK to save the new or edited chord diagram.

Showing string pitches and fret numbers

The Guitar page of House Style ▸ Engraving Rules contains options to show string pitches at the left-hand side of horizontal guitar scale diagrams, and fret numbers below the diagrams – see **Engraving Rules options** on page 617.

Sharing guitar scale diagrams

Any guitar scale diagram you create or edit is saved in your personal library of scale diagrams, which is a file called Scale library.scl, found in a folder called Scale Diagrams inside your user-level application data folder – see **User-editable files** on page 642. You can send this file to your colleagues or friends if you want to share your scale libraries with them.

2.17 Hairpins

📖 **2.21 Lines**.

Notations

Hairpin is the colloquial term for a line that represents a gradual change of dynamic, typically over a relatively short space of time, while text such as *cresc.* or *dim.* is favored for changes of dynamic over longer time spans.

Creating and extending hairpins

Select the note where you want the hairpin to begin and type **H** for a crescendo, or **Shift-H** for a diminuendo. As with other lines, you can extend and retract the right-hand end of the hairpin using **Space** and **Shift-Space** respectively.

Use **Alt**+←/→ to move between a hairpin's handles; you can use ←/→ (with **Ctrl** *or* ⌘ for larger steps) to make fine adjustments to the position of each end of the hairpin.

Hairpins often have an explicit dynamic at the left- or right-hand end, or both ends:

Simply create the dynamic using Expression text, and Sibelius will automatically adjust the length of the hairpin to accommodate the dynamic. You can even drag a dynamic into the middle of a hairpin, and Sibelius automatically breaks the hairpin:

p———*f*———*ff*

Hairpins can be angled by dragging either end of the hairpin, but it is generally recommended that hairpins should be horizontal wherever possible.

Types of hairpin

Create ▸ Line also contains dashed, dotted and "from/to silence" hairpins, and **Create ▸ Symbol** contains suitable "exponential" symbols to add to the end of crescendos if required.

Hairpins over two systems

When a hairpin is split over two systems, Sibelius draws the hairpin in two halves, the vertical position of each of which can be adjusted independently of the other.

Hairpin apertures

By default, Sibelius makes the aperture (that is, the distance between the two lines at the open end of the hairpin) the same, regardless of the length of the hairpin. In some published music, however, the aperture of the hairpin widens slightly the longer the hairpin is, and Sibelius allows you to reproduce this appearance. You can adjust the aperture of all hairpins using the settings in **House Style ▸ Engraving Rules**, or an individual hairpin using the **Lines** panel of Properties – read on.

Adjusting hairpin apertures globally

The **Lines** page of **House Style ▸ Engraving Rules** has the following options for hairpin apertures:

- Small aperture *n* spaces: the aperture for hairpins that are shorter than the length specified in Large aperture if wider than *n* spaces
- Large aperture *n* spaces: the aperture for hairpins that are longer than the length specified in Large aperture if wider than *n* spaces
- Continuation small aperture *n* spaces: the aperture at the end of the first segment of a *crescendo* hairpin over a system or page break, or the aperture at the beginning of the second segment of a *diminuendo* hairpin over a system or page break
- Continuation large aperture *n* spaces: the aperture at the beginning of the second segment of a *crescendo* hairpin over a system or page break, or the aperture at the end of the first segment of a *diminuendo* hairpin over a system or page break.

Adjusting hairpin apertures individually

If you want a particular hairpin to have a non-standard aperture, you can change it using the options on the Lines panel of Properties (⊞ **5.17 Properties**). Hairpin end apertures and Hairpin continuation apertures control the four possible points of a hairpin, shown here split across a system or page break:

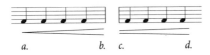

a.　　　　*b.*　*c.*　　　　*d.*

- Closed (*a.* in the above example) is the closed end of the hairpin, and can be set larger than 0 if desired, to make the hairpin open at one end
- Open (*d.* in the above example) is the open end of the hairpin; to override the default value, switch on the Open checkbox
- Small (*c.* in the above example) is the segment of the hairpin that uses the Small continuation aperture (as defined in House Style ▸ Engraving Rules); this only has an effect if the hairpin is split across a system or page break
- Large (*b.* in the above example) is the segment of the hairpin that uses the Large continuation aperture; this only has an effect if the hairpin is split across a system or page break.

Interpretation during playback

You can adjust the playback of an individual hairpin using the Playback panel of the Properties window – see **Hairpins** on page 262.

Default position

Sibelius automatically positions hairpins below instrumental staves, and above vocal staves. You can adjust the default position of each type of hairpin using House Style ▸ Default Positions – ⊞ **8.12 Default Positions**.

2.18 Instruments

📖 2.29 Staves, 3.8 Instrument names, 8.14 Edit Instruments.

Instruments or staves?

In the slightly technical meaning of "instrument" used in Sibelius, an instrument is one or more staves with a single name appearing at the left. So a piano with two staves counts as one instrument because its name only appears once, between the staves. This also means that Violin 1 counts as one instrument, even though there will typically be many violinists. Even if the Violin 1's divide onto two staves, the name Violin 1 still only appears once between them, so it's still only one instrument as far as Sibelius is concerned. Singers are also instruments. If there is a single percussion staff, it counts as just one instrument, even though it may be used for snare drum, cymbals, tom-toms, etc. simultaneously.

Creating instruments

At any time you can create an instrument that isn't already in your score – just choose **Create ▸ Instruments** (shortcut I).

This is the same as the dialog you get if you click **Change Instruments** in the **File ▸ New** dialog when creating a new score.

The dialog is split into two halves: the left half is for choosing new instruments to add to the score, and the right half shows you the staves already in the score and allows you to delete them, reorder them, and add extra staves to existing instruments.

To add a new instrument:

- Set the **Choose from** list to the option that most closely matches the kind of ensemble you're writing for, because different ensembles contain different instruments and often in a slightly different order:
  - **All instruments** lists all 600-odd instruments Sibelius knows about
  - **Common instruments** omits esoterica like flageolets and bass viols

- Band instruments includes all the instruments you would find in drum corps, marching, military, brass or wind bands
- Jazz instruments lists all the instruments you typically find in jazz combos and big bands
- Orchestral instruments has all the woodwind, brass, percussion and strings you'd normally find in an orchestra
- Rock and pop instruments has guitars, keyboards, singers, and so on
- World instruments lists ethnic instruments by geographical region.

- Choose the instrumental family from the Family list, e.g. woodwind, brass, strings, etc.
- Select the instrument you want to add from the Instrument list; click Add to add it to the Staves in Score list, where it will appear with a + before its name, to indicate it's new. It is listed in the position in which it will appear in the score when you click OK. You can add several adjacent instruments quickly by dragging down the Instruments list with the mouse before clicking Add.
- If you change your mind, you can select a staff in the Staves in Score list and click Delete from Score to remove it
- You can also select a staff and use the Up and Down buttons to move it in the vertical order. All staves of a single instrument (e.g. both staves of a piano or harp, or all Violin I staves) always move together.
- If you want to make one or more of the staves small, e.g. for a solo instrument, select it in the Staves in Score list and switch on the Small staff checkbox.
- When you click OK, Sibelius makes all the necessary changes to the score, adding, removing, and/or reordering staves.

You can also use this dialog to add extra staves to existing instruments in your score – see **Multi-staff instruments** in ▢ **2.29 Staves** for more details. When you add a new instrument to your score, Sibelius automatically creates a dynamic part for that instrument too – ▢ **7.1 Working with parts**.

Deleting instruments

To delete instruments, choose Create ▸ Instruments, select the staff or staves you want to delete from the Staves in Score list, and click Delete from Score; or alternatively, select them throughout the score as a passage by triple-clicking in the score, and hit Delete.

In either case, you will be prompted that this will also delete all music on them; if you want to proceed, click Yes, then click OK to close the dialog.

System separators

System separators are thick double lines drawn between systems, normally at the left-hand side, to make the format clearer. Right system separators (drawn at the right margin) are very rarely required but, true to Sibelius's unrelenting comprehensiveness, are nonetheless available should you hanker after them.

You can switch system separators on or off using Draw left/right separator on the Instruments page of the House Style ▸ Engraving Rules dialog. You can also set the minimum number of staves a system should have before the separators will appear, and the distance of the separators from the margin.

Because this option is copied into parts, you can also use it to control automatically which parts have separators; e.g. if you want them to appear only in complex percussion parts containing (say) 3 or more staves, you can set the minimum number of staves to 3 in the score, and all the parts will also get the same setting.

Standard instrument orders

Different kinds of music use standard vertical orders in which instruments usually appear. For example, in orchestral music woodwind goes at the top, followed by brass, percussion, singers, keyboards and strings. Within each section the order is standard too, as shown on Sibelius's Instruments *dialog.*

There are a few exceptions to these standard orders:

* *Music where a soloist is predominant and so goes on the top staff*

* *Percussion: the order of instruments within the percussion section can vary from score to score*

* *Music for two orchestras, choirs etc.*

Instrument ranges

Sibelius can draw notes in shades of red if they're too high or low for an instrument's range (switch on **View ▸ Note Colors ▸ Notes out of Range** – 📖 **5.23 View menu**). Each instrument has two ranges: the "professional" range, and the "comfortable" range, both of which you can adjust.

The professional range, generally speaking, defines the absolute highest and lowest notes playable on a particular instrument; notes outside this range are colored bright red. The comfortable range defines the highest and lowest notes that a typical non-professional player routinely uses; notes outside this range but within the professional range are colored dark red.

Of course, most instruments do not have a clearly-defined range (think of singers, for example). Commonly used optional adaptations to instruments, such as the double bass low C string, the flute low B and piano high C (as opposed to A) tend to be included in the professional range but not the comfortable one.

If you want to adjust the ranges of instruments in your score, 📖 **8.14 Edit Instruments**.

Transposing instruments

Sibelius takes care of all the complications surrounding transposing instruments for you:

* You can input music either at transposed pitch or at sounding (concert) pitch. To switch instantly between the two representations at any time, simply choose **Notes ▸ Transposing Score** (shortcut **Ctrl+Shift+T** *or* ⇧⌘T) or click the appropriate toolbar button.

* When copying music between transposing instruments, Sibelius automatically transposes the music as necessary so that it always *sounds* the same. This saves big headaches when copying (say) from Clarinet in A to Horn in F.

* When you look at a part for a transposing instrument from a sounding pitch score, you don't even need to think about transposing the part – Sibelius does it for you automatically

* You can input music from a MIDI keyboard either by playing how it sounds or how it's written – e.g. you can play transposed parts into Sibelius to produce a combined sounding pitch score. Just switch on **Input written pitches** on the **Note Input** page of **File ▸ Preferences** (in the **Sibelius** menu on Mac).

Accidentals and key signatures for transposing instruments

Sibelius will, by default, notate transposing instruments correctly using appropriate accidentals for the remote key. If you had, say, an A flat written for alto saxophone in F major and then switched on transposing score, Sibelius would correctly notate that note as F natural in D major.

In key signatures that change sign when transposed, potential problems with enharmonic spelling can arise. For example, a score in F sharp major with a part for clarinet in B flat would end up in A flat major when transposed. Under normal circumstances Sibelius would only need to transpose notes up by a major 2nd for the clarinet in B flat, but here the transposition degree changes to a diminished 3rd (i.e. F sharps become A flats as opposed to G sharps).

Sibelius has an option to take care of this rather mind-bending detail automatically for you: switch on **Adjust note spelling in transposing instruments in remote keys** on the **Clefs and Key Signatures** page of **House Style ▸ Engraving Rules**.

Normally this option should be switched on, but if your score contains special-case spellings that you would not write under normal circumstances, you may find that switching off this option remedies problems in the resulting transposition. For example, an A double-flat on a clarinet in B flat in F sharp major does not transpose nicely up a diminished 3rd! (It would become C *triple*-flat, so rarely used that there is currently no accepted standard as to how this should actually be notated.)

In the situation where a transposing instrument's part could be written using either sharps or flats, Sibelius allows you either to use the key signature resulting from transposing the concert pitch key, or to simplify the key signature using its enharmonic equivalent.

By way of example, consider a piece in B major that has a part for Clarinet in B flat. The composer may wish to write that part in C sharp major using seven sharps, or simplify the key signature to D flat major as it has only five flats. By default, Sibelius will simplify remote key signatures when this happens. However, if you wish to use the unsimplified form, switch off **Respell remote key signatures in transposing score** on the **Clefs and Key Signatures** page of **House Style ▸ Engraving Rules**.

Multiple players and divisi...

Wind instruments frequently use two or more numbered players, e.g. Trumpets 1, 2 and 3. Strings often divide onto two staves ("divisi") or sometimes onto several staves numbered by string desks. Choral staves frequently divide onto two staves (semichorus or Dec and Can). There are two ways to handle these situations, depending on the case:

...easy case

If your score is consistent throughout as to which players use which staves, then there's no problem. For instance, if all three trumpets in a score are always on the same staff, just create a single Trumpet instrument and rename it (say) "Trumpets 1.2.3" at the start.

Similarly, if trumpets 1+2 are always together on one staff and trumpet 3 always has a separate one, just create two separately-named instruments (called "Trumpet 1.2" and "Trumpet 3"), or else create a single instrument ("Trumpets") and add a second staff to it.

...more complex case

Complications only arise if players hop around from staff to staff mid-score, because then you'll want to change the names at the left-hand side mid-score.

For instance, all three trumpets may play in unison on a single "Trumpets 1.2.3" staff in some places, they may divide onto two staves ("Trumpets 1.2" and "Trumpet 3") elsewhere, and in complex passages they may even split onto three separate staves.

Because the name at the left-hand side will need to change mid-score, you should create a separate Trumpet instrument for every different name that you want to use – so in a complex score for three trumpets you might create five instruments called Trumpets 1.2.3, Trumpets 1.2, Trumpet 1, Trumpet 2 and Trumpet 3. Then simply write the music on the appropriate staff, and hide the spare staves when not in use (💭 **2.29 Staves**).

Indicate where the staves divide or join, or where the players change, using the Technique text style to write (e.g.) "1.2" or "a 2" or "div." or "unis."

Where the number of staves changes, you should put a system break, otherwise you will find partially-used staves appearing, which looks odd.

If you want to produce separate parts for individual players, 💭 **7.4 Extracting parts**.

Doubling instruments

Doubling instruments are two or more instruments played by the same person. In nearly all cases, you should use Create ▸ Other ▸ Instrument Change wherever the player changes instrument (see below).

One possible exception is for unpitched percussion, e.g. triangle, snare drum and bass drum on the same staff. This is discussed in detail in 💭 **2.26 Percussion**.

Instrument changes

Sibelius makes it easy to change instruments at any point along a staff using Create ▸ Other ▸ Instrument Change. First consider whether you want the instrument change to take effect up until the end of the score (or up to an existing instrument change later in the score), or only temporarily for a specific passage.

* To change instrument temporarily, first select the passage for which you want the instrument change to take effect; Sibelius will automatically revert to the original instrument at the end of the selection.

* To change instrument permanently, select a single note after which you want the instrument change to take effect, or make no selection (in which case you can click to place the instrument change in a moment).

* Once you have selected where you want the instrument change to begin, and optionally where you want it to end, choose Create ▸ Other ▸ Instrument Change (shortcut Ctrl+Shift+Alt+I *or* ⇧⌥⌘I). The dialog shown below appears.

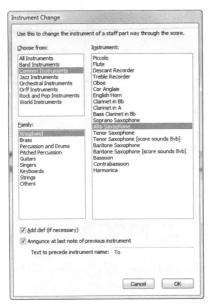

- Choose the instrument you want to change to from the list. The two extra options you can set are as follows:
  - If **Add clef (if necessary)** is switched on, Sibelius will create a clef change at the point where the instrument change occurs, if the clef of the new instrument is different to that of the original instrument
  - If **Announce at last note of previous instrument** is switched on, Sibelius will create a warning, "To [instrument]", at the start of the rests preceding the change. If you want Sibelius to use a word other than "To" before the instrument's name in the warning, change **Text to precede instrument name**.
- Now click **OK**. If you didn't have a selection before you opened the dialog, your mouse pointer will now be blue, and you can click in the score to place your instrument change; otherwise, Sibelius automatically creates the instrument change (or changes) at the selection.

Sibelius always does the following for you when you create an instrument change:

- Changes the playback sound of the staff as appropriate
- Changes the instrument name on subsequent systems (which you can edit if you wish). If you don't want the instrument name to change, choose **House Style ▸ Engraving Rules** (shortcut **Ctrl+Shift+E** *or* ⇧⌘E), go to the **Instruments** page, and switch off **Change instrument names at start of system after instrument changes**.
- Writes the name of the new instrument above the top of the staff where it starts playing (you can edit this in place if you wish, or change the default instrument change name in **House Style ▸ Edit Instruments** – 📖 **8.14 Edit Instruments**)
- Changes the transposition of the staff, if appropriate (e.g. if switching from a B♭ to A clarinet), showing an appropriate change of key signature if **Notes ▸ Transposing Score** is switched on
- Changes the staff type, if appropriate (e.g. number of staff lines, tab or normal notation, etc.).

The pictures below show how instrument changes appear in your score, in this case when changing from Clarinet in B♭ to Alto Saxophone (in E♭). On the left, **View ▸ Hidden Objects** is switched on (so you can see exactly where the instrument changes as a gray rectangle), and **Notes ▸ Transposing Score** is switched off (i.e. the music is in sounding pitch); on the right, **Notes ▸ Transposing Score** is switched on.

When you switch **Notes ▸ Transposing Score** on or off, note that the instrument change may take up more or less space. If you find the spacing looks odd, try selecting the affected bars and choosing **Layout ▸ Reset Note Spacing** (shortcut **Ctrl+Shift+N** *or* ⇧⌘N).

Editing instrument changes

You can move the instrument change along the staff by dragging either the gray rectangle or the key signature to the left or right, or using the ←/→ keys. If a clef change was created alongside the instrument change, note that it will not move when you move the instrument change itself – they are separate objects. (This also means that if you delete the instrument change, the clef will remain, and vice versa.)

The text marking above the instrument change can be moved independently of the instrument change itself, by selecting it and moving it with the mouse or arrow keys. You can edit the text by double-clicking it, just like any other text object; you can also hide the text by selecting it and choosing **Edit ▸ Hide or Show ▸ Hide** (shortcut **Ctrl+Shift+H** *or* ⇧⌘H).

You can also copy, paste and delete instrument changes just like any other object in Sibelius.

Instrument changes and dynamic parts

By default, instrument changes created in the full score will appear in dynamic parts, but you can delete them in the parts if you want to without affecting the full score. Instrument changes you create in dynamic parts, conversely, will not appear in the full score. This allows you to create multiple dynamic parts for different instruments or different transpositions – see **Parts in different transpositions** on page 548.

2.19 Jazz articulations

📖 **2.3 Articulations**, 📖 **2.21 Lines**.

There are a number of special notations used for wind and brass instruments in jazz ensembles, all of which are simple to create in Sibelius.

Plops, scoops, doits and falls

The fifth Keypad layout (shortcut F11) provides a quick and easy way to create four common kinds of special effects:

| Plop | Scoop | Doit | Fall |

- A plop (shortcut 5) is used to approach a target note from a higher indefinite starting pitch
- A scoop (shortcut 7), sometimes also known as a rip, is used to approach a target note from a lower indefinite starting pitch
- A doit (shortcut 9), sometimes also known as a lift, starts on a definite pitch and slides upward to an indefinite ending pitch
- A fall (shortcut 8), sometimes also known as a fall-off or spill, is a downward drop from a specific note to an indefinite ending pitch.

If you add any of these jazz articulations to a chord, Sibelius will automatically add it to all notes of the chord, taking into account factors like backnotes (where one or more notes is on the opposite side of the stem), rhythm dots, and so on.

To adjust the horizontal position of an individual plop, scoop, doit or fall, select it and type Shift+Alt+←/→ *or* ⇧⌥←/→ (to select the jazz articulation without using the mouse, use Alt+←/→ *or* ⌥←/→ with the note selected).

If your score is played back by a device that supports the playback of these symbols, Sibelius will play them back. You can change the sound ID changes that they give rise to on the **Symbols** page of Play ▶ Dictionary (📖 **4.9 Playback dictionary**).

Shakes

A shake is a rapid oscillation between the original note and the next highest note in the overtone series, or sometimes an even wider interval for a more dramatic effect, normally played on a brass instrument.

The symbol for a shake is a wavy line, which can be created from the **Create ▶ Line** dialog. If you need to create a lot of shakes, you may find it helpful to assign a keyboard shortcut to the wavy line, called **Vibrato**, which can be found in the **Line styles** category (📖 **5.12 Menus and shortcuts**). You may even prefer the look of the fatter **Wide vibrato** line.

Flip or turn

A flip, also sometimes known as a turn, is an upward gliss to a neighboring or indefinite pitch followed by a downward gliss, played when moving from a higher pitch to a lower one.

Flips use the same kind of line as guitar bends (📖 **2.15 Guitar notation and tab**), so to create one, select the note on which you want the flip to start and hit J.

Bend or smear

A bend, also sometimes known as a smear, is where the player starts the note flatter than written, and slides up to the correct pitch. Add a bend using the symbol on the fourth **More ornaments** row towards the bottom of **Create ▸ Symbol** (shortcut Z).

Long falls

A long fall is, as its name suggests, like a regular fall, only the effect is supposed to last longer, and perhaps the target pitch is lower than for a regular fall.

To create a long fall, use the wavy glissando line in **Create ▸ Line** (shortcut L).

Engraving Rules options

To adjust the default position of plops, scoops, doits and falls, choose **House Style ▸ Engraving Rules** (shortcut **Ctrl+Shift+E** *or* ⇧⌘E), and go to the **Jazz Articulations** page. Here you will find a comprehensive set of options for the horizontal and vertical positions of these jazz symbols relative to noteheads, with separate settings for notes on lines and spaces.

Notations

2.20 Key signatures

📖 **5.20 Transposing**.

The key signatures that appear at the start of each system are automatic. They are adjusted to suit the current clef, transposed for transposing instruments and omitted from those instruments that don't usually have them (e.g. most percussion).

The only key signatures you have to specify are the one at the start plus any key changes that occur in the music.

Creating key signatures

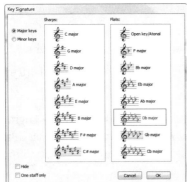

Choose **Create ▸ Key Signature** (shortcut K) and click the key signature you want. Switch between major and minor keys using the radio buttons to the left of the dialog. (The distinction between major and minor keys is primarily so Sibelius knows how best to spell accidentals inputted from MIDI – for instance, in A minor it prefers writing D♯ to E♭, whereas in C major it prefers E♭ to D♯.)

If you select, say, a note or rest and then create a key signature, Sibelius automatically places it after the selected object.

If you create a key signature change in the middle of a piece, Sibelius automatically precedes the change with a double barline, which you can delete if you feel particularly strongly about that kind of thing.

If you want to change key signature for a number of bars and then return to the original key, simply select the bars in which you want the new key to take effect before you create it. Sibelius will create your new key signature at the start of the selection, and restore the original key signature at the end of the selection.

If you want to transpose your music as well as change the key signature, use **Notes ▸ Transpose** instead – 📖 **5.20 Transposing**.

To create a key signature at the beginning of your score, make sure nothing is selected, then choose **Create ▸ Key Signature**, choose the key signature and click at the start of the score. You can also use this method to create a key change with the mouse anywhere in the score.

If your score is a transposing score, choose a key signature in sounding pitch – it will automatically be transposed for transposing instruments.

Moving and deleting key signature changes

You can move key changes with the mouse or arrow keys.

To delete the key signature at the start of a score, either choose it in the **File ▸ New** dialog when creating the score, or else create an **Open key/Atonal, C major**, or **A minor** key signature and put it on top of the existing one.

To delete a key signature elsewhere (i.e. a key change), select the key change and hit **Delete**. To delete a change of key signature that happens at the start of a system, delete the cautionary key change at the end of the previous system.

Cautionary key signatures

If a new section, song or movement in a score starts in a new key, you often want to omit the cautionary key signature that would otherwise appear at the end of the preceding system. It's easiest to do this when you create the key signature at the start of the new movement: just switch on **Hide** in the **Create ▸ Key Signature** dialog.

To hide the cautionary key signature after creating it, select it and choose **Edit ▸ Hide or Show ▸ Hide** (shortcut **Ctrl+Shift+H** *or* ⇧⌘H). In either case, ensure that the preceding system ends with a system or page break, otherwise if the score reformats the hidden key change may end up mid-system and it won't be clear where it occurs. For more information about hiding objects, ▭ **5.9 Hiding objects**.

Open key/Atonal

Some transposing scores that are apparently in C major have no key signatures in the transposing instruments either. The composer has omitted all key signatures because the key changes too often, the music is in a scale or mode other than major or minor (the only two scales for which key signatures are designed to be used), or the music has no obvious tonal center.

To use this notation, choose **Open key/Atonal** at the top right of the **Create ▸ Key Signature** dialog.

You can switch back to music with key signatures later in the score by creating a normal key signature (e.g. C major). A classic case of this is Stravinsky's Rite of Spring, which is mostly atonal but partly in keys – mostly the transposing instruments don't have key signatures, but sometimes they do.

If your score uses an **Open key/Atonal** key signature, you will need to show accidentals where appropriate. There are a number of different approaches to how accidentals should appear:

- At the first occurrence of a sharpened or flattened note in a bar, but not at subsequent repetitions of that pitch within the same bar: this is what Sibelius does by default
- At every sharpened or flattened note, wherever it appears: use **Plug-ins ▸ Accidentals ▸ Add Accidentals to All Sharp and Flat Notes** to achieve this
- On every note, including naturals: use **Plug-ins ▸ Accidentals ▸ Add Accidentals to All Notes**.

▭ **6.1 Working with plug-ins** for more information.

Instruments without key signatures

Unpitched percussion staves never have key signatures, Timpani and Horn usually don't, and Trumpet and Harp sometimes don't. Although Sibelius has alternative instruments in the **Create ▸ Instruments** dialog for all these common exceptions, if you want to specify that some other instrument doesn't have a key signature:

- Select a bar in the instrument in question, and choose House Style ▸ Edit Instruments
- Click Edit Instrument, click Yes when asked if you want to proceed, then in the dialog that appears click Edit Staff Type
- On the General page of the Edit Staff Type dialog, switch off Key signatures / Tuning
- Click OK, then OK again, and finally Close.

For further information about editing instruments, ⊞ **8.14 Edit Instruments**.

Enharmonic key signatures

Occasionally a score will have sharp and flat key signatures simultaneously in order to simplify the keys of transposing instruments. For example, if a score is in B major (sounding pitch), with 5 sharps, trumpets in B♭ will often be written not in C♯ major (7 sharps) but in the enharmonically equivalent and easier-to-read D♭ major (5 flats). Sibelius does this for you automatically when the Respell remote key signatures in transposing score option is switched on in the Clefs and Key Signatures page of the House Style ▸ Engraving Rules dialog.

Another useful trick can be employed for non-transposing instruments, such as harp. For example, in your B major score, you'd ideally want the harp to be written in C♭ major. To do this:

- Create a C♭ major key signature in each of the harp staves using the One staff only option (see below)
- Select the harp staves, and choose Plug-ins ▸ Accidentals ▸ Simplify Accidentals, which rewrites the harp staves in C♭ major, but leaves all the other staves alone.

Multiple key signatures

In some contemporary scores, different key signatures are used in different instruments (not to be confused with the more common case of transposing instruments having different key signatures). To create a key signature that only applies to one staff, switch on One staff only in the Create ▸ Key Signature dialog when creating it. This option can also be useful when writing in keys with many accidentals (e.g. F♯ major), where some of the instruments in your score may idiomatically benefit from being written in the enharmonic equivalent using flats (e.g. G♭ major).

The note spacing of other staves in the system may be affected by the insertion of a key signature on a single staff; to correct this, select the bar and choose Layout ▸ Reset Note Spacing (shortcut Ctrl+Shift+N *or* ⇧⌘N).

Engraving Rules options

The Clefs and Key Signatures page of the House Style ▸ Engraving Rules dialog (shortcut Ctrl+Shift+E *or* ⇧⌘E) has the usual round-up of the arcane and the obscure. The main option you might be interested in is Cautionary naturals, which adds cautionary naturals to key changes to cancel sharps/flats in the previous key.

With this option off, cautionary naturals appear only when changing to C major, A minor or Open key/Atonal, since (if you think about it) without cautionary naturals in these cases, the key change would be a bit hard to see.

2.21 Lines

  📖 **2.2 Arpeggios, 2.17 Hairpins, 2.28 Slurs, 5.7 Filters and Find, 8.15 Edit Lines.**

The **Create ▸ Line** dialog (shortcut L) contains special lines used in music such as trills, slurs, hairpins, glissandi and so on for entry in your score. You can also edit existing lines and design new ones – 📖 **8.15 Edit Lines.**

Creating lines

All lines are created in the same way:

* Lines are either created automatically at the position of the selected note/rest, or can be placed with the mouse:
  * If you want the line to be automatically positioned, either select the note/rest where you want the line to start, or select a passage of notes over which you want the line to last
  * If you want to place the line with the mouse, make sure nothing is selected – hit **Esc**
* Choose **Create ▸ Line** (shortcut L). The dialog is split into two halves: *staff lines* (which apply only to a single staff) on the left, and *system lines* (which apply to all staves and appear in all parts) on the right.
* Select the line you want to create and click **OK**. The line will either be placed automatically in the score at the selected object/passage, or the mouse pointer will change color to show that it is "loaded" with an object – click in the score to create the line.
* To extend the line rightwards a note at a time, hit **space**; to retract the line leftwards again, type **Shift-space**. You can also drag either end of a line with the mouse. System lines cannot be extended and retracted using the keyboard.
* When either end of a line is selected (shown by a small blue box), you can also make small adjustments to its position using the arrow keys (with **Ctrl** *or* ⌘ for larger steps).

Slurs

Slurs are a special kind of line – 📖 **2.28 Slurs.**

Hairpins

Hairpins are likewise special enough to have their own topic – 📖 **2.17 Hairpins.**

Rit. and accel.

Various kinds of *rit.* and *accel.* lines are available in the **System lines** pane of the **Create ▸ Line** dialog. To create them in your score, simply click and drag.

Because they are system lines, *rit.* and *accel.* lines are repeated in your score in the same way as other system objects, e.g. Tempo text, and are included in every part.

In keyboard and vocal music, *rit.* and *accel.* are normally written in italics. In choral music, this is written on each singer's staff, rather than just at the top. To notate this, create an italic *rit./accel.* line on the top staff and use Expression text to write the directions on the other staves.

In solo keyboard music, the *rit./accel.* instructions normally go between the staves. To notate this, simply create a *rit./accel.* line above the top staff and drag it down between the staves.

To adjust how *rit./accel.* lines affect playback, see **Rit. and accel.** on page 264.

Trills

To create a trill, select it from the **Create ▸ Line** dialog, then click and drag in your score to extend the trill line rightwards from the *tr* symbol. If you want a trill without a wiggly line, click and drag the trill's handle in the score as far as it will go to the left.

To adjust how trills play back, see **Trills** on page 263.

Pedaling

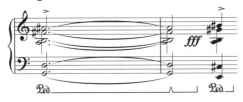

In addition to a standard pedal line, the **Create ▸ Line** dialog includes various other lines to allow you to write the "notch" repedaling notation. You can also create pedal marks with no lines where the pedal up is denoted by an asterisk from the dialog.

To adjust how pedal lines play back, see **Pedaling** on page 265.

Positioning hairpins, trills and Ped
Hairpins should go below the staff, along with other dynamics, unless they are in voice 1 or 3 of multiple voices, or there are lyrics below. They go between the staves of keyboard instruments when they apply to both hands. Hairpins should not normally be diagonal.
Trills go above the staff, except sometimes when they are in voice 2 or 4.
Pedaling invariably goes below the lowest piano staff.

1st, 2nd and 3rd endings (1st/2nd/3rd-time bars)

The 1st, 2nd and 3rd endings (1st/2nd/3rd-time bars) within the **System Line** pane of the **Create ▸ Line** dialog appear at the top of the system and apply to all instruments.

In large scores, one or more duplicates appear in the middle of the system as well (e.g. above the strings in orchestral scores) for clarity, as happens with tempo text and rehearsal marks. You can adjust the positions where these duplicates appear, or delete the duplicates individually – 📖 **8.1 Layout and formatting**.

These repeat ending lines play back – see **1st and 2nd ending lines** on page 288.

You can create arbitrary *n*th-ending lines simply by creating a new line based on an existing one and changing the text at the start of the line, and they will all play back as expected – 📖 **8.15 Edit Lines**.

Octave (8/15) lines

These lines are predominantly used to avoid multiple leger lines on a staff. While frequently used in keyboard music, these lines seldom occur in music for other instruments. *8va* and *15ma* (for one and two octaves upwards, respectively) and *8vb* and *15mb* (for one and two octaves downwards, respectively) are included in the **Staff lines** pane of the **Create ▸ Line** dialog.

If you prefer not to use Italianate terminology, you can modify the line so that it simply says *8* rather than *8va*, or you could modify the *8vb* line to say *8va* or *8va bassa* – 📖 **8.15 Edit Lines**.

Gliss. and port.

Usually a *gliss.* line is straight and includes the word *gliss.* at an angle along its length (although Sibelius automatically omits the word if the line isn't long enough), or sometimes the line is wiggly instead. Portamento (*port.*) is similar but is usually only represented by a straight line.

If you want to change the thickness of the wiggles used by the wavy *gliss.* line, edit the line (📖 **8.15 Edit Lines**) and choose another kind of line from the **Style** drop-down menu.

In some scores you may need a *gliss.* line that does not include any text along the line, even where the line is long enough for the text to be included; for example, if you have many glissandos in your score but only want to mark the first few explicitly with the text. To do this, edit the *port.* line and remove the text, and use that as a textless *gliss.* line – 📖 **8.15 Edit Lines**.

To adjust how these lines play back, see **Gliss. and port.** on page 265.

Some printer drivers have a bug that makes angled text or wiggly lines print at the wrong angle; if you find this happens, 📖 **5.16 Printing**.

Arpeggio lines

Arpeggios (for keyboard and harp) are created from the fifth Keypad layout – 📖 **2.2 Arpeggios**.

Brackets for keyboard music and double-stops

Brackets for showing where notes spanning two staves should be played by one hand in keyboard music, and for showing where notes should be double-stopped on string instruments, are found in the **Staff Line** pane of **Create ▸ Line**. When you create these lines, click and drag to create these lines at the desired length. Make sure you drag *upwards* to ensure that the bracket points in the same direction as shown in the dialog.

Rectangle

A rectangle, which is required for the "frame" notation used by modern classical composers such as Lutoslawski, is included in the **Staff Line** pane of the **Create ▸ Line** dialog. (To the uninitiated, a rectangle or "frame" drawn around a group of notes usually indicates that they should be repeated over and over again in free rhythm.)

To input a rectangle, first ensure nothing is selected in your score (hit **Esc**), then simply select the rather squat rectangle from the **Create ▸ Line** dialog, click in the score where one corner of the rectangle is to go, and drag out the opposite corner. If you draw the rectangle around some notes, it will expand and contract to enclose the notes if the note spacing changes.

Beam line

The **Staff lines** pane of the **Create ▸ Line** dialog includes a beam that you can draw onto notes to create obscure, special effects.

Dashed lines

These are for showing the extent of a marking such as *cresc.* Use these lines instead of typing a row of hyphens, since the lines will automatically stretch or contract if the spacing of the score changes, whereas a row of hyphens will stay a fixed length.

Guitar lines

Lines for all the common guitar techniques on both tab and notation staves can be found at the bottom of the **Staff lines** pane of the **Create ▸ Line** dialog, plus a complete set of string indicator lines (a circled numeral followed by a horizontal line with a hook at the right-hand end), suitable for positioning both above and below the staff. ☐ **2.15 Guitar notation and tab**.

Hauptstimme and Nebenstimme

Used mostly by the composers of the Second Viennese School, Hauptstimme lines denote the most prominent instrument in a passage; nebenstimme lines denote the second most promiment instrument.

Default positions

The default vertical positions of lines relative to the staff, and the default horizontal positions relative to notes, are defined in **House Style ▸ Default Positions**. ☐ **8.12 Default Positions**.

Reset Position

Layout ▸ Reset Position (shortcut **Ctrl+Shift+P** *or* ⌂⌘P) aligns the ends of lines with notes, and moves them to their default vertical position. ☐ **8.1 Layout and formatting**.

Reformatting of lines

As you've probably learned to expect by now, lines behave themselves very intelligently if the note spacing changes or if the music reformats. Basically, both ends of a line are independently attached to a note or other rhythmic position, so if you change the spacing of notes then any lines in the vicinity will expand or contract accordingly.

Try this yourself: simply put a hairpin under some notes, and try dragging one of the notes left and right to see what happens. Moreover, Sibelius will automatically split lines across two or more systems, or join the bits back together again, if the music reformats more drastically. See below for further details about this.

A side-effect of lines' smart behavior is that you don't need to spend ages cleaning up lines in instrumental parts – Sibelius will already have taken care of it for you.

Lines over two or more systems

To input a line that splits across two or more systems using the mouse, such as this slur:

do not input two separate lines! Instead, simply input one line as normal, selecting the note and typing S at point 1, and then hitting **space** until the slur extends to point 2. Even when creating lines with the mouse, you don't need to drag horizontally along the upper staff – just go straight to point 2 without passing GO and Sibelius will take care of the rest.

Sibelius in fact does lots of clever stuff in such cases – if you draw an *8va* across more than one system, Sibelius will put a cautionary *(8)* at the start of the second system. You can modify what it writes for the cautionary by editing the line (📖 **8.15 Edit Lines**). Similarly, a crescendo hairpin split between systems will have an open end at the left-hand side of the second system.

With horizontal lines such as 8va, Sibelius also lets you move the second half of the line up and down independently of the upper half, which is useful in case you need to avoid a high note. Simply select the portion of the line you wish to adjust and move it up and down. This does *not* apply to hairpins; if a hairpin goes over more than one system, you cannot adjust the vertical position of the hairpin independently on subsequent systems, as the hairpin will go diagonal instead.

If a line goes over more than two systems, you can only adjust the vertical position of the portion on the original system, and all subsequent systems together (in other words, you cannot adjust each subsequent system independently).

To adjust the horizontal position of the ends of the split portions of lines over more than one system, see the Lines page of the House Style ▸ Engraving Rules dialog (shortcut Ctrl+Shift+E *or* ⇧⌘E):

* The RH end option controls the spacing between the right-hand end of the line and the end of the system
* The LH end checkbox controls whether the continuation of a system line starts aligned with the start of the key signature. It defaults to off, which aligns with the end of the key signature.

Hiding lines

To hide a line, mainly required for adding hidden hairpins to tweak playback, select the line and choose Edit ▸ Hide or Show ▸ Hide (shortcut Ctrl+Shift+H *or* ⇧⌘H). For more information about hiding objects, 📖 **5.9 Hiding objects**.

2.22 Lute tablature

📖 **2.15 Guitar notation and tab**.

Sibelius supports a wide range of lute tablature styles, and several different tunings. By default, all the lute tablature is in the French/English style, but Italian and Spanish styles are also available by selecting appropriate instruments.

Creating lute tablature

Inputting lute tablature is just the same as inputting other forms of tab (📖 **1.7 Guitar tab input**), with the slight complication that you use the numbers on the main keyboard to represent the tablature letters; e.g. 0 produces a, 2 produces c, 5 produces f, and so on.

When starting a new score, you'll probably find it easiest to use the Lute tablature manuscript paper – 📖 **2.23 Manuscript paper**.

Different styles of lute tablature

The notational conventions of the three supported styles of lute tablature are as follows:

- *French/English*: the lowest string of the lute is the bottom line in the tab staff, and letters between the courses are used to represent the notes.
- *Spanish*: the lowest string of the lute is the bottom line of the tab staff, and numbers on the strings (rather like modern guitar tab) are used to represent the notes.
- *Italian*: identical to the Spanish style, except that the lowest string of the lute is the *top* line of the staff, not the bottom one.

German lute tablature (which uses letters to represent notes, but does not include staff lines at all) is not supported by Sibelius.

To create any of the supported kinds of lute tablature, simply choose your desired lute from the Create ▸ Instruments dialog – 📖 **2.18 Instruments**.

Rhythms

When writing rhythms above lute tablature staves, note values of eighth notes (quavers) and shorter are often left unbeamed. Sibelius automatically beams these notes together, but you can quickly separate them again by selecting the passage in which you want to separate them (e.g. you could triple-click the lute staff to select it throughout the score), then hit F9 to choose the third Keypad layout, and hit 7 on the numeric keypad.

You cannot notate a backwards tail, i.e. half note (minim) – this will appear as a tailless stem, like a quarter note (crotchet).

If you want to remove the stem and beam/flag from a selected note or passage (because it's a repeated note value), choose notehead number 8 from the Notes panel of Properties. (Choose notehead number 0 to bring the stem and beam/flag back again.)

Diapasons

Diapasons are extra strings not notated on the staff itself. In Italian style lute tablature, diapasons are written above the staff, in between the top line of the staff and the bottom of the stems that show the rhythm of the music; use Technique text (shortcut **Ctrl+T** *or* ⌘T) to write these letters.

In French style lute tablature, the diapasons are written directly underneath the staff; use Percussion stickings text (choose **Create ▸ Text ▸ Other Staff Text ▸ Percussion stickings**) to write them in your score.

Notations

2.23 Manuscript paper

Each time you start a new score you can choose to write it on a particular type of manuscript paper. This just means an empty score set up with a useful layout so you can use it as a template. The preset manuscript paper choices have various combinations of instruments, along with other less obvious settings to improve the look and playback of your score.

You do not have to use the instruments exactly as provided – feel free to delete instruments or add new ones.

It's better to use a manuscript paper containing instruments than to start with a blank page, even if the instrumentation isn't exactly right, because various other options are already set for you in the manuscript papers appropriate for the particular type of music.

Types of manuscript paper

There are more than 60 predefined manuscript papers supplied with Sibelius, including:

* **Blank** has no preset instruments
* **Piano**
* *Bands:* a wide range of manuscript papers suitable for concert band, wind band, marching band, school bands, brass band, drum corps, military band and other ensembles
* *Orchestra:* Classical, Romantic, Modern, concert, string and film orchestras are all included. The **Orchestra, film** manuscript paper was designed by *The Simpsons* composer Alf Clausen and Kyle Clausen.
* *Choir:* various **Choir** manuscript papers are included, some (called **reduction**) with the singers reduced onto two staves ("closed score"), some with organ or piano accompaniment.
* *Voice + keyboard*
* *Jazz:* a number of suitable templates using "handwritten" house styles, including **Lead sheet**, **Big band**, and **Jazz quartet** – 🕮 **8.8 House Style™**
* *Guitar:* various manuscript papers for notation and tab, including **Lute tablature**
* Brass and wind groups of various sizes
* String quartet and string orchestra (also usable for string quintet)
* Various other ensembles such as handbells, percussion corps, salsa band, pop group and Orff classroom groups.

Using the options in the **File ▸ New** dialog (shortcut **Ctrl+N** *or* **⌘N**), you can choose any of these manuscript papers, then add and remove instruments, change house style, add time and key signatures, tempo marks, and even create a title page.

If you want to create an educational worksheet from scratch, it's usually easiest to start off not by using **File ▸ New**, but by choosing a template from **File ▸ Worksheet Creator** – 🕮 **5.25 Worksheet Creator**.

Creating your own manuscript paper

If you often need to set up unusual groups of instruments and/or options, you can create your own manuscript paper to save you time starting new scores. Like real manuscript paper, you can choose different paper sizes, shapes and staff sizes, and have the manuscript paper pre-printed with particular instruments. However, you can also include more sophisticated settings, such as those in the **House Style** menu. This means you can get a consistent appearance without having to set up all the options each time.

* Create a score with all the settings you want to be included in the manuscript paper – e.g. page size/shape, staff size, instruments, Engraving Rules options, text styles, music font, noteheads
* Save it anywhere you like, using whatever name you want to call the manuscript paper (e.g. **Choir, Big paper, Sketches**)
* Then choose **File ▸ Export ▸ Manuscript Paper**
* You can then delete the original file you saved if you like – it will still remain as manuscript paper
* Next time you start a new score, your new manuscript paper will appear in the **Manuscript Paper** list.

If you want to create a new manuscript paper to match an existing score (e.g. if you've set up special text styles etc.), export the house style from that score, create a new score, import the house style you exported, and then export as manuscript paper. ☐ **8.8 House Style™** for details on exporting/importing a house style.

If you ever want to rename or delete manuscript paper, you will find the manuscript paper files in a folder called **Manuscript paper** within Sibelius's application data folder (see **User-editable files** in ☐ **9.1 Working with files**).

2.24 Multirests

📖 **2.5 Bars and bar rests, 3.5 Bar numbers, 7.1 Working with parts, 8.4 Auto Breaks**.

A multirest is an abbreviation for several consecutive bar rests, with the number of bars written above. Multirests are normally only found in instrumental parts, though they do very occasionally appear in full scores (e.g. Sibelius's *Tapiola*, bars 28–29).

Using multirests

Multirests are really just a display option in Sibelius – you can view empty bars either as individual bar rests or consolidated into multirests.

To display bar rests as multirests, choose Layout ▸ Auto Breaks and switch on Use multirests. Sibelius does this automatically for you in parts. There is also a special shortcut for switching Use multirests on and off – Ctrl+Shift+M *or* ⇧⌘M.

Sibelius automatically splits multirests at time signatures, rehearsal marks, key changes, clef changes, tempo marks and so on. If you need to split a multirest manually, see **Forcing a multirest to split** below.

Creating a multirest

Creating a multirest is the same as creating lots of single bar rests: choose Create ▸ Bar ▸ Other; type in the Number of bars you want, click OK, then click where you want to put the multirest.

Alternatively, you can just copy an existing multirest selecting it as a system passage using Ctrl+click *or* ⌘-click, then using Alt+click *or* ⌐-click.

Inputting into a multirest

Multirests work just like normal bar rests – you can input notes into them, or copy music into them. As you input notes into a multirest, Sibelius will strip bars off it to put the notes into, and reduce the length of the multirest accordingly.

Changing the length of a multirest

To adjust the number of bars in a multirest, switch off Use Multirests in Layout ▸ Auto Breaks to turn it back into separate bar rests, then add or delete bars. Finally, switch on Use Multirests in Layout ▸ Auto Breaks again.

Forcing a multirest to split

Sibelius can automatically split multirests for you – see **Auto layout of multirests** below.

If you need to force a multirest to split:

- Switch off Use Multirests in Layout ▸ Auto Breaks
- Select a barline and choose Layout ▸ Break ▸ Split Multirest; a small multirest symbol cut in half will appear on the screen above the barline if View ▸ Layout Marks is on
- Switch on Use Multirests again, and the multirest will now split at the chosen barline.

If after switching off **Use Multirests** in **Layout ▸ Auto Breaks** you select a *passage* and choose **Layout ▸ Break ▸ Split Multirest**, the passage will be split at both ends to become a separate multirest (when **Use Multirests** is switched back on). If there are any notes, text or other objects in the passage, they will still split up the multirest.

Preventing a multirest from splitting in parts

Multirests in parts are automatically split by system objects. If you do not want the object to be visible in the part, you can prevent the multirest from being split by selecting the item *in the part* and choosing **Edit ▸ Hide or Show ▸ Hide** (shortcut **Ctrl+Shift+H** or ⇧⌘H) – 📖 **7.1 Working with parts**.

Determining what causes a multirest to split

Sometimes you may find that a multirest splits unexpectedly in a part. Normally this happens because a system text object has become attached to the wrong place; to fix it, select the object in question, hit **W** to switch back to the full score, then cut the object to the clipboard with **Ctrl+X** *or* ⌘X, then paste it to the right bar with **Ctrl+V** *or* ⌘V.

If you can't see why a multirest is split, try selecting the bars in question, then run **Plug-ins ▸ Proof-reading ▸ What Is Where**. Check the resulting output for system text items, as this is normally the cause. Once you have identified what's causing the split, repair it using the above steps.

Hiding a multirest

To hide a multirest, simply select it and hit **Delete**. This deletes the multirest symbol but leaves the implied bars intact. (What this actually does is to delete the first bar rest which is "inside" the multirest.)

Deleting a multirest

To delete a multirest entirely, **Ctrl**-click *or* ⌘-click it to make a system passage (surrounded by a purple double-box), then hit **Delete**.

Auto layout of multirests

For information about how to automatically split multirests, 📖 **8.4 Auto Breaks**.

Showing bar numbers on multirests

Sibelius can show the bar numbers of the bars enclosed in a multirest as a range of bar numbers above or below the multirest – see **Appearance and frequency** in 📖 **3.5 Bar numbers**.

Engraving Rules options

The **Bar Rests** page of the **House Style ▸ Engraving Rules** dialog (shortcut **Ctrl+Shift+E** *or* ⇧⌘E) has various self-explanatory options.

Most notably, you can choose to notate multirests as H-bars, narrow H-bars (to leave space on either side for last-minute additions in session parts), in the "old style" of funny little rectangles, or completely blank (for annotations in jazz parts).

| *H-bar* | *Narrow H-bar* | *Old style* | *Blank* |

Parts often include a number above all bar rests, whether they are a single bar or many bars in length. To draw 1 above all single bar rests, switch on **Show '1' above bar rests** in the **Bar Rests** page of the **House Style ▸ Engraving Rules** dialog. This option is also available in the **Multiple Part Appearance** dialog – ⌨ **7.1 Working with parts**.

Another useful option on the **Bar rests** page is **Draw H-bar using a symbol**: this uses a stretched symbol rather than drawing a rectangle to produce the thick bar of an H-bar. This option is switched off by default, but you may want to switch it on when using the Reprise or Inkpen2 fonts, as it will give multirests a handwritten appearance. (Beware though that bugs in some printer drivers may make H-bars misprint or even possibly cause a crash when printing if this option is switched on – so test to see whether it works with your printer before using it routinely.)

Sibelius allows you to set how far multirest H-bars should be offset into a bar. To change this value, edit **Distance from multirest to barline**. The default is 1 space, and entering larger numbers will increase the gap at either side of the multirest in respect to the barlines either side of it.

Multirests can be scaled so that they are proportionally wider as their duration increases. Sibelius allows you to set how many extra spaces it should add to a multirest spanning ten bars. To alter this, change **Extra space for 10-bar multirests**. The default is **12** which means Sibelius will add 12 spaces for a ten bar multirest, and proportionally more the longer a multirest is. The scale used is logarithmic so that multirests won't become dramatically wider as the number of bars increases. If you wish to switch off this feature completely, enter 0.

You can also edit the **Multirests (numbers)** and **Multirests (tacet)** text styles that are used to write the numbers and text above multirests, to change, for example, their vertical position – ⌨ **3.9 Edit Text Styles**.

Positioning multirest numbers below the H-bar

Multirest numbers normally go above the H-bar, however if you want to position the numbers *below*, you should change **Vertical position relative to staff** of the **Multirests (numbers)** text style in **House Style ▸ Default Positions** to (say) -6.

2.25 Noteheads

📖 **2.6 Beam groups, 2.26 Percussion, 2.30 Stems and leger lines, 8.16 Edit Note-heads**.

Sibelius includes numerous special notehead shapes such as diamond, cross and slash, and you can create your own custom noteheads, too. You can also control whether or not particular notehead shapes play back, transpose, have stems or leger lines, and so on (📖 **8.16 Edit Noteheads**).

Noteheads are distinct from note values – a cross notehead can be applied equally to an eighth note (quaver), a half note (minim) or a double whole note (breve), and will slightly change its appearance accordingly.

Choosing a notehead

To change the notehead type of existing music, select a note or passage and use the drop-down menu on the **Notes** panel of the Properties window. You can also choose the notehead by holding down **Shift+Alt** *or* ⇧⌥ and typing numbers from the row along the top of the main keyboard (not the numeric keypad); see below for the notehead numbers. If the notehead you want is numbered higher than 9 (say, notehead type 13), type both digits quickly one after another. If you're not sure what you're looking for, type **Shift-+/−** to cycle forward and back through the complete choice of noteheads.

You can also choose the notehead type as you create notes: simply choose the desired type from the Properties window or type the shortcut before entering the pitch of the note. The chosen notehead type will be used by all subsequent notes until you change it again.

Since noteheads are customizable, the shortcuts listed in this topic (and throughout the Reference) may not be correct if you have edited existing notehead types.

Common noteheads

Cross noteheads (shortcut **Shift+Alt+1** *or* ⇧⌥1) indicate notes of uncertain pitch, usually for unpitched percussion. A cross half note (minim) can be written as a normal half note with a cross through it in avant garde notation, or as a diamond in drum set (kit) notation (shortcut **Shift+Alt+5** *or* ⇧⌥5).

Diamond noteheads (shortcut **Shift+Alt+2** *or* ⇧⌥2) usually indicate notes that are fingered but not played, such as a string harmonic (see **Harmonics** in 📖 **4.2 Interpretation of your score**), or (in avant garde music) piano keys depressed silently. For guitar harmonics, quarter notes (crotchets) and shorter notes are written with a black filled-in diamond (shortcut **Shift+Alt+6** *or* ⇧⌥6).

Slashes indicate the rhythm of chords improvised to chord symbols in jazz, rock and commercial music. Two types of slash are provided, one with a stem (shortcut **Shift+Alt+4** *or* ⇧⌥4) and one without (shortcut **Shift+Alt+3** *or* ⇧⌥3). These noteheads don't play back, and don't transpose. They are usually written only on the middle line of the staff.

Headless notes (shortcut **Shift+Alt+7** *or* ⇧⌥7) indicate pure rhythms in contemporary music, either because a previous note or chord is being repeated, or because (like the cross notehead) the pitch is indefinite or is improvised. Headless whole-notes (semibreves) are hard to see.

Stemless notes (shortcut **Shift+Alt+8** *or* ⇧⌥8) are useful for arhythmic music such as plainchant.

Silent notes (shortcut **Shift+Alt+9** *or* ⇧⌥9) look exactly like normal noteheads, but they don't play back, which can be useful in certain situations.

Cue-size noteheads (shortcut **Shift+Alt+10** *or* ⇧⌥10) are used to mix normal- and cue-sized noteheads within the same chord (for normal cue notes, see below). Beware that using this notehead type doesn't make associated objects such as accidentals small too.

Noteheads with slashes through them (shortcuts **Shift+Alt+11/12** *or* ⇧⌥11/12) are used for things like rim-shots in percussion notation.

The arrow down (shortcut **Shift+Alt+13** *or* ⇧✲13) and arrow up (shortcut **Shift+Alt+14** *or* ⇧✲14) noteheads, which are only suitable for notes with stems pointing up and down respectively, are used to denote unspecified extremely low or high notes. These noteheads are drawn without leger lines.

Noteheads **16–23** are used for shape note music, also known as "sacred harp" music, formulated in an American song book by B.F. White and E.J. King in 1844. The technique is called "fasola" (i.e. *fa – so – la*, a kind of solmization), whereby differently-shaped noteheads are used for different degrees of the scale. Use Plug-ins ▸ Notes and Rests ▸ Apply Shape Notes to create this notation automatically – see **Apply Shape Notes** on page 501.

Notehead **24** is an alternative cross notehead with a smaller half note (minim) notehead, occasionally used instead of notehead 1. Notehead **29** is another alternative cross notehead, with a bolder cross.

Notehead **25** is used for Kodály stick notation.

Notehead 26 is used in marching percussion, generally meaning all drums playing in unison.

Noteheads **27** and **28** are alternative slash noteheads, sometimes used instead of noteheads 3 and 4.

Notehead **30** is sometimes used in percussion notation to represent a "ping," a specific kind of rimshot.

Different sizes of noteheads

You should only create small noteheads with notehead type **10** if normal and small noteheads are needed in the same chord. To make a single note or whole chord cue-sized, use the cue button (shortcut **Enter**) on the second Keypad layout (shortcut **F8**) instead, as this will also make the stem and any accents and articulations small – 📖 **2.14 Grace notes**.

If you prefer a slightly larger notehead design throughout a score, you can use the supplied Blank (larger notes) manuscript paper – 📖 **2.23 Manuscript paper** – or you can import the Standard (larger notes) house style into an existing score – 📖 **8.8 House Style™**.

Notes in parentheses

You can add parentheses (round brackets) to any notehead (including grace notes) using the button on the second Keypad layout (shortcut **F8**). The parentheses will automatically adjust to enclose accidentals, etc.

Note names inside noteheads

In music for students beginning to learn an instrument, it may be useful to show the name of the note inside the notehead itself. To do this, see **Add Note Names to Noteheads** on page 505.

2.26 Percussion

📖 **2.25 Noteheads**, **2.34 Tremolos**.

This topic only covers writing for unpitched percussion instruments. Writing for pitched percussion instruments is very much like writing for other pitched instruments, so doesn't require any special knowledge.

Unpitched percussion can be notated in a variety of ways, depending on the nature of the music and ensemble being written for. For example, in rock, jazz and commercial music, different pitches and noteheads are used to notate different unpitched instruments on the same staff; this is usually called a *drum set* (or drum kit).

In music for orchestra, band, drum ensemble or drum corps there are further possibilities:

• each instrument (or set of instruments) may have a different staff (e.g. cymbal, bass drum, triangle); or

• only one staff is used, with text showing where the player switches from one instrument to another; or

• each percussion player has their own staff or set of staves; this is useful for creating separate parts for individual percussionists to play from.

Sibelius has all the most common pitched and unpitched percussion instruments built-in, and makes it easy to notate all of the above.

Unpitched percussion instruments

Each unpitched percussion instrument built into Sibelius has its own *drum map*, meaning a list of correspondences between each percussion sound it uses (e.g. cowbell, bass drum) and the position on the staff and type of notehead (e.g. normal, cross, diamond) uses to notate it.

For most unpitched percussion instruments, this drum map is very simple. For example, the percussion instruments that use 1-line staves are typically set up to produce the desired sound when you put a normal, cross or diamond notehead on the staff line itself.

Some percussion instruments, however, are more complex, and have more staff lines, and more noteheads. For example, drum set, marching snare drum, bass drum and cymbal instruments use five-line staves, and different noteheads at different positions on the staff produce different sounds.

Because there are dozens of unpitched percussion instruments built into Sibelius, it's impractical to describe in detail the specific drum maps used by each instrument. So, to look at the drum map for a particular instrument:

• Select a bar in the instrument in question, if you are already using it in your score

• Choose **House Style ▸ Edit Instruments**

• If you selected a note or bar, you will see that the instrument is selected; if no instrument is selected, select it from the **Instruments in family** list

- Click **Edit Instrument**; if you are prompted that editing this instrument will change the score, click **Yes**
- Now click **Edit Staff Type**, and choose the **Percussion** page.
- The area at the top of the dialog shows which noteheads are mapped; to see which sound is produced by a specific notehead, select it and look at the **Sound** read-out below. You can also see here which key on your MIDI keyboard to play to input this note – see **Note input for unpitched percussion** below.

For more information about this dialog, and about editing existing percussion instruments and defining your own, ⎕ **8.14 Edit Instruments**.

Drum set notation, however, is sufficiently standardized that we can look at it in detail – read on.

Drum set notation

To create a drum set staff in Sibelius, choose **Create ▸ Instruments** (shortcut I), and select either **Drum Set** or **Drum Kit** (which are identical other than the name).

The **Drum Set** and **Drum Kit** instruments use a notational system based on the recommendations of the Percussive Arts Society (in Norman Weinberg's book, *Guide To Standardized Drumset Notation*), as follows:

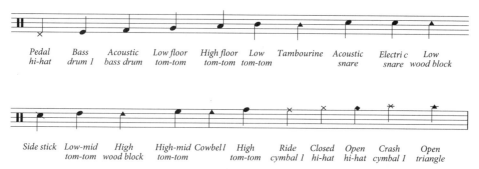

Note input for unpitched percussion

When inputting into percussion staves, you can use any of Sibelius's input methods, but if the percussion instrument uses different types of noteheads, it is quicker to use step-time or Flexi-time input than to use mouse or alphabetic input.

Consider the following simple example, for kick and snare drums with open and closed hi-hats on a regular drum kit:

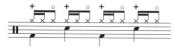

The quarter notes (crotchets) are in voice 2 and use the default notehead, and the eighth notes (quavers) and sixteenth notes (semiquavers) are in voice 1, and use the cross notehead. (If you don't use the cross notehead, the notes won't play back as hi-hats.)

If you input this music with the mouse or using alphabetic input, you will need to change the voice 1 notes to use the cross notehead after inputting them:

- Select the bars where you want to change the notehead ($\square$ **1.9 Selections and passages**)
- Either filter for a specific voice, e.g. Edit ▸ Filter ▸ Voice 1, which is what we want in the above example, or filter for the specific pitch you want to change using Edit ▸ Filter ▸ Advanced Filter. The pitch filter treats percussion clefs as treble clef, so:
  - ○ In 1-line staves, the pitch of the single staff line is B4 (because this line corresponds to the middle line of a 5-line staff)
  - ○ In 2-line staves, the pitches are (from bottom to top) G4 and D5
  - ○ In 3-line staves, the pitches are E4, B4 and F5
  - ○ In 4-line staves, the pitches are F4, A4, C5 and E5
  - ○ In 5-line percussion staves, the middle line is B4.

  To find out more about using Sibelius's filtering features, $\square$ **5.7 Filters and Find**.

- Change the notehead by typing Shift+Alt+*n* or ⇧⌥*n*, where *n* is a number on the main keyboard (not the numeric keypad); in the example above, we need to type Shift+Alt+1 *or* ⇧⌥1. Alternatively, you can choose the notehead from the menu in the Notes panel of Properties ($\square$ **2.25 Noteheads**).

If you input this music using a MIDI keyboard in step-time or Flexi-time, however, Sibelius automatically maps the pitch of the notes you play on your MIDI keyboard onto the appropriate pitch, and also chooses the correct notehead (and articulation, if specified). If you play a pitch for which there is more than one notehead mapped in the staff type, Sibelius will choose the first notehead listed in the drum map.

You can choose whether to use the pitch mappings determined by the instrument itself, or the pitches used by your particular MIDI device (i.e. your keyboard or sound module). This is determined by the option under Percussion Staves on the Note Input page of File ▸ Preferences (in the Sibelius menu on Mac).

By default, Sibelius is set to The instrument, which means that it expects you to play the pitches set in the instrument definition. With this setting chosen, a 1-line staff is treated as the middle line of a 5-line staff (i.e. pitch B4), a 2-line staff is the 2nd and 4th lines (i.e. pitches G4 and D5), a 3-line staff is the 1st, 3rd and 5th lines (i.e. pitches E4, B4, and F5), and a 4-line staff is the spaces (F4, A4, C5, and E5). Hence a note on the line of a 1-line staff can be inputted by playing the B above middle C.

If you would rather play the key on your MIDI keyboard that corresponds to the sound you want, set the Percussion Staves option to The MIDI device's drum map. You will hear the correct sound as you input it, and Sibelius will automatically translate the pitch you play into the drum set staff.

Playback of unpitched percussion

Although it is possible to position any notehead at any position on an unpitched percussion staff, Sibelius will only play back those noteheads that are specifically mapped in the instrument definition – see **Percussion page** on page 627.

Different staves for different instruments

In orchestral scores, it's common to use a different one-line staff for each unpitched percussion instrument used, like this:

A wide range of individual percussion instruments is accessible from the **Create ▸ Instruments** dialog. For example, to notate a bass drum, cymbals and triangle in your score:

- In the **Create ▸ Instruments** dialog, choose the **Percussion/Drums** family and add **Cymbals, Triangle** and **Bass drum** instruments
- Click **Create** and the instruments are added to your score.

All of these instruments play back automatically with the correct sound. Notice how stems on 1-line staves point upwards.

Creating your own drum map

If you want to write multiple percussion instruments on the same staff using sounds, noteheads or staff positions that aren't defined in any of the built-in instruments, you will need to create your own instrument with its own drum map.

For example, if you want to write:

- Choose **House Style ▸ Edit Instruments**
- From the **Common instruments** ensemble, select the **Percussion and Drums** family, then select **Drum set (basic)** from the **Instruments in family** list. (It doesn't really matter which instrument you choose, as we're going to edit it in a moment anyway, but we'll choose this one because it has the right number of staff lines, and not too many existing noteheads in its drum map.)
- Click **New Instrument**, and answer **Yes** when asked if you want to create a new instrument based on this one
- Change **Name in dialogs** to something like **Bass drum, Cymbal, Triangle,** so you'll be able to find it again later
- Change **Full name in score** to something like **Bass drum\n\Cymbal\n\Triangle** (\n\ tells Sibelius to put the next word on a new line)
- Click **Edit Staff Type**, and go to the **Percussion** tab in the dialog that appears
- In our example we need only three pitches on the staff to be mapped to particular sounds: we'll use the top line for the triangle, the middle line for the cymbals, and the bottom line for the bass drum; select each of the other unwanted pitches and click **Delete** to remove them

Notations

- For each of the remaining pitches, select the notehead, then choose the correct sound from the **Sound** drop-down menu.
- You might also want to change the **Notehead** for a particular instrument, or even specify a different sound when a particular **Articulation** is used with a notehead, but this isn't necessary
- When you've set the sounds, click **OK** to confirm the changes to the staff type
- Click **OK** to confirm the changes to your new instrument.
- Make sure your new **Bass drum, Cymbal, Triangle** instrument is in the **Common instruments** ensemble: move it to the **Instruments in family** list from the **Instruments not in ensemble** list by clicking **Add to Family**, then click **Close** to close the **Edit Instruments** dialog
- Now choose **Create ▸ Instruments**, select your new instrument from the list, and click **Add to Score** to create it, then click **OK**
- Input the music on the staff using the three pitches defined in the staff type; you can use voices if you like – ☐ **2.36 Voices**.

Single staff for each player

If your score requires more than one percussionist, or if one percussionist is expected to change between instruments, it is useful to notate all the percussion on a single staff, with text indicating where the changeover occurs. In Sibelius this is done using instrument changes – ☐ **2.18 Instruments**.

There are many predefined percussion instruments set up with the appropriate sounds; e.g. the Cymbal [1 line] instrument plays with a cymbal sound. You can of course create new percussion instruments if required.

Percussion symbols

Sibelius comes with many useful symbols that graphically represent instruments, types of beaters and various other playing techniques for a wide range of pitched and non-pitched percussion instruments. To add such a symbol to your score, choose **Create ▸ Symbol** (shortcut Z) and click on your desired symbol from a choice of drums, metallic and other instruments, beaters and techniques –☐ **2.31 Symbols**.

Removing borders from percussion beater symbols

Sibelius allows you to remove the borders around percussion beater symbols if you wish:

- Choose **House Style ▸ Edit Symbols**
- Click on the empty box symbol at the far right of the first row of beaters
- Click **Edit**, enter 0 into the **Number** field, then click **OK**.

Buzz rolls (Z on stem)

Used to indicate multiple stroke rolls in percussion writing, Sibelius allows you to add a buzz roll symbol to any note or chord. Choose the third Keypad layout (shortcut **F9**) and hit **6**. For more detailed information on buzz rolls, ☐ **2.34 Tremolos**.

2.27 Repeat bars

The repeat bar sign indicates that the bar in which it appears is a repetition of the previous bar:

A hangover from the days of hand-copied music, this sign is still commonly used in rhythm section parts (for drums, guitar, etc.) because it is easier for players to read than many copies of the same music in successive bars.

Different versions of the sign are used to show that the last two or four fully written-out bars should be repeated, e.g.:

Creating repeat bars

Repeat bars are created from the fifth Keypad layout (shortcut F11). To input a repeat bar while inputting notes, i.e. if the note input caret is visible (🕮 **1.1 Note input**):

* Hit F12 to choose the fifth Keypad layout (🕮 **1.2 Keypad**)
* Hit 1 on the numeric keypad for a one-bar repeat, 2 for a two-bar repeat, or 4 for a four-bar repeat
* The required repeat bar sign is created at the caret position; if the caret is in the middle of a bar that already contains notes in the same voice as the repeat bar sign you are creating, they will be deleted. When creating two- or four-bar repeat bars, any notes in the same voice in subsequent bars spanned by the repeat bar will also be deleted.
* To input more repeat bars, simply hit 1, 2 or 4 again as many times as required.

You can also create lots of repeat bars in a single operation: select the passage you want to show repeat bars, then hit F12 to choose the fifth Keypad layout and type 1, 2 or 4. Any "left-over" bars (e.g. if you have nine bars selected and create four-bar repeats) will be unchanged.

Copying repeat bars

Repeat bars can be copied like any other object, and can also be repeated quickly using Edit ▸ Repeat (shortcut R).

Deleting repeat bars

To delete a repeat bar, simply select the bar and hit Delete (which empties the bar, and leaves a bar rest). Creating a note in the same voice as the repeat bar will also delete the repeat bar.

Numbering repeat bars

Sibelius automatically numbers repeat bars every four bars. The first repeat bar is always numbered "2" (to denote that it is the second time the music is played). You will find options to control this automatic numbering on the Bar Rests page of House Style ▸ Engraving Rules:

- **Number repeat bars every** *n* **bars** allows you to choose whether repeat bars should be numbered every one, two, four (the default) or eight bars
- **Show bar numbers in parentheses** determines whether or not the numbers should be drawn in parentheses (round brackets)
- You can choose to restart the numbering at **Special barlines** (e.g. double barlines, repeat barlines) and **Rehearsal marks** if you wish.

To change the font and size of the numbers on repeat bars, edit the Repeat bar numbers text style (⬜ **3.9 Edit Text Styles**). To change the position of the numbers, use **House Style ▸ Default Positions** (⬜ **8.12 Default Positions**).

Two- and four-bar repeats are not numbered in the same way: instead, they simply show "2" or "4" above the repeat bar sign.

Formatting of repeat bars

Sibelius will never allow a system or page break to fall in the middle of a two- or four-bar repeat. You can select any of the barlines in the middle of two- or four-bar repeats in your score and create a system or page break (⬜ **8.5 Breaks**), and the layout mark will appear above the barline (if **View ▸ Layout Marks** is switched on), but the break will only take effect if you delete the repeat bars.

Cueing in repeat bars

You may sometimes need to cue the melody or rhythm played by another instrument for the benefit of the performer playing the repeated bars, in which case use an otherwise unused voice for these notes. Make sure that the **Play on pass** checkboxes on the **Playback** panel of Properties are switched off for any such notes to avoid interfering with the playback of the repeat bar – see **When to play back notes** on page 291.

Repeat bars on keyboard instruments

It is conventional to show repeat bars in both staves of keyboard and other grand staff instruments: to achieve this, either create the repeat bars in each staff separately, or copy them from one staff to the other.

Playback of repeat bars

When Sibelius encounters a repeat bar, it automatically plays back the music of the previous one, two or four fully written-out bars. Be aware that if a repeat bar also includes notes in another voice that are set to play back, Sibelius will play only those notes, and ignore the repeat bar sign.

You may sometimes want to e.g. change the dynamics of repeated bars, like this:

Sibelius will play back dynamics over repeat bars, but any instructions that would result in a change of sound (e.g. "pizz." or "mute") will only take effect on the first note following the repeat bars.

2.28 Slurs

📖 **2.21 Lines**.

Slurs are used to indicate phrasing and playing technique. Slurs that indicate phrasing are sometimes called phrase-marks, but since phrase-marks are just big slurs, we'll use the word "slur" to cover both. This terminology is also fairly standard in music engraving.

Like other kinds of objects in Sibelius (e.g. tuplets), slurs are *magnetic*, which means that they are positioned intelligently, snapping to notes and avoiding any articulations that are present on the notes at the start or the end of the slur.

It is also possible to create a *non-magnetic* slur, which doesn't snap to notes or get positioned automatically, but which can still be useful in certain situations.

Creating and extending slurs

To create a magnetic slur, either:

- Select a note (or grace note) and type **S**. This draws a slur to the next note; or
- Select the passage of notes (on a single staff) you want to be slurred and type **S**, which draws a slur over all the selected notes.

You can then extend the slur to the following note by hitting **Space** (by analogy with creating lyrics), or contract it back again with **Shift-Space**.

These keys move the right-hand end because it is selected. Look for the small square "handle" – slurs have handles when selected; if one end of the slur is selected, only that end gets a handle). This use of **Space** and **Shift-Space** also works for other lines.

You can also select and move the left-hand end in the same way, either with the arrows, mouse or by typing **Space/Shift-Space**.

As you extend and retract the slur, you may find that it flips to the other side of the notes. If the stems of all of the notes under the slur point upwards (i.e. they are all

> **Positioning slurs**
> *Slurs typically go at the stem end in two or more voices.*
>
> *When a slur starts on a tied note, the slur should start at the first of the notes that are tied together. Similarly, if a slur ends on a tied note, the slur should end on the last of the tied notes.*
>
> *To make slurs more visible, the very ends and the highest or lowest point of the arch should avoid touching a staff line.*

below the middle line of the staff), Sibelius positions the slur below the notes, curving downwards. If, however, any of the stems of the notes under the slur point downwards, Sibelius positions the slur above the notes, curving upwards.

Should you decide that you want to fly in the face of centuries-old convention regarding slur placement, you can of course flip the slur after you have created it by selecting it and choosing **Edit ▸ Flip** (shortcut **X**).

Slur handles

Although Sibelius's default settings produce pleasing slur shapes in most situations, you may occasionally find that you need to adjust an individual slur in order to make it as graceful as possible. When you select a slur, a gray frame appears showing you the slur's handles:

(If you would prefer slur handles to be visible all the time, switch on **View ▸ Handles** – 📖 **5.23 View menu.**)

Holding down **Alt** *or* ⌥ and typing ←/→ moves through the six handles as follows: the left end of the slur, the left-hand curve point, the bottom middle of the slur, the top middle of the slur, the right-hand curve point, and the right end of the slur.

With any handle selected, you can use the arrow keys (with **Ctrl** *or* ⌘ for bigger steps) to adjust its position:

- If you move the left- or right-hand end with the arrow keys, you can move its position relative to the note to which it is attached, but it will not attach to another note; to re-attach the slur, use **Space** or **Shift-Space**.
- Moving the bottom middle handle of the slur changes its vertical position relative to the notes to which it is attached, but without changing the curvature.
- Moving the top middle handle of the slur up or down changes the height of the slur while retaining its relative curvature. You can also alter the angle of the slur's curvature by moving the top middle handle left or right.
- Moving the left-hand or right-hand curve point changes the curvature of the slur, allowing you to make fine adjustments to the slur's contour.

You can also move the slur's handles using the controls on the **Lines** panel of Properties:

- **End X** and **Y** show the offset of the left or right end of the slur, if selected, measured in spaces. (Normally both **X** and **Y** will read 0.)
- **Slur left curve X** and **Y** and **Slur right curve X** and **Y** express the position of the left-hand and right-hand curve points, if they have been manually adjusted. The **X** value is expressed as a percentage of the length of the slur, and the **Y** value is expressed in spaces. You can reset the position of either curve point by switching off the appropriate checkbox.

Finally, you can change the shape of a slur by dragging any of its handles with the mouse.

To reset a slur's shape, select the slur line itself and choose **Layout ▸ Reset Design** (shortcut **Ctrl+Shift+D** *or* ⇧⌘D); to reset the position of a single handle, select just that handle and choose **Reset Design**. This also "unflips" a slur, if you flipped it with **Edit ▸ Flip**.

To reset the position of the left or right end of a slur, select any part of the slur and choose **Layout ▸ Reset Position** (shortcut **Ctrl+Shift+P** *or* ⇧⌘P).

Slur thickness

Slurs are tapered at each end, and thicker in the middle. You can change their default thickness on the Slurs page of House Style ▸ Engraving Rules:

- To change the default width of the tapered ends of slurs, change **Outline width** *n* **spaces**.
- **Middle thickness** *n* **spaces** determines the thickness of the slur at its thickest point. The value represents the thickness of the slur's width, less the minimum thickness of the slur (so a value of, say, 0.5 spaces produces a slur that is just over half a space thick – which is very thick indeed!).

You can also adjust the thickness of an individual slur if you wish, by selecting the slur and adjusting the **Slur thickness** control on the **Lines** panel of Properties.

Slur shoulder

The *shoulder* of a slur controls the rate of onset of the slur's curvature, and this value is varied according to the length of the slur: longer slurs require a larger shoulder, so that they approach their full height more quickly than shorter slurs.

You can adjust the default range of shoulder values used on the **Slurs** page of House Style ▸ Engraving Rules: change **Shoulder for short slurs** *n*% and **Shoulder for long slurs** *n*% to alter subtly the rate of onset of slurs' curvatures.

Slur height

Sibelius by default draws slurs so that a short slur (defined as a slur of two spaces in length) will be one space high, and scales the height using an exponential function that approaches an asymptote as the slur lengthens; in practice, slurs will never be taller than four spaces with the default values.

You can adjust the default height of slurs on the **Slurs** page of House Style ▸ Engraving Rules, by changing the **Height scale** value: a value of 200% produces slurs that tend towards eight spaces tall; a value of 50% produces slurs that tend towards two spaces tall.

Conversely, you may want to ensure that long slurs do not take up too much vertical space and end up looking too "loopy": switch on **Limit height for long slurs** and set **Maximum height** *n* **spaces** to a suitable value. This is useful if you generally want quite curvy slurs, but want to ensure that longer slurs do not get excessively curvy.

Slurs over two systems

When a slur is split over two systems, Sibelius draws each half of the slur as a separate arc, allowing you to adjust the position of both segments of the slurs fully, as if they were two separate slurs.

Adjusting the shape and position of a slur that crosses a system break is therefore the same as adjusting a regular slur, except that you can use Alt+←/→ *or* ⌥←/→ to move between all the handles, on both sides of the system break.

It is also possible to draw the slur over the system break as a single arc, drawing half of the slur on the first system, and the second half of the slur on the second system. However, this appearance is very rarely used in published music. Nevertheless, should you want to use it, switch on **Clip at end of systems** on the **Slurs** page of House Style ▸ Engraving Rules.

Slurs over more than two systems

When a slur is split over three or more systems, Sibelius draws the slur as the appropriate number of arcs, but it is not able to provide complete control over the positioning and curvature of all of the slur's segments. You can edit a slur over three or more systems as follows:

- Moving the left end point of the first segment of the slur only moves that end point; moving the left end point of any other segment of the slur moves that end point of all segments of the slur other than the first segment.
- Moving the right end point of the first segment of the slur moves the right end point of all segments of the slur, except for the segment on the last system; moving the right end point of the last segment of the slur moves only that end point.
- Moving the left or right curve point or the top middle handle of the first segment of the slur adjusts the curvature of all segments of the slur, except for the segment on the last system; moving the left or right curve point or the top middle handle of the last segment of the slur adjusts the curvature of that segment only.
- Moving the bottom middle handle of the slur on the first segment changes the vertical position of the slur on all systems except the last system; moving the bottom middle handle of the last segment of the slur adjusts the vertical position of that segment only.

In some circumstances, it may be necessary to use separate slurs on each system in order to achieve the ideal appearance.

S-shaped slurs

Sometimes in keyboard music you need to write an S-shaped slur with two arcs, flowing above and below the notes.

To create an S-shaped slur, simply input a normal slur, then drag the left-hand or right-hand curve handle above or below the curvature of the slur, as appropriate.

Slurs on cross-staff notes

Magnetic slurs do not attach to cross-staff notes. The slur will naturally go to where the note would be on the original staff, but you can drag the slur's end to the note's actual position.

Non-magnetic slurs

Although we don't recommend it except for special circumstances, you can also create less intelligent "non-magnetic" slurs by creating a slur *with nothing selected* with the mouse from the **Create ▶ Line** dialog. Non-magnetic slurs don't snap to notes, and nor do they avoid beams and articulations, but they can be useful in some situations.

Non-magnetic slurs appear in red when selected, as a hint that you should probably use a magnetic one instead.

If you use **Layout ▶ Reset Position** (shortcut **Ctrl+Shift+P** *or* ⇧⌘P) to reset the position of a slur, this also turns it into a magnetic slur if it was non-magnetic.

Dashed and dotted slurs

Create dashed or dotted slurs by choosing them from the **Create ▸ Line** dialog (shortcut L). If you create them with no note selected, they are non-magnetic; use **Layout ▸ Reset Position** to make them magnetic.

You can change the appearance of dashed slurs by editing the length of the dash and the gaps between them – 🕮 **8.15 Edit Lines**.

Slurs in lyrics

If you want to print a tiny slur after a word in lyrics (e.g. at the end of a line of block lyrics in hymns), don't use a real slur – instead, use the elision character. 🕮 **3.3 Lyrics** for more details.

To add slurs to vocal staves (to show the underlay of the lyrics more clearly), use the **Plug-ins ▸ Text ▸ Add Slurs to Lyrics** plug-in (🕮 **6.1 Working with plug-ins**).

Copying slurs

When you copy a passage containing slurs in Sibelius, the slurs are also copied along with the notes. Sibelius retains any adjustments you have made to the shapes of the copied slurs.

You can also use the **Copy Articulations and Slurs** plug-in to copy slurs in a particular rhythmic pattern to other similar phrases in the score – see page 502.

Engraving Rules options

The **Slurs** page of **House Style ▸ Engraving Rules** (shortcut **Ctrl+Shift+E** *or* ⇧⌘E) has a number of reassuringly obscure options concerning slurs, in addition to those discussed variously above:

- For slurs that are positioned near noteheads:
  ○ **Horizontally *n* spaces from note center** determines the default horizontal position of the end point of a magnetic slur, relative to the width of the notehead
  ○ **Vertically *n* spaces from notehead** determines the default vertical position of the left and right end point of a magnetic slur, relative to the top or bottom of the notehead
  ○ **Vertically *n* spaces extra to avoid tie** determines the extra gap above or below the notehead, to ensure that the end point of a magnetic slur does not collide with a tie
- For slurs that are positioned near stems:
  ○ **Horizontally *n* spaces from stem** determines the default horizontal position of the end point of a magnetic slur, to the left or right of the stem of the note to which it is attached
  ○ **Vertically *n* spaces beyond stem** determines the default gap above or below the end of the stem and the end point of a magnetic slur; a negative value moves the end point of the slur towards the notehead
  ○ **Vertically *n* spaces beyond stem (eighth notes or shorter)** is the value Sibelius uses for the gap between the end point of a magnetic slur and the stem of the note to which it is attached, if the note has a flag or is beamed
- **Minimum distance *x* spaces from staff line** prevents the ends of slurs touching staff lines
- The **Avoiding articulation** options specify the distance between ends of slurs and articulations on the same note.

Notations

2.29 Staves

📖 **2.15 Guitar notation and tab, 2.18 Instruments, 2.26 Percussion, 7.1 Working with parts, 5.8 Focus on Staves, 8.14 Edit Instruments**.

To move or align staves, 📖 **8.10 Staff spacing**.

Creating staves

To create a staff for a new instrument, choose **Create ▸ Instruments** (shortcut I) – 📖 **2.18 Instruments**.

Multi-staff instruments

Many instruments can have more than one staff:

- Keyboard instruments – left hand and right hand
- Wind instruments – when there are several players
- Percussion – e.g. celesta, complicated marimba writing
- Singers – sometimes when divided
- Strings – often when divisi.

To add another staff to an instrument:

- If you want to add a staff throughout the score, make sure you have nothing selected; if, on the other hand, you want the new staff to appear only from a certain point in the score, select the bar at which you want it to start.
- Choose **Create ▸ Instruments** (shortcut I)
- In the **Staves in score** list, select the staff next to which you want to add a new staff
- Click **Above** or **Below**
- Click **OK**.

You can add further staves in the same way. A single instrument can have any number of staves (even 5, or 47391082), though you will seldom need more than two or three. If the number of staves used for an instrument changes throughout your score, you may need to adjust some playback settings – 📖 **4.1 Working with playback**.

All of an instrument's staves share its name, which is vertically centered on the staves.

Ossias

An ossia is a small bar or so of music above a normal-sized staff to show an alternative way of playing something. Ossias are incredibly easy to create with Sibelius. Simply:

- Select the passage you want to create an ossia above, e.g. click a bar (you can select just a few notes, if you like; it doesn't have to be a whole number of bars)
- From **Create ▸ Other ▸ Ossia Staff**, choose **Ossia Above**, or **Ossia Below**.
- The ossia bar(s) automatically appear, already made small for you. Now you can copy the music from the original (with Alt+click *or* ⌥-click) and amend as necessary to make your ossia.

What creating an ossia really does is to create a small staff above/below the selected one, with instrument changes before and after the ossia to hide the staff lines on either side of it. You can drag these instrument changes to adjust the width of the ossia.

Creating an ossia this way always creates an extra staff. If you create two ossias on the same system using the method described above, you will find it difficult to line them up, because Sibelius will have created a second extra staff above the selected one. Instead, create the second ossia using an instrument change to whatever instrument the ossia belongs to, then back to No instrument (hidden) at the end (📖 **2.18 Instruments**).

Systems indented at the left-hand side

Systems are automatically indented as necessary to fit in full instrument names, e.g. at the start and at new sections. You can also indent the first staff of parts automatically – 📖 **7.1 Working with parts**.

To indent any system manually, simply drag the initial barline (to the left of the clef) or the left-most end of the staff rightwards.

The indent is set for that particular barline only, so to keep the format the same you're recommended to put a system or page break at the end of the preceding system, if there is one. (If you don't do this, then if that barline ends up in the middle of a system Sibelius will put a gap before it to produce a divided system, like a coda – which is ingenious but may come as a surprise.)

To reset the indentation of a staff that you have dragged, select the initial barline or the leftmost end of the staff and choose Layout ▸ Reset Position (shortcut **Ctrl+Shift+P** *or* ⇧⌘P).

Systems indented at the right-hand side

It is occasionally useful to be able to make a system stop short of the right margin, e.g. for music examples, worksheets or exam or test papers. To do this:

• First, it's a good idea to force a system break after the bar that will be at the end of the shortened system, by selecting the barline and typing **Return** (on the main keyboard)

• Now switch on View ▸ Handles, which makes finding the handle you need to use easier

• Select the gray handle that is drawn just to the right of the barline at the right-hand side of the system. The handle turns purple to show that it's selected.

• Drag the handle leftwards, or use the shortcuts ←/→ (with **Ctrl** *or* ⌘ for larger steps), to increase the right-hand indent for that system. You can now switch View ▸ Handles off again.

To reset a system to its default width, select the handle and choose Layout ▸ Reset Position (shortcut **Ctrl+Shift+P** *or* ⇧⌘P).

Hiding staves

There are two ways of hiding staves in Sibelius, each with very different purposes:

• If you want to hide staves with music on them temporarily, e.g. when editing scores for large ensembles and want to work on particular staves without being distracted by all of the others, or if you want to prepare a special version of your score with hidden staves which play back, use View ▸ Focus on Staves – 📖 **5.8 Focus on Staves**

- If, on the other hand, you want to hide staves that have no music on them, to save space on the page and make your score easier to read, use Layout ▸ Hide Empty Staves – read on.

Usefully, Sibelius shows you where staves are hidden in your score by drawing a dashed blue line across the page if View ▸ Layout Marks is switched on – 🕮 **8.5 Breaks**.

Save trees – hide empty staves

If a staff only contains bars rest, you can hide it from that particular system, as is done in large scores:

- Double-click the staff to select it all (or select several staves as a passage)
- Choose Layout ▸ Hide Empty Staves (shortcut Ctrl+Shift+Alt+H *or* ⇧⌥⌘H).

You can also do this to several staves, or a passage lasting as many bars as you like, or even to the whole score. Staves will be hidden only on systems where they have no music, or where all the music is hidden (e.g. cue passages).

To hide empty staves throughout the score, simply choose Edit ▸ Select ▸ Select All (shortcut Ctrl+A *or* ⌘A) and choose Layout ▸ Hide Empty Staves – all unused staves throughout the score will disappear and the whole score will instantly reformat to fit on fewer pages, possibly saving several grateful trees.

When using Layout ▸ Hide Empty Staves, if you include keyboard staves then you may end up with just one hand hidden, which looks odd. So either check the keyboard part afterwards and re-show the hidden keyboard staff if this occurs, or (if, say, you're hiding staves throughout a score and can't be bothered to check the keyboard staves afterwards) don't include keyboard staves when hiding staves.

You can't, of course, hide the only staff in a system, since there has to be at least one staff to show that there's a system there at all. If you want actually to delete all the bars from a single staff, you should instead select the bars as a system passage and hit Delete.

Show hidden staves

To re-show staves that you've previously hidden using Layout ▸ Hide Empty Staves:

- Click a bar where you want to show the staves
- Choose Layout ▸ Show Empty Staves (shortcut Ctrl+Shift+Alt+S *or* ⇧⌥⌘S)
- In the dialog that appears, click OK to show all hidden staves, or select the particular staves you want to show.

This shows staves that were hidden using Layout ▸ Hide Empty Staves (because they contain no music), but it doesn't show:

- staves that were hidden using an instrument change to No instrument (hidden) – to make these reappear, use another instrument change to revert to the original instrument
- staves that were hidden using Focus on Staves – to make these reappear, switch off View ▸ Focus on Staves.

Deleting staves permanently

If you want to get rid of a staff (and any music on it) permanently, choose **Create ▸ Instruments** (shortcut I), select the staff (or staves) you want to delete from the **Staves in Score** list, and click **Delete from Score**, then click **OK**. Alternatively, you can triple-click on a staff in the score to select it throughout, then hit **Delete**.

Staff size

The staff size determines the size of everything in the score. If you double the staff size, all text, lines and so on will double too. If your score looks too cramped or spaced out, you can alleviate this by changing the staff size; ⚏ **8.6 Document Setup**.

Small staves

To make a staff go smaller than other staves, choose **Create ▸ Instruments**, select the staff in question in the **Staves in score** list, and switch on the **Small staff** checkbox, then click **OK**.

By default, small staves are 75% of normal size, but you can adjust this on the **Staves** page of the **House Style ▸ Engraving Rules** dialog (shortcut **Ctrl+Shift+E** *or* ⇧⌘E).

Staves with gaps in

Penderecki, Stockhausen and some other contemporary composers like to have no staff lines in bars where an instrument isn't playing. This gives scores a scrap-book (sometimes called "cutaway") look, with passages of music dotted about on the page. In choral music, preces and responses are often written similarly.

This is easy to achieve in Sibelius using instrument changes, as follows:

- First, preferably switch on **View ▸ Hidden Objects** (shortcut **Shift+Alt+H** *or* ⇧⌥H) if it's not already switched on; instrument changes will now appear as gray rectangles (with this option switched off they don't appear at all!)

- Select the passage of music during which you want the staff lines to disappear: for example, if you want them to disappear at the start of a bar, select that bar; if you want them to disappear after a particular note, select that note. Extend the selection to the point at which you want the staff lines to reappear again using **Shift-→** (hold **Ctrl** *or* ⌘ to extend by whole bars).

- Choose **Create ▸ Other ▸ Instrument Change**. In the dialog that appears, set **Choose from** to **All instruments**, **Family** to **Other**, and then select **No instrument (hidden)** from the list of instruments.

- Click **OK** and Sibelius creates two instrument changes: at the start of the selection it creates an instrument change to **No instrument (hidden)**, hiding the staff lines; and at the end of the selection it creates an instrument change back to the original instrument.

- In case Sibelius didn't position either instrument change precisely to your liking, you can select the gray instrument change rectangle and nudge it left and right with the ←/→ keys (with **Ctrl** *or* ⌘ for larger steps), or drag it with the mouse.

Creating an incipit

Although the incipit of a piece of music must strictly speaking refer to its first few notes, incipits occur in many types of scores, typically as a short fragment of music preceding the first full system, often indented both at the left- and right-hand sides of the page.

Incipits can represent a number of things: for example, a plainsong tone preceding a choral movement; a chart showing which handbells are used in a composition; or even a riff or collection of chord symbols used in a specific pop song.

Regardless of its content, you can create any kind of incipit like this:

- Add a suitable extra instrument to your score (e.g. **treble staff** from the Others family)
- Write the required music for the incipit
- Indent the staff at the left- and right-hand sides (see **Systems indented at the left-hand side** and **Systems indented at the right-hand side** above)
- Use Layout ▸ Hide Empty Staves to hide all the other staves on the first system (see **Save trees – hide empty staves** above)
- Use Create ▸ Other ▸ Bar Number Change to create a bar number change to bar 1 at the start of the second system, so that the piece itself starts with the correct bar number.

Creating prefatory staves

Prefatory staves are commonly used in modern performing editions of early music, and typically show the original clef, key signature, time signature for each staff; they may also show the first note on each staff, written in its original note value and at the appropriate position for the original clef.

Unlike an incipit, which typically appears as a single staff above the first full system of music, prefatory staves occur at the start of the first system, with a gap between the prefatory staves and the first full bar of music.

To create prefatory staves:

- Input the prefatory music into the first bar of the score (which you will probably need to input as an irregular bar), using notes and/or symbols.
- Select the barline at the end of the prefatory bar, and choose Layout ▸ Break ▸ Split System. This repeats the clefs, bracketing and so on at the start of the second bar. To close up the gap after the incipit, select the barline after the gap and choose Layout ▸ Reset Position.
- Select the barline before or after the prefatory bar and open the Bars panel of Properties; here you can adjust whether clefs, key signatures, brackets and the barline itself will appear. Change Gap before bar to adjust the size of the gap after the prefatory staves from this panel.
- When creating the new clefs and key signatures in the first bar proper, remember to switch on Hide, and for time signatures, remember to switch off Allow cautionary.
- Finally, use Create ▸ Other ▸ Bar Number Change to create a bar number change to bar 1 at the start of the first full bar of music, so that it starts with the correct bar number.

Comparing two staves

If you need to compare two staves in the same file to determine any differences between them, use the Plug-ins ▸ Analysis ▸ Compare Staves plug-in – 📖 **6.1 Working with plug-ins**.

2.30 Stems and leger lines

Flipping stem direction

The rule for stem-directions (see box) is almost completely rigid. About the only stem direction you should ever reverse is for notes on the middle staff line.

To reverse a note's stem, select it and choose Edit ▸ Flip (shortcut X). This also flips any ties as necessary (although you can also flip ties independently if you wish).

Don't confuse flipping stems with writing ordinary music in two voices. If you write in two voices the stems are automatically reversed for you (📖 **2.36 Voices**).

To flip the stems of all notes joined by a beam, you need only flip the stem of one of the notes. (Beware that you should select a note whose stem direction has not been altered by the presence of the beam.)

If you need to flip the stems of a beamed group in a situation where multiple voices are present, select the first stem of the beamed group.

Stems on the middle line

Stems on the middle line of the staff usually point downwards (see **Stem directions** box on the left), but the exceptions to this are vocal and choral music, where stems on the middle line often point upwards, and percussion music written on 1-line staves, on which stems always point up.

Sibelius automatically does this for appropriate instruments. To change this, edit the instrument – 📖 **8.14 Edit Instruments**.

Forcing stem direction

In rare cases (e.g. bagpipe music), you may wish to specify that stems always point up or down, regardless of the pitch of the notes. You can edit an instrument to do this – 📖 **8.14 Edit Instruments**.

Adjusting stem-lengths

Normally you should never change the lengths of stems, as the rules for stem-lengths are almost totally rigid and so are followed religiously by Sibelius. But there are occasions when a stem has to be lengthened in order, for instance, to avoid a collision between a beam and a grace note, or to allow room in avant-garde music for a special symbol to go on the stem; or shortened to avoid collisions in tight situations, particularly when using multiple voices.

To adjust a stem's length, simply drag the end of the stem, or click the end and adjust it with the arrow keys. Ctrl+↑/↓ or ⌘↑/↓ adjusts in steps of 0.25 spaces. It often helps to zoom in close on the stem so you can see more clearly what you're doing.

You can move individual stems right back to the notehead, resulting in a stemless note. However, it's preferable to use proper stemless notes instead – 📖 **2.25 Noteheads**.

You can even move a stem past the notehead to go backwards, which makes the stem end up on the wrong side of the note – though this is not very useful.

Stemless notes

To create stemless notes, use notehead 8 – select the note(s) or passage you want to make stemless and type Shift+Alt+8 *or* ⇧⌥8 (on the main keyboard).

> **Leger lines**
>
> *Leger lines for successive notes above or below the staff should never touch, even if the note values are very short.*
>
> *To prevent leger lines from touching, select the affected passage and increase the spacing between the notes slightly.*

Stem symbols

In contemporary music, symbols are sometimes added to stems to indicate special playing techniques; 📖 **2.31 Symbols**. However, Sibelius will automatically position and play tremolos and buzz rolls for you; 📖 **2.34 Tremolos**.

Hiding leger lines

Sibelius adds leger lines automatically when you create notes above or below the staff. If you want to hide leger lines, you can do it using either of two approaches: to hide all the leger lines on a particular instrument, switch off the **Leger lines** option in the instrument's staff type (📖 **8.14 Edit Instruments**); if you want to hide leger lines in a particular passage of notes, use a notehead type with the **Leger lines** option switched off (📖 **8.16 Edit Noteheads**).

Engraving Rules options

On the **Notes and Tremolos** page of the **House Style ▸ Engraving Rules** dialog (shortcut Ctrl+Shift+E *or* ⇧⌘E) you will find these exciting options:

* **Leger lines *x* spaces thick** allows you to change the thickness of leger lines; the default is 0.16 spaces. Leger lines are normally slightly thicker than staff lines.

* **Leger lines extend beyond noteheads by *x*% of its width** allows you to change the length of leger lines; the default is 28%.

On the **Beams and Stems** page of the **House Style ▸ Engraving Rules** dialog (shortcut Ctrl+Shift+E *or* ⇧⌘E) you will find even more exciting options:

* **Stems *x* spaces thick** allows you to change the thickness of stems; the default is 0.1 spaces

* **Minimum length *x* spaces** allows you to specify a minimum length for all stems, enabling you to override (say) the short stems on high/low notes in 2 voices. By default it is set to 2.75.

* **Adjust for cross-staff and between-note beams** ensures that the stem is always on the correct side of the notehead. This option is switched on by default, and should only be switched off in scores created in older versions of Sibelius in which you have fixed by hand problems with stems appearing on the wrong side of the notehead, e.g. in complex cross-staff beaming.

* **New stem length rule** makes the stems of notes on or either side of the middle staff line 0.25 spaces longer than with the option off, which many engravers and publishers prefer. This option is switched on by default.

2.31 Symbols

📖 **8.11 Music fonts**, **8.17 Edit Symbols**.

All of Sibelius's standard music symbols are available not only from the Keypad and menus, but also from the large **Create ▸ Symbol** dialog, which also includes many extra symbols. Like text and lines, symbols can attach either to a single staff, or to the system.

The difference between symbols and other objects is that you can position symbols anywhere you like. This enables you to override any of Sibelius's positioning rules by putting a symbol such as a sharp exactly where you want it, even in weird places where sharps shouldn't go.

The disadvantage of symbols is that their IQ is not as high as that of other objects. For instance, if you put a sharp symbol next to a note, it won't move vertically if the note is dragged up or down, nor will the note play as a sharp, and nor will it change to a natural (or whatever) if the music is transposed. The moral of this is: don't use a symbol where a normal object will do equally well.

Symbols are still smart in other ways, though – they attach to staves and rhythmic positions, so that they stay in the right place in parts (📖 **8.7 Attachment**).

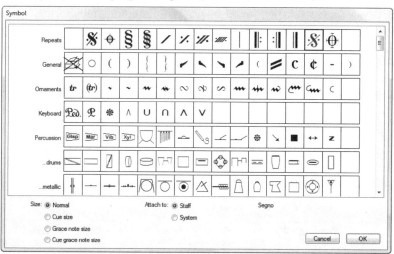

Creating a symbol

- Select the note next to which you want to add a symbol, then choose **Create ▸ Symbol** (shortcut Z for "zymbol")

- Select a symbol from the dialog and, if necessary, adjust the size of the symbol using the four size options. (Symbols automatically shrink when attached to a small staff, so you should normally leave the size at **Normal** when putting a symbol on a small staff.)

- Choose whether you want to attach the system to the **Staff** or the **System**. You only need to create a system symbol if you want it to appear all your parts (e.g. a fermata (pause) over a barline, or a coda or segno symbol) or when using symbols that control how repeat structures behave (e.g. segno and coda symbols).

- Click **OK**, and the symbol is created in the score next to the selected note. (Double-clicking the symbol in the dialog does the same as clicking **OK**.)

Alternatively, you can place symbols with the mouse. To do this:

- Ensure that nothing is selected (hit **Esc**), then choose **Create ▸ Symbol**
- Select a symbol and click **OK**
- The mouse pointer changes color, and you click in the score to position the symbol.

Symbols can be copied and deleted just like other objects.

Moving symbols

It's often useful to "nudge" symbols around in tiny steps using the arrow keys; holding down **Ctrl** *or* ⌘ moves in bigger steps, exactly one space in size. **Layout ▸ Reset Position** (shortcut **Ctrl+Shift+P** *or* ⇧⌘P) returns a symbol to its default position.

Editing symbols

For details on editing existing symbols and creating new ones, 📖 **8.17 Edit Symbols**.

Playback of symbols

Although most symbols don't play back, a handful (such as scoops and falls) will play back if your current playback device supports it. You can set up playback for other symbols using the **Play ▸ Dictionary** dialog – 📖 **4.9 Playback dictionary**.

Notable symbols

The **Create ▸ Symbol** dialog is grouped according to categories, and each symbol shows its name when selected in the dialog. Some of the less obvious symbols are as follows:

Category	Symbols	Meaning
Repeats	∕ ∕. ∕∕.	Repeat the last groups of eighths (quavers), usually found in handwritten music; repeat last bar; repeat last two bars. Also includes various barline symbols, useful for scores where some staves have independent barlines. Two kinds of coda and segno symbols are provided, one pair in a design usually used in Japan.
General	( ) ⌐ ↗ ↘	Parentheses (round brackets) for placing around symbols (e.g. accidentals, 8va, trills); keyboard brace; bracket/winged repeat ends
Ornaments		Includes mordents, turns, and so on, but these do not play back automatically; to create trills that play back, 📖 **2.21 Lines**; to play back mordents and turns, 📖 **6.1 Working with plug-ins**. Further ornament symbols are found in the **More ornaments** rows further down the dialog (see below).
Keyboard	𝄟. ✳ ∪ ∧	Pedal symbols that you can use to change the appearance of the pedal line (📖 **2.21 Lines**); heel and toe symbols for organ pedals (left and right foot)
Percussion		These rows include most symbols provided in the well-known Ghent™ font. The first row includes symbols for various percussion instruments.
...beaters	🖋 🖋 🖋	Includes sticks for various instruments (pictured left are soft, medium and hard beaters)
Guitar	🎸 ∨ ∨	Includes frames for various numbers of strings; vibrato bar scoop; vibrato bar dip

Category	Symbols	Meaning
Articulation		The first two rows are ordered according to relative proximity to the notehead (e.g. a staccato dot goes nearer to a notehead than a down-bow symbol); the symbols on the first row go above the note, and those on the second row, below the note. The third row contains other articulations:
	● ● ● ⎛	Multiple staccatos, for use on repeated notes written as a one-note tremolo; snap pizzicato for stringed instruments, mainly used by Bartók, and sometimes drawn the other way up
	, ✓ //	Comma and tick, indicating a breath, usually in choral music (the comma also indicates a short silence on instruments like the piano, which can't literally breathe); cesuras in two different thicknesses
	➚ ⌣ ❙	Stress and unstress marks (above and below), used by Schoenberg; "notch" staccato, sometimes used in early music
Accidentals		The first nine symbols in both rows (unbracketed and bracketed) are ordered from flattest to sharpest, including microtones; remember that as these are symbols they're not automatically transposed, nor do they play back, so use a normal accidental if possible.
	♭♭ ♭♭	*1½ half-steps (semitones) flat*
	♭	*1¼ half-steps (semitones) flat, or occasionally 1½ half-steps flat*
	♭ ♭ ◀	*½ half-step (semitone) flat*
	♮	*¼ half-step (semitone) flat or ½ half-step flat*
	♮	*¼ half-step (semitone) sharp or ½ half-step sharp*
	♯ ♯ ♯	*½ half-step (semitone) sharp*
	♯	*1¼ half-steps (semitones) sharp, or occasionally 1½ half-steps sharp*
	♯	*1½ half-steps (semitones) sharp*
		Alternative symbols for microtones are available on the **More accidentals** row further down the dialog.
Notes	♪♪♩ ♩	These notes are not used by Sibelius to draw ordinary notes; they are provided purely in case you want to write notes in totally weird places. Sibelius draws notes using a notehead (from the **Noteheads** row), with tails (from the **Notes** row) for short notes.
	↘↘	Tail aficionados might like to examine closely how we've constructed the tails of sixteenth notes (semiquavers) and shorter notes, such that the tail nearest the notehead is of slightly greater curvature. (Tail non-aficionados will have no idea what we're talking about.)
	╲ ⌢ ◄ ●	Grace note slash for acciaccatura stem; *laissez vibrer* tie symbol (preferable to using a real tie in some circumstances), which can also be used for ties going into 2nd endings (2nd-time bars) and codas; tremolo stroke; rhythm dot
	▌	Cluster symbol; by stacking several of them vertically you can make a cluster chord of any size
Noteheads		To change noteheads, don't use symbols – 📖 **2.25 Noteheads**. Also contains "stalk" symbols for altered unisons – 📖 **2.1 Accidentals**. More uncommon noteheads for avant garde and modern classical music can be found in the **Round noteheads** row further down the dialog.
Rests		All standard rests, including old-style multirests; also includes constituent parts of H-bars – 📖 **2.24 Multirests**

Category	Symbols	Meaning
Conductor		Put these at the right-hand end of a staff (e.g. in choral music) to show it's going to divide on the next system. They can stick out into the right margin of the page. You can also use the arrows individually, pointing the other way around to show that two staves are going to join together again.
		Beat, left-hand beat, right-hand beat, long beat. The leftmost symbol is the only standard one; the others are used occasionally (e.g. by Lutoslawski), but their meanings vary somewhat. Beat marks appear in the full score to tell the conductor how to beat in tricky circumstances; they also sometimes appear in parts so the performers know when to wait for a beat.
		Double and triple beats (for a single beat, use one of the above arrows or a simple vertical line). They appear over sequences of music to indicate how the conductor will group them; they are schematic drawings of the shape outlined by the conductor's baton. Used e.g. in Boulez's *Le Marteau sans maître*. The lower set is for compound beats. Further conductor symbols are found on the **More conductor** row further down the dialog.
Clefs		Contains all standard clefs – 📖 **2.11 Clefs**. The *8* and *15* are separate symbols (at the right of the second row), which you can alter in order to change all appropriate clefs at once. More uncommon clefs (e.g. upside down and back-to-front treble and bass clefs) are found on the **More clefs** row further down the dialog.
Octaves		Used in *8va* etc. lines – 📖 **2.21 Lines**
Layout Marks		Used by Sibelius to show page/system breaks etc. – it's unlikely you'll want to use these.
Techniques		This row contains a myriad exciting and unusual symbols:
	⌐ ⌐ ⌐	Lift (doit) and fall for jazz notation; mute, for stringed instruments
	● ◑ ○	Wind instrument fingerings: open hole, half-hole and closed hole
		Attach to the stem of a note or chord. They mean: whispered or *sprechstimme*; swished (or some similar action on percussion instruments); *sul ponticello* (played on the bridge); harp "buzz" (when the pedal is changed while the respective string is still vibrating), also used by Penderecki to notate an unmeasured string tremolo played as fast as possible. A slightly different "z" stem marking for buzz rolls is available from the third Keypad layout.
		"Exponential" crescendo curves that fit onto short and long crescendo hairpins – 📖 **2.17 Hairpins**.
Accordion	⊖	25 treble coupler diagrams and 21 bass coupler diagrams for accordion music, plus empty diagrams and blobs that you can superimpose to produce further combinations
Handbells		All of the symbols commonly used in handbell music are to be found here
More ornaments		More than 50 additional ornament symbols, including *pincé*, shake, *port de voix*, cadence, cadence coupée, etc., are provided in these four rows.
Clusters		Symbols for white note and black note clusters for intervals between a second and an octave.
Special stems		A variety of alternative stem symbols for use with stemless notes, to show different playing techniques.
Prolations	○ ⊙ ¢ ℂ	Symbols for *tempus perfectus, tempus imperfectus, prolatio perfectus* (major prolation), *prolatio imperfectus* (minor prolation), etc. for use in editions of medieval music.
Miscellaneous		Leger line symbols of various widths (normal, whole note, cue note) are provided; line these up with the regular stave lines to ensure that they look as good as possible
Note names		Special noteheads that show note names inside the notehead shape. To use these, 📖 **6.8 Other plug-ins**.

2.32 Ties

Ties are used in music to indicate that two notes of identical pitch are joined to each other to form one longer note. Notes at the end or middle of a tie should not be replayed. Ties are distinctly different than slurs, which are used to show phrase structures and, in the case of wind or string instruments, group notes together that should be played within one single movement of the bow or in one continuous breath – 📖 **2.28 Slurs**.

Ties versus slurs

Never use a slur instead of a tie – slurs looks similar, but won't behave like a tie in playback or if you transpose the music. Likewise you should never use a tie instead of a slur, as it is then possible to tie notes to nothing (i.e. neither to another note nor a rest), resulting in notes being held indefinitely during playback.

Creating ties

Ties are input from the first Keypad layout. Simply select a note and then choose the tie from the keypad (shortcut **Enter**). To add a tie to all the notes of a chord, double-click it (or choose **Edit ▸ Select ▸ Select More**, shortcut **Ctrl+Shift+A** *or* ⌥⌘A) before selecting the tie from the Keypad.

You can edit the size and position of ties in a number of ways:

- To flip a tie to curve upwards instead of downwards (or vice versa), select it and choose **Edit ▸ Flip** (shortcut **X**); to reset it to its original direction, choose **Layout ▸ Reset Position** (shortcut **Ctrl+Shift+P** *or* ⌥⌘P)

- Select either end (use **Alt+←/→** *or* ⌥←/→ to select either end using the keyboard) and drag the end, or type **Shift+Alt+←/→** *or* ⌥⌥←/→; hold down **Ctrl** *or* ⌘ for larger steps. Sibelius always ensures the tie remains horizontal and symmetrical.

- You can also adjust the position of the ends of ties and their "shoulders" individually via the **Notes** panel of the Properties window (📖 **5.17 Properties**). To adjust them throughout the score, see **Engraving rules options** below.

- You can also select and drag the middle of the tie (or move it with ↑/↓) to make it more or less arched

- To reset the shape of a tie after adjusting its curvature, choose **Layout ▸ Reset Design** (shortcut **Ctrl+Shift+D** *or* ⌥⌘D).

Ties across breaks

If a tie crosses a page or system break, the tie will be drawn in two segments, each of which looks like a complete tie. You can adjust both the end points and the curvature of each segment of the tie independently of the other, but note that you cannot move either segment of the tie vertically without also moving the other segment.

If you prefer to display ties over breaks as a single broken tie, switch on **Clip at end of systems** on the Ties 1 page of **House Style ▸ Engraving Rules**.

Ties across changes of time signature

In some published music, if a tie crosses a time signature change, the tie is broken on either side of the time signature. To achieve this, see **Using layers to break ties across time signatures** on page 425.

Laissez vibrer ties

In percussion and piano music, you can create a *laissez vibrer* effect by tying a note/chord to a rest in the normal way (using **Enter** on the numeric keypad) to indicate that the note/chord is to be held until it dies away. Playback also implements this (by sending a NoteOn but no NoteOff); the way this sounds (particularly if the note is subsequently re-played) may depend on the sophistication of your MIDI playback device. If you don't like the playback effect this produces, use the *laissez vibrer* symbols from the **Notes** rows of the **Create ▸ Symbol** dialog (shortcut Z) instead.

Ties in arpeggiated music

In keyboard and harp music it's common to see figures such as the one shown on the right. To achieve this, simply enter the notes as usual, adding a tie to each one. You can then simply extend each tie as far as necessary to meet the destination note.

Beware that Sibelius does not "know" that these ties should be attached to their respective destinations, so it will not automatically adjust their length if the layout or spacing changes. So you may wish to adjust the length of the ties once the layout of your score is finalized.

Positioning ties

Although ties may superficially look like slurs, the engraving rules concerning how they are positioned are not the same.

Ties are flatter than slurs, and always have their ends close to the noteheads they're tying – never at the stem end of a note.

To make ties more visible, the very ends and the highest or lowest point of the arch should avoid touching a staff line.

If ties occur together with slurs, ties should always be positioned nearest the notes.

Notes tied into 2nd ending (2nd-time) bars

When notes are tied over into a 2nd ending (2nd-time bar), you need to draw ties at the very start of the 2nd ending. To achieve this, you should use the above-mentioned *laissez vibrer* symbols, or a non-magnetic slur (📖 **2.28 Slurs**), although neither of these methods will play back correctly.

Engraving rules options

There is a bewildering array of options concerning ties on the **Ties 1** and **Ties 2** pages of **House Style ▸ Engraving Rules** (shortcut Ctrl+Shift+E *or* ⇧⌘E). Many of the options are unavailable unless **Tie position rule** on **Ties 1** is set to **Optical ties**. Unless you have a good reason not to, you should use Optical ties.

The other options on **Ties 1** are as follows:

- The settings under **Shape** determine the default amount of shoulder Sibelius should give to ties. You can think of the shoulder as the steepness of the curvature of the tie: a larger shoulder makes flatter ties. Sibelius can automatically increase the shoulder of longer ties, which prevents long ties from having too great a curvature.

- Normally, ties that cross a system or page break are drawn as two complete ties, one on either side of the break. If you would prefer Sibelius to draw ties over breaks as two halves of the same tie instead, switch on **Clip at end of systems**.

- The options in **Thickness** allow you to specify the default outline thickness and middle thickness of ties, in a similar manner to slurs (⊞ **2.28 Slurs**).

- **Ties Above/Below on Notehead Side** determines whether or not ties, when drawn curving away from the stem (as opposed to towards the stem), should go between the noteheads or above or below them. By default, Sibelius draws ties on single notes above or below (**Use on single notes** on), and ties in chords between noteheads (**Use on chords** off). The other options in this section allow you to specify the distance of the tie relative to the notehead when not drawn between the notes, with separate settings for above and below.

The options on **Ties 2** continue in a similar vein:

- **Ties Above/Below on Stem Side** determines whether or not ties should be positioned specially when they are forced to draw curving towards the stem, which commonly happens in music that uses multiple voices. Some publishers prefer the innermost tie (i.e. the one closest to the ends of the stems) to be positioned higher than normal, so that it can also be a little longer. Sibelius's default settings are designed to keep ties looking as symmetrical as possible, so it doesn't treat chords specially (**Use on chords** off), but does move ties on single notes (**Use on single notes** on), using the other options that allow you to specify the horizontal and vertical distance that the innermost tie should be moved.

- **Ties Between Notes** are the options that apply when ties are not positioned above or below when on the notehead side, or when they are moved as a result of the settings under **Ties Above/Below on Stem Side**. You can determine how Sibelius decides the direction of curvature of ties in chords, and specify how you want Sibelius to position the left- and right-hand ends of ties. As aforementioned, Sibelius's default settings are designed to keep ties looking symmetrical, so both **Align left ends of ties between chords** and **Align right ends of ties between chords** are on by default, which (particularly in conjunction with the **Ties in Spaces** options – see below) make ties look good even in complex chords involving intervals of a 2nd or other clusters.

  Ties start after rhythm dots does as its name suggests, and is also on by default (though note that ties forced onto the stem side do not start after rhythm dots: instead, they typically go above the rhythm dot and hence can start to the left of the dot). The other options allow you to control precisely the distances Sibelius uses when positioning ties between notes and chords.

- **Ties in Spaces** determines whether or not Sibelius should **Prefer one tie per space**. This is useful, as it prevents ties from appearing "bunched up" in chords of more than two notes that contain intervals of a 2nd or other clusters of notes. If this option is switched on, Sibelius will ensure that only one tie falls within a single space on the staff, by displacing the other ties according to the limits defined by the two **Maximum** options. It's advisable to only allow a maximum of **1** tie to be positioned beyond the notehead end of the chord, but you could allow more to be positioned on the stem side (Sibelius's default value is **2**).

If you have strong feelings about how ties should be positioned, you are encouraged to experiment with these settings to determine the best combination for your own tastes. Once you have set the options correctly, you should seldom need to edit ties by hand (but if you encounter cases that need manual adjustment, use the **Notes** panel of the Properties window).

2.33 Time signatures

Creating time signatures

- Select a note, rest, line or other object in your score
- Choose **Create ▸ Time Signature** (shortcut **T**) and click the time signature you want; click **Other** and use the drop-down lists to create more complex time signatures
- Click **OK** or hit **Return**; the time signature is created at the beginning of the following bar.

To create a time signature at the start of your score, it's easiest to choose it on the **File ▸ New** dialog when you first create the score. To create or change it subsequently, make sure that nothing is selected (hit **Esc**), then choose **Create ▸ Time Signature**, select the time signature you want and click **OK**. The mouse pointer turns colored to show that it "contains" an object – click at the start of the score to place the initial time signature.

Pick-up (upbeat) bars

If your score starts with a pick-up (upbeat) bar, it's easiest to specify this at the same time as creating the initial time signature. Click **Start with bar of length** in the **Create ▸ Time Signature** dialog, and choose the length of the bar from the list, or type it on the numeric keypad (with **Num Lock** on). You can choose more than one note value if you want a pick-up (upbeat) bar with a peculiar length such as a half note (minim) plus an eighth note (quaver).

You will notice that pick-up (upbeat) bars correctly show the number of beats in each bar as rests, divided according to the **Beam and Rest Groups** settings you made when creating the time signature.

Should you forget to create a pick-up bar at this stage, you can create it as an irregular bar later – 📖 **2.5 Bars and bar rests**.

When music starts with a pick-up bar, it's normal to number the first complete bar as bar 1, rather than bar 2 as it would otherwise be. Sibelius does this for you by automatically numbering the pick-up bar as bar 0.

Rebarring music

If you put a time signature into some existing music, Sibelius splits the existing music up into new bar-lengths, with ties across barlines where necessary, unless you switch off the **Rewrite bars up to next time signature** option in **Create ▸ Time Signature**.

Sibelius only rebars the music up to the next time signature change in your score, if there is one. However, if you start by selecting a passage before creating a time signature, Sibelius will restore the original time signature at the end of the selection, and only rewrite music up to that point. This is very useful when you want to change the barring of a few bars in the middle of the score.

In the unlikely event that you have copied some bars into a score that don't match the prevailing time signature and you would like to rebar them accordingly, select the time signature and delete it. When asked if the bars following should be rewritten, click **No**, then reinsert the same time signature, ensuring that **Rewrite bars up to next time signature** is switched on.

Cautionary time signatures

Allow cautionary allows a cautionary time signature to appear at the end of the preceding system if the time signature is being put (or subsequently ends up) at the end of a system. You'd normally want to switch off this box if putting a time signature at the start of a new piece, song or movement within a larger score. (The same goes for cautionary key signatures and clefs.)

Complex time signatures

To create a time signature other than the most common ones illustrated on the **Create ▸ Time Signature** dialog, click **Other** and pick the numbers you want from the lists provided.

If you want the groups shown as an additive time signature, such as 3+2/2/8, simply type **3+2+2** into the box for the top of the time signature instead of picking a number from the list. On Mac, you must use the **+** key on the numeric keypad, not on the main keyboard.

Alternatively, if you want the time signature written as 7/8 but to have 2+2+3 (or any other text) written above the time signature in the same font, add the extra text using the **Time signatures (one staff only)** text style – see **Multiple time signatures** below.

Beam and rest groups

Sibelius automatically groups beats appropriately for each time signature you create. You can, however, change these settings for yourself by clicking **Beam and Rest Groups** in the **Create ▸ Time Signature** dialog, or you can change the beam groups in existing music in the **Notes ▸ Reset Beam Groups** dialog. For more details, ☐ **2.6 Beam groups**.

Irregular bars and free rhythm

To create a bar of irregular length (i.e. length different to that specified by the prevailing time signature), ☐ **2.5 Bars and bar rests**.

For other cases of music with free rhythm, ☐ **2.13 Free rhythm**.

Multiple time signatures

Occasionally scores have two simultaneous time signatures with the same bar-length, such as 2/4 against 6/8. To input this sort of case:

• Create a 2/4 time signature and input the 2/4 music as normal

• Input the 6/8 music as triplet eighths (quavers), but use the **Create ▸ Tuplet** dialog at least for the first tuplet, switching on **None** and switching off **Bracket**, so it won't show that they're triplets

• You can copy the first 6/8 bar as a quick way to get the triplet rhythm for subsequent bars

• When all of the music has been inputted, delete the 2/4 time signature and drag the first note rightwards until there's enough space for a replacement time signature

• Type the 2/4 and 6/8 using text – start with nothing selected and use **Create ▸ Text ▸ Other staff text ▸ Time signatures (one staff only)**

• Click where you want to put the time signature to type it in as text, with a **Return** (on the main keyboard) after the top number.

In cases where two or more time signatures with different bar lengths are required, such as 4/4 and 5/4:

- Calculate the lowest common multiple between the two time signatures – in this case, 20/4 – and create that as the time signature
- When all of the music has been inputted, delete the 20/4 time signature and drag the first note rightwards until there's enough space for a replacement time signature
- Type the 4/4 and 5/4 using text – to do this you'll need to create a new text style (see above)
- Add the extra barlines using the vertical line from the **Create ▸ Line** dialog.

This method has the advantage of ensuring that systems end at coinciding barlines.

If simultaneous time signatures always have barlines in different places, adopt the same procedure, but remove the barlines in one staff (see **Hiding barlines on some staves only** in ▭ **2.4 Barlines**), then use the vertical line from the **Staff lines** pane in the **Create ▸ Line** dialog to draw in suitable barlines where you want them.

Alternating time signatures

To write music in e.g. alternating 2/4 and 3/4 time, signaled by a 2/4 3/4 composite time signature:

- Input a 2/4 time signature and copy it to alternate bars
- Do the same for a 3/4 time signature in the remaining bars
- Input the music
- Then delete all the time signatures except the initial 2/4 (saying **No** when asked if you want to rewrite the music)
- Finally write a 3/4 time signature immediately after the initial 2/4 using text, as described in **Multiple time signatures** above.

Modifying time signatures

You can copy and delete time signatures like other objects. You can also drag time signatures left and right to move them – even to fairly silly places. We don't recommend you drag time signatures out of the bar they belong to.

Big time signatures etc.

Big time signatures between staves are often used in large modern scores where the meter changes frequently.

On the **Time signatures** page of the **House Style ▸ Engraving Rules** dialog (shortcut Ctrl+Shift+E *or* ⇧⌘E), click either **Time signatures (large)** or the even larger **Time signatures (huge)**. These are actually text styles that time signatures can use instead. These affect all time signatures throughout the score.

To alter the size, font and positioning of big time signatures, click **Edit Text Style**; ▭ **3.9 Edit Text Styles**. This also lets you adjust which staves big time signatures go above.

The other exciting **House Style ▸ Engraving Rules** option confers upon you the ability to adjust the default gap before time signatures.

2.34 Tremolos

📖 **2.26 Percussion**.

Tremolos are an abbreviation for rapidly repeated notes. A one-note tremolo is for a single repeated note; a two-note tremolo represents two alternating notes; a buzz roll is a special kind of tremolo used for unpitched percussion.

One-note tremolos

Adding one tremolo stroke to a quarter note (crotchet) or longer note indicates that it is to be played as two eighth notes (quavers). Adding two strokes means it should be played as four sixteenth notes (semiquavers), and so on. Three and four strokes are also used to mean that the note should be reiterated as fast as possible (an "unmeasured" tremolo), e.g. to indicate a drum roll.

On an eighth (quaver) or shorter note, one tremolo stroke means it should be divided into two, two strokes means it should be divided into four, and so on.

One-note

One-note tremolos are notated as strokes on the stem of a note or chord, e.g.

To write this, choose the number of strokes you want the note to have from the third Keypad layout (either before or after you create the note).

To add tremolos to a note or chord after creating it, select the note/chord and choose the number of strokes from the third Keypad layout (type **1/2/3/4/5** for 1/2/3/4/5 strokes).

You can remove the tremolos by choosing the same Keypad button.

The number of divisions per note in a one-note tremolo is sometimes indicated by placing multiple staccatos above the note, in addition to strokes through the stem. You can add multiple staccatos as symbols – 📖 **2.31 Symbols**.

Two-note

Two-note tremolos are notated as beam-like strokes between two notes or chords, e.g.

On the first note/chord, simply choose the number of strokes you want from the third Keypad layout (type **1/2/3/4/5** for 1/2/3/4/5 strokes), then click the two-note tremolo button shown on the left (shortcut **Enter**). You can do this before or after creating the second note.

Each of the notes is written as if it lasted for the whole length of the tremolo, i.e. it looks as if the note-lengths are doubled. Sibelius automatically doubles the note values for you. So to write a two-note tremolo that lasts for a half note (minim) you would write two quarter notes (crotchets) and then use the third Keypad layout to add the tremolo:

Two-note tremolos

These are beams between two notes or chords that indicate that they should be repeatedly played alternately. Multiple strokes mean exactly the same as for one-note tremolos.

Before   *After*

Notations

You can switch off the tremolos by choosing the same buttons from the Keypad again.

Two-note tremolos can be written between staves (by crossing one or other note onto the other staff – 📖 **2.7 Beam positions**), and across barlines.

To adjust the angle of a two-note tremolo, drag the stems of the notes at either side. If the two-note tremolo is between two whole-notes (semibreves), drag the tremolo line itself (this has the same effect as dragging the stem of the first note – were it to have one!)

The **Notes and Tremolos** page of the **House Style ▸ Engraving Rules** dialog (shortcut **Ctrl+Shift+E** *or* ⇧⌘E) contains three options governing the appearance of two-note tremolos, should you be struck by a desire to change them:

| Between stems | Touching stems | Outer tremolo touching stems |

Buzz roll (Z on stem)

Buzz rolls are notated by adding a Z symbol to the stem of a note or chord to indicate a multiple stroke roll, as used in percussion writing (see right). To add a buzz roll to a note or chord after creating it, select the note or chord and, from the third Keypad layout (shortcut F9), hit 6. Sibelius plays buzz rolls back as fast tremolos. 📖 **2.26 Percussion**.

The tribulations of tremolo notations

With two-note tremolos, the odd convention of writing each note with the total length of the tremolo produces various anomalies.

In the 19th century, a crazy convention was in operation whereby the note values were only doubled if the tremolo lasted for a quarter note (crotchet) or more. Thus you could find pairs of eighths (quavers) tremoloing, and also half notes (minims), but never quarter notes (crotchets). This was bananas.

However, another idiosyncrasy that survives to the present day is as follows: if you want to notate a two-note tremolo lasting for two 4/4 bars, you write two whole-notes (semibreves) with a tremolo across the barline, rather than doubling the note values to two double whole notes (breves). Most people go a lifetime without noticing this weird exception – what sheltered lives they lead.

2.35 Triplets and other tuplets

📖 **5.7 Filters and Find**, **5.9 Hiding objects**.

"Tuplets" are rhythms like triplets, which are played at some fraction of their normal speed.

(Tuplet is not a nice word, though alternatives like "irrational rhythm" aren't too terrific either. Opinion is divided as to whether "tuplet" rhymes with "duplet" or with "couplet.")

Creating tuplets quickly

- Input or select the first note (only) of the tuplet, which must be of the unit length of the tuplet (see box).

  For instance, if you want a triplet with a total length of a half note (minim), the first note you input must be a quarter note (crotchet).

- Type **Ctrl+3** or **⌘3** for a triplet – which, let's face it, is what you're probably after – or **Ctrl+2–9** or **⌘2–9** for anything from a duplet to a nonuplet

- The tuplet will appear, with the correct number of rests. Add the other notes in the normal way.

The tuplet has the format and bracket options last set on the Create ▸ Tuplet dialog (see **Creating tuplets slowly** below).

> **Tuplets with a single number**
> *The simplest case is the triplet; **3** over ♩♩♩ means 3 quarter notes (crotchets) compressed into the time of 2 quarter notes. The quarter note is the "unit" of the tuplet in this case.*
>
> *Where numbers other than 3 are used, the tendency is to squash into the next lowest power of 2 units – so 5 means 5 in the time of 4, 15 means 15 in the time of 8, and so on. The exceptions to this rule are 2 and 4, which normally mean 2 in the time of 3 and 4 in the time of 6.*
>
> *When triplets are being used a lot, 3 is often written over the first few and left off after that. If your whole score is written like this, you should probably use a different time signature!*

Creating tuplets slowly

- Input or select the first note (only) of the tuplet, which must be of the unit length of the tuplet

- Choose **Create ▸ Tuplet**

- Type in any number or ratio, as complex as you like (e.g. **13**, or **99:64**)

- Click **Number** to write just a single number (or the first number of the ratio), **Ratio** to write a ratio (e.g. **5:3**), **Ratio+note** to write e.g. **5:3♪**, and **None** to write no number at all

- By default, Sibelius creates tuplets with **Auto Bracket** switched on; this means that the triplet bracket disappears if there is a beam joining exactly the same notes as the bracket would join, and if the tuplet is at the beam end of the notes. If you want explicitly to specify that your tuplet should or should not be bracketed, choose one of the other options.

- Switch on **Full duration** if you want the bracket to extend up to the next note/rest (see box on next page)

- Click **OK**; the tuplet will appear and you can input the remaining notes as normal.

Editing tuplets .

A number of plug-ins are provided for editing existing tuplets – 📖 **6.14 Tuplets plug-ins**.

Copying tuplets

You can select a tuplet's bracket or number and copy it onto another note to turn that note into a tuplet.

You can also, of course, copy passages containing tuplets. The only thing you can't copy is part of a tuplet, such as just the first note of a tuplet, as that would produce a chunk of fractional rhythm that wouldn't make much sense. If you get an unexpected warning that you're copying part of a tuplet, make sure you've selected the tuplet number or bracket as well as the notes within it.

Deleting tuplets

To delete a tuplet, select the number or bracket and hit **Delete**. This deletes not only the number and bracket, but also the notes. This is because without the tuplet, the notes would no longer add up.

> **Tuplet brackets**
>
> *A bracket is often written over the notes within the tuplet. The number used to be written above or below the bracket, but to conserve space it goes in a gap in the center of the bracket nowadays.*
>
> *In older scores you will often find a slur used instead of a bracket, even when the notes are not meant to be played smoothly; nowadays a slur is only used when slurring is specifically intended.*
>
> *A few composers, such as Britten and Holloway, write just a bracket on its own to mean a triplet.*
>
> *In modern scores tuplet brackets are often extended rightwards, nearly up to the start of the note/rest following the tuplet. This looks cleaner when notating, say, simultaneous triplet quarter notes (crotchets) and sextuplet eighth notes (quavers), because it means the brackets will all end in the same place.*

Setting the unit length

Sometimes the first note of the tuplet is not the same as the unit length: a triplet that is three quarter notes (crotchets) long may start with an eighth note (quaver), for instance. If this is the case, you should input a first note with the unit length you want (here, a quarter note) so Sibelius knows how long the rhythm lasts, then input the tuplet, then change the note value of the first note afterwards.

Special tuplets

There are cases where you would write a tuplet with a single digit that denotes something other than what it would ordinarily mean; for example, in 6/8, you might see this:

This is actually a 7:6 ratio tuplet. To obtain this, use the **Create ▸ Tuplet** dialog, type **7:6** (to tell Sibelius what the tuplet really is), and set **Format** to **Number** (which tells Sibelius only to write the 7 in the score).

Some composers write 7 meaning 7:8 and 15 meaning 15:16, since this way the note values are much closer to how they sound than in the standard notation, so to write this you would choose a ratio of (say) **7:8** and set **Format** to **Number**.

Moving tuplets

Tuplets are "magnetic" – that is, automatically positioned – like slurs (📖 **2.21 Lines**). Sibelius decides whether the tuplet should go above or below the notes, and at what angle. The tuplet number and bracket move automatically to avoid collisions with notes at either end of the tuplet, and articulations on notes in the tuplet. Try dragging the first note in a tuplet up and down and see what happens! This means that if you transpose your music, the tuplet number and bracket move automatically to ensure they do not collide with the notes.

If you disagree with where Sibelius puts the tuplet by default, you can flip it to the other side of the notes by selecting the number (or bracket) and choosing **Edit ▸ Flip** (shortcut **X**).

You can also move the whole tuplet up and down by dragging the number (or the middle of the bracket if there is no number) or using the arrow keys. You shouldn't try to drag a tuplet to the other side of the notes – use **Edit ▸ Flip** (shortcut **X**) instead.

You can adjust the angle of the bracket and number by moving either tip of the bracket.

To restore the default position of a tuplet if you move it, select it and choose **Layout ▸ Reset Position** (shortcut **Ctrl+Shift+P** *or* ⌃⌘P).

Nested tuplets

Nested tuplets (meaning tuplets within tuplets) are much beloved of composers like Brian Ferneyhough, and can be a little tricky to sight-read. Sibelius automatically notates nested tuplets of just about any depth or complexity, and they even play back correctly.

Input nested tuplets just like normal tuplets, but input the outermost (i.e. widest) tuplet first, and work your way in.

Ratio tuplets

In modern notation you can write things like 5:4 meaning "5 in the time of 4." You can use this to make simple tuplets more explicit – e.g. writing 3:2 for a triplet – or to specify more unusual rhythms like 5:3. The second number must be more than half and less than twice the first number.

Hidden tuplets

You can write "hidden" tuplets either by hiding the bracket and number (📖 **5.9 Hiding objects**), or by switching off the bracket and the number from the **Create ▸ Tuplet** dialog when you create them. This makes the notes end up spaced in a different proportion from other staves in the score without anything else to indicate that a tuplet was present. This is useful for quick flourishes of notes and other examples of "free rhythm" where it would be tedious to notate an exact rhythm in the score. You can also use it to write mixed time signatures such as 4/4 against 6/8. 📖 **2.13 Free rhythm**, **2.33 Time signatures**.

Changing the appearance of tuplets already in your score

If, after creating a number of tuplets, you decide that you would like to change the way they are printed, you can do so using filters and the **Properties** window.

For example, to hide the brackets and numbers of tuplets already in your score:

- Choose **Edit ▸ Filter ▸ Tuplets**
- All the tuplet brackets and numbers in your score will now be selected. Now:
  ○ To hide all the tuplet brackets and numbers, simply choose **Edit ▸ Hide or Show ▸ Hide** (shortcut **Ctrl+Shift+H** *or* ⌃⌘H) or choose **Hide** from the menu on the **General** panel of the Properties window
  ○ To change the appearance of the tuplet, use the options on the **Notes** panel of the Properties window.

Filters are an extremely powerful way of changing lots of objects in your score in a single operation – 📖 **5.7 Filters and Find**.

Horizontal tuplet brackets

If you want your tuplet brackets to always be horizontal, choose **House Style ▸ Edit Lines**, select the tuplet bracket line in the **Staff lines** list, click **Edit**, and in the **Edit Line** dialog, switch on the **Horizontal** option (📖 **8.15 Edit Lines**). Beware, however, that forcing tuplet brackets to be horizontal will disable some of their "magnetic" behaviors.

Tuplets over barlines

Although Sibelius cannot automatically notate tuplets over barlines, the effect can be achieved easily enough, as follows:

- Create an irregular bar of twice the length of the prevailing time signature: choose **Create ▸ Bar ▸ Other** (shortcut **Alt+B** *or* ⌥B)
- Write the music for the two bars that contain the tuplet which crosses the barline
- Add a suitable barline – in the example above you would choose **Create ▸ Barline ▸ Normal** and click in the appropriate place
- If you are using bar numbers you should also create a bar number change in the next bar to compensate for the missing "real" bar; choose **Create ▸ Other ▸ Bar Number Change**.

Tuplet design and Engraving Rules options

You can change the design of tuplet numbers and brackets from the **House Style ▸ Edit Text Styles** and **House Style ▸ Edit Lines** dialogs. If you're changing the font of tuplet numbers, it's normal to use a medium italic serif font. 📖 **3.9 Edit Text Styles**, **2.21 Lines**.

A number of options concerning the appearance and positioning of tuplets are found on the **Tuplets** page of the **House Style ▸ Engraving Rules** dialog:

- **Rotate single digits** controls whether the single-digit tuplet numbers (e.g. triplets) should be drawn at the same angle as the bracket; single digits can look better drawn upright, so this option is switched off by default. Tuplet text consisting of multiple digits (e.g. **12** or **3:2**) has to be drawn at the same angle as the bracket to align with it, and are unaffected by this option.
- The **Position on Notes** options allow you to choose the default position of tuplets with and without brackets. By default, **Always above on vocal staves** is switched on, since this ensures that tuplet brackets and numbers don't interfere with lyrics below the staff.
- **Vertical Distance from Notes** controls the default distance tuplets are drawn from notes.

2.36 Voices

What voices are

Music usually has a single "voice" (or "layer") of notes, chords and rests on each staff. The stems point up or down according to the pitch of the note.:

When music is in two voices, however, the staff has two independent streams of music that can have different rhythms. The two voices are distinguished by drawing the stems upwards in *voice 1* and downwards in *voice 2*.:

Notice that there are also two different sets of rests, the higher ones belonging to voice 1 and the lower ones to voice 2. Usually, for simplicity, people only write one rest where two identical ones occur in both voices.

In guitar and organ music and occasionally elsewhere, you can also have a third voice (with stems up again) and even a fourth (with stems down again).

Using voices

Sibelius allows four independent voices per staff, which are color-coded: voice 1 is dark blue, voice 2 is green, voice 3 is orange and voice 4 is pink.

Notes, of course, can only be in a single voice, but staff-attached text and lines can either be in a single voice, a combination of voices, or all voices: this doesn't affect the visual appearance of the score, but can be useful for playback (e.g. to make a hairpin apply to all voices in the staff).

You can use the mouse to click the voice buttons on the Keypad to change voice, or you can use the **Edit ▸ Voice** submenu, or the keyboard shortcuts **Alt+1/2/3/4** *or* ⌥1/2/3/4 (for "all voices" use **Alt+5** *or* ⌥5).

To set the voice of a note (either a selected note, or a note you are about to create), click the appropriate voice button on the Keypad, or use the appropriate keyboard shortcut.

To make text or a line apply to all voices, simply type **Alt+5** *or* ⌥5 (or click the **All** button on the Keypad). If, however, you need it to apply to a combination of voices, you must click the buttons on the Keypad with the mouse rather than use the shortcuts; so if text or a line is in voice 1, and you click the voice 2 button on the Keypad, that object will then belong to *both* voice 1 and voice 2 (and will be colored light blue in the score to show this).

You cannot automatically create text or lines in a combination of voices: they are always created in a single voice initially, and you can edit their voices afterwards.

Other objects such as clefs, key signatures, system text (e.g. title, tempo markings) and system lines (e.g. *rit./accel.* lines, 1st- and 2nd-endings) always apply to all voices, and so are always light blue (for staff objects) or purple (for system objects) when selected. It doesn't matter which voice is chosen when you create these objects.

Viewing voice colors

It is often useful to see to which voice notes belong at all times, not just when selected. To see this, switch on **View ▸ Note Colors ▸ Voice Colors.**

Starting off an extra voice of notes

To start off an extra voice with the keyboard, or using step-time input:

- Select a note, rest or other object (such as text or a line) at the point where you want the new voice to start
- Type **N** (the shortcut for **Notes ▸ Input Notes**) followed by **Alt+2** *or* ⌥2 for voice 2; the caret goes green
- Input the note as normal, and it appears in voice 2; the rest of the bar is filled with the appropriate rests
- Now you can continue adding notes in voice 2 as normal.

To start off an extra voice with the mouse:

- With nothing in your score selected, choose the voice button, note value and any other note properties from the Keypad
- Click in the score where you want the new voice to begin; Sibelius inputs the note, and fills up the rest of the bar with rests in the new voice
- Now you can continue to input notes in the new voice as normal.

To start off Flexi-time recording in an extra voice, choose the desired voice in the **Notes ▸ Flexi-time Options** dialog (shortcut **Ctrl+Shift+O** *or* ⇧⌘O). If the voice already exists in the score, you can just select a rest in that voice and then start Flexi-time as normal – 📖 **1.4 Flexi-time™**.

Bars partially in two voices

If you don't want two voices right to the end of a bar, **Delete** any unwanted rests at the end, to hide them.

If you want voice 2 to start part-way through a bar that already contains notes in another voice, simply input the voice 2 note at the point where you want it to start using the mouse. Alternatively, input rests in voice 2 from the start of the bar, followed by the notes, and **Delete** the rests afterwards.

In either case, the notes in voice 1 will revert to having stems both up and down where you deleted the rests.

Deleting voice 2

You can remove parts of bars of voice 2 by deleting rests, as described above. However, if you want to delete a whole bar of voice 2, you should just put a bar rest into voice 2 from the second Keypad layout, then **Delete** it.

You can also use filters to remove a passage in a particular voice – 📖 **5.7 Filters and Find**.

Merging voices

If you want to merge all the notes in a passage in multiple voices into a single voice, simply select the passage and choose the desired voice from the Keypad or Edit ▸ Voice (shortcut Alt+1/2/3/4 *or* ⌥1/2/3/4):

Before *After*

You can't merge voices with tuplets in – Sibelius will omit one of the voices where the tuplet occurs.

Merging staves using voices

If you want to reduce the music from two (or more) staves, each of which uses a single voice, onto a single staff using multiple voices, you should use the Arrange feature (📖 **5.1 Arrange™**) unless you need to have total control over the resulting reduction, in which case proceed like this:

Imagine you want to reduce two violin staves onto a single violin staff. Here's how you do it:

• Create the new (destination) violin staff

• Select the original (source) staff that you want to end up in voice 1 (stems up) on the destination staff as a passage selection (i.e. surrounded by a single light blue box)

• Alt+click *or* ⌥-click the music into the destination staff

• Select the other source staff, the one you want to end up in voice 2 (stems down) on the destination staff as a passage selection

• Now choose Edit ▸ Filter ▸ Voice 1 (shortcut Ctrl+Shift+Alt+1 *or* ⇧⌥⌘1); your passage selection will be converted to a multiple selection (the light blue box will disappear and only the note-heads will be colored blue)

• Choose Edit ▸ Voice ▸ Voice 2 (shortcut Alt+2 *or* ⌥2); all of the selected notes in the source staff are swapped into voice 2

• Finally, Alt+click *or* ⌥-click the music into the destination staff.

The important step in the above procedure is the filter operation (📖 **5.7 Filters and Find**): this converts the passage selection into a multiple selection. If you were to copy a passage selection of voice 2 notes onto another staff, the existing music on the destination staff would be overwritten – this is because passage selections always *overwrite* existing music, whereas multiple selections *add* to the existing music. For more information on this kind of operation, 📖 **1.9 Selections and passages**.

Splitting voices

Sometimes it is useful to split a passage written in a single voice into two or more voices, for example if you have played polyphonic music into a single voice using Flexi-time, or imported a MIDI file.

Figure 1   Figure 2

Figure 3

To split the music in *Figure 1* above into two voices (to produce *Figure 3*), do the following:

* Select the music you want to split as a passage
* Choose Edit ▸ Filter ▸ Bottom Note or Single Notes (shortcut Ctrl+Alt+B *or* ⌥⌘B), then choose voice 2 on the Keypad or Edit ▸ Voice ▸ 2 (shortcut Alt+2 *or* ⌥2); your music will now look like *Figure 2*
* Finally, change the note values to consolidate unnecessarily tied notes (or use the Combine Tied Notes and Rests plug-in – see **Combine Tied Notes and Rests** on page 519); you should end up with *Figure 3*.

You can't split voices with tuplets in – Sibelius will omit one of the voices where the tuplet occurs.

Voices 3 and 4

Add voices 3 and 4 just like voice 2. If you want three voices, you can use voices 1+2+3 or 1+2+4 depending on the stem directions you want the voices to have. The stems of voices 1 and 3 point upwards, and those of voices 2 and 4 point downwards.

There are no particular rules for how to position three or more voices, so you may need to move notes horizontally to avoid collisions. See **Crossing voices** below.

Swapping voices

If you start creating music into the wrong voice, then instead of scrapping it and starting again you can just select the music as a passage and swap the voices round.

The various options are in Edit ▸ Voice. You're only likely to want to swap voices 1 and 2, for which you can type the shortcut Shift-V.

Copying voices

To copy a single voice from a staff containing notes in more than one voice, select the passage you want to copy and use, say, Edit ▸ Filter ▸ Voice 2 (shortcut Ctrl+Shift+Alt+2 *or* ⇧⌥⌘2) to filter only the notes in voice 2. Now you can Alt+click *or* ⌥-click them into another staff as normal.

Sibelius copies notes and rests *into the same voice as the voice they came from*. However, if you want to copy from one voice to another...

Copying from one voice to another

Use Plug-ins ▸ Notes and Rests ▸ Paste Into Voice – see **Paste Into Voice** on page 503.

If you want to copy from one voice to another manually, do this by swapping voices. For instance, suppose you want to copy some voice 1 notes into voice 2 elsewhere:

- Swap voices 1 and 2 in the original you're copying, so that the notes you're copying end up in voice 2. Do this by selecting the music as a passage and choosing Edit ▸ Voice ▸ Swap 1 and 2 (shortcut Shift-V).
- Select the voice 2 notes to be copied by selecting a passage and filtering to get voice 2, as described in **Copying voices** above
- Copy the notes, which will end up in voice 2 as that's the voice they came from
- Swap voices 1 and 2 back again in the original passage.

Rests

When rests appear in multiple voices, Sibelius automatically draws them above or below their normal positions so it's clear to which voice they belong. You can drag the rests up or down further or move them with the arrow keys if they start getting in the way of other voices.

A subtlety: when you delete rests (e.g. in voice 2) they are hidden but not completely removed, and so can cause the note spacing to be wider than normal if the hidden rests are shorter than other simultaneous note values. This is unlikely to cause any problems, but if you are concerned about it, switch on View ▸ Hidden Objects and Delete the hidden rests (shown in gray).

Hiding voices

In some situations you might wish to hide notes in one or more voices, e.g. if you want your score only to show a written tune but want it, say, to play back with hidden harmonies. To do this, add the harmonies in a different voice than the melody, then use filters (📖 **5.7 Filters and Find**) to select all the notes in the extra voice(s), and choose Edit ▸ Hide or Show ▸ Hide (shortcut Ctrl+Shift+H *or* ⇧⌘H) to hide them.

Crossing voices

Although voice 1's notes are usually higher than voice 2's, this is not obligatory; the voices can cross – and if they contain chords they can even interlock. Sibelius automatically tries to position the two voices so that no collisions occur. However, with three or more voices, collisions are likely as there are no hard-and-fast rules regarding where to put the third or fourth voice.

Should you want to adjust the horizontal position of notes, rests and chords in these cases:

- Select the note, chord or rest you want to move
- Open the General tab of the Properties window
- Type the distance (in spaces) you want to move the note into the X box – positive numbers for rightwards, negative for leftwards
- If you need to move only the rhythm dots attached to a note, you can select them and drag them left or right with the mouse.

Engraving Rules options

The rules for positioning notes in multiple voices are very complex and best not contemplated by humans. Sibelius, however, includes three alternative rules for voice positioning, available on the Notes and Tremolos page of the House Style ▸ Engraving Rules dialog (shortcut Ctrl+Shift+E *or* ⇧⌘E). The default Version 2 rule is recommended, but should you feel the urge to use one of the older rules, you can choose them from this dialog.

3. Text

3.1 Working with text

📖 **3.2 Common text styles**, **3.9 Edit Text Styles**, **5.7 Filters and Find**.

This topic explains in detail the different methods of creating and editing text in Sibelius. For a simple introduction, refer to the Handbook.

Creating text fast

There are several quick ways to create text:

- Preferably, first select a note near where you want the text to appear, then type the keyboard shortcuts **Ctrl+E** *or* ⌘E, **Ctrl+T** *or* ⌘T and **Ctrl+L** *or* ⌘L to get the three most common text styles, namely **Expression**, **Technique** and **Lyrics line 1**

- Other text styles with shortcuts are: **Lyrics line 2** (shortcut **Ctrl+Alt+L** *or* ⌥⌘L) and **Tempo** (**Ctrl+Alt+T** *or* ⌥⌘T)

- If you have a note or other object selected, Sibelius will automatically create the text at that point in the score; if you have nothing selected, the mouse pointer will change color to show that it "contains" an object, and you can click in the score to place the text

- For standard words like *cresc.*, use the menus of useful words – see **Word menus** below

- If the same text is used over and over again, just copy it with **Alt+click** *or* ⌥-click, or "multicopy" it, holding **Shift** to put the copied text at its default vertical position (e.g. to put the same dynamics on every instrument) – 📖 **1.9 Selections and passages**

- You can copy text to the clipboard and then paste it elsewhere in the same score, into another score, or even to/from another program – see **Copying lines of text and text between programs** below

- You can also "copy" the caret itself to start a new piece of text. Find some text on the screen in the style you require, double-click it to make the caret appear, then **Alt+click** *or* ⌥-click somewhere else to start some new text in the same style.

Word menus

To save you time, Sibelius has built-in menus of useful words to type when creating text. Each text style has its own appropriate word menu. For instance, Expression produces a menu of dynamics (etc.), and Chord symbols gives various bits from which you can make up any chord symbol.

To obtain the word menu, simply right-click (Windows) *or* **Control**-click (Mac) while creating or editing text. Some of the words and characters on the menus have keyboard shortcuts; 📖 **5.12 Menus and shortcuts** or the menus themselves for a full list.

You can edit the word menus, assign your own keyboard shortcuts to the words, change the display size of each menu, or create your own new ones – see **Creating and modifying word menus** below.

Text editing

The text editing keys are similar to other programs. The main shortcuts are as follows:

- To edit an existing text object, double-click it, or hit **Return** (on the main keyboard)
- To stop editing text, hit **Esc**
- To select all text in the current text object, type **Ctrl+A** *or* **⌘A**
- For a new line while editing, hit **Return** (on the main keyboard)
- To make text bold/non-bold, click **B** (shortcut **Ctrl+B** *or* **⌘B**) in the **Text** panel of the Properties window. This (and italic/underlining) affects text you are about to type, a chunk of text you have selected, or the whole text object (or text objects) if it's selected
- To make text italic/non-italic, click **I** (shortcut **Ctrl+I** *or* **⌘I**) in the **Text** panel of the Properties window
- To reset a text style's font to its default while editing it, type **Ctrl+Alt+Space** *or* **^⌥-Space**
- To make text underlined/non-underlined, click **U** (shortcut **Ctrl+U** *or* **⌘U**) in the **Text** panel of the Properties window. Underlining text is very rare in music.
- To change the font or point size of text, change the value in the **Text** panel of the Properties window (although you should normally edit the text style instead)
- There are various other editing shortcuts: 📖 **5.12 Menus and shortcuts** for full details.

If you just want to change the font/bold/italic/underlining/point size of a small amount of text, it's fine to use the options on the **Text** panel of the Properties window. However, if you need to make more widespread adjustments, there are much more efficient ways:

- If you want to change all of the text in your score to use another font (e.g. to change the title, instrument names, lyrics, technique instructions etc. to another font in a single operation), choose **House Style ▸ Edit All Fonts**, and choose a new **Main Text Font**
- If you want to change all the text throughout the score in just one particular text style, you should edit the text style itself instead (📖 **3.9 Edit Text Styles**), because this will automatically change all existing text and also all new text you create in that style thereafter. For example, if you decide you want your lyrics in a different font, you should edit the text style rather than changing all the existing words manually.
- If you want to change quite a lot of text, but not all of it, e.g. to have a chorus in italics, define a new text style based on the most similar existing one and use that text style instead (see **Changing the text style of existing text** below if you have already entered the text in your score).

Selecting a line of text

To select all text in a particular text style along a staff, select a single text item and then choose **Edit ▸ Select ▸ Select More** (type **Ctrl+Shift+A** *or* **⇧⌘A**). This allows you to:

- move all the items together with the mouse or arrow keys
- copy the text to the clipboard for pasting elsewhere in the score, or into another program (see below)
- line them up if they end up out of alignment, e.g. lyrics and chord symbols: use **Layout ▸ Align In a Row** (shortcut **Ctrl+Shift+R** *or* **⇧⌘R**) or **Layout ▸ Reset Position** (shortcut **Ctrl+Shift+P** *or* **⇧⌘P**) – 📖 **8.1 Layout and formatting**.

Copying lines of text and text between programs

You can copy text objects in Sibelius in a variety of ways:

- within the same score or different scores, either using Alt+click *or* ⌥-click (optionally holding Shift to put the text at that text style's default vertical position) or using Edit ▸ Copy and Edit ▸ Paste – the latter method is especially useful with lyrics (📖 **3.3 Lyrics**)

- into another program (e.g. Microsoft Word): simply select the text to be copied, use Edit ▸ Copy (shortcut Ctrl+C *or* ⌘C) to copy it to the clipboard, switch to the other program, and use Edit ▸ Paste (shortcut usually Ctrl+V *or* ⌘V) to paste the text.

If you copy several text objects into another program at once, they will be pasted one after another, with a space in between each; for lyrics, separate syllables of the same word are pasted with hyphens in between – 📖 **3.3 Lyrics**. When copied into another program, fonts etc. are ignored, so dynamics and notes in metronome mark (which use the music text font, as defined in the House Style ▸ Edit All Fonts dialog) will not appear as such when pasted into, say, a Word document unless you correct the font afterwards.

To copy text into Sibelius from other programs:

- Select the text and copy it to the clipboard with Edit ▸ Copy (shortcut normally Ctrl+C *or* ⌘C)

- Switch to Sibelius and create a suitable text caret, e.g. select a note and type Ctrl+T *or* ⌘T for Technique text

- Choose Edit ▸ Paste (shortcut Ctrl+V *or* ⌘V) to paste the text.

Pasting lyrics into Sibelius from other programs is slightly different – 📖 **3.3 Lyrics**.

Changing the text style of existing text

You can change the text style of an existing text object. Select the text and open the Text panel of the Properties dialog, where you can change the text style from a drop-down menu, with the following limitations:

- You cannot change staff text into system text, and vice versa; and

- You cannot change lyrics into any non-lyrics text style, and vice versa.

Hiding text

To hide text, which is mainly used for hidden dynamics and other playback markings, select the text you want to hide and choose Edit ▸ Hide or Show ▸ Hide (shortcut Ctrl+Shift+H *or* ⇧⌘H). For more details, 📖 **5.9 Hiding objects**.

Any text following a tilde character (~) is automatically hidden by Sibelius and will not print. This is normally only used to write MIDI messages (📖 **4.17 MIDI messages**).

Reset Position

Layout ▸ Reset Position (shortcut Ctrl+Shift+P *or* ⇧⌘P) resets text to its default position.

Reset Design

If you want to change a text object back to its default font or size (set in House Style ▸ Edit Text Styles), for example if you have changed the font or made some text italic, select it and choose Layout ▸ Reset Design (shortcut Ctrl+Shift+D *or* ⇧⌘D).

Text at the left of the system

If you want to put text to the left of a system, you're probably specifying which players are playing an instrument, in which case, 📖 **2.18 Instruments**.

However, if you have a special reason to write text to the left of the system, it's fine to do so but you should put a system break at the end of the preceding system, to ensure that the text remains where it is if the music reformats. 📖 **8.5 Breaks**.

Text between staves

When you create text between staves using the mouse, such as for keyboard dynamics, Sibelius guesses which staff you intend to attach it to depending on the default vertical position of the text style (📖 **8.12 Default Positions**). This usually produces the right result – for example, if you create lyrics between staves, Sibelius decides to attach them to the upper staff, because lyrics normally belong to the staff above. But if you put text between two staves, make sure that it's attached to the correct one (📖 **8.7 Attachment**), otherwise the text will misbehave if you move the staff or create a part.

Avoid putting one piece of text between two separate instruments but applying to both (which is in any case not good notation). Otherwise, if you have separate parts for the instruments, only one of them will get the text. It's fine to write one piece of text between the two hands of a keyboard instrument, though, because both hands will end up in the same part.

Multiple pieces of text

You often need pieces of text side by side over different notes, such as fingerings or syllables of long-drawn-out words like *cres – cen – do*. In all cases like this you must use separate pieces of text: don't just type it all as one bit of text with spaces in between. The reason is that if the music reformats you'll want the separate bits to move closer together or further apart.

When typing a long word as separate syllables over several bars, use a dashed line from the **Create▸ Line** dialog (shortcut L) instead of hyphens. Then as the spacing between syllables changes, more or fewer dashes will appear. (This is how hyphens in lyrics work, in fact.)

Creating special objects with text

One of Sibelius's obscure but occasionally useful features is the ability to create special cases of objects such as rehearsal marks, time signatures and bar numbers, using the **Create▸ Text ▸ Special Text** styles.

This otherwise incomprehensible concept is best illustrated by example:

Supposing you want your score to start with a special rehearsal mark called START. Sibelius won't let you input this as a normal rehearsal mark because it's not in alphabetical or numerical sequence. The complicated way round this would be to create a whole new text style for large boxed text, and use it to type the word START.

But in fact, all you have to do is use **Create ▸ Text ▸ Special Text ▸ Rehearsal mark**. This creates a piece of text that is not a real rehearsal mark, but uses the same text style as rehearsal marks and so will look (and in many ways behave) just like a rehearsal mark. When you type START with the **Rehearsal mark** style, the text will appear big and bold in a box, will be duplicated lower down the score (e.g. above the strings), and will also automatically appear in all parts. Neat, huh?

There are various text styles that can be used to create special objects in this way:

- **Time signatures**: for creating weird Ferneyhoughesque time signatures such as 5/6 (this will create the time signature in every staff)
- **Rehearsal marks**: for writing special rehearsal marks that are not in sequence (though there is automatic provision for restarting the rehearsal mark sequence).

From here on it gets more tenuous:

- **Page numbers**: for obscure things like writing folio numbers in an edition of early music
- **Tab letters/numbers**: not all that useful as it's not clear why you'd want special ones
- **Tuplets**: for unusual formats such as "3 in 2."

Creating and modifying word menus

Choose the **Word Menus** page of the **File ▸ Preferences** dialog (in the **Sibelius** menu on Mac; shortcut **Ctrl+,** *or ⌘,*), to see this dialog:

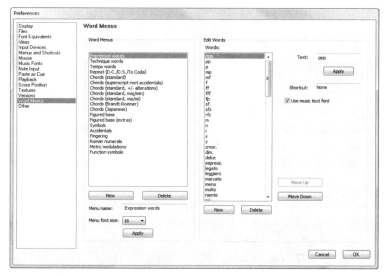

- Click an existing word menu to edit it, or enter the name for a new word menu in **Menu name** and click **New** below the list of word menus
- To change the name of a new or existing word menu, enter the new name into **Menu name** and click **Apply**
- To add a new word to the menu, click the **New** button below the **Words** list, and then type it into the **Text** box and click **Apply**
- To change a word in the menu, select it in the list, edit it in the **Text** box and click **Apply**
- To change the order of how words appear in the menu, use **Move Up** and **Move Down**
- When creating or changing words you can also assign a keyboard shortcut: click in the **Shortcut** box and type the shortcut. You can assign any shortcut you like, but be careful not to use any key combinations that are already being used by your operating system (for example, you should not use **Ctrl+F4** on Windows or **⌥⌘M** on Mac).

- Click **Use music text font** in the unlikely event that you're typing music characters from the music text font (as defined in the **House Style ▸ Edit All Fonts** dialog – 🕮 **8.11 Music fonts**). This is for things like *mf*. When editing a word menu the characters are shown in a plain text font, so they may not look how they will when you create them from the word menu (e.g. in the **Chord symbols** or **Figured bass** word menus)
- To delete a word from the list, select it, then click **Delete** below the list of words
- To delete an entire word menu, select it, then click **Delete** below the list of word menus.
- To change the display size of the word menu, choose the desired font size from **Menu font size**.
- When you're finished, click **OK**.

If you've created a new word menu and you want to assign it to a text style, go to the **General** tab of that text style's **Edit Text Style** dialog (🕮 **3.9 Edit Text Styles**) and set **Word menu** to the menu you created.

To customize shortcuts other than for word menus, 🕮 **5.12 Menus and shortcuts**.

Special characters

In addition to words, many of the word menus also include special characters, such as *f* or ♪.

Most of these characters are taken from the music text font (e.g. Opus Text), regardless of the font you're using for standard characters. You can change the font used – 🕮 **8.11 Music fonts**. Figured bass characters are taken from the Opus Figured Bass font.

Creating text in complex scripts

Sibelius uses the Unicode™ standard character set, which means you can write text in any script in Sibelius, provided you have fonts that contain the required characters. Unicode guarantees that text in complex scripts is automatically translated between Mac and Windows.

When creating text in e.g. western European languages that use the Roman alphabet with diacritics, some of these accented characters are available on the word menus – 🕮 **5.12 Menus and shortcuts** for a full list of accented letter shortcuts.

To write text in non-Roman alphabets (e.g. Japanese, Cyrillic, Greek, Korean, etc.), you will in general need to use a dedicated input method for the appropriate alphabet, because many of these alphabets have more characters than fit on a physical computer keyboard. Input methods are software programs provided by your operating system that map sequences of keypresses onto specific characters from a non-Roman alphabet. The workings of input methods vary depending on the alphabets for which they are designed.

On Windows, different input methods are provided using software components called Input Method Editors (IMEs). An introduction to the IMEs provided by Windows can be found here:

http://www.microsoft.com/globaldev/handson/user/IME_Paper.mspx

On Mac OS X, input methods are chosen from the input menu, which can be enabled as follows:

- Run **System Preferences** and double-click **International**

- Click the **Input Menu** tab and find the alphabet you want to use in the list of input methods, then switch on its checkbox

- Make sure that **Show input menu in menu bar** is switched on.

- A menu that uses a national flag as its icon now appears in your menu bar, as shown on the right, and you can switch to any of the enabled input methods by choosing it from this menu.

Note that the font you use for your text in Sibelius must contain the characters of the alphabet you wish to use, or else you will only see empty rectangles in place of the characters you are expecting. On the **Word Menus** page of **Sibelius ▸ Preferences**, you can switch on **Automatically switch font to match chosen input source (in the input menu)**, which allows Mac OS X to automatically set the font most suitable for your chosen alphabet. This option is switched off by default.

Mac OS X also provides a useful window called the Character Palette that allows you to enter special characters visually. To enable it:

- Go to the **Input Menu** page of **International**, and in the list of available input methods, switch on **Character Palette**.

- Choose **Show Character Palette** from the input menu on the main menu bar.

- The Character Palette window will now appear.

- Choose the character you wish to enter and click **Insert**. The character will be added to the text object you are currently editing in Sibelius using the current font. If you find that the current font does not contain the desired character, undo and then click **Insert with Font** instead.

3.2 Common text styles

📖 **3.1 Working with text**, **3.3 Lyrics**, **3.4 Figured bass and Roman numerals**, **3.5 Bar numbers**, **3.6 Page numbers**, **3.7 Rehearsal marks**.

Sibelius includes many text styles for use in your score. This topic describes many of these text styles in detail, though several of them are important enough that they have their own topics – see the list above.

So what is a text style, anyway?

There are many different kinds of text in used in scores, such as: lyrics, which go below the staff; expression markings, which are italic and normally go below the staff (except when there are lyrics present, in which case they go above the staff); titles which are big, bold and centered at the top of the page; and so on.

Each kind of text may use a different font, formatting (such as bold, italic and, rarely, underlined), justification (such as left-, center- or right-alignment), and positioning (such as whether the text should appear above or below one staff or all staves, or perhaps at the top or bottom of the page). These settings together are what make up a *text style*.

Because Sibelius has text styles for each of the kinds of text you will need to write in your score, you don't need to set any of this up for yourself: simply choose the appropriate text style, and Sibelius will produce text that looks right, and that goes in the right place on the page.

The other advantage of text styles is that if you want to change something about the appearance of text in your score – for example, you want to make all your lyrics bigger, or make your tempo instructions use a different font – you need only change the text style itself, and Sibelius will automatically update all the text in the score that uses that text style.

To find out how to edit any of Sibelius's existing text styles and create new ones, 📖 **3.9 Edit Text Styles**.

Three types of text

There are three types of text in Sibelius (try saying that three times quickly!):

* *Staff text:* text that applies to a single staff, typically directions for a single instrument
* *System text:* text that applies to all staves in the score (though it may only be displayed above one or two of them), and which will appear in all parts (if there are any) – typically tempo or rehearsal directions
* *Blank page text:* text that can only be created on a blank page, typically performance directions or other front matter.

Important text styles

The table below lists the most important text styles and what they are used for.

	Name	Used for...
Staff text	Expression	...writing dynamics and expressive markings such as ***mp***, *cresc.* and *legato* *Shortcut:* **Ctrl+E** *or* ⌘**E**
	Technique	...writing playing techniques such as "mute," "pizz.", etc. *Shortcut:* **Ctrl+T** *or* ⌘**T**
	Lyrics line 1, Lyrics line 2 etc.	...writing lyrics in vocal music – 📖 **3.3 Lyrics** *Shortcut:* **Ctrl+L** *or* ⌘**L** (Line 1), **Ctrl+Alt+L** *or* ⌥⌘**L** (Line 2)
	Plain text	...writing blocks of lyrics, editorial commentaries, etc.
	Roman numerals	...writing chord symbols with inversions in Roman numerals – 📖 **3.4 Figured bass and Roman numerals**
	Figured bass	...figuring continuo instruments in Baroque music – 📖 **3.4 Figured bass and Roman numerals**
	Fingering	...writing fingerings in e.g. keyboard, brass or string music
	Guitar fingering (p i m a)	...writing fingerings in guitar music
	Boxed text	...writing certain playing techniques, e.g. in percussion
	Small text	...writing certain playing techniques
	Nashville chord numbers	...writing e.g. 6/3
	Footnote	...writing editorial commentaries at the bottom of a *single* page (not the same as **Footer**)
System text	Title	...writing the title of the piece or movement
	Subtitle	...writing subtitles (e.g. for a particular movement)
	Composer	...writing the name of the composer (usually all in CAPITALS) or arranger/orchestrator (not in capitals)
	Lyricist	...writing the name of the lyricist, poet, or other source of text
	Dedication	...writing a dedication (e.g. *To the choir of St. John's*)
	Tempo	...writing tempo markings such as **Andante** *Shortcut:* **Ctrl+Alt+T** *or* ⌥⌘**T**
	Metronome mark	...writing metronome marks and metric modulations
	Copyright	...writing copyright lines in your score
	Header etc.	...writing a header *on every page*
	Footer etc..	...writing a footer *on every page* (not the same as **Footnote**)
	Rit./Accel.	...writing particular tempo instructions
Blank page text	Composer (on blank page)	...writing the name of the composer on a title page at the start of the score
	Dedication (on blank page)	...writing a dedication on a title page at the start of the score
	Plain text (on blank page)	...writing instrumentation, performance directions, etc. on blank pages
	Subtitle (on blank page)	...writing a subtitle on a blank page
	Title (on blank page)	...writing the title of the work on a title page at the start of the score

Text

Positioning Expression and Technique text

Expression text goes below the staff it applies to, but above in staves with lyrics. Technique text goes above the staff. For music in two voices, both Expression and Technique text goes above the staff for Voice 1 and below for Voice 2. If Expression or Technique text applies to both hands of a keyboard instrument, it should go between the staves.

The left-hand side of Expression text normally goes just to the left of the note to which it applies.

If f has to be written on a staff (which is best avoided), the crossbar should be positioned over a staff line for clarity. Similarly, p on a staff should be centered on a space.

Expression

For writing dynamics and other similar instructions to players, e.g. *legato, lively, marcato*, normally written in italics. Expression text is positioned below the staff for instrumental staves, and above the staff for vocal staves with lyrics.

Dynamics such as *mf* or *sfz* are special bold italic characters that use a special "music text" font (📖 **8.11 Music fonts**), normally Opus Text. You can create these characters from the word menu (right-click *or* Control-click), or by holding down Ctrl *or* ⌘ and typing the letters, e.g. Ctrl+MF *or* ⌘MF to produce *mf*. The exception is *z*, for which you must type Ctrl+Shift+Z *or* ⇧⌘Z (because Ctrl+Z *or* ⌘Z is the shortcut for Edit ▸ Undo).

All common expression markings can be created quickly from the word menu, to save you typing them.

Although nearly all dynamics you create in your score are played back automatically, beware that the words *cresc.* and *dim.* do not play back (because it's unclear by how much or for how long you want to get louder/softer) – if you need them to play, create hairpins as appropriate and hide them (📖 **2.17 Hairpins**). A couple of special effects, e.g. *fp*, don't play back quite correctly, but you can achieve the right effect using MIDI messages if playback of this particular marking is very important to you.

Dynamics only apply to a single staff (except in keyboard music – 📖 **4.1 Working with playback**), but you can quickly add dynamics to multiple staves in a couple of ways:

- Copy the dynamic with Edit ▸ Copy (shortcut Ctrl+C *or* ⌘C), then select the staves you want to copy the dynamic to and type Ctrl+V *or* ⌘V to paste it to all selected staves. This is called "multicopying" – 📖 **1.9 Selections and passages**

- Select the dynamic and use Alt+click *or* ⌥-click to copy it onto other staves; you can hold down Shift while you Alt+click *or* ⌥-click to put each dynamic at its default vertical position; to align them later, select the bar in which they occur, then choose Edit ▸ Filter ▸ Dynamics (shortcut Shift+Alt+D *or* ⇧⌥D) and use Layout ▸ Align in a Column (shortcut Ctrl+Shift+C *or* ⇧⌘C).

Technique

This is for writing technical instructions that are not normally written in italics, e.g. mute, pizz., a2, solo, tremolo. You can also write musical symbols such as accidentals in Technique text using the word menu, which is useful for things like harp music.

Metronome mark

Metronome marks look something like ♩ = 72, and are often accompanied by a tempo marking (see **Tempo** below). To write a metronome mark:

- Select an object (e.g. a note or rest) in your score where you want the metronome mark to go, normally the first note of a bar, and choose Create ▸ Text ▸ Metronome mark; a flashing caret appears. (If nothing is selected in your score, choose **Create ▸ Text ▸ Metronome mark**, then click in your score to place the text.)

- Write notes in metronome marks by right-clicking (Windows) *or* **Control**-clicking (Mac) to get the word menu. You can alternatively use the **Ctrl** *or* ⌘ key in conjunction with the numeric keypad.
- You can then type = 60 or whatever in the normal way. Hit **space** on either side of the = sign.

When typing a metronome mark after a tempo mark, e.g. **Allegro** ♩ = 60, you are not advised to input it using two separate bits of text (Tempo text plus Metronome mark text), or the two separate text objects could collide if the notes in the bar get too close together. Instead, write all the text in the Tempo text style, and when you get to the metronome mark, switch off **Bold** and preferably choose a smaller point size on the **Text** panel of the Properties window.

Sibelius includes a plug-in that allows you to add metronome marks to your score by tapping the desired tempo with the mouse – see **Set Metronome Mark** on page 508.

Metric modulations

Metric modulations (also sometimes known as *l'istesso tempo* markings, meaning "the same tempo") are used to illustrate the relationship between note values in different tempos, e.g.:

Metric modulations are also frequently used to show a "swing" feel, e.g.

To create a metric modulation, choose **Create ▸ Text ▸ Other System Text ▸ Metric modulation**. The word menu for this text style contains all the most common metric modulations and swing markings, both with and without parentheses. This text style uses the Opus Metronome font.

Typography of tempo and metronome text

Sudden changes of tempo should begin with a capital letter to startle you: **Molto vivace, Tempo I, Più mosso.** *Gradual changes of tempo begin with a lower-case letter: poco rit., accel.*

If tempo text or a metronome mark is above a time signature, the left-hand sides of both should be aligned.

Tempo

Tempo text usually appears at the start of the score, e.g. **Allegro non troppo**, and is often accompanied by a metronome mark (see above). It's quickest to create these from the **File ▸ New** dialog when first setting up your score, though you can easily add them later: simply choose **Create ▸ Text ▸ Tempo**.

Sibelius knows the meaning of a wide variety of tempo markings and will play them back even if you don't create a metronome mark – 📖 **4.9 Playback dictionary**. As usual, right-clicking (Windows) *or* **Control**-clicking (Mac) while creating Tempo text gives a menu of useful words.

To create *rits.* and *accels.*, we recommend you don't type them as text, but use *rit./accel.* lines instead (📖 **2.21 Lines**), as these play back. Beware that **A tempo** and **Tempo I** don't play back, so create a metronome mark (which you can hide if you want) to revert to the original tempo.

In large scores, text in the Tempo and Metronome mark styles automatically appears not just at the top, but duplicated lower down as well (normally above the keyboard or strings). The copies mimic each other whenever you edit one of them – for instance, if you edit one piece of tempo text, all copies will change simultaneously.

However, each piece of text can be dragged up and down independently, and indeed Sibelius will often move copies up and down automatically (via Magnetic Layout) to avoid collisions with high or low notes, etc.

To delete all copies of the Tempo text at once, delete the top one. To delete one of the lower copies, simply select it and hit **Delete**; to bring it back, select the *top* one and choose **Layout ▸ Reset Design** (shortcut **Ctrl+Shift+D** *or* ⇧⌘D).

You can alter how many copies of the text you would like to appear, and above which staves – 📖 **3.9 Edit Text Styles** and **8.8 House Style™**. Other system objects behave similarly, such as rehearsal marks.

Lyrics

The text styles in the **Create ▸ Text ▸ Lyrics** submenu are a bit special – 📖 **3.3 Lyrics**.

> **Rules for fingering**
>
> *In keyboard music, fingerings for the right hand go above the notes, and for the left hand go below the notes. Triplets and other tuplets should be moved to the other side of the notes if necessary, to avoid collisions.*
>
> *Fingerings are centered horizontally on the notes. Successive fingerings don't need to line up in a row – they should go up and down following the pitch of the notes, so that they are fairly near each note.*

Title, Subtitle, Composer, Lyricist, Dedication

It's quickest to create most of these from the **File ▸ New** dialog when first setting up your score, though you can easily add them later. By default, these text styles are left-, center- or right-aligned on the page, which means you can only drag text in these styles up and down, not left or right.

You can put titles above any system in your score, not just at the start – you might want a new title at the start of a new section, song or movement, say – though if you do this it is best to put a system or page break at the end of the previous system to keep the sections separated.

Occasionally (e.g. for high-volume copying work) you may want these text styles to go at a fixed position on the page rather than relative to the top staff. To achieve this, set the **Vertical Posn** tab for each style in the **House Style ▸ Edit Text Styles** (shortcut **Ctrl+Shift+Alt+T** *or* ⇧⌥⌘T) dialog to a fixed **mm from top margin**.

Fingering

(In **Create ▸ Text ▸ Other Staff Text**.) This is for keyboard, brass and string fingerings. Hit **Return** (on the main keyboard) after each number. Hitting **space** advances to the next note.

Sibelius can add brass and string fingering automatically, and reposition fingerings to avoid notes – 📖 **6.1 Working with plug-ins**.

Small text and Boxed text

These are for other technique-like instructions. Boxed text is useful for important instructions such as changes of instrument.

Copyright

A copyright line is normally written on the first page of a score. This text style (choose **Create ▸ Text ▸ Other system text ▸ Copyright**) goes at the bottom of the page, centered, and appears in all parts. The © symbol is available from the word menu.

You should create the text on the first bar of the score – though it will appear at the bottom of the page, it will in fact be attached to the first bar, which will ensure it always remains on the first page even if the score reformats.

Footnote

This positions text at the bottom of the page. To create a footnote, select a note in the staff and bar you want the footnote to refer to, then choose **Create ▸ Text ▸ Other Staff Text ▸ Footnote**. The caret will nonetheless appear at the foot of the page.

You can refer to the footnote with an asterisk or numeral using (say) Technique text above the staff. The footnote you type will always stay on the same page as the bar it's referring to. It will also appear only in the part of the staff in question.

Header and Header (after first page)

Headers are text that goes at the top of every page – e.g. the name of the piece, or instrument in a part.

Header (within **Other System Text**) produces the same text on every page; if you change the header on any page, it automatically changes on all other pages. Headers and footers appear on the page where you place them and all subsequent pages, but not previous pages. So you should normally place the header/footer on the first page, so they appear throughout. **Header (after first page)** works the same but is always shown hidden on the first page, to avoid colliding with the title. Headers are system text and so appear in all parts.

Footer

Footers are text that goes at the bottom of every page. **Create ▸ Text ▸ Other System Text ▸ Footer (outside edge)** goes on the right of right-hand pages and the left of left-hand pages; **Footer (inside edge)** goes on the inside edge.

As with headers, you should normally create the footer on the first or perhaps the second page; it will automatically appear on all subsequent pages (but not previous ones). If you change the footer on any page, it automatically changes on all other pages. Footers are system text and so appear in all parts.

Plain text

To create plain text in your score, for example to type miscellaneous performance instructions or blocks of lyrics, use **Create ▸ Text ▸ Other Staff Text ▸ Plain text**.

3.3 Lyrics

📖 **3.1 Working with text**, **3.9 Edit Text Styles**.

Lyrics are words written under notes to be sung by a singer. There are three ways of creating lyrics:

* typing them in directly;
* copying lyrics syllable by syllable into Sibelius from a word processor or other program;
* automatically flowing lyrics into the score from a text file, with Sibelius automatically allocating syllables to notes for you.

Lyrics in a "block," for extra verses at the end of a song or hymn, are created differently because they don't align with the notes – see **Blocks of lyrics** below.

Typing lyrics

To type lyrics directly into Sibelius:

* Input the notes for which you want to write lyrics
* Select the note where you want the lyrics to start and choose **Create ▸ Text ▸ Lyrics ▸ Lyrics line 1** (shortcut **Ctrl+L** *or* ⌘L)
* Start typing lyrics
* Hit – (hyphen) at the end of each syllable within a word
* Hit **space** at the end of each word
* If a syllable lasts for two or more notes, hit **space** or – once for each note
* If a word is followed by a comma, period or other punctuation, type it *before* hitting **space**.

If you need more than one word per note or an elision, see **Several words per note and elisions** below.

Editing lyrics

You can edit lyrics much like other text. You can alter them, move them, copy them and delete them.

To edit a lyric, double-click it, or select it and hit **Return** (on the main keyboard). You can use the arrow keys and **Backspace** to move between words and syllables.

If you delete a syllable, this also deletes any lyric line or hyphens to the right of it (which are attached to the syllable).

You can move a syllable left or right by one note by selecting it (so it goes dark blue, not so the caret appears) and hitting **space** or **Shift-space**. Similarly you can extend or retract a lyric line or row of lyric hyphens by selecting the right-hand end and hitting **Space** or **Shift-space**.

Text

Lyrics normally go beneath the staff. They are only written above a staff if two staves are sharing the same set of lyrics (e.g. in a hymn), or if a staff has two voices with different lyrics.

Syllables sung to different notes are separated by one or more hyphens. If the last syllable of a word continues over several notes, a "lyric line" is drawn after the final syllable along the notes sung to that syllable. Any punctuation after the final syllable comes before the lyric line.

Verses, choruses and translations

It is common for vocal music to have two or more lines of lyrics under the same music. Usually this is denoted by the verse number being written before the first word or syllable of each verse, e.g. "1. The"

In this example, you would type "1. The" as a single text object using a non-breakable space (see **Several words per note and elisions** below).

To input a second line of lyrics, simply choose Create ▸ Text ▸ Lyrics ▸ Lyrics line 2 (shortcut Ctrl+Alt+L *or* ⌥⌘L) and create them in the same way as other lyrics; they will automatically appear beneath the line 1 lyrics.

For translations that require a second line of lyrics, use Lyrics line 2 and edit its text style to use italics (🕮 **3.9 Edit Text Styles**), or you can switch to and from italics temporarily by typing Ctrl+I or ⌘I while entering lyrics. For choruses in line 1, you could instead use Create ▸ Text ▸ Lyrics ▸ Lyrics (chorus), which is set to use italics.

Sibelius has predefined text styles for five verses of text. Lyrics for lines 3, 4 and 5 can be obtained from the Create ▸ Text ▸ Lyrics submenu. You can create even more verses of lyrics using House Style ▸ Edit Text Styles (shortcut Ctrl+Shift+Alt+T *or* ⇧⌥⌘T) – 🕮 **3.9 Edit Text Styles**.

If you want to quickly add verse numbers to your score after inputting the lyrics, use the Plug-ins ▸ Text ▸ Add Verse Numbers plug-in – 🕮 **6.1 Working with plug-ins**.

Copying lyrics into Sibelius

You can copy and paste lyrics between other programs (such as word processors) and Sibelius, from one part of a score to another in Sibelius, or from one score to a different one.

The text you are copying can either be plain, unhyphenated text or already have hyphens between syllables, e.g.:

Ma-ry had a lit-tle lamb,
its fleece was white as snow.

If the text doesn't already have hyphens in, Sibelius will work out how to split it into syllables for you.

You can tell Sibelius which language your lyrics are typically in, and set up a couple of other options, on the Others page of File ▸ Preferences (in the Sibelius menu on Mac). Similar options are also found in the Create ▸ Text ▸ Lyrics ▸ From Text File dialog (see **Creating lyrics from a text file** below).

To copy lyrics text into Sibelius:

- Select the text you want to copy:
  - If you are copying within Sibelius, select the lyrics you want to copy: either use a lasso selection (🕮 **1.9 Selections and passages**) or select a single syllable and choose Edit ▸

Select ▸ **Select More** (or type **Ctrl+Shift+A** *or* ⇧⌘A) to select a line of lyrics, then choose **Edit** ▸ **Copy** (shortcut **Ctrl+C** *or* ⌘C)

∘ If you are copying from another program, select the text you want to copy and in that program's menus choose **Edit** ▸ **Copy** (shortcut normally **Ctrl+C** *or* ⌘C) to copy it to the clipboard

- Select the note where you want to start pasting lyrics, then choose **Create** ▸ **Text** ▸ **Lyrics** ▸ **Lyrics line 1** (shortcut **Ctrl+L** *or* ⌘L); a flashing caret appears
- To paste a syllable, type **Ctrl+V** *or* ⌘V, which pastes text up to the next space or hyphen (i.e. one note's worth)
- You can then edit the pasted text as if you typed it in yourself, or hit **space** or – (hyphen) to extend the word or syllable over more than one note
- When you want to input the next word or syllable, type **Ctrl+V** *or* ⌘V again
- If you make a mistake, you can choose **Edit** ▸ **Undo** (shortcut **Ctrl+Z** *or* ⌘Z), which will remove the last pasted word or syllable from the score and put it back on the clipboard so that you can paste it again.

If the text you had copied had extra hyphens or spaces between words or syllables, or had syllables lasting more than one note, this is ignored when pasting. This is useful if, say, you're copying lyrics from one staff to another in Sibelius and the rhythms are different.

Tip: When pasting lyrics like this, you can just type **Space** every syllable, even in the middle of a word – Sibelius will still write a hyphen where required.

Copying a whole line of lyrics

A quick way of copying a whole line of lyrics to somewhere else in your score where the rhythm of the words *is the same*:

- Select the original row of lyrics by selecting one word or syllable, then choosing **Edit** ▸ **Select** ▸ **Select More** (shortcut **Ctrl+Shift+A** *or* ⇧⌘A)
- Choose **Edit** ▸ **Copy** (shortcut **Ctrl+C** *or* ⌘C)
- Select the first note of the destination passage, where you want to paste the lyrics
- Choose **Edit** ▸ **Paste** (shortcut **Ctrl+V** *or* ⌘V), without choosing **Create** ▸ **Text** ▸ **Lyrics** ▸ **Lyrics line 1** first, to paste all the lyrics at once.

The destination lyrics may collide, in which case afterwards select the destination notes as a passage, and choose **Layout** ▸ **Reset Note Spacing** (shortcut **Ctrl+Shift+N** *or* ⇧⌘N).

Copying lyrics from one line (or verse) to another

It's fairly common for songs to have identical lyrics in similar phrases in different verses, so you may find it useful to copy the lyrics you have already written from one verse to another. Say you want to copy the lyrics using the text style **Lyrics line 1** to **Lyrics line 3**:

- Make a passage selection around the music containing the lyrics you want to copy
- Choose **Edit** ▸ **Filter** ▸ **Advanced Filter** (shortcut **Ctrl+Shift+Alt+F** *or* ⇧⌥⌘F)
- On the dialog that appears, switch off all the **Find** options apart from **Text**
- From the list of text styles on the right, click **None** and then choose **Lyrics line 1**

- Click **Select**
- Copy the lyrics to the clipboard using **Edit ▸ Copy** (shortcut **Ctrl+C** *or* **⌘C**)
- Select the note from where you want the copied lyrics to start from and choose **Edit ▸ Paste** (shortcut **Ctrl+V** *or* **⌘V**)
- From the **Text** panel of the Properties window, change the text style of the copied lyrics from **Lyrics line 1** to **Lyrics line 3**
- Choose **Layout ▸ Reset Position** (**Ctrl+Shift+P** *or* **⇧⌘P**).

Copying lyrics from Sibelius

It can be useful to copy and paste lyrics from Sibelius, either into a different program (e.g. a word processor) or into, say, a block of lyrics at the end of the score in Sibelius (see **Blocks of lyrics** below). To do this:

- Select the lyrics you want to copy (e.g. select a passage or the whole score and then choose **Edit ▸ Filter ▸ Lyrics**) and choose **Edit ▸ Copy** (shortcut **Ctrl+C** *or* **⌘C**) to copy them to the clipboard
- Now paste the lyrics to the desired location:
  - To paste the lyrics in Sibelius, create a suitable text caret, e.g. for a block of lyrics, choose **Create ▸ Text ▸ Other Staff Text ▸ Plain Text** and click in the score, then choose **Edit ▸ Paste** (shortcut **Ctrl+V** *or* **⌘V**) to paste the lyrics
  - To paste the lyrics into another program, switch to it and choose **Edit ▸ Paste** (shortcut normally **Ctrl+V** *or* **⌘V**).

The pasted text will contain hyphens between syllables, so you should remove these.

If you want to save all the lyrics from your score quickly, use **Plug-ins ▸ Text ▸ Export Lyrics –** 📖 **6.1 Working with plug-ins**.

Creating lyrics from a text file

Sibelius can read lyrics from a text file and flow them into your score automatically, working out how to hyphenate the words and mapping them onto the notes on a staff, including *melismas,* meaning a single syllable or word sung to more than one note, indicated by a slur over the notes.

First, go through your score and check that you have created slurs in all the places you expect Sibelius to produce melismas.

Next you need to ensure that your lyrics are in a plain text file. If you are using Microsoft Word, choose **File ▸ Save As**, and set the document type to **Plain text** (or **Text only** on Mac); if you are using another application, the steps will probably be similar, but may not be identical.

Once you're ready, select the bars in the staff or staves to which you want to add lyrics, then choose **Create ▸ Text ▸ Lyrics ▸ From Text File**. A simple dialog appears, as shown on the right.

- Choose the text file containing the lyrics by clicking **Browse**

- **Lyrics are in** should be set to the language used by your lyrics (choices are English, French, German, Italian, Spanish and Latin); Sibelius should guess the language automatically, but if it makes a mistake, correct the setting here before proceeding

- **Automatically syllabify ambiguous words** determines what Sibelius should do when it encounters words that can be hyphenated in multiple ways (e.g. "everything" can be hyphenated as "ev-er-y-thing" or "ev'-ry-thing"). When switched on, Sibelius examines both the phrase structure of the music to which the lyrics are being added, and the phrasing of the text itself, in order to try and determine the most musically satisfying result. If this option is switched off, Sibelius will prompt you to choose the appropriate syllabification for each ambiguous word.

- **Lyrics text style** determines which text style Sibelius should use for the lyrics it adds to the score

- **Delete existing lyrics text** will remove any lyrics in the selected passage in the chosen text style before adding new lyrics; this option is useful if you find yourself using this feature successively, e.g. after fixing an error in the music or adding a slur to correct a melisma

- **Use apostrophes to show combined syllables** option tells Sibelius to show where it has chosen to combine two syllables into one for ambiguous words, e.g. if it splits "everything" into three syllables rather than four, with this option switched on it will write "ev'-ry-thing", and with this option switched off it will write "eve-ry-thing." It is more usual to use an apostrophe in this situation, so it is recommended to leave this option switched on.

- If **Warn when lyrics won't fit the music** is switched on, Sibelius will prompt you if it determines that you either have too many lyrics to fit the available notes, or vice versa, and it will give you the option to proceed if you wish.

When you click **OK**, Sibelius will add the lyrics to the selected passage in the score. If Sibelius is unable to determine how best to deal with ambiguous words, it will prompt you to help it: the **Choose Syllabification** dialog will appear, showing the word in question and allowing you to choose between the different ways of hyphenating it; hover your mouse pointer over the combo box to see a tool tip that shows the word in context. You can switch on **Syllabify similar words consistently** to prompt Sibelius to use the same hyphenation pattern for words with similar characteristics (e.g. the same suffix).

If your lyrics switch between different languages, you can add a special command to your text file that tells Sibelius where to use the hyphenation rules for another language: just put the name of the language inside curly braces, e.g. {English} or {German}.

To force a word to hyphenate in a particular way, simply add the hyphens to the word or words in question in the text file containing the lyrics you want to add.

In some languages, such as Spanish and Italian, it is common to elide the end of one word with the beginning of the next, treating those two syllables as one (e.g. "donde irà" in Spanish may be sung as three syllables rather than four, i.e. "don-de i-rà"). Sibelius will do this for you automatically where appropriate.

Splitting words into syllables

When you split a word of lyrics with hyphens it's important to split between the correct letters, otherwise the syllables can be hard to read. A rule of thumb (though there are exceptions) is as follows:

- Put standard prefixes and suffixes (e.g. un-, -ing, -ed, -ly) as separate syllables
- If there is a single consonant between two syllables (e.g. labor), split *before* it (la-bor)
- If there are two consonants between two syllables (e.g. better, Batman), split between them (better, Bat-man).

As there are exceptions, if in doubt, ensure that each syllable can be read and pronounced correctly on its own; for example, "laughter" should be split "laugh-ter" rather than "laug-hter" because "laug" doesn't produce the right sound when read on its own.

Of course, when all else fails you can always look it up in a dictionary!

Checking lyrics hyphenation

Because it's all too easy for you to split up the syllables of a word incorrectly if you're typing them in, Sibelius includes a handy plug-in for checking the hyphenation of lyrics in your score – see **Check Lyrics Hyphenation** on page 516.

Sharing lyrics

If two staves have identical or near-identical rhythms, you can write a single line of lyrics between them applying to both; where the rhythms differ slightly you should position syllables horizontally between the two notes (as in "–ry" and "on" in the illustration).

Lyrics in two voices

In choral music it is common for two vocal lines to share the same staff (e.g. soprano and alto on a single staff). Often only one set of lyrics is required for music of this kind since the rhythms of the two lines tend to be similar; if the rhythms are dissimilar for extended passages, it is clearer to write each vocal line on a separate staff.

On the other hand, if a staff has two singers with significantly different rhythms or lyrics for only a few bars, you should write an extra line of lyrics above for voice 1 and a separate line of lyrics below for voice 2. The extra line of lyrics can appear just for a few notes, though if it isn't present for the whole system, then it's clearest if the extra line of lyrics occurs only where the music splits into two voices:

When adding lyrics to music in two voices, you can choose the voice into which you want to create lyrics before you start:

- Create all the notes (both voices 1 and 2)

- To create the lyrics for voice 1 above the staff, choose **Create ▸ Text ▸ Other staff text ▸ Lyrics above staff**
- To add lyrics in voice 2, select the first note in voice 2 to which you want to add lyrics, then choose **Create ▸ Text ▸ Lyrics ▸ Lyrics line 1** (shortcut **Ctrl+L** *or* ⌘L).

Several words per note and elisions

In sung dialog (such as recitative) you often find several words sung to one long note. But if you type a space or hyphen after the first syllable, the caret would immediately move onto the next note.

So instead use the special keypresses **Ctrl+space** *or* ⌕-space and **Ctrl+–** (hyphen) *or* ⌕–, which produce non-breaking spaces and hyphens (i.e. without moving onto the next note). These keypresses are also occasionally useful when creating other kinds of text, such as chord symbols.

Similarly, in Italian and some other languages, two elided syllables are often written on the same note with an elision character in between, e.g. Ky – ri – e̯ e – lei – son. To achieve this, simply type _ (underscore) while creating lyrics to get an elision character.

You can also use the elision character as a slur in block lyrics, e.g. at the end of a line of a hymn.

> ### Punctuation in lyrics
> *When using a poem for lyrics, include capitals (at the start of lines) and punctuation (at the end of lines and elsewhere) exactly as in the original text. Punctuation at the end of words goes before the lyric line.*
>
> *If you repeat part of a sentence that isn't repeated in the original text, put a comma before the repetition, e.g. "My sister, my sister, my sister is a thistle-sifter."*

Slurs and beams

Where multiple notes are sung to the same syllable, you can join them with a slur to make it clearer where syllables start and end. Use **Plug-ins ▸ Text ▸ Add Slurs to Lyrics** to do this automatically. Because unnecessary slurs can clutter the music, a good policy is only to use slurs if the word-setting is complex or potentially confusing. Phrase-marks should not be used in vocal music.

In older scores, notes sung to separate syllables were never beamed together, to make it clearer which syllable went with which note. This convention has all but died out (because it makes rhythms harder to read) but should you need it in a score, use the **Plug-ins ▸ Text ▸ Traditional Lyrics Beaming** plug-in to do it automatically.

For more information about these plug-ins, 📖 **6.12 Text plug-ins**.

Hanging punctuation

If you type the word "Oh," as lyrics, then Sibelius will center the letters themselves under the note and ignore the width occupied by the comma, which "hangs" to the right. Similarly, if a verse starts with "1. The" then the word "The" is centered and the "1." hangs to the left. These are examples of a typographical nicety called *hanging punctuation*.

If you don't want Sibelius to allow for hanging punctuation, switch off **Hanging punctuation** on the **Text** page of the **House Style ▸ Engraving Rules** dialog (shortcut **Ctrl+Shift+E** *or* ⇧⌘E).

Horizontal position

The horizontal position of lyrics is controlled by Sibelius according to complex rules. While you type each syllable in, Sibelius adjusts its precise position according to how wide the syllable is and how many notes it lasts for:

- Lyrics are centered if a word or syllable is followed by another word or syllable on the next note

- Lyrics are not centered if a word or syllable is followed by:
  - A new word, two or more notes later; the word is left-aligned with the note to which it's attached, with a lyric line trailing.
  - A new syllable, two or more notes later; by default, the syllable is left-aligned with the note to which it's attached, followed by one or more hyphens; but the syllable will be centered if **Center all syllables followed by hyphens** on the **Text** page of the **House Style ▶ Engraving Rules** dialog is switched on.

Once you've typed lyrics in, you can drag individual syllables left and right like other text if you need to adjust their position.

Syllables are attached to the notes they are written under, so if you adjust the note spacing they move as well. Additionally, if you pull two syllables joined by hyphens apart, more hyphens will appear the farther apart they get, and the hyphens will shift about so as to remain precisely centered between the syllables.

If you want to adjust the horizontal spacing of lyrics yourself, select the bar or passage in question, and use **Shift+Alt+←/→** *or* ⌥⌘←/→ to narrow or widen the spacing accordingly (**Ctrl+Shift+Alt+←/→** *or* ⌥⌘←/→ move in bigger steps) – ⌑ **8.9 Note spacing**.

To reset the spacing to its default, simply select the relevant passage and choose **Layout ▶ Reset Note Spacing** (shortcut **Ctrl+Shift+N** *or* ⌥⌘N).

The behavior of this function is determined by the **Allow space for lyrics** option in **House Style ▶ Note Spacing Rule**, which must be switched on for **Layout ▶ Reset Note Spacing** to avoid lyric collisions. If you switch off this option, Sibelius will completely ignore lyrics when respacing your music, so we recommend you leave it switched on.

Particularly long center-aligned syllables on the first note of a bar can overhang the preceding barline, which may, in passages with tight spacing, cause a collision with the lyric at the end of the previous bar; if you would prefer to disable this behavior, switch off **Allow first syllable to overhang barline** in the **House Style ▶ Note Spacing Rule** dialog.

Sometimes allowing space for wide lyrics can make the note spacing rather uneven; this is one of the bugbears of music engraving, and improving it requires something of a compromise between how best to space the lyrics and how best to space the notes. For examples and advice on this, ⌑ **8.9 Note spacing**.

Lyric hyphens

Where syllables are split between notes, a hyphen is normally drawn between those syllables; where syllables are sung over many notes, more than one hyphen appears, depending on the distance between the syllables.

Single hyphens for syllables on adjacent notes are precisely centered between the syllables. Multiple hyphens are governed by the options on the **Text** page of the **House Style ▶ Engraving Rules** dialog – see **Engraving Rules options** below.

In the English language, it's often acceptable for the hyphen between syllables to disappear in tight spacing situations (e.g. where words such as, say, "little" occur on adjacent, short notes). In other languages, however, the absence of a hyphen can change the meaning of the text completely. Sibelius will always try to leave sufficient room for a single hyphen between two syllables, but in tight spacing situations this may not always be possible. (If you don't want Sibelius to try and ensure that a hyphen will always appear, switch off **Allow extra space for hyphens** in the **House Style ▸ Note Spacing Rule** dialog).

Where words are split over system breaks, opinion is divided over whether a hyphen should appear at the start of the second system as well as at the end of the first. Sibelius accommodates both conventions: if you want hyphens to appear at the start of systems, switch on the option in the **House Style ▸ Engraving Rules** dialog. Sibelius cannot, however, guarantee that a hyphen will appear at the start of the second system, even if **Allow hyphens at start of systems** is switched on. If you find that a hyphen does not appear when required, increase the space before the first note on the system after the break a little, and the hyphen will then appear.

If you find that a hyphen is not correctly centered between two syllables, select it and choose **Layout ▸ Reset Position** (shortcut **Ctrl+Shift+P** or ⇧⌘P). You can also move hyphens about – click the (rightmost) hyphen and drag left or right.

Vertical position

Sibelius puts lyrics at a standard vertical position beneath the staff. However, you can move syllables individually up and down like other text.

To move a line of lyrics, click one of the lyrics and choose **Edit ▸ Select ▸ Select More** (shortcut **Ctrl+Shift+A** *or* ⇧⌘A) to select the whole line, then move the lyrics with the arrow keys (**Ctrl+↑/ ↓** *or* ⌘↑/↓ for big steps). Alternatively, after selecting a line of lyrics like this you can align them in a row using **Layout ▸ Align In a Row** (shortcut **Ctrl+Shift+R** *or* ⇧⌘R), move them back to their default vertical position using **Layout ▸ Reset Position** (**Ctrl+Shift+P** *or* ⇧⌘P), or **Delete** them.

To align all the lyrics in your score quickly, use the **Plug-ins ▸ Text ▸ Align Lyrics** plug-in – 📖 **6.1 Working with plug-ins**.

To change lyrics' default vertical position, 📖 **8.12 Default Positions**.

Text style

You can change the appearance of lyrics in a variety of ways:

- Use **House Style ▸ Edit Text Styles** (shortcut **Ctrl+Shift+Alt+T** *or* ⇧⌥⌘T) to change lyrics text styles globally (e.g. if you want all lyrics in your score to be in a particular font, or all italic) – 📖 **3.9 Edit Text Styles**
- Any change you make to the appearance of lyrics via the Properties window (📖 **5.17 Properties**) while editing lyrics applies to all subsequent text you create, e.g. if you change to an italic font and then hit **space** to move on to the next word, the next word and all subsequent ones will be italic until you explicitly switch it off again or stop typing lyrics.

If you want to change the appearance of your lyrics back to their default settings (i.e. those set in **House Style ▸ Edit Text Styles**), select them and choose **Layout ▸ Reset Design** (shortcut **Ctrl+Shift+D** *or* ⇧⌘D).

After changing the font or size of lyric – whether by editing the text style, using **House Style ▸ Edit All Fonts** or importing a house style (📖 **8.8 House Style™**) – you may want to choose

Layout▶ Reset Note Spacing (shortcut Ctrl+Shift+N or ⇧⌘N), as the lyrics will probably require more or less horizontal space than previously.

Blocks of lyrics

Extra verses of a song or hymn can be written as blocks of words at the end of the score. These aren't the same as normal lyrics because they don't align with notes.

To type a block of lyrics, use Create▶ Text▶ Other System Text▶ Block lyrics. Simply type the lyrics, and hit Return (on the main keyboard) at the end of each line, or copy the lyrics from elsewhere in the score if you can (see **Copying lyrics from Sibelius** above). It's convenient if you type each verse as a separate text object, so that you can move them around separately.

Stem directions

Notes on the middle staff line normally have stems pointing down; however, when there are lyrics the stem is often drawn pointing up so as to avoid colliding with the words. By default, Sibelius observes this convention; if you would prefer it not to, see **Stems on the middle line** on page 177.

Engraving Rules options

On the Text page of the House Style▶ Engraving Rules dialog (shortcut Ctrl+Shift+E *or* ⇧⌘E) you can set the position of lyric lines and spacing of hyphens, and some other options besides:

* **Use text hyphens (not symbols)** makes Sibelius draw lyrics hyphens with the font used for creating lyrics, rather than using a special symbol from the Create▶ Symbols dialog. This option is switched on by default.
* **One hyphen maximum** forces only one lyric hyphen to appear, even if syllables are spaced a long way apart. This option is switched off by default.
* **Hyphens allowed at start of systems** controls whether a lyric hyphen can appear at the start of a system if there is a syllable on the first note. This option is switched off by default.
* **Hanging punctuation** controls whether Sibelius takes account of hanging punctuation when positioning lyrics (see **Hanging punctuation** above).
* **Center all syllables followed by hyphens** center-aligns melismatic syllables (i.e. held over more than one note) which are followed by hyphens, rather than left-aligning them as per the default behavior. This option is switched off by default.
* **Center all syllables containing East Asian characters** is switched on by default. The rules for aligning lyrics in Western alphabets are not appropriate for East Asian languages, where most lyrics are single characters.
* **Draw slurs between East Asian characters** draws small slurs beneath any lyric items containing more than one East Asian character, between the first and the last East Asian character in the syllable, making it clear that they should all be sung to the same note. This option is switched on by default.

3.4 Figured bass and Roman numerals

📖 **3.1 Working with text**.

Figured bass, or thoroughbass, is commonly used in music of the Baroque period. Figures are added to the bass line only where specific inversions and chromatic alterations are required; if no figures are present, it is assumed that the player should play the notes of the triad formed by the bass note and the third and fifth above it, according to the key signature.

Roman numerals are normally used for harmonic analysis. Sibelius allows you to create chord names using either the alphabetic or numeric convention to indicate inversions. For example, Sibelius can display a second inversion tonic chord as Ic or I$^6_4$.

Creating figured bass

Sibelius includes a comprehensive set of symbols for figured bass in the font Opus Figured Bass, which is similar in appearance to Times.

To input figured bass:

- Input the notes onto the bass or continuo staff
- Select the first note, then choose **Create ▸ Text ▸ Other Staff Text ▸ Figured bass**
- To enter numbers with no accidental alterations, type the numbers from the keyboard in the normal way
- To enter numbers followed by a natural, use the lower case letters along the row **W** to **O**, where each letter corresponds to the number above it on the keyboard (e.g. **W** is 2♮). To add the natural on the left side of the number (e.g. ♮2), hold down **Shift** whilst typing the appropriate key.
- To enter numbers followed by a sharp, use the letters **S** to **K**, where each letter corresponds to the number above it (e.g. **S** is 2♯). To add the sharp on the left side of the number (e.g. ♯2), hold down **Shift** whilst typing the appropriate key.
- To enter numbers followed by a flat, use the letters **X** to **M**, where each letter corresponds to the number above it (e.g. **X** is 2♭). To add the flat on the left side of the number (e.g. ♭2), hold down **Shift** whilst typing the appropriate key.
- Hit **Return** (on the main keyboard) for a new line in a column of figures
- Type **Ctrl** *or* ⌘ with the number keys on the main keyboard to add numbers with slashes. The only exception to this rule is 7̸, whose shortcut is **Shift-7**.
- To move on to the next note or beat, hit **space**.

Other special characters include:

[3]	Q	[5]	Shift-Q	(3)	P
(5)	Shift-P	(2)	A	(4)	Shift-A
9♯	L	♯9	Shift-L	3+	Z
5+	Shift-Z	(8)	=	6+	,
7+	Shift-,	[7]	;	♭9	Shift-;
+7	Shift-.				

- You will find various other characters available in the word menu (right-click on Windows *or* Control-click on Mac), which also lists further keyboard shortcuts
- Hit **space** to advance to the next note or beat, whichever comes first.

The Opus Figured Bass font was designed by Tage Mellgren (**www.editionglobal.com**).

Creating Roman numerals

To input Roman numerals, choose **Create ▸ Text ▸ Other Staff Text ▸ Roman Numerals**.

To enter chords containing only alphabetic characters, just type the letters of the chord as you would normally.

Entering chords including numbers is a little more involved, but once you know how it works, it is a simple process. Let's say we want to enter the chord $V^6_{\flat 3}$, where the 6 is the superscript number and the 3 is the subscript number:

- First type the root of the chord alphabetically as you would normally (e.g. **V**)
- If the superscript number has an accidental, hit **X** (sharp), **Y** (flat) or **Z** (natural) as appropriate, otherwise, go on to the next step
- If the subscript number has an accidental, type **Shift-X** (sharp), **Shift-Y** (flat) or **Shift-Z** (natural) as appropriate, otherwise go on to the next step
- If you have entered accidentals for either of the subscript or superscript numbers, advance the caret along by typing **Shift-.**.
- If the chord includes a superscript number, enter it by typing the number (e.g. **6**)
- If the chord includes a subscript number, enter it by typing the number while holding down **Shift** (e.g. **Shift-3**)
- To enter superscript numbers with a slash, type the letters **M** to **U**, where **M** is the number **1**, **N** the number **2** etc. If you wish to enter a subscript number, hold down the **Shift** key while typing the appropriate letter.
- To move on to the next note or beat, hit **space**.

Function symbols

Function symbols are used to describe the harmonic structure of music, using symbols such as T to mean tonic, D to mean dominant, and so on.

Use **Create ▸ Text ▸ Other Staff Text ▸ Function symbols** to create function symbols:

* Hit **space** to advance to the next note or beat.
* If the function symbol requires brackets, **U** and **I** draw square brackets, while **Shift-U** and **Shift-I** draw parentheses.
* If the function symbol contains a subscript number below the main symbol, type this first, by holding down **Alt** *or* ⌥ and typing the number **1–9**, then the main symbol.
* The main symbols are all on the keys you would expect, e.g. **d, D, t, T, s, S, g, G**. Baseline and superscript 𝕊 characters are on **a** and **A**. ⅅ is on **Shift-F**; ⅅ is on **Alt+F** *or* ⌥F; ⅅ is on **Alt+D** *or* ⌥D.
* If a function symbol has two rows of numbers *following* the main symbol, type the upper (super-superscript) number first, then the lower (superscript) number. If the number(s) following the main symbol are followed "<" or ">", type all the numbers before "<" or ">".
* For superscript numbers, type **1–9** on the main keyboard. Superscript "v" is produced by typing **v**. "<" and ">" characters suitable for following superscript numbers are produced by typing **,** (comma) and **.** (period).
* For super-superscript numbers, type **Shift-1** to **Shift-9** on the main keyboard. Super-superscript "v" is on **V**. "<" and ">" characters suitable for following super-superscript numbers are produced by typing **<** and **>**.

3.5 Bar numbers

Scores can have bar numbers that appear automatically, normally above the first bar on each system. You can adjust their frequency and appearance to suit your preferences.

To see bar numbers on every bar on the screen only so it's easier to find your way around a large score, just switch on View▸ Staff Names and Bar Numbers; this also usefully indicates the name of each staff at the left-hand side of the screen – 📖 **5.23 View menu**.

All of the options you need to adjust bar numbers printed in your score are found on the Bar numbers page of House Style ▸ Engraving Rules (shortcut Ctrl+Shift+E *or* ⇧⌘E).

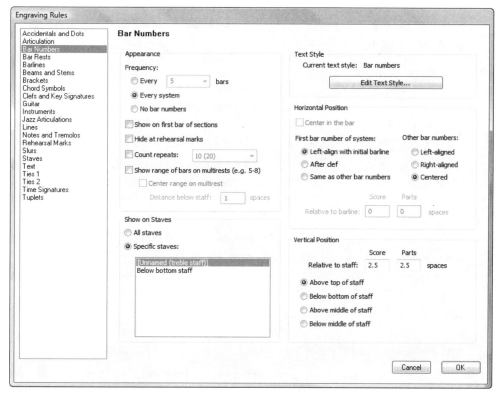

Appearance and frequency

The options in the Appearance group are as follows:

- The choices under Frequency allow you to choose whether you want to see bar numbers Every *n* bars, Every system (the default), or No bar numbers. You can use Every *n* bars to make bar numbers appear at any interval; typical values in published music are 1, 5 and 10. Writing bar numbers on every bar is a convention often used in music examples, handbell music, music for children (who may be reluctant or unable to count), and parts for session musicians (who may be reluctant or unable to count).

- Show on first bar of sections, which is switched off by default, determines whether the bar number is shown on the first bar of the score, and on any subsequent bars that follow a Section end (provided the bar is at the start of a system). Switch this option on if you set bar numbers to appear on every bar; otherwise, no bar number will appear on the first bar of the score.

- **Hide at rehearsal marks** tells Sibelius to automatically hide bar numbers that fall on the same barlines as rehearsal marks, to ensure they don't collide.

- **Count repeats,** which is switched off by default, determines whether Sibelius should take repeats into account when numbering bars – see **Bar numbers in repeat structures** below.

- Show range of bars on multirests (e.g. 5–8) allows you to use a convention most often seen in commercial, film and TV music, whereby the bars
enclosed in a multirest are numbered above or below the multirest, as
shown on the right. If the other bar numbers in your score are not centered,
but you want the bar number ranges to be drawn in the center of and below the multirest, switch on **Center ranges on multirest.** Specify how far below the multirest the range should appear by setting **Distance below staff** *n* spaces.

Show on Staves options

The options under Show on Staves allow you to choose which staves Sibelius should draw bar numbers on. This is similar to how the House Style ▸ System Object Positions dialog works for other system objects such as rehearsal marks and Tempo text (📖 **8.12 Default Positions**), but it's specifically for bar numbers.

Normally bar numbers go above the top staff of the score and above one or more other instrumental families in orchestral and band music, or sometimes below the bottom staff of the score. Choose the Specific staves radio button, then select the staff or staves on which you want bar numbers to appear:

- To select more than one staff in the list, hold down Ctrl *or* ⌘ and click: you can select up to five staves, including the top staff and Below bottom staff.

- To put bar numbers below the bottom staff, see **Placing bar numbers below the bottom staff** below.

- To put bar numbers between the staves of a keyboard instrument (which is occasionally done), select the top staff in the Selected staves list, then position the bar numbers below the top staff – see **Vertical Position options** below.

It's very rare for bar numbers to appear on all staves of a score, but if you want to do this, choose the All staves radio button. If you're only doing this so that you can see what bar you're working on at all times, there's an easier way: just switch on View ▸ Staff Names and Bar Numbers (📖 **5.23 View menu**).

Text Style options

If you wish to change the font or point size used by the bar numbers in your score or dynamic parts, click Edit Text Style. This shows a special version of the Edit Text Style dialog with only the options appropriate for bar numbers shown – 📖 **3.9 Edit Text Styles**.

Horizontal Position options

Switching on Center in the bar disables all the other options under Horizontal Position, and also applies to any bar number changes you create (see below). If your bar numbers aren't centered,

Sibelius allows you to choose the positions of bar numbers at the start of the system separately from other bar numbers.

By default, **First bar number of system** is set to **Left-align with initial barline**. If you choose **After clef**, Sibelius will place the bar number to the right of the clef, and if you choose **Same as other bar numbers**, Sibelius will follow the option set for **Other bar numbers**.

Other bar numbers are by default set to be **Centered**, which means that they will appear centered above barlines. Choosing **Left** will align the left-hand side of the bar number with the barline, and choosing **Right** will align the right-hand side of the bar number with the barline at the *end* of the bar.

Vertical Position options

The options under **Show on Staves** determine on which staves bar numbers should appear (see **Show on Staves options** above), and the options under **Vertical Position** determine the positioning of bar numbers relative to the chosen staves.

The **Above top of staff**, **Above middle of staff**, **Below middle of staff**, **Below bottom of staff** options are identical to those found in House Style ▸ Default Positions (□ **8.12 Default Positions**), and determine whether the value for **Relative to staff** *n* **spaces** is measured from the middle line, or the top or bottom line, of the staff.

Placing bar numbers below the bottom staff

In some kinds of music, such as film scores, it is common for bar numbers to appear below the staff, and are also often centered on every bar. To achieve this:

- Choose **House Style ▸ Engraving Rules** and select the **Bar numbers** page
- Under **Appearance**, choose **Every** *n* **bars**, and set *n* to be 1
- Under **Show on Staves**, choose **Selected staves**, and select only **Below bottom staff** (use **Ctrl**+click *or* ⌘-click to deselect any other staves).
- Under **Horizontal Position**, switch on **Center in the bar**
- Under **Vertical Position**, choose **Below bottom of staff**, and set the **Score** value of **Relative to staff** *n* **spaces** to (say) 3 spaces
- Click **OK**.

If you want a similar look in your dynamic parts, then view one of your parts and repeat the above procedure in the part. Then, while still viewing the part, choose **House Style ▸ Export House Style** and export the house style of that part. Use the **Multiple Part Appearance** dialog to import this house style into your other parts – see **Exporting house styles from parts** on page 548 for more details.

Bar numbers in repeat structures

When a score contains repeats, it is most common for the bars to be numbered as if they are all played once straight through; in other words, the fact that some of the bars are repeated is not reflected in the way they are numbered.

However, it is not unheard of for scores to have their bars numbered according to the actual order in which they are played, and Sibelius makes this easy: switch on **Count repeats** on the **Bar num-**

Text

bers page of **House Style ▸ Engraving Rules**, and choose the desired format from the drop-down menu:

- **10**: bar numbers are only drawn once, but any bar numbers after repeated sections take the number of repeated bars into account
- **10 (20)**: bar numbers for repeated bars are drawn in parentheses; this is the default option
- **10/20**: the repeated bar numbers are drawn after a slash
- **10–20**: the repeated bar numbers are drawn after a dash.

The effect of each of these options is shown below:

10	*1*	*2*	*3*	*4*	*11*	*12*	*15*	*16*	*17*
10 (20)	*1 (5) (9) (13)*	*2 (6) (10) (14)*	*3 (7)*	*4 (8)*	*11*	*12*	*15*	*16*	*17*
10/20	*1/5/9/13*	*2/6/10/14*	*3/7*	*4/8*	*11*	*12*	*15*	*16*	*17*
10–20	*1–5–9–13*	*2–6–10–14*	*3–7*	*4–8*	*11*	*12*	*15*	*16*	*17*

If you are using **Bar number** as the format for your rehearsal marks (on the **Rehearsal marks** page of **House Style ▸ Engraving Rules**), note that **Count repeats** will also change the display of rehearsal marks.

Selecting bar numbers

You can select bar numbers like any other object, but beware that while you can move and hide selected bar numbers (see below), you can't copy bar numbers, nor can you delete them. (You can, however, copy and delete bar number *changes* – see **Bar number changes** below.)

To quickly select a group of bar numbers, you can:

- Select a single bar number, then choose **Edit ▸ Select ▸ Select More** to select all bar numbers along that system; or
- Select a passage of music, then choose **Edit ▸ Filter ▸ Bar Numbers** to select only the bar numbers in those bars; or
- Make a marquee selection, using **Shift**-drag *or* ⌘-drag.

Once you have a range of bar numbers selected, you can move or hide them; see below.

Moving bar numbers

Bar numbers can be moved horizontally or vertically – just select one or more bar numbers and then drag them with the mouse or nudge them with the arrow keys (with **Ctrl** *or* ⌘ for bigger steps). To reset bar numbers to their original positions, select them and choose **Layout ▸ Reset Position** (shortcut **Ctrl+Shift+P** *or* ⇧⌘P).

If your bar numbers are also shown above or below other staves in your score, dragging one bar number also changes the position of that bar number above or below the other staves on which it appears.

Hiding bar numbers

To hide bar numbers, simply select the bar numbers in question, then choose **Edit** ▸ **Hide** or **Show** ▸ **Hide** (shortcut **Ctrl+Shift+H** *or* ⇧⌘H).

For more information about hiding objects, ▢ **5.9 Hiding objects**.

Bar number changes

To make bar numbers re-start at a particular number (e.g. at the start of a new section, song or movement), or to change to a different bar number format (e.g. to number added bars "1a, 1b, 1c," etc.), you can create a bar number change:

- If you want to re-start bar numbers at a particular bar, select the bar in which you want the bar numbers to restart, or ensure you have nothing selected, then choose **Create** ▸ **Other** ▸ **Bar Number Change**; or

- If you want to change the bar numbers of a range of bars, select the bars whose numbers you want to change, then choose **Create** ▸ **Other** ▸ **Bar Number Change**. (This is particularly useful for changing bar number format; Sibelius will helpfully reset the sequence back to the original format at the end of the selected passage.)

In either case, you will then see the following dialog:

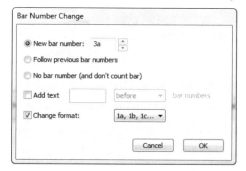

The radio button options are as follows:

- **New bar number** allows the user to specify a particular new bar number to re-start from; set this to 1 if you want to restart bar numbering at the start of a new movement
- **Follow previous bar numbers** is most useful in conjunction with the **Change format** option below; it allows you to continue an existing sequence using a new format. For example, if the bar number of the bar prior to the bar number change is 2, and you choose **Follow previous bar numbers** and set **Change format** to 1a, 1b, 1c..., the bar number change will appear as "2a."
- **No bar number (and don't count bar)** allows you to specify that Sibelius should completely skip the bar to which this bar number change is attached, useful if you need to, say, split a bar over a system break by way of two irregular bars, and want to ensure that the second irregular bar doesn't upset the subsequent bar numbers. It produces a bar number change that is only visible when **View** ▸ **Hidden Objects** is switched on, and displays a bar number inside square brackets.

The difference between **Follow previous bar numbers** and **New bar number** is that a bar number change set to **Follow previous bar numbers** will update as you drag it around; in our example above, you could drag the "2a" bar number to the right, and it would change to "3a", "4a", "5a", etc., whereas a bar number change set to a specific **New bar number** will always be the same. Like **Follow previous bar numbers**, bar number changes set to **No bar number (and don't count bar)** update dynamically as you drag them around the score.

When you change bar number format, you will normally want to set **Follow previous bar numbers**, and to select the passage of bars you want to renumber so that Sibelius can automatically reset the numbering at the end of the passage.

The **Add text** checkbox allows you to specify some text to be added before or after the bar numbers; you could tell Sibelius to add the text " new" (note the leading space) to appear after the bar number, producing bar numbers like 1 new, 2 new, 3 new, etc. Alternatively you could add the text "orig " (note the trailing space) to appear before the bar number, producing bar numbers like orig 1, orig 2, orig 3, etc.

Change format allows you to specify a new bar number format:

- **1, 2, 3...**: the standard bar number format, using numbers only
- **1a, 1b, 1c...** and **1A, 1B, 1C...**: this format is most commonly used in music for theatre productions, where last-minute alterations (such as adding extra bars in the overture to allow the actors more time to get to their marks) cannot be allowed to interfere with the bar numbering of the rest of the show. So inserted bars are usually numbered after the original bar they follow; if you insert four bars after the old bar 2, the new bars would be numbered 2a, 2b, 2c, 2d, and the next bar would still be numbered 3. This format is also sometimes used to number the bars in 2nd endings (2nd time bars).
- **a, b, c...** and **A, B, C...**: this format is most commonly used for introductory passages, e.g. the first eight bars of a song before the vocalist comes in are numbered a–h, and the ninth bar is numbered 1.

Notice that when you set the bar number format to anything other than 1, 2, 3..., Sibelius always shows the bar numbers on every bar, overriding whatever general choice you may have made in the **Frequency** options on the **Bar numbers** page of **House Style ▸ Engraving Rules**.

You can copy and delete bar number changes (unlike normal bar numbers), and you can also move a bar number change horizontally and vertically up to three spaces away from the barline to which it belongs – if you move it further, it will snap to the nearest bar.

Go to Bar

To jump quickly to any bar, choose **Edit ▸ Go to Bar** (shortcut **Ctrl+Alt+G** *or* ⌥⌘G), type in the bar number and click **OK**. Two subtle things to know about this feature:

- You can type in bar numbers in any of the supported formats, and if Sibelius is unable to find a bar number that matches exactly, it will instead take you to the closest one it can find.
- If the same bar number occurs multiple times in your score (because, say, you have several movements in the same file), Sibelius will search forwards from the beginning of the score or the current selection; to go to the next matching bar number, simply choose **Edit ▸ Go to Bar** again and click **OK** without changing the bar number you're looking for.

First bar number

If you are inputting a section from a longer score, you may want to start with a bar number other than 1. To do this, input a bar number change at the start (see above).

Pick-up (upbeat) bars

If your music starts with a pick-up (upbeat) bar, it's normal to number the first complete bar as bar 1, rather than bar 2 as it would otherwise be. Sibelius automatically numbers pick-up bars as bar 0.

Bar numbers in parts

You can use different text styles for bar numbers in your score and parts as Sibelius has unique text styles for the score (Bar numbers) and parts (Bar numbers (parts)).

If you wish to change the appearance of bar numbers in all of your parts simultaneously rather than having to edit each individual part, use the House Style page of the Multiple Part Appearance dialog (📖 **7.3 Multiple Part Appearance**).

Text

3.6 Page numbers

Sibelius numbers the pages in your score automatically, by default following the centuries-old conventions (in books as well as music) that right-hand pages are always odd-numbered and left-hand pages are always even-numbered, and that the first page should not show a page number.

In double-sided printouts, page numbers are normally positioned on the outside edge of the page (i.e. the edge furthest from the binding), and in single-sided printouts they are normally positioned on the right-hand edge (or sometimes in the center, though this is considered in typographic circles to be in poor taste!); this makes the page number appear nearest to your thumb when you flick through a score, maximizing their visibility. Whatever the binding, page numbers usually go at the top of the page.

Because Sibelius follows these conventions for you, you will rarely need to do anything at all with page numbers in your score, but if you're working with complex layouts involving blank pages at the start of the score or multiple pieces in the same file, you may find that you want to change the page numbering: that's where **Create ▸ Other ▸ Page Number Change** comes in.

Page Number Change

Using a page number change, you can switch to one of several page number formats, restart page numbering at any point, and even hide subsequent page numbers. First, select something (e.g. a bar) on the page on which you want the page number change to take effect, then choose **Create ▸ Other ▸ Page Number Change**. The following dialog appears:

- **New page number** allows you to specify the first page number in the sequence; if you switch this checkbox off, the page number change that's created will simply follow the existing sequence
- You can choose from one of four **Format** options:
  - **1, 2, 3...** is the default Arabic numeral format
  - **a, b, c...** and **A, B, C...** use lower and upper case alphabetic schemes respectively, and are useful for front matter
  - **i, ii, iii...** and **I, II, III...** use lower and upper case Roman numerals, and are also useful for front matter.
- Finally you can choose which of the page numbers affected by the page number change should be visible:

- Show page numbers will show all page numbers (until the next page number change)
- Hide first page number will hide the first page number of the page number change, and show all subsequent ones (until the next page number change)
- Hide page numbers will hide all page numbers (until the next page number change).
- Hide page numbers until after next page of music is useful for situations in which your score starts with one or more blank pages, and you want page numbers to appear from the *second* page of music onwards.

When you click OK, Sibelius creates the appropriate page number change. Notice that Sibelius also creates a page break at the end of the page; this is because you have told Sibelius that you want a page number change in a specific place, so it has to fix the layout of the score to ensure that the page number change will stay on the right page.

If you want to change the page number on a blank page (created using a special page break – 📖 **8.5 Breaks**), make sure you have nothing selected before you choose Create ▸ Other ▸ Page Number Change, then after clicking OK in the dialog, click on the blank page from which you want the page number change to take effect.

Selecting page numbers

Although you cannot select the automatic page numbers that Sibelius creates by default, you can select page numbers produced via page number changes.

To select all the page number changes in a score, you can e.g. select the whole score with Edit ▸ Select ▸ Select All (shortcut Ctrl+A *or* ⌘A), then choose Edit ▸ Filter ▸ Page Number Changes. You can then hide or delete the selected page number changes – see below.

Hiding page numbers

If you decide to hide page numbers after creating a page number change, you don't need to create the page number change again: simply select one of the page numbers affected by the page number change, and choose Edit ▸ Hide or Show ▸ Hide (shortcut Ctrl+Shift+H *or* ⇧⌘H).

If you want to hide only the first page number in a page number change, be sure to select that page number; selecting any other page number will result in all page numbers affected by the page number change being hidden.

For further information about hiding objects, 📖 **5.9 Hiding objects**.

Deleting page numbers

You cannot delete automatic page numbers (though you can hide them), but you can delete the page numbers produced via page number changes – simply select them (see above) and hit Delete. Deleting the page break to which a page number change is attached will also delete the page number change, but the reverse isn't true (i.e. if you delete the page number change, the page break will not be deleted).

If you don't want any page numbers to appear in your score, select a bar on the first page, then use Create ▸ Other ▸ Page Number Change and switch on Hide page numbers.

Page numbers in parts

Normally instrumental parts are numbered from page 1, independently of the score. This is what Sibelius does by default, but you can make your parts use the same page numbers as the score if you wish using the options on the Layout page of Multiple Part Appearance – 📖 **7.3 Multiple Part Appearance**.

You can also create a page number change in a part, which will affect only the part in which it is created.

Showing the page number on page 1

By default, Sibelius will number your score from page 1, and will not show a page number on the first page, though if you have View ▸ Hidden Objects switched on you will see a gray "1" in the top right-hand corner of the page. To make the first page number visible, should you want to, use Create ▸ Other ▸ Page Number Change to create a page number change to page 1 on the first page of the score, and choose Show page numbers.

First page number

Here are a few recommendations for what the first page number of your score should be in different situations, should you wish to become an expert on the matter:

* If your score is to start with a left-hand page, create a page number change to page 2 on the first page (or leave it at 1 if your Sibelius file includes a title page).
* If your score has no cover (i.e. the front page has music on), then the front page is page 1.
* If your score is "self-covering" – i.e. the front page is a cover but is made of the same paper as the rest of the score – then that cover is treated as page 1; so if your music starts on the first left-hand page, create a page number change to page 2, unless your score includes a title page.
* If your score has a separate cover made of card, then page 1 is normally the first right-hand page inside the cover.

Remember that page 1 normally doesn't have a number printed on it.

Positioning page numbers relative to the margin

By default, page numbers are aligned with the page margins on both left- and right-hand pages. However, some publishers prefer page numbers on left-hand pages to be aligned with the left-hand side of the staff instead; if you want to use this convention:

* Choose House Style ▸ Edit Text Styles
* Choose Page numbers from the list of text styles, and click Edit
* In the System Text Style dialog that appears, choose the Horizontal Posn tab, then switch on the (not quite self-explanatory) At left of page, align to 'No names' staff margin option
* Click OK and Close.

Page numbers in single-sided scores

If you intend your score to be printed single-sided rather than double-sided, you should change the position of your page numbers so that they always appear on the right-hand side of the page:

* Choose House Style ▸ Edit Text Styles

- Choose **Page numbers** from the list of text styles, and click **Edit**
- In the **System Text Style** dialog that appears, choose the **Horizontal Posn** tab, and set **Align** to page to **Right**
- Click **OK** and **Close**.

Page numbers in text

Page numbers are sometimes shown as part of a running header or footer. If you want to do this, you can add the current page number to a header or footer (or indeed to any other text) using the \$PageNum\ wildcard. For example:

- First you need to hide Sibelius's automatic page numbers. Select the first bar of the score and choose **Create ▸ Other ▸ Page Number Change**.
- Click the **Hide page numbers** radio button, then click **OK**. (Switch on **View ▸ Hidden Objects**, if it's not switched on already, and you'll notice that the page numbers are still there, only now they're all hidden.)
- Now either edit your existing header text, or use **Create ▸ Text ▸ Other System Text ▸ Header (after first page)** to create a new one.
- Add \$PageNum\ to the header, e.g. your header may look like this when editing it: \$Title\ – \$Composer\ – p.\$PageNum\, which produces something like "Symphony no. 40 – Mozart – p.15". The results are only visible when you stop editing it and Sibelius automatically substitutes the wildcards.

For more information about wildcards, ▢ **3.10 Wildcards**.

Go to Page

To jump quickly to any page, choose **Edit ▸ Go to Page** (**Ctrl+Shift+G** *or* ⇧⌘G), type in the page number and click **OK**. You can type in a page number in any of the formats that Sibelius understands.

3.7 Rehearsal marks

Rehearsal marks are large letters or numbers that pinpoint important places in the music. They are automatically lettered or numbered in sequence by Sibelius – you only have to indicate where they go. This means that you can create and delete rehearsal marks freely without having to worry about re-lettering or renumbering them yourself.

Creating rehearsal marks

- Choose **Create ▸ Rehearsal Mark**. The following dialog appears:

- **Consecutive** means that the rehearsal mark that's created will continue in the sequence already established (or become the first rehearsal mark in the sequence), using the format specified in **House Style ▸ Engraving Rules** (see below). Normally this is what you will want, so this is what you get when you type the shortcut **Ctrl+R** *or* ⌘**R**, without Sibelius showing you the dialog.

  For example, if you put several consecutive rehearsal marks along a staff, they will appear as **A B C D E**. If you then delete **B**, the subsequent marks will be automatically changed from **C D E** to **B C D** to maintain the sequence. Similarly, if you create a new rehearsal mark between two others, the subsequent marks will be adjusted.

- **Start at** allows you to create a rehearsal mark out of sequence, and to restart the sequence from a particular point. Simply type the mark you want into the box; Sibelius will continue the sequence thereafter for **Consecutive** rehearsal marks – e.g. if you ask it to start with **Y2**, it will follow this with **Z2**, then **A3, B3**, etc.

- **New prefix/suffix** allows you to add some fixed text before or after the rehearsal mark, so you can produce special sequences of rehearsal marks like **A1, A2, A3, A4**, or **1A, 2A, 3A, 4A**, etc. that differ from the standard sequence (you can set a prefix or suffix for all rehearsal marks if need be – see **Engraving Rules options** below). Type your desired **Prefix** or **Suffix** into the boxes provided. The **Override defaults** option allows you to choose whether the prefix/suffix specified here should be used instead of the default prefix/suffix defined in **House Style ▸ Engraving Rules**; if you want to replace the default prefix and suffix, switch this option on.

- Now click **OK**:
  - If no note is selected, the mouse pointer will change color and you should click above a barline to place the rehearsal mark
  - If a note is selected, the rehearsal mark is automatically positioned above the barline at the start of the next bar.

Editing rehearsal marks

You can drag, copy and delete rehearsal marks in the normal ways. As you drag them, they snap to barlines horizontally.

As with tempo text, large scores often have more than one of each rehearsal mark – say, one above the system and another above the strings in orchestral music.

If you delete the top rehearsal mark, any duplicates lower down the system will delete with it. You can move the vertical position of each rehearsal mark down the system independently, though because Magnetic Layout will ensure rehearsal marks do not collide with anything, you shouldn't need to do this.

You can alter which staves rehearsal marks and other system objects appear above – see **System Object Positions** on page 610.

If you need to move a rehearsal mark slightly left or right of the barline to avoid an obstacle, select the rehearsal mark and edit its X value on the **General** panel of the Properties window.

Engraving Rules options

You can choose the format in which all rehearsal marks appear from the **Rehearsal marks** page of the **House Style ▸ Engraving Rules** dialog (shortcut **Ctrl+Shift+E** *or* ⇧⌘E). The choice is:

- A-Z, A1-Z1, A2...
- A-Z, AA-ZZ, AAA...
- 1, 2, 3...
- Bar number
- Hide all

The format changes for all existing rehearsal marks, so after changing to the third format the sequence Y Z AA BB would become 25 26 27 28.

(Slight fun: set rehearsal marks to **Bar number** format. Create a rehearsal mark, and watch what happens when you drag it from bar to bar.)

The **Prefix** and **Suffix** options allow you to specify text to be placed before and after the automatic part of all rehearsal marks. This is useful if the font you are using for rehearsal marks has special characters for drawing fancy boxes around letters and numbers; Sibelius's own Reprise Rehearsal is one such font (try importing one of the **Reprise** house styles, for example).

The font, size, box and so on is controlled by clicking the **Edit Text Style** button. ⬚ **3.9 Edit Text Styles**.

Rehearsal marks are automatically shrunk to a smaller size than the score in parts. You can control the size they end up at by editing the **Rehearsal marks** text style. Choose **House Style ▸ Edit Text Styles** (shortcut **Ctrl+Shift+Alt+T** or ⇧⌥⌘T on Mac), select the **Rehearsal marks** text style and click **Edit**. Adjust the **Parts** size on the **General** page of the **Text Style** dialog as required. For information on working with parts, ⬚ **7.1 Working with parts**.

Text

3.8 Instrument names

 2.18 Instruments, 8.14 Edit Instruments.

Each instrument has two names – the full name that is normally before the first system, and the short name (abbreviation) that is normally before subsequent systems. If you change one you should also adjust the other. The names will change throughout the score, not just on the system where you make the modification.

Editing instrument names

You can edit the name of any instrument in your score – to use a foreign language, for instance, or to name a singing character such as Wozzeck instead of Baritone. Just click the name at the left of one of the systems, and edit it like any other text.

Editing an instrument's name doesn't change an instrument from one kind to another, so changing "Violin" to "Flute" doesn't make it a flute. Similarly, changing "Horn in F" to "Horn in E♭" doesn't change the transposition and make it an E♭ instrument. To make this kind of change, use **Create ▸ Other ▸ Instrument Change** instead – **2.18 Instruments**.

You can edit the instrument name at the start of a system following an instrument change just like any other instrument name – see **Instrument names and instrument changes** below.

If you have several identical instruments in your score and you want to make all their names the same, it may be quicker to use **House Style ▸ Edit Instruments** rather than editing each name individually – **8.14 Edit Instruments**.

Hiding instrument names

If you don't want instrument names to be shown at all, switch them off from the **House Style ▸ Engraving Rules** dialog (see **Format and style of names** below).

If you want to remove the instrument name just for a single instrument, select the name and hit **Delete** – if you subsequently want to restore the instrument name, you need to double-click where the name should be, and the caret will reappear to allow you to type the name back in.

Moving instrument names

You can move an instrument name with the mouse, which will move all instances of the name. However, it's normal to adjust the position of instrument names by changing their alignment – see **Format and style of names** below.

Format and style of names

To alter the format of instrument names, choose **House Style ▸ Engraving Rules** (shortcut Ctrl+Shift+E *or* ⇧⌘E) and select the **Instruments** page.

The various options let you choose whether to use the full name, short name or no name at the start of the score, at subsequent systems, and at any new section (see below).

Recommended settings are as follows:

- For scores with lots of instruments (e.g. orchestral or band), specify full names at the start (and maybe at new sections), and full or short names subsequently.

- For scores for solo instrument and scores for a few instruments with no hidden staves, specify full names at the start (and maybe at new sections), and no names subsequently.

- For parts, scores for solo instrument, and music examples, you could specify no names throughout. In parts, by default Sibelius puts no names next to the systems, and instead writes the instrument name at the top of the page.

Instrument names are governed by a text style, so their font, size, etc. can be adjusted like other text styles by choosing House Style ▸ Edit Text Styles (shortcut Ctrl+Shift+Alt+T *or* ⇧⌥⌘T). Select Instrument names from the list on the left, and then click Edit. You can adjust the horizontal alignment of instrument names from the Horizontal Posn tab (🕮 **3.9 Edit Text Styles**), and you can adjust how far away from the initial barline they appear by altering the Gap between instrument names and initial barline option on the Instruments page of House Style ▸ Engraving Rules.

Instrument names are traditionally centered in a column, but this can make some names end up far from the staff they refer to if other names on the system are much wider. So instrument names are sometimes right-aligned instead (or very occasionally, such as in band music, they are left-aligned). Sibelius's manuscript papers are set up with sensible instrument name settings for you, so if you use a suitable manuscript paper to create your score you don't need to worry about this.

Here are some more advanced instrument name formats:

You can write this at the start of your score simply by double-clicking the name to edit it. (You might also want to edit the short form of the name on a subsequent page.)

To achieve this, simply double-click the instrument name and hit **Return** (on the main keyboard) between each name.

In this instance, create a single flute, then add an extra staff below (🕮 **2.29 Staves**), and then edit the instrument name: type "1 **Return Return** Fl. **space space Return Return** 2". The 1 and 2 are correctly positioned vertically but will get slightly mispositioned if you change the gap between staves from the default.

You can get this effect by creating the name in a right-justified text style with line spacing set to 50%; type "1 **Return** Clarinet **space space space Return** 2." As you need to set the Instrument names text style to have line spacing of 50%, other instrument names that span more than one line will need an extra **Return** between lines to space them correctly.

Here "Violin I" is the instrument name, and "*divisi*" has simply been added by typing Expression text in the margin. Beware that this "*divisi*" is attached to the first bar of the staff, so reformatting the score might move it. For this reason, create a system break at the end of the previous system to make sure it doesn't get displaced.

In some choral scores, no instrument names are used to the left of systems. Instead they are typed in capitals in Technique text above each staff (starting over the clef) at the start of the piece, and then wherever the singers used on the system change. This convention is often used in early music editions and in scores where the same staves occur on most systems. Instrument names for choral singers are usually written in capitals.

Instrument names at new sections

Scores that include several pieces, songs or movements can be regarded as having several "sections," each often starting with a new title. At new sections you often write full instrument names, even if short names or no names are used elsewhere. To do this:

* Select the final bar of the preceding section
* Choose **Window ▸ Properties** (shortcut **Ctrl+Alt+P** *or* ⌥⌘P), open the **Bars** panel, then switch on **Section end**
* On the **House Style ▸ Engraving Rules** dialog, **Instruments** page, set the behavior of names **At new sections** to **Full** (or maybe **Short**).

For more information on scores with multiple sections, ▯ **9.3 Splitting and joining scores**.

Instrument names and instrument changes

When you create an instrument change on a staff, by default the instrument name at the start of the next system is updated to show the name of the new instrument. If you don't want Sibelius to do this, choose **House Style ▸ Engraving Rules**, choose the **Instruments** page, and switch off **Change instrument names at start of systems after instrument changes**.

Instrument names in dynamic parts

It is uncommon for instrument names to be printed at the left-hand side of every staff in instrumental parts; instead, they tend to be printed at the top left-hand corner of the first page, and thereafter as part of a running header. With dynamic parts, Sibelius handles all of this for you using wildcards (▯ **3.10 Wildcards**), so you can leave the header alone. However, if you're not used to working with wildcards and try to edit the headers, it's possible for you to undo Sibelius's hard work and end up with a mess. There are three common problems:

All parts show the same instrument name at the top left corner of the first page

This happens if you directly edit the existing text object at the top left-hand corner of the first page of the full score or any of the parts, which you should avoid doing. The wildcard used for the text at the top of the first page is \\$PartName\\, which takes its value from the **Part name** field in **File ▸ Score Info** dialog. So to fix this, you simply need to repair the text object:

* Switch to the full score if necessary by hitting **W**
* Double-click the text object at the top left-hand corner of the first page to edit it
* Delete the existing text and replace it with the string **\\$PartName**, then hit **Esc** to stop editing
* Notice that the text now says "Full Score"
* If the text is shown in the score but you wish it to be hidden there, choose **Edit ▸ Hide or Show ▸ Show in Parts**.

If you want to change this text in any of the parts, the secret is to edit the **Part name** value in **Score Info**. There are two ways of doing this:

- Either single-click the name of the part in the Parts window and type the new name, hitting **Enter** when you're finished; or
- View the part in question, then choose **File ▸ Score Info** and edit **Part name** there.

No instrument names appear in the parts

If you can't see the instrument name at the top left-hand corner of the part's first page or in the header on subsequent pages, try these steps:

- First, make sure **View ▸ Hidden Objects** is switched on; then look at the start of the score. The instrument name should be visible, either in gray (meaning that it's hidden) or black (meaning that it's shown).
- If the instrument name is there but grey, select it, then choose **Edit ▸ Hide or Show ▸ Show in Parts**, which will hide it in the score but show it in all the parts.
- If no instrument name is there, then you've somehow deleted the required text object. To put it back:
  - Make sure you can see the first bar of the full score or part
  - Select the first bar of the score or part so that it is surrounded by a single blue box
  - Choose **Create ▸ Text ▸ Special Text ▸ Instrument name at top left**
  - A flashing cursor appears: type **\\$PartName** and hit **Esc**.

In multi-staff parts, the instrument name is missing from the left of each staff

By default, Sibelius doesn't show instrument names to the left of each staff in dynamic parts, because most parts only contain a single staff. However, in cases where you have multiple staves in the same part, you may then wish to show instrument names at the start of the first (and perhaps subsequent systems). To achieve this:

- View the part in which you want instrument names to appear
- Choose **House Style ▸ Engraving Rules** and go to the **Instruments** page
- Set instrument names to appear in **Full** at **Start of score** (and **Short** subsequently, if you wish), and click **OK**.

If you have many parts in which you need instrument names to appear, rather than repeating this process in each part individually it may be quicker to export a house style from this part and import it into the others – see **Exporting house styles from parts** on page 548.

For more information about working with dynamic parts, 📖 **7.1 Working with parts**.

Nameless staves

To create nameless staves from the **Create ▸ Instruments** dialog, select the **All instruments** ensemble, and choose the **Others** family, which includes **treble staff** and **bass staff**. These staves are not intended to represent any particular instrument.

If, however, you simply want to have no instrument names for all the instruments in your score, change the options on the **Instruments** page of the **House Style ▸ Engraving Rules** dialog (see **Format and style of names** above).

3.9 Edit Text Styles

📖 **3.1 Working with text**, **8.12 Default Positions**.

This topic tells you how to change a text style's font, size, alignment and other features.

You can redefine not only normal types of text, but also things like rehearsal marks, tuplet numbers, bar numbers, page numbers and instrument names. Any change you make is instantly reflected in all text of that style wherever it appears in your score.

If you want to make quick changes to the font of all the text styles in your score, use the **House Style ▸ Edit All Fonts** dialog; if, on the other hand, you need to adjust individual text styles, use the **House Style ▸ Edit Text Styles** dialog.

Edit All Fonts dialog

To change all the fonts used in your score, choose **House Style ▸ Edit All Fonts**. What this dialog actually does is change the fonts used by lots of text styles, all at once.

• **Main Text Font**: this is the font family used by text styles like Title, Composer, Tempo, Expression, Technique, Lyrics line 1, and so on. Changing this setting can dramatically alter the appearance of your score.

• **Main Music Font**: this is the font family used for the musical symbols in your score, such as notes, rests, clefs, time signatures, and so on. 📖 **8.11 Music fonts**.

• Music Text Font: this is the font used for text instructions that use special symbols, such as dynamics (e.g. *mf*). It's a good idea for the music text font to be from the same family as the music font: if you choose Opus, Helsinki or another "engraved" music font, choose Opus Text, Helsinki Text, or that specific music font's equivalent, if available; if you choose Reprise, Inkpen2 or another "handwritten" music font, choose Reprise Text or Inkpen2 Text.

When you click OK, Sibelius updates the appearance of your score instantly. If you don't like the result, simply choose **Edit ▸ Undo** (shortcut **Ctrl+Z** *or* **⌘Z**).

After changing the music font, you may find that selecting the whole score and doing **Layout ▸ Reset Note Spacing** (shortcut **Ctrl+Shift+N** *or* **⇧⌘N**) improves the appearance of the score, if the new fonts you've chosen are significantly wider or narrower than the ones you were using previously. The same is true if your score uses lyrics and you change the main text font.

Edit Text Styles dialog

To change or create a text style, choose **House Style ▸ Edit Text Styles** (shortcut **Ctrl+Shift+Alt+T** *or* **⇧⌥⌘T**). A handy tip is that if you select a text object in the score before you choose **Edit Text Styles**, Sibelius will automatically select the appropriate text style in the dialog, so you don't need to hunt through the list to find it.

Let's assume you want to modify an existing staff style, such as **Technique**; click **Technique** in the list, then click **Edit**.

If, on the other hand, you want to create a new text style based on Technique, select it in the list, then click **New**. Choose a text style similar to the one you want to create, e.g. if you want a new lyrics text style, base it on an existing **Lyrics line 1** style. You'll be asked if you really want to create a new text style based on this existing style; click **Yes**.

Whether you're editing an existing text style or creating a new one, you'll get a tabbed dialog looking rather like this:

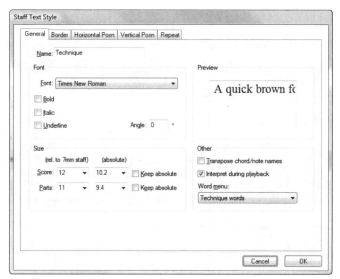

Notice that the dialog's caption (in its title bar) tells you what kind of text style you're editing; it will say **Staff Text Style**, **System Text Style** or **Blank Page Text Style**. You can't change whether an existing text style is staff, system or blank page text, and nor would you want to – but note that when you create a new text style based on an existing one, the new style will be of the same type (staff, system or blank page) as the existing style.

When you're satisfied with the style settings, click **OK** and they will apply instantly to your score, changing any existing text in that style.

General tab

Name is the name of the style, which you can change if you like. Changing it does not create a new style, it just renames the current one. You'd want to do this if you were putting one of the styles to a new use; for instance, if you don't want to use Technique at all but you do want a similar style called "Stage directions," you can just edit the name of Technique to describe the new purpose. Otherwise, you should create a new style based on Technique, as described above. Special styles such as Bar numbers will still behave in their special ways even if you change the name.

Font allows you to choose the font, surprisingly. Click on a font in the list to change font. You can also make the font **Bold**, **Italic** or **Underlined**. Underlining is exceedingly rare in music, so don't do it unless you really mean it. See below for advice on fonts and styles to use in music.

Angle lets you write text at an angle, which is again a rare requirement. Some printer drivers have a bug that makes angled text print at the wrong angle; if this happens, click **Substitute Arpeggios, gliss., etc.** on the **File ▸ Print** dialog.

Size is the point size of the text, which Sibelius allows you to set independently in a score and parts (☐ **7.1 Working with parts**). Text in music is mostly proportional to the staff size: if the staff size is large, so are all dynamics, lyrics and so on. So the left-hand number is a relative size: it's the size the text would appear if the staff size were 0.28" (7mm). It is normally easiest to specify text sizes in music for a standard staff size like this. The right-hand number is the absolute size, that is, how large the text will actually turn out for the current staff size. You can change either number, and the other will change automatically.

Keep absolute allows you to create text styles that always remain at the same size, regardless of the size of the staff. This can be useful for, say, applying a fixed size to titles in parts, or for making rehearsal marks always appear at the same size so they don't look funny above small staves.

Transpose chord/note names is only used by things like chord symbols, and tells Sibelius to change them when the music is transposed.

Interpret during playback specifies whether or not text objects using the text style being edited will be interpreted by the playback dictionary during playback – ☐ **4.9 Playback dictionary**.

Word menu lets you choose the list of useful words that will appear when you right-click (Windows) *or* **Control**-click (Mac) while typing text in the style. ☐ **3.1 Working with text**.

Point sizes

In all typesetting, text sizes are specified in points (pt), which are equal to 1/72 inch (approx. 0.35mm). Since letters vary in size – even capital letters vary in height slightly – the measurement used to specify the size is the distance from the top of the highest letter to the bottom of the lowest. This is about one-and-a-half-times the height of capital letters. The size of text in books is normally around 10 pt.

Border tab

Circled draws a circle around the text. Text in circles is rare in music (other than for specifying guitar strings), though it is occasionally used for bar numbers and even rehearsal marks.

Boxed draws a box around the text. This is more common than circles, and is used for rehearsal marks, and less commonly for bar numbers and for important instructions to players.

Sibelius even lets you have text inside a circle *and* a box – though this is a very, very, very rare requirement.

The thickness of the line used to draw the box and circle is controlled by **Text borders** on the **Text** page of the **House Style ▸ Engraving Rules** dialog (shortcut **Ctrl+Shift+E** *or* ⇧⌘E).

Erase background is for text that falls over staff lines or barlines. It is primarily intended for guitar tab numerals, but you could switch this option on for (say) dynamics, if you sometimes need them to go across a barline.

Position specifies where and how big the circle or box is to be, and the size of the area erased by **Erase background**. Sibelius fills in sensible default values for you.

Horizontal Position tab

Because staff text can only be attached to rhythmic positions in a bar, the options under **Align to note** are the only options available for staff text. System text can be either attached to rhythmic positions (e.g. **Tempo**) or to the page (e.g. **Header (after first page)**), so either **Align to note** or **Align to page** can be chosen. Blank page text can never be attached to rhythmic positions in a bar (because there are no bars on blank pages!), so only **Align to page** can be chosen.

For text that uses **Align to note**, **Left / Centered / Right** specify how the text is to be positioned relative to where it is created. These options also affect the alignment of multiple lines of text in the same text object. Left alignment is the usual setting. However, you may want to align certain types of text differently – such as fingerings, which are often centered above notes.

To set the horizontal distance of the text from where it is created, ⌐ **8.12 Default Positions**.

The **Align to page** options (only for system and blank page text) align the text to the left/center/ right of the page as you'd expect – for instance, the title of a piece is almost always centered on the page. But you can also choose **Inside / Outside edge**, which are used for double-sided printing, and are best explained by an example: when printing single-sided, page numbers are usually put at the right-hand side; but when printing double-sided, page numbers usually go on the right of right-hand pages and the left of left-hand pages – that is, on the outside edge.

Page-aligned text always attaches to the first bar in a system (e.g. **Title** text) when created, or the first bar on the page if the text is aligned to the page vertically (e.g. **Footer**).

If the text is set to **Align to page**, there are three further options:

- **At left of page, align to 'No names' staff margin** is intended for page numbers – ⌐ **3.6 Page numbers**.
- **Snap to margin** prevents the text from being dragged away from the margin to which it is aligned.
- **Relative to first page margins only** tells Sibelius that it should always align this text to the margins of the start of the score, ignoring any margin changes later on (produced via special page breaks – ⌐ **8.5 Breaks**). This is useful for headers, footers and page numbers.

Vertical Position tab

To set the vertical distance of the text from where it is created, ⌐ **8.12 Default Positions**.

Line spacing sets the distance between lines of text when you hit **Return** (on the main keyboard) at the end of a line. It is expressed as a percentage of the point size. 120% is a normal setting for books, but 100% is more suitable for text in music. Incidentally, line spacing is known in printers' jargon as *leading* (to rhyme with "heading"), from the time when extra strips of lead had to be put in between lines of text to space them out. Those were the days.

Snap to top or bottom of page is useful for positioning text that is in a fixed position on the page, such as page numbers, headers, footers and footnotes. If you switch this on, you can then set the **mm from top/bottom margin** for the text style, and you can enter different values for the score and parts if you wish (1 inch = 25.4mm) – ⌐ **7.1 Working with parts**.

Titles, rehearsal marks, bar numbers, composer name and so on should normally be positioned relative to the top staff rather than the page margin. You can also specify that this kind of text should be positioned **Relative to first page margins only**, again ignoring any margin changes produced via special page breaks.

Multiple system object positions, available only for system text, lets you write the text above more than one staff. For instance, titles only go above the top staff (so click just **Top staff**), whereas rehearsal marks in orchestral scores normally go both above the top staff and also above the strings (so click **Top staff** and **2nd position**). You can set which staves constitute the 2nd, 3rd and 4th positions with the **House Style ▸ System Object Positions** dialog – 📖 **8.8 House Style™**.

Bottom staff is occasionally required for putting rehearsal marks below the bottom staff. To do this, you'll also need to switch on **Below bottom staff** in the **House Style ▸ System Object Positions** dialog.

Repeat tab

This is only available for system text, and is useful only for headers, footers, copyright lines and the like. It makes the text you type appear on multiple pages.

It's fairly common for publishers to have different headers or footers on left and right pages – for instance, you might have the name of an anthology or album on each top left page and the name of the current piece or song on each top right page.

Deleting text styles

The **Delete** button on the **House Style ▸ Edit Text Styles** dialog deletes the selected text style or styles, you'll be startled to hear. Predefined text styles, and text styles that are currently in use in the score, cannot be deleted.

Tasteful fonts

In music it's usual to use just one font family for all text, with the possible exception of titles and instrument names. A font family consists of variants on one basic font – normally bold, italic and bold italic versions, though some font families also have *heavier* (thicker-lined) and *lighter* (thinner-lined) fonts, and/or *condensed* (squashed) fonts. You should use only two or at most three font families in any one score.

By default, all the text styles use the Times New Roman font family (unless you use manuscript paper or a handwritten house style based on the Reprise or Inkpen2 fonts), because Times looks good and will already be installed on your computer. If you substitute another family, you are very strongly advised to use serif fonts, with the possible exception of one or two text styles specified below. *Serif fonts* (such as the one used in this paragraph) have pointed cross-strokes called *serifs* at the tips of the letters, unlike *sans serif* fonts. Serif fonts are used in most books and newspapers for most of the text whereas sans serif fonts are mainly used for titles, if at all.

You are recommended to keep approximately the same point size for each text style as Sibelius's defaults (unless otherwise stated below), although when changing font you may want to adjust the point size slightly because some fonts look a bit larger or smaller than others of the same point size.

If you intend to change the main text font when creating a new score, it's better to start with a Georgia or Arial house style than Times, as both Georgia and Arial are more similar in size to most other fonts than Times. This should ensure that your main text font doesn't end up too big in proportion to the rest of the score.

Here's some advice on redesigning the main text styles in good taste:

- **Expression**: use an *italic non-bold* font (except for dynamics such as ***mf***, which should use a special music text font such as Opus Text).
- **Technique**: use a non-italic non-bold font.
- **Lyrics line 1**: Times New Roman and Times have the virtue of being unusually narrow, so using them for lyrics causes least disruption to the note spacing. Another classic font for lyrics is Plantin, used by Oxford University Press.

  If you're writing a second line of lyrics for a translation or a chorus, it's normal to use italics. For second, third etc. verses, use non-italics.
- **Chord Symbol**: by default this uses the specially-designed font Opus Chords (or Reprise Chords or Inkpen2 Chords, depending on the house style). You could substitute another medium font, possibly a sans serif one, but beware that some chord symbols require special characters not provided in ordinary text fonts.
- **Title, Subtitle, Composer, Lyricist, Dedication**: for the main title and perhaps subtitle, you can set the font and size to almost anything you like. For the composer, lyricist and dedication, you should normally use the same font and a similar size to Technique, but with the dedication normally in italics.
- **Tempo** and **Metronome mark**: the sizes of these styles vary quite widely from score to score. Tempo is almost always in a bold font and larger than Metronome mark, which is usually in a non-bold font.
- **Instruments**: you may just be able to get away with a tasteful sans serif font, but proceed with caution.
- **Bar numbers**: usually in italics. You can add a box to draw attention to the numbers, but in this case use a non-italic font. (Italics might crash into the box.)
- **Page numbers**: use a non-bold non-italic font. 📖 **3.6 Page numbers** for advice on positioning.
- **Rehearsal marks**: preferably use a bold font for clarity, but not italics (they might collide with the box). It often looks good to use the same font as the main title, even if it is an unusual font. You can omit the box, but to do so is outdated for the very good reason that rehearsal marks without a box are not visible enough.
- **Time signatures**: by default these use the Opus, Helsinki, Reprise or Inkpen2 font. You could substitute another standard music font, or even a bold text font. If you try this, you may need to adjust the line spacing on the **Vertical posn** tab.
- **Tuplets**: an italic serif font is normal, though non-italic and/or sans serif are sometimes seen in modern scores that use lots of tuplets.
- Other text styles: preferably match similar text styles above, e.g. you should make **Boxed text** and **Footnote** identical or similar to **Technique**.
- Symbols styles (e.g. **Common symbols, Percussion instruments**): these styles specify the font used for music symbols, so they're not like other text. 📖 **8.11 Music fonts** for advice, and don't change these styles unless you know what you're doing.

3.10 Wildcards

A wildcard is a code in a text object that inserts some special text from somewhere else. Sibelius has various useful wildcards that allow you to do things like include a piece's title and page number in a header, that will automatically update if you change the title (and hence can be used in your own manuscript paper).

What wildcards look like

Wildcards in Sibelius begin with \$ and end with \ – e.g. \$Title\. When you are editing a text object containing a wildcard, you will see the code itself (as shown below left). When you stop editing the text, you'll see the text that the wildcard refers to instead (as shown below right).

Available wildcards

The following wildcards produce the text typed in the File ▸ Score Info dialog (📖 **9.1 Working with files**), and some of them are also set on the final page of the File > New dialog when creating a new score:

- \$Title\
- \$Subtitle\
- \$Composer\
- \$Arranger\
- \$Artist\
- \$Copyright\
- \$PartName\
- \$InstrumentChanges\
- \$Lyricist\
- \$Copyist\
- \$Publisher\
- \$Dedication\
- \$OpusNumber\
- \$ComposerDates\
- \$YearOfComposition\
- \$MoreInfo\

All of these wildcards can be set to different values in the full score and each of the dynamic parts, if you like. Sibelius uses this ability to good advantage to make sure that each of your dynamic parts is named correctly – see **Part name and Instrument changes** below.

These additional wildcards are also available:

- \$DateShort\: the current short date in the format chosen by your operating system's regional settings (e.g. dd:mm:yyyy)

- \\$DateLong\\: the current long date in the format chosen by your operating system's regional settings (e.g. dd MMMM yyyy)
- \\$Time\\: the current time in the format hh:mm:ss (24 hour)
- \\$User\\: the username of the person currently logged on to this computer
- \\$FilePath\\: the filename and path of the current score. (This will not work until a score has been saved.)
- \\$FileName\\: the filename of the current score *without* its path. (This will not work until a score has been saved.)
- \\$FileDate\\: the date and time that the score was most recently saved, in the format stipulated by your system's locale (e.g. dd MM yyyy hh:mm:ss)
- \\$PageNum\\: the current page number.

Part name and Instrument changes

In a full score, \\$PartName\\ defaults to "Full Score", while \\$InstrumentChanges\\ provides a list of all the instruments used in the score (it lists the initial instrument of each staff, and all instrument changes that occur on each staff), separated by carriage returns.

In a dynamic part, both \\$PartName\\ and \\$InstrumentChanges\\ provide a list of all the instruments used in the part, separated by carriage returns.

In addition, there are two further equivalent wildcards, \\$HeaderPartName\\ and \\$HeaderInstrumentChanges\\, which separate each instrument name with a comma rather than a carriage return.

So why are there so many nearly identical wildcards?

- Sibelius uses \\$PartName\\ for the instrument name (or names) that appear at the top left-hand corner of the first page of each dynamic part (and the full score, though this text is hidden in the full score by default)
- Sibelius uses \\$HeaderPartName\\ for the instrument name (or names) that appear in the running header on page 2 onwards of each dynamic part (and the full score, though again this text is hidden in the full score by default)
- It is conventional for parts containing doubling instruments that are to be played by a single performer to be given a name like "Reeds 1". To do this, you should set **Part name** in **File ▸ Score Info** for the part in question to "Reeds 1", which will update the text at the top left-hand corner of the first page and in the running header. Sometimes you would also want to show the actual list of instruments used in the part, and this is where \\$InstrumentChanges\\ comes in handy. In the images below, fragments on the left shows what you should type into the text object at the top left-hand corner of the first page; the fragments on the right show what you will see when you finish editing the text. In both cases, you can see what is entered in **File ▸ Score Info**.

In the bottom pair of fragments, notice how the \\$PartName\\ wildcard is bold, and the corresponding "REEDS 1" text is also bold. Read on to find out how you can apply other kinds of formatting to wildcards.

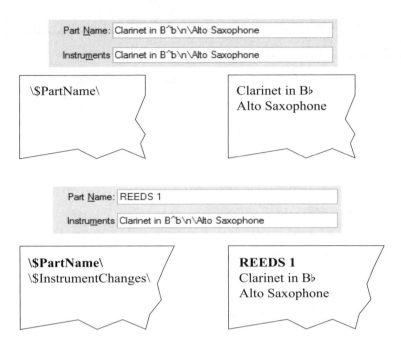

Using wildcards

You can use wildcards in any text object, and any number of wildcards within the same run of text. For example, if you created a text object that read **\$Title\ – Last edited by \$User\ on \$FileDate**, it might evaluate to "Firebird – Last edited by Igor Stravinsky on 16 May 1910 02:15:28."

You can also change the formatting of wildcards; for example, if you have a text object that reads **\$Title\ – \$Composer** and wanted the title of the score to be bold:

* Edit the text (e.g. by hitting **Return**, **F2** or by double-clicking it)
* Select just the **\$Title** wildcard (e.g. using **Shift+←/→**)
* Type **Ctrl+B** *or* **⌘B** (or switch on **B** in the **Text** panel of Properties) to make it bold.

You can use the same procedure to e.g. make a wildcard italic, change its font, make it larger, and so on.

Some further hints for the successful use of wildcards:

* Wildcards themselves are case-insensitive, so **\$TITLE**, **\$title** and **\$Title** are all equivalent. Furthermore, the case of the wildcard itself has no effect on the case of the substituted text.
* However, wildcards never have spaces in them, so if you type **\$Composer Dates** instead of **\$ComposerDates**, the wildcard won't work.
* If you use a wildcard and it evaluates to nothing, e.g. if you type **\$Title** but haven't entered anything into the **Title** field in **File ▸ Score Info**, then when you stop editing the text object, it may disappear altogether. So it's a good idea to make sure that you have provided a value for the wildcard to show before you attempt to use it.

- You shouldn't type the wildcards themselves into dialogs anywhere, e.g. don't type them into any of the fields in File ▸ Score Info. Only type them directly into text objects in the score. This means that you can't, for example, use one wildcard to define another wildcard (though it's a mystery why you should want to do this).

Adding formatting changes to Score Info

Sibelius allows you to add line-breaks and changes of font, character and style at any point within text in the File ▸ Score Info dialog. Most changes of format are simply sandwiched between backslashes – e.g. \n\.

• \B\ – bold on	• \b\ – bold off
• \I\ – italic on	• \i\ – italic off
• \U\ – underline on	• \u\ – underline off
• \n\ – new line	• \f\ – change to the text style's default font

- \f*fontname*\ – change to given font name (e.g. \fArial\ to switch to Arial)
- \s*height*\ – set the font size to *height* x 1/32nd spaces (e.g. \s64\ to set font height to two spaces)
- ^ – use the Music text font (as set in House Style ▸ Edit All Fonts) for the next character.

For example, suppose you were working on an arrangement of a piece by another composer and wanted to include both your names in the Composer field of the Files ▸ Score Info dialog on separate lines. You could enter something like this: J.S. Bach\n\arr. Aran Gerr which, if referred to by the wildcard \$Composer\ in a piece of text in the score, would evaluate to:

"J.S. Bach
arr. Aran Gerr"

3.11 Font equivalents

For advanced users only

If you open a score that uses a font that is not installed on your computer, Sibelius will substitute a similar font instead. This works both for text fonts (e.g. if you don't have Helvetica, Arial is used instead) and music fonts (e.g. if you don't have Petrucci, Opus is used instead).

You can control which fonts are substituted by using the **Font Equivalents** page of the **File ▸ Preferences** dialog (in the **Sibelius** menu on Mac):

Suppose you were given a file by a user that contained the font Didot, which you don't have on your own computer. You could tell Sibelius to replace the font with Palatino Linotype, after which it will always use Palatino Linotype in place of the missing Didot font on any score you might open in the future that includes it. To enter a missing font name and set up equivalents for it:

• Enter the name of the missing font you wish to substitute into the **Font** field on the left, or choose from a list of fonts by clicking the **Choose** button. When you have entered the font's name, click the **Add Font** button. The font will be added to the list of fonts on the left.

• To set a substitute for the font, select the missing font from the list on the left and, into the field labeled **If font is not available, replace it with one of these**, enter the name of the font you wish Sibelius to substitute for it, or use the **Choose** button to select from a list of fonts installed on your computer. When you have entered the name of the substitute font, click the **Add Substitute** button. Sibelius will add the font to the list of substitutes on the right.

• To add additional substitutes for a font, carry out the above step as many times as necessary.

To adjust the precedence of font substitutes, use the **Move Up** and **Move Down** buttons on the right to shift items in the list of font substitutes up and down. Sibelius will always favor the font at the *top* of the list to those lower down; i.e. if the topmost font is installed it will use it, otherwise it will see if the next font in the list is installed and use that, etc.

To remove a font or substitution from either list, select the font you wish to remove and click the appropriate **Remove** button.

You can also use third-party music fonts in Sibelius. For details on how to tell Sibelius about such fonts, see **Using fonts not supplied with Sibelius** in 🕮 **8.11 Music fonts**.

4. Playback & video

4.1 Working with playback

📖 **4.3 Mixer**, **4.8 Live Playback**, **4.4 Sibelius Sounds Essentials**, **4.17 MIDI messages**.

Sibelius will play back your scores beautifully with a minimum of fuss. You don't need to be a MIDI wizard or a sequencer expert to get great playback from Sibelius: it's as simple as hitting play!

This topic introduces various playback features in bite-sized chunks, and tells you which other topics to read for further information.

Playback devices and playback configurations

Sibelius requires one or more *playback devices* to produce sound. A playback device is a software device (e.g. virtual instrument, software synthesizer) or hardware device (e.g. soundcard, external MIDI sound module) that can produce one or more sounds. You may have many different playback devices available on your computer, and you can use them with Sibelius in any combination, which you set up by way of a *playback configuration*.

To find out more about the different types of playback device and how you set up your own playback configurations using **Play ▸ Playback Devices**, 📖 **4.12 Playback Devices**.

Sibelius also comes with its own set of built-in sounds called Sibelius Sounds Essentials. For more details, 📖 **4.4 Sibelius Sounds Essentials**.

Controlling playback

You control playback using the Playback window (shown on the right), or the corresponding commands in the **Play** menu or their keyboard shortcuts. To show the Playback window if it's not already visible, choose **Window ▸ Playback** (shortcut **Ctrl+Alt+Y** *or* ⌥⌘Y).

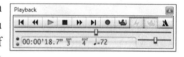

Playback line

The *playback line* is a green line that follows the music during playback, and which shows where Sibelius will play back from when you next start playback. You can control the position of the playback line when not playing back using the Playback window. If you want to hide the playback line when you're not playing back, switch off **View ▸ Playback Line**.

Following the score during playback

Sibelius automatically follows the score during playback, and automatically zooms out, so that you can see the music as it plays. You can navigate around the score during playback just the same as when playback is stopped, including changing the zoom level (and Sibelius will remember your chosen zoom level next time you play back).

You can change this behavior using the options on the **Score Position** page of **File ▸ Preferences** (in the **Sibelius** menu on Mac) – 📖 **5.15 Preferences**.

Playback

Playback during input and editing

Notes play back as you input them, click them and drag them. If you find this annoying, switch off **Play notes as you edit** on the **Note Input** page of **File ▸ Preferences** (in the **Sibelius** menu on Mac).

Choosing sounds

Sibelius automatically chooses the best available sounds for playback from the playback devices you have available, using a unique way of categorising and organising sounds called SoundWorld™ (📖 **4.18 SoundWorld™**).

To change sounds, use the Mixer window, which you can hide or show by choosing **Window ▸ Mixer**, or by typing **Ctrl+Alt+M** *or* **M** (📖 **4.3 Mixer**).

You can also change sounds halfway along a staff using instrument changes (see **Instrument changes** on page 137).

Interpretation of your score

Sibelius is designed to automatically interpret all the notations and markings in your score (📖 **4.2 Interpretation of your score**); normally you don't even need to adjust their effect, but you can if you want to, using **Play ▸ Dictionary** (📖 **4.9 Playback dictionary**).

Sibelius can also produces a remarkably human interpretation of your score using Espressivo™ and Rubato™, which you can control via **Play ▸ Performance** (📖 **4.5 Performance**).

You can even record your own interpretation using Live Tempo (📖 **4.7 Live Tempo**).

All Notes Off

Play ▸ All Notes Off (shortcut **Shift-O**) switches all notes that are currently playing off. This may be necessary:

* If your computer, soundcard or playback device gets overloaded by fast-forwarding or rewinding (which it may do if your device is not very fast or if you're fast-forwarding or rewinding through complex music)
* If you stop playback while the sustain pedal is depressed.

If you hear a note hanging while the score is playing, you can even type **Shift-O** during playback – Sibelius will clear all notes and resume playback.

The most common cause of hanging notes is dangling ties (i.e. a note with a tie not followed by another note of the same pitch). Sibelius includes a plug-in to check your score and eliminate any troublesome dangling ties – see **Remove Dangling Ties** on page 504.

4.2 Interpretation of your score

📖 **2.21 Lines, 2.26 Percussion, 4.6 Repeats, 4.9 Playback dictionary**.

Our philosophy in designing Sibelius's playback features is that you should be able to write a score just as you would on manuscript paper, using normal notation and no special commands, and play it back well without any further setting up.

To achieve this:

* Sibelius chooses the best available sound for each instrument by default
* Whenever you play back a score, Sibelius reads more or less anything you've written in the score, in whatever format you put it. Sibelius even interprets markings such as *ff*, pizz., or *accel.*, and you can change these settings and add your own via Sibelius's built-in playback dictionary.

What Sibelius reads

Almost all of the notation in a score should play back correctly right away. Sibelius interprets the following:

* Notes, chords, rests, accidentals, ties, grace notes
* Clefs, key signatures, time signatures
* Instruments – these determine the sounds used, which you can change if you like
* Standard articulations, e.g. accent, staccato, marcato, etc.
* Tremolos and buzz rolls (z on stem)
* Text specifying dynamics such as *pp*, *sfz*, *loud*
* Tempo marks such as **Allegro**, metronome marks such as ♩ = 108, metric modulations such as ♩ = ♪, and pauses (fermatas)
* Other text, e.g. *con sord.*, *pizz.*, *legato* – 📖 **4.9 Playback dictionary** for full details on playback of text
* Repeats, including 1st and 2nd endings (1st- or 2nd-time bars), repeat barlines, codas, segnos – 📖 **4.6 Repeats**
* Lines such as slurs, trills, octave (*8va*) lines, pedaling, *rit./accel.*, gliss., hairpins
* Guitar tab and notations such as bends and slides
* Special noteheads used for percussion
* Transposing instruments (which always play at their correct sounding pitch)
* Text MIDI messages entered for advanced playback control – 📖 **4.17 MIDI messages**
* Hidden objects, e.g. hidden metronome marks, notes or dynamics, or whole staves – 📖 **3.1 Working with text, 5.9 Hiding objects, 5.8 Focus on Staves**.

Dynamics

Dynamics consist of discrete Expression text instructions like *mf* and hairpins, which are lines that specify a gradual change of dynamic – see **Hairpins** below.

Because staff objects only apply to the instrument and voice(s) they're attached to, it's particularly noticeable in playback if dynamics are attached to the wrong staff, as the instruments will play with incorrect dynamics (▥ **8.7 Attachment**). For instruments with multiple staves, such as keyboard instruments, see **Instruments with multiple staves** below.

To change the staff to which a dynamic is attached, move it over the staff you want it to be attached to so that the gray attachment arrow jumps onto the new staff, and then reposition it to the correct location. (You can only change the attachment of an object in the full score: if you drag an object in a dynamic part, it won't re-attach.)

To change the voice(s) to which a dynamic applies, select it and click the voice buttons at the bottom of the Keypad (shortcut Alt+1/2/3/4 *or* ⌥1/2/3/4 to assign it to another voice; Alt+5 *or* ⌥5 makes the dynamic apply to all voices). If you want to make a dynamic apply to other combinations of voices, click the voice buttons at the bottom of the Keypad window (▥ **1.2 Keypad**).

Dynamics created using Expression text (see **Expression** on page 212) are interpreted according to the appropriate entry in the playback dictionary (▥ **4.9 Playback dictionary**) – e.g. *fff* equates to the maximum dynamic. But this isn't quite the end of the story – the actual playback dynamic of a note also depends on the level of Espressivo and any articulations (such as accents) present.

Hairpins

When you input a hairpin, by default Sibelius automatically works out its end dynamic. If there's an actual dynamic (e.g. *ff*) written at the right-hand end, it uses that; if no dynamic is specified, Sibelius increases or decreases the dynamic by one level (e.g. a crescendo hairpin that starts at a prevailing *mp* will go to *mf*, while a diminuendo hairpin that starts at a prevailing *ff* will go to *f*).

If you want to specify the end dynamic more precisely, either as an explicit dynamic or as a percentage change to the initial dynamic, select the hairpin whose end dynamic you want to change, and open the **Playback** panel of the Properties window (shortcut Ctrl+Alt+P *or* ⌥⌘P). Change the drop-down from auto, which is the default, to choose a new percentage value, and whether that value is a percentage Change from the initial dynamic or a percentage of the Maximum velocity. If you specify a particular final dynamic for a hairpin in Properties, that dynamic will always be used, even if you add, remove or change an Expression text object at the end of the hairpin.

In the real world, different kinds of instruments handle gradual changes of dynamic in different ways. Percussive instruments (such as piano, timpani, harp, etc.) can only change dynamic at the start of a note, while sustaining instruments (such as most wind, brass and string instruments) can change dynamic during the course of a note.

Sibelius will play dynamics as realistically as your playback device will allow. For many playback devices, including the supplied Sibelius Sounds Essentials sample library, Sibelius will play a smooth change of dynamic over the duration of the hairpin, when written for instruments that make a sustaining sound (e.g. wind, brass, strings and singers). Other devices, including most MIDI sound modules and soundcards, are not set up this way, and on those devices, Sibelius can only specify the dynamic at the start of the note, and can't vary the dynamic mid-note.

If Sibelius does not automatically play back hairpins on sustaining instruments on your particular playback device, you can add MIDI messages to change the volume using a plug-in – see **Cresc./Dim. Playback** on page 510.

Like Expression text (see **Dynamics** above), all staff lines, including hairpins, only affect the playback of the instrument and voice(s) to which they are attached.

Trills

By default, trills alternate 12 times per second with an interval of a diatonic step – i.e. either a half-step (semitone) or a whole step (tone), depending on the pitch of the note relative to the current key signature.

To change the playback of an individual trill, select it, then change the controls on the **Playback** panel of the Properties window:

- To specify an interval in half-steps (semitones), switch off **Diatonic**, then set **Half-steps** to the desired interval. (To make a trill do a one-note tremolo in percussion, select the trill and set **Half-steps** to 0.)
- To change the speed of the trill, set **Speed** to the desired number of notes per second
- Switch on **Play straight** if you don't want Sibelius to make tiny variations in the rhythm of the trill. It's a good idea to leave this switched off, as playing the notes "straight" can make the trill sound very mechanical.
- Switch on **Start on upper note** if you want the trill to start on the upper note rather than the lower note.

You can write a small accidental as a symbol above the trill to indicate the interval, but Sibelius won't read it directly.

Other ornaments don't play back automatically, but Sibelius includes a plug-in to play back mordents and turns – see **Ornament Playback** on page 511.

Tempo

To change the tempo of your score, use a piece of Tempo text – such as **Allegro**, **Slow**, **Presto**, and so on – or use a metronome mark – such as ♩ = 120 – which should be written in Metronome mark text. To find out how to type these markings into your score as text, see **Tempo** on page 213 and **Metronome mark** on page 212. To change how fast Sibelius thinks tempo marks like **Allegro** are, ▦ **4.9 Playback dictionary**.

You can also adjust the tempo of your score during playback using the tempo slider in the Playback window, but don't try to use this as the main way of setting the tempo, because the position of the tempo slider won't be remembered next time you open the score.

Metric modulations

Sibelius plays back metric modulations provided they are typed using a system text style (e.g. Tempo or Metronome mark) – see **Metric modulations** on page 213 for details on how to create them.

Sibelius understands complex formats like ♩ = ♩. ♪ etc.; any number of notes (with or without dots) linked with ties or + signs are allowed. The only limitation is that Sibelius relies on the entries in the Play ▸ Dictionary dialog used for playback of regular metronome marks to recognize metric modulations. This means that if you need a metric modulation with a combination of notes with ties or + signs on the *left*-hand side of the = sign, you will need to define new words in the dictionary for each type of metric modulation you want to use (🕮 **4.9 Playback dictionary**).

Rit. and accel.

Sibelius plays *rits.* and *accels.* using special lines (🕮 **2.21 Lines**).

Rit./accel. lines allow you to specify the amount of *rit./accel.* and where the *rit./accel.* ends, namely at the end of the line. The line can be either a visible dashed line or an invisible one which merely tells Sibelius how long to *rit./accel.* for (visible as a continuous gray line when View ▸ **Hidden Objects** is switched on). You can also specify the final tempo of the *rit./accel.* from the **Playback** panel of the Properties window (🕮 **5.17 Properties**):

- **Final tempo**: specified either as an absolute tempo in beats per minute, or a percentage of the initial tempo (by default it is 75% for any *rit.* line, and 133% for any *accel.* line)
- You can also specify how the tempo changes during the *accel.* or *rit.*:
  - **Early**: changes the tempo most rapidly at the start of the line
  - **Late**: changes the tempo most rapidly towards the end of the line
  - **Linear**: changes the tempo at a constant rate along the duration of the line.

If you want to return to the original tempo after an *accel.* or *rit.*, you should write some Tempo text, such as **A tempo** in Tempo text, at this point. However, Sibelius doesn't automatically interpret **A tempo** (because it's often unclear which tempo it should return to), so you will also need to create a hidden metronome mark (see **Metronome mark** on page 212).

You can also adjust the playback of *rit.* and *accel.* instructions by recording a Live Tempo performance – 🕮 **4.7 Live Tempo**.

Fermatas (pauses)

Sibelius plays fermatas (pauses) using articulations added from the fourth (F10) Keypad layout (🕮 **2.3 Articulations**).

When you want to specify a pause, make sure to create a fermata on every staff, particularly if the rhythms differ between staves; Sibelius can only work out how best to play the pause if a fermata is present on all staves that have notes. If a fermata is absent from one or more staves, Sibelius will simply play the rhythm on those staves as written, and then hold the last note that coincides with the fermata(s) on the other staff or staves.

The length of a fermata is determined either by the default setting on the **Articulations** page of Play ▸ Dictionary (🕮 **4.9 Playback dictionary**), or by the settings on the **Playback** panel of Properties, which override the defaults if present. To adjust the playback of an individual pause:

- If each staff has a different rhythm, select the note with a fermata that *ends* last (not the fermata itself) and switch on the **Fermata** checkbox in the **Playback** panel of Properties
- Set **Extend duration** to the desired percentage of the duration of the written note value (e.g. to make a fermata on a whole note (semibreve) last for eight quarter note beats, type **200**)

* If you want the fermata to be followed by a gap before the next note, set **Add gap** to the percentage of the duration of the written note value (e.g. for a one quarter note gap following a fermata on a whole note, type **25**).

You can also adjust the playback of fermatas by recording a Live Tempo performance – 📖 **4.7 Live Tempo**.

Gliss. and port.

Gliss. and *port.* lines (📖 **2.21 Lines**) play back, defaulting to an appropriate kind of glissando for the instrument to which they apply, e.g. passing through chromatic steps for wind instruments, but a continuous slide for strings. If you want to change the way a line plays back, select it and use the **Playback** panel of the Properties window:

* **Glissando type** provides different kinds of glissando. Normally you can leave this set to Instrument default.
* For the **Continuous** glissando type (a smooth slide), the way the gliss. is played is specified as follows:
  ○ **Early**: plays the *gliss.* quickest at the start of the line
  ○ **Late**: plays the *gliss.* quickest towards the end of the line
  ○ **Linear**: plays the *gliss.* at a constant speed from beginning to end.

Harmonics

Although Sibelius does not play back harmonics automatically, you can easily make them play back using the **Playback ▸ Harmonics playback** plug-in (📖 **6.1 Working with plug-ins**), or by using hidden notes and silent noteheads.

Natural harmonics (e.g. on brass instruments) are normally denoted by an "o" symbol above the note. To make the harmonic play back, make the printed pitch use a silent notehead, and add the sounding pitch of the harmonic using a hidden note in another voice – for more details, 📖 **5.9 Hiding objects** and **2.25 Noteheads**

Artificial harmonics (e.g. on stringed instruments) are denoted by a diamond notehead a perfect fourth or fifth above the written pitch. Use a silent notehead for the written pitch, and a diamond notehead for the harmonic. You will probably want to make the diamond notehead silent, too – 📖 **8.16 Edit Noteheads**. As before, add the sounding pitch of the harmonic using a hidden note in another voice.

Pedaling

Pedaling plays back, as long as it's written using lines (not symbols or text). It will apply to both staves of the instrument, provided **Use same slot for all staves of keyboard instruments** is switched on, which it is by default, on the **Playback** page of **File ▸ Preferences** (in the **Sibelius** menu on Mac).

Instruments with multiple staves

If an instrument normally uses two staves, such as a piano or harp, you need only create dynamics attached to the top staff, and they will apply to both staves on playback if they are in between the staves. Beware that this also applies to any instrument you create with two staves (e.g. if you create a flute with two staves, dynamics between the two staves will apply to both).

Playback

In the rare case where you don't want a dynamic to apply to both staves of a keyboard instrument, position it close to one staff, or outside the staves (i.e. above the right-hand staff or below the left-hand staff). If you don't want dynamics to apply to both staves anywhere, switch off the **Affect adjacent staff** option in the **Play ▸ Performance** dialog. In this dialog you can also adjust the threshold for how far away from the staff a dynamic has to be in order for Sibelius to make it apply to the adjacent staff. For more details, ☐ **4.5 Performance**.

Where the number of staves used for an instrument changes, such as where an instrument divides into staves for separate players or later rejoins, you may need to put a hidden dynamic and/or playing technique (e.g. pizz., mute) at the start of the next system to match the dynamic/technique prevailing just before the staves changed. This is because playback effects are tracked along each staff – Sibelius doesn't know if a player moves from one staff to another.

Silent notes and ignoring text/lines

You can make any object (e.g. dynamics, notes) be ignored during playback by switching off all of its **Play on pass** checkboxes on the **Playback** panel of the Properties window – ☐ **4.6 Repeats**.

Alternatively, you can prevent particular noteheads playing by using the silent notehead type (shortcut **Shift+Alt+9** *or* ⇧⌥9) – ☐ **2.25 Noteheads**.

You can also specify that all text in a certain text style should have no effect on playback by switching off the **Interpret during playback** option on the **General** page of **Edit Text Style** – ☐ **3.9 Edit Text Styles**.

4.3 Mixer

Sibelius's Mixer window allows you to modify sounds for playback, including volume and pan, and adjust settings in the virtual instruments and effects used in your current playback configuration.

To show or hide the Mixer, choose **Window ▸ Mixer**, or use shortcut **Ctrl+Alt+M** (Windows) *or* **M** (Mac), or click the toolbar button shown on the right. The Mixer window has several sections, as follows:

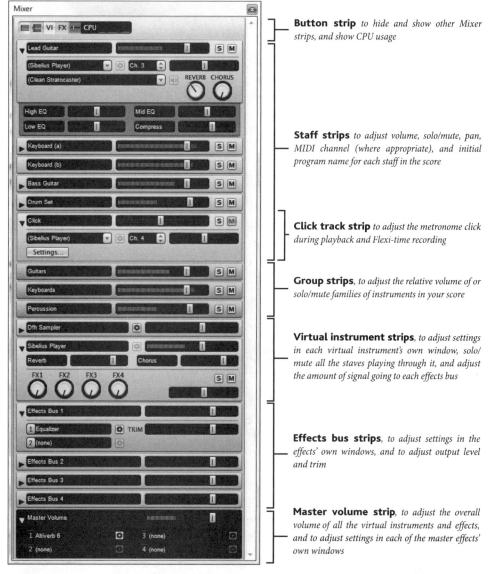

Button strip *to hide and show other Mixer strips, and show CPU usage*

Staff strips *to adjust volume, solo/mute, pan, MIDI channel (where appropriate), and initial program name for each staff in the score*

Click track strip *to adjust the metronome click during playback and Flexi-time recording*

Group strips, *to adjust the relative volume of or solo/mute families of instruments in your score*

Virtual instrument strips, *to adjust settings in each virtual instrument's own window, solo/ mute all the staves playing through it, and adjust the amount of signal going to each effects bus*

Effects bus strips, *to adjust settings in the effects' own windows, and to adjust output level and trim*

Master volume strip, *to adjust the overall volume of all the virtual instruments and effects, and to adjust settings in each of the master effects' own windows*

Though the Mixer's width is fixed, you can change its height by dragging its bottom edge (Windows) or bottom right-hand corner (Mac), and you can hide and show each type of strip individually using the buttons on the button strip, so it doesn't have to be as tall as shown here.

Button strip

The button strip at the top of the Mixer allows you to hide and show each of the other types of strip:

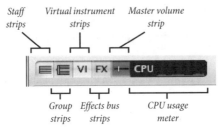

By default, only the staff and master volume strips are shown when you first open the Mixer. The buttons for virtual instruments strips and effects bus strips are disabled if your current playback configuration doesn't use any virtual instruments or effects.

The CPU usage meter in the button strip gives you an indication of the processor usage of the audio system, i.e. all the virtual instruments and effects in your current playback configuration (but not overall processor usage of your whole computer). If this meter goes into the red during playback, it means that it is taking your computer longer to render the required audio than it is taking to play it, which means it is likely you will hear glitches or stuttering during playback.

If this happens, you can always export an audio file of your score, which will play back without glitches (📖 **9.10 Exporting audio files**), but to reduce glitches during playback, see **How to get the best out of virtual instruments and effects** on page 343.

Staff strips

Each staff in your score has its own staff strip:

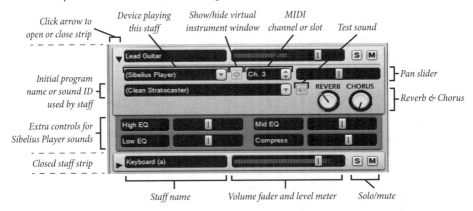

You can open or close each staff strip by clicking the arrow at the left-hand side of the strip. To open or close all staff strips, hold down **Shift** and click the arrow; to open or close all Mixer strips of all kinds, hold down **Ctrl** *or* ⌘ and click an arrow at the left-hand side of any strip.

The controls in each staff strip work as follows:

- The staff name read-out shows you the name of the staff, as it appears in **Create ▸ Instruments**; this isn't editable. If you want to edit the instrument name, 📖 **3.8 Instrument names**.

- To adjust the volume, simply drag the fader left (to reduce it) or right (to increase it). The fader has a "sticky" position at the default volume (100, out of 127), and you can also reset it to its default volume by double-clicking the fader. During playback, the fader background lights up to show you the level of playback on that staff. This allows you to correct the relative balance of staves without having to write louder dynamics for loud instruments and softer ones for soft instruments. Most devices play all instruments at roughly the same volume by default, so you should give (say) a complete Violin I section a volume somewhat higher than a solo flute.

- To hear just one staff, click the solo button (**S**). The mute buttons for all staves are then disabled (so they look like this: **M**). You can solo other staves simultaneously by clicking their solo buttons. When you switch all the solo buttons off again, the mute buttons are re-enabled. See **Mute and solo** on page 274.

- To mute a staff, click the mute button (**M**). Click once to set the staff to be half-muted (**M**) and click twice to set it to be fully muted (**M**). A third click makes it unmuted again. See **Mute and solo** on page 274.

- To adjust the pan position of the staff – that is, its stereo position from left to right – first open the strip by clicking the disclosure arrow, then simply drag the pan slider left or right. The slider has a "sticky" position in the middle. It sounds best if you don't position staves too far to the left or right.

  Beware that some virtual instruments (e.g. Vienna Symphonic Library Vienna Instruments) don't respond to this pan slider, so if you are using such a virtual instrument, you'll hear no effect when changing pan here. You can change the pan of the audio output of that virtual instrument instead – see **Virtual instrument strips** on page 272.

- The device menu allows you to change the device used to play the initial sound on a given staff, but it is recommended that you don't change this here: instead, use the **Preferred Sounds** page of **Play ▸ Playback Devices** to tell Sibelius you would prefer it to use another device instead, as this choice will be saved in your playback configuration and therefore apply to all scores – see **Preferred Sounds page** on page 329.

  If you do decide to change the device used to play back a staff, notice that the menu contains a list of all the devices in your playback configuration, and an extra entry (**Auto**) at the top of the list. If you want to tell Sibelius to choose the device automatically again, choose (**Auto**).

  Once you explicitly choose a device for a given staff, the name of the device no longer appears in parentheses, and the menu of sound IDs or program names below will only show you those sounds provided by the specific device you have chosen.

  You can change the device for all staves by holding down **Shift** when you choose a device from the device menu; normally you should only choose (**Auto**) when you do this, which resets all staves back to automatic device allocation.

- The button to the right of the device menu (⚙) is only enabled if the device currently being used for this staff is a virtual instrument; clicking it shows the virtual instrument's window. Click this button again to hide the window.

- The MIDI channel or slot control shows a read-out of the channel being used for this staff, but you won't normally be able to edit it. You don't need to change this anyway, because Sibelius intelligently works out which channel or slot to use for each staff. You can only change the MIDI channel used by a staff if you have chosen a specific device for that staff, and if that device is using a manual sound set (see **Manual Sound Sets page** on page 326).

• The sound read-out shows you the program name or sound ID used by the staff at the start of the score. If the staff contains any objects that change the playback sound after the first bar – e.g. instrument changes, text instructions for playing techniques, etc. – this read-out doesn't update. Hold your mouse pointer over the read-out to see a tooltip that shows the sound ID and program that Sibelius is actually using for this staff.

By default, this read-out shows the program name used by the staff. If you would prefer to see the sound ID instead whenever possible (for more information about sound IDs, ☐ **4.18 SoundWorld™**), change the Display option on the Playback page of File ▸ Preferences (in the Sibelius menu on Mac) – see **Playback preferences** on page 333.

Notice that, by default, the sound name is displayed in parentheses: this denotes that the choice of sound is automatically determined by Sibelius. Once you choose a specific program name or sound ID from the menu, the sound name is displayed without parentheses.

To change the initial sound of a staff, click the arrow to open the sound menu:

　◦ If program names are displayed, you will see a hierarchical menu. If no specific device is chosen for the staff, the first level of the menu shows the names of the sound sets in your current configuration, and the second level then displays the names of the groups into which the program names are divided (e.g. **Strings, Woodwind**, etc.); the third level displays the instrument families (e.g. **Violin, Flutes**, etc.); finally, the fourth level shows the program names themselves. When you choose a specific program, Sibelius will also set that staff to always play back through the device on which that program is available.

　◦ If sound IDs are displayed, you will see a different hierarchical menu, listing all of the sound IDs in the S3W and any additional sound IDs provided by the devices in your current play-back configuration. If a specific device has already been chosen for the staff, then the menu includes only those sound IDs provided by the sound set used by that device.

As with the device menu, you can reset a staff to choose sounds automatically once more by choosing **(Auto)** from the menu. You can reset all staves to automatic sound allocation by holding **Shift** and choosing **(Auto)** from the menu.

You can also change the sounds used for different instruments in your score by editing the instrument definition itself in House Style ▸ Edit Instruments; this approach is recommended if you want to adjust the sound of (say) several identical instruments in your score in one place, or if you want to export this setting so that you can import it into another score via a house style (☐ **8.14 Edit Instruments**).

• The button to the right of the sound menu (🔊) allows you to test the current sound choice for that staff.

• If the staff is playing back using the built-in Sibelius Player, up to six additional faders may appear, depending on the sound. These faders allow you to adjust subtle aspects of the sound, such as intonation, timbre, distortion (for guitars), tremolo speed (for vibes and electric keyboards), and so on. To reset one of these additional faders to its default value, simply double-click it. These six faders respond to MIDI controllers 91, 93, 74, 71, 73 and 72 respectively.

During playback, you can only adjust the volume (including solo and mute), pan and extra Sibelius Player sound controls (if they appear) for each staff; in order to change any of the other settings the score must not be playing back.

Click track strip

The click track strip is always found at the bottom of the staff strips:

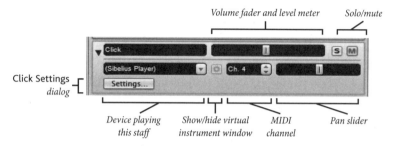

The click track strip is very similar to the other staff strips, except that instead of choosing an initial sound ID, you can click **Settings** to show the **Click Settings** dialog, as shown on the right.

- **Subdivide beats** is useful in some time signatures such as 6/8, where it will click lightly on every eighth note (quaver)

- **Stress irregular beat groups** accents beats in the bar depending on the beat groups defined for irregular time signatures such as 7/8 (☐ **2.33 Time signatures**).

- You can also choose the percussion sounds used by the click track on the first beat of the bar and subsequent beats, either by sound ID or program name, depending on your choice on the **Playback** page of **File ▸ Preferences** (in the **Sibelius** menu on Mac).

In addition to the solo and mute button on the click track strip itself, you can also mute and unmute the click track staff by clicking the **Click When Playing** button in the Playback window.

Group strips

Group strips allow you to adjust the relative volume and pan of each family of instruments used in the score. This makes it very convenient to e.g. boost the volume of the strings relative to the volume of the woodwinds, and so on. The controls in group strips are as follows:

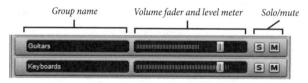

- At the left of the strip is a read-out of the group name. Sibelius determines which staves will be included in each group, and you can't edit the name of the groups.

Playback

- To adjust the volume of all the staves in the group, simply drag the fader left or right (as for **Staff strips** above). Sibelius maintains the relative balance of all the instruments in the group as you adjust the volume.
- To solo all the staves in a group, click the solo button (as for **Staff strips** above).
- To mute or half-mute all the staves in a group, click the mute button (as for **Staff strips** above).

If you have staff strips visible while you work with the group strip, you will see that changes made in the group strip are reflected in each staff strip.

Virtual instrument strips

Each virtual instrument in your playback configuration has its own strip:

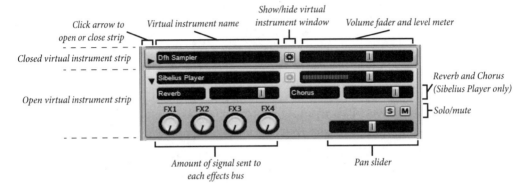

- A read-out of the name of the virtual instrument is shown at the left-hand side.
- To show a virtual instrument's window in order to adjust its settings, click ⚙. Click it again to hide the window. If you make any changes in the virtual instrument's window that you want to have remembered next time you use Sibelius, remember to save your playback configuration in Play ▸ Playback Devices (see **Editing a playback configuration** on page 325).
- You can adjust the output level of each virtual instrument by dragging its volume fader.
- Sibelius Player has built-in reverb and chorus effects, and the return levels of these effects can be adjusted using the **Reverb** and **Chorus** faders that appear in Sibelius Player's own virtual instrument strip.
- To solo or mute all the staves being played by a virtual instrument, click the solo or mute button in the virtual instrument strip. The solo and mute buttons in the affected staff strips reflect the changes made in the virtual instrument strip.
- The four knobs allow you to determine how much signal should be sent from this virtual instrument to each of the four effects buses. Simply drag around in a circle to increase or decrease the amount sent to each bus. The knob marked **FX1** sends to Effects Bus 1, **FX2** to Effects Bus 2, and so on. What this means is that you can send the output from different virtual instruments to different effects buses. If you want the same effect to be applied to all virtual instruments, use the master insert effects instead (see **Master volume strip** below).
- Some virtual instruments (e.g. Vienna Symphonic Library Vienna Instruments) do not respond to MIDI pan messages, so in order to pan them to the left or right, you can adjust the pan slider in the virtual instrument strip instead. For other virtual instruments this is unnecessary.

Effects bus strips

Sibelius provides four effects buses, each of which is able to load up to two effects, which you specify on the Effects page of Play ▸ Playback Devices – see **Effects page** on page 330. Each bus has its own strip:

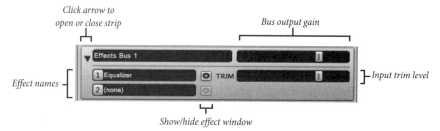

Click arrow to open or close strip

Bus output gain

Effect names

Input trim level

Show/hide effect window

In its closed state, the strip shows a read-out of the name of the bus and a fader to adjust the gain of the bus's output going into the mix.

If you open the strip by clicking the arrow, you will see an extra fader labeled TRIM. This adjusts the input levels going into the effects bus. You won't normally need to adjust this, as nearly every effect has its own gain control in its own window, but this is provided for the benefit of those effects that do not have such a control.

At the left of the open strip is a read-out of each of the effects in the bus. To show an effect's window in order to adjust its settings, click ⚙. Click it again to hide the window. If you make any changes in the effect's window that you want to be remembered next time you use Sibelius, don't forget to save your playback configuration in Play ▸ Playback Devices (see **Editing a playback configuration** on page 325).

Master volume strip

At the very bottom of the Mixer window is the master volume strip, which allows you to adjust the volume of all the virtual instruments and effects from a single fader, and to make changes to the master insert effects, which also apply to the output of all the virtual instruments and effects you are using:

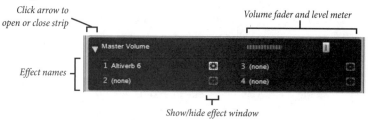

Click arrow to open or close strip

Volume fader and level meter

Effect names

Show/hide effect window

When the master volume strip is closed, the only control is the volume fader. During playback, the fader background lights up to show you the output level. Note that this fader only affects virtual instruments, so if any of the staves in your score are playing back through your soundcard's built-in synthesizer or an external MIDI device, this fader will have no effect on their volume.

If you open the strip by clicking its arrow, you can show the window of each of the four master insert effects by clicking 🔧. For information about master insert effects, see **Effects page** on page 330.

Mute and solo

For the purposes of trying out individual instruments or groups of instruments, any staff can play back at full volume, at half volume or be completely muted (silent). Simply click the mute button (Ⓜ) for the staff in question to cycle through the different mute settings.

A good use of this is to produce "music minus one" recordings: putting one instrument into the background helps people learn their part from memory. Making a solo instrument totally silent is useful for practicing your own part while Sibelius plays the accompaniment, or for playing back music written for bagpipe or accordion.

You can solo a particular staff (muting all the other staves) by clicking the solo button (Ⓢ). You can add further staves by clicking their solo buttons.

To play back just some of the instruments in the score, you can alternatively select the required instruments as a passage before you play (📖 **1.9 Selections and passages**). If you play back a selection of staves in your score, the mute setting of those staves is ignored – so if you're working on a string quartet score and mute the violin staff, but then select, say, that violin staff and a cello staff to play them both back, they will both sound. Sibelius assumes that if you specifically select a staff to play it back, you actually want to hear it, even if it's muted.

Controlling the Mixer using an input device

If you have an external MIDI input device, such as a dedicated control surface or controller keyboard with extra faders, knobs or other controls, you can use your device to control the Mixer directly. For more information, see **Input maps** on page 60.

SoundStage

Given that you have only two ears (probably), your brain works wonders at conjuring up a three-dimensional image from just two sound sources. So the fact that your playback device can only play back in stereo is hardly a restriction, as long as you can recreate the sounds that would go into your ears if live players were really in front of you. The three-dimensional impression created by well-prepared stereo sound is sometimes called a "soundstage" – and Sibelius's SoundStage feature recreates this automatically.

Imagine you want to recreate the soundstage you'd hear when in the audience of a concert hall, with an orchestra playing on the stage. A number of factors come into play:

- Each instrument is at a slightly different distance from you, and different parts have varying numbers of players. This affects the relative volume of the instruments.
- Each instrument is at a slightly different left-to-right position relative to you.
- The acoustics of the building generate reverb, from which you can hear not only the size but also the shape of the building.
- Instruments that are closer to you produce less reverb than others. This is because more of their sound travels directly to your ears rather than bouncing off the walls. (You can probably imagine

this if you mentally compare the "dead" sound of someone speaking on a normal telephone with the rather more echoey sound of a speaker-phone.)

• An instrument that is a long way off, such as an off-stage trumpet, sounds very reverberant because none of its sound travels directly to your ears; conversely, however, the instrument sounds soft, so its volume is low.

You don't need to switch SoundStage on or off – it's always on. Whenever you create instruments, Sibelius automatically positions them in 3D space for you as they would be on a concert stage – not only in stereo (i.e. with suitable pan positions), but also with subtle adjustments to the volume settings to imitate how far or near instruments are.

Sibelius's SoundStage setting covers standard layouts for orchestra, brass band, choir and string ensemble – and work well for just about any other combination, in fact.

Improving playback with lots of instruments

Playback may produce an organ-like effect with large numbers of instruments. This is a pain as it's a giveaway that the sound is not a real recording.

There are four main causes of this problem, which are fairly easy to avoid:

• *Incorrect balance.* For instance, if you set all the volumes in an orchestral score to maximum, you may find that some instruments are too loud and others are swamped.

• *Not enough expression.* Try setting the Espressivo option in the Play ▸ Performance dialog to Espressivo or Molto espressivo. This will introduce gradations of volume that will help separate the different lines of music, even in a large score. In general, the more instruments that are playing, the more Espressivo you should add (📖 **4.5 Performance**).

• *Phasing* – an annoying "badly-tuned-radio" sound caused by two identical instruments playing the same sound in unison. If two staves in your score often double one another, such as Violins 1 and 2, use the Play on pass checkboxes on Properties (📖 **5.17 Properties**) to silence one of the staves while they are doubled. This should produce a significant improvement.

• *Not enough different pan positions.* The ear will find it hard to separate the different instrumental sounds. Change the pan positions accordingly.

4.4 Sibelius Sounds Essentials

📖 **4.1 Working with playback**, **4.3 Mixer**, **4.5 Performance**, **9.10 Exporting audio files**.

Sibelius comes with Sibelius Sounds Essentials, a high-quality sound library consisting of carefully chosen instruments from the award-winning Garritan Personal Orchestra, Garritan Concert & Marching Band and Garritan Jazz and Big Band, and Tapspace's Virtual Drumline. The result is a versatile collection of sounds well-suited for every genre of music.

You can add further sound libraries for use with Sibelius, including the full versions of all of the sound libraries from which the sounds in Sibelius Sounds Essentials are taken. Choose **Help ▸ Sibelius Sounds** to be taken to our web site for more information.

Sibelius Sounds Essentials plays back through the built-in Sibelius Player, a sample player virtual instrument, based on the technology behind the Structure sampler for Pro Tools, developed by Digidesign's world-beating Advanced Instrument Research group.

Computer requirements

Be aware that sound libraries can take up a large amount of hard disk space, so ensure that you have plenty available, and that loading many sounds simultaneously requires more RAM. See **How to get the best out of virtual instruments and effects** on page 343 for advice applicable both to Sibelius Player and other virtual instruments.

Setting up Sibelius Sounds Essentials

Sibelius is set to play back through Sibelius Sounds Essentials by default, but if you switch to another set of playback devices you may need to switch back to Sibelius Sounds Essentials, as follows:

- Choose **Play ▸ Playback Devices**
- From the **Configuration** menu at the top of the dialog, choose **Sibelius Sounds**.
- You will see **Sibelius Player** in the **Active devices** list on the right-hand side of the **Active Devices** page of the dialog. **Sound set** will be set to **Essentials**.
- Click **Close**.

As soon as you open a score, Sibelius automatically loads the necessary sounds in the background. Depending on the number of instruments in your score, this takes anywhere from a few seconds to half a minute or so, during which time you can input and edit in your score as normal. If you try to start playback before all of the sounds have been loaded, you will see a progress bar while the remaining sounds are loaded, and playback will then begin.

How Sibelius Player works

Sibelius Player can play up to 128 different sounds at once, though the maximum number depends on the available resources of your computer. For example, if your computer has less than 1GB RAM, Sibelius will limit the number of available channels to 32; if your computer has 2GB RAM,

Sibelius will allow 64 channels; if you have more than 2GB RAM, Sibelius will allow 128 channels. You can adjust this limit if you like on the **Playback** page of **File ▸ Preferences** (in the **Sibelius** page on Mac), though if you increase the maximum number, beware that your computer may not be able to handle all the sounds, resulting in stuttering playback and considerably slower performance for Sibelius and your computer as a whole.

Normally the number of available channels will exceed the number of sounds required by all but the largest of scores, but it's nevertheless worth understanding how Sibelius allocates sounds to channels.

A staff in your score may potentially use more than one sound due to things like instrument changes (e.g. if a staff starts out as a clarinet, but later changes to a saxophone sound) or changes in playing technique (e.g. if a violin staff starts arco but later plays pizzicato), which may increase the total number of sounds used in your score above the number of available channels, depending on whether or not Sibelius can play the sounds using the same channel.

Sounds can share a channel if they are accessed by a *switch*, meaning that Sibelius can either play a specific note to trigger a change in sound (known as a *keyswitch*) or set a MIDI controller to a specific value, or play a note at a certain velocity, and so on. Several of the sounds in Sibelius Sounds Essentials work this way: for example, the violins from Garritan Personal Orchestra can switch between arco, pizzicato and unmeasured tremolo by way of keyswitches, and the trumpet from Garritan Jazz and Big Band can switch between normal and muted playing in the same way.

If you need to change to a completely different sound – e.g. from clarinet to saxophone – this normally requires an extra channel.

What this means in practice is that, if your score uses more sounds that each require a separate channel than the maximum number of available channels, Sibelius will make some compromise decisions for you about how best to play it back. For staves that are in the same instrumental family (e.g. woodwind, brass, strings) it will double up staves onto the same slot so that they all use the same sound – so you may end up with clarinets, oboes and bassoons all playing back with (say) a bassoon sound.

Included sounds

The sounds included with Sibelius Sounds Essentials are as follows:

Name	Techniques/instruments	Range
From Garritan Personal Orchestra		
Piccolo Lite	*Params:* Intonation, Timbre	D5 to C8
Flute Solo Lite	*Params:* Intonation, Timbre	B3 to A7
Flute Solo 2 Lite	*Params:* Intonation, Timbre	G3 to A7
Oboe Solo	*Params:* Intonation, Timbre	B♭3 to A6
Oboe Solo 2	*Params:* Intonation, Timbre	B♭3 to A6
English Horn Solo	*Params:* Intonation, Timbre	E3 to C6
B♭ Clarinet Solo	*Params:* Intonation, Timbre	G2 to C7
B♭ Clarinet Solo 2	*Params:* Intonation, Timbre	G2 to C7
Bass Clarinet Solo	*Params:* Intonation, Timbre	B♭1 to F5
Bassoon Solo	*Params:* Intonation, Timbre	B0 to E5
Bassoon Solo 2	*Params:* Intonation, Timbre	B♭1 to E5

Playback

Name	Techniques/instruments	Range
Contrabassoon Solo	*Params:* Intonation, Timbre	A0 to F3
French Horn	*Params:* Intonation, Timbre *Keyswitches:* open (C0); mute (D0)	E1 to F5
French Horn 2	*Params:* Intonation, Timbre	E1 to F5
Trumpet Solo	*Params:* Intonation, Timbre *Keyswitches:* open (C0); mute (D0)	C3 to F6
Trumpet Solo 2	*Params:* Intonation, Timbre	E3 to F6
Tenor Trombone Solo	*Params:* Intonation, Timbre *Keyswitches:* open (C0); mute (D0)	E1 to F5
Tuba Solo	*Params:* Intonation, Timbre	B♭0 to B4
Concert Piano Lite		A0 to C8
Hauptwek All Stops		C2 to G6
Harp Lite		C1 to G7
Basic Orchestral Percussion	*Sounds:* Bass drum hit (B1); Bass drum hit 2 (C2), Bass drum roll (C#2); Timpani hit (D2–G3); Side drum hit, snares off, left (G#3); Side drum hit, snares off, right (A3); Side drum hit, snares off, roll (A#3); Side drum hit, snares on, left (B3); Side drum hit, snares on, right (C4); Side drum hit, snares on, roll (C#4)	
Violin Solo Lite	*Params:* Intonation, Timbre *Keyswitches:* arco (C–1); pizzicato (F–1), tremolo (G–1)	G3 to C8
Violin Solo 2 Lite	*Params:* Intonation, Timbre	G3 to C8
Violin Ensemble Lite	*Params:* Intonation, Timbre *Keyswitches:* arco (C–1); pizzicato (F–1), tremolo (G–1)	G3 to A8
Viola Solo Lite	*Params:* Intonation, Timbre *Keyswitches:* arco (C–1); pizzicato (F–1), tremolo (G–1)	C3 to C7
Viola Solo 2 Lite	*Params:* Intonation, Timbre	C3 to C7
Viola Ensemble Lite	*Params:* Intonation, Timbre *Keyswitches:* arco (C–1); pizzicato (F–1), tremolo (G–1)	C3 to A6
Cello Solo Lite	*Params:* Intonation, Timbre *Keyswitches:* arco (C–1); pizzicato (F–1), tremolo (G–1)	C2 to E6
Cello Solo 2 Lite	*Params:* Intonation, Timbre	C2 to E6
Cello Ensemble Lite	*Params:* Intonation, Timbre *Keyswitches:* arco (C–1); pizzicato (F–1), tremolo (G–1)	C2 to E6
Double Bass Solo Lite	*Params:* Intonation, Timbre *Keyswitches:* arco (C–1); pizzicato (F–1), tremolo (G–1)	C0 to C5
Double Bass Solo 2 Lite	*Params:* Intonation, Timbre	C0 to C5
Double Bass Ensemble Lite	*Params:* Intonation, Timbre *Keyswitches:* arco (C–1); pizzicato (F–1), tremolo (G–1)	C0 to G4
Full String Ensemble Lite	*Params:* Intonation, Timbre *Keyswitches:* arco (C–1); pizzicato (F–1), tremolo (G–1)	C1 to D7

From Garritan Jazz and Big Band

Name	Techniques/instruments	Range
Alto Saxophone	*Params:* Intonation, Timbre	C#3 to F6
Tenor Saxophone	*Params:* Intonation, Timbre	G#2 to C6
Baritone Saxophone	*Params:* Intonation, Timbre	C2 to C6
Jazz Trumpet	*Params:* Intonation, Timbre *Keyswitches:* open (C1); straight mute (D1); harmon mute (F1)	E3 to B♭6

Name	Techniques/instruments	Range
Jazz Trombone	*Params:* Intonation, Timbre *Keyswitches:* open (C0); straight mute (D0); harmon mute (F0)	B♭0 to C6
Brush Drum Kit Lite	*Sounds:* High Q (D♯1), Slap (E1), Scratch Push (F1), Scratch Pull (F♯1), Sticks (G1), Square Click (G♯1), Metronome Click (A1), Metronome Bell (A♯1), Loose Kick (B1), Tight Kick (C2), Side Stick (C♯2), Long snare swirl (D2), Claps (D♯2), Rim Shot with brushes (E2), Short snare swirl (E2), Snares on with brushes (E2), Low Floor Tom (F2), Hi-Hat Closed (F♯2), High Floor Tom (G2), Hi-Hat Pedal (G♯2), Low Rack Tom (A2), Hi-Hat Open (A♯2), Mid Rack Tom (B2), High Mid-Rack Tom (C3), Medium Crash (C♯3), Hi Tom (D3), Medium Ride (D♯3), Sizzle Cymbal (E3), Ride bell with brush (F3), Ride bell with handle (F♯3), Ride bell (G3), Cowbell (G♯3), High Crash (A3), Vibraslap (A♯3), High Ride (B3), High Bongo (C4), Low Bongo (C♯4), Muffled Slap (D4), Conga (D♯4), Tumba (E4), High Timbale (F4), Low Timbale (F♯4), High Agogo (G4), Low Agogo (G♯4), Cabasa (A4), Maracas (A♯4), Low Whistle (B4), High Whistle (C5), Short Guiro (C♯5), Low Guiro (D5), Claves (D♯5), High Woodblock (E5), Low Woodblock (F5), High Cuica (F♯5), Low Cuica (G5), Mute Triangle (G♯5), Open Triangle (A5), Shaker (A♯5), Jingle Bell (B5), Bell Tree (C6), Castanets (C♯6), Mute Surdo (D6), Open Surdo (D♯6), Ride bell (E6)	
Latin Percussion Lite	*Sounds:* Bata Low Open (C2), Bata Low Muff (C♯2), Bata Low Slap (D2), Bata Mid Open (E♭2), Bata Mid Muff (E2), Bata Mid Slap (F2), Bata High Open (F♯2), Bata High Muff (G2), Bata High Slap (A♭2), Bongo Low Open (A2), Bongo Low Muff (B♭2), Bongo Low Slap (B2), Bongo High Open (C3), Bongo High Muff (C♯3), Bongo High Slap (D3), Cajone Low (E♭3), Cajone Slap (E3), Cajone Stick Hit (F3), Conga Low (F♯3), Conga Open (G3), Conga Muff (A♭3), Conga Slap (A3), Djembe Open (B♭3), Djembe Muff (B3), Djembe Slap (C4), Quinto Open (C♯4), Quinto Muff (D4), Quinto Slap (E♭4), Super Tumba Low (E4), Super Tumba Open (F4), Super Tumba Muff (F♯4), Super Tumba Slap (G4), Surdo Open (A♭4), Surdu Muff (A4), Timbales Low (B♭4), Timbales High (B4), Timbales Edge (C5), Tumba Low (C♯5), Tumba Muff (D5), Tumba Open (E♭5), Tumba Slap (E5), Udu Long (F5), Udu Short (F♯5), Cabasa Short (G5), Cabasa Long (A♭5), Cabasa Snap (A5), Maracas 1 Short (B♭5), Maracas 1 Long (B5), Maracas 2 Short (C6), Maracas 2 Long (C♯6), Shaker Short 1 (D6), Shaker Short 2 (E♭6), Egg (E6), Egg 1 (F6), Egg 2 (F♯6), Egg Shake (G6), Shekere Low (A♭6), Shekere High (A6), Shekere Short 1 (B♭6), Shekere Short 2 (B6)	

From Garritan Concert & Marching Band

Name	Techniques/instruments	Range
Trumpet Ensemble Lite	*Params:* Intonation, Timbre	E3 to B♭6
Mellophone Ensemble Lite	*Params:* Intonation, Timbre	B♭1 to F5
Euphonium Ensemble Lite	*Params:* Intonation, Timbre	E1 to F5
Baritone Ensemble Lite	*Params:* Intonation, Timbre	E2 to F5
Sousaphone Ensemble Lite	*Params:* Intonation, Timbre	B♭0 to F4
Tuba Ensemble Lite	*Params:* Intonation, Timbre	B♭1 to F4
Trombone Ensemble Lite	*Params:* Intonation, Timbre	E1 to F5

From Sibelius Sounds Choral (sounds from Garritan)

Name	Techniques/instruments	Range
Sopranos 1 Ahs Lite	*Params:* Intonation, Timbre	G3 to C6
Altos 1 Ahs Lite	*Params:* Intonation, Timbre	E3 to G5
Tenors 1 Ahs Lite	*Params:* Intonation, Timbre	G2 to C5
Basses 1 Ahs Lite	*Params:* Intonation, Timbre	C2 to G4

Playback

Name	Techniques/instruments	Range
From Garritan World Music		
Ewe Drum Ensemble	*Sounds are on white notes only*	C2 to B4
Djembe Ensemble	*Sounds are on white notes only*	C3 to C4
Taiko Drums		
From Tapspace Virtual Drumline		
Marching Snares (Manual)	*All with snares on:* sustained roll (E6); RH hits (G♯5); LH hits (F♯5); RH shots (G5); LH shots (F5); RH rims (E♭5); LH rims (D♭5); ride cymbal (E3); bell of ride cymbal (D3); cymbal crash (C3)	
Marching Snares (Auto RL)	*All with snares on, automatic RL switching:* sustained roll (B5); rim shots (C5); main hits (B4); rims (A4); ride cymbal (E3); bell of ride cymbal (D3); cymbal crash (C3)	
Marching Tenor Drums (Manual)	*Sounds:* Spock 1 RH Hits (E5); Spock 1 LH Hits (E♭5); Spock 2 RH Hits (D5); Spock 2 LH Hits (D♭5); Drum 1 RH Hits (C5); Drum 1 LH Hits (B4); Drum 2 RH Hits (B♭4); Drum 2 LH Hits (A4); Drum 3 RH Hits (A♭4); Drum 3 LH Hits (G4); Drum 4 RH Hits (F♯4); Drum 4 LH Hits (F4); Sustained buzz roll spock 1 (B♭3); Sustained buzz roll spock 2 (A3); Sustained buzz roll drum 1 (A♭3); Sustained buzz roll drum 2 (G3); Sustained buzz roll drum 3 (F♯3); Sustained buzz roll drum 4 (F3); Spock 1 RH shot/rim (E3); Spock 1 LH shot/rim (E♭3); Spock 2 RH shot/rim (D3); Spock 2 LH shot/rim (D♭3); Drum 1 RH shot/rim (C3); Drum 1 LH shot/rim (B2); Drum 2 LH shot/rim (B♭2); Drum 2 RH shot/rim (A2); Drum 3 RH shot/rim (A♭2); Drum 3 LH shot/rim (G2); Drum 4 RH shot/rim (F♯2); Drum 4 LH shot/rim (F2)	
Marching Tenor Drums (Auto RL)	*Automatic RL switching:* Spock 2 shots/rims (D♭6); Spock 2 hits (B5); Spock 1 shots/rims (A♭5); Spock 1 hits (G5); Drum 1 shots/rims (G♭5); Drum 1 hits (E5); Drum 2 shots/rims (D♭5); Drum 2 hits (C5); Drum 3 shots/rims (B♭4); Drum 3 hits (A4); Drum 4 shots/rims (F♯4); Drum 4 hits (F4); Roll Spock 2 sustained buzz (A3); Roll Spock 1 sustained buzz (F3); Roll Drum 1 sustained buzz (D3); Roll Drum 2 sustained buzz (B2); Roll Drum 3 sustained buzz (G2); Roll Drum 4 sustained buzz (E2)	
Marching Bass Drums (Manual)	*Sounds:* Drum 1 RH hits (E5); Drum 1 LH hits (E♭5); Drum 2 RH hits (D5); Drum 2 LH hits (C♯5); Drum 3 RH hits (C5); Drum 3 LH hits (B4); Drum 4 RH hits (B♭4); Drum 4 LH hits (A4); Drum 5 RH hits (A♭4); Drum 5 LH hits (A4); Drum 5 RH hits (A♭4); Drum 5 LH hits (G4); Drum 6 RH hits (F♯4); Drum 6 LH hits (F4); Unison RH hits (E4); Unison LH hits (E♭4); Unison RH rims (D4); Unison LH rims (C♯4); Unison sustained roll (A♭3)	
Marching Bass Drums (Auto RL)	*Automatic RL switching:* Unison sustained roll (B6); Drum 1 hits (G5); Drum 2 hits (E5); Unison rims (D5); Drum 3 hits (C5); Unison hits (B4); Drum 4 hits (A4); Drum 5 hits (F4); Drum 6 hits (D4)	
Marching Cymbals	*Unison cymbal section:* hi hat choke (B♭5); sizzle/suck A (C♯5); sizzle (D5); vacuum suck (C5); crash choke fat (B4); flat crash (B♭4)	

Name	Techniques/instruments	Range
Unpitched Concert Percussion	*Sounds:* Brake drum RL (C7); wind chimes (B6); Finger cymbal (A6); Triangle roll (G6); Triangle hit sustain/muted (F6); Bell plate (E6); Suspended cymbal cresc. **mp** (D6); Suspended cymbal cresc. *f* (C6); Suspended cymbal crash (B5); Suspended cymbal crash choke (A5); Suspended cymbal w/stick tip (ride) (G5); Hand cymbals choke (F5); Hand cymbals crash (E5); Concert snare drum roll (D5); Concert snare drum hits RL (C5); Tambourine fist hits (B4); Tambourine roll shaken (A4); Tambourine thumb roll (G4); Tambourine finger hits RL (F4); Temple block high RL (E4); Temple block med-high RL (D4); Temple block med RL (C4); Temple block med-low RL (B3); Temple block low RL (A3); Concert tom high RL (G3); Concert tom med-high RL (F3); Concert tom med-low (E3); Concert tom low RL (D3); Impact drum hits RL (C3); Tam-tam hit *p* (B2); Tam-tam hit *f* (A2); Concert bass drum roll (G2); Concert bass drum hit RL (F2)	
Woodblock	*Sounds:* High Woodblock (E5), Low Woodblock (F5)	
General MIDI Drum Set	*Sounds:* Bass Drum 2 (B1), Bass Drum 1 (C2), Side Stick (C#2), Snare Drum 1 (D2), Hand Clap (E♭2), Rim Shot (E2), Low Tom 2 (F2), Closed Hi-hat (F#2), Low Tom 1 (G2), Pedal Hi-hat (A♭2), Mid Tom 2 (A2), Open Hi-hat (B♭2), Mid Tom 1 (B2), High Tom 2 (C3), Crash Cymbal 1 (C#3), High Tom 1 (D3), Ride Cymbal 1 (E♭3), Chinese Cymbal (E3), Ride Bell (F3), Tambourine (F#3), Splash Cymbal (G3), Cowbell (A♭3), Crash Cymbal 2 (A3), Vibra Slap (B♭3), Ride Cymbal 2 (B3), High Bongo (C4), Low Bongo (C#4), Mute High Conga (D4), Open High Conga (E♭4), Low Conga (E4), High Timbale (F4), Low Timbale (F#4), High Agogo (G4), Low Agogo (A♭4), Cabasa (A4), Maracas (B♭4), Short Whistle (B4), Long Whistle (C5), Short Guiro (C#5), Long Guiro (D5), Claves (E♭5), High Wood Block (E5), Low Wood Block (F5), Mute Triangle (F#5), Open Triangle (G5)	
Marimba		C2 to C7
Vibraphone	*Params:* Fan Level, Fan Speed Sustain; Damped	F3 to F6
Xylophone		F4 to C8
Glockenspiel		F5 to C8
Crotales (one octave)		C6 to C7
Chimes		C4 to G5
Timpani	*Params:* Bass EQ, Mid EQ, High EQ	C2 to C4
From other providers		
Handbells (Garritan)		C4 to C7
Recorder (Garritan)	*Params:* Intonation, Timbre	C0 to G9
Electric Stage Piano	*Params:* Delay Mix, Key Off Level, Tremolo Depth, Tremolo Rate, Chorus Mix	C–1 to G9
Soft B Organ	*Params:* Lo Level, Hi Level, Rotary Mix, Rotary Speed, Percuss Level, Percuss Length	C–1 to G9
Electric Clavichord	*Params:* Amp Mix, Echo Mix, Cutoff, Release	C–1 to G9
Nylon Guitar	*Params:* Fret Noise, Release, Cutoff, High EQ	C–1 to B5
Clean Electric Guitar	*Params:* High EQ, Mid EQ, Low EQ, Compress	C2 to F#6
Delay Electric Guitar	*Params:* High EQ, Compress, Mid EQ, Delay Rate, Low EQ, Delay Feedback	C2 to F#6
Distorted Electric Guitar	*Params:* High EQ, Compress, Mid EQ, Distortion Headroom, Low EQ, Distortion Drive	C2 to F#6

Name	Techniques/instruments	Range
Overdriven Electric Guitar	*Params:* High EQ, Compress, Mid EQ, Overdrive Headroom, Low EQ, Overdrive	C2 to F#6
Flange Electric Guitar	*Params:* High EQ, Compress, Mid EQ, Flange Rate, Low EQ, Flange Mix	C2 to F#6
Tremolo Electric Guitar	*Params:* High EQ, COmpress, Mid EQ, Tremolo Rate, Low EQ, Tremolo Depth	C2 to F#6
Bass Guitar	*Params:* High EQ, Low EQ, Cutoff, Velocity Sens., Compress, Release	C0 to B4
Slap Bass		C–1 to B4
Upright Bass	*Params:* High EQ, Mid EQ, Low EQ, Compress	C1 to C5
Sitar		C2 to C6
Atmosphere pad	*Params:* Attack, Release, Cutoff, Velo	C–1 to G9
New Age pad	*Params:* Attack, Release, Cutoff, Resonance	C–1 to G9
Lead Charang	*Params:* Dirt Mix, Delay Mix, Cutoff, Resonance, Attack, Glide Time	C–1 to G9
Synth Bass	*Params:* Bass, Treble, Cutoff, Resonance, Attack, Release	C–1 to G9
Synth Bass 2	*Params:* Bass, Treble, Cutoff, Resonance, Attack, Release	C–1 to G9
Bass and Lead	*Params:* High Gain, High Freq, Cutoff, Resonance, Filter Env., Sample Start	C–1 to G9
Brass Section	*Params:* Attack, Release, Cutoff, Resonance, Delay	C–1 to G9
Synth Brass	*Params:* Attack, Release, Cutoff, Resonance, Delay	C–1 to G9
Synth Brass 2	*Params:* Attack, Release, Cutoff, Resonance, Delay	C–1 to G9
Polysynth Pad	*Params:* Attack, Release, Cutoff, Resonance	C–1 to G9
Synth Voice	*Params:* Ooh-Aah Crossfade, Air, Cutoff, Sample Start, Attack, Release	C–1 to G9
Bright	*Params:* Attack, Release, Cutoff, Resonance, Delay	C–1 to G9
Echoes	*Params:* Attack, Release, Cutoff, Filter Envelope, Delay	C–1 to G9
Oohs	*Params:* Attack, Release, Cutoff, Filter Envelope, Delay	C–1 to G9
Metallic Shimmer	*Params:* Attack, Release, Cutoff, Decay, Delay	C–1 to G9
Sci-fi	*Params:* Attack, Release, Cutoff, Resonance	C–1 to G9
Warm Pad	*Params:* Attack, Release, Cutoff, Resonance, Delay	C–1 to G9
Bowed Pad	*Params:* Attack, Release, Cutoff, Resonance, Delay	C–1 to G9
Sweep Pad	*Params:* Phaser Mix, Delay Mix, Cutoff, Resonance, Attack, Release	C–1 to G9
Rain Synth	*Params:* Attack, Release, Cutoff, Resonance, Delay	C–1 to G9
Soundtrack Synth	*Params:* Phaser, Delay, Cutoff, Filter Envelope, Attack, Release	C–1 to G9
Sawtooth	*Params:* Glide Time, Delay Mix, Cutoff, Resonance, Attack	C–1 to G9
Square	*Params:* Glide Time, Delay Mix, Cutoff, Resonance, Attack	C–1 to G9
909 Drive Kit	*Params:* Delay Time, Delay Mix, Distortion Drive, Distortion Mix *Sounds:* Rimshot 2 (G1), Claps 2 (G#1), Tight Kick 2 (A1), Metronome Bell (A#1), Loose Kick (B1), Tight Kick (C2), Side Stick (C#2), Rimshot (D2), Claps (D#2), Snare Drum (E2), Low Floor Tom (F2), Hi-Hat Closed (F#2), High Floor Tom (G2), Hi-Hat Pedal (G#2), Low Rack Tom (A2), Hi-Hat Open (A#2), Mid-Rack Tom (B2), High Mid-Rack Tom (C3), Low Crash (C#3), High Rack Tom (D3), Low Ride (D#3), High Crash (A3), High Ride (B3), Ride Bell (B3)	

Name	Techniques/instruments	Range
909 Clean Kit	*Params:* Delay Time, Delay Mix, Distortion Drive, Distortion Mix *Sounds:* Rimshot 2 (G1), Claps 2 (G♯1), Tight Kick 2 (A1), Metronome Bell (A♯1), Loose Kick (B1), Tight Kick (C2), Side Stick (C♯2), Rimshot (D2), Claps (D♯2), Snare Drum (E2), Low Floor Tom (F2), Hi-Hat Closed (F♯2), High Floor Tom (G2), Hi-Hat Pedal (G♯2), Low Rack Tom (A2), Hi-Hat Open (A♯2), Mid-Rack Tom (B2), High Mid-Rack Tom (C3), Low Crash (C♯3), High Rack Tom (D3), Low Ride (D♯3), High Crash (A3), High Ride (B3), Ride Bell (B3)	
808 Clean Kit	*Params:* Delay Time, Delay Mix, Distortion Drive, Distortion Mix *Sounds:* Claps 2 (G♯1), Tight Kick 2 (A1), Metronome Bell (A♯1), Loose Kick (B1), Tight Kick (C2), Side Stick (C♯2), Rimshot (D2), Claps (D♯2), Snare Drum (E2), Low Floor Tom (F2), Hi-Hat Closed (F♯2), High Floor Tom (G2), Hi-Hat Pedal (G♯2), Low Rack Tom (A2), Hi-Hat Open (A♯2), Mid-Rack Tom (B2), High Mid-Rack Tom (C3), Low Crash (C♯3), High Rack Tom (D3), Low Ride (D♯3), High Ride (E3), Cowbell (G♯3), Muffled Slap (D4), Conga (D♯4), Tumba (E4), High Timbale (F4), Low Timbale (F♯4), Zap (G4), Zappy (G♯4), Hat 1 (A♯4), High Woodblock (D♯5)	
808 Drive Kit	*Params:* Delay Time, Delay Mix, Distortion Drive, Distortion Mix *Sounds:* Claps 2 (G♯1), Tight Kick 2 (A1), Metronome Bell (A♯1), Loose Kick (B1), Tight Kick (C2), Side Stick (C♯2), Rimshot (D2), Claps (D♯2), Snare Drum (E2), Low Floor Tom (F2), Hi-Hat Closed (F♯2), High Floor Tom (G2), Hi-Hat Pedal (G♯2), Low Rack Tom (A2), Hi-Hat Open (A♯2), Mid-Rack Tom (B2), High Mid-Rack Tom (C3), Low Crash (C♯3), High Rack Tom (D3), Low Ride (D♯3), High Ride (E3), Cowbell (G♯3), Muffled Slap (D4), Conga (D♯4), Tumba (E4), High Timbale (F4), Low Timbale (F♯4), Zap (G4), Zappy (G♯4), Hat 1 (A♯4), High Woodblock (D♯5)	
Club Kit	*Params:* Delay Time, Delay Mix, Distortion Drive, Distortion Mix *Sounds:* Claps 2 (G♯1), Tight Kick 2 (A1), Metronome Bell (A♯1), Loose Kick (B1), Tight Kick (C2), Side Stick (C♯2), Rimshot (D2), Claps (D♯2), Snare Drum (E2), Low Floor Tom (F2), Hi-Hat Closed (F♯2), High Floor Tom (G2), Hi-Hat Pedal (G♯2), Low Rack Tom (A2), Hi-Hat Open (A♯2), Mid Rack Tom (B2), High Rack Tom (C3), Low Crash (C♯3), Low Tom (D3), Low Ride (D♯3), Hi-Hat Open (E3), Cowbell (F♯3), Muffled Slap (A3)	
Fusion Kit	*Params:* Delay Time, Delay Mix, Distortion Drive, Distortion Mix *Sounds:* Tight Kick 2 (A1), Metronome Bell (A♯1), Loose Kick (B1), Tight Kick (C2), Side Stick (C♯2), Rimshot (D2), Claps (D♯2), Snare Drum (E2), Low Floor Tom (F2), Hi-Hat Closed Pedal (F♯2), High Floor Tom (G2), Hi-Hat Pedal (G♯2), Low Rack Tom (A2), Hi-Hat Open (A♯2), Mid-Rack Tom (B2), High Mid-Rack Tom (C3), Low Crash (C♯3), High Rack Tom (D3), Low Ride (D♯3), Splash Cymbal (A3), Hi-hat Open (B3)	
Goa Kit	*Params:* Delay Time, Delay Mix, Distortion Drive, Distortion Mix *Sounds:* Tight Kick 1 (A1), Metronome Bell (A♯1), Loose Kick (B1), Tight Kick (C2), Side Stick (C♯2), Rimshot (D2), Claps (D♯2), Snare Drum (E2), Low Floor Tom (F2), Hi-hat Closed Pedal (F♯2), High Floor Tom (G2), Hi-Hat Pedal (G♯2), Mid-Rack Tom (A2), Hi-Hat Open (A♯2), High Mid-Rack Tom (B2), High Tom (C3), Low Crash (C♯3), Low Rack Tom (D3), Low Ride (D♯3), Splash Cymbal	

Playback

4.5 Performance

📖 **4.1 Working with playback**.

Sibelius contains such advanced features to improve the playback of your scores that we prefer to think that it doesn't just play back – it performs!

Options controlling the style of performance are all available from the Play ▸ Performance dialog, and are described below. These also affect the results you get when exporting a MIDI file (📖 **9.9 Exporting MIDI files**), an audio file (📖 **9.10 Exporting audio files**), or a Scorch web page (📖 **9.11 Exporting Scorch web pages**).

Espressivo™

Espressivo (Italian for "expressively") is a unique feature that enables Sibelius to play back scores adding its own expression, like a human performer. Sibelius still obeys the dynamics and articulations you write in the score, but adds a whole lot of further phrasing and interpretation over and above these.

If you play back a score that uses several instruments – or even a full orchestra – Espressivo produces independent expression for every single instrument.

In the Play ▸ Performance dialog, the Espressivo drop-down menu gives five different degrees of expression for different styles of music:

* Meccanico ("mechanically") plays the score absolutely literally, with no dynamics or articulations except where marked
* Senza espress. ("without expression") adds only tiny fluctuations of volume and slight accents at the start of bars and note-groups as a human performer will naturally do even when trying to play with no expression
* Poco espress. ("slightly expressively") has slight dynamics following the contour of the music, suitable for a fast, fairly mechanical style (such as Baroque music)
* Espressivo is the default option, with more dynamics added
* Molto espress. ("very expressively") produces lots of expression, which can be too over the top for some kinds of music. It works well for large groups of instruments, as it helps to separate the different lines.

Rubato™

Rubato is the rhythmic counterpart to Espressivo. Sibelius can subtly vary the tempo of your score to add greater expression, in much the same way as a human performer would.

In the Play ▸ Performance dialog, you can choose six different degrees of Rubato from the menu, which are suitable for different styles of music:

* Meccanico: the default option, this plays the score absolutely literally, with no gradations of tempo except where marked by Tempo text, metronome marks, or *rit./accel.* lines

- **Senza Rubato**: plays the score like a real performer trying to keep the tempo absolutely strict, so there are some barely perceptible tempo fluctuations
- **Poco Rubato**: adds a small amount of rubato, so the tempo of your score will vary a little over the course of a phrase
- **Rubato**: produces moderate gradations of tempo
- **Più Rubato**: adds quite a lot of rubato
- **Molto Rubato**: adds the maximum amount of rubato, so Sibelius will exaggerate the rhythmic phrasing. This can sound over the top for some kinds of music.

The recommended setting for rubato in your score is **Rubato** (the middle setting). Higher settings than this can produce an extreme effect in which playback may "lurch" in particularly busy passages.

Rubato may only be slight in music that is repetitive or uniform, as Sibelius bases it on the shapes of phrases. The effect of rubato is also lessened the greater the number of instruments in your score, as heavy rubato is less appropriate (and unlikely to be conductable!) for large ensembles.

An alternative to Sibelius's automatic Rubato feature is to record your own interpretation of the nuances of tempo in your score, using Live Tempo – 📖 **4.7 Live Tempo**.

Rhythmic feel™

Sibelius can play back with a wide range of "rhythmic feels" suitable for different styles of music, from jazz to Viennese waltz. Some rhythmic feels involve adjusting the notated rhythm, some adjust the beat stresses, and some do both.

The **Rhythmic Feel** options in the **Play ▸ Performance** dialog are as follows:

- **Straight** – the default setting
- **Light / Regular / Heavy swing** – a jazz convention in which two notated eighth notes (quavers) are performed approximately as a triplet quarter note plus eighth note (triplet crotchet plus quaver)
- **Triplet swing** – swings two eighth notes (quavers) as an exact triplet quarter note plus eighth note (crotchet plus quaver)
- **Shuffle** – a light sixteenth note (semiquaver) swing
- **Swung sixteenths** – as for **Regular swing** but swings sixteenth notes (semiquavers) rather than eighth notes (quavers)
- **Dotted eighths (quavers)** – effectively a very extreme swing; we're not quite sure why you'd want this, but here it is anyway
- **Notes Inégales** – triplet quarter note plus eighth note (triplet crotchet plus quaver), similar to **Triplet swing**, for an effect used in some early music (although the conventions required for really authentic *notes inègales* are more complex than this)
- **Light / Viennese waltz** – shortens the first beat of the bar (to a lesser and greater degree respectively), for a characteristic waltz feel
- **Samba** – a sixteenth note (semiquaver) feel, stressing the first and fourth beats
- **Rock / Pop** – stresses the first and third beats of a 4/4 bar, lightens the stress on the second and fourth, and lightens further still on off-beats, Rock more so than Pop

Playback

- **Reggae** – a sixteenth note (semiquaver) pattern with a strong emphasis on the 3rd and 4th sixteenths
- **Funk** – similar to Pop, but makes the second beat of the bar (in 4/4) slightly early.

You can switch rhythmic feel on or off, or even change from one rhythmic feel to another, for different parts of your score by adding text indications such as "Swing" or "Straight" in Tempo text (which you can hide if necessary) – 📖 **Playback dictionary**.

You might think that you need an option to swing both eighth notes (quavers) and sixteenth notes (semiquavers) at the same time, but if you think about it, they can't be swung simultaneously – since if you have sixteenths against eighths, the sixteenths would have to be extra-long in an on-quaver and short in an off-quaver. What you probably want instead is that in places where the fastest notes are eighths, playback should swing eighths, and where the fastest notes are sixteenths, it should swing sixteenths. To do this, put suitable hidden text markings where the music changes between passages of eighths and sixteenths – 📖 **Playback dictionary**.

Incidentally, the option **Only change beats** on the Play ▸ Performance dialog should be ignored, since each of the preset rhythmic feels switches it on or off as appropriate. It controls whether the rhythmic feel only changes the stress or rhythm of notes that fall on the beat; e.g. **Viennese waltz** turns this option on, but the swing options turn it off. There's no reason to change this, but feel free to experiment if you're particularly bored.

Reverb

Reverb, short for reverberation, means echo – strictly speaking, the spread-out echo you hear in a room, rather than the delayed one you hear in the Swiss Alps. Sound reaches our ears via many routes, some (e.g. a direct path from a performer to your ear) more direct than others (e.g. bouncing off the wall before arriving at your ear). Sounds that take a longer route to our ears are attenuated more than those that take a direct route, but the time and volume differences involved are so small that we don't perceive each reflected sound as a copy of the original; rather, we perceive the effect of the entire series of reflections as a single sound. The most realistic simulations of reverb are produced by *convolution*, which take a recorded "impulse response" (a recording of the reverberation of a space, such as a concert hall, in response to an ideal sound, or "impulse") and combines it with the audio input, producing an output signal that simulates playing your input sound in a specific room or environment. Convolution reverb is much more complex than other kinds of digital reverb, which typically use multiple feedback delay circuits to produce a large, decaying series of copies of the original signal.

The built-in Sibelius Player has two reverbs: a high-quality convolution reverb, which produces the best sound quality but uses more processing power; and a standard stereo reverb, which doesn't sound quite as good, but is more conservative in its demands on your computer. By default, convolution reverb is used for playback; to use the standard reverb, go to the **Playback** page of File ▸ **Preferences** (in the **Sibelius** menu on Mac) and switch off **Use convolution reverb**.

Adding reverb can have a dramatic effect on making your scores sound lifelike, as the human ear is almost as sensitive to the acoustics of a room as it is to the sound within it. Music for small ensembles may benefit from a small amount of reverb, characteristic of playing in a medium-sized room, whereas large orchestral works can be given extra depth by greater reverb settings.

Sibelius's **Play ▸ Performance** dialog gives seven preset degrees of reverb from **Dry** to **Cathedral**. Each preset produces sound of a different character in the Sibelius Player, so it's worth trying out a couple of the presets with each score. You can adjust the mix of reverb against the so-called *dry* signal, i.e. that which has not been passed through the reverb effect, using the Reverb fader on the Sibelius Player's strip in the Mixer – see **Virtual instrument strips** on page 272.

For the benefit of other playback devices, Sibelius's seven presets are also mapped onto different values for the standard MIDI reverb controller (91): **Dry** sends no reverb, and **Cathedral** sends almost maximum reverb. Most soundcards and sound modules, and some MIDI keyboards, can add reverb, though different devices may react differently to the reverb settings.

Some MIDI devices can do a range of other reverb effects, such as plate reverb, hall reverb, etc., though Sibelius's presets cannot map onto these settings: see your MIDI device's manual for details.

Note durations

You can adjust the length of notes on playback by setting **Unslurred notes**. By default, Sibelius plays unslurred notes at full length, so the playback effect is always smooth (legato). If you lengthen notes beyond 100% so they overlap, this produces enhanced legato on some MIDI devices but may cause problems on others where a pitch is repeated – the overlap can cause the second note to play very short, or you might find that some notes "hang" (continue playing indefinitely).

You can adjust the length of notes under slurs using the **Staff Lines** page of **Play ▸ Dictionary** – ⊞ **4.9 Playback dictionary**.

The **Play ties between different voices** option (switched on by default) tells Sibelius not to replay the second note of a tied pair if the second note is in a different voice from the first note, which happens frequently in music for keyboard instruments.

Dynamics between keyboard staves

Sibelius automatically plays back dynamics between the two staves of keyboard instruments (or other instruments with multiple staves, e.g. a flute with two staves) – see **Instruments with multiple staves** on page 265.

Play ▸ Performance allows you to set the minimum distance away from the staff that a dynamic must be before it will apply to the adjacent staff (i.e. the staff below if it is attached to the upper staff, or the staff above if it is attached to the lower staff).

If you don't want dynamics to apply to both staves of keyboard instruments, switch off the **Affect adjacent staff** option.

Repeats

The **Play repeats** option determines whether Sibelius will play back any of the repeat markings in your score; it is switched on by default, and this is usually the most useful setting. ⊞ **4.6 Repeats**.

The **Gap after final barlines** option determines how long Sibelius should pause after each final double barline in a score that contains multiple songs, pieces or movements.

ReWire

The **ReWire** options are explained in **Fixed tempo and Tempo track mode** on page 351.

Playback

4.6 Repeats

📖 **2.4 Barlines, 2.21 Lines, 2.31 Symbols, 3.1 Working with text, 4.1 Working with playback, 4.9 Playback dictionary, 5.17 Properties.**

Like other kinds of playback, Sibelius understands repeat markings in your score and plays them back automatically. Sibelius can also play very complicated repeat structures.

Various kinds of object can affect the playback of repeats: barlines; lines such as 1st- and 2nd-endings; text such as **D.C. al Coda** or *1st time **mf**;* and symbols for codas and segnos. MIDI files saved from Sibelius also incorporate repeats in exactly the same way as playback.

Playing repeats

Repeats are only played back if **Play repeats** is switched on in the **Play ▸ Performance** dialog. This option is switched on by default, but if you find that repeats don't play back, you should check this first.

Repeat barlines

To create a start or end repeat barline, select the barline where you want the repeat to go, and choose **Create ▸ Barline ▸ Start Repeat** or **End Repeat**. For more details, 📖 **2.4 Barlines**.

By default, repeat barlines only repeat once (i.e. any passage with an end repeat barline at the end of it will be played twice). If you want a repeated section to play back more than twice, select the end repeat barline and switch on more of the **Play on pass** checkboxes in the **Playback** panel of the Properties window (see below); if you switch on, say, checkboxes 1, 2 and 3, that section will *repeat* three times and hence be played back *four* times in total. However, if an ending line (see below) is also present at the same bar, its playback properties take precedence, so the barline will only repeat as many times as dictated by the ending line.

1st and 2nd ending lines

For information on creating these lines, 📖 **2.21 Lines**.

Ending lines with brackets that are open at the right-hand end automatically set the **Last time ending** option; this tells Sibelius that it has finished playing all of the ending lines preceding that one. If you have multiple sets of ending lines in your score, to get correct playback you must ensure that the last ending of each repeated section has an open right-hand end:

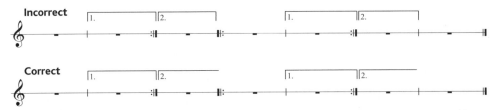

Sibelius sets the playback properties of these lines automatically when you create them; it reads the numbers under the bracket and sets the **Play on pass** checkboxes (see **Properties** below) appropriately. For example, an ending line with the text 1.–3. will set checkboxes **1**, **2**, and **3** automatically; a line with the text 1, 3, 5 will set checkboxes **1**, **3** and **5**; and so on.

Codas

Codas – music that comes at the very end of a song with a repeating structure – are normally separated from the preceding music by a gap. To create a coda:

- Create the bars where the coda music will go
- Select the barline just before the coda
- Choose **Create ▸ Barline ▸ Double** (because codas are normally preceded by double barlines, to show the end of the previous section)
- You would also normally add a text direction here informing the player what to do when they get to this double barline the first time through – see **Dal segno (D.S.) and da capo (D.C.)** below
- Choose **Layout ▸ Break ▸ Split System**. This creates a gap after the selected barline. You can drag the barline at the start of the second half of the system in order to increase or decrease the gap (to remove the gap entirely, select the barline after the gap and choose **Layout ▸ Reset Position**). To control whether the clef, key signature etc. are repeated after the gap, select the barline at the end of the first bar after the gap and open the **Bars** panel of the Properties window (📖 **5.17 Properties**).
- To write the word **CODA** above the start of the coda, hit **Esc** to make sure nothing is selected. Then choose **Create ▸ Text ▸ Tempo** (shortcut **Ctrl+Alt+T** *or* ⌥⌘T) and click above the start of the coda. Right-click (Windows) *or* **Control**-click (Mac) to see the word menu, which includes the coda symbol, then type the word **CODA** in the normal way.

Dal segno (D.S.) and da capo (D.C.)

The Italian term "dal segno" literally means "from the sign." In most music you will see either **D.S. al Fine** (which means "go back to the 𝄋 sign and play the music again until you come to the bar marked **Fine**, then stop") or **D.S. al Coda** (which means "go back to the 𝄋 sign and play the music again until you come to the bar marked **To Coda**, then jump to the coda").

Similarly, "da capo" literally means "from the head," i.e. the start of the song or piece. Just as with D.S., in most music you will either see **D.C. al Fine** or **D.C. al Coda**.

You may also see simply **D.C.** or **D.S.** in the final bar of a score, which means to repeat from the start of the score or the 𝄋 sign respectively, then stop at the end.

In music, these instructions always appear at the end of the bar from which you have to jump back (either to the 𝄋 sign or to the start of the piece). To input these instructions:

- Select the barline where the player has to jump back in the song
- Choose **Create ▸ Text ▸ Other System Text ▸ Repeat (D.C./D.S./To Coda)**. (It's important to use this text style rather than Tempo because it automatically attaches to the end of the bar.)
- A flashing caret appears. Now right-click (Windows) *or* **Control**-click (Mac) to see the word menu, which includes the text you need – enter it in the score simply by clicking it in the menu. If you type the words yourself, be sure to use the correct case (i.e. type "Fine", not "fine", as the latter won't play back correctly).

Creating a segno

If the player has to jump back to a segno, you do of course need to put the segno symbol in the right place. To do this:

- Select the note at the start of the bar to which the player has to jump back
- Choose **Create ▸ Symbol** (shortcut Z for "zymbol")
- The segno symbol (𝄋) is right at the top of the dialog, in the row labeled **Repeats**. Click it once to select it, and make sure the **Attach to** option is set to **System**.
- Click OK, and the segno is created in your score.

Fine and To Coda

The final special pieces of text used in repeat structures are **Fine** (which shows where the player should stop playing the song if they've previously jumped back from a **D.S.** or **D.C.** instruction), and **To Coda** (which shows where the player should jump forward to the coda, if they've previously jumped back from a **D.S. al Coda** or **D.C. al Coda** instruction).

Both of these instructions occur at the end of bars, and are entered the same way as **D.S.** and **D.C.** – see **Dal segno (D.S.) and da capo (D.C.)** above.

Repeat bars

To create a repeat bar, 📖 **2.5 Bars and bar rests**. Sibelius does not play back repeat bars automatically, but you can easily achieve the effect for yourself. We'll assume you want to write a pattern in the first bar of a drum staff, then tell the drummer to repeat it for the next few bars:

- Input the first bar of the pattern as normal
- Select the first bar and hit R (the shortcut for **Edit ▸ Repeat**) to repeat it in the next bar
- With the copied bar selected, type Alt+2 *or* ⌥2 to set all the music into voice 2; you'll probably now have a bunch of rests in voice 1 too
- Now choose **Edit ▸ Filter ▸ Voice 2** (shortcut Ctrl+Shift+Alt+2 *or* ⇧⌥⌘2) to filter just the voice 2 notes
- Choose **Edit ▸ Hide or Show ▸ Hide** (shortcut Ctrl+Shift+H *or* ⇧⌘H) to hide the voice 2 notes.
- Select one of the voice 1 rests, and type F9 to choose the second Keypad layout, then 0 on the keypad to turn the voice 1 rests into a bar rest
- Select the whole copied bar again, and type R repeatedly to make as many copies as you need
- Finally, select all the repeated bars, open the **Bars** panel of Properties, and choose the repeat bar symbol from the drop-down list to turn the normal bar rests in voice 1 into repeat bar symbols.

You can even automatically number the repeated bars using the **Plug-ins ▸ Text ▸ Number Bars** plug-in.

Properties

The **Playback** panel of the Properties window contains the main controls for adjusting the playback effect of lines, text and even notes.

• **Play on pass**: these checkboxes control whether the selected object will be played on a given pass through the score, up to a total of eight repeats. For repeat barlines and 1st and 2nd ending lines, Sibelius sets these properties automatically (see **Repeat barlines** and **1st and 2nd ending lines** above). For text, you can set this option yourself (see **When to play back text and lines** below).

- **Last time ending** applies only to ending lines with open right-hand ends (i.e. no hook at the right-hand end) – see **1st and 2nd ending lines** above.
- **Jump at bar end** tells Sibelius whether to obey a jump (e.g. from a text instruction such as **D.C. al Coda**) at the precise point in the bar the text is attached to, or at the end of the bar (the default option). You only need to switch off this option if you need a repeat instruction to be obeyed in the middle of a bar.

When to play back text and lines

The Play on pass checkboxes can be used to tell Sibelius when staff text that affects playback (typically Expression and Technique) should play back. For example, you could create Technique text such as "To sax (2nd time only)", and switch on the 2 checkbox under Play on pass, which will make Sibelius switch to a saxophone sound the second time it plays back that bar; similarly, you could create some Expression text "*1st, 3rd, 5th times:* $\boldsymbol{mf}$ " (switching on Play on pass checkboxes 1, 3, and 5) and another object "*2nd, 4th times:* $\boldsymbol{pp}$" (switching on checkboxes 2 and 4) at the start of a repeated section, and Sibelius will obey the dynamics appropriately. In a similar vein, you could create a staff line (such as a hairpin or glissando) and set it to play back only on a single pass through the score.

System text (typically in the Tempo or Repeat (D.C./D.S./To Coda) text styles) is unaffected by the state of the Play on pass checkboxes: Sibelius decides intelligently when to take notice of these instructions. Similarly, system lines other than repeat endings, e.g. *rit./accel.*, always play back on every pass through the score.

When to play back notes

The Play on pass checkboxes also apply to notes, which opens up some exciting possibilities: for songs which have, say, different rhythmic underlay in the vocal line in different verses, you could create cue-sized notes that follow the rhythm of the verse 2 lyrics, and set them to play on the second pass only; for jazz, you could create a little solo passage in the horns that should only play back on the repeat; and so on.

You can even make a note totally silent by switching off *all* of the Play on pass checkboxes! (If you need to make just one notehead of a chord silent, you can use a silent notehead instead – 📖 **2.25 Noteheads**.)

Skipping bars

In some circumstances, you may not want a particular bar to play back at all. For example, your score may start with a prefatory staff (such as a "handbells used" chart), or you may have a guitar fill box on one page of your score, and you would prefer these bars not to play back.

This is easy to arrange, using system text to form a pair of "markers" – one text object to set the place you want to jump *from*, and another to set the place you want to jump *to*:

- Decide on a name for your pair of markers; it doesn't matter what it is. For the sake of argument, let's use the word "cat".

- At the end of the bar immediately preceding the bar(s) you don't want to play, create a new Repeat (D.C./D.S./To Coda) text object, consisting of the words "jump to" and the name of your marker, e.g. jump to cat
- At the start of the bar you want playback to jump to, create a new Tempo text object, consisting of the word "marker" and the name of your marker, e.g. marker cat.

You will probably not want either text object in your marker pair to appear when you print, in which case you can either select them and hide them (using Edit ▸ Hide or Show ▸ Hide) or by inserting a tilde character (~) at the start of each text object, which will hide it.

Sibelius will *always* obey a marker pair when it encounters it during playback, i.e. like all system text objects, they ignore the Play on pass checkboxes.

Optional endings & Repeat to fade

In sheet music for some pop songs, you will sometimes see alternative endings; one will typically be **Repeat to fade**, and the other will be **Optional ending** (the idea being that those musicians who can't magically make their own performances repeat to fade use the optional ending instead).

You can make Sibelius play these back in a number of ways; here is one way to play using the optional ending:

- Use ending lines with closed right-hand ends for both the **Repeat to fade** and **Optional ending** bars
- Set the **Repeat to fade** ending line to play back (say) twice using the controls in the Playback panel of Properties; ensure the Last time ending checkbox is switched off
- Select the **Optional ending** line and switch on the Last time ending option in the Playback panel of Properties.

When you play back the score, Sibelius will play the **Repeat to fade** ending twice, then play the **Optional ending** bars to finish.

Alternatively, here's how to simulate a repeat to fade:

- Set the final section to repeat a number of times by selecting the end repeat barline and adjusting the Play on passes checkboxes in the Playback panel of Properties
- Create a diminuendo hairpin over the length of the repeated section, and set it to play back during the last repetition of the closing section; in the same panel, set its dynamic change to be 100% of maximum
- Hide the hairpin by selecting it and choosing Edit ▸ Hide or Show ▸ Hide (shortcut Ctrl+Shift+H *or* ⇧⌘H).

Finding problems in complex repeat structures

In scores with complex repeat structures, it can be useful to switch on timecode Above every bar in Play ▸ Video and Time ▸ Timecode and Duration. In repeated sections, you will see more than one timecode stacked vertically, one for each pass; by looking at the timecodes you can therefore tell at a glance what order and how many times Sibelius will play back the bars in your score. For more details, 🕮 **4.11 Timecode and hit points**.

4.7 Live Tempo

Live Tempo is an easy way to finely control the tempo of your score during playback, allowing you to provide your own interpretation of your music simply by tapping on your computer keyboard, MIDI keyboard, or MIDI foot pedal.

When you record a performance using Live Tempo, Sibelius responds the way a real group of musicians would, by reading the markings in the score and interpreting your input. If you want to subdivide the beat to provide more accuracy for a *ritardando*, or if you want to speed up and start tapping only one beat per bar, Sibelius will follow you. You can even stop tapping whenever you like, and Sibelius will keep playing back at the last tempo you reached, until you start tapping again or until it encounters a change of tempo in the score.

You might even say that using Live Tempo, you are the conductor, and Sibelius is your orchestra.

Setting up for Live Tempo recording

In order to record your performance, you need to choose your input device. Although you can freely switch between your computer keyboard, MIDI keyboard and MIDI foot pedal at any time, you are advised to choose one input device and stick to it, at least during a single Live Tempo recording.

Before you record, you should calibrate your input device, so that Sibelius can determine the latency in your computer's playback system, and your own response speed (which is latency of a different kind!).

Open the score in which you want to record a Live Tempo performance, and choose **Play ▸ Calibrate Live Tempo**. The following dialog appears:

Simply choose the input device you want to calibrate from the radio buttons at the top of the dialog, then click **Start Calibration**. You will hear a click: simply tap along in time with the click, pressing any key on your computer keyboard, any key on your MIDI keyboard, or your MIDI foot pedal.

If Sibelius doesn't receive any beats, it will tell you, so you can fix the problem (e.g. ensure that your MIDI device is properly connected) and try again. Normally, however, you will simply find that the **OK** button becomes enabled, and you can click it to continue.

Once you have calibrated your input device, you don't need to do it again, provided you always use the same input device and the same playback configuration (i.e. the same playback devices). If, however, you want to record Live Tempo using a different input device, or if you switch to a different playback configuration, you are advised to use **Play ▸ Calibrate Live Tempo** before recording your Live Tempo performance.

Live Tempo Options

Before you start your recording, choose **Play ▸ Live Tempo Options** to review the settings you can change to help Sibelius interpret your performance:

- **Count-in** allows you to specify how many beats you will provide to Sibelius to establish the tempo before playback begins. By default, Sibelius expects one bar's worth of beats (e.g. in 3/4, you tap three times, and on the fourth tap, Sibelius starts playing), but you can change this. If your score begins with a pick-up (upbeat) bar, the count-in includes the pick-up (e.g. if your score is in 4/4 and begins with a quarter note (crotchet) pick-up, Sibelius will begin playing on your fourth tap, assuming you have specified a one-bar count-in).
- The **Allow beat multiples** option determines whether Sibelius is allowed to interpret your taps as subdivisions (e.g. tapping eighth notes (quavers) in 4/4) or multiple beats (e.g. tapping once per bar in 3/4). This option is switched on by default.
- **Sensitivity** is the most important setting, and also the most dependent on personal taste. When the slider is set towards the left, Sibelius will follow your individual taps less closely, instead smoothing them out to establish a more consistent beat; when the slider is set towards the right, Sibelius will follow your individual taps more closely, so the tempo adjustment is more immediate.

Once you're happy with the settings, click **OK**. Now you're ready to record your performance.

Depending on factors like the number of instruments and the general range of tempos in the score, you may find that you need to visit **Live Tempo Options** a couple of times in order to try out different settings. The choices you make here are saved in the score.

Recording a Live Tempo performance

You are recommended to switch on View ▸ Panorama before you record Live Tempo, because there is a special Live Tempo display that only appears in Panorama – see **Live Tempo display** below.

Once you have calibrated your input device and reviewed the Live Tempo options for your score, set the playback line to the position from which you want Live Tempo recording to begin (e.g. type Ctrl+[*or* ⌘[to move the playback line to the start of the score), then click the red Record Live Tempo button on the Playback window (shown above right) or choose Play ▸ Record Live Tempo.

If you haven't yet calibrated an input device, Sibelius will warn you that you may get unexpected results unless you do, and ask if you want to calibrate an input device now: you are recommended to click Yes, which will take you directly to the Calibrate Live Tempo dialog (see above).

Otherwise, the playback line will turn red, and Sibelius will wait for your first tap. Depending on how many beats or bars of introduction are set in Play ▸ Live Tempo Options, Sibelius will start playing back and following your tempo.

During Live Tempo recording, Sibelius's playback may sound a little lumpy (particularly if you have set the Sensitivity slider towards the right in Live Tempo Options). This is because it has to guess how long each beat will be in order to play back in time with your taps. When you play back your Live Tempo recording, the tempo changes will sound smoother.

If you want to stop tapping at any point but keep playback going (e.g. because you have established the tempo you want), simply stop tapping: Sibelius will keep going at the speed you have reached. When you want to join in again, simply start tapping again: Sibelius will start following you once more.

Live Tempo recording will continue until you reach the end of the score, unless your score contains multiple songs, movements or pieces, in which case it will continue until the next final barline or *Fine* marking.

If you want to stop recording Live Tempo before the end of the score, simply hit Esc or click the stop button in the Playback window.

Live Tempo display

You can see a graphical representation of the tempo adjustments recorded via Live Tempo by switching on View ▸ Panorama. When you record Live Tempo, View ▸ Live Tempo is switched on, showing a graph above the top staff in the score:

The vertical lines in the graph align with the barlines in the score. A horizontal line runs down the middle of the graph, which represents the default tempo at that point in the score. The variations in tempo produced by your Live Tempo recording relative to the default tempo are shown as a line that runs either above or below the horizontal line on the graph. (In the picture above, the graph shows the tempo getting faster than the regular playback tempo, then getting slower again.)

When you make a passage selection in your score, the graph reflects the selection, blocking out the sections in the graph that correspond to the selected bars. This allows you to see where Live Tempo data will be cleared if you use Play ▸ Clear Live Tempo.

Playing back a Live Tempo performance

To play back your Live Tempo performance, simply ensure that the blue Play Live Tempo button on the Playback window (shown on the right) or **Play ▸ Live Tempo** is switched on before you start playback.

Your Live Tempo performance is preserved when you export a MIDI or audio file, publish your score on SibeliusMusic.com, or export a Scorch web page, provided **Play ▸ Live Tempo** is switched on.

Clearing Live Tempo

To clear a whole Live Tempo performance, choose **Play ▸ Clear Live Tempo** with nothing selected, and answer **Yes** when asked if you want to remove the Live Tempo data from the entire score.

If you want to clear the tempo changes created by recording Live Tempo in a passage, simply select those bars and choose **Play ▸ Clear Live Tempo**. This removes the Live Tempo data from the selected passage. If you are in Panorama and **View ▸ Live Tempo** is switched on, you will see that the graph is cleared for those bars.

When you play back your score having cleared Live Tempo from a passage, the effect is as if you had stopped tapping for that passage during the Live Tempo recording: Sibelius will continue playing back at the same speed as was reached at the last point that has Live Tempo data, until the next Live Tempo data or the next marking in the score that changes the tempo, whichever comes first.

Subdividing the beat and multiple beats per tap

If **Allow beat multiples** is switched on in **Live Tempo Options**, Sibelius will allow you either to subdivide the beat, or to provide fewer taps in the bar than there are beats.

In a simple meter (e.g. 2/4, 3/4, 4/4), Sibelius allows you to subdivide the beat in multiples of two, e.g. in 4/4, two eighth note (quaver) taps per beat, or even four 16th note (semiquaver) taps per beat. In a compound meter (e.g. 6/8, 9/8, 12/8), Sibelius allows you to subdivide the beat in multiples of three or six, e.g. three eighth note (quaver) taps ber beat in 6/8.

Typically you subdivide the beat when you want to speed up or slow down. For example, if you are approaching a *ritardando* towards the end of a movement or piece in 4/4, you may decide to start subdividing the quarter note (crotchet) beat so that when you start to slow down, you have greater control over the rate of tempo change by beating in eighth notes (quavers). You don't need to warn Sibelius about this: as soon as you start tapping around twice as fast as you were previously, the program will interpret that as subdivision, and act accordingly. For best results, you should start to subdivide the beat *before* you try to change tempo.

The approach is similar for tapping less often than the number of beats in the bar. In a simple duple meter, e.g. 4/4, if you simply start tapping around half as fast as you were previously, Sibelius will interpet that as beating in half notes (minims). In a simple triple meter, e.g. 3/4, if you likewise tap around a third as fast as you were previously, Sibelius will interpret that as beating in dotted half notes (dotted minims). Sibelius assumes that you will never tap less frequently than once per bar: if you do, it will assume that you have stopped tapping altogether.

Irregular or complex time signatures

For irregular time signatures such as 5/4, or complex time signatures such as 3+2/8, Sibelius examines the beam group settings for the time signature in order to interpret your tapping during Live Tempo recording. If you find that you want to divide the bar differently than the way Sibelius expects, use Notes ▸ Reset Beam Groups to change the beam groups used by that time signature.

For irregular bars (i.e. bars that do not contain a time signature, but whose duration does not match that of the prevailing time signature), Sibelius examines the bar to see whether it has a regular or irregular beat pattern, and then interprets your tapping accordingly.

Pauses (fermatas)

Pauses (fermatas) can occur either in the middle of a phrase, as a point of emphasis or repose, or at the end of a phrase. A pause at the end of a phrase may sometimes be followed by a short articulatory gap, such as an upbeat, before the start of the next phrase.

By default, Sibelius plays back pauses by extending the length of the paused note, and then continues at the original tempo (unless there is a new tempo marking following the pause). When you encounter a pause during Live Tempo recording, Sibelius will extend the pause until you tap again, to signal the next beat.

You can, however, adjust the playback of notes with pauses on them, either using the Play ▸ Dictionary dialog, which changes the default behavior of pauses in your score, or using the controls on the Playback panel of Properties, which changes the behavior of an individual pause. If you specify that a pause should be followed by a gap using either of these methods, Sibelius will respect this during Live Tempo recording: you tap once to begin the pause, tap again to begin the gap following the pause, and a third time to signal the next beat.

Repeated sections

If a section of your score is repeated (e.g. by a repeat barline or a D.C. al Coda marking), you can record a different Live Tempo performance for each pass through the music, and this is reflected in the graph shown in Panorama. If you clear Live Tempo from a repeated passage, however, the Live Tempo data is cleared from all passes.

Adding tempo markings

If you add a new Tempo text marking or metronome mark to a passage of the score for which a Live Tempo performance has been recorded, the actual playback speed of the score will not change at that point if Play ▸ Live Tempo is switched on: the Live Tempo performance takes precedence over the tempos marked in the score. You will, however, see that the Live Tempo graph updates to show how the recorded Live Tempo performance corresponds to the new written tempo.

To make a new tempo marking in the score take effect, you must clear the Live Tempo data – see Clearing Live Tempo above.

Live Tempo and ReWire

You cannot use Live Tempo and ReWire at the same time: Live Tempo is disabled when Sibelius is running in ReWire mode.

4.8 Live Playback

📖 **1.4 Flexi-time™**, **4.1 Working with playback**, **4.5 Performance**, **9.5 Opening MIDI files**.

In real life, a musical performance never precisely matches what is notated in the score; there are all manner of nuances of tempo, dynamic and rhythmic flexibility that cannot easily be reproduced even by smart features like Espressivo, Rubato and Rhythmic feel (📖 **4.5 Performance**).

So if you provide Sibelius with an actual, human performance – either from a real-time recording using Flexi-time (📖 **1.4 Flexi-time™**) or by importing a MIDI file (📖 **9.5 Opening MIDI files**) – it can preserve it for you using Live Playback.

Live Playback stores exactly how you play each note (even individual notes in chords), right down to the tiniest variations in velocity (how loud a note is), duration (how long you played it for), and start position (how much it deviates from precisely where the beat is).

You can also edit your performance, or create a Live Playback performance for music that you have inputted in other ways (e.g. using step-time or alphabetic input, or from scanning printed sheet music) using the **Playback** panel of the Properties window, or the **Play ▸ Transform Live Playback** dialog.

Hearing Live Playback

Live Playback is switched on by default in all new scores. To switch it on or off, choose **Play ▸ Live Playback** (shortcut **Shift**-L), or click the button in the Playback window (shown on the left), which lights up when Live Playback is on, and is black when it's off. When you save and re-open your score, Sibelius remembers whether you had it switched on or off.

Live Playback is totally separate from Sibelius's own interpretation of your score. For example, when **Play ▸ Live Playback** is switched on (and when Live Playback data is stored in your score), Sibelius plays back the score exactly as it was originally performed. Items added to the score that would usually affect dynamics or timing – such as dynamics, hairpins, other text directions (such as MIDI messages), and options such as Espressivo, Rubato and Rhythmic Feel – are not played back, unless they apply to notes with no Live Playback data.

So if you, say, import a MIDI file and then add a dynamic to one of the staves using Expression text (📖 **3.1 Working with text**), it won't be played back unless you switch off **Play ▸ Live Playback** (shortcut **Shift**-L).

Conversely, if you input a score using step-time or alphabetic input and then play it back, you'll hear no difference between playback with Live Playback switched on or off, because no Live Playback data is stored in your score – see **Creating Live Playback data** below.

Tempo instructions – such as Tempo text, metronome marks, and *rit./accel.* lines – and repeats are always observed, whether or not Live Playback is switched on.

Viewing Live Playback velocities

To see the Live Playback velocities stored in your score, switch on **View ▸ Live Playback Veloci-ties**. This option is only available when **Play ▸ Live Playback** is switched on. Notes that have Live Playback data (and have the Properties checkbox **Live velocity** switched on) display a vertical column above the staff, a little like the columns you see in a bar graph. The height of the column represents the maximum possible velocity (127), and the colored section rising from the bottom of the column represents the Live Playback velocity of the note or chord in question. Sibelius can display Live Playback velocities for single notes and chords, in any number of voices, as follows:

Voice 1 single note

The velocity of single notes is always shown.

Voice 1 chord

When no notes are selected or all notes are selected, the highest and lowest velocities are shown (highest in dark blue, lowest in light blue). Selecting an individual notehead always shows just that notehead's velocity.

Voices 1 & 2 single notes

When unselected, the voice 1 velocity is shown in blue; the voice 2 velocity is shown in green.

Voices 1 & 2 chords

When unselected, the velocity of the note with the highest velocity in each voice is displayed.

Voices 1–4

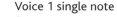

Voices 3 and 4 have a separate column, and behave like voices 1 and 2.

Editing Live Playback

There are three main ways of editing Live Playback data:

• By directly editing the values stored for each note in the **Playback** panel of the Properties window

• By dragging the vertical bars shown when **View ▸ Live Playback Velocities** is switched on

• By using the **Play ▸ Transform Live Playback** dialog.

Properties

You can use the **Playback** panel of the Properties window (shortcut **Ctrl+Alt+P** *or* ⌥⌘P) to edit the Live Playback data for individual notes, multiple selections, or selected passages. These controls are only available when **Play ▸ Live Playback** is switched on.

• **Live velocity** is in the range 0–127; 127 is the loudest, 0 is the softest

Playback

- **Live start position** is measured in *ticks*; 256 ticks = 1 quarter note (crotchet). A negative value causes the note to sound earlier than its notated position in the bar (e.g. –64 will cause it to sound one sixteenth note (semiquaver) earlier than notated), and a positive value causes the note to sound later (e.g. 128 will cause it to sound one eighth note (quaver) later than notated). You can even set a note to sound in a bar different to its notated position, but typically you would only make small adjustments that affect the "feel" of the rhythm, e.g. how loose or tight it sounds.
- **Live duration** is also measured in ticks. You can set a note to have an arbitrary duration, and changing the duration here will not affect its notated appearance (so you can have a written half note (minim) that only sounds for a quarter note (crotchet), or even a written quarter note that sounds as long as a half note).

To edit Live Playback data for an individual note, simply select the note and adjust the values in the Playback panel. You can select individual noteheads in chords and adjust their data independently.

If you select a passage or multiple selection, the options in the **Playback** panel will normally display --, showing that different values are stored for different notes in the selection (unless all the notes in the selection have identical data, in which case that will be shown). When you change Live Playback data for a selected passage or multiple selection, you are effectively making the data identical for all selected notes.

You can override any or all of the Live Playback parameters for individual notes simply by switching off the appropriate checkbox in the **Playback** panel of Properties – see **Switching Live Playback on and off for sections of a score** below.

To perform more sophisticated transformations on the data across a selected passage (i.e. to manipulate it in ways other than simply switching it on or off, or setting it to a constant value across the whole passage), see **Transform Live Playback** below.

Editing Live Playback velocities

You can drag the vertical bars drawn when View ▸ Live Playback Velocities is switched on in order to edit velocities graphically. It's a good idea to zoom in close before editing velocities so you can see what you're doing more clearly.

- To edit the velocity of an individual note (or note within a chord), select the note, then click and drag the vertical bar up and down.
- To set the same velocity for all the notes in a passage, select the passage in which you want to set the velocities, then click one of the vertical bars; all of the other vertical bars will be set to the new value.
- To set different velocities across a range of notes, don't make a passage selection: instead, click on the vertical bar of the first note whose velocity you want to edit, and – keeping the mouse button held down – drag it across the vertical bars on subsequent notes. As the mouse pointer moves over the vertical bars, the velocities are set according to the height at which the mouse pointer crosses them. It's possible to create expressive curves across a passage in this way. (Beware that if the passage contains chords, all of the notes in the chord will be set to the same velocity.)
- If you want to edit the velocities for notes only in (say) voice 2, select the passage, filter voice 2 (🕮 **5.7 Filters and Find**), then use either of the methods just mentioned.

- To change how far above or below the staff the vertical bars appear, hold **Ctrl** *or* ⌘ and drag one of the vertical bars with the mouse. This changes the position of the vertical bars throughout the score for that staff, and they can be dragged up to 20 spaces above or below the staff.

As with every operation in Sibelius, if you change your mind after editing velocities, simply choose **Edit ▸ Undo** (shortcut **Ctrl+Z** *or* ⌘Z).

Transform Live Playback

The **Play ▸ Transform Live Playback** dialog (shortcut **Ctrl+Shift+Alt+L** *or* ⇧⌥⌘L) allows you to apply sophisticated transformations to the Live Playback data in your score.

To use this dialog, select the passage you want to transform and choose **Play ▸ Transform Live Playback** (if you don't make a selection, you are asked if you want the operation to apply to the whole score).

The dialog is split into two pages, **Velocities** and **Timings**. You can set up one transformation on either or both of these pages, so you can transform velocities and timings simultaneously if you like. The options are as follows:

- Velocities tab:
  - **Leave unchanged**: select this option if you only want to perform a transformation on the **Timings** tab
  - **Constant velocity** (range 0-127): sets all the notes in the selection to the same velocity
  - **Louder**: adds the specified velocity to all the notes, up to the maximum value (127)
  - **Softer**: subtracts the specified velocity from all the notes, down to a minimum of zero
  - **Crescendo/Diminuendo**: specify the desired velocity of the first and last notes in the selection, and Sibelius will scale the velocities of the intervening notes to produce a crescendo or diminuendo
  - **Scale dynamic range**: compresses or expands the velocities of the notes in the selection so they range between the specified minimum and maximum; this allows you to make the dynamic range narrower or wider.
- Timings tab:
  - **Leave unchanged**: select this option if you only want to perform a transformation on the **Velocities** tab

○ **Scale live durations**: scales the durations of all the notes in the selection by the specified percentage, allowing you to make their live durations longer or shorter

○ **Set live durations** *n*% **of the notated durations**: changes the live durations of the selected notes to a percentage of their *notated* durations (i.e. regardless of their current live durations)

○ **Constant live durations**: sets the live duration of every note to the specified number of ticks (256 ticks = 1 quarter note (crotchet))

○ **Move earlier**: reduces the start position of the notes by the specified number of ticks; you can use this option to make the music sound "ahead of the beat"

○ **Move later**: increases the start position of the notes by the specified number of ticks; you can use this option to make the music sound "behind the beat"

○ **Scale start positions relative to notation**: allows you to exaggerate or reduce the effect of the start positions in the selected passage. The **Keep durations constant** option (switched on by default), as the name suggests, allows you to choose whether to keep the original durations. The musical effect of rescaling the notes' start positions makes the music sound more or less behind or ahead of the beat, i.e. "tighter" or "looser."

To apply the chosen transformations, click **OK**, then type **P** to hear the results.

Creating Live Playback data

If you didn't create your score using Flexi-time or by importing a MIDI file, no Live Playback data will exist. You can easily create Live Playback data, however, as follows:

• Select the passage of music you want to create Live Playback data for

• Open the **Playback** panel of the Properties window

• Switch on the checkboxes next to **Velocity**, **Position** and **Duration**. Sibelius automatically creates Live Playback data with sensible defaults (all start positions are set to 0, durations are set to the equivalent number of ticks for the notated duration, and velocities are set to 80).

You can then edit the Live Playback data in the normal way.

Switching Live Playback on and off for sections of a score

Naturally you can switch **Play ▸ Live Playback** on and off to switch between the Live Playback interpretation of the score and Sibelius's own interpretation. However, in some circumstances you may wish to switch off the Live Playback data for part of a score. To do this:

• Select the passage in which you want the Live Playback data to be switched off

• Open the **Playback** panel of the Properties window

• Switch off the checkboxes next to **Live velocity**, **Live duration** and **Live start position**.

You can switch these options off independently, with different effects on the resulting playback. If you switch off both the **Live duration** and **Live start position** checkboxes, then Sibelius's own smart Rubato and Rhythmic feel playback options will play back; if you switch off the **Live velocity** checkbox, Sibelius will use Espressivo for playback, and respond to Expression text, etc. This means that you can pick and choose which parts of the Live Playback performance you want to retain, and which parts you want to leave up to Sibelius's own interpretation.

4.9 Playback dictionary

📖 **4.1 Working with playback**, **4.17 MIDI messages**, **4.18 SoundWorld™**.

Sibelius reads and interprets not only text (such as *mf*, *pizz.* and *legato*) when playing back, but also many other markings in your score, including lines (e.g. octave lines, slurs, trills, pedal markings), articulations (e.g. staccato, tenuto, accent), and symbols.

Though you won't normally need to do so, you can modify exactly what effect these markings have on playback using Sibelius's **Play ▸ Dictionary** dialog, and even add your own markings to the dictionary. The dialog has six pages, each dealing with a different kind of item that can affect playback:

- **Staff Text**, for playing instructions that apply only to a single staff, e.g. *ff*, *legato*
- **System Text**, for instructions that apply to all instruments, e.g. **Fast**, **Swing**, **Adagio**
- **Staff Lines**, for lines that apply to a single staff, e.g. trills, octave (*8va*) lines, slurs, hairpins
- **Articulations**, e.g. staccato, tenuto. Note that one-note tremolos and buzz rolls are also handled on this page.
- **Noteheads**, for effects produced by noteheads, e.g. harmonics, ghost notes
- **Symbols**, e.g. scoops, falls, mallets and beaters for percussion.

Each of these pages is described in detail below.

Staff Text page

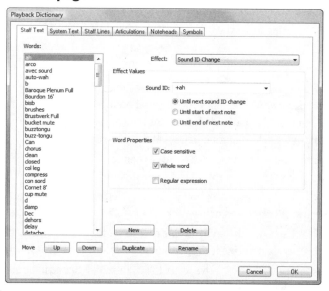

The words are listed at the left-hand side of the dialog. You can change the order of words in the list by clicking the **Up** and **Down** buttons; though this has no effect on how Sibelius handles them in playback, it is useful to be able to add words in alphabetical order, and in any case you may be able to derive some limited amusement from clicking these buttons.

To edit a word, click **Rename**, which shows a simple dialog in which you can change the text. To add a new word, select a word that has a similar effect to the one you wish to create, and click **New**, which shows a simple dialog in which you can specify the new word. To make a copy of an existing word, click **Duplicate**. To remove a word altogether, click **Delete**.

Each word can also have a combination of the following options set:

* **Case sensitive**: in most cases, you will not want your word to be treated as case sensitive (i.e. you want "swing," "Swing" and "SWING" to be equivalent), so this should normally be switched off

* **Whole word** means that the word is not an abbreviation. However, most musical terms can be abbreviated, so it is common to switch this option off. For example, Sibelius will change to a pizzicato string sound when confronted with any word beginning with the letters "pizz," so that "pizz," "pizz." (with a period) and "pizzicato" will all produce the same effect. ("pizza" will also work, but is unlikely to occur in your score.) Don't put a period (full stop) at the end of your word in this dialog if it's an abbreviation. If your word is not an abbreviation, switch this on instead.

* Regular expressions allow sophisticated matching of patterns inside text strings, but aren't for the faint of heart. You'll normally never need to switch on **Regular expression** – but if you're curious, see **Regular expressions** below.

To determine the playback effect of a particular word, select it, then choose the type of **Effect** from the list on the right. The **Effect Values** group below updates to show what you can change for each type of **Effect**:

* **Control change** sets a MIDI controller to a certain value:
  * **MIDI controller** specifies the number of the MIDI controller to change (e.g. controller 1 is modulation, controller 64 is sustain pedal, controller 91 is reverb, etc.)
  * **Controller value** specifies the value to set the chosen MIDI controller to; 0 is the minimum and 127 is the maximum.

* **Dynamic** allows you to change the prevailing dynamic; this is the effect used for text such as *mf*, *ff* and *loud*:
  * **Dynamic** specifies the volume at which the following music should be played, using a range between 0 and 127. Depending on the playback device, this may be played using note velocity, or MIDI expression (controller 11), or modulation (controller 1), or something else.
  * **Attack** specifies the sharpness of the attack of notes at this dynamic, using a range between 0 and 127. Depending on the playback device, this may or may not have an audible effect.
  * **Sound ID change** allows you to specify an optional sound ID change in addition to the change in dynamic; see **Sound ID changes** below

* **Dynamic change** allows you to change the dynamic for one note or for the following music, relative to the current dynamic (rather than setting it to an absolute level, as **Dynamic** does):
  * **Dynamic *n*% of current dynamic** allows you to specify the change in dynamic in terms of a percentage of the prevailing dynamic
  * **Attack *n*% of current attack** allows you to specify the change in attack in terms of a percentage of the prevailing attack
  * **Sound ID change** allows you to specify an optional sound ID change in addition to the change in dynamic; see **Sound ID changes** below

○ Change for is a list containing two choices, either **one note only** (meaning the dynamic only affects the note to which the text instruction is attached) or **all subsequent notes** (meaning that the change "sticks" until the next dynamic is encountered)

• **Dynamic envelope** is for effects where the dynamic increases and decreases over time, e.g. *sfz* or *fp*:

○ **Initial dynamic** specifies the dynamic at the start of the note

○ **Decay** determines the length of time over which the dynamic returns either to its original level or to the optional **End dynamic**, expressed as a percentage of the length of the note

○ **End dynamic** optionally specifies the dynamic at the end of the note.

• **Program change** allows you to change MIDI program number, in order to change the sound used by a staff. In general you shouldn't use this mechanism: either use instrument changes (□ **2.18 Instruments**) or a sound ID change (see below). But should you have a good reason to use it:

○ **Program** specifies the program number, using a range between 0 and 127

○ **Send bank change** allows you to choose whether or not a MIDI bank change message should be sent in addition to the program change. If you switch this on, **Bank High** and **Bank Low** are then enabled.

○ **Bank High** and **Bank Low** allow you to set the most significant ("high") and least significant ("low") bits required to effect a MIDI bank change message.

• **Sound ID change** allows you to add or remove techniques from the present sound. You can choose one or more sound ID elements from the menu – see **Sound ID changes** below.

System Text page

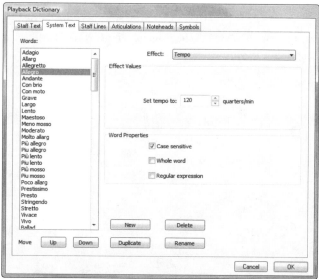

The System Text page has similar controls to the Staff Text page (see **Staff Text page** above), but the types of **Effect** are different:

• **Metronome** is used to specify the meaning of the characters to the left of the equals sign in a metronome mark. For example, in the metronome mark "♩ = 120", the quarter note (crotchet)

Playback

character is actually a letter "q" in Sibelius's music fonts, so **q =** is defined to use the **Metronome** effect and is set to **1 beats (quarters)**. Similarly, in "♪ = 160" the eighth note (quaver) is a letter "e", so **e =** is defined to mean **0.5 beats (quarters)**. However, because all the standard note durations (including dotted notes) are defined for you, you'll never need to set up any more **Metronome** words – unless you invent some new note durations, of course.

- **Repeat** is used to specify the kind of effect a word should have on the playback of repeated sections in the score. For example, a word defined to have the **Repeat** effect **D.C. al Coda** will tell Sibelius to jump to the start of the score and keep playing until it finds a word defined to have the **Repeat** effect **To Coda**, which in turn causes Sibelius to jump to the place in the score where it finds a word defined to have the **Repeat** effect **Coda**, signifying the start of the coda itself. **Repeat** words are the only predefined ones to use the **Regular expression** option – see **Regular expressions** below. As with **Metronome** words, you won't need to set up any **Repeat** words, because all the common ones are already set up for you. For more information about how Sibelius plays back repeats, 📖 **4.6 Repeats**.

- **Rhythmic Feel** words change the rhythmic feel setting of the score at the specific point at which the word is encountered. For example, the word "Swing" is defined to set rhythmic feel to **Regular Swing**. For more information about rhythmic feel, 📖 **4.5 Performance**.

- **Rit./Accel.** words allow you to specify a *rit.* or *accel.*, though it is recommended that you use the lines provided for this purpose instead, as they provide greater control – see **Rit. and accel.** on page 264. Should you decide you do want to define a **Rit./Accel.** word, set **Scale tempo to** n**%** **of current tempo** to an appropriate value, and set **Over** n **beats (quarters)** to the length of time following the text that you want the change of tempo to occur.

- **Tempo** words allow you to set a specific tempo. For example, "Allegro" is defined to **Set tempo to 120 quarters/min**, while "Lento" is defined to **Set tempo to 60 quarters/min**.

- **Tempo Scale** words allow you to scale the current tempo by a specified percentage. For example, "Slower" is defined to scale the tempo to 90% of the original tempo, while "Faster" sets the tempo to 110% of the original tempo.

Staff Lines page

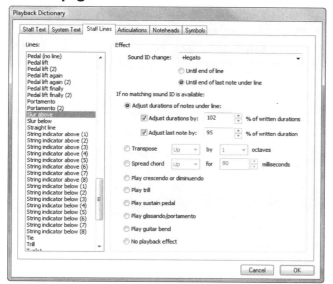

The **Staff Lines** page allows you to specify a **Sound ID change** for each type of line that exists in your score. For example, you might specify a sound ID change of **+legato** for a slur, which would automatically choose a special, smooth violin sound on your playback device if you then put a slur on a violin staff in your score, and a different smooth trumpet sound if you then put a slur on a trumpet staff, and so on – see **Sound ID changes** below

Failing that, if Sibelius is unable to find a suitable sound to play the specified sound ID change, or if no sound ID change is specified, it will do whichever of the default effects is specified under **If no matching sound ID is available**. The choices are as follows:

- **Adjust durations of notes under line** is useful for slurs, which typically lengthen the notes under them to make them legato, with the exception of the last note under the slur, which is shortened (so that it is separated from the next note). To change these options:
  - If you want to change the lengths of the notes under the line, switch on **Adjust durations by** *n%*; durations greater than 100% increase the duration, and less than 100% reduce it
  - To shorten the last note under the line, switch on **Adjust last note by** *n%*.
- **Transpose** *up/down 1/2* **octaves** is used by octave (*8va, 15mb*, etc.) lines. Simply set whether you want the notes under the line to be transposed up or down, and by one or two octaves.
- **Spread chord** *up/down* **for** *n* **milliseconds** is for arpeggio (spread chord) lines, or lines you want to behave like arpeggio lines.
- **Play crescendo or diminuendo** is for hairpins. You can determine the precise playback effect of an individual hairpin by selecting it in the score and using the options on the **Playback** panel of Properties (see **Hairpins** on page 262).
- **Play trill** is for trills. You can specify the playback speed and interval of an individual trill by selecting it in the score and using the options on the **Playback** panel of Properties (see **Trills** on page 263).
- **Play sustain pedal** is for pedal lines.

- **Play glissando/portamento** is for *gliss.* and *port.* lines. You can specify the playback speed and interval of an individual line by selecting it in the score and using the options on the **Playback** panel of Properties (see **Gliss. and port.** on page 265).

- **Play guitar bend** is for bend lines (see **Bend** on page 123).

- **No playback effect** means that Sibelius will simply ignore the line during playback.

Any one of these options can be applied to any line, so you can make a slur behave like an octave line, or a guitar bend behave like an arpeggio line, if you really like.

Note, however, that those lines that have individually adjustable playback via the **Playback** panel of the Properties window – i.e. hairpins, trills, *gliss.* and *port.* lines – can only be adjusted in the Properties window if they are based on the appropriate type of line. In other words, although you can tell Sibelius to make, say, a **Box** line play back as a hairpin, it will always play back in the default way, and you won't be able to adjust its effect on playback in the Properties window.

Articulations page

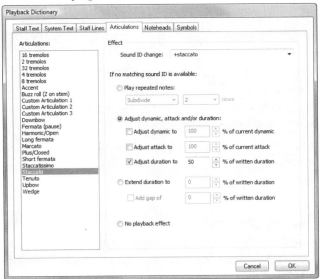

The **Articulations** page allows you to specify a **Sound ID change** for each type of articulation or tremolo. For example, you may specify upbow and downbow articulations to give rise to **+upbow** and **+downbow** sound ID changes, which would automatically choose special upbow and downbow sounds from your playback device, if available – see **Sound ID changes** below.

Failing that, if Sibelius is unable to find a suitable sound to play the specified sound ID change, or if no sound ID change is specified, it will do whichever of the default effects is specified under **If no matching sound ID is available**. The choices are as follows:

- **Play repeated notes** is for tremolos and buzz rolls (z on stem). You can determine whether it should be played measured – in which case choose **Subdivide** and set *n* **times** to the appropriate value – or **Unmeasured**, which means to play the note repeatedly as fast as possible.

- **Adjust dynamic, attack and/or duration** is for most other articulations. For example, by default, staccatos shorten a note by 50%, accents boost the dynamic by 50%, and downbows both boost the dynamic by 10% and shorten the note a little, too.
  - ○ To change the dynamic of the note on which the articulation occurs, switch on **Adjust dynamic to *n*% of current dynamic** and set the value appropriately.
  - ○ To change the attack of the note on which the articulation occurs, switch on **Adjust attack to *n*% of current attack** and set the value appropriately.
  - ○ To change the duration of the note, switch on **Adjust duration to *n*% of the written duration**. This isn't intended to be used for fermatas (pauses) – they have their own special options.
- **Extend duration by *n* times written duration** is for fermatas. By default, a regular fermata is set to 1.5 times written duration, a long (square) fermata is set to 1.75 times written duration, and a short (triangular) fermata is set to 1.25 written duration, but you can change these settings if you like. You can also optionally **Add gap of *n*% of written duration**, which will add the specified amount of silence following the fermata before the next note.
- **No playback effect** means that Sibelius will simply ignore the articulation during playback.

As with staff lines, you can apply any one of these options to any articulation, so you can make a staccato behave like a fermata if you like.

Noteheads page

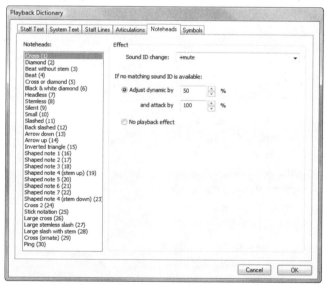

The **Noteheads** page allows you to specify a **Sound ID change** for each type of notehead in your score. For example, you might define a diamond notehead to give rise to the sound ID change **+harmonic**, which would automatically choose a harmonic sound on your playback device if one is available – see **Sound ID changes** below.

Failing that, you can define each notehead to have a default playback effect. In the case of noteheads, you can only specify a given notehead to adjust the current dynamic; this is useful for so-

Playback

called "ghost" notes in guitar music, which are normally written with a cross notehead and sound much quieter than normal notes.

Symbols page

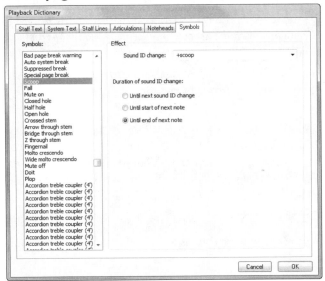

The Symbols page allows you to specify a Sound ID change for each type of symbol in your score. For example, a fall symbol can give rise to a sound ID change +fall, which will automatically trigger (say) a trumpet fall sound in your playback device, if one is available – see **Sound ID changes** below. No other playback effects are available for symbols.

Sound ID changes

For an introduction to sound IDs, 📖 **4.18 SoundWorld™**.

Sound ID changes allow you to add or remove one or more playing techniques from the current sound on a staff at any point. For example, the word "pizz" may be defined to produce a sound ID change of +pizzicato, while "arco" may be -pizzicato. You can also define something in the dictionary to add one element and subtract another simultaneously, such as -mute +sul ponticello.

To define a sound ID change, you can either type the sound ID elements you want to add or remove into the box, or choose them from the menu of common sound ID elements provided.

To add an element, put + directly before it, with no space between; to remove an element, put – directly before it, with no space between. To remove all current elements, type [reset] (include the square brackets).

On the **Staff Text** and **Symbols** pages, you can specify whether the sound ID change should take effect Until the next sound ID change, Until the start of the next note, or Until the end of the next note. Normally a sound ID change takes effect until another instruction to the contrary (e.g. the instruction "mute," or a symbol denoting "snares on" for side drum), but occasionally you may want a sound ID change to take effect for a single note (e.g. scoop or fall symbols, or a text indication above a single note on an unpitched percussion staff).

Similarly, on the **Staff Lines** page you can specify whether the sound ID change should take effect **Until end of line** (which is suitable for e.g. trill lines) or **Until end of last note under line** (which is suitable for e.g. slurs, octave lines, hairpins, and so on).

Note that simply defining a new sound ID change in **Play ▸ Dictionary** does not guarantee that it will be played back – Sibelius can only play those effects that are available in the devices in your current playback configuration – but the beauty of sound IDs is that they are device-independent, so the sound may be available on another computer or using a different configuration later, at which point Sibelius will play it back automatically.

When dictionary items take effect

When you insert words from the playback dictionary in your score using text, be aware that Sibelius treats words from the **Staff Text** and **System Text** pages differently.

Words entered in system text (e.g. tempo markings or rhythmic feel) take effect at the start of the bar to which they are attached.

Words entered in staff text (e.g. dynamics and words such as *pizz.*) take effect on the note to which they are attached; staff lines similarly affect playback from the point at which they are attached to the point at which they end.

Regular expressions

Regular expressions define, using symbols that have special meanings, patterns to match within a text string. Sibelius uses regular expressions to match terms used for playing back repeat structures such as **D.C. al Fine** and **D.S. al Coda** (📖 **4.6 Repeats**).

You can use regular expressions in the playback dictionary yourself, but you should exercise extreme caution in doing so – it's all too easy to create one that breaks playback of every other word in your score (e.g. the regular expression **a** matches any string that has an "a" in it, and ^. or $ will match anything at all).

- ^ means the match must occur at the start of the string, e.g. **^In the beginning**; see below
- $ means the match must occur at the end of the string, e.g. **Amen$**; see below
- . means match any single character, e.g. **c.t** (which would match **cat**, **cbt**, **cct**, **cdt** and so on!); to search for a literal period (full stop), use **\.**
- * matches any number of occurrences of the previous character (or choice of characters surrounded by square brackets [ ]). This can also include no occurrences, so the regular expression **a*** is matched by the string **b**, in addition to **a**, **aaaaa**, and so on. A useful regular expression is **.***, which means "match anything", so you can do **^begin.*end$**, which matches anything that is surrounded by **begin** and **end**
- + matches one or more occurrences of the previous character, so the regular expression **a+** is matched by the strings **a**, **aaaaa** and **baaa**, but not **b** or an empty string

- [ ] are the grouping operators, meaning "match any character in the group," so you can find digits with [0-9]. Punctuation characters lose their special meaning when within these brackets, so you can write things like D[.$S]* al Coda
- \x*NN* matches the hexadecimal character *NN*
- (*x*)|(*y*) are exclusive choice operators, where the string must match either *x* or *y*. You can use these to match whole words, e.g. (apple)|(banana)

Regular expressions match any part of the string, so a matches (say) a long string and cat. To explicitly match a alone, you need to add the start and end anchors: ^a$

Many punctuation characters (. $ ^ [ ] ( ) * + \) have special meaning in regular expressions, and to match them literally (i.e. to match a string containing one of these characters), they need to be preceded by \

Copying playback dictionary entries to other scores

Once you've edited entries in the playback dictionary, you can transfer your updated dictionary into other scores. Simply export the house style from the score in which you edited the dictionary, then import it into the new score – 📖 **8.8 House Style™** for more details – or save your score as a manuscript paper – 📖 **2.23 Manuscript paper**.

4.10 Video

📖 **4.1 Working with playback**, **4.11 Timecode and hit points**.

This topic explains how you can attach a digital video to your score, giving you the ability to write to picture using Sibelius.

Being able to compose directly to synchronized video is extremely useful both to professional composers and in education. Many school music syllabi include modules where students are required to compose music to video, and Sibelius provides an integrated platform on which to score, realize and print their work.

Adding a video

To add a video to your score:

- Choose **Play ▸ Video and Time ▸ Add Video**. A dialog appears asking you to locate the video file you want to add to the score. Once you've found the file, click **Open**.
- The video will now appear in Sibelius's Video window, along with the filename of the video in the title bar of the window.

Removing a video

To remove a video from your score:

- Choose **Play ▸ Video and Time ▸ Remove Video**
- Sibelius will warn you that the video will no longer be associated with the score and allow you to cancel the operation if you so wish.

Synchronization

Once a video has been added to a score, it will maintain synchronization with the score at all times during playback, and will also update the video whenever the position of the playback line changes. This means you can easily jump to a particular point in the video using the Playback window's timeline slider, as well as the Rewind and Fast-forward buttons.

When pressed once, Rewind and Fast-forward (shortcuts [and]) move by exactly 0.2 seconds; hold them down to accelerate. With some computers and video formats, you may find rewinding video is rather slower than fast-forwarding. For pinpoint accuracy when moving through the video, use **Shift-[** and **Shift-]** to advance through the video a single frame at a time.

Example videos

A variety of short videos for students to compose music to is available for download from **www.sibeliuseducation.com**.

File formats

Sibelius will play any video file format supported by your operating system. On Windows this will normally include .avi, .mpg, .wmv and, if you have QuickTime installed, .mov files. Mac users should be able to play .avi, .mpg and .mov files. Sibelius also requires that you have the necessary codecs installed on your system in order to play back the video file you have selected, so you may

Playback

find that some files fail to play back, even though they use one of these file extensions, and other files with the same extension play without problems. However, if this happens you will probably find that the video also fails to play in other video players on your computer as this is due to a lack of the required codec. If Sibelius cannot recognize the format of a file, it will notify you and the video will not be attached to the score.

Saving and opening scores with video files

When you save a score with a video added, Sibelius saves the file location of the video in the score. If you need to give your score to another Sibelius user, you must also supply them with the video file itself if you want them to be able to view it (the video is not embedded in the Sibelius file).

When opening a score with a video added, Sibelius first looks for the video file in the folder it was opened from. If it can't find the video file, it will ask you whether you wish to locate the video file manually. If you click Yes, a dialog appears in which you can set the new path of the file. If you click No, then Sibelius won't attempt to play the video.

Hiding and showing the Video window

When you add a video to a score, Sibelius will automatically show the Video window. If you wish to hide or show the Video window, choose Window ▸ Video (shortcut Ctrl+Alt+V *or* ⌥⌘V). There is also a button on the toolbar that will switch the Video window on and off.

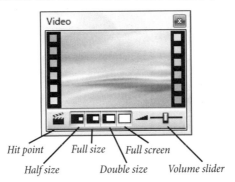

Hit point / Full size \ Full screen
Half size   Double size   Volume slider

Hiding the Video window does not remove the video from the score. In fact, the video will still continue to play back along with the score whilst remaining invisible, so you will still be able to hear the video's soundtrack. If you wish to remove the video from the score permanently, see **Removing a video** above.

Setting the volume level of the video

Sibelius allows you to adjust the volume of the video's soundtrack independently of the score by changing the position of the volume slider at the bottom of the Video window. When set to its left-most position, the soundtrack of the video will be completely silent.

Setting the size of the Video window

The Video window has four size presets so that you can select the most suitable dimensions for the video. These four buttons can be found at the bottom of the Video window (see above) and options are also in the Play ▸ Video and Time submenu. The video can be set to Half Size, Full Size or Double Size, or alternatively can be in Full Screen mode (see below).

Full screen mode

Using full screen mode for videos can be useful, but you should be aware that precisely what happens depends almost entirely on the codec used by the video itself and the behavior of the hardware or software being used to render the video.

- If you have a dual-display system, you may find that you are unable to choose which display you want the video to appear on, in which case it may be impossible for you to watch the video on one display and the score on the other. You may also experience problems such as Sibelius's play-back line not drawing properly, or the Video window appearing frozen on one display with the video itself running full screen on the other, etc.
- On Windows, if you are using a QuickTime codec to play back your video, it will play in full screen on your *primary* display, regardless of the display the Video window happens to be on
- On Windows, if you are using Windows Media to play back your video, switching to full screen mode will play the video at full screen on the display on which the Video window was previously located. If you click on the Video window or stop playback on Sibelius, the video will immediately exit full screen mode: this is a feature of the Windows Media codec.

On single-display systems, full screen mode works largely without problems. However, if you do encounter problems, you can normally restore the window back to its previous size by hitting **Esc**.

Windows Media and QuickTime

On Windows, some videos play back better using Windows Media and others with QuickTime. Sibelius allows you to choose your preferred player from the **Display** page of **File ▸ Preferences**. If you do not have QuickTime installed, you will not be able to choose this option.

If you attach a video that is not supported by your chosen video player, Sibelius will try to use the other player, overriding your setting. This may happen if, say, you try to play a QuickTime .mov file using Windows Media.

Sibelius will display the name of the video player it is using in parentheses in the title bar of the Video window after the video's filename.

Translucency of the Video window

Sibelius allows you to make the Video window translucent along with the other tool windows. This setting can be found on the **Display** page of **File ▸ Preferences** (in the **Sibelius** menu on Mac). Unlike the other tool windows, however, it is possible to switch off the Video window's translucency independently. This is sometimes necessary as some hardware configurations and codecs may cause flickering or ghost images in the Video window during playback when it is translucent.

For more information about translucent windows, ⌨ **5.6 Display settings**.

Start time

You can set the video to start playing from some point other than the start, in order to (say) skip a trailer that you are not scoring in Sibelius. You can also tell Sibelius only to begin playing the video back from a certain point in the score. There are three settings in **Play ▸ Video** and **Time ▸ Timecode and Duration** that allow you set up the exact correlation between the score and video, as follows:

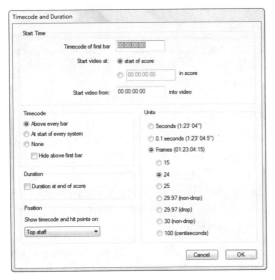

- **Timecode of first bar:** this setting tells Sibelius the time position of the first bar.
- **Start video at:** this is the time position at which you want the video to start playing back in the score. This is expressed as an absolute time, so the position must always be higher than or equal to the **Timecode of first bar.** If you want the video to begin playing back at the very start of the score, then choose **start of score.**
- **Start video from:** this setting is used when you want the video to start playing back from a point other than its very beginning. For example, if you had a video file that starts with two seconds of lead-in tape, you would probably want to ignore the first two seconds completely and tell Sibelius only to start playing the video from after that point. To do this, you would set **Start video from** to two seconds.

The dialog can understand a variety of formats. 1'00", 00:01:00:00 and 1:00' are all equivalent to "one minute." Additionally, Sibelius will interpret any single whole number entered into any of these fields as seconds, so entering 18 will always evaluate to 00:00:18:00. When entering values involving frames, you should ensure you use the same frame rate as selected in **Frames.**

For further information on working with timecode and hit points, 🕮 **4.11 Timecode and hit points**.

Adding your music to video files

Both Windows and Mac OS X come with inexpensive or free software that enable you to add the music you've written in Sibelius to the video file itself. First you need to export your score as an audio file in Sibelius – 🕮 **9.10 Exporting audio files**. Then you can import the file Sibelius creates, along with the video file you wrote the music to, into your movie editor.

Windows Movie Maker is included on all Windows systems, and iMovie comes free with most Apple computers (visit **www.apple.com/ilife/imovie** for more information).

If you would like to have a go at composing some music to your own visuals for a bit of fun, visit www.picasa.com and download the free software that allows you to quickly generate smart video slideshows from your own digital photo albums.

Playing back an audio track in sync with your score

You can use Sibelius's video feature to play an audio track back in sync with your score, which can be useful for transcription, or even for adding real recorded audio to the playback of your score (e.g. a recording of an acoustic instrument or singer playing the melody).

To add an audio track, choose Play ▸ Video and Time ▸ Add Video, and in the dialog that appears set the file type menu to All files. You can then choose any audio file in a suitable format (e.g. .wav, .mp3, .aiff, etc.), and it will be linked to your score. Notice that when you add an audio track to your score, the Video window shrinks down so that only the buttons and the slider to control the volume are visible.

You can use Plug-ins ▸ Other ▸ Set Metronome Mark to match the tempo of your score to the tempo of your audio track. Beware, however, that when you adjust the tempo of your score using the tempo slider in the Playback window, the pitch of the audio track will change as it is sped up or slowed down.

Playback

4.11 Timecode and hit points

📖 **4.1 Working with playback**, **4.10 Video**.

Timecode means the position in time of a point in a score or video. It is usually measured from the start of the score, or in film/TV scoring from the start of the reel or some other convenient point.

When you play back a score, a timecode read-out is displayed in the Playback window, together with a read-out of the current tempo in beats per minute.

Sibelius can also display timecode automatically as text above every barline in your score. It calculates the time position of barlines based on the number of bars, bar lengths and metronome marks up to that point. Timecode is particularly useful for working out precise timings of particular passages of music, or for synchronizing musical events with hit points (events in a film).

Sibelius does not synchronize playback with or display an incoming SMPTE or MTC data stream. This functionality is provided by professional sequencers such as Pro Tools, which can be used to play back music in this way if you export it from Sibelius as a MIDI file (📖 **9.9 Exporting MIDI files**). Sibelius will, however, synchronize playback with digital video files which can easily be attached to any Sibelius score (📖 **4.10 Video**).

Timecode read-out

During playback, timecode and tempo readouts appear on the Playback window:

You can switch the Playback window on and off using **Window ▸ Playback** (shortcut **Ctrl+Alt+Y** *or* ⌥⌘Y) or with the toolbar button ▶ . The timecode display (on the bottom left) shows the time elapsed since the start of the score (rather than the time elapsed since playback started) – in other words, it shows the absolute "score time" values specified by **Play ▸ Video and Time ▸ Timecode and Duration** (see below), rather than "real time."

Timecode and Duration dialog

The Play ▸ Video and Time ▸ Timecode and Duration dialog contains various options relating to time, which are saved in the score.

Notating timecode in the score

To write timecode in your score, switch on **Above every bar** or **At start of every system**. To change the staff it appears above, choose from the list under **Position**. This automatically displays timecode as text over every barline in your score; to move the timecode higher or lower, choose **House Style ▸ Default Positions** and adjust the vertical position of the **Timecode** text style accordingly (□ **8.12 Default Positions**).

Units

Timecode can be displayed in several formats:

- **Frames** (e.g. 01:23:04:13), which is the standard format used for film/TV scoring
- **0.1 seconds** (e.g. 1:23'4.5"), which is more legible but not quite as precise
- **Seconds** (e.g. 1:23'4), which is rather imprecise but useful for rough timings.

If your score includes repeats, repeated bars will show two or more timecodes in a pile, one for each "pass" of the music – □ **4.6 Repeats**.

Timecodes are printed when you print your score, but by default are not displayed in parts. If you wish to switch timecode on in parts, use the **House Style** page of the **Multiple Part Appearance** dialog (□ **7.3 Multiple Part Appearance**).

Because film and video can run at different speeds, timecode can be calculated based on the number of frames per second. **15, 24, 25, 29.97 (non-drop), 29.97 (drop)** and **30 (non-drop)** are all used in various kinds of film or video, and **100 (centiseconds)**, while not a standard film or video speed, is included as you may find it useful.

Start time

Timecode of first bar specifies the timecode of the start of the score (in the format Hours:Minutes:Seconds:Frames).

This is used as an offset for all displayed times (i.e. both for the timecode read-out during playback in the Playback window, and any timecode text in the score). If you are using a frame-based timecode format, the frames value of the start time is interpreted according to the current frames per second setting in the dialog.

Changing the Timecode of first bar has two uses:

* If your score is intended for film/TV work, the start time is often required to specify the location of a particular cue in the film
* If your score is part of a larger work, such as one movement of a symphony, set the start time of the score to the end time of the previous movement (given as the duration on the last page of the previous movement). Then all timecodes will be relative to the start of the symphony rather than the start of this movement.

For details of the Start video at and Start video from options, ☐ **4.10 Video**.

Duration at end of score

This calculates and writes the duration of your score on the last page, e.g. 4'33", in whatever format you have chosen for units.

If you set a start time for the score, it is added to the duration – so if you split a work into two files and set the start time of the second to the duration of the first, then the duration of the second file tells you the cumulative time up to that point. (See **Start time** above.)

How timecode and duration are calculated

The timecode and duration of score values take account of repeats (☐ **4.6 Repeats**), tempo text (e.g. **Allegro**) and metronome marks (☐ **3.1 Working with text**), fermatas (pauses) and *rit./accel.* lines (☐ **2.21 Lines**) – and are instantly updated whenever you create or edit these. Try it and see!

However, timecode values *do not* take account of adjustments to playback speed made with the tempo slider.

Hit points

Hit points are time references in the score that pinpoint important events that occur in a film or video, to make it easier for you to write music that fits in with these points. Sibelius allows you to add named hit points that even move around to show the corresponding point in the film or video if the timings in your score change.

How to add hit points to your score

When you add a hit point to your score, it will be added at the current position of the playback line. Suppose you had a video where an important event happens at 04'32": you would use the timeline slider on the Playback window to navigate to this point in the video, and then use the rewind and fast-forward buttons to advance in either direction in finer (0.2 second) steps if necessary.

When the frame you wish to mark is showing in the Video window, click the **Add Hit Point** button  on the Video window, or choose **Create ▸ Other ▸ Hit Point**. A hit point will be added above that point in the score.

You can also add hit points to your score using the **New** button in **Play ▸ Timecode and Duration ▸ Hit Points**. Adding hit points this way will always add them at the very beginning of the score, regardless of the current position of the playback line, and you can then type in the timecode position you want (see below).

You can move the hit points up or down in the score by changing the **Vertical position** of the **Hit points** text style in House Style ▸ Default Positions – ▢ **8.12 Default Positions**.

Editing the time position and name of hit points

You can edit any hit point in your score by choosing **Play ▸ Video and Time ▸ Hit Points** (shortcut **Shift+Alt+P** *or* ⇧⌥P). This dialog lists all the hit points in your score:

Timecode	Bar.beat.100ths	Name
00:00:27:00	12.2	Piano Drop 01
00:00:40:01	16.4	Piano Drop 02
00:00:50:12	20.2	Piano Drop 03
00:01:00:19	23.3.5	Piano Drop 04
00:01:07:23	26.1.5	Piano Drop 05

New
Delete
Delete All
Shift All

Display in score:
☑ Timecode
☑ Bar.beat.100ths
☑ Name

Cancel
OK

- The **Timecode** column shows the absolute time position at which each hit point falls. The format of this display will depend on the timecode setting you have chosen in **Play ▸ Video and Time ▸ Timecode and Duration**. This field is editable by double-clicking the time value you wish to change.

- The **Bar.beat.100ths** column shows the location of the hit point in the score in terms of bars, beats and hundredths of a beat. For instance, **64.2.96** would be bar 64, beat 2.96. If a hit point falls precisely on a beat, the hundredths value will be omitted. You cannot change this value manually, but it will update automatically if you reposition the hit point by editing its **Time**.

- The **Name** column shows the name of each hit point in your score. You can edit the name of any hit point by double-clicking its current name. Note that you must press **Return** after entering a new name to enter it into the table.

Deleting existing hit points

If you wish to remove a hit point from the score, you can do so from **Play ▸ Video and Time ▸ Hit Points**. Select the hit point you wish to delete, then click **Delete**. If you wish to delete all hit points from your score, click **Delete All**.

Playback

Fit selection to time

If you want to make a particular hit point arrive at a specific point in the score, you need to adjust the tempo of the score. Sibelius has a plug-in to perform the necessary calculations for you – see **Fit Selection to Time** on page 498.

Shifting all hit points

There may be some instances where your score's hit points fall out of sync with the video if you have made changes to the score start time or video start time settings. In order to rectify this problem, you can offset all the hit points you have created by the same time value by clicking Shift All in Play ▸ Video and Time ▸ Hit Points. You can enter any positive or negative offset using a variety of formats (1'00", 00:01:00:00 and 1:00' are all equivalent to "one minute"). Also, Sibelius will interpret any whole number entered into any of these fields as seconds, so entering -4 will always evaluate to -00:00:04:00. When entering values that specify frames, you should ensure you use the same frame rate as selected in the Frames section of Play ▸ Video and Time ▸ Timecode and Duration (see above).

Showing hit points on a staff

Some composers find it useful to relate the position of each hit point to the closest beat position in the music, often by adding cross noteheads to a single line staff at the top or bottom of the score. Sibelius has a plug-in to do this for you – see **Add Hit Point Staff** on page 496.

Text styles

Timecodes are written using the Timecode text style, and hit points using the Hit points text style. Their height above the staff is determined by the value of the relevant text style's vertical position in House Style ▸ Default Positions (📖 **8.12 Default Positions**). You can also adjust the vertical position of the score's duration as it appears below the final bar of the score by editing the Duration at end of score text style.

4.12 Playback Devices

MIDI setup for Windows, **MIDI setup for Mac** in Handbook; ▯ **4.3 Mixer**, **4.4 Sibelius Sounds Essentials**, **4.15 Working with virtual instruments**.

This topic introduces the concept of playback configurations, and tells you how to set up configurations using the Play ▸ Playback Devices dialog.

Playback devices

A *playback device* is a hardware or software device that provides one or more sounds. There are several types of playback device, including:

- Virtual instruments that use VST or Audio Unit technology, including the built-in Sibelius Player
- Internal MIDI hardware, such as some soundcards' built-in synthesizers
- External MIDI hardware, such as sound modules and keyboards with sounds built in.

Sibelius can play back using any combination of hardware and software playback devices, even within the same playback configuration.

If you have any external MIDI devices (e.g. sound modules or synthesizers) that you want to use for playback in Sibelius, you need to connect them to your computer before Sibelius can "see" them – see **MIDI setup for Windows** or **MIDI setup for Mac** in the Handbook.

If you're not familiar with MIDI terminology, ▯ **4.13 MIDI for beginners**.

For an introduction to virtual instruments and effects, ▯ **4.14 Virtual instruments for beginners**.

Playback configurations

A *playback configuration* is a collection of settings that determines which of the playback devices available on your system should be used for playback, which *sound set* each of them should use, and how to use their particular capabilities (e.g. that you prefer to use the violin sound from one device, and the brass sounds from another), so that Sibelius can work out which sounds to use for each of your scores with as little intervention from you as possible.

You can set up as many playback configurations as you like, each one suitable for different purposes, and switch between them at any time. For example, you may want to use your computer's built-in sounds while composing or arranging so that you don't have to wait for large samples to load before you can get working, but need to be able to switch easily to using an orchestral sample library to produce an audio demo or rehearsal CD. This can be achieved simply by creating two playback configurations and switching between them.

When you switch between playback configurations, you don't need to make any changes to your score: Sibelius automatically works out the best way to play back your score using the current playback configuration, so you never need to laboriously re-assign playback sounds.

Playback

323

Sound sets

A *sound set* is a file that lists all of the sounds available on a particular virtual instrument or MIDI device, and tells Sibelius what real instrumental sounds those sounds correspond to, so that Sibelius can automatically make the best possible use of them.

Note that the choice of available sound sets will be different based on the type of device you have selected, and Sibelius does not come with sound sets for every possible MIDI device or virtual instrument. If your device isn't listed in the **Sound set** column of the **Active devices** list on the **Active Devices** page of **Play ▸ Playback Devices**, a sound set file may be available from the support pages of the Sibelius web site – choose **Help ▸ Online Support**.

If you have a device for which no sound set is available, you can still use it with Sibelius, by creating a *manual sound set*. A manual sound set is like a miniature sound set that describes a very specific set of sounds. For example, if you have a virtual instrument that provides a single piano sound, you don't need a complete sound set file; instead, you create a manual sound set to tell Sibelius that this device can only play a piano sound. Alternatively, you may be using a virtual instrument that can provide many sounds, but for which no sound set is available, in which case you can create a manual sound set that tells Sibelius what sound is available on every channel provided by the device.

You can even create your own sound set file using the separate Sound Set Editor application, available for download from the online support pages.

Default playback configurations

Sibelius creates three default playback configurations for you:

* **Sibelius Sounds**: chosen by default, this configuration uses the built-in Sibelius Player to play back the included high-quality Sibelius Sounds Essentials sample library (📖 **4.4 Sibelius Sounds Essentials**). Depending on your computer's available resources, this configuration can play up to 128 different instruments simultaneously.
* **General MIDI (enhanced)**: this configuration uses a high-quality General MIDI-compatible virtual instrument from M-Audio, and can play up to 32 different instruments simultaneously.
* **General MIDI (basic)**: this configuration uses your computer's built-in sounds. On Windows, this uses the Microsoft GS Wavetable Synth, which can play up to 16 different instruments simultaneously. On Mac, this uses two instances of Apple's DLS Music Device, allowing up to 32 different instruments simultaneously.

If you have upgraded from Sibelius 5, and still have the version of Sibelius Sounds Essentials that was included with Sibelius 5 installed on your computer, Sibelius will also create two further playback configurations for you: **Sibelius Essentials (16 sounds, Kontakt)** and **Sibelius Essentials (32 Sounds, Kontakt)**. These configurations allow you to use the old version of Sibelius Sounds Essentials in Sibelius 6 if you want to, though you are recommended to use the new **Sibelius Sounds** playback configuration instead. (When you first open a Sibelius 5 score that was set to use Sibelius Sounds Essentials in Sibelius 6, Sibelius automatically sets it to use the new **Sibelius Sounds** playback configuration and hence the new version of the supplied sample library.)

Creating a new playback configuration

To create a new playback configuration, choose an existing entry from the **Configuration** menu upon which to base your new one. Click **New**, and you will be prompted to choose a name: type one and click **OK**. Depending on the devices in use, you may find that Sibelius is busy for a few moments after you click **OK**.

Changing the current playback configuration

To use a different playback configuration, choose **Play ▸ Playback Devices**, and choose an item from the **Configuration** list at the top of the dialog. You may find that Sibelius is busy for a few moments, particularly if the new configuration uses one or more virtual instruments.

Renaming and deleting playback configurations

To rename an existing configuration, simply choose it from the list at the top of the dialog, then click **Rename**. Similarly, to delete an existing configuration, choose it from the list, then click **Delete** and answer **Yes** when prompted. You can neither rename nor delete any of the playback configurations Sibelius creates by default.

Editing a playback configuration

To make changes to an existing playback configuration, you work with the four pages of the **Play ▸ Playback Devices** dialog, which are discussed in detail below.

You cannot edit the default playback configurations, except for changing the sound sets used by the active devices on the **Active Devices** page, and adding or removing separate effects on the **Effects** page. To edit one of the defaults, create a new configuration based on it – see above.

Notice that when you make any changes in the dialog, an asterisk is appended to the name of the configuration in the menu at the top. To save your configuration, simply click **Save**.

Active Devices page

On the **Active Devices** page, you can choose which of the devices available on your system should be used by this configuration:

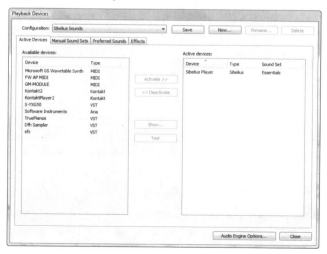

- The **Available devices** box on the left lists the playback devices available on your system. This box is disabled (grayed out) if the current playback configuration is one of the defaults created by Sibelius. Each device is listed by its **Name**, and is one of the following **Type**s:

  - The built-in Sibelius Player is recognised as type **Sibelius**.
  - Kontakt Player and the full Kontakt sampler from Native Instruments show as type **Kontakt**. On Mac, Sibelius will also show whether the virtual instrument uses VST or Audio Unit technology.
  - Garritan software instruments, such as Garritan Personal Orchestra and Authorized Steinway, use the ARIA sample player, and show as type **Aria**. On Mac, Sibelius will also show whether the virtual instrument uses VST or Audio Unit technology.
  - All other virtual instruments on Windows, and some on Mac, show as type **VST**.
  - Some virtual instruments on Mac use Apple's Audio Unit technology, and show as type **AU**.
  - Normal MIDI devices, such as internal soundcard synths or external keyboards and sound modules, show as type **MIDI**.

  To activate a device in the current configuration, select it in the **Available devices** list and click **Activate**. When you activate the Sibelius Player or a **MIDI** device, it is moved from **Available devices** to the **Active devices** list on the right. But when you activate a **Kontakt, Aria, VST** or **AU** device, it remains in the **Available devices** list and is *copied* to the **Active devices** list: you can therefore activate more than one instance of a virtual instrument, but you can only ever have one instance of the Sibelius Player or a MIDI device.

- The **Active devices** box on the right lists the playback devices that are activated, i.e. available for Sibelius to use during playback. In addition to the **Name** and **Type** columns in common with the **Available devices** list, there is an extra **Sound set** column. You can click on the sound set column to choose between the available sound sets. If no suitable sound set is available for the device you are using, set **Sound set** to (none), and then use the **Manual Sound Sets** page to tell Sibelius how to play back using this device – see below.

  You can rename the devices in the **Active devices** list by double-clicking their names; Sibelius will append the original name of the device to the name you choose. This can be helpful if you are using multiple instances of the same virtual instrument, each loaded with a different sound set or individual sound.

  To deactivate a device, select it in the **Active devices** list and click **Deactivate** to remove it from the list.

Manual Sound Sets page

Sibelius Player, **Kontakt**- and **Aria**-type virtual instruments, and **MIDI**-type devices, provide special functions that allow Sibelius to load sounds automatically into them, if a suitable sound set is available. If no sound set is available, or if a device is a regular **VST**- or **AU**-type virtual instrument, you have to tell Sibelius which sounds are available, by creating a miniature sound set for each virtual instrument, using the **Manual Sound Sets** page.

Once you have told Sibelius which sound is available on each channel of your device, it can treat that device like any other, and automatically route the playback of each staff to the most appropriate available sound.

The options on the **Manual Sound Sets** page are as follows:

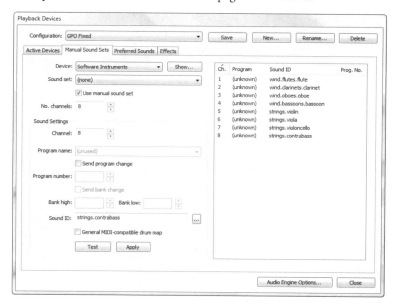

- First choose the virtual instrument from the **Device** menu at the top of the dialog. You can create a manual sound set for any type of device with any kind of sound set, except for the built-in Sibelius Player; in addition, manual sound sets are unavailable by default for **Kontakt**-type devices because it is recommended to allow Sibelius to load the sounds itself. To create a manual sound set for a **Kontakt**-type device, switch on **Allow manual sound sets** on the **Playback** page of **File ▸ Preferences** (in the **Sibelius** menu on Mac).

- If you are creating a manual sound set for a virtual instrument, click **Show** to make its interface appear in another window; this button is disabled for **MIDI**-type devices. There is tremendous variation in how the interfaces of virtual instruments appear and behave, so it's impractical to attempt to provide any help for working with them. Refer to the documentation that accompanied your virtual instrument for help working out which things to click on. Leave the window open – you'll need it again in a minute.

- If you have already chosen a sound set for this device on the **Active Devices** page, it will now be chosen in the **Sound set** menu; if not, you can choose it here now. If no suitable sound set is available, choose **(none)**.

- Switch on **Use manual sound set** to tell Sibelius that it should follow the choices you make here. If you switch this option off, your manual sound set will not be used, but the settings will be saved as part of the playback configuration, so that you can restore them again later.

- If your device has a sound set, **No. channels** will be set to the appropriate number of different channels, slots or sounds the device can play at once. Some virtual instruments are designed to emulate only a single instrument, such as a specific electric piano or synthesizer, in which case they can normally play only one sound at once, and therefore **No. channels** should be set to **1**. Other virtual instruments, particularly those supplied with sample libraries, can play a number of sounds simultaneously, so **No. channels** may need to be set to **8** or **16**. Notice that the table on the right of the dialog is updated with the appropriate number of channels chosen here.

If **No. channels** is not automatically set correctly for your device, set it manually.

- Now go back to your virtual instrument's interface and load a sound, or set it to an appropriate preset. If your virtual instrument can play back multiple sounds simultaneously, start by loading a sound into the first channel or slot. If you are working with a MIDI device, set the first channel to use an appropriate patch, if necessary.

- Now look at the **Sound Settings** options on the **Manual Sound Sets** page. Either click on the first row in the table on the right or use the **Channel** spin control next to choose a channel.

- If you have chosen a sound set for this device, the **Program** menu will be enabled and the **Sound ID** menu will be disabled.

  - If **Program** is enabled, choose the name of the program you have loaded into your device, then click **Apply**.

  - Switch on **Send program change** if your device has a sound set chosen but you know that it requires an explicit program change message to be sent at the start of playback (in which case Sibelius will send the program change stipulated by the sound set), or if you have no sound set chosen and know that the sound you want can be chosen with a specific program change when starting playback (in which case the **Program number** control will become enabled, and you can specify the program change to send).

  - If **Send program change** is switched on, you can also switch on **Send bank change** if necessary; as before, if your device has a sound set, switching on **Send bank change** will send the bank change stipulated by the sound set, and if it does not, you can specify the **Bank high** and **Bank low** components of the bank change message to send when starting playback.

  - If **Sound ID** is enabled, choose the sound that most closely matches the sound you have loaded into your device by clicking ... to see a menu. For example, if you have loaded a violin ensemble sound, choose **strings.violin.ensemble** from the menu; if it's a Steinway piano sound, choose **keyboard.piano.grand.steinway**. Be as specific as the menu allows, as this will help Sibelius to use the sound most appropriately. Once you have chosen the closest match, click **Apply**.

  - Switch on **General MIDI-compatible drum map** instead of choosing a single sound ID or program name if you know that the program on that channel is an unpitched percussion map that matches the General MIDI standard. If the device is not General MIDI-compatible, you will need a sound set file for your device in order to be able to address its unpitched percussion sounds.

- You will see that the first row of the table on the right of the dialog is updated. If your device can handle another sound simultaneously, repeat the above steps until you have loaded as many sounds as needed and set up their mappings in the manual sound set.

Don't forget to click **Save** at the top of the dialog to avoid losing what you've just done!

Sibelius needs to be given a sound ID (or program name if a sound set is available) in order to be able to route playback to a channel automatically. If you don't want Sibelius to route each staff in your score to a channel automatically – because you have (say) a pre-existing template that you use for all your projects and you're comfortable assigning staves to channels by hand – you can set up an empty manual sound set. Simply set **No. channels** to the appropriate number and switch on **Use manual sound set**, but make no other choices.

To make Sibelius use those channels in playback, you must open each staff's strip in the Mixer in turn, and explicitly choose the device it should use (so that the device's name does not appear in parentheses), then explicitly choose the channel using the arrows at the right-hand side of the channel read-out. For more details, see **Staff strips** on page 268.

Preferred Sounds page

Having chosen which devices to use for playback, and set up any manual sound sets as necessary, you can now tell Sibelius which devices to use for which kinds of sounds. For example, if you prefer the brass sounds of one device and the string sounds of another, you can tell Sibelius to use these devices for these kinds of sounds whenever possible.

Setting up the **Preferred Sounds** page is completely optional: Sibelius is designed to choose the best available sound in any given situation. So you can ignore this page of the dialog altogether and just let Sibelius get on with sorting out which of your sounds to use.

But if you want to do so, you can set your preferences on the **Preferred Sounds** page of Play ▸ **Playback Devices**:

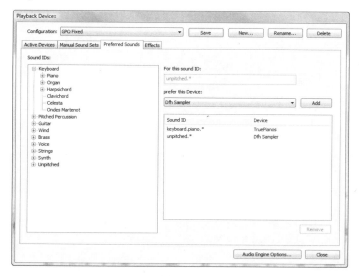

- Using the **Sound IDs** tree view on the left of the dialog, select the group of sounds for which you want to specify a preferred device. When you select a branch of the tree, you also implicitly select all sub-branches within it. This means that if you select, say, **Strings**, you are also selecting **Strings.Violin** and everything underneath it, as well as **Strings.Violoncello** and everything within that.
- Once you have chosen the appropriate branch, you will see that **For this sound ID** shows the complete sound name you have chosen. Now make your choice from the **Prefer this device** list and click **Add** to set your preference.
- Notice that the preference you have set up is now shown in the list on the right of the dialog. If you want to remove any of your existing choices, simply select them in the list and click **Remove**.

You can be as specific as you like in your preferences: if you generally want brass sounds to be played by a particular device, just select **Brass** and set a preference; if, on the other hand, you always want to use a particular device that closely emulates the sound of a Hammond B3 organ when your score uses such an instrument, choose **keyboard.organ.drawbar.percussive.with rotary speaker**, and then set a preference for that sound only.

As with the settings on the other pages of this dialog, don't forget to click **Save** to save your changes.

Effects page

The **Effects** page allows you to load effects into the various buses provided:

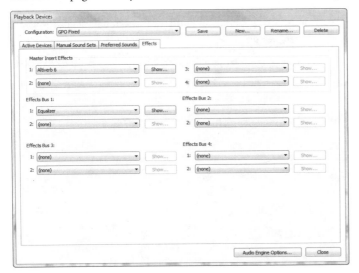

Master Insert Effects are effects that are applied to the entire audio signal just before it is output by your sound device and, shortly afterwards, makes its way to your ears. Effects such as compressors and limiters can usefully be added as master insert effects, as you would normally want them to apply to all of the sound produced by all the virtual instruments you are using. You may also want to use reverb as a master insert effect, though doing it this way means that you cannot alter the amount of reverb virtual instrument by virtual instrument. You can chain up to four master insert effects: the audio signal is passed through each effect, one after the other.

Sibelius also provides four effects *send buses*, which can be used to direct some of the audio signal to one or more effects. These buses are *post-fader*, meaning that the amount of signal sent to the effect depends on the level of the volume fader for the output of the virtual instrument. You choose how much of each virtual instrument's output signal is sent to each of the send buses using the controls in the Mixer window (**4.3 Mixer**). You can chain up to two effects in each of the four send buses.

You can use the send buses to add effects to the output of individual virtual instruments. For example, you may have a guitar virtual instrument and want to add a stomp box effect: load the stomp box effect into one of the send buses, and send some of the output from your virtual instrument to that send bus.

Adding an effect to your playback configuration is very simple: simply choose it from the drop-down list for the appropriate slot in whichever bus you want it to appear. To show an effect's graphical interface, click the **Show** button. Any changes you make in the effect's interface are saved when you save your configuration.

Note that effects can only affect the sound produced by virtual instruments, because the sound produced by MIDI devices isn't part of the same audio stream (indeed, for external MIDI devices the sound is never inside your computer at all). Furthermore, the built-in Sibelius Player includes two master effects – reverb and chorus – of its own, which do not appear here on the **Effects** page, and which only apply to sounds played by the Sibelius Player.

Audio Engine Options

To set up the audio interface Sibelius should use for playback, click **Audio Engine Options** at the bottom of **Play ▶ Playback Devices**. This dialog appears:

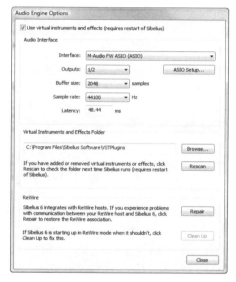

- Choose the device you want to use for playback from the **Interface** drop-down. On Windows, you may see the same device listed several times, with different acronyms in parentheses at the end:

  ○ If you see a device with **(ASIO)** at the end of its name, use this one. ASIO (which stands for "Audio Stream Input/Output") provides a low latency interface, and so is ideal when you are using virtual instruments and effects for playback and input.

  ○ Devices with **(DS)** at the end of their name use Microsoft's DirectSound technology. DirectSound doesn't provide such low latency as ASIO, but is recommended if no ASIO device is available. Depending on the specific hardware, a DirectSound device may or may not provide low enough latency for use when inputting via Flexi-time.

  ○ Devices with **(MME)** at the end of their name use Microsoft's MultiMedia Extension technology, a predecessor of DirectSound and ASIO. Some inexpensive soundcards or built-in sound hardware (in laptops or low-end desktop computers) only support MME, which will generally work adequately for playback, but will definitely not provide low enough latency for use when inputting via Flexi-time.

On Windows, Sibelius will automatically choose an ASIO device if one is available; it will otherwise choose a DirectSound device, or a MME device as a last resort.

On Mac, practically every device supports Mac OS X's built in Core Audio standard, so you will normally only see **(CoreAudio)** at the end of each device's name. Core Audio is similar to ASIO in that it provides a low latency interface. Sibelius will use the device chosen on the **Output** tab of the **Sound** pane of System Preferences by default.

* On Windows, when you are using an ASIO device, the **ASIO Setup** button is enabled. Clicking this button opens your device's ASIO control panel, where you can modify various comfortingly technical settings specific to your device.

* **Outputs** allows you to choose which of your device's outputs to use for playback. Most soundcards have a single pair of stereo outputs, so you will see only **1/2** in this menu. If you have a soundcard or other audio interface with multiple pairs of outputs, each pair will be listed here.

* **Buffer size**, as you might expect, determines the size of the buffer provided by your audio interface for data to be streamed into, which has an effect on the latency of the device: the larger the buffer, the higher the latency. The buffer sizes provided by your hardware may vary, but for most ASIO and Core Audio devices, a reasonable buffer size is 1024 samples.

* **Sample rate** is the frequency at which the audio is played back through the audio interface. Normally this should be set to **44100Hz**.

* **Latency** is the amount of time, in milliseconds, it takes for the audio device to play a note after Sibelius tells it to. You can't edit the latency directly; it's calculated by the combination of buffer size and sample rate.

* On Windows, you will also see an option to choose the folder from which Sibelius should load virtual instruments and effects (by default, **C:\Program Files\Sibelius Software\VSTPlugins**). You can change this by clicking **Browse** if you already have virtual instruments and effects in another location on your computer. (On Mac, all virtual instruments and effects live in a single location specified by Mac OS X, so there is never any need to change it.)

* Click **Rescan** if you find that virtual instruments or effects you expect to appear in **Playback Devices** are not appearing. When you next restart Sibelius, it will re-examine each of the virtual instruments and effects in the specified folder. Beware that this can take a little while! (Sibelius automatically detects newly-installed virtual instruments or effects without requiring you to click **Rescan**.)

* The options in the **ReWire** group are explained in 📖 **4.16 ReWire**.

The **Use virtual instruments and effects** option at the top of the dialog allows you to disable Sibelius's support for virtual instruments and effects altogether. If you want only **MIDI**-type devices to appear in **Play ▸ Playback Devices**, switch this option off, then restart Sibelius.

Click **Close** once you have finished making changes in the **Audio Engine Options** dialog.

Presets for virtual instruments and effects

Some virtual instruments and effects have a number of built-in presets provided by their designers. You can see which presets are available by opening the menu at the top left-hand corner of the virtual instrument or effect's window:

If the menu is empty or only contains a single item, then the virtual instrument or effect you are using doesn't provide any presets. If you choose a preset from the menu and want to ensure that your choice is remembered, don't forget to save your playback configuration in **Play ▸ Playback Devices**.

To the right of the menu are two further buttons, to load and save **.fxp** VST preset files. Saving a preset file saves the state of the virtual instrument or effect to disk, and loading it again restores the virtual instrument or effect to the same exact state. This is useful if you need to adjust a virtual instrument or effect's settings, and then use those same settings in another playback configuration within Sibelius, or even in another application.

Playback preferences

The **Playback** page of **File ▸ Preferences** (in the **Sibelius** menu on Mac) provides the following options:

- In the **Default Playback Configuration** group, you can tell Sibelius always to load a specific playback configuration when you start the program.

- In the **Opening Files** group, you can determine what Sibelius should do when opening a score that uses a different playback configuration than the currently chosen one. By default, **Let me choose whether to change to the new configuration** is chosen, which means that Sibelius will show you a message box when you open a score, allowing you to switch to the configuration the score was last saved with (click **Yes**) or stick with your current configuration (click **No**). You can alternatively choose **Always change to the new configuration** or **Never change to the new configuration**.

- The options in the **Sample Player Options** group apply to the built-in Sibelius Player, and to the **Kontakt**- and **Aria**-type sample players:

  ○ Switch off **Load sounds immediately** if you don't want the sounds required to play your score to be loaded until you either start playback or select a note.

333

- ○ **Re-use already loaded sounds** tells Sibelius not to reload every single sound when you switch between different scores. You should leave this switched on.
- The options in the **Sibelius Player Options** group apply only to the built-in Sibelius Player:
  - ○ **Maximum number of channels** determines how many simultaneous sounds Sibelius Player can load – see **How Sibelius Player works** on page 276.
  - ○ **Use convolution reverb (sounds better, uses more CPU)** specifies that Sibelius should use the high-quality convolution reverb built-in to Sibelius Player during playback; **But not during Flexi-time input (for lowest latency)** tells Sibelius to use the standard reverb during recording to improve latency – see **Reverb** on page 286.
  - ○ **Unload sounds when switching between scores** tells Sibelius to unload all sounds from Sibelius Player when switching scores. You only need to switch this option on if you are switching between two or more large scores that share very few instruments in common, and are concerned about memory usage.
- In the **Kontakt and Kontakt Player** group, switch on **Allow manual sound sets** if you want to control the loading of sounds into Kontakt Player or the full Kontakt package yourself. Unless you know what you're doing, you should leave this switched off.
- In the **Display** group, you can tell Sibelius whether you want it to display **Sound IDs** or **Program names** (the default setting). If you choose to display program names, Sibelius will show them in the Mixer and **House Style ▸ Edit Instruments** dialogs whenever possible.
- In the **Slot and Channel Sharing** group:
  - ○ Switch off **Use same slot for all staves of keyboard instruments** to adjust the sound, volume or pan of each staff of a multiple staff instrument (e.g. piano, organ, etc.) individually.
  - ○ Switch on **Use same slot for similar instruments** to limit the number of slots or channels Sibelius uses to play back your score. With this option switched on, Sibelius will actively try to make similar instruments (e.g. all woodwinds, all brass, all strings) share the same slot or channel.
  - ○ **Use variant sounds for identical instruments** tells Sibelius to try and find different equivalent sounds when you have several instruments that use the same basic sound (e.g. first and second violins in an orchestral score, or four alto saxophones in a big band score) to reduce the homogeneity of the sound. The effectiveness of this option depends on the capabilities of the playback devices you are using.
  - ○ Switch off **Automatically allocate slot for click track** if you never use Flexi-time recording or never want to hear a metronome click during playback. When this option is switched off, Sibelius will not reserve a slot or channel for the click track, freeing it up for another sound (and preventing Sibelius from loading an otherwise unnecessary percussion patch). However, if you subsequently start Flexi-time recording or unmute the click track during playback, Sibelius will not load an appropriate click sound unless you switch this option back on. It is therefore recommended that you leave this option switched on.

- In the **MIDI Messages** group:

  ○ **Send reset controllers at start**: tells Sibelius whether to reset all the MIDI controllers when it starts playback; if you use the Proteus 2, switch this option off

  ○ **Send bank high (controller 0)** and **Send bank low (controller 32)**: these options tell Sibelius whether to send bank numbers when sending program change messages; if you use the Roland SC-88 or Korg 05RW, you might want to switch this option off if you find that sending bank messages changes the mode of the MIDI device or chooses a non-GM bank. (These settings give global control over whether Sibelius sends bank messages, but you can also change this on a staff-by-staff basis from the **Window ▸ Mixer** window – ⮂ **4.3 Mixer**.)

  ○ **Send program changes**: tells Sibelius whether to send program changes when it starts playback. You might want to switch this option off if you need to specify the patch used by a particular MIDI channel in your score (e.g. if you are using a program like Gigasampler for playback).

  ○ **Convert Live Playback velocities to dynamics on sustaining instruments** means that Live Playback velocities are converted to dynamics rather than to attack for sustaining instruments use the modulation wheel for volume (e.g. in Garritan Personal Orchestra).

  ○ **Send note offs for all notes** is a special "brute force" option for badly-behaved playback devices that do not respond to the standard MIDI messages for stopping playback. If you find that notes are often left sounding when you stop playback, try switching this option on: Sibelius will then send an explicit note off message for each note that is sounding at the moment you stop playback.

- In the **Error Reporting** group, you can decide whether Sibelius should **Warn when MIDI devices return errors**. Switching this option off suppresses the errors returned by the operating system's MIDI system. It is recommended that you leave this option switched on, as the error messages can be very useful in troubleshooting problems with playback and note input from external MIDI devices. On Windows, errors relating to playback include the code **MMSYSTEM/OUT**, while errors relating to input say **MMSYSTEM/IN**.

If you see an error message when starting Sibelius or during playback, you should try to obtain a driver update from the manufacturer of your soundcard or other audio device. If no update is available, or if it makes no difference, check to see if you actually experience any problems with playback or input: some of the error messages are harmless, and if that applies to you, you can either suppress individual error messages by switching on **Don't say this again** when they appear, or suppress them altogether by switching off **Warn when MIDI devices return errors** instead.

Playback

4.13 MIDI for beginners

This topic assumes that you know very little about anything at all. (It was originally entitled "MIDI for idiots," which could give offense but does have certain poetic qualities.) Read this topic if you know little or nothing about MIDI. Skip this topic if you know quite a lot about MIDI.

For information on plugging your MIDI devices into your computer and setting it up, ⌨ **4.12 Playback Devices**, and **MIDI setup for Windows** and **MIDI setup for Mac** in the Handbook.

Basic question – what is MIDI?

MIDI stands for Musical Instrument Digital Interface. It is a standard, not a thing* – the universal standard for connecting electronic musical instruments together. MIDI keyboards, synthesizers, sound modules, samplers and other electronic music gadgets can all be plugged into one another with MIDI cables, and can also be plugged into your computer. Soundcards, software synthesizers and virtual instruments are also MIDI compatible, and as they're already in your computer you don't need to attach cables at all in order to play music back.

MIDI is supposed to make your life easy, in the same way that plugging a printer into your computer is now quite easy. Remember the good old days, when you couldn't even work your printer without a computing degree, and the manual disconcertingly included a complete circuit diagram in case you needed to solder on extra components? Ah, those were the days!

Unfortunately, in the sphere of MIDI those days are still with us. People using MIDI devices are still expected to have a working knowledge of technicalities like MIDI channels, program numbers, banks and worse – knowledge that in most cases can and should be hidden from everyone except the experts.

(*This superficially obvious point does need spelling out, as we have on a number of occasions been asked questions such as: "How big is a MIDI?")

Program numbers and General MIDI

The sounds available from MIDI devices are referred to by numbers, typically in the range 0 to 127. The piano sound might be number 0, and the flute sound number 73. It would be nice if these were called instrument numbers or sound numbers, but in practice they're called *program numbers* for obscure historical reasons. (They are sometimes called "program changes," "patch numbers" or "voice numbers" instead, confusingly.)

Until recently program numbers weren't standardized. Though program 0 happens to be a piano sound on most devices, program 73 might be anything. Before standardization, you used to have to tell computers the program numbers you wanted for each instrument in each score, which could be very tiresome. Also, if you played the same score on other MIDI devices, you might get the wrong sounds – not very satisfactory.

Fortunately a standard list of 128 sounds has emerged, called General MIDI (known as GM to its friends). These sounds start with piano as program number 0, and pass through most of the instruments you can think of, with a very final gunshot as program number 127. Virtually all soundcards and a lot of new MIDI devices follow this standard, maybe with extra sounds too. Professional MIDI devices are less likely to be General MIDI compatible.

More recently, the MIDI manufacturers have got together again and ratified some additions to the General MIDI standard, resulting in General MIDI 2, or GM2 for short. GM2 adds an extra 128 sounds to the standard set, among other things, but it isn't yet in very widespread usage. You can usually tell if your own MIDI device is GM- or GM2-compatible by seeing if it includes the appropriate logo on its front panel.

Within Sibelius program numbers works like this: whenever you create a flute staff Sibelius normally sets it to program number 73, which is the General MIDI program number for a flute sound. When you play back the score on any General MIDI-based device, this produces the right sound. It's as simple as that.

Moreover, if you connect a different device and tell Sibelius what type of device it is, Sibelius will alter the program number to produce that device's best flute sound. Sibelius can be used with any MIDI device.

Counting from 0

A pointless complication of MIDI is that some manuals list program numbers in the range 0-127 and others in the range 1-128. (This is because for obscure technical reasons, computer programmers count from 0, so when designing the internal workings of MIDI devices they tend to get carried away and forget that normal people count from 1.)

The annoying consequence of this is that sometimes when setting up MIDI devices you find you get the wrong sound and have to add or subtract 1 from a program number to correct the problem. Sibelius almost always makes the adjustment for you, so try not to think about this.

Banks: variants of sounds

Some MIDI devices can play back hundreds of different sounds, even though program numbers only go up to 127. This limitation is overcome by arranging the extra sounds in groups or *banks* of program numbers. To access these, you specify the bank number as well as the program number.

A bank number consists of 2 values, though often MIDI devices only specify one of the values (the other one being implicitly 0).

Channels

If you've had enough of MIDI technicalities, you can skip this bit.

Channels are often the first thing you're told about MIDI, but with Sibelius they are largely irrelevant. Most MIDI devices can only play back up to 16 different sounds at once (that is, only 16 different timbres), even though the maximum number of notes that can play at once might be 32 or more. You can think of the MIDI device as containing 16 staves called *channels* that can only play one timbre at a time. Sibelius, or whatever else is plugged into it, produces different timbres by saying which channel each note or chord is playing on. Some other things like the overall volume control (shown as a fader on Sibelius's Mixer window), pan (= stereo) position and piano pedaling also apply to the channel, not to individual notes.

Other MIDI terms

Some other MIDI terms that we won't explain here but are in the **Glossary** are: *aftertouch, control change, NoteOn, NoteOff, pan position, pitch bend, track, velocity, volume.*

MIDI files

MIDI files are music files in a standard format – sometimes called the *Standard MIDI File* (SMF) format, in fact. Almost all music programs and some keyboards can save (export) MIDI files and open (import) them. Nowadays, you can even buy MIDI files of your favorite music on floppy disk from your local music shop. The Internet is also full of MIDI files, but beware that many of these infringe copyright and so are illegal.

You can use MIDI files as one way to transfer music between Sibelius and virtually any other music program. However, MIDI files are designed for playing music back rather than notating and printing it. Hence they don't include lots of notational information, such as slurs, articulations and page layout. Even the distinction between F♯ and G♭ is ignored.

These restrictions mean that MIDI files are not a terrific way of transferring music notation from one computer program to another, though it's the only universal standard.

Fortunately, however, Sibelius does a good job of turning MIDI files into notation or vice versa in a matter of seconds; 📖 **9.5 Opening MIDI files** and **9.9 Exporting MIDI files**. But don't expect miracles: converting a score into MIDI and back again is rather like converting a complex text document to ASCII (plain text) format and back again – the basic information is retained but layout and other niceties are lost.

If you want to convert music into Sibelius from Finale, if you export a MusicXML file from Finale, Sibelius can transfer much more information than can be done with MIDI files – 📖 **9.6 Opening MusicXML files**.

4.14 Virtual instruments for beginners

Music making has been revolutionized by the advances in computer technology over the past two decades, and nowhere is that more evident than the rise of virtual instruments – computer programs that emulate the performance of a real instrument – which have now all but replaced dedicated hardware devices (such as MIDI synthesizers and sound modules).

Taking advantage of the rapidly increasing power of the computers we have on our desks and in our studios, virtual instruments are attractive because they allow an almost infinite range of sounds to be produced by the same hardware. With nearly every hardware device, your choice of sounds is limited to those that the original manufacturer included; when you are working in the software realm, your sonic palette is limited only by the range of virtual instruments at your disposal, and you can always install a new one.

There are literally thousands of virtual instruments of one kind or another that you can use with Sibelius, but this landscape can be confusing and intimidating to the beginner. Let's try and sketch out a map.

What is a virtual instrument?

As we've already touched upon, a virtual instrument is a computer program that emulates the performance of a real instrument, be it an electronic instrument like an analog or digital synthesizer, or (perhaps of most interest to us) an acoustic instrument.

Generally speaking, virtual instruments perform this emulation by one of two means: playback of sampled sounds, or sound synthesis. A "sample" is simply a digital recording of a sound, in this case usually a single note, and it is the most straightforward way to reproduce the sound of an acoustic instrument (because the original recording was of that acoustic instrument). "Synthesis" means that the sound is produced by mathematical means rather than from a recording, and is either based on a model that describes the actual sound (e.g. additive synthesis), or on a model that describes the production mechanism of sound (e.g. modeled synthesis).

Sample-based virtual instruments

A good example of a sample-based virtual instrument is the built-in Sibelius Player: it is able to load collections of samples (normally called "libraries") and play music back with them, loading up to 128 different "programs," or sounds, at once.

In the olden days of MIDI, a single "program" would only mean a single sound – e.g. a violin *arco* sound would be one program, and a violin *pizzicato* sound would be another. In the world of sample-based virtual instruments, however, a single program may include many related sounds – to continue the violin example, not only *arco* and *pizzicato* but also other playing techniques (sometimes known generically in the world of virtual instruments as "articulations") such as *legato, staccato, spiccato, col legno,* tremolo, and so on – all of which are loaded into the same channel and arranged in *layers,* meaning that they are part of the same program but hidden away until called upon.

You switch between the different layers using a variety of special techniques, such as playing a very high or (more usually) very low note on your MIDI keyboard (this is known as a "keyswitch," because the sound switches at the press of a specific key), or adjusting a continuous MIDI controller (e.g. using the modulation wheel on your MIDI keyboard). The most sophisticated sample-based virtual instruments can assign any sound to any combination of keyswitches, MIDI controllers, and even esoterica like MIDI breath controllers (which makes the wearer look as if he is playing an invisible harmonica).

Fortunately, Sibelius's playback engine is powerful enough that it knows how to insert keyswitch notes, modify MIDI controllers and so on for many of the popular sample-based virtual instruments in order to select the most appropriate sound at every point, so you don't normally need to worry about this.

Other sample-based virtual instruments include the famous Vienna Symphonic Library, Garritan Personal Orchestra, EastWest Quantum Leap Symphonic Orchestra, Sonivox Symphonic Orchestra, Miroslav Philharmonik – and that's just a handful of the ones dedicated to reproducing the traditional orchestra! In addition there are virtual instruments targeted at every group of instruments and genre of music, from marching bands and battery percussion (e.g. Virtual Drumline from Tapspace) to beautiful pianos (e.g. Synthogy Ivory) to ethnic and rare instruments (e.g. EastWest Quantum Leap Ra) to massed choirs (e.g. EastWest Symphonic Choirs) to traditional swing and big bands (e.g. Garritan Jazz & Big Band, Sonivox Broadway Big Band) to 1960s beat combos (e.g. EastWest Fab Four), and so on. Fortunately you can use practically any of these virtual instruments with Sibelius, so the possibilities are almost limitless!

Sample-based virtual instruments tend to require a lot of hard disk space and a lot of RAM to use them effectively. Some of the samples are so large that you can only use a few sounds at the same time on a single computer (and it can take upwards of 10 minutes even to load them all from disk before you can play anything!), so it is important to strike the right balance between sound quality and pragmatism. For some hints on these considerations, see **How to get the best out of virtual instruments and effects** below.

Synthesis-based virtual instruments

Although synthesis-based virtual instruments have long been fantastic at reproducing the analog and digital synthesizers of the 1970s and 1980s – in some cases improving upon the original hardware versions – and are also able to faithfully reproduce some other famous sounds, such as the Hammond organ, it is only recently that great improvements in physical modeling techniques have begun to bear fruit in producing really convincing renditions of acoustic instruments.

Synthesis-based virtual instruments are attractive because they do not require huge libraries of samples in order to produce great sound: instead of recording musicians playing each note with each desired articulation, these virtual instruments build a complex mathematical model of how the sound is produced, and the result is a faithful simulation of the actual sound. Modeled instruments can respond in real time to the way they are played by the performer almost as well as the instruments they simulate; this approach can also take account of subtle factors like sympathetic reverberation and combinations of harmonics in ways that simply playing samples cannot. By tweaking the model in small ways to account for, say, differences in the design of similar instruments from different manufacturers (such as the differences between pianos from Steinway and Bechstein), it's possible to produce a wide variety of sounds without having to go and record every note of every instrument.

Some of the more impressive virtual instruments to take this physical modeling approach include Pianoteq (which models a number of modern grand and period pianos), Lounge Lizard (which models Wurlitzer and Rhodes electric pianos) and String Studio (which models a variety of stringed instruments, including guitar, clavinet, and harp).

An interesting kind of hybrid virtual instrument is also emerging, combining both samples and synthesis to produce virtual instruments that capture the real character of sampled sounds without the requirement for large libraries of samples. A great example of a virtual instrument that takes this approach is Synful Orchestra.

Synthesis-based virtual instruments, particularly those that employ physical modeling, tend to require more CPU power than sample-based virtual instruments, but they also require substantially less hard disk space, and somewhat less RAM.

Virtual instrument technologies

There are a number of confusingly-named technologies used by both sample- and synthesis-based virtual instruments; some are specific to Windows PCs, others are specific to Macs, and still others only allow their virtual instruments to work with certain software packages.

Sibelius currently supports virtual instruments that follow the VST and Audio Units standards. VST stands for "Virtual Studio Technology," and was invented by Steinberg. VST virtual instruments (sometimes shortened to "VSTi") can be used on both Windows and Mac. Audio Units (sometimes shortened to AU) were invented by Apple, and Audio Unit virtual instruments can only be used on Mac.

There are several other virtual instrument formats, including RTAS (Real Time Audio Suite) and TDM (Time Division Multiplexing), both of which are formats used by Digidesign Pro Tools, DXi (DirectX Instrument) and MAS (MOTU Audio System). At present Sibelius doesn't support any of these. However, most virtual instruments are available in both VST and Audio Unit formats.

Although there are significant differences between VST and AU (and indeed the other formats) as technologies, as far as the user is concerned there is no practical difference.

Virtual instruments as "plug-ins"

You will commonly hear virtual instruments that adopt the VST standard in particular called "VST plug-ins." The word "plug-in" is used to describe any piece of software that can operate inside another software environment (a "program within a program," if you like). For simplicity, however, when you see the word "plug-in" in this Reference, it will only mean the plug-ins you can run from Sibelius's Plug-ins menu (📖 **6.1 Working with plug-ins**), and not to virtual instruments.

In addition to being used within another so-called "host" application, such as Sibelius or Pro Tools, many virtual instruments also operate in so-called "stand-alone" mode, meaning that they can be run on their own with no need for a host, which is ideal for live performance.

Effects

Sibelius can also use effects in addition to virtual instruments, so you should know a bit about effects. Effects are computer programs that process an audio signal in order to change one or more characteristics of a sound. Like virtual instruments, sometimes they emulate devices from the real world, such as guitar amplifiers or tube compressors, and sometimes they emulate naturally-occurring sound phenomena, such as reverb.

Here are some of the common kinds of effects you may come across:

* *Filter* effects attenuate (reduce) some frequencies in the audio signal, while letting other frequencies through unchanged. In truth, most effects (including many of those listed below) are filters of one sort or another, but when people talk about "filters" they tend to mean things like *wah-wah*, which produces its characteristic sound by varying the frequencies that can pass the filter, and *equalization* or "EQ" effects, which attenuate certain ranges of frequencies and boost others. Using EQ you can compensate for imperfections in an audio signal or unbalanced frequency response in audio reproduction equipment.

* *Compressors* compress the dynamic range of an audio signal, making the quiet sounds louder and the loud sounds quieter. The goal is to achieve a more uniform, consistent sound. Compression is especially useful for drums, bass guitars and other rock instruments, though most records – whether in rock and pop, jazz or classical music – make use of this effect. You may also come across *limiters*, which are simply compressors that provide a greater amount of compression, and which are designed to prevent distortion (or "clipping") at high volumes .

* *Distortion* effects alter the original shape of the waveforms that comprise the audio signal. Although distortion is generally undesirable, it is what gives electric guitars their characteristic, aggressive sound. The more extreme kinds of distortion effects emulate the loud, harmonically rich sound of amplifiers, speaker cabinets and fuzz boxes, but subtler distortion effects can also be useful, such as those that mimic the attractive warmth of sound produced by old-fashioned vacuum tube (valve) amplifiers or analog tape.

* *Delay* effects take the audio signal as an input, then play it back again after a specified (usually quite short) period of time. The delayed sound may be played back multiple times, or played back into the delay again, creating the sound of a repeating, decaying echo. Don't confuse delay with reverb (see below).

* *Modulation* effects multiply the incoming audio signal, either with copies of itself or with other waveforms. Common modulation effects include *chorus*, *flanging* and *phasing*. Chorus effects mix the incoming audio signal with one or more delayed, pitch-shifted copies of itself, simulating the sound of several instruments or voices where there is really only one. Flanging produces a "whooshing" sound by mixing the audio signal with a slightly-delayed copy of itself, varying the delay continuously. It is so named, legend has it, because it was discovered by accident when a tape machine was being used to produce a delay effect in one of the Beatles' recording sessions, and somebody touched the rim of the tape reel (called a "flange"), changing the pitch slightly. Phasing is similar, except that it passes the input audio signal through a filter simultaneously rather than after a varying delay. The filter itself responds differently to different frequencies, resulting in tiny delays of varying lengths at different frequencies. The result is a sound with a less pronounced "whooshing" characteristic than is typically produced by flanging.

* *Reverberation* effects, or "reverb" for short, simulate the way that sounds reflect off the different surfaces in a room. Sibelius's built-in Sibelius Player includes two high-quality reverb effects, which you can read about in **Reverb** on page 286.

If your head is spinning after all this, don't worry. Start small by experimenting with reverb, which is perhaps the effect that makes the biggest difference to the sounds produced by virtual instruments. Sibelius Player has its own reverb, but you can also add a separate reverb effect if you like. Once you feel comfortable with reverb, you might want to dabble with compression, which smooths out the dynamic range. You could even try adding a limiter set to -3dB or -6dB, to ensure that your overall mix doesn't clip. (See, you're already an expert!)

If you want to try effects out, you can download many free ones from the web, including the Kjaerhus Classic series (**www.kjaerhusaudio.com**; Windows only) or Smartelectronix's free Audio Unit effects (**mda.smartelectronix.com/effects.htm**; Mac only).

But beware! If you get deeply into the world of effects, pretty soon you'll find yourself talking about the "warmth" and "touch-sensitivity" of sound, spouting jargon like "riding the gain," enthusing about "slapback echoes"... and then there will truly be no hope for you.

How to get the best out of virtual instruments and effects

The downside of using virtual instruments is that they are yet another thing to use up your computer's resources, on top of essentials like running the operating system and, more importantly still, Sibelius. You will find that the more sample-based virtual instruments you want to install, the more hard disk space you will need; and the more sample-based virtual instruments you want to run simultaneously, the faster the processor and the greater the amount of RAM you will need. (With synthesis-based virtual instruments there is less dependence on hard disk space and RAM, and a greater dependence on processor speed.)

Providing enough disk space is a simple problem to solve: hard disks are inexpensive, capacious and easy to add (you don't even need to open up your computer if you have a USB 2.0 or Firewire connector). It's usually recommended to install samples on a separate drive from your operating system and applications, as this improves disk-streaming performance.

The RAM requirements get complicated more quickly, not to mention technical – so if talk of "32-bit this" and "64-bit that" frightens and confuses you, then skip down a couple of paragraphs: the most important recommendation for RAM is that you should buy as much as you can afford, and ideally 2GB or more.

Most Windows computers sold for the past decade or so have used 32-bit microprocessors, which can address a maximum of 4GB RAM (they won't "see" any more than that, even if you install it), but Windows itself is only able to make limited use of memory above 2GB, so this is the recommended maximum. Once you take away the memory required to run your operating system and Sibelius, you will find you have approximately 1GB RAM left into which you can load samples. The situation is similar on Macs: though theoretically Mac OS X can easily address more than 2GB RAM, at the time of writing only one Mac in the current range will accept more than 2GB RAM (the Mac Pro desktop), and that is really a 64-bit computer, which complicates things still further.

Computers that use 64-bit processors can in theory address up to 16 *exabytes* of memory (that's more than 16 million GB!), though in practice the most any computer available today will accept is 32GB. However, in order to take advantage of the extra power of a 64-bit processor, you also need a 64-bit operating system, and all your applications, including the virtual instruments themselves, also need to be updated to take advantage of the greater capacity. So at the moment the benefits are largely theoretical, and it may yet be another couple of years before support for these kinds of systems is commonplace.

As a result of the above complications, true power users of virtual instruments often have several computers ganged together in their studios, each running different virtual instruments, all controlled from yet another computer. This is definitely not something for the faint of heart (or those without deep pockets) to attempt.

If your eyes have glazed over reading the above, pull yourself together now, because here's where things get interesting again.

What all this means to mere mortals like us is that there are limits on how many virtual instruments, or how many sounds, can be used simultaneously on one computer, because a great deal of computational work is required to play them back.

Assuming you have a recent computer with 2GB RAM, a rough estimate would be that you could play around 32–40 simultaneous sounds in real time, though this is highly dependent on the nature of the sounds you are using.

There are a couple of neat tricks you can use with Sibelius to improve on this, however. Firstly, you can very easily switch between different sets of virtual instruments, so you can use a lightweight combination for inputting, editing and aural proofing, then switch to a more complex and demanding combination when you want to hear that special performance. Secondly, even if your computer struggles to keep up with the demands of playback in real time, you can use Sibelius's File ▸ Export ▸ Audio feature to export an audio file of your score, and Sibelius will effectively play the score back internally, slower than real time, allowing your computer to keep up – 📖 **9.10 Exporting audio files**.

In addition to concerns about hard disk space, RAM and processor speed, to consider using virtual instruments exclusively you will also very probably need a high quality audio interface or pro audio soundcard; this is especially important on Windows PCs (the audio hardware built into today's Macs is adequate for playback), particularly if you want to use virtual instruments to produce sound during note input as well as playback.

When you input notes using a MIDI controller keyboard, especially in Flexi-time, you need to hear almost instantaneous feedback (otherwise you will end up playing out of time to compensate for the delay in hearing what you are playing). The delay between telling the computer to play a note and you actually hearing it is called "latency," and a latency of more than around 20ms is too high and will lead to input errors.

To reduce latency you have to reduce the amount of time it takes to get the MIDI note input messages into your computer and, crucially, the audio out again. A high quality audio interface or soundcard can reduce latency to 5ms or less. Soundcards primarily intended for playing video games are not particularly suitable for real-time audio applications and use with virtual instruments; instead, look for cards specifically intended for audio applications. For Windows soundcards, ASIO support is essential (ASIO is another of Steinberg's technologies, and provides good support for low-latency playback). Soundcards with good ASIO support include products manufactured by M-Audio, Digidesign, Presonus, RME, Echo Digital, and others. An entry-level pro audio sound card, such as M-Audio's Audiophile 2496, will cost considerably less than $200, and can usually coexist peacefully alongside your existing sound hardware, but will perform much better than even a high-end gaming-focused soundcard that costs twice as much.

For further information

There are hundreds of web sites and other resources available that can help you deepen your understanding of the world of virtual instruments and effects. Here are just a few of them:

- Virtual Instruments magazine (**www.virtualinstrumentsmag.com**)
- Sound on Sound magazine (**www.soundonsound.com**)
- KVR Audio, a great source of free virtual instruments and effects, and up-to-date information about commercial products (**www.kvraudio.com**)
- Northern Sound Source, one of the largest music technology and composer forums on the web (**www.northernsounds.com**)
- BigBlueLounge.com, another of the largest music and audio production resource and communities on the web (**www.bigbluelounge.com**).

Playback

4.15 Working with virtual instruments

This topic provides some examples of how to use different virtual instruments with Sibelius.

If you need an introduction to the world of virtual instruments, 📖 **4.14 Virtual instruments for beginners** before you get started. If you are not yet familiar with the Play ▸ Playback Devices dialog, 📖 **4.12 Playback Devices**.

There are two kinds of virtual instruments discussed in this topic:

* those that can play back different sounds simultaneously, which we will call *multi-channel virtual instruments*, including Kontakt, Steinberg Halion, MOTU MachFive, EastWest Play, etc.

* those that can play back only a single sound at once, which we will call *single-channel virtual instruments*, including TruePianos, Pianoteq, Garritan Authorized Steinway, Lounge Lizard, etc.

The built-in Sibelius Player, and sample libraries that use Kontakt Player or ARIA players, fall into the former group, but is treated specially, because Sibelius can load sounds automatically into this virtual instrument. For all other virtual instruments, whether they are multi-channel or single-channel, you have to load the sounds yourself.

Sibelius Sounds Essentials

Sibelius Sounds Essentials is the library of sounds that comes with Sibelius, and plays back using the built-in Sibelius Player – 📖 **4.4 Sibelius Sounds Essentials**.

Other Kontakt- and ARIA-based sound libraries

There is a growing number of sample libraries available that use Kontakt Player and ARIA, all of which can be used within Sibelius. These libraries have the advantage that Sibelius is able to load the sounds required to play back your score automatically, provided a sound set is available.

The most popular such libraries include Garritan Personal Orchestra, Garritan Jazz and Big Band, Garritan Concert and Marching Band, Tapspace Virtual Drumline, Vir2 VI.ONE, and more.

The simplest way to get started with one of these libraries is to choose one of the existing playback configurations, e.g. Sibelius Essentials (16 sounds), then click New and type a new name, e.g. GPO. Then change the Sound set column to the appropriate choice for the library you are using, and click Close.

For further information:

* *Garritan libraries:* see the Garritan Wiki at http://www.garritan.info/.
* *Virtual Drumline:* see http://www.tapspace.com/support/.

Combining different sound libraries

You may find it useful to combine sounds from multiple sound libraries within the same playback configuration. For example, Garritan Personal Orchestra does not provide any vocal sounds, so for a score consisting of orchestra plus chorus, you may wish to use the sounds from Sibelius Sounds Choral in conjunction with your orchestral sounds.

To do this, simply create a new playback configuration with at least one instance of GPO's sample player (which could be either ARIA or Kontakt Player 2, depending on your version of GPO), set to the appropriate sound set; then activate Sibelius Player, and set it to use the **Choral** sound set (or perhaps the **Essentials Choral Combo** sound set). Sibelius will automatically choose to play the vocal staves using Sibelius Sounds Choral, and the rest of the staves using GPO.

Alternatively, you may wish to combine two libraries whose sounds overlap to some extent. For example, Garritan Jazz and Big Band does not provide as many keyboard and guitar sounds as Sibelius Sounds Essentials, so let's imagine that you want to combine the electric guitar sounds from Sibelius Sounds Essentials with the Jazz and Big Band sounds.

To do this, create a playback configuration with at least one instance of Jazz and Big Band's sample player (which could be either ARIA or Kontakt Player 2), set to the **Garritan JABB** sound set; then activate Sibelius Player, and set it to use the **Essentials** sound set.

Now, to tell Sibelius to use the guitars from Sibelius Sounds Essentials, choose the **Preferred Sounds** page of **Play ▸ Playback Devices**, and using the hierarchical list of sound IDs on the left-hand side of the dialog, select **Guitar ▸ Electric**. On the right-hand side, choose **Sibelius Player**, and click **Add**. Finally, click **Close**.

Treating Kontakt-type devices the same as other virtual instruments

By default, Sibelius always loads sounds into Kontakt Player and the full Kontakt sampler automatically. If you want Sibelius to treat Kontakt-type devices the same as other virtual instruments, switch on **Allow manual sound sets** on the **Playback** page of **File ▸ Preferences** (in the **Sibelius** menu on Mac).

When this option is switched on, you can choose Kontakt Player 2 and switch on **Use manual sound set** on the **Manual Sound Sets** page of **Play ▸ Playback Devices**, in order to follow any of the procedures described below.

Using a multi-channel virtual instrument with a sound set

In order for Sibelius to take best advantage of the advanced features of today's sample libraries, including keyswitches to choose between playing techniques and automation of controllers to manipulate the quality of the sound (e.g. dynamics) it's recommended to have a sound set for the library. Let's assume you're using the sounds from Vienna Symphonic Library (VSL) Special Edition via the Vienna Ensemble application, which allows you to load up to 16 Vienna Instruments at once (subject to your computer having sufficient memory).

To get started, create a new playback configuration: on the **Active Devices** page of **Play ▸ Playback Devices**, click **New** and give your configuration a name, then select **Vienna Ensemble** in the **Available devices** list and click **Activate** to add it to the **Active devices** list. Choose the **VSL Ensemble Special Edition** sound set from the menu in the **Sound set** column.

Now choose the **Manual Sound Sets** page. This is where you tell Sibelius which sound is loaded into each channel of Vienna Ensemble. Click **Show** to show its main window, and proceed to load the desired sound into each channel. In the **Manual Sound Sets** page, switch on **Use manual sound set**, then ensure **No. channels** is set to the appropriate value. Now for each channel, choose the appropriate **Program** from the list provided, and click **Apply** after each one. When you have finished loading sounds into Vienna Ensemble and choosing the same program for each channel in the **Manual Sound Sets** page, click **Close**.

Sibelius will now automatically route playback of each staff in your score to the appropriate program loaded into Vienna Ensemble, and will be able to take advantage of the keyswitches and other controller information defined in the sound set.

If you want to manually assign a specific staff to a particular channel, you can do so using the Mixer: first expand the staff strip, then choose the device from the device menu (so that its name is not shown in parentheses), then choose the desired sound from the sound menu. You can also use the arrows to the right of the channel number to change the channel directly.

For further information about using VSL Special Edition with Sibelius, see www.sibelius.com/helpcenter/en/a555.

You can also find information about using Synful Orchestra, another multi-channel virtual instrument, with Sibelius here: www.sibelius.com/helpcenter/en/a554

Sound sets for other multi-channel virtual instruments are available from the web site of Jonathan Loving at http://jonathanloving.googlepages.com/, but please note that Sibelius technical help cannot provide support for these third-party sound sets.

Using a multi-channel virtual instrument without a sound set

It is also possible to use a sample library such as EastWest Quantum Leap Symphonic Orchestra (EWQLSO to its friends) without a sound set, although this precludes Sibelius from automatically issuing keyswitch notes and other automation data. Provided you know the capabilities of your sample library and are comfortable doing the extra programming by hand (e.g. adding ~N*x,y* MIDI messages for keyswitch notes, and using **Plug-ins ▸ Playback ▸ Add Continuous Controller Changes** for automation data), this can work quite successfully.

The procedure to set this up is the same as in **Using a multi-channel virtual instrument with a sound set** above, until the point at which you show the sampler's interface and load the programs into each channel. On the **Manual Sound Sets** page of **Play ▸ Playback Devices**, switch on **Use manual sound set**: note that the **Program** menu is disabled, because you don't have a sound set.

If you want Sibelius to attempt to route each staff to each channel automatically, you must now choose an appropriate sound ID for each channel. For example, if you have a sectional violin sound loaded into the first channel, choose a sound ID of **strings.violin.ensemble**; if you have an oboe sound loaded into the second channel, choose **wind.oboes.oboe**, and so on. Click **Apply** after choosing each sound ID, then click **Close** when you are finished.

If, on the other hand, you are happy to allocate each staff manually, simply make sure that **Use manual sound set** is switched on, and that the correct number of channels is chosen, then click **Save** and **Close**. When you now play back, you will most likely hear nothing but silence, since Sibelius doesn't know which sound is provided by which channel. Using the Mixer, you must now explicitly choose the device to be used by each staff (so that the device's name is not shown in parentheses), and then set the channel using the arrows to the right of the channel number.

The biggest drawback of using a sample library with no sound set is that you cannot play back unpitched percussion without a sound set unless the unpitched percussion program is mapped the same way as General MIDI percussion. To play back other unpitched percussion, you must create a sound set file, at least for those programs.

Using a multi-channel virtual instrument with multiple programs per channel

Some samplers allow you to set up *banks*, which allow access to multiple programs on the same channel, switching between these programs using MIDI program changes. This means that you can, for example, set up different playing techniques for the same instrument (e.g. for a violin bank you may have legato bowing, staccato bowing, tremolando and pizzicato programs loaded, accessible via program changes 1 through 4).

As before, you have to load each bank directly in the sampler's interface manually.

If you want Sibelius to route playback automatically, there are two approaches: if you have a sound set file, Sibelius can not only route each staff to the correct channel automatically, but also switch between the different playing techniques for you; if you don't have a sound set, you can choose the appropriate sound ID for the basic sound on each channel, and then use explicit MIDI messages in the score to switch playing techniques (e.g. ~P2 for staccato bowing).

(An aside about creating a sound set for an arrangement of banks: you must decide before you begin which bank will be loaded into which channel in your sampler, so that you can set up the channel mask appropriately for each program. In our example, let's assume that the violin bank is loaded into channel 3: this means that each violin program accessible within the bank must also have a channel mask set that allows these programs only on channel 3.)

If you want to route playback yourself, then you need only ensure that **Use manual sound set** is switched on, and that you have the appropriate number of channels chosen. If your banks require a specific program change to be sent at the start of playback to ensure the default program is selected, you can achieve this by switching on **Send program change** and setting the **Program change** value accordingly.

Now you must use the Mixer to explicitly choose the appropriate device for each staff (so that its name does not appear in parentheses), and set the channel using the arrows to the right of the channel number read-out. To switch to other programs within the bank, you'll need to use explicit MIDI messages in the score.

Using single-channel virtual instruments

Single-channel virtual instruments can only provide one instrumental sound at once, but are otherwise identical in operation to multi-channel virtual instruments.

For example, you may have a virtual instrument that provides an excellent piano sound, e.g. Garritan Authorized Steinway, and want to use it in conjunction with (say) Sibelius Sounds Essentials. To achieve this, create a new playback configuration based on the default **Sibelius Sounds** configuration, then activate the Steinway. In the right-hand **Active devices** list, set **Sound set** to (none), then choose the **Manual Sound Sets** page. Switch on **Use manual sound set**, and set **Sound ID** to something appropriate, e.g. keyboard.piano.grand, then click **Apply**. Finally, go to the **Preferred Sounds** page, and choose Keyboard ▶ Piano ▶ Grand from the hierarchical list on the left, before choosing **Steinway** from the **prefer this device** menu and clicking **Add** to confirm your choice. Now click **Close** to complete your configuration.

When you play back your score, Sibelius will use Garritan Authorized Steinway for any piano instruments, and Sibelius Sounds Essentials for the other instruments.

349

Using soundfonts with virtual instruments

Soundfonts are collections of sampled sounds, usually in one of two formats (SF2 and DLS). Initially intended to provide a way of changing the sounds available on soundcards from some manufacturers, it is now possible to use soundfonts without the need for a specific soundcard.

Many soundfonts are available for download from the web. The most useful ones are complete General MIDI banks, which require no special configuration in Sibelius.

There is no built-in support for soundfonts in Windows, but the simplest way to use soundfonts in Sibelius is to use a multi-channel virtual instrument that can load and play them back. For example, RGC Audio's *sfz* (freeware; available for download from **http://www.project5.com/products/instruments/sfz_player/default.asp**) can load SF2 and DLS soundfonts.

Mac OS X includes built-in support for soundfonts. To use a soundfont on Mac OS X:

- Copy the **.sf2** or **.dls** file into the **/Library/Audio/Sound/Banks** folder on your hard disk
- Choose a playback configuration that includes the built-in **DLSMusicDevice** in the list of **Active devices** in **Play ▸ Playback Devices** (e.g. Sibelius's standard **Default** configuration)
- Show the **DLSMusicDevice**'s interface, e.g. via the Mixer, and choose the desired soundfont from the **Sound Bank** menu.

You can only use a single soundfont bank in each instance of the **DLSMusicDevice**, but you can activate multiple instances of the **DLSMusicDevice** in **Play ▸ Playback Devices**, and set each one to use a different sound font.

4.16 ReWire

ReWire is a so-called *virtual audio cable* that allows you to route the audio from Sibelius's playback into a Digital Audio Workstation (DAW), such as Pro Tools. It also provides you with a means to synchronize Sibelius's playback with your DAW's playback.

This opens up many possibilities for using Sibelius together with other audio software. For example, you can add an acoustic solo instrument line to your score's playback by routing the audio from Sibelius to your DAW and recording the audio there. Alternatively, you can augment a project started in your DAW with material written in Sibelius, the project in each application automatically staying in sync with the other.

Synth and mixer applications

In the ReWire standard there are two kinds of applications: *synth applications*, which produce audio to feed to *mixer applications*, which provide the capability of manipulating, editing and outputting the audio. You can also think of the synth application as a *slave* or *client* and the mixer application as the *master* or *host*.

Sibelius is a synth application, and as such it can feed audio to your chosen mixer application, which will typically be a DAW like Pro Tools, Logic, Cubase, or Digital Performer. In return, the mixer application provides timing information that allows Sibelius to stay in sync during playback.

ReWire basics

The basic process of setting up a ReWire connection between Sibelius and another application is to run the mixer application first, add a stereo audio or aux channel, then load Sibelius as a multi-channel ReWire instrument. The mixer application then automatically launches Sibelius, which starts up in a special ReWire mode, whereby all audio playback is routed to the mixer application rather than to your soundcard.

When Sibelius is running in ReWire mode, the ReWire logo shown on the right appears in the blue panel at the bottom of the Playback window. (If you go to Play▸ Playback Devices and click Audio Engine Options, you will see that the audio interface controls are disabled: this is because Sibelius is simply passing its audio on to the mixer application.)

Now when you start playback in Sibelius or your DAW, both applications will play back. To terminate the ReWire connection, quit your DAW and then quit Sibelius, or remove the ReWire track from your DAW's project window, then quit Sibelius.

Fixed tempo and Tempo track mode

Although ReWire is an ingenious way to pass audio and synchronization data between applications, it does not provide complete synchronization information: the mixer application only reports the playback position to the synth application in terms of beats from the start of the project, and does not provide tempo information. Sibelius has to map this information to the corresponding time in the score, but this means making one of two assumptions about how the ReWire mixer application is set up:

- *Fixed tempo*: the project in the mixer application doesn't have a tempo map, and is just playing back at a fixed tempo (e.g. if you created a new project in Pro Tools and didn't set up any tempo changes)
- *Tempo track*: the project in the mixer application has tempo changes set up at the same time as the Sibelius score, so the tempo at any point is the same in both Sibelius and the ReWire host.

You can change between these two modes using the options in Sibelius's **Play ▶ Performance** dialog, and this choice is saved in your score.

By default, Sibelius assumes that the mixer application is running without a tempo map, i.e. in fixed tempo mode. This is useful for e.g. simply taking the audio out of Sibelius and into your DAW in order to record (say) a vocal or solo instrument track over the top of it.

However, if you want to mix MIDI or virtual instrument tracks in your DAW with Sibelius's playback, then both applications must share the same tempo track. Export a MIDI file from one application and import it into the other to ensure that the project in your DAW and your Sibelius score are using the same tempo track, then choose **Play ▶ Performance** in Sibelius and select the **Tempo track** option.

Setting up ReWire with Pro Tools

You can use ReWire to connect Sibelius to any version of Pro Tools, as follows:

- Choose **Track ▶ New** and specify one **Instrument** track (or audio or **Auxiliary Input** track), and click **Create**
- In the Mix window, click the **Insert** selector on the track and choose **Multichannel plug-in ▶ Instrument ▶ Sibelius (stereo)**
- Sibelius will launch
- Check that the correct output (**Mix L – Mix R**) is chosen in the ReWire plug-in window in Pro Tools
- In Sibelius, open the appropriate score, or start a new one
- Start playback in either Pro Tools or Sibelius: both applications will start playing back
- If you intend to use **Tempo track** mode in Sibelius (see above), export a MIDI file from your Sibelius score or your Pro Tools session and import it into the other application to ensure both applications are using the same tempo track.

For more detailed information, consult the Pro Tools DigiRack Plug-ins Guide for your version of Pro Tools.

Setting up ReWire with other applications

You can use ReWire to connect Sibelius to a variety of DAWs, including Cubase, Logic, Digital Performer, Reaper, and even Garageband on Mac. Please refer to the documentation supplied with your DAW for instructions for setting up ReWire connections.

Troubleshooting

If Sibelius does not appear as a ReWire device in your DAW, choose **Play ▶ Playback Devices** in Sibelius and click **Audio Engine Options**. Click the **Repair** button to fix the ReWire association, then quit and restart your DAW.

If the ReWire connection appears to be working correctly (e.g. both applications start and stop playback correctly) but you find that you are hearing no audio from Sibelius in your DAW, check that the current playback configuration in Sibelius is set to use virtual instruments: the host application will not receive any sound from MIDI devices, whether they are internal (e.g. your computer's built-in soundcard) or external (e.g. a sound module).

If you find that Sibelius continues to start up in ReWire mode even after you have quit your DAW, choose **Play ▸ Playback Devices** and click **Audio Engine Options**, then click **Clean Up**. Now restart Sibelius, and it should start up and operate normally once more.

4.17 MIDI messages

For advanced users only

📖 **4.9 Playback dictionary**

MIDI is that most rare of beasts, a standard set by a number of different manufacturers that is universally implemented and supported. This sounds too good to be true, and it is, because in order to understand exactly how MIDI works, you need to be able to speak Martian.

MIDI devices (such as your computer's soundcard or your MIDI keyboard) send and receive MIDI messages, which consist of a *status byte* and one or two *data bytes*. MIDI bytes can have a decimal value of 0-127. In order to be device-independent, numbers in MIDI messages (including program changes) always count from 0, even if your MIDI device's manual counts from 1.

MIDI messages are classified either as *channel messages*, which affect a single channel (in Sibelius, this translates to the staff to which they are attached), or *system messages*, which affect all channels (in Sibelius, all staves).

Channel messages carry the majority of the musical data (e.g. which notes to play, how long they should last, which sound to use), while system messages are used for more technical things like synchronization with other MIDI devices.

Sibelius supports all MIDI messages (including control changes, pitch bend, SYSEX, and so on).

Creating MIDI messages in Sibelius

Because Sibelius reads almost all markings in your score and automatically turns them into appropriate MIDI messages when playing back (📖 **4.2 Interpretation of your score**), you'll generally only need to enter messages manually in Sibelius in very specific circumstances. These include changing the sound of a staff mid-way through a score, e.g. when, say, a clarinetist doubles on saxophone in the same piece, or if you need to use a different sound for different timbres on the same instrument, e.g. muted and unmuted. The clearest way to do this is to define a new word in the playback dictionary (📖 **4.9 Playback dictionary**).

However, you can also tell Sibelius to send any MIDI message you like at any point, by typing it in as text using the simple MIDI message commands described below.

These MIDI messages can be appended to ordinary text and are hidden, so if you write **2nd time molto vibrato ~C1,90** in, say, a repeated section of your music, Sibelius will reset controller 1 (modulation) to zero to silence the staff at the exact point where **2nd time molto vibrato** appears on the printout. **~C1,90** is automatically hidden (and will disappear completely if View ▸ Hidden Objects is switched off – so it's a good idea to switch this on before working with MIDI messages).

If you need to mute lots of staves, you can of course copy **2nd time molto vibrato ~C1,90** using Alt+click *or* ⌥-click to save you retyping, or you can add it to the word menu obtained when you right-click (Windows) *or* Control-click (Mac), and assign it a keyboard shortcut at the same time – 📖 **3.1 Working with text**.

When you import a MIDI file, you can choose to have MIDI messages in the file written into your score, in which case any control changes etc. will appear as if you'd typed them in yourself.

Should I use the dictionary or MIDI messages?

Most situations are more conveniently dealt with using the Play ▸ Dictionary dialog. Only the most esoteric adjustments require MIDI messages, typically to exploit subtle behaviours of specific devices. Certainly if you want your score to play back acceptably on other devices, you should avoid using MIDI messages wherever possible.

Syntax

You can type MIDI messages into your score using any staff text style – typically Technique or Expression text. MIDI messages can be written on their own, or put at the end of any other text (such as "mute").

Messages take the form: ~ followed by a single command letter, followed by one or more numbers, which are usually separated by commas.

E.g. ~C64,127

(~ is informally called a "swung dash" or "tilde," but the technical term is *twiddle.*)

Although using decimal (e.g. 0-127) is the most human-readable way of specifying the values, some manuals for MIDI devices specify values for MIDI messages in other ways, which can also be entered directly in Sibelius. Values can be specified using seven decimal bits (preceded by b, e.g. b0111101) or hexadecimal up to 7F (preceded by h, e.g. h5C), but unless you're a computer, you won't want to think about this for too long.

Note that:

• MIDI messages are case sensitive (i.e. you must type capitals or small letters as indicated) – so ~C0,0 is correct but ~c0,0 won't work

• Hex digits themselves (e.g. 5C) are case insensitive, but the h that precedes the digit must always be lower case

• You can write multiple messages in the same piece of text, separated by a space or Return (on the main keyboard), and with just one tilde at the start, e.g.: ~P43 A65 C64,127

• If you like you can also put spaces or Returns around commas and numbers.

You may wish to switch off the Transpose chord/note names option in House Style ▸ Edit Text Styles for your chosen text style to prevent the capital letter at the start of MIDI messages (e.g. ~C) being transposed as if it were a chord symbol – ⌨ **3.9 Edit Text Styles**.

Channel messages

Channel messages are split into two types: *channel voice messages*, which carry the musical data; and *channel mode messages*, which affect how the MIDI device responds to the musical data.

Let's examine each of the channel messages in turn:

Program and bank changes

A program change controls which sound is used to play subsequent notes on a particular channel. Sibelius automatically sends the correct program change for each staff, as set in the Window ▸

4. Playback & video

Mixer window, when it starts playing. However, if you want to change the sound a staff uses midway through your score, you can use a program change message.

Sibelius also allows you to change the bank and program in the same MIDI message. If your playback device only supports General MIDI sounds, you'll never need to use a bank and program change together, but if it has a wider selection of sounds (such as General MIDI 2 or Roland JV-1080), you may want to use a sound from a different bank.

There are three kinds of program change message, as follows:

- Program change only: ~P *program* e.g. ~P76
- Program and bank change, sending bank number: ~P *bank,program* e.g. ~P24,76
- Program and bank change, specifying MSB and LSB for bank number: ~P *MSB,LSB,program*, e.g. ~P64,2,36

(For an explanation of MSB and LSB, see **Bank numbers** below.)

In all of the above cases, the value of *program* assumes your MIDI device counts program numbers from 0 rather than 1 (⌨ **4.13 MIDI for beginners**). If your MIDI device counts from 1, use ~p instead of ~P.

With a message in the form ~P *bank,program*, only the LSB is sent if *bank* is less than 128. If *bank* is greater than 128, MSB and LSB are sent according to the formula *bank* = (MSB x 128) + LSB.

With a message of the form ~P *MSB,LSB,program*, if you specify a value of −1 for either *MSB* or *LSB*, that byte will not be sent; this allows you to specify sending just the MSB or LSB (if you don't want to send either, just use a simple program change).

You can find out whether your device counts from 0 or 1 and the values for *MSB* and *LSB* in its documentation. MSB and LSB may also be listed as Coarse and Fine, or CC (Control Change) 0 and 32, respectively.

This is quite a lot to get your head around, so let's take a couple of examples:

Let's say that we want to change the sound of one of our staves to that of a dog's bark midway through our score, using the Roland SC-88 sound module. The SC-88 manual lists "Dog, PC = 124, CC00 = 001." Roland devices count program numbers from 1 (since their manuals list the first GM sound, Acoustic Grand Piano, as program number 1). The SC-88 is peculiar in that it can do weird things using the LSB. It uses this to determine whether Roland SC-55 compatibility mode is used (which is mostly the same as the SC-88 but has fewer sounds available). For this reason, the LSB should normally be 0, and the MSB determines the bank to use.

To change to a dog sound mid-score, enter ~p1,0,124, ~p128,124 or ~P1,0,123 – each of these does exactly the same thing. You could also define a word in the playback dictionary to do the same thing: add an entry **dog**, and specify **Value** to be **123** and **Unit** to be **128**.

By contrast, devices that use Yamaha's XG standard keep the MSB constant (at 0) and change the LSB according to the type of variant of the basic bank 0 sound (e.g. LSB 1 = panned, 3 = stereo, etc.). Program numbers count from 1. To access the sound "PianoStr" (bank 40), a variant of the basic piano sound (bank 0 program 1) use ~p0,40,1.

Bank numbers

Bank numbers are calculated from two other numbers, known as the Most Significant Byte (MSB) and Least Significant Byte (LSB, sometimes called Coarse and Fine, or CC (Controller Change) 0 and 32, respectively). The formula for calculating bank numbers is (MSB x 128) + LSB. These values will be given in the manual for your MIDI device. For example, your MIDI device's documentation might say something like:

Bank number	MSB	LSB
Bank 0	64	0
Bank 1	64	1
Bank 2	64	2

So to calculate the bank number for bank 2 in the above example, the calculation is (64 x 128) + 2, which gives a bank number of 8194, which is the number you can use in a ~P *MSB,LSB,program* MIDI message (see above).

Some manuals will present bank numbers as single values rather than as separate MSB and LSB, in which case you don't need to get your calculator out.

Control changes

Control changes are used to control a wide variety of functions in a MIDI device. Although the function of each control change is clearly defined, not all MIDI devices support every control change. These are split up into groups, including:

- Control changes 0–31: data from switches, modulation wheels, faders and pedals on the MIDI device (including modulation, volume, expression, etc.)
- Control changes 32–63: optionally send the LSB for control changes 0-31 respectively
- Control changes 64–67: switched functions (i.e. either on or off) such as portamento, sustain pedal, damper (soft) pedal, etc.
- Control changes 91–95: depth or level of special effects such as reverb, chorus, etc.
- Control changes 96–101: used in conjunction with control changes 6 and 38 (Data Entry), these can be used to edit sounds
- Control changes 121–127: channel mode messages (see **Channel mode messages** below).

The syntax for control changes is ~C*byte1,byte2*, where *byte1* is the number of the control change (from 0–127) and *byte2* is the control value (also from 0–127).

For full details of the control changes supported by your MIDI device, consult the manufacturer's manual.

The most commonly used control changes are as follows:

Pitch bend

Pitch bend normally allows you to alter the pitch of a note by up to a whole step (tone) up or down, although there are a couple of ways to increase this range – see below.

The syntax of pitch bend is ~B0,*bend-by*, e.g. ~B0,96.

Bend-by is a number between 0 and 127, where each integer represents 1/32nd of a half-step (semitone). ~B0,64 produces a note at its written pitch; values lower than 64 flatten the note, and values higher than 64 sharpen it. To make a note sound one half-step (semitone) higher than written, use ~B0,96; to make it sound one half-step (semitone) lower, use ~B0,32.

You could, for example, use this control change to make a note play back sharp or flat without adding an accidental, e.g. if you want to make *ficta* – editorial accidentals above the staff – play back, you can insert the accidental from the Create ▸ Symbol dialog, and then use a MIDI message of e.g. ~B0,96 to play the note a semitone sharp. Don't forget to use ~B0,64 to return the channel to its normal tuning on the next note! This is, in fact, what the Add Ficta Above Note plug-in does for you – 📖 **6.1 Working with plug-ins**.

You can also use the pitch bend control change to create a portamento or glissando effect by creating a number of MIDI messages one after another. The pitch bend does not last for just one note – it remains indefinitely, so you usually put a pitch bend in the opposite direction on the next note to revert to normal pitch.

If you want finer control over the pitch bend, you can change the initial byte, also in the range 0– 127, to give very small deviations in temperament (1/128 x 32 half-steps) e.g. ~B127,64 will sharpen the written note by a small amount.

To create a pitch bend effect over an interval wider than a whole step (tone), you can either use the portamento control change (see **Control changes** below) to make a pitch bend, or use the following method:

* First, set up the range over which the pitch bend can operate: insert the MIDI messages ~C101,0 C100,0 C6,*half-steps* in your score, where *half-steps* is the total range of the pitch bend in half-steps (semitones), from 0-12. For example, to set up pitch bend with a maximum range of an octave, use ~C6,12. (It's best to put these messages at the start of your score.)
* When you want to add a pitch bend to your score, insert a ~B0,*bend-by* command as usual, except that now you must divide the *bend-by* parameter into the number of half-steps (semitones) set up with your ~C6 command, e.g. if you entered ~C6,12, each half-step (semitone) adds or subtracts 5.3 (64 divided by 12) to *bend-by*. So to bend upwards by four half-steps (semitones), you would enter ~B0,85.

This method requires that your MIDI device supports standard "Registered Parameter Messages" (RPMs), which is common but not universal. If you intend to use other RPMs in the same score, you should remember to "close" the parameters, by adding ~C101,127 ~C100,127 after the ~C6,*half-steps* message.

Aftertouch

Aftertouch refers to the amount of pressure used when e.g. a key on a MIDI keyboard is pressed. This information can be used to control some aspects of the sound produced by playback, e.g. vibrato on a violin sound. The precise effect of this controller is dependent on the MIDI device used.

Aftertouch can be applied either to a particular note (*polyphonic aftertouch*), or to all notes on a channel (*channel aftertouch*). Polyphonic aftertouch is not as widely implemented in MIDI devices as channel aftertouch.

The syntax is as follows:

- Channel aftertouch: ~A *pressure* e.g. ~A64
- Polyphonic aftertouch: ~a *pitch,pressure* e.g. ~a60,64

Modulation

Control change 1 controls the vibrato "wobble" generated by a modulation wheel. For lots of wobble, use ~C1,127; for no wobble, use ~C1,0.

Breath

Control change 2 is only recognized by certain MIDI devices, such as wind synthesizers, and corresponds to the "breath pressure" used to play a note.

Portamento

Portamento is a smooth "glide" from one note to another (rather like a glissando played on a trombone). This effect is actually controlled by two control changes: ~C5,*0–127* controls the length of time taken to perform the portamento (0 is fastest, 127 is slowest), and ~C84,*0–127* determines the distance of the portamento (values below 60 start below the note, values above 60 start above the note; the precise interval depends on the MIDI device).

So you must first "set up" the portamento effect with a ~C5 message, and then attach the ~C84 message to the note on which the portamento occurs.

This control change is not supported by all MIDI devices.

Volume

Control change 7 determines the volume of a given note, e.g. ~C7,127 is the loudest and ~C7,0 is the softest.

In MIDI, *volume* is not the same as *velocity*. Velocity is set when the note is played (part of the NoteOn message – see above), and is analogous to, for example, how hard you strike a note on the piano. Sophisticated MIDI devices will play the same pitch with a different timbre depending on the velocity of the note. Volume, on the other hand, is like an overall volume control knob on an amplifier. So a trumpet playing a fortissimo note (i.e. with a high velocity) but with low volume still sounds like a trumpet playing fortissimo, but with the volume turned down.

The faders in the **Window ▸ Mixer** window change the volume controller to specify the volume of staves in the score. You should only need to enter this MIDI message manually in your score if you want to achieve a change of dynamic over the course of a held note – the **Cresc./Dim. Playback** plug-in enters these messages for you (📖 **6.1 Working with plug-ins**).

Pan

Control change 10 determines the pan position of a particular channel, e.g. ~C10,0 is absolute left, ~C10,64 is center, and ~C10,127 is absolute right.

You don't need to use this MIDI message unless you need to change the pan position of an instrument during playback – the initial pan position is set in the **Window ▸ Mixer** window.

Playback

Expression

Control change 11 takes a fraction of the channel volume specified by controller 7, so ~C11,127 uses 100% of the channel volume, ~C11,64 uses 50% of the channel volume, and so on. Functionally ~C7 is intended to act something like a volume knob and ~C11 is a way of temporarily tweaking the "main" volume.

Sustain pedal

Sibelius automatically products MIDI messages for the sustain pedal if you use the Ped. lines from the **Create ▸ Line** dialog (📖 **2.21 Lines**). However, if you want to make playback of your score sustain without using these lines, use ~C64,127. Switch the pedal off again with ~C64,0. Values between 0 and 127 produce half-pedaling on some MIDI devices.

Soft pedal

Control change 67 simulates the effect of using the *una corda* (left) pedal on a piano: to switch on the soft pedal, use ~C67,127; to switch it off, use ~C67,0. This control change does not work on all MIDI devices.

Channel mode messages

You'll probably never need to use control changes 121–127 in Sibelius, but just in case:

- ~C121: resets all controllers
- ~C122: Local Control on/off
- ~C124–127: Omni mode on/off, Mono/Poly mode

NoteOn/NoteOff

These messages control which pitch is played, how loud the note is, and how long it lasts for. You should never need to use these messages in Sibelius, because you can make notes play just by inputting notes (and hiding them if appropriate).

However, for completeness' sake, they can be entered in the form: ~N*note,velocity* for NoteOn, and ~O*note,velocity* for NoteOff. (You must insert a NoteOff message, or your note will sound forever!)

note is the MIDI key number (e.g. 60 is middle C) and *velocity* is a value between 0 and 127 (127 is the loudest). With NoteOff, many MIDI devices ignore the velocity but some interpret it as the abruptness with which the note is released; if in doubt, use (say) 64.

System messages

These don't need a channel, so the staff they are attached to only determines which MIDI device they are sent to.

System messages are split into three types: *system common messages, system real-time messages,* and *system exclusive messages.* Typically, only the last two are useful in Sibelius – the first one is largely connected with synchronizing MIDI with clock-based MIDI components. It is therefore not currently possible to enter system common messages in Sibelius.

System exclusive messages are used to send data that is specific to the particular MIDI device you are using, and they may vary from device to device.

To enter system messages in your score:

- System exclusive: ~X *bytes* e.g. ~Xh40, h00, hf7. Normally you should put hf7 at the end to terminate the system exclusive, unless you're going to follow it with a D command containing more data.

- System exclusive continuation data (without any "command" byte): ~D *bytes* e.g. ~Dh40, h00, h7f

- System real-time: ~S *bytes*. These messages are useful for syncing Sibelius's playback with other sequencers or samplers. The three most useful commands are ~ShFA (sequencer start), ~ShFB (sequencer continue/pause), and ~ShFC (sequencer stop).

Hiding MIDI messages

Any text that begins with a tilde (~) is automatically hidden by Sibelius, so you don't need to worry about hiding MIDI messages individually. Only the ~ and the messages after it are hidden, so you can still read preceding instructions to the players such as "mute" that are meant to be visible. When you edit the text the ~ message reappears.

The MIDI messages are displayed in gray if **View▸ Hidden Objects** (shortcut **Ctrl+Alt+H** *or* ⌥⌘H) is switched on.

Further information

If this topic hasn't exhausted your appetite for strings of letters and numbers, you can find more information on MIDI messages at **http://www.harmony-central.com/MIDI/**

4.18 SoundWorld™

For advanced users only.

SoundWorld is a standard developed by Sibelius for naming and classifying sound timbres. This replaces the messy patchwork of patch numbers and (often cryptic) names used by MIDI keyboards, sound modules and sound libraries to specify their sounds. Instead you can choose the sounds you want using standardized, user-friendly names. Because the names are independent of a particular playback device, Sibelius can play a score which was originally created for different devices than the ones in your system. Also, if a sound is not available in the current playback configuration Sibelius can intelligently find the best alternative and use that instead. It can also play instrumental techniques (such as slurs and accents) using specialized sounds if they are available, rather than just approximating them by changing duration or volume.

If you want to find out how SoundWorld works, read on. You don't need to understand this to use Sibelius, but you may be interested all the same.

Sound IDs, SoundWorlds and sound sets

SoundWorld refers to each sound using a structured name called a sound ID, such as **woodwind.flutes.flute, woodwind.flutes.piccolo.flutter-tongue** or **strings.violin.ensemble.pizzicato**. Notice how each sound ID usually starts with an instrument family then the instrument name, sometimes followed by playing techniques specific to that instrument.

A SoundWorld simply means a collection of sound IDs, organized into a tree structure. The specific SoundWorld that Sibelius uses is called the Sibelius Standard SoundWorld (or S3W for short), which is a fairly comprehensive list of sounds available on leading sound libraries and MIDI devices. As more sounds become available, new sound IDs will be added to S3W.

To play a particular sound ID, Sibelius needs to know which sounds are available on its playback devices. To find out, for each device Sibelius has a sound set, an XML file that lists all the sound IDs the device can play and the MIDI messages (e.g. program changes, controller changes, even keyswitches) needed to play them. A sound set also lists various other capabilities of the device, such as how many sounds it can play simultaneously and whether there are any special channels (e.g. the percussion-only channel 10 on General MIDI devices).

Where sound IDs appear in Sibelius

Sound IDs can appear in Sibelius wherever you specify sounds. For example:

- Each instrument has a preferred sound ID, which you can change in **House Style ▸ Edit Instruments**
- The Mixer shows the sound ID of each staff in the score
- Each notehead on a percussion staff has a preferred sound ID, which you can change by editing the instrument
- All playing techniques and articulations for instruments are described by sound IDs, which you can change in **Play ▸ Dictionary**.

How Sibelius chooses which sound ID to use

To play a staff, Sibelius starts with its initial sound ID (as shown in the Mixer): for instance, a solo violin by default starts with the sound ID **strings.violin**. Markings in the score, such as articulations, slurs, text instructions for specific playing techniques like pizz. and so on, all modify the sound ID by adding or subtracting elements of it. These changes are specified in the playback dictionary. In the example below you can see the changes to the sound ID above the staff, and the resulting sound IDs below the staff:

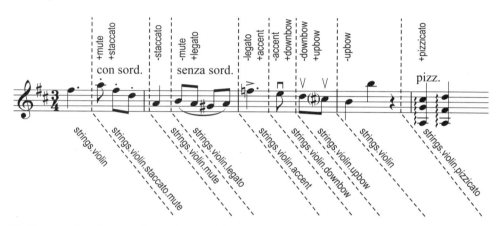

Sibelius now has the sound IDs that would produce ideal playback. However, it is very common that a sound ID is not available to be played, either because you don't have the sound on any playback devices, or there aren't enough available slots or channels to play every required sound ID at once. Sibelius then has to find the best possible alternative sound given the limitations.

As an example, suppose Sibelius wants to play **strings.violin.staccato.mute** (as shown above) but this isn't available. To find the best alternative sound ID, Sibelius uses a substitution rule which relies entirely on the tree structure of all the sound IDs in the SoundWorld. It makes use of the fact that, say, **strings.violin.staccato.mute** is a type of violin staccato sound (a child of **strings.violin.staccato**), which is in turn a type of violin sound (a child of **strings.violin**). The rule also relies on an order of priority between siblings such as (say) **strings.violin** and **strings.viola**.

So, starting from the unavailable **strings.violin.staccato.mute**, Sibelius first tries to find its first descendant sound ID that is available, which means trying its first child (which might be **strings.violin.staccato.mute.stradivarius**), then the first child of that sound ID; when it reaches a sound ID with no children, Sibelius tries its first sibling instead and *its* children. If no descendants of the original ID are available, it then tries its parent, in this case **strings.violin.staccato**, followed by the parent's first child and other descendants in the same way; then eventually the grandparent **strings.violin**, and so on until it reaches the first sound that can actually be played. S3W has been structured so that this will be the *closest possible* approximation to the original sound.

Playback

Structure of the tree of sound IDs

Why is the sound ID we're looking for called **strings.violin.staccato.mute** and not **strings.violin.mute.staccato**? To make substitution work well, one convention adopted in S3W is that different types of playing techniques appear in sound IDs in a specific order as follows, in descending order of priority:

* Macro quality (e.g. **pizzicato, pizzicato.snap, pizzicato.secco, bisbigliando, col legno, snares on, snares off,** etc.)
* Ensemble (i.e. the presence of the element **ensemble** means that the sound is an ensemble sound; its absence means that the sound is a solo sound)
* Duration (e.g. **staccato, staccato.wedge, staccato.detaché, spiccato, portato, legato**)
* Attack/dynamics (e.g. **accent, crescendo, diminuendo, fortepiano, sforzato, sforzato.sforzatissimo, non vibrato, vibrato,** etc.)
* Micro quality (e.g. **sul tasto, sul pont, sul tasto.flautando, mute, mute.harmon, mute.cup, mute.straight, open,** etc.)
* Ornament (e.g. **trill, tremolo, mordent, turn, flutter-tongue, glissando, scoop, fall,** etc.)
* Players (e.g. **2 players,** meaning an **ensemble** sound of a specific number of players)
* Repetition speed (e.g. **slow, fast**)
* Length modifier (e.g. **long, short**)
* Variant *n* (e.g. **strings.violins.violin.solo.1** and **strings.violins.violin.solo.2,** for sounds that are almost identical but which nevertheless need unique sound IDs)

So duration elements (like **staccato**) are more important than micro quality elements (like **mute**) and are listed first in the sound ID. This means that when Sibelius has to find a substitute for **strings.violin.staccato.mute,** it will find **strings.violin.staccato** before it finds **strings.violin.mute**; so if both are available it will actually choose the former, which is a better substitute.

Additionally, the techniques in each group of elements listed above are treated as mutually exclusive. This means that if a staff is currently using **strings.violin.pizzicato** and a text instruction "*col legno*" is reached, Sibelius knows to replace the **pizzicato** element with **col legno** (rather then add **col legno** to the end), producing **strings.violin.col legno** (rather than the impossible **strings.violin.pizzicato.col legno**).

5. Power tools

5. Power tools

5.1 Arrange™

📖 **5.2 Edit Arrange Styles**.

Arrange™ is designed to assist students with arranging and orchestration, and to save time for professionals who already know what they want to do.

It intelligently copies music from any number of staves into any other number of staves, deciding (if necessary) which instruments to use. It can be used to produce piano reductions, and to "explode" chords onto multiple staves. Most importantly of all, this sophisticated feature even helps you arrange and orchestrate for a wide variety of styles and ensembles, from choral music to band and orchestral scoring.

You can be as specific or unspecific as you like as to how you want to arrange. For example, if you already know which instruments you want to use, you can use Arrange just as a quick way to copy music onto them, e.g. to split up chords onto brass intelligently. However, students and others can use the numerous ready-made Arrange styles to experiment with arrangement and orchestration at any level.

Summary

Arrange is, in effect, a special kind of copy and paste operation:

* Copy the music you want to arrange to the clipboard using **Edit ▶ Copy** (shortcut **Ctrl+C** *or* ⌘**C**). It's important that the source material should use a constant number of voices (i.e. either all in one voice throughout, or all in two voices throughout, but not alternating between one and two voices in different bars). Don't copy unpitched percussion staves as Arrange only handles pitched material.

* Select the staves into which you want to paste the resulting music, either elsewhere in the same score or in another score. You don't have to select the right number of bars in the destination staves – it's sufficient just to select a single bar.

  If you want to arrange a passage starting mid-bar, create suitable rests in all the destination staves so that you can select the precise point at which you want the arranged music to be pasted.

  If you select a range of adjacent staves using **Shift**-click, Arrange will also arrange onto any hidden staves which may lie in the range. If you don't want this to happen, select the staves to arrange onto one by one with **Ctrl+click** *or* ⌘**-click**.

* Choose **Notes ▶ Arrange** (shortcut **Ctrl+Shift+V** *or* ⇧⌘**V**)

* The **Arrange Style** dialog appears; choose the desired style from the drop-down list, and click **OK**.

A progress bar appears, and within a few seconds, Sibelius has completed the arrangement for you, choosing which music is best suited to which instruments, and transposing the music by octaves as necessary to suit their ranges.

If you haven't already done so, try out Arrange by opening the example score **Arrange** in the **Other** folder within the **Scores** folder and following the instructions at the top of the score. This should give you a flavor of what Arrange can do.

The above is just a brief summary of Arrange – keep reading to understand the different ways to use this feature before you try it out in practice.

Using Arrange musically

Like composing, arranging and orchestration are advanced musical skills that inevitably require human involvement. Hence the Arrange feature is not intended to produce a completely finished result all by itself. It is up to you to:

• Choose the passage you arrange carefully – a phrase or less is usually best (more detail below). You don't have to arrange all the source staves at once – you could arrange the right hand of a piano piece onto woodwind and the left hand onto strings, if you know that's what you want.

• Consider adapting your source music before arranging to make it more suitable for the instruments you are using – Arrange never alters your basic material, and something which suits a piano may not be suitable for arranging onto a wind band or string section without adaptation. See **Preparing music to be arranged** below for advice on how to improve your basic material, and **After arranging music** for some tips on what to do after arranging.

• Choose the Arrange style and the staves you select carefully; Arrange styles to use for different ensembles are detailed later. If you don't like the arrangement, choose **Edit ▸ Undo** and try again with a different Arrange style and/or selected staves.

• Vary the Arrange style and selected staves often to produce an interesting arrangement – don't always arrange onto all instruments at once!

• You should also modify the results of Arrange as appropriate, such as adjusting octaves or applying orchestration techniques such as "dovetailing" music from one instrument to another.

It's important for you to understand that Arrange keeps the same instrumentation and pitch throughout each passage you arrange – for example, if a line of notes starts very high and goes very low or vice versa, Sibelius won't "dovetail" (jump) it from one instrument to another, or change its octave mid-passage. Arrange will however vary the instrumentation between each passage you arrange as it sees fit.

Because of this, you should normally arrange no more than (say) a phrase of music at a time, otherwise the results may force some instruments into difficult or unplayable ranges. Arranging short passages allows Sibelius to change the instrumentation and pitch, to keep the music within the range of the instruments (and also to keep the arrangement sounding interesting). Sibelius warns you if the passage you arrange is probably too long.

How Arrange arranges

Specifically, Arrange does the following (except for the special **Explode** and **Reduction** styles, explained later):

• Chooses appropriate instruments to arrange onto from the destination staves you selected. Most or all of the selected staves are normally used, unless the Arrange style is for a specific choice of instruments (e.g. the **Family** and **Mixed Ensemble** styles described below) in which case any others you've selected are ignored.

* Sibelius divides the music up among the instruments, normally with a single line of notes per staff if possible

* Some of the music may be transposed by octaves to get it into an instrument's comfortable playing range or for coloristic effect. (You can set playing ranges yourself, which will affect how Sibelius arranges music – 🕮 **2.18 Instruments**.)

* Sibelius may put different kinds of material onto different kinds of instrument (e.g. fast music on woodwind, slow music on strings), depending on the Arrange style you choose. In particular there are **Block** and **Mixed** styles of orchestration, explained below.

* Sibelius may orchestrate using appropriate doublings, e.g. piccolo an octave above flute. Again this depends on the Arrange style.

Other than splitting it up and transposing it, Arrange will not change the source music.

Arrange styles

The specific way in which Sibelius arranges your music is determined by the Arrange style. The Arrange style specifies which instruments can be used, instrumental doublings, and which kinds of material go onto different instruments.

A wide-ranging list of over 130 Arrange styles is supplied, and you can even create your own (🕮 **5.2 Edit Arrange Styles**). In basic terms, the styles encompass explode and reduction operations, and arranging/orchestrating for a wide variety of ensembles, from choir to band.

The Arrange styles are named as follows:

* first, they mostly specify the kind of ensemble or instruments they will arrange onto (e.g. **Orchestra, Band,1 Family: Brass**);

* second, they may name the particular style of arrangement (e.g. **Impressionist** or **Film**);

* third, they specify any particular instruments that are included or omitted (e.g. **no trumpets**, or **solo woodwind and strings**);

* and fourth, some styles state whether they will use a **Block** or **Mixed** orchestration (see below).

Each Arrange style also has a more detailed description on the right-hand side of the Arrange dialog when you select the style; this gives useful information and advice about what the style does and how best to use it.

Block and Mixed styles

Arrange styles designed for orchestration are of two types – **Block** and **Mixed**:

* **Block** puts different kinds of musical material onto different families of instruments. The material is split up according to its speed – so in an orchestral arrangement, the woodwinds could play, say, the fastest music, and the brass could play the slowest. Typically the tune is faster than the accompaniment, but by no means always.

  In many cases we have provided two styles for the same families, e.g. one with woodwind playing the faster music, and an alternative one with woodwind playing the slower music.

- **Mixed** styles allow instruments in different families to double each other, so instruments with similar ranges, such as violins and flutes, play the same material.

Where neither **Block** nor **Mixed** is stated, the Arrange style will produce a **Mixed** orchestration.

Explode

To "explode" chords (i.e. separate out their notes) onto a larger number of staves:

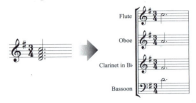

- Select the material you want to explode (which can be in one or more staves), and copy it to the clipboard by choosing **Edit ▸ Copy** (shortcut **Ctrl+C** *or* ⌘C)
- Select the staves you want to explode onto (either elsewhere in the same score, or in a different score). Choose **Notes ▸ Arrange** (shortcut **Ctrl+Shift+V** *or* ⇧⌘V)
- Choose the **Explode** Arrange style, and click **OK**. Sibelius will then instantly explode the music onto the destination staves.

If there are fewer staves than notes, Sibelius will put two notes on a staff in separate voices. If you subsequently want to merge these two voices into chords in a single voice, simply select the passage and choose, say, **Edit ▸ Voice ▸ 1** (shortcut **Alt+1** *or* ⌥1).

Sibelius will also transpose notes by octaves if necessary to make them playable on the destination instruments.

If you explode a long passage, Sibelius may warn you saying "We recommend you arrange no more than a few bars at a time" – ignore this and click **Yes**.

If you are exploding music from a single staff onto a maximum of four staves and want greater control over precisely how Sibelius distributes music to each of the destination staves (in particular if you do not want the music transposed by octaves), use **Plug-ins ▸ Composing Tools ▸ Explode** instead – see **Explode** on page 497.

Reduction

To reduce music from multiple staves onto a smaller number of staves (sometimes called "imploding" as the counterpart of "exploding"):

- Select the material you want to reduce and copy it to the clipboard using **Edit ▸ Copy** (shortcut **Ctrl+C** *or* ⌘C)
- Select the staves you want to reduce onto (either elsewhere in the same score, or in a different score). Choose **Notes ▸ Arrange** (shortcut **Ctrl+Shift+V** *or* ⇧⌘V).

- Choose one of the **Reduction** Arrange styles, and click **OK**.

Several **Reduction** styles are provided that are intended for slightly different uses; read the description of each style to find out which one is most suitable for the result you are looking for.

For keyboard reduction, the most suitable style will depend on the complexity of the source material. For most purposes we recommend the **Keyboard reduction: Up to 2 voices per staff** style, but if you find the resultant reduction too complex, try the **1 voice per staff** style instead; you should also consider omitting any staves in the source passage which would be too hard to play on a keyboard instrument.

If you reduce a long passage, Sibelius may warn you saying "We recommend you arrange no more than a few bars at a time" – ignore this and click **Yes**.

After using one of the **Reduction** styles, you may find a number of duplicate dynamics are placed on top of one another in the resulting music (because they appeared on separate source staves); if so, select the music as a passage and choose **Edit ▸ Filter ▸ Dynamics** (shortcut **Shift+Alt+D** *or* ⇧⌥D), then hit **Delete** to remove them. (In rare cases you may also find redundant slurs after making a reduction, in which case use filters to remove them too.)

If the music you want to reduce includes triplets or other tuplets, or if you want greater control over how Sibelius should reduce your music, use **Plug-ins ▸ Composing Tools ▸ Reduce** instead – see **Reduce** on page 500.

Arranging for families of instruments

The **1 Family** and **2 Families** styles will only arrange onto the instruments specified in the name of the style – so, for example, you could choose all the staves in an orchestral or band score and then use the **1 Family: Woodwind** Arrange style, and music will only be arranged onto the woodwind instruments. However, if you select (say) all woodwind staves except flutes, flutes will not be used.

These styles are also suitable for arranging music for smaller ensembles, e.g. wind quartet, brass quintet or string orchestra.

The **2 Families** styles are provided in both **Block** and **Mixed** configurations, to give different textures and colors.

Arranging for orchestra

The **Orchestra** styles are grouped according to musical style. A variety of styles for music ranging from **Baroque** to **Modern**, with **Impressionist** and **Film** along the way, is provided.

Most of the **Orchestra** styles produce tuttis if you select all the staves, although you can select any number of destination staves; hence if you select only, say, the flute, clarinet and viola staves as the destination passage, only those instruments will be used when you Arrange. To avoid getting tutti orchestration throughout, we recommend you vary the staves you select and the Arrange style you use!

Other styles, such as the **Family** and **Mixed Ensemble** styles, can be used for orchestra as they use smaller groups of instruments to produce particular coloristic effects. You don't have to select particular staves when using these styles – you can just select all of them, and the style will only use

Power tools

the instruments it's designed for. Read the description of each Arrange style carefully to see which instruments it expects to use.

Try out some of the more exotic styles – you may find some very attractive results with more unusual instruments.

None of the styles include unpitched percussion, although a few styles do use pitched percussion instruments for added color (e.g. timpani in the **Romantic** styles, and mallet percussion in the **Modern** styles). You can of course omit pitched percussion by not selecting any pitched percussion destination staves.

Arranging for band

The **Band** styles are equally suitable for wind bands, concert bands, symphonic bands, school bands, marching bands and drum corps. Read the descriptions: some of the styles produce tuttis, and some use combinations of fewer instruments. Many of the styles include mallet percussion, but unpitched percussion instruments are not included.

The **Brass Band** styles, as the name suggests, are for arranging onto standard brass bands.

Read **Arranging for orchestra** above for general advice about using a variety of instruments and Arrange styles (including **Family** and **Mixed Ensemble** styles) to produce the most interesting arrangement possible.

Arranging for mixed ensembles

The **Mixed Ensemble** styles are mainly provided as ready-made orchestrations for use with orchestra, band or other large ensembles. They use just a few instruments each. As with the **Family** styles, use them for variety to avoid arranging onto all the instruments too much of the time!

Arranging for choir

The **Choir** styles produce various standard choral effects, such as sopranos doubled by tenors at the octave, or the melody on one of the inner voices with the other parts providing an accompaniment, and so on. The styles can be used to arrange onto any combination of voices, so you can create arrangements for SSAA or TBB choirs just as easily as SATB settings.

If you want to create a piano reduction of choral music, simply use the appropriate **Keyboard reduction** Arrange style.

Arranging for jazz ensembles

Different **Jazz** styles for a variety of ensembles, including quintet (which can also be used to arrange for quartet and trio), big band, and trad jazz band, are provided. The **Family** styles are also suitable for big band and jazz band. Again, vary the style and the staves you select, to produce an interesting arrangement.

Arranging for rock and pop ensembles

The **Rock** and **Pop** styles include standard guitar/bass/keys combinations (although they don't arrange onto drums). Give the styles that include an orchestra a try!

Arranging for solo instrument(s)

The Solo with accompaniment styles put the melody onto a solo instrument and the remaining music onto other instruments. To use the styles, you must select the accompanying instruments as specified by the style (guitar, harp, keyboard or strings) and also select the solo instrument staff. You can select more than one solo instrument staff (e.g. Flute and Clarinet), in which case they will end up doubling each other.

The plain Solo styles are provided as a quick way of putting the melody onto a single specified instrument. The accompanying music is not used (and can be arranged separately onto any other instruments using other Arrange styles).

All of these styles assume that the melody is the fastest music in the source material, which is typically but by no means always the case; if not, you can use filters instead, e.g. to select the topmost line of notes from the source music (☐ **5.7 Filters and Find**).

Arranging for other ensembles

If the ensemble you want to arrange for is not listed, e.g. cello sextet, simply choose the Standard Arrangement style, which produces reasonable results on any combination of instruments.

Preparing music to be arranged

It's worth spending a little time optimizing your music before you use the Arrange feature to improve the results.

Sibelius doesn't change the source music (other than transposing it by octaves to suit the destination instruments), so you should make any other adjustments required to make it more appropriate to the instruments you want to arrange onto. Though you can do this after arranging, it's better to do it beforehand so you don't have to make the same changes on several different instruments. Some things to bear in mind:

- Try to make the source music have a constant number of voices on each staff. (It can change number of voices between different passages that you're arranging separately.) For example, in this case:

where voice 2 is only used occasionally in the right hand, you should separate off the bottom notes of the voice 1 chords into voice 2. To do this, select the affected passage (here, in the upper staff) and choose Edit ▸ Filter ▸ Bottom Note and then swap the music into voice 2 by choosing Edit ▸ Voice ▸ 2 (shortcut ⌥2 *or* Alt+2), which will leave you with:

This ensures that Sibelius will put the new voice 2 line of notes into the same instrument(s). If you don't do this then Sibelius will first warn you, and will then put the two notes originally in voice 2 into a separate instrument with rests on either side. This is because Sibelius treats voice 2 as running throughout the passage, and it will add rests where there are no voice 2 notes to create a continuous "line of notes."

- The Arrange styles such as **Orchestra: Baroque** are designed for music of that period – you can't make jazz music sound Baroque just by orchestrating it onto Baroque instruments!

- You may wish to split existing music into different voices to make it more suitable for the instruments you're arranging for. For example, an "oom-pah-pah" bass figure works best if the "oom" lasts for the duration of the bar in, say, voice 2, while the "pah-pah" chords are in voice 1:

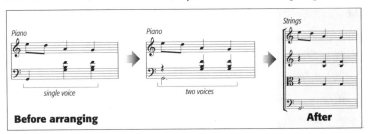

- Arrange copies dynamics and other staff objects (such as symbols, lines and so on) – but it doesn't copy system objects (such as key signatures and time signatures). If the music you are arranging contains changes in time signature, you should create the time signature changes in the destination point (preferably before rather than after arranging).

- Delete unnecessary objects. For example, if you're arranging piano music for wind instruments, you should delete any pedal lines before you start – but don't delete things like dynamics, slurs and trills, which you'll want copied to the destination staves.

- Delete any octave (8va) lines in your score and make them explicit – in other words, by transposing the music by the appropriate number of octaves – before you arrange. This is because octave lines are rarely used for most non-keyboard instruments, and Sibelius ignores octave lines when trying to decide which instruments best suits the range of the notes.

- If you're feeling very adventurous, you could try using **Edit ▸ Filter ▸ Advanced Filter** to, say, select just the first beat of every bar in your source music before you arrange. By copying just some of the music in the source passage, you can quickly create light accompanimental textures.

After arranging music

- Arrange tries to keep music within each instrument's range, but in some cases this isn't possible: so if you end up with some notes out of range, you should either dovetail those notes onto another instrument with a more suitable range, or change the octave of the notes out of range.

- If you end up with a lot of notes out of range, you're probably trying to arrange too much music at once. Try arranging a phrase at a time, as this will reduce the amount of cleaning up you will have to do afterwards.

- If a particular staff requires two voices, after arranging you will find that Sibelius has written the music in two voices throughout the destination passage (even if the voices are mostly in unison). Voice 2 may be above voice 1 for all or part of it, so you may need to swap the voices using **Edit ▸ Voice ▸ Swap 1 and 2** (shortcut **Shift-V**). If the voices are in unison or homophony, you may want to make it look cleaner by merging most or all of the music on that staff into a single voice; just select the music as a passage and choose Edit ▸ Voice ▸ 1 (shortcut Alt+1 *or* ⌥1).

- If you try arranging some music and find that some instruments end up playing unsuitable material (e.g. fast low notes on Horn), Undo it and arrange again, either omitting those instruments from the selection so they won't be used, or else using a different style. For example, with the styles for 2 families of instruments in blocks, there are alternative versions provided with (say) the brass playing the faster notes or the slower notes.

5.2 Edit Arrange Styles

📖 **5.1 Arrange™**.

For advanced users only

More than 130 predefined Arrange styles are supplied with Sibelius, but should you want to define your own, this topic will tell you how.

In order to create effective Arrange styles, you first need to understand how Sibelius's Arrange feature works.

How it works

Sibelius's Arrange algorithm is complex, but it basically involves splitting the selected music into separate monophonic "lines of notes," each consisting of single notes and rests. These are then distributed among the chosen destination staves, possibly transposed by octaves, doubling other staves (in unison or octaves), or using multiple voices as necessary.

Sibelius determines the lines of notes as follows:

• Any voice on any staff that contains one or more note (or rest, or bar rest) is treated as one or more lines of notes

• If the number of notes in the voice is not constant (for example, if a passage of thirds is followed by a passage of single notes), Sibelius puts upper notes of chords into more lines than lower notes

• Each line of notes also includes all other objects attached to that staff or voice, so all notes retain any articulations, ties, notehead types, etc., plus objects such as text and lines.

These lines of notes are then arranged to fit the destination staves according to the selected Arrange style. Arrange styles specify "groups of instruments" into which similar music will be arranged.

These general principles apply:

• Sibelius will try to put all of the source music into the selected staves, which may result either in a lot of doubling (if there are too few lines of notes for the number of staves selected) or many staves with multiple voices (if there are too many lines of notes for the number of staves).

• Sibelius will only assign one line of notes to each group, unless there are fewer lines than groups – for example, in an extreme case, if the source music consists of a single monophonic line, which is subsequently arranged for full orchestra, Sibelius will not compose music to accompany the single line; it will simply double it across all the staves

• Sibelius adjusts the pitch of each line of notes to fit the comfortable range of the destination instrument. (Optionally, the user can also specify that Sibelius should "stretch" the source music across a determined range of pitches – see below.)

When arranging, Sibelius sorts the lines of notes in four basic ways, determined by the Arrange style:

- *Fastest to slowest*: the lines of notes with the shortest average note values are given to the first listed group of instruments, with the last listed group getting the lines of notes with the longest average note values

- *Highest to lowest*: the lines of notes with the highest average pitch are given to the first group of instruments, etc.

- *Busiest (playing the most notes)*: the lines of notes with the most notes are given to the first listed group of instruments, and the lines with the fewest notes to the last listed group

- *Busiest (playing most of the time)*: the lines of notes that play for the longest proportion of the total duration of the source material are given to the first listed group of instruments, etc.

Editing Arrange styles

- Choose **Notes ▸ Edit Arrange Styles**:
  - To edit an existing style, select it from the drop-down list and click **Edit**
  - To create a new style, select the most suitable existing style on which to base your new style, then click **New**
- This dialog appears:

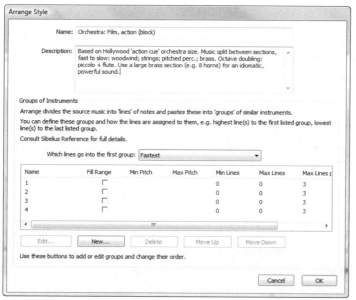

At the top of the dialog you can edit the **Name** for the style and write a suitable **Description** if you like. The lower half of the dialog lists the groups of instruments into which Sibelius will arrange the music.

- Remove an existing group of instruments by selecting its name and clicking **Delete**; change the ordering of the groups by selecting one and clicking **Move Up** or **Move Down**

Power tools

- To add a new group of instruments, click **New**, and choose the instruments to include in the group:

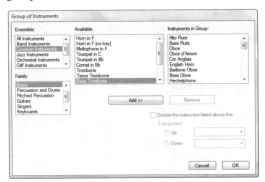

You can approach this in a variety of ways; you might place melodic instruments (e.g. high woodwinds and strings) in one group, and supporting instruments (e.g. brass, horns and lower strings) in another.

You can also specify that an instrument should double the instrument listed above at a specified interval (e.g. if you want your flute doubled at the octave by a piccolo, or if you want particular instruments to play in thirds).

If you want to have two instruments doubling a single instrument, for example, if you want your flutes doubled by piccolo and clarinet, the instruments would be listed in the **Instruments in Group** field as follows:

Flute	*not set to double*
Piccolo	*doubles up one octave*
Clarinet	*doubles at the unison*

In other words, you can have multiple instruments doubling the same instrument. The instrument that will be doubled when you switch on the **Double the instrument above this** option will be the *first* instrument above the selected instrument that is *not* set to double another instrument.

Even if you don't specify instruments to double each other, they may end up doubling anyway (if you arrange lines of notes onto a larger number of staves).

- When you've finished adding instruments to the group, click **OK**
- Give the group a name (e.g. **Vln1+Fl**) by double-clicking the blank space in the **Name** column
- If you want to specify a range of pitches into which Sibelius should arrange the music for that group, set **Fill range** to **Yes** and then choose the **Min Pitch** and **Max Pitch** as appropriate. Sibelius will then transpose the music by octaves so that it's in the stated range, and so that the different instruments in the group collectively fill the entire range.

Fill range is useful if, say, your source material is a piano piece, which of necessity uses a narrow range for chords (generally a compass of less than a tenth in each hand), and you want the music to be played by a string section across its entire range; or to ensure that the material ends up in a particular range, e.g. high woodwind, even if the instruments could play it at other pitches.

- **Min Lines** determines the minimum number of lines of notes that may be assigned to the selected group. The default setting of **0** is recommended; this means that the group does not have to play at all times.

- **Max Lines** determines the maximum number of lines of notes that may be assigned to the selected group. The default setting (blank) allows any number of lines to be assigned to the group.

  You should only change this setting if you want particular effects, e.g. setting **Max Lines** to **1** forces all the instruments in the group to double the same material.

- **Max Lines per Staff** and **Max Voices per Staff** control the distribution of lines of notes among the instruments within the group. The default settings (of **2** and **2** respectively) are suitable for most kinds of music.

  Generally, Sibelius will only use multiple voices on the same staff if it has to, for example if there are more lines of notes assigned to a particular group than there are staves within the group.

  If **Max Lines per Staff** is set to a greater number than **Max Voices**, then Sibelius will merge lines of notes into chords in the same voice. (Obviously, there's little point in setting **Max Lines per Staff** to a smaller number than **Max Voices**.) If you only want single notes on each staff, set both these options to **1**.

  Some useful settings for these options:

Keyboard	Max Lines per Staff = 4, Max Voices = 2
Single woodwind	Max Lines per Staff = 1, Max Voices = 1
Double woodwind	Max Lines per Staff = 2, Max Voices = 2
Brass	Max Lines per Staff = 2, Max Voices = 2
Strings	Max Lines per Staff = 2, Max Voices = 2
Singers	Max Lines per Staff = 1, Max Voices = 1

- All the instruments in a group are assigned similar music. The way in which lines of notes are assigned to groups is defined by the **Which lines go into the first group** option; for example, if this is set to **Highest**, the highest lines go to the first listed group, the second highest to the next listed group, and so on. Change the order of the groups of instruments by clicking **Move Up** or **Move Down**. (See below for more detail on this.)

- When you have finished defining your Arrange style, click **OK**.

Arrange styles are automatically saved in the **Arrange Styles** folder within your user application data folder, so if you like, you can share them with other users simply by sending them the appropriate *.sar* files from that folder – **User-editable files** in 📖 **9.1 Working with files**.

If you are creating styles for other people to use, you should include *all possible appropriate instruments* in each style (we've done this in the predefined styles). For example, a brass Arrange style should preferably include rare instruments like piccolo trumpet and horns with crooks, in case someone else wants to arrange for these.

Which lines go into the first group

The Arrange styles provided are suitable for most kinds of arrangement, but should you need to define your own, it's important to understand how the distribution of lines of notes affects the resulting arrangement.

Power tools

The four methods of sorting the lines of notes – which are determined by the **Which lines go into the first group** option – give rise to very different distributions of the music. In general terms:

- If sorting by pitch (i.e. **Highest**), the groups should be disposed such that the instruments in each group should be able to play in the correct register, e.g. the first group would be high instruments (such as violins and flutes), a second group medium instruments (e.g. violas, clarinets, horns), and a third group bass instruments (e.g. cellos, bassoons, trombones). Sorting by pitch allows conventional doublings in a "mixed" orchestration (e.g. violins doubled by flutes and clarinets, violas doubled by oboes, cellos doubled by bassoons, etc.) to be set up most easily. Typically this kind of Arrange style should contain three or four groups. The **Mixed** styles are defined like this.

- If sorting by speed (i.e. **Fastest** or **Busiest**), each group should contain a spread of instruments able to play across the entire range of pitches, such as instruments from the standard instrumental families (woodwind, brass and strings). This allows for a "block" orchestration, in which each family plays a particular kind of material (e.g. woodwinds play the fastest music, brass play the slowest music). Typically this kind of Arrange style should contain two or three groups. The **Block** styles are defined like this, sorting by **Fastest**, which is our recommended setting for block orchestration.

- If in doubt about which method of sorting to use, **Highest** (i.e. mixed orchestration) generally gives the best default results.

5.3 Classroom Control

If you are an educator running Sibelius in one or more classrooms or labs in your school, college or university using Sibelius's Licence Server, you can use the Classroom Control feature to perform useful classroom management tasks from your own workstation. You can get files from other copies of Sibelius on the network, send files to particular students, "freeze" copies of Sibelius to focus the attention of the class on you, and more.

Classroom Control is only available if you are running a network site license of Sibelius.

Setting the teacher password

Before you can use Classroom Control, you must change the teacher password for your network site license. This is done in the Licence Server Control Panel, which should be installed on your workstation, or on the server on which the Sibelius Licence Server itself is installed.

For security purposes, the default password is not printed here, and is instead printed in your Licence Server User Guide, along with instructions for changing the password.

Logging in to Classroom Control

To get started with Classroom Control, run Sibelius on your workstation. Your copy of Sibelius must be one of the networked copies of your network site license. Choose **File ▸ Classroom Control**, and you are invited to log in:

(If you cannot see the **File ▸ Classroom Control** menu item, your copy of Sibelius is not part of a network site license. Contact your network manager or system administrator for further assistance.)

Type the password you have set in the Licence Server Control Panel, and click **OK**. If you switch on **Keep me logged in on this computer**, Sibelius will save your password and not ask you to provide it when you use Classroom Control in subsequent sessions. You should only switch this on if you are confident that students do not have access to your workstation.

Keep your password secure

Be aware that the **File ▸ Classroom Control** menu item appears in the menus of all copies of Sibelius running on your network. In order to guard against mischievous students being able to log in to Classroom Control, it is important that you choose a strong password in the Licence Server Control Panel, and don't share it with your students.

Power tools

Using Classroom Control

Once you have logged in by providing your teacher password, the following dialog appears:

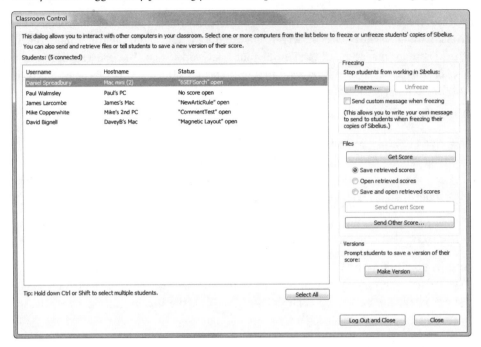

The table on the left of the dialog lists information about each copy of Sibelius that is currently running on your network:

- **Username** lists the long form of the user's account name, if available, or the short username used by that user to log in to the computer if not.
- **Hostname** lists the hostname of the computer a given user is currently logged into; if no hostname is available, you will see a numeric IP address instead.
- **Status** lists the filename of the score the user is working on, or **No score open** if the student does not currently have a file open; if you have frozen this copy of Sibelius, it will say **Frozen**.

To perform classroom management functions, select one or more rows from the table, or click the **Select All** button at the bottom of the window to select all of the rows with one click.

To close the Classroom Control dialog, click **Close**. Clicking **Log Out and Close** closes the dialog and makes Sibelius forget the teacher password, so that you will be prompted to enter it next time you choose **File ▸ Classroom Control**; this is more secure, but marginally less convenient.

The classroom management options on the right are split into three groups, described below.

Freezing and unfreezing

Freezing allows you temporarily to lock Sibelius on a user's computer. When you select one or more users from the list and click **Freeze**, the copy of Sibelius running on each of the selected computers will show a message informing the user that their copy of Sibelius has been frozen by their teacher. You can choose to send a custom message (e.g. "10 minutes left!") by switching on the **Send custom message when freezing** option before you click **Freeze**: you will then be prompted to provide a message to be displayed to the affected users. To unlock a frozen copy of Sibelius, select it in the table and click **Unfreeze**.

If you try to close the Classroom Control dialog while some copies of Sibelius on the network are still frozen, Sibelius will prompt you to unfreeze them.

Getting and sending scores

The options in the **Files** group allow you to get the currently open score from any user's computer, or send a score from your own workstation to any of the other computers on the network. This is useful for, say, showing one student's work on the digital projector or interactive whiteboard connected to your own workstation, or for distributing a worksheet or exercise to the students in your class.

Before you get a user's score, first decide what you want to do with it, and set the radio buttons in the **Files** group appropriately: choose **Save retrieved scores** if you don't want to look at the score now, but instead simply want to save it on your own workstation; choose **Open retrieved scores** if you just want to take a look at the score, but don't necessarily want to save it on your own workstation; or choose **Save and open retrieved scores** if you want to look at the score now and save it on your workstation. If you choose to save the score, Sibelius will create a folder inside your **Scores** folder named after the user whose score you are retrieving, and save the score in there.

To get scores that are currently open on other computers on the network, simply choose one or more rows in the list on the left, then click **Get Score**. A progress bar appears while Sibelius requests the scores from each selected copy of Sibelius, and transfers them over the network; depending on the size of the scores and the speed and congestion of your network, this may take a few seconds. If you chose to open, or save and open, the retrieved scores, Sibelius opens each score as it arrives over the network.

You can also send a score to one or more copies of Sibelius on the network: if a score is currently open in your copy of Sibelius, clicking **Send Current Score** will send it over the network to the copies of Sibelius you have selected in the list at the left, automatically opening it on each copy. If no score is open, or if you want to send a different score than the one you are currently looking at, click **Send Other Score**, which shows a standard file selection window. Choose the file you want to send, and click **Open**. The file is sent over the network and opened on each selected client copy.

Making versions

If your students are working on a long-term project, such as exam coursework, you will find Sibelius's versioning features a very useful way for students to keep track of their progress. From the Classroom Control dialog, you can click **Make Version**, which will prompt the selected users to provide a comment about their current work and save their score. You may want to click this button, for example, a few minutes before the end of a lesson in order to be sure that each student has saved his or her work correctly, and been given the opportunity to provide a comment about the progress in that session.

For more information about versions, 📖 **5.22 Versions**.

5.4 Color

📖 **5.10 Highlight**.

Sibelius allows you to color most objects in your scores. This is very useful for producing more eye-catching scores – for example, you might want to color all the tempo directions or rehearsal marks a particular color to make them stand out for the conductor or performers – and also has educational applications: you could use different colors to differentiate between different fingerings or chord diagrams, or color each pitch on a notation staff differently to help students learn to read music.

How to color an object

Changing the color of an object is simple:

* Select the object (or objects) you want to color
* Choose **Edit ▸ Color** (shortcut **Ctrl+J** *or* ⌘J)
* A standard color picker dialog appears: choose the color you want and click **OK**.

To color another object the same color as the last color you applied, select the object and choose **Edit ▸ Reapply Color** (shortcut **Ctrl+Shift+J** *or* ⇧⌘J).

You can color objects individually, or a whole bunch of selected objects at once. For example, to change the color of all the notes in a bar, select the bar so that it's surrounded by a single light blue box, then choose **Edit ▸ Color**. You can also use filters (📖 **5.7 Filters and Find**) to select, say, all the lyrics in your song and color them all at once.

Resetting an object's color

To reset the color of an object to black, select it and choose **Layout ▸ Reset Design** (shortcut **Ctrl+Shift+D** *or* ⇧⌘D).

Viewing notes in color

Whether you can see notes whose color you have changed depends on the option you have chosen in the **View ▸ Note Colors** submenu. If you have **Voice Colors** switched on, all notes will be colored according to this option, and not according to any individual colors you have chosen. User-chosen colors are only visible if either **None** or **Notes Out of Range** are switched on. 📖 **5.23 View menu**.

Printing in color

You can print your score in full color if desired – simply ensure that the **Print in color** option in the **File ▸ Print** dialog is switched on. If you have a black-and-white printer, colored objects will print in shades of gray. If this option is switched off, all colored objects will be printed in black – 📖 **5.16 Printing**.

Which objects can be colored?

With a few exceptions, you can change the color of anything you can select, including notes, lines, text, chord diagrams, symbols, and more.

When coloring notes, the following constituent parts are drawn in the same color as the notehead itself: accidentals; articulations; rhythm dots; brackets; and ties.

The following parts ignore the chosen color of the notehead and are always drawn in black: beams; leger lines; stems; acciaccatura slash; tremolos; and flags/hooks.

Which objects cannot be colored?

- Individual noteheads in chords (if you color one notehead of a chord, all the other noteheads will be colored the same)
- Instrument names to the left of the system
- Bar numbers (although you can color bar number *changes* if you want)
- Initial clefs at the start of systems (although you can color clef *changes* if you want)
- Initial key signatures at the start of systems (although you can color key signature *changes*)
- Note names denoting the tuning of tab staves at the start of systems
- Normal barlines (although you can color special barlines, such as repeat, double and final barlines)
- Staff lines.

Storing colors in the Windows color picker

If you want to retain a number of colors so you can re-use them later, you can store them in the **Custom colors** section of the color picker. This is not as straightforward as it may seem, as the new color is always stored as the *first* custom color (which overwrites your new color on the right side of the dialog) unless you've previously selected a custom color.

If you want to go through a score looking for several colors you've already used and add them to the custom colors list:

- Select the object that uses the color you want to store
- Choose **Edit ▸ Color** (shortcut **Ctrl+J**)
- Type **Alt+C** to select the first custom color
- Use the arrow keys to move the focus to the custom color slot in which you want to store the object color
- Click **Add to custom colors.**

Storing colors in the Mac color picker

To add a custom color on Mac:

- Select the object that uses the color you want to store
- Choose **Edit ▸ Color** (shortcut ⌘J)
- Click and hold down the left mouse button in the box showing the color of the object at the top of the dialog
- Drag the mouse down into one of the custom color boxes at the bottom of the dialog.

Power tools

5.5 Comments

Comments are "sticky notes" that you can create in your score, to serve as reminders of things you need to do, or possibly as a handy way to communicate with people you collaborate with, whether it's your teacher or student, arranger or editor.

Creating a comment

To add a comment to your score, simply click the comment button on the toolbar (shown on the right), choose **Create ▸ Comment**, or use the keyboard shortcut **Shift+Alt+C** *or* ⇧⌥C. Click where you want the comment to go, type the text you want to appear in the comment, and hit **Esc**.

If you had any music selected before you created the comment, the comment will automatically appear attached to the top staff in the selection, and the text of the comment will show the names of the selected staves, and the bars selected. This is handy for making a reminder specific to particular bars in particular instruments.

Editing a comment

To edit a comment, simply double-click the main part of the comment. Editing a comment is just like editing any other text in your score: you can change the font, formatting (e.g. bold, italic) and size of an individual comment using the controls in the **Text** panel of Properties.

If you want to change the default font, size or formatting for comments in your score, choose **House Style ▸ Edit Text Styles** and edit the **Comment** text style (☐ **3.9 Edit Text Styles**).

Resizing a comment

As you type, Sibelius will automatically ensure that your comment is large enough to display all of the text you enter, but comments can also be resized by grabbing hold either of the bottom edge of the comment or the right-hand edge of the comment, clicking and dragging.

Comments can also be minimized by double-clicking the bar that shows your name and the date on which the comment was created or last edited. A minimized comment looks like this:

Comment colors

Sibelius automatically assigns a color for the comments added to the score by each individual user, allowing you to see at a glance which comments have been added by different people. You cannot edit the color chosen for each user by default, but you can change the color of an existing comment by selecting it and choosing **Edit ▸ Color** (📖 **5.4 Color**).

Deleting comments

To delete a comment, simply select it and hit **Delete**. If you want to delete many comments quickly, select the passage in which you want to delete the comments, or select the whole score, and choose **Edit ▸ Filter ▸ Comments**, then hit **Delete**.

Viewing comments

You can choose whether or not comments should be visible in your score by choosing **View ▸ Comments**, which toggles all comments on or off. If you open a score that contains comments but **View ▸ Comments** is switched off, Sibelius will ask you whether you want to show the comments in the score.

Printing comments

To print comments, make sure **View ▸ Comments** is switched on, and that any other options in the **View** menu that you do not want to be included in your print-out are switched off. Now choose **File ▸ Print**, and make sure that **Print View menu options** is switched on (on the **Sibelius** page of the dialog on Mac).

Changing the username displayed in a comment

By default, Sibelius uses the name associated with the user account with which you are logged in to your computer. Sometimes this may result in a name like **Default User** appearing in your comments. To change the name displayed in a comment, choose **File ▸ Preferences** (in the **Sibelius** menu on Mac), and go to the **Other** page, where you will find options to specify the appearance of comments in your scores:

- Switch off **Show username in comments** if you only want to see the date and time the comment was created or last edited.

- Switch on **Override default username** if you want to change the username that appears in each comment you subsequently create.

- Switch off **Show date and time in comments** if you only want to see the username in the header of each comment.

- If you have both username and date and time set to show in the title bar of comments, the **Order of text in comment header** option allows you to specify whether the username or the date and time should be shown first. If the width of a comment is insufficient to show both the username and date, Sibelius will only show whichever is set to appear first, and hide the other.

5.6 Display settings

📖 **5.23 View menu**.

It's worth spending a few moments setting Sibelius's display to suit your preferences and to make sure it runs as quickly and smoothly as possible on your computer.

Screen resolution

Sibelius requires a minimum screen resolution of 1024 x 768 pixels, and we recommend a higher resolution where possible. To change your screen resolution:

- On Windows:
  - ◦ Minimize any open programs, then right-click on the desktop, and choose **Properties** from the context menu
  - ◦ Click the **Settings** tab
  - ◦ Drag the **Screen Resolution** slider right to increase the screen resolution, and click **Apply** to try out your changes. If your computer is more than a couple of years old, you may need to reduce the **Color Quality** value in order to display higher resolutions – but see **Number of colors** below.
- On Mac:
  - ◦ From the dock, launch **System Preferences**, and click the **Displays** icon
  - ◦ Choose a new screen resolution from the available list; your Mac is automatically set to use the new resolution.

Depending on your computer's graphics card, higher resolutions may cause screen redraw to slow down a bit; if you find this to be the case, try reducing the number of colors used in your display, as this reduces the work that your graphics card has to do.

Number of colors

On Mac, Sibelius should look good at any "color depth" (number of colors), from 256 colors right up to millions of colors. You should only have to change the number of colors used by your display if you find redraw particularly slow at a certain color depth.

On Windows, however, we recommend that you set your display to a color depth of at least 16-bit color. This is because some of the buttons on the Keypad may display incorrectly on displays using 256 (or fewer) colors.

To change the color depth used by your display, follow the same procedure described in **Screen resolution** above.

Textures

Within Sibelius, both the virtual paper and desk use high-quality textures to make them easier on the eye. You can easily change the textures from a huge range of papers, woods, marbles and so on, using the **Textures** page of **File ▸ Preferences** (in the **Sibelius** menu on Mac).

By choosing from the **Edit textures for** menu you can set the textures for the **Score**, **Parts**, editing **Ideas**, and viewing read-only **Versions** independently.

There are some fun textures to choose between – try **Tiger skin** for your desktop, or **Paper, coffee-stained** for your paper if you've been up all night writing music! Perhaps more useful is the **Paper, graph** texture, which is very good for visually aligning objects in your score – the grid lines are 1 space apart when viewed at 100%.

If screen redraw seems particularly slow, try switching on the **Alternative texture drawing** option in this dialog, then quit and restart Sibelius; this may make Sibelius faster on some computers, but slower on those with limited memory. (This option is not available on Mac when smoothing is switched on.)

If screen redraw is still slow, you will probably find that switching textures off (by setting the options to **Use color, not texture**) makes screen redraw quicker.

You can even add your own textures to Sibelius if you like – just create a folder called **Textures** inside your computer's application data area (see **User-editable files** on page 642), and drop some suitable Windows bitmap (BMP) files into it. When you next run Sibelius, the new textures will be available on the **Textures** page of the **File ▸ Preferences** dialog.

Smoothing

On Windows, you can set how and to what extent Sibelius should smooth the appearance of your score as it appears on your display by choosing **File ▸ Preferences** and selecting **Display**.

You can choose a smoothing preset from the Settings menu (Sibelius will use **Smooth and Fast** by default), or you can change the settings individually, i.e. whether or not to smooth **Slurs and ties**, **Beams**, **Angled lines** (e.g. hairpins) and **Straight lines** (e.g. staff lines). Smoothing of symbols and text can either be switched off, use the system default or be switched on. The system default can be changed by clicking the **Effects** button on the **Appearance** page of your system's **Display properties**. (Choose **Start ▸ Settings ▸ Control Panel** and double-click **Display**.)

On Mac, Sibelius uses Mac OS X's built-in Quartz display, which is always beautifully smooth. No options are necessary for Quartz display, so the **Smoothing** options do not appear on Mac.

Speed tips

Here are a few ways you can improve the speed at which Sibelius runs on your computer:

- If dragging the paper seems slow, try **Alternative texture drawing** or switch off the paper and desk textures (see **Textures** above). You could also try changing the smoothing level and color depth, and switch on **Translucent Windows**.
- On Windows, using Adobe Type 1 (PostScript) versions of the Opus, Reprise, Inkpen2 and Helsinki fonts can also slow down the time it takes to redraw the screen – so wherever possible use TrueType fonts. (These are installed by default, so unless you've specifically changed the fonts Sibelius should use, you don't need to worry about this.)

Power tools

- If selecting objects seems slow, close up any open "panels" on the Properties window you're not specifically using, or hide it completely by choosing **Window▸ Properties** (shortcut **Ctrl+Alt+P** *or* ⌥⌘P).

- Once you've memorized everything on the Keypad, hiding it by switching off **Window▸ Keypad** (shortcut **Ctrl+Alt+K** *or* ⌥⌘K) will provide a small speed increase.

- You will also find that switching off rulers in the **View▸ Rulers** submenu speeds things up too.

- As you are inputting or editing, Sibelius always checks to make sure that what you hear when you click on a note is the best available sound (e.g. if you click on a staccato note, Sibelius will try to play a staccato sound if one is available). If your playback device provides lots of different playing techniques, working out which sound to play at any given moment can take a little while, particularly if you are working with a large score. So consider either switching off **Play notes as you edit** on the **Note Input** page of **File▸ Preferences** (in the **Sibelius** menu on Mac), or switching to a playback configuration that uses simpler playback devices; e.g. choose **Play▸ Playback Devices**, and choose **General MIDI (enhanced)** from the **Configuration** menu at the top of the dialog, then click **Close**. You can switch back to your more capable playback configuration when you've done the majority of the input and editing work.

Translucent windows

You can switch on the **Translucent tool windows** option on the **Display** page of **File▸ Preferences** (in the **Sibelius** menu on Mac) to make the Navigator, Keypad, Mixer, Video and Properties windows translucent so that you can see your music through them. If you experience flickering or other problems during playback, switching on **Except video window** to prevent the video window from being translucent should resolve this issue (📖 **4.10 Video**).

Sibelius also allows you to set how transparent windows should be using the **Translucency** slider. A value of **0%** means the windows are completely opaque, whilst **100%** makes them rather uselessly invisible.

Using translucency usually speeds up screen redraw, so we recommend that you switch this option on.

Multiple monitors

You can run Sibelius across multiple monitors, which is very useful as you can, say, have a different score open on each monitor, or even view two pages of the same score across both displays.

5.7 Filters and Find

📖 **1.9 Selections and passages**.

One of Sibelius's smart features is the ability to find objects with particular characteristics – such as all hairpins, or the top notes only from a passage of chords, or all text in the Expression text style that says *cresc.*, or all eighth note (quaver) middle Cs in voice 2 that have a down-bow and a marcato.

You can either select all the objects that match the characteristics you choose using options from the **Edit ▸ Filter** submenu, or find each matching object in turn using the **Edit ▸ Find** (shortcut **Ctrl+F** *or* ⌘**F**) and **Edit ▸ Find Next** (shortcut **Ctrl+G** *or* ⌘**G**) functions. Having done that, you can do anything you like with the selection – edit it, copy it, delete it or whatever.

How to use filters

- Select the passage of music you want to select objects from, or the whole score (**Ctrl+A** *or* ⌘**A**)
- Choose one of the "quick filters" from the **Edit ▸ Filter** menu, or choose **Advanced Filter** (shortcut **Ctrl+Shift+Alt+F** *or* ⇧⌥⌘**F**) to select more complex characteristics (details below)
- You can then do what you like with the selection – e.g. delete it, copy it, move it with the arrow keys, add articulations, change note value
- Alternatively, you may want to choose another characteristic from the **Edit ▸ Filter** menu to narrow down the selection further (see below).

Quick filters

The **Edit ▸ Filter** menu contains a selection of standard filters for quick access. The first group of quick filters is for the various kinds of text in your score:

- **Bar Numbers**: selects all bar numbers and bar number changes
- **Chord Symbols**: selects all chord symbols (and legacy chord symbols)
- **Comments**: selects all "sticky note" comments
- **Dynamics**: selects all Expression text and hairpins (shortcut **Shift+Alt+D** *or* ⇧⌥**D**)
- **Expression Text**: selects all text in the Expression style
- **Lyrics**: selects all lyrics
- **Page Number Changes**: selects all page number changes
- **Rehearsal Marks**: selects all rehearsal marks
- **Staff Text**: selects all text in any staff text style (e.g. Technique, Expression, Plain text, Boxed text)
- **System Text**: selects all text in any system text style (e.g. Tempo, Plain system text), if you have a system selection
- **Technique Text**: selects all text in the Technique style.

The next group of quick filters is for non-text objects:

- **Grace Notes**: selects all grace notes, including acciaccaturas, appoggiaturas and stemless grace notes
- **Hairpins**: selects all hairpin lines

- **Hidden Objects**: selects all hidden objects, of any kind
- **Instrument Changes**: selects all instrument changes
- **Notes and Chords**: selects all notes and chords (along with their accidentals, articulations, etc.), but doesn't select other objects such as text
- **Pedal Lines**: selects all kinds of keyboard pedal lines
- **Repeat Bars**: selects all 1-bar, 2-bar and 4-bar repeats
- **Rests**: selects all rests, but doesn't select notes or other objects
- **Slurs**: selects all slurs (magnetic and non-magnetic)
- **Symbols**: selects all symbols (including system symbols, if you have a system selection)
- **Tuplets**: selects tuplet brackets and numbers; useful for hiding, showing, or resetting the position of tuplet brackets in a single operation.

The **Edit ▸ Filter ▸ Voices** submenu allows you to select objects in specific voices:

- **Voice 1/2/3/4** (shortcuts **Ctrl+Shift+Alt+1/2/3/4** or ⇧⌥⌘1/2/3/4): selects all objects in that voice (e.g. notes, rests, text, lines, etc.), including objects that are not exclusively in that voice – for example, if you filter Voice 1, text objects that apply to, say, both voices 1 and 2 will also be selected. This is particularly useful for copying a single voice onto another staff, since you want associated objects such as dynamics to be copied with the notes.
- **Voice 1/2/3/4 Only**: selects objects that are *only* in that voice, so it will not select objects that are in multiple voices – for example, if you filter **Voice 2 Only**, text objects that apply to both voices 1 and 2 will *not* be selected. This is mainly used for *deleting* a particular voice from a passage, since you would not generally want to delete any object that also applies to a remaining voice on that staff.

Edit ▸ Filter ▸ Notes in Chords (For Copying) and **Notes in Chords (For Deletion)** contain identical sets of filters, but with one crucial difference: filters for copying include tuplet numbers and brackets, while filters for deletion do not. When copying music including tuplets, tuplet numbers and brackets must be included in the selection, otherwise the pasted notes will use the wrong duration; conversely, when deleting music including tuplets, tuplet numbers and brackets must be *excluded* from the selection, otherwise the entire tuplet will be deleted, including any other notes in those tuplets that were not originally included in the filtered passage. The quick filters in these two submenus are as follows:

- **Top/2nd/3rd/Bottom Note**: selects only the specified notehead from chords in all voices in the staff; if you choose the **Top Note** or **Bottom Note** filters, single notes will also be selected. This is useful if you want to delete notes from chords but leave, say, the melody intact. **2nd** and **3rd** mean the second or third notehead counting down from the top, not up from the bottom.
- **Top/2nd/3rd/Bottom Note or Single Notes** (shortcuts **Ctrl+Alt+1/2/3/B** or ⌥⌘1/2/3/B): if a passage contains both chords and single notes, this filter will select the specified notehead from chords *and* the single notes in all voices, so you end up with a continuous line of music. This feature is useful for arranging from a keyboard sketch, where you want to copy lines of music onto other staves.

Finally, at the bottom of the **Edit ▸ Filter** submenu you will find **Player 1/2 (For Deletion)**, which are designed to make it easy to separate a staff for (say) Flutes 1 and 2 into individual parts for each player. You can also use it to separate two players from one staff onto separate staves in a score, in complex situations not handled by other filters such as where the music is sometimes in one voice and sometimes in two. See **Extracting individual players** on page 555.

Using filters for copying and deleting

The chief uses of filters are for copying and deleting music, which is reflected in the range of quick filters built into Sibelius. The distinction between using filters for copying and deleting may be less than obvious at first, so let's take a real-world example.

You have a passage for, say, two flutes written on the same staff in two voices, and you decide that what you actually want is for Flute 2's line to be played by a clarinet. To do this quickly, select the passage in the flute staff, then choose **Edit ▸ Filter ▸ Voice 2**, which will select all of Flute 2's notes and any associated dynamics, slurs and so on. Now simply copy the music into the clarinet staff with **Alt+click** *or* ⌥-click, and swap the new clarinet music into voice 1 with **Alt+1** *or* ⌥1. To delete the Flute 2 music from the flute staff subsequently, select the passage again and choose **Edit ▸ Filter ▸ Voice 2 Only**. This selects all the notes, but only the dynamics and so on that apply *only* to voice 2, so when you **Delete**, you don't lose text (etc.) that should also apply to voice 1.

When you delete a voice, hit **Delete** twice – the first **Delete** turns the notes into rests, and the second **Delete** deletes these rests.

Advanced Filter dialog

If you want to apply a more complex filter, such as one using a combination of characteristics, you should use the **Edit ▸ Filter ▸ Advanced Filter** dialog (shortcut **Ctrl+Shift+Alt+F** *or* ⇧⌥⌘F), which allows you to select or deselect any objects in the selected passage or the whole score.

The dialog is split into two sections: on the left are general values that need to be set for the filter operation such as whether to **Find in** the whole score or a selected passage, which general object types to include (**Text**, **Lines** etc.), and which voices to include; on the right are detailed values for each general object type – these are in six pages, selected from the **View** list box, and explained in detail below.

The four **Voice** boxes indicate which voices in your score will be filtered; by default, all four voices are filtered.

If you select a passage or multiple selection before choosing **Edit ▸ Filter ▸ Advanced Filter**, you will be able to choose whether your filter applies to the **Selection** or the **Whole score**. If you don't select anything before filtering, it will automatically apply to the whole score.

Build up as complex a filter as you like by using the six pages of options accessed via the **View** list at the left. Switch on the **Find** box for a particular page to add it to the filter; switch it off again to remove it. Obviously enough, at least one of the **Find** boxes must be switched on to perform a filter operation!

Clicking **Reset** in the dialog sets all the filter options back to their defaults, so you can start afresh.

Power tools

The options on the **Notes and Chords** page are as follows:

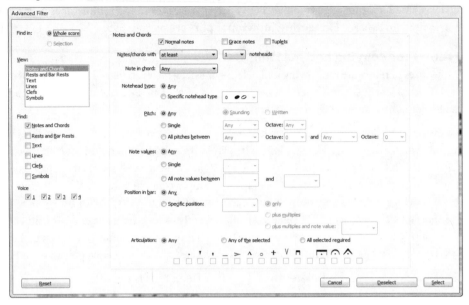

- At the top of the dialog, choose whether you want to filter **Normal notes** (meaning non-grace notes, but including cue-sized notes) and/or **Grace notes.**

- Whether you should switch **Tuplets** on depends on whether you are making a filter for copying or for deletion. If you are selecting notes for copying elsewhere, switch **Tuplets** on; if you are selecting notes in order to delete them, switch **Tuplets** off; if you are deselecting notes from chords in order to copy the remaining selected notes, switch **Tuplets** off; if you are deselecting notes from chords in order to delete the remaining selected notes, switch **Tuplets** on.

- **Notes/chords with** *at least/at most/exactly n* **noteheads**: filters chords with the specified number of notes.

- **Note in chord** *Top note/2nd from Top/3rd from Top/Bottom Note*: filters the specified note.

- **Notehead type**: filters **Any** notehead type by default, but allows you to choose a **Specific notehead type**, which is useful when e.g. working with unpitched percussion staves.

- **Pitch**: filters only notes of the specific **Single** pitch or a range of pitches (**All pitches between**), and optionally in a specified octave. You can choose to filter **Sounding** or **Written** pitch; by default, Sibelius filters notes of **Any** sounding pitch, so you don't need to worry about transposing instruments. If you filter for a specific pitch or range of pitches, enharmonically equivalent notes are treated separately, so if you want to select both (say) F♯4 and G♭4, you must filter **All pitches between** these two pitches.

- **Note values**: selects only notes/rests of the specific **Single** duration or a range of lengths (**All note values between**). Pick note values from the list or type them on the numeric keypad (with **Num Lock** on). Ties are ignored for this purpose, so a half note (minim) tied to an eighth note (quaver) is treated as two separate notes. By default, Sibelius filters notes of **Any** duration.

- **Position in bar**: by default, filters notes at **Any** rhythmic position, but optionally filters notes and chords at a **Specific position** after the start of the bar. Leave the **Specific position** box empty to filter just notes/rests at the start of bars. If you choose quarter note (crotchet), only notes that are one quarter note into the bar (i.e. begin on the second quarter note) will be filtered. If you also choose **Plus multiples**, every note on a quarter note (crotchet) beat is filtered. If you instead choose **Plus multiple and note value**, every note on a quarter note beat *plus* multiples of the specified duration is filtered.

- **Articulations**: filters notes and chords according to their articulations. If **Any** is selected then a note/chord will be filtered whether or not it has articulations; if **Any of the selected** is selected, a note/chord will only be filtered if it has *any* of the specified articulations; if **All selected required** is selected, a note/chord will only be filtered if it has *all* of the specified articulations.

The **Rests and Bar Rests** page contains several of the same options as the **Notes and Chords** page for finding rests of particular durations, and you can switch on **Find bar rests** to select or deselect bar rests.

The **Text** page allows you to find a particular word (e.g. "legato," "mf") to filter all matching text in the selection; by default, this field is case insensitive (so "legato", "Legato", "LEGATO" will all be matched), but you can switch on **Case sensitive** if you want to consider case. You can optionally specify one or more text styles to filter – click on the text style to add it to the selection, and click on it again to remove it from the selection. The **All** or **None** buttons should be fairly self-explanatory! If you want to filter for system text styles, make sure you are filtering the whole score, or have a system selection before you open the dialog.

The **Lines** page makes it possible to select or deselect one or more types of line. You can also filter for all kinds of line if you like by switching on **All lines**. If you want to filter for system lines, make sure you are filtering the whole score, or have a system selection before you open the dialog.

The **Clefs** page is for selecting or deselecting clef changes (but not initial clefs at the very start of the score, as these aren't objects that can be selected). You can filter for clef changes to a specific clef or clefs, or for all clef changes by switching on **All clefs**.

The **Symbols** page allows you to select or deselect a single staff or system symbol, or all symbols (by switching on **All symbols**). If you want to filter for a system symbol, make sure you are filtering the whole score, or have a system selection before you open the dialog.

Once you have set the options you want, check that the appropriate **Find** boxes are selected, then click **Select** to select all objects in the selection or whole score that match the filter characteristics, or **Deselect** to remove all objects that match the filter characteristics from the selection.

Selecting objects with characteristics x *and* y

Let's suppose you want to select all half note (minim) middle Cs in a passage, in order to put an accent on them. Think of this as selecting everything that is both a half note and a middle C.

To do this, you select all half notes and then filter all middle Cs from those, like this:

- First, select a passage
- Choose **Edit ▸ Filter ▸ Advanced Filter** (shortcut **Ctrl+Shift+Alt+F** *or* ⇧⌥⌘F)
- From **Note values** choose a half note
- By **Pitch**, choose **Single**, then from the first list choose **C**, and from the **Octave** list choose **4**
- Click **Select**, and the filter is performed on your score, leaving only middle C half notes selected
- Add accents using the first Keypad layout.

Power tools

Selecting objects with characteristic x *or* y

Let's suppose you want (for some unearthly reason) to select all notes in a passage that are either half notes (minims) *or* middle Cs, to put an accent on them. This sort of case is rather unlikely, and so there is no direct way to do it. However, the indirect method is:

- Select a passage, then using the Edit ▸ Filter ▸ Advanced Filter dialog, select all half notes
- Put an accent on them using the first Keypad layout
- Select the passage again, then using Edit ▸ Filter ▸ Advanced Filter select all middle Cs
- Put an accent on them, too.

Finding objects

Finding works in much the same way as filtering, except that it selects matching objects one by one rather than all at once. The Edit ▸ Find dialog is very similar to the Advanced Filter dialog. To find objects:

- Choose Edit ▸ Find (shortcut Ctrl+F *or* ⌘F) and choose the combination of characteristics you want to find in your score – see **Advanced Filter dialog** above for details on how to use this dialog
- Click Find to find the first object in your score that matches the criteria you have chosen; if no matching objects are found, Sibelius pops up a message telling you so.

Once you've set up a Find operation, you can use Edit ▸ Find Next (shortcut Ctrl+G *or* ⌘G) to find the next matching object in your score.

The search order is as follows:

- The search starts at the beginning of the score, with the first bar in the top staff
- Sibelius searches to the very end of that staff (at the end of the score), then moves down to the next staff and searches from the start of the score in that staff to the very end again, and so on
- If the end of the score is reached (i.e., the end of the bottom staff), you are asked if you want to stop the search, or continue searching from the top staff at the beginning of the score.

Finding and replacing text

If you want to find and replace particular text in your score, use the Plug-ins ▸ Text ▸ Find and Replace Text plug-in – see **Find and Replace Text** on page 527.

Finding motives (motifs)

If you want to find a particular melodic or rhythmic motive in your score, use the Plug-ins ▸ Analysis ▸ Find Motive plug-in – see **Find Motive** on page 486.

5.8 Focus on Staves

📖 **2.29 Staves, 4.1 Working with playback, 5.13 Panorama**.

When working on scores for large ensembles such as orchestra or band, it's often useful to see just one or a few staves that you're working on; for example, you might want to see just the string staves, or just the horns. This works particularly well in conjunction with View ▸ Panorama.

Similarly, sometimes it's useful to prepare scores where some staves with music on are hidden for the purposes of playback; for example, you might want to prepare a simple lead sheet for printing, but want to hear a hidden accompaniment during playback.

Sibelius's View ▸ Focus on Staves (shortcut Ctrl+Alt+F *or* ⌥⌘F) feature allows you to accomplish both of these tasks with ease.

Choosing which staves to work on

Using Focus on Staves is very easy:

- Select the staff or staves you want to see (i.e. leave all the staves you want to be hidden unselected). You only have to select a single bar in each staff you want to focus on: use **Shift**-click to select adjacent staves, or **Ctrl**+click or **⌘**-click to select non-adjacent staves (📖 **1.9 Selections and passages**). To focus on a single staff, you need only have a note or other object selected.

- Click the toolbar button (shown on the right), or choose View ▸ Focus on Staves (shortcut Ctrl+Alt+F *or* ⌥⌘F)

- Instantly, the staves you didn't want to focus on are hidden

- You can now work on the remaining staves in exactly the same way as normal, inputting and editing notes, adding text, and so on

- Try switching on View ▸ Panorama, which lays out the staves as a single continuous system on an infinitely-wide page, ignoring the layout of the score (📖 **5.13 Panorama**)

- To leave focus mode, simply click the toolbar button or type the shortcut again, or switch off View ▸ Focus on Staves.

If your initial selection of staves included any staves hidden with Layout ▸ Hide Empty Staves (📖 **2.29 Staves**), these staves will be shown when View ▸ Focus on Staves is switched on, and will disappear again when you switch it off if they're still empty.

Sibelius remembers the last combination of staves you chose to focus on, so you can focus on the same staves again simply by switching on View ▸ Focus on Staves with nothing selected.

Playback

If you start playback while Focus on Staves is switched on, all the staves in your score will sound, not just the ones you're focused on. This can be very useful, as it allows you to create scores in which staves cannot be seen, but do play back – such as a hidden realization or lead sheet accompaniment.

Power tools

If you don't want to hear the hidden staves during playback, use the Mixer window to mute them (📖 **4.3 Mixer**).

Because the View ▸ Focus on Staves setting is saved in your score, you can use this feature to great effect with Sibelius Scorch (📖 **5.19 SibeliusMusic.com**), producing versions of your scores that play back one way, but print another.

Selections and passages

When View ▸ Focus on Staves is switched on, dashed blue lines may appear between the focused staves, showing you where staves are present but not shown. (Notice that the same dashed lines appear when you use the Layout ▸ Hide Empty Staves feature – 📖 **2.29 Staves** for more details.)

Beware that when you make a selection across multiple staves when View ▸ Focus on Staves is switched on, any such hidden staves between the visible staves you have selected will also be selected. This can have unintended side-effects: for example, when you copy such a passage elsewhere in the score, you will find that music on the hidden staves has also been copied.

Because of this, we recommend that you should:

* Leave View ▸ Layout Marks on so that you can see where staves are hidden before doing any copying;
* Preferably only copy single-staff passages, to avoid copying music you cannot see;
* Switch off View ▸ Focus on Staves if you want to do complex copying operations involving multiple staves, unless you can see that no hidden staves are included in the selection.

Multirests

If you switch on Use Multirests when focusing on staves, it's exactly the same as switching on multirests when you're not using Focus on Staves. In other words, you'll only see a multirest if you have at least two consecutive bars rest in *all* the staves in the score (not just in the staves you're focusing on).

Possible confusions

Don't confuse Focus on Staves with Layout ▸ Hide Empty Staves (📖 **2.29 Staves**). Focus on Staves can hide staves with music on, affects staves on every page, and is normally used temporarily (unless you're hiding an accompaniment or realization for playback purposes). Layout ▸ Hide Empty Staves works on individual systems, only works with staves which are empty or in which all items are hidden, and is primarily intended for saving space in full scores.

5.9 Hiding objects

It can be useful for certain objects to be present in parts but hidden in your scores. For example, you often want cue passages to appear in parts, but these should be hidden in the full score.

Or you may want some music to be played back that isn't visible, such as a jazz or figured bass realization.

Sibelius allows you to hide any object, and to control whether that object should be visible in the score, or in parts, or in neither.

Hiding an object

To hide an object, select it and choose one of the options in **Edit ▸ Hide or Show**, as follows:

- **Hide/Show** (shortcut **Ctrl+Shift+H** *or* ⇧⌘H): hides or shows an object in the current score or part
- **Show in Score**: shows an object in the full score only (and hides it in all parts)
- **Show in Parts**: shows an object in all parts (and hides it in the score)
- **Show in All**: shows an object both in the full score and all of the parts.

Hide/Show is duplicated on the **General** panel of the Properties window; select the object you want to hide or show and choose the appropriate option from the drop-down menu.

When you hide an object or select a hidden object, it will be shown in a pale color on the screen. Once you deselect the object, it will disappear, although you can choose to see all hidden objects in gray – see **Viewing hidden objects** below.

What can be hidden

Any object in your score can be hidden, including notes, rests, text, time and key signature changes, lines, and so on. Hiding a note also hides any associated accidentals, beams, stems and articulations. (But you can hide accidentals, flags, and beams independently if necessary – 📖 **2.1 Accidentals** and **2.6 Beam groups**.)

For details on hiding particular objects, see the relevant topic in this Reference, so to find out about hiding lines, 📖 **2.21 Lines**.

Some uses for hidden objects:

- *Notes*: create cue passages that are hidden and silent in the full score, but that appear in parts (📖 **2.14 Grace notes**); have "improvised" solos and realizations that play back but aren't visible.
- *Text*: hide metronome marks or dynamics that still play back; add directions for players that aren't visible in the score but are shown in parts; add notes to the conductor that appear in the score but not in parts
- *Lines*: add markings, e.g. hairpins or *accel./rit.* lines, which play back but are hidden.

Power tools

Viewing hidden objects

To be able to see hidden objects on the screen, switch on **View ▸ Hidden Objects** (shortcut Ctrl+Alt+H *or* ⌥⌘H); this option is switched off by default. When this option is switched on, hidden objects appear in light gray in your score (but they do not print – see **Playing and printing hidden objects** below). Hidden objects can then also be selected and edited in exactly the same way as normal ones.

When **View ▸ Hidden Objects** is switched off, hidden objects in your score are completely invisible and cannot be selected or edited individually (although they do show up if you make a passage or system selection – say, if you type Ctrl+A *or* ⌘A to select all – and you can still move between hidden and visible objects using the arrow and Tab keys).

This option also controls whether or not various objects that are not normally notated are shown. For example:

- invisible barlines (🕮 **2.4 Barlines**) are shown as a gray barline
- key changes (🕮 **2.20 Key signatures**) and instrument changes (🕮 **2.18 Instruments**) that result in no accidentals appearing are shown as a gray rectangle
- rests and bar rests that are hidden by the instrument's staff type, such as in some guitar tab instruments, appear in gray.

Note also that if you delete a rest it is initially hidden, so it will appear in light gray if **View ▸ Hidden Objects** (shortcut Ctrl+Alt+H *or* ⌥⌘H) is switched on. If you delete it again, it then disappears entirely.

Hidden objects in parts

When an object is hidden in the full score but visible in a part, or vice versa, and **View ▸ Differences in parts** is switched on, the visible version of it will appear in orange (to show it's not identical in the score and part); the hidden version will appear in gray as usual when **View ▸ Hidden Objects** is switched on, but will turn a pale orange when selected.

Playing and printing hidden objects

By default, hidden objects *don't* print and *do* play back, regardless of whether **View ▸ Hidden Objects** is switched on or off. You might not want certain hidden objects to play back, for example a cue passage that is hidden in the full score but shown in parts; if so, use silent noteheads or switch off the objects' **Play on pass** checkboxes in the Properties window – 🕮 **2.25 Noteheads** and **4.6 Repeats**.

If you want to print hidden objects, e.g. to help with proof-reading, switch on **View ▸ Hidden Objects** and then print your score, making sure to switch on **Print View menu options** in the **File ▸ Print** dialog (🕮 **5.16 Printing**).

5.10 Highlight

📖 **5.4 Color**.

Sibelius allows you to draw highlights on your music to remind you of sections you are working on, or simply to draw attention to a particular feature of your score.

Creating a highlight

To create a highlight in your score, either:

- Choose **Create ▸ Highlight**, then click and drag along the passage you want to highlight; or
- Select a passage, then choose **Create ▸ Highlight** to create a highlight for the duration of that passage. You can only highlight a passage in a single staff at once, so if you choose a passage containing multiple staves, the highlight will only appear on the top staff in the selection. (Though you can highlight the other staves individually.)

Highlights are yellow by default, but you can change their color after creating them just like other objects – 📖 **5.4 Color**.

Selecting highlights and highlighted objects

You can select, move and delete highlighted notes or other objects just the same as any other. To select the highlight itself click its edge, so you can move, copy and delete it.

Moving a highlight

- To move a highlight left or right, click on the top or bottom edge of the highlight and drag with the mouse, or use the ←/→ keys (with **Ctrl** *or* ⌘ for larger steps)
- To adjust the length of a selected highlight, click on the left or right line of the box around the highlight and drag the mouse, hit **space** to extend it by a note (**Shift-space** retracts by a note), or use the ←/→ keys (with **Ctrl** *or* ⌘ for larger steps).

Deleting a highlight

To delete a highlight, click the edge of the highlight and hit **Delete**; to remove all the highlights in a score, use the **Plug-ins ▸ Other ▸ Remove All Highlights** plug-in (see page 507).

Viewing highlights

You can specify whether highlights are displayed in your score by choosing **View ▸ Highlights**.

Printing highlights

You can choose whether or not to print highlights.

- If you don't want to print them, make sure that the **Print View menu options** setting in the **File ▸ Print** dialog (shortcut **Ctrl+P** *or* ⌘P) is switched off when you print your score
- To print highlights, switch on **View ▸ Highlights** (and switch off any other **View** menu options that you don't want to be printed), then print your score, making sure that the **Print View menu options** setting in the **File ▸ Print** dialog (shortcut **Ctrl+P** *or* ⌘P) is switched on.

For further information about printing, 📖 **5.16 Printing**.

Power tools

5.11 Ideas

When writing music you often come up with a bit of melody, rhythm, accompaniment or chord progression with some potential. Arrangers and copyists may use and reuse a large number of specific chunks of notation, such as text markings, specific chord symbols or diagrams, and so on.

We call these fragments *ideas*: snippets of any length, any kind and for any number of instruments. Just tap a key to capture an idea and store it for later. Once you've captured an idea you can edit it, tag it with your own keywords (e.g. *canon, lyrical, riff*) to help find it again, or even color-code it. The Ideas window lets you browse and search through all the available ideas, and even play them back. Using an idea is as simple as pasting from the clipboard; Sibelius even transposes them into the right key and range.

You can import and export sets of ideas to share with others – even via the Internet. If you're a teacher or educator, you can save a set of ideas inside a score in order to create a compositional worksheet for your students.

Furthermore, Sibelius comes with more than 2000 built-in ideas, spanning many instruments and musical genres, so if you're stuck for inspiration or are looking for something stylish to kickstart your creative process, you'll find something suitable in seconds.

What's in an idea

An idea can consist of practically anything you can write in Sibelius. You can select any amount of music – from a single note on one staff up to hundreds of bars on any number of staves – and capture it as an idea. You can also select other kinds of objects – such as lines, symbols, text objects and even imported graphics – and capture them as ideas, with or without notes.

As well as music, an idea also contains *tags*. Tags are how you label your ideas using keywords to describe each idea so that you can easily find it later on. This is useful when you have thousands of ideas to sift through! In addition to the tags that you specify, Sibelius automatically tags each idea with other information, including:

- Key signature
- Time signature
- Tempo
- Length of the idea, in bars
- Instruments used in the idea
- Creation date
- Modification date

You can search for ideas using any of the tags you have chosen yourself or the ones Sibelius adds automatically. You can also assign a specific color to any idea.

Ideas window

The main way of working with ideas is the Ideas window, which you can show and hide by choosing Window ▸ Ideas (shortcut Ctrl+Alt+I *or* ⌥⌘I), or by clicking the toolbar button shown on the right.

The Ideas window has two views, *compact* and *detailed*. By default, it opens in compact view, which looks like this:

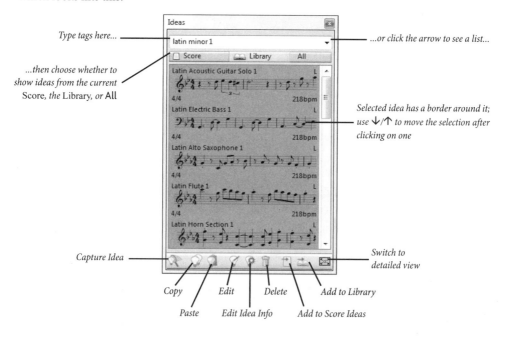

Type tags here...

...or click the arrow to see a list...

...then choose whether to show ideas from the current Score, the Library, or All

Selected idea has a border around it; use ↓/↑ to move the selection after clicking on one

Capture Idea

Switch to detailed view

Copy   *Edit*   *Delete*   *Add to Library*

Paste   *Edit Idea Info*   *Add to Score Ideas*

Power tools

To search for ideas, you simply type one or more tags into the box at the top of the window. If you don't know what to type, click the little arrow at the right of the window, and a drop-down menu will appear, listing the most frequently used tags in the available ideas. You can simply click one of the tags in the list to add it to the box. Once you have one or more words in the box, you can still pull down the menu again, and Sibelius will show you the tags that occur most often in ideas that also use the tags you've already chosen. Each time you add a word to the box and hit **Return**, Sibelius updates the list of ideas in the main part of the window.

The **Score** and **Library** buttons allow you to choose whether you want the ideas shown in the window to come from the current score, or the *library*, which is a repository of ideas available to every score you work on (including the built-in ideas, and other ideas you put into the library), or both (see **Where ideas are saved** below). Notice that if the score you're working on has no ideas in it, the **Score** button will be disabled, and you won't be able to switch off the **Library** button.

The main part of the window shows you the ideas that match the tags you typed, with the most relevant ideas at the top, or, if you haven't typed anything into the box at the top of the window, it shows all available ideas (from the score and/or library), with the most recently captured or edited ideas at the top of the list. Ideas are always shown at sounding pitch.

Each listed idea shows a small preview of the music or other objects contained within it; normally you will see two or three bars of the top staff. Important tags are shown in the four corners around the notation preview: at the top left, the idea's name; at the top right, the letter L appears if the idea is located in the library rather than the current score; at the bottom left, the time signature of the idea; and at the bottom right, the tempo of the idea. If you hover your mouse over the idea, a tool tip appears showing the other tags, including instrumentation. If you don't want to see the notation preview, you can switch off **Show notation preview in Ideas window compact view** on the **Ideas** page of **File ▸ Preferences** (in the **Sibelius** menu on Mac), in which case you will see just the name of the idea and its tempo.

Each idea is shown on a colored background, which you can change to categorize them further. (New ideas you capture yourself have a white background by default.)

You can right-click (Windows) *or* **Control**-click (Mac) on an idea in the list to see a menu that includes a number of useful options. These do the same as the buttons at the bottom of the window, as follows:

- **Copy**: copies the selected idea to the clipboard, so that you can paste it into your score; see **Pasting an idea** below
- **Paste**: pastes the current clipboard contents into the score; if you have a selection in the score, the clipboard contents will be pasted directly at that position; if there is no selection, the mouse pointer will turn blue and you can click in the score to paste at that position
- **Edit**: edits the selected idea; see **Editing an idea** below
- **Edit Idea Info**: allows you to edit an idea's tags and color, as well as see the tags that Sibelius has automatically given to the idea
- **Delete**: deletes the selected idea from the collection of ideas saved in the score or in the library, as appropriate
- **Add to Score Ideas**: only enabled if the selected idea is in the library, this allows you to copy the idea from the library to the collection of ideas in the current score
- **Add to Library**: only enabled if the selected idea is in the collection of ideas in the score, this allows you to copy the idea from the current score to the library
- **Detailed View**: switches the window to detailed view, which looks like this:

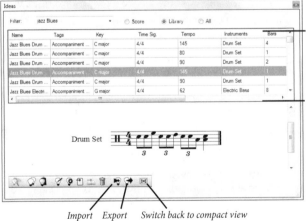

Click the column names to sort the list by that column; drag columns left and right to re-order them

Drag the divider up and down to change the height of the list and preview panes

Import   Export   Switch back to compact view

Detailed view offers much the same functionality as compact view, but (not surprisingly) with more detail. Instead of seeing a short notation preview for each idea, you can see a complete preview of one idea in the pane at the bottom of the window. The list in the upper pane of the window shows you all the tags belonging to each idea, and can be sorted by clicking on any of the column headings. You can change the width of the columns (or indeed the order of the columns) by dragging them around. You can also change the height of the two panes in the window by dragging the divider in between them up or down.

Notice that you can only change the height of the Ideas window in compact view, but in detailed view you can resize the window in both directions.

Detailed view adds two extra buttons not present in compact view, for importing and exporting ideas – see **Where ideas are saved** below.

Auditioning ideas

If you want to hear what an idea sounds like, simply click on it in the Ideas window and hold your left mouse button to audition it; Sibelius will play the idea as a loop, repeating it up to eight times. If you would prefer Sibelius to play your idea just once instead of as a loop, switch off **Automatically repeat ideas when auditioned** on the **Ideas** page of **File ▸ Preferences** (in the **Sibelius** menu on Mac).

Capturing an idea

You create an idea by selecting some music in the score and choosing **Edit ▸ Capture Idea** (shortcut **Shift-I**). You can capture an idea from any kind of selection, including:

- Passage selections of any numbers of bars and staves. If you have a system passage selection, beware that system objects (such as time signatures, repeat barlines, Tempo text, etc.) will be excluded from the idea – ideas can't contain system objects. Also, you cannot capture an idea from a selection that includes discontiguous staves.

- A single selected object, e.g. a note, text object, line, etc. Again, beware that you cannot capture a system object as an idea.

- Multiple selections of notes, e.g. the first and third beats of a bar, selected via **Ctrl**+click *or* ⌘-click, or by a filter. Multiple selections are turned into passage selections when they are captured as ideas, so you will find that when you edit or paste your idea, it is padded out with appropriate rests.

- Multiple selections of things other than notes, e.g. a series of Expression text objects and hairpins, selected via **Ctrl**+click *or* ⌘-click, or by a filter.

(For more information about different kinds of selections, ▢ **1.9 Selections and passages**.)

There are certain obvious things you can't capture as ideas. For example, you can't capture an accidental, beam or articulation without capturing the note or notes to which it's attached. A good rule of thumb is that if you can copy and paste it, you can capture it as an idea.

If the Ideas window is shown, and provided you don't have any tags typed into the box at the top of the window, you will see your idea appear at the top of the window. Sibelius automatically chooses a name for your idea (taken from the score's title or filename, plus a number to ensure it's unique). You can change the name later if you like.

Finding an idea

To find an idea, type one or more tags into the box at the top of the Ideas window, then choose an idea from the list.

Power tools

As you type in the box, Sibelius drops down the menu below so that you can see tags that match what you have typed (e.g. if you type "cl" you may see "clarinet", "closed", "classical", and as soon as you add "a", "closed" will disappear from the list). You can either keep typing, or use the arrow keys or the mouse to select one of the tags from the list. As soon as you have chosen a tag or hit **space** to show that you have finished typing one tag, the list of ideas in the main part of the window is updated.

You can then type another tag. When you add a second tag, only those ideas that match both your original tag *and* your new tag will be shown in the list. As before, when you start to type into the box, the menu drops down to show you the possible tags that match the letters you have typed so far.

Each time you add another tag, the choice of ideas in the main part of the window is reduced accordingly to show only those ideas that match all the tags you have typed into the box. You can then select the idea you want in the list by clicking on it.

Ideas are listed in the main part of the Ideas window in descending order of relevance. If the tag you typed is in the idea's **Name**, then it is considered highly relevant; if the tag occurs in the general list of **Tags**, then it is considered quite relevant; if the tag occurs in the tags generated automatically by Sibelius, it is considered a little relevant.

Pasting an idea

Before you can paste an idea, you have to copy it to the clipboard. To do this, simply select it in the Ideas window, then either type **Ctrl+C** *or* **⌘C**, or click the **Copy** button at the bottom of the window, or right-click (Windows) *or* **Control**-click (Mac) and choose **Copy** from the context menu.

Pasting an idea into a score is just like any other kind of pasting: either select the place in the score where you want the idea to appear, then choose **Edit ▸ Paste** (shortcut **Ctrl+V** *or* **⌘V**); or make sure you have nothing selected, then choose **Edit ▸ Paste**, and click in the score where you want the idea to go. You could also click the **Paste** button at the bottom of the Ideas window.

As with any other kind of pasting, you can use multicopy to paste lots of copies of an idea (see **Multicopying a passage** on page 58), or choose **Edit ▸ Repeat** (shortcut **R**) immediately after pasting to repeat the idea after itself.

Unlike normal pasting, when pasting an idea Sibelius does some extra things for you by default: namely, it transposes the idea to match the prevailing key of the score at the point where you paste, and it also transposes by octaves to ensure that the music fits the playable range of the instrument into which you paste the idea.

When Sibelius transposes an idea to match the current key, it simply transposes all the notes up or down by the same interval, meaning that if your idea is in a major key and you paste into a minor key, the pasted idea will still "sound" major (though you can do modal transposition if required using the Transform Scale plug-in – see **Transform Scale** on page 534). If you would rather Sibelius didn't transpose your ideas at all, switch off Transpose to match current key signature on the Ideas page of File ▸ Preferences (in the Sibelius menu on Mac).

Similarly, if you don't want Sibelius to try and make your idea fit the range of the instrument you're pasting into, switch off Transpose by octaves to fit within instrument range in the same place.

When you paste an idea that uses an unpitched percussion instrument onto a different unpitched percussion staff in your score, Sibelius will automatically create an instrument change at the start of the pasted idea (and restore the original instrument at the end of the idea), so that the playback of the idea is correct. If you don't want Sibelius to do this, switch off **Create instrument changes for unpitched ideas**.

If you want to keep track of where you have used ideas in your score (or if you're a teacher and you want to see where students have used them), switch on **Create colored highlight**, which is also on the **Ideas** page of File ▸ **Preferences** (in the **Sibelius** menu on Mac). This creates a highlight in the idea's background color where you paste it.

Built-in ideas

Sibelius includes more than 2000 ideas, designed to provide inspiration to composers of all ages, and covering as wide a range of genres as possible at a basic level.

Each idea has a unique name, normally the genre name, followed by the instrument (or instruments) in the idea, followed by a number. In general, the higher the number, the more complex the music in the idea. The built-in ideas are also color-coded by genre (as shown in the list below).

To find ideas in a specific genre, first type one of the following tags:

- African (peach)
- Chill Out (pastel green)
- Classical (lime green)
- Concert Band (bright green)
- Country (yellow)
- Dance (gray)
- Film (light blue)
- Folk (olive)
- Funk (gray-pink)
- Garage (misty blue)
- Groovy (pastel pink)
- Hip-hop (pastel blue)
- Jazz (mid-pink)
- Latin (orange)
- Marching Band (turquoise)
- Modern Classical (dull green)
- Motown (beige)
- Pop (bright blue)
- Reggae (violet)
- Rock (bright pink)

You can then further narrow down the matches using tags like the following:

- *Instrument*, e.g. guitar, drum, piano
- *Tempo*, e.g. fast, slow, moderato
- *Idea type*, e.g. melody, accompaniment, rhythm
- *Complexity*, e.g. basic, moderate, complex
- *Mood*, e.g. happy, sad, reflective
- *Characteristics*, e.g. exciting, lively, relaxed, majestic, major, minor, swing, dramatic, humorous

Type one or more tags from one or more of these categories and you'll soon find ideas that suit your purpose.

Some further hints for using the built-in ideas in your own scores:

Power tools

- The ideas vary in length, typically between two and eight bars. The longer ideas are suitable for e.g. demonstrating particular points of composition, style or playing technique, while the shorter ideas are more suitable for adapting, repeating or otherwise using in your own compositions.

- Nearly all of the ideas are for single instruments (as specified in their names), and will work best when pasted onto that instrument, or a closely related one. However, you can paste an idea onto any staff in your score, and Sibelius will transpose it to fit the instrument's range as appropriate, so don't be afraid to experiment.

- All of the ideas within each genre have been designed to work together, though they do not necessarily share the same harmonic structures or chord sequences. Ideas with the same number for different instruments, e.g. **Reggae Bass 1** and **Reggae Keyboard 1**, will generally fit together.

- The built-in ideas have been designed to sound at their best when played back through Sibelius Sounds Essentials (📖 **4.4 Sibelius Sounds Essentials**) with Play ▸ Live Playback switched on (📖 **4.8 Live Playback**), but you can of course play them back on any device.

Using ideas in your teaching

If you are a teacher, you have probably already come up with dozens of ways to use Sibelius's ideas features creatively in your teaching, but here are a few practical suggestions about how your students can get the best out of it:

- *Audition notated ideas:* Students who are not good readers of music notation will find that the ability to audition ideas simply by clicking on them in the Ideas window will spark their creativity.

- *Create ostinatos in ABA form:* Show them how to create an appropriate instrument in the score using **Create ▸ Instruments** (shortcut I), then paste an idea onto the staff. Show them how to quickly repeat an idea after pasting it using **Edit ▸ Repeat** (shortcut R). With these simple techniques, students will quickly be able to build up their own compositions using the built-in ideas provided.

- *Keep track of their creativity with colored highlights:* You may find that switching on **Create colored highlights** (on the **Ideas** page of **File ▸ Preferences**, in the **Sibelius** menu on Mac) helps students to see the patterns produced by using ideas together, and you can also see where students have used ideas or created their own music by the presence or absence of these highlights.

- *Create score templates:* You can create simple projects for your students by setting up a score template that includes some carefully chosen ideas. For example, you could create empty staves for a small jazz combo (drums, keyboard, bass, and a lead instrument like a saxophone). You could then take appropriate ideas from the built-in library and add them to the score (by selecting them and choosing **Add to Score** in the Ideas window) to give the students the raw material to build a 12-bar blues, e.g. a few bass lines, some keyboard riffs, and a handful of drum patterns. If you switch on **Show ideas from this score only** (on the **File** page of **File ▸ Score Info**) then students will only be able to choose from the ideas you have selected for them when working with this file.

- *Improvise a melody:* Encourage your more able students to try improvising a melody in the lead instrument after they have constructed a suitable bass, piano and drums backing using the supplied ideas.

Sibelius's ideas feature also lends itself to:

- Elements of music study
- Using ideas as a call and/or response
- Experimenting with changing instrument sounds
- Aural training through loop recognition and dictation
- Students capturing their own ideas to make a resource bank for younger students
- Helping students to create music in the pop/dance music genre.

A number of the built-in ideas (particularly those tagged "Classical") have been designed as very specific starting points for composition tasks, covering a large number of composition topics for GCSE and AS / A2 Level Music.

For more guidance, visit **www.sibeliuseducation.com**.

Limiting access to the library

If you never want to see ideas from the library when working on a specific score (e.g. if you are preparing a lesson for your students in which they should be allowed to work only with a set of ideas determined by you and saved within the score itself), switch on **Show ideas from this score only** on the File page of File ▸ **Score Info**.

When this option is switched on, the **Library** button in the Ideas window is switched off and disabled, so that only those Ideas saved in the score itself will be visible when working on that score.

Editing an idea

You can edit both the music and the tags of ideas.

To edit an idea's tags, select it in the Ideas window, then click the **Edit Idea Info** button at the bottom of the window, or right-click and choose **Edit Idea Info** from the context menu. The dialog shown on the right appears.

You can edit the idea's **Name** and **Tags** simply by typing into the boxes provided. To change the background color of the idea, click **Color** and choose the colour from the picker that appears.

You can also see all the automatic tags that Sibelius has created in this dialog, though you can't edit them; they are automatically updated if you edit the music in the idea.

To edit the music in an idea, select it in the Ideas window, then click the **Edit Idea** button at the bottom of the window, or right-click and choose **Edit Idea** from the context menu.

A new window will appear, as if you had opened another score. Your idea is shown in Panorama (📖 **5.13 Panorama**), and you can edit it just like any other score

When you have finished editing your idea, simply save it by choosing File ▸ **Save** (shortcut **Ctrl+S** *or* ⌘S), then close the window by choosing File ▸ **Close** (shortcut **Ctrl+W** *or* ⌘W) to return to your original score.

Power tools

If you want to discard any unsaved changes in your idea, simply choose **File ▸ Close**, then click **No** when asked if you want to save your changes.

Where ideas are saved

An idea can be saved either in the current score, or to the library. When an idea is saved in a score, it can only appear in the Ideas window when that score is open, and when the **Score** button is switched on. When an idea is saved in the library, it can appear in the Ideas window when any score is open, provided the **Library** button is switched on.

By default, when you capture an idea, it is added to your current score, which means that it is available only to that score, unless you select it and click **Add to Library** in the Ideas window. If you would prefer all your ideas to go directly to the library instead, set **Add captured ideas to Library** on the **Ideas** page of **File ▸ Preferences** (in the **Sibelius** menu on Mac).

The library is a big repository of ideas you may want to keep for use in many different scores, rather than a single score; it is also where all the built-in ideas are saved; if you don't want to see them, and only want to see your own ideas in the library, switch off **Show built-in ideas**.

The built-in ideas are saved inside the Sibelius program folder (Windows) or application package (Mac) and you shouldn't interfere with them. Ideas that you save to the library yourself are saved in a folder called **Ideas** in your user account's application data folder, but you should never need to interfere with these files directly (see **User-editable files** on page 642), because Sibelius has built-in features to import and export them for sharing them with other users.

Sharing ideas

If you want to share your ideas with others, there are two ways to achieve this: either save the ideas you want to share to a specific score, and then distribute that score (this is useful for setting projects for students – see **Using ideas in your teaching** above); or export a selection of ideas as an .ideas file that can be imported into someone else's ideas library.

To save ideas to a score, select the ideas you want to travel with the score and click the **Add to Score** button at the bottom of the Ideas window, or right-click and choose **Add to Score** from the context menu. You can only select multiple ideas at once if you're using the detailed view of the Ideas window, so you may find that most useful for this kind of operation. Check that the right ideas are in the score by switching off the **Library** button in the Ideas window, which will then only show those ideas saved in the score.

To export a selection of ideas, you need to be using the detailed view of the Ideas window. Select the ideas you want to export in the usual way – using **Shift**-click to select a continuous range of ideas from the list, or **Ctrl**+click *or* ⌘-click to select multiple ideas dotted around the list – then click the **Export** button at the bottom of the window, or right-click (Windows) *or* **Control**-click (Mac) and choose **Export** from the context menu. You will be prompted for a filename and a location to save the ideas; when you click **Save**, an .ideas file is saved to your chosen location. You can then send that .ideas file to somebody (e.g. by email) or upload it to SibeliusEducation.com.

Importing ideas

To import ideas into your library, e.g. if you have received an .**ideas** file from another Sibelius user, switch to the Ideas window's detailed view, then click **Import**. You are prompted to choose the .**ideas** file you want to import; click **Open** and a simple dialog appears, allowing you to specify whether the incoming ideas should be added to the library or to one of the scores you currently have open.

Power tools

5.12 Menus and shortcuts

Nearly every function of Sibelius can be performed using just the keyboard. Once you've learned the keyboard shortcuts for the features you use most often, you'll find using Sibelius much quicker and easier.

You can find most of the shortcuts in Sibelius's menus; they're referred to in this Reference each time we mention a feature that has a shortcut; there's a comprehensive list of shortcuts on the next few pages; and the essential shortcuts are also listed on the back cover of the Handbook.

You can customize most of the keyboard shortcuts if you want, and you can also enable or disable particular features in Sibelius's menus, which is useful in schools – see below.

For details of the conventions used in this Reference for naming menus and shortcuts, refer to the beginning of the separate Handbook.

Shortcut patterns

Here are some general patterns to shortcuts that make them easier to remember:

- Standard operations common to all programs (e.g. New, Copy, Print, Find, Save, Undo) use standard shortcuts, which are mostly Ctrl or ⌘ plus the initial letter of the operation (the notable exceptions being Undo, which is Ctrl+Z or ⌘Z, and Paste, which is Ctrl+V or ⌘V)
- Most Create menu shortcuts (other than text) are a single letter, usually the initial letter (e.g. L for Line, K for Key Signature)
- Create▸ Text menu shortcuts are Ctrl or ⌘, or Ctrl+Alt or ⌥⌘, plus the initial letter (e.g. Ctrl+E or ⌘E for Expression, Ctrl+T or ⌘T for Technique, Ctrl+Alt+T or ⌥⌘T for Tempo)
- Most Notes, Layout and House Style menu shortcuts are Ctrl+Shift or ⇧⌘ plus the initial letter. For Layout▸ Reset... options they use the initial letter of the thing to be reset (e.g. Ctrl+Shift+P or ⇧⌘P for Reset Position)
- Tool window shortcuts are Ctrl+Alt or ⌥⌘ plus the initial letter (or a letter from the name) of the window you want to show or hide
- Ctrl or ⌘ with the arrow keys or Home/End/Page Up/Page Down means "large steps," e.g. with a note selected, Ctrl+↑ or ⌘↑ transposes by an octave; with a bar selected, Ctrl+Shift+Alt+→ or ⇧⌥⌘→ increases note spacing by a large amount
- Shift with arrows or mouse click means "extend selection," e.g. with a bar selected, Shift-↑ extends the selection to the staff above.

Windows/Mac differences

Sibelius and the keyboard shortcuts are virtually identical on Windows and Mac. The Command key (⌘) on Mac keyboards is equivalent to the Ctrl key on Windows keyboards, and the Option key (⌥) on Mac is equivalent to the Alt key on Windows. As a result, almost all shortcuts are interchangeable as long as, for example, ⌘ is substituted for Ctrl as appropriate. There are a few exceptions, but these are clearly explained where they arise.

Likewise, older designs of the standard Mac mouse only have one button, so Mac users may need to use Control-click to access the context-sensitive menus, while Windows users and Mac users with a multi-button mouse use right-click.

School features

Sibelius comes with a ready-made educational feature set called School features, which disables all of the program's advanced features. To use this feature set, select the Menus and Shortcuts page of File ▸ Preferences (in the Sibelius menu on Mac), select School features from the list, then click OK.

The features that remain enabled are the main ones likely to be used by students (e.g. inputting of notes and other common objects, basic playback, printing), but with more advanced features (or features you don't want students to waste time playing around with!) disabled, e.g. most House Style and Layout menu features, advanced playback features, plug-ins, and Help menu web links.

Sibelius doesn't prevent students going into the Preferences dialog themselves to switch the disabled features back on, but you can threaten them with punishment if they try this.

You can also use School features as the basis for your own custom feature set – see **Enabling and disabling features** below.

Notebook (laptop) features

Sibelius comes with a feature set especially designed for laptop users who don't have a keypad on their computer. To use this feature set, choose File ▸ Preferences and select the Menus and Shortcuts page. Select Notebook (laptop) features from the list, then click OK. See **Accessing numeric keypad functions on a notebook (laptop)** on page 18 for more information.

Customizing keyboard shortcuts

You can customize the existing shortcuts in Sibelius as you like. For instance, if you use lots of triplets and find Ctrl+3 *or* ⌘3 a pain to type, you could assign a single key, preferably an unused one, such as U.

To get started, choose the Menus and Shortcuts page of File ▸ Preferences (in the Sibelius menu on Mac) to see this dialog:

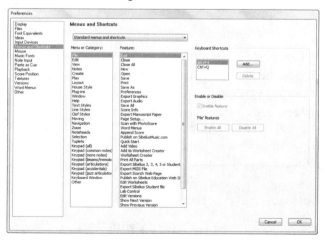

Before you can define a new shortcut, you need to create a new *feature set*, a specific set of keyboard shortcuts and enabled features (see **Enabling and disabling features** below). By default, Sibelius uses the **Standard menus and shortcuts** feature set (though other sets are also included – see above), but you can have as many different feature sets as you like. Let's create one:

* Pull down the list at the top of the dialog and click **Add feature set** to create a new feature set

* In the **New Feature Set** dialog, type a suitable name. The **Base on default set** option (switched on by default) is recommended: this retains all of Sibelius's standard shortcuts and allows you to add to them – if you switch this option off, you'll have to define every single shortcut from scratch.

* Click **OK**, and your new feature set is automatically chosen in the **Menus and Shortcuts** dialog

* If you need to delete or rename a feature set, choose **Edit feature sets** from the list. You can also duplicate an existing feature set, which is useful for e.g. basing a new set on the **School features** set supplied.

Now you can get down to the serious business of defining your own shortcuts:

* All of the features for which you can customize shortcuts are organized according to their **Menu or Category**; choose the appropriate option in the list – for example, choose **Tuplets**

* The **Feature** list shows the available features within the chosen menu or category; choose **Triplet**

* In the **Keyboard Shortcuts** box at the right, any current shortcuts for that function are displayed; the standard shortcut for creating a triplet will be shown

* You can select the existing shortcut and click **Delete** to remove it, but there's seldom need as you can define multiple shortcuts for the same feature (the first shortcut listed is the one that will be shown in Sibelius's menus, if that feature has a menu item). So let's just add another shortcut – click **Add**

* The **Add Keyboard Shortcut** dialog appears. Type your own shortcut (in this case, just **U**), then click **OK**. You can type a single key or a combination (such as **Ctrl+Alt+U** *or* ⌥⌘U), but single key shortcuts will reduce your stress levels enormously.

* If the shortcut you choose is already used by another feature, Sibelius will ask if you want to override it

* When you have finished customizing shortcuts, click **OK** to close the **Menus and Shortcuts** dialog.

Here are a few things to bear in mind when customizing shortcuts:

* You can theoretically reassign keys on the Keypad (this could be useful for emulating other music programs), but the Keypad on the screen won't magically rearrange itself to show this: so if you make 3 on the Keypad the shortcut for a triplet, you don't get a little triplet drawn there

* On Mac, you can't assign a number of combinations, since they are intercepted by the operating system, including: ⇧⌘0–9, F1–F12, ⌥⌘T, ⌘M and ⌘H.

* On Windows, the main keys that cannot be assigned are **Alt+F**, **Alt+E**, **Alt+V**, **Alt+N**, **Alt+C**, **Alt+P**, **Alt+L**, **Alt+S**, **Alt+U**, **Alt+W**, **Alt+H** – these are the shortcuts for each of Sibelius's menus. You should also not attempt to re-assign other standard Windows shortcuts such as **Ctrl+F4**, **Alt+F4**, **Ctrl+Esc**, **Ctrl+Tab**, **Alt+Tab** and so on.

To customize shortcuts for items in word menus, 📖 **3.1 Working with text**.

Finding unused keyboard shortcuts

There are various possible keyboard shortcuts left unused by Sibelius's standard set. Generally speaking, most of the combinations of single letters, Ctrl *or* ⌘ plus letters, and Ctrl+Shift *or* ⇧⌘ plus letters (and a smaller number of Ctrl+Shift+Alt *or* ⇧⌥⌘ plus letters) are already used by default, but without affecting these you could use:

* Ctrl+Shift *or* ⇧⌘, or Ctrl+Shift+Alt *or* ⇧⌥⌘, plus the numbers on the main keyboard
* Ctrl *or* ⌘, Ctrl+Shift *or* ⇧⌘, or Ctrl+Shift+Alt *or* ⇧⌥⌘ plus most of the function keys
* Single-key shortcuts using punctuation keys (e.g. , . / # ; etc.)

Enabling and disabling features

As well as allowing you to customize keyboard shortcuts, the Menus and Shortcuts page of the Preferences dialog also allows you selectively to disable individual features, which may be useful in schools when you don't want students to be able to use particular functions of the program.

To do this, create a feature set (e.g. based on the supplied School features set – you can't disable features in the default feature set) – see **Customizing keyboard shortcuts** above. Then choose the feature you want to disable from the Feature list and switch off the Enable feature option. Disabled features do not disappear from Sibelius's menus, but they are grayed out and cannot be accessed by their keyboard shortcuts.

Sharing feature sets

Feature sets are saved in the Menus and Shortcuts folder inside your system's application data folder (see **User-editable files** on page 642), and have the file extension .sfs. You can transfer feature sets from one computer to another simply by copying this file, then choosing the copied feature set on the second computer from the Menus and Shortcuts page of the File ▸ Preferences dialog (in the Sibelius menu on Mac).

Feature set files are platform-dependent; that is, a feature set created on Windows will not work on Mac, and vice versa (because the keys on Windows and Mac keyboards are different).

Restoring default keyboard shortcuts

To restore keyboard shortcuts to their default settings, simply reselect the Standard menus and shortcuts feature set in the Menus and Shortcuts page of File ▸ Preferences (in the Sibelius menu on Mac), and click OK.

Power tools

Feature	Windows shortcut	Mac shortcut
Files		
New	Ctrl+N	⌘N
Open	Ctrl+O	⌘O
Close	Ctrl+F4 / Ctrl+W	⌘W
Close All	Ctrl+Alt+W	⌥⌘W
Save	Ctrl+S	⌘S
Save As	Ctrl+Shift+S	⇧⌘S
Creating notes		
Input Notes	N	N
♪ / ♪ / ♪ / ♩ / ♩ / ♩ / o	1/2/3/4/5/6 (on keypad)	1/2/3/4/5/6 (on keypad)⌥
♮ / ♯ / ♭ (on/off)	7/8/9 (on keypad)	7/8/9 (on keypad)
> . − (on/off)	/ * -	= / *
Rhythm dot	. (period)	. (period)
Create note	A/B/C/D/E/F/G or play note/chord on MIDI keyboard	A/B/C/D/E/F/G or play note/chord on MIDI keyboard
Create rest	0 (on keypad)	0 (on keypad)
Add Interval above	1/2/3/4/5/6/7/8/9 (on main keyboard)	1/2/3/4/5/6/7/8/9 (on main keyboard)
Add Interval below	Shift+1/2/3/4/5/6/7/8/9 (on main keyboard)	⇧1/2/3/4/5/6/7/8/9 (on main keyboard)
Add Pitch above	Shift+A-G	⇧A-G
Tie (on/off)	Enter (on keypad)	Enter (on keypad)
Start a new voice	N Alt+2/3/4	N ⌥2/3/4
Flexi-time™		
Flexi-time	Ctrl+Shift+F	⇧⌘F
Stop Flexi-time	Space	Space
Flexi-time Options	Ctrl+Shift+O	⇧⌘O
Editing notes		
Re-input Pitches	Ctrl+Shift+I	⇧⌘I
Edit pitch	A/B/C/D/E/F/G or play note/chord on MIDI keyboard	A/B/C/D/E/F/G or play note/chord on MIDI keyboard
Edit note value: ♪ / ♪ / ♪ / ♩ / ♩ / ♩ / o; start/stop re-inputting pitches	1/2/3/4/5/6 (on keypad)	1/2/3/4/5/6 (on keypad)
Edit accidental: ♮ / ♯ / ♭ (on/off)	7/8/9 (on keypad)	7/8/9 (on keypad)
Edit articulation(s): > . − (on/off)	/ * -	= / *
Turn into rest(s)	Delete / Backspace	Delete / Backspace
Turn into individual rest(s)	0 on first Keypad layout	0 on first Keypad layout
Respell Accidental	Return (on main keyboard)	Return (on main keyboard)
Cross note/chord/rest to staff above/below	Ctrl+Shift+↑/↓	⇧⌘↑/↓
Standard notehead	Shift+Alt+0 (on main keyboard)	⇧⌥0 (on main keyboard)
Change notehead	Shift+Alt+0/1/2/3... (or two digits)	⇧⌥0/1/2/3... (or two digits)
Next notehead/bar rest type	Shift+=	⇧=
Previous notehead/bar rest type	Shift+−	⇧−
Swap voices 1 and 2	Shift+V	⇧V
Transpose	Shift+T	⇧T
Arrange	Ctrl+Shift+V	⇧⌘V

Feature	Windows shortcut	Mac shortcut
Keyboard window		
Toggle QWERTY input	Shift+Alt+Q	⇧⌥Q
Up octave (in QWERTY input)	X	X
Down octave (in QWERTY input)	Z	Z
C (in QWERTY input)	A	A
C♯ (in QWERTY input)	W	W
D (in QWERTY input)	S	S
E♭ (in QWERTY input)	E	E
E (in QWERTY input)	D	D
F (in QWERTY input)	F	F
F♯ (in QWERTY input)	T	T
G (in QWERTY input)	G	G
A♭ (in QWERTY input)	Y	Y
A (in QWERTY input)	H	H
B♭ (in QWERTY input)	U	U
B (in QWERTY input)	J	J
C above (in QWERTY input)	K	K
Creating objects		
Create menu	Shift+F10 / right-click (with nothing selected)	Control-click (with nothing selected)
Bar at end	Ctrl+B	⌘B
Single bar (in mid-score)	Ctrl+Shift+B	⇧⌘B
Other bar (multiple/irregular)	Alt+B	⌥B
Clef	Q	Q
Chord Symbol	Ctrl+K	⌘K
Comment	Shift+Alt+C	⇧⌥C
Instruments	I	I
Instrument Change	Ctrl+Shift+Alt+I	⇧⌥⌘I
Key signature	K	K
Line	L	L
Slur/flipped slur	S/Shift+S (then space to extend)	S/⇧S (then space to extend)
Crescendo/diminuendo hairpin	H/Shift+H (then space to extend)	H/⇧H (then space to extend)
Rehearsal mark	Ctrl+R	⌘R
Symbol	Z	Z
Time signature	T	T
Triplet	Ctrl+3 (on main keyboard)	⌘3 (on main keyboard)
Tuplet	Ctrl+2–9 (on main keyboard)	⌘2–9 (on main keyboard)
Creating text		
Expression	Ctrl+E	⌘E
Lyrics line 1	Ctrl+L	⌘L
Lyrics line 2	Ctrl+Alt+L	⌥⌘L
Technique	Ctrl+T	⌘T
Tempo	Ctrl+Alt+T	⌥⌘T

Power tools

Feature	Windows shortcut	Mac shortcut
Editing text		
Start editing	**Return** (on main keyboard) / **F2** / double-click	**Return** (on main keyboard) / double-click
Stop editing	**Esc**	**Esc**
Move left/right a character	←/→	←/→
Move left/right a word	**Ctrl**+←/→	⌥←/→
Move to start/end of line	**Home/End**	*none*
Move to start/end of text	**Ctrl**+**Home/End**	⌘←/→
Select word	double-click	double-click
Select next/previous character	**Shift**+←/→	⇧←/→
Select to end/beginning of word	**Ctrl**+**Shift**+←/→	⇧⌥←/→
Select to end/beginning of text	**Ctrl**+**Shift**+**Home/End**	⇧⌘←/→
Select All text	**Ctrl**+**A**	⌘A
Delete previous/next character	**Backspace** / **Delete**	**Backspace**
Delete previous/next word	**Ctrl**+**Backspace/Delete**	⌥-**Backspace/Delete**
Replace selected text	type new text	type new text
New line	**Return** / **Enter**	**Return** / **Enter**
Bold/italic/underline on/off	**Ctrl**+**B/I/U**	⌘B/I/U
Default font	**Ctrl**+**Alt**+**Space**	^⌥-**Space**
Advance to next note/beat (lyrics/chord symbols/figured bass/fingering)	space	space
Hyphens to next note (lyrics)	– (hyphen)	– (hyphen)
Elision (lyrics)	_ (underscore)	_ (underscore)
Non-breaking space/non-breaking hyphen (lyrics/chord symbols)	**Ctrl**+**space/hyphen**	⌥-**space/hyphen**
Word menu	**Shift**+**F10** / right-click	Control-click
f / m / n ?p / r / s / z (Expression text)	**Ctrl**+**F/M/N/P/R/S**, **Ctrl**+**Shift**+**Z**	⌘F/M/N/P/R/S, ⇧⌘Z
cresc. / *dim.* (Expression text)	**Ctrl**+**Shift**+**C/D**	⇧⌘C/D
♪ / ♪. / ♪ / ♩ / ♩. / 𝅝 / 𝅗𝅥 / ♯ / ♭	**Ctrl**+1/2/3… (on keypad)	⌘1/2/3… (on keypad)
à / è / ì / ò / ù	**Ctrl**+**Shift**+**Alt**+**A/E/I/O/U**	⌥` followed by letter (e.g. ⌥`A)
á / é / í / ó / ú	**Ctrl**+**Shift**+**A/E/I/O/U**	⌥E followed by letter
ä / ë / ï / ö / ü	**Alt**+number from **Character Map**	⌥U followed by letter
â / ê / î / ô / û	**Alt**+number from **Character Map**	⌥I followed by letter
ç / Ç	**Alt**+number from **Character Map**	⌥C / ⇧⌥C
Other special characters	**Alt**+number from **Character Map**	use **Keyboard Viewer** utility
" / " (smart quotes)	**Alt**+2 / **Shift**+**Alt**+2	⌥] / ⇧⌥]
' / ' (smart single quotes)	**Alt**+' / **Shift**+**Alt**+'	⌥[/ ⇧⌥[
… (ellipsis)	**Alt**+0133 (on keypad)	⌥;
©	**Ctrl**+**Shift**+**C**	⇧⌘C
✗ (Lyricist/Title/Copyright)	**Ctrl**+**Shift**+**P**	⇧⌘P
℥ (Tempo)	**Ctrl**+**Shift**+4 ($)	⇧⌘4 ($)
⊕ (Tempo)	**Ctrl**+0 (zero)	⌘0 (zero)
← / → (in metric modulations)	**Ctrl**+[/]	⌘[/]
Harp pedal diagrams (Technique text)	**Ctrl**+**Alt**+7/8/9/+ (on keypad)	⌥⌘7/8/9/+ (on keypad)

Feature	Windows shortcut	Mac shortcut
Guitar tab		
Change fret	0/1/2/3… (or two digits, on main keyboard)	0/1/2/3… (or two digits, on main keyboard)
Move left/right through bar	←/→	←/→
Move up/down a string	↑/↓	↑/↓
Move to top/bottom string	Ctrl+↑/↓	⌘↑/↓
Bend	J (then **space** to extend)	J (then **space** to extend)
Pre-bend / slide / notehead in parentheses	— / . (period) / 1 on second Keypad layout	* /. (period) / 1 on second Keypad layout
Quarter-tone sharp (shown as 0.5)	= (on main keyboard)	= (on main keyboard)
Playback & video		
Play or Stop	Space	Space
Replay	Ctrl+Space	⌥-Space
Play From Selection	P	P
Rewind/fast-forward (in 0.2 second steps)	[/]	[/]
Move backward/forward by a single frame	Shift-[/]	⇧[/]
Stop	Esc	Esc / ⌘.
All Notes Off	Shift+O	⇧O
Move Playback Line to Start	Ctrl+[	⌘[
Move Playback Line to End	Ctrl+]	⌘]
Move Playback Line to Selection	Y	Y
Go to Playback Line	Shift+Y	⇧Y
Live Playback	Shift+L	⇧L
Transform Live Playback	Ctrl+Shift+Alt+L	⇧⌥⌘L
Mixer (show/hide)	Ctrl+Alt+M	M
Hit Points	Shift+Alt+P	⇧⌥P
Editing objects		
Undo	Ctrl+Z	⌘Z
Redo	Ctrl+Y	⌘Y
Undo History	Ctrl+Shift+Z	⇧⌘Z
Redo History	Ctrl+Shift+Y	⇧⌘Y
Cut	Ctrl+X	⌘X
Copy	Ctrl+C	⌘C
Copy to where you click	Alt+click	⌥-click
Copy to where you click, putting copy at default vertical position	Shift+Alt+click	⇧⌥-click
Capture Idea	Shift-I	⇧I
Paste	Ctrl+V	⌘V
Paste as Cue	Ctrl+Shift+Alt+V	⇧⌥⌘V
Repeat (note/chord/passage/text/line/etc.)	R	R
Delete	Backspace / Delete	Backspace (←) / Delete
Delete Bars	Ctrl+Backspace	⌘← (Backspace)
Flip (stem, slur, tuplet, tie, etc.)	X	X
Voice 1/2/3/4/All Voices	Alt+1/2/3/4/5 (on main keyboard)	⌥1/2/3/4/5 (on main keyboard)
Hide/Show	Ctrl+Shift+H	⇧⌘H
Color	Ctrl+J	⌘J

Power tools

Feature	Windows shortcut	Mac shortcut
Re-apply Color	Ctrl+Shift+J	⇧⌘J
Change Chord Symbol	Ctrl+Shift+K	⇧⌘K
Change Chord Diagram	Ctrl+Shift+Alt+K	⇧⌥⌘K

Navigation

Feature	Windows shortcut	Mac shortcut
Select first object on page (if nothing selected)	Tab	Tab
Select next/previous object	Tab/Shift+Tab	Tab/⇧-Tab
Select previous/next note/chord/rest	←/→	←/→
Select start of previous/next bar	Ctrl+←/→	⌘←/→
Select end/mid-point/whole of line	Alt+←/→	⌥←/→
Select note/rest above/below (in chord or adjacent staff)	Alt+↑/↓	⌥↑/↓
Move score	drag Navigator/paper	drag Navigator/paper
Go up/down a screenful	Page Up/Down	⇞/⇟ or Page Up/Down
Go left/right a screenful or page	Home/End	↖/↘ (⇧↖) or Home/End
Go up/down a little	Alt+Page Up/Down	⌥⇞/⇟ or ⌥Page Up/Down
Go left/right a little	Alt+Home/End	⌥↖/↘ or ⌥Home/End
Go to top/bottom of page	Ctrl+Page Up/Down	⌘⇞/⇟ or ⌘-Page Up/Down
Go to first/last page	Ctrl+Home/End	⌘↖/↘ (⇧⌘↖) or ⌘-Home/End
Go to selection start	Shift+Home	⇧↖ or ⇧Home
Go to selection end	Shift+End	⇧↘ or ⇧End
Go To Bar	Ctrl+Alt+G	⇧⌥G
Go To Page	Ctrl+Shift+G	⇧⌘G
Zoom in/out	Ctrl+=/− or +/− on keypad (or click/right-click with zoom tool)	⌘=/− or +/− on keypad (or click/⌥-click with zoom tool)
100% zoom	Ctrl+1	⌘1
Fit to page zoom	Ctrl+0	⌘0

Moving objects

Feature	Windows shortcut	Mac shortcut
Move object(s) (in larger steps; 1 space by default)	↑/↓/←/→ (Ctrl+↑/↓/←/→)	↑/↓/←/→ (⌘↑/↓/←/→)
Move objects, snapping to good positions while moving	Shift-drag	⇧-drag
Move staff/staves up/down (in larger steps; 1 space by default)	Alt+↑/↓ (Ctrl+Alt+↑/↓) or drag	⌥↑/↓ (⌥⌘↑/↓) or drag
Move staff/staves up/down independently (in larger steps; 1 space by default)	Shift+Alt+↑/↓ (Ctrl+Shift+Alt+↑/↓) or Shift+drag	⇧⌥↑/↓ (⇧⌥⌘↑/↓) or ⇧-drag
Move note/rest/accidental/rhythm dot/end of tie (in larger steps; 1 space by default)	Shift+Alt+←/→ (Ctrl+Shift+Alt+←/→)	⇧⌥←/→ (⇧⌥⌘←/→)
Move line (either end) or lyric to next/previous note	space/Shift+space	space/⇧-space

Multiple selections & passages

Feature	Windows shortcut	Mac shortcut
Select bar	click staff (avoiding notes etc.)	click staff (avoiding notes etc.)
Select bar in all staves	Ctrl+click staff	⌘-click staff
Select all bars in staff (on one system)	double-click staff	double-click staff
Select all bars in all staves (on one system)	Ctrl+double-click staff	⌘-double-click staff
Select all bars in staff throughout score	triple-click staff	triple-click staff
Edit ▸ Select ▸ Select Bars	Ctrl+Alt+A	⌥⌘A
Select System Passage	Shift+Alt+A	⇧⌥A

Feature	Windows shortcut	Mac shortcut
Extend passage to object	Shift+click	⇧-click
Extend passage by a note/rest	Shift+←/→	⇧←/→
Extend passage by a bar	Ctrl+Shift+←/→	⇧⌘←/→
Extend passage by a staff	Shift+↑/↓	⇧↑/↓
Select All of score	Ctrl+A	⌘A
Select all noteheads in chord (**Select More**)	Ctrl+Shift+A or double-click	⇧⌘A or double-click
Select all text on staff in same style (**Select More**)	Ctrl+Shift+A	⇧⌘A
Select objects with marquee	Shift+drag on paper	⌘-drag on paper
Add/remove object to/from selection	Ctrl+click	⌘-click
Select Graphic	Alt+G	⌥G
Select None	Esc	Esc / ⌘.

Filters and Find

Advanced Filter	Ctrl+Shift+Alt+F	⇧⌥⌘F
Filter Dynamics	Shift+Alt+D	⇧⌥D
Filter Voice 1/2/3/4	Ctrl+Shift+Alt+1/2/3/4	⇧⌥⌘1/2/3/4
Filter Top/2nd/3rd/Bottom Note or Single Notes	Ctrl+Alt+1/2/3, Ctrl+Shift+Alt+B	⌥⌘1/2/3, ⇧⌥⌘B
Find	Ctrl+F	⌘F
Find Next	Ctrl+G	⌘G

Layout

Document Setup	Ctrl+D	⌘D
Hide Empty Staves	Ctrl+Shift+Alt+H	⇧⌥⌘H
Show Empty Staves	Ctrl+Shift+Alt+S	⇧⌥⌘S
System Break on/off	Shift+Return (on main keyboard)	⇧-Return (on main keyboard)
Page Break on/off	Ctrl+Return (on main keyboard)	⌘-Return (on main keyboard)
Special Page Break	Ctrl+Shift+Return (on main keyboard)	⇧⌘-Return (on main keyboard)
Lock Format	Ctrl+Shift+L	⇧⌘L
Unlock Format	Ctrl+Shift+U	⇧⌘U
Make Into System	Shift+Alt+M	⇧⌥M
Make Into Page	Ctrl+Shift+Alt+M	⇧⌥⌘M
Align in a Row/Column	Ctrl+Shift+R/C	⇧⌘R/C
Reset Note Spacing	Ctrl+Shift+N	⇧⌘N
Reset Position	Ctrl+Shift+P	⇧⌘P
Reset Design	Ctrl+Shift+D	⇧⌘D
Reset to Score Position	Ctrl+Shift+Alt+P	⇧⌥⌘P
Reset to Score Design	Ctrl+Shift+Alt+D	⇧⌥⌘D
Condense/expand note spacing (in larger steps)	Shift+Alt+←/→ (Ctrl+Shift+Alt+←/→)	⇧⌥←/→ (⇧⌥⌘←/→)
Use Multirests (in Auto Breaks) on/off	Ctrl+Shift+M	⇧⌘M

House Style™

Engraving Rules	Ctrl+Shift+E	⇧⌘E
Edit Text Styles	Ctrl+Shift+Alt+T	⇧⌥⌘T

Power tools

Feature	Windows shortcut	Mac shortcut
View & Window menus		
Panorama	Shift-P	⇧P
Focus on Staves	Ctrl+Alt+F	⌥⌘F
Hidden Objects (show/hide)	Ctrl+Alt+H	⌥⌘H
Object Rulers (show/hide)	Shift+Alt+R	⇧⌥R
Staff Rulers (show/hide)	Ctrl+Shift+Alt+R	⇧⌥⌘R
Transposing Score	Ctrl+Shift+T	⇧⌘T
Navigator (show/hide)	Ctrl+Alt+N	⌥⌘N
Keypad (show/hide)	Ctrl+Alt+K	⌥⌘K
Keyboard (show/hide)	Ctrl+Alt+B	⌥⌘B
Fretboard (show/hide)	Ctrl+Alt+E	⌥⌘E
Playback (show/hide)	Ctrl+Alt+Y	⌥⌘Y
Mixer (show/hide)	Ctrl+Alt+M	M
Ideas (show/hide)	Ctrl+Alt+I	⌥⌘I
Parts (show/hide)	Ctrl+Alt+R	⌥⌘R
Compare (show/hide)	Ctrl+Alt+C	⌥⌘C
Video (show/hide)	Ctrl+Alt+V	⌥⌘V
Properties (show/hide)	Ctrl+Alt+P	⌥⌘P
Hide/Show Tool Windows	Ctrl+Alt+X	⌥⌘X
Switch between full score and part	W	W
Next Part	Ctrl+Alt+Tab	⌥⌘~
Previous Part	Ctrl+Shift+Alt+Tab	⇧⌥⌘~
Full Screen (Windows only)	Ctrl+U	*none*
Menus and dialogs		
Go into menu	Alt+underlined letter	*none*
Choose from menu	underlined letter	*none*
Choose from dialog	Alt+underlined letter	*none*
Move to next/previous box in dialog	Tab/Shift-Tab	Tab/⇧-Tab
Select consecutive items from list	Shift+click or drag	drag
Select separate items from list	Ctrl+click	⌘-click
OK (or default button)	Return/Enter	Return/Enter
Cancel	Esc	Esc / ⌘.
Keypad layouts	F7–F12	F7–F12
Next Keypad layout	+ (on keypad)	+ (on keypad)
Back to first Keypad layout	F7 / Shift-+	– (on keypad) / F7
Contextual edit menu	Shift+F10 / right-click on selected object(s)	Control-click on selected object(s)
Change window	Ctrl+Tab	⌘~
Hide application	*none*	⌘H
Minimize window	*none*	⌘M
Miscellaneous		
Sibelius Reference	F1	⌘?
Print	Ctrl+P	⌘P
Preferences	Ctrl+,	⌘,
Quit/Exit	Alt+F4 / Ctrl+Q	⌘Q

5.13 Panorama

📖 **5.8 Focus on Staves**, **5.23 View menu**.

Panorama is an alternative way of viewing your score. Instead of being laid out on the screen in pages, exactly as it will be printed out, you can view your score as a single system of music, laid out on an infinitely-wide piece of paper. This kind of view is sometimes called *scroll view* or *galley view* in other programs.

Using Panorama allows you to concentrate on inputting and editing without thinking about the page layout. Note input in Panorama is also very convenient, particularly if you have more than one system per page in normal view; Panorama eliminates the vertical movement of music from system to system, and so the score only ever moves horizontally. This reduces the disorientation you can sometimes feel when working quickly in normal view.

Switching on Panorama

To switch on Panorama, simply choose View ▸ Panorama (shortcut **Shift-P**), or click the toolbar button shown on the right. When viewing your score like this, Sibelius also does the following:

- Disables the Navigator, because there's only one page
- Switches on View ▸ Scroll Bars
- Switches on View ▸ Staff Names and Bar Numbers.

To switch off Panorama, simply choose View ▸ Panorama again.

If you switch off scroll bars or **Staff Names and Bar Numbers** while in Panorama, Sibelius only changes the settings for as long as you're in Panorama, but remembers them the next time you use Panorama.

Moving around in Panorama

Working in Panorama is as close as possible to working in normal view; you can use all the same navigation shortcuts (e.g. **Home**, **End**, **Page Up** *or* ⇞, **Page Down** *or* ⇟, etc.) and features like zoom. Try the **Fit page height** zoom level, which is particularly useful as it makes sure that you can see all of the staves on the screen at once.

Notice that as you drag the start of the music off the left-hand side of the screen, you will see a useful reminder of the current clef and key signature on each staff, drawn in light blue.

Inputting and editing in Panorama

Inputting and editing in Panorama is practically the same as in normal view. There are a few things you can't do in Panorama, because they don't make sense when there are no pages:

- You cannot see or input page-aligned text (such as **Title**, **Header (after first page)**, etc.) in Panorama
- If **View ▸ Layout Marks** is switched on, Sibelius draws layout marks above barlines, and though you can create system or page breaks if you want to, you won't see their effect in Panorama

Power tools

- Scores cannot be printed in Panorama (because few printers can handle infinitely-wide paper!), so when you choose File ▸ Print, Sibelius will print the score in normal view instead
- Layout ▸ Hide Empty Staves cannot be used to hide staves on specific systems in Panorama, because there is only a single system; so any staves that are hidden in normal view will appear in Panorama
- Edit ▸ Go to Page and Create ▸ Other ▸ Page Number Change are disabled
- Layout ▸ Align Staves is disabled
- When you choose File ▸ Export ▸ Graphics, you can only export a Graphic selection, and not specific systems or pages – 📖 **9.8 Exporting graphics**.

Note spacing in Panorama

In Panorama, Sibelius uses a fixed justification factor in its note spacing; in other words, Sibelius loosens the note spacing by a fixed amount, specified by an option on the Display page of File ▸ Preferences (in the Sibelius menu on Mac), rather than the variable justification factor on every system in normal view required to make the music fit the width of the page.

Notice, though, that any manual adjustments you make to note spacing are shown in Panorama, so if you widen the spacing of a bar in normal view (e.g. to avoid collisions between chord symbols), those adjustments will be shown in Panorama as well. Be aware also that if you adjust the note spacing in Panorama, the adjusted spacing may be narrower or wider when you switch back to normal view, because Sibelius then has to justify the spacing to make the music fit the width of the page.

Staff spacing in Panorama

In Panorama, Sibelius uses the space between systems as defined on the Staves page of House Style ▸ Engraving Rules, multiplied by a fixed justification factor as specified by an option on the Display page of File ▸ Preferences (in the Sibelius menu on Mac). Because there is no fixed page height, Sibelius ignores the value of Justify staves when page is x% full, with the result that staves can sometimes appear closer together in Panorama than in normal view. If you find them too close together, change the value in Preferences.

Usefully, however, you can adjust the distance between staves in Panorama without it affecting normal view, which you may want to do if notes or other objects above or below the staff collide with other objects: just drag or otherwise nudge them in the usual ways (📖 **8.10 Staff spacing**).

Using Panorama with Focus on Staves

When you use View ▸ Focus on Staves to look at just a couple of staves from your score, the layout in normal view can be a little odd due to the other staves missing; try switching on View ▸ Panorama at the same time, which makes Focus on Staves considerably more convenient. 📖 **5.8 Focus on Staves**.

Opening scores in Panorama

When you save a score, Sibelius remembers whether or not Panorama was switched on, and when you re-open it later on, it will automatically switch on Panorama if required. You can tell Sibelius to always use Panorama or normal view instead if you prefer on the Files page of File ▸ Preferences (in the Sibelius menu on Mac) – 📖 **5.15 Preferences**.

5.14 Order

📖 **9.4 Importing graphics**.

Order refers to the order in which objects in your score are drawn on the screen. Normally, the staff lines are drawn first, then objects like clefs, notes, ties, slurs and so on are drawn from left to right, just as if you were writing them out on paper yourself. Sometimes, though, it is useful to be able to change the order in which objects are drawn; for example, if you want an imported graphic to appear behind the notes but in front of the staff, or if you want to create special effects like ties breaking either side of a time signature.

Layers

Sibelius provides 32 *layers*: objects in layer 1 are drawn first of all (and therefore behind all other objects), and objects in layer 32 are drawn last (and therefore in front of all other objects). Each type of object has a default layer, controlling its place in the draw order, which can be edited in Layout ▸ Magnetic Layout Options (see **Magnetic Layout Options** on page 567).

Layers are not to be confused with voices – 📖 **2.36 Voices**.

Changing the draw order of an object

To change the draw order of an object, select it and choose the appropriate option from the Edit ▸ Order submenu:

- **Bring to Front**: moves the object to layer 32, in front of all other objects
- **Bring Forward**: moves the object to the next layer (e.g. if the object is currently on layer 14, this moves it to layer 15)
- **Send Backward**: moves the object to the previous layer (e.g. from layer 18 to layer 17)
- **Send to Back**: moves the object to layer 1, behind all other objects
- **Reset to Default**: moves the object back to its default layer.

You can also move an object between layers using the **General** panel of Properties: switch on the **Custom order** checkbox, then either type the desired layer number, or use the paddle controls to move the object through the draw order. Switch off **Custom order** to reset the object back to its original layer.

You may find that as you change an object's draw order, you see no visible change on the screen. That's because most objects default to layers around 10–12.

Using layers to break ties across time signatures

One useful application for custom orders is to allow ties on tied notes or chords to break on either side of a time signature, like this:

To achieve this, simply input the music as normal, then:

- Choose **House Style ▸ Edit Text Styles**
- Select the **Time signatures** text style, and click **Edit**
- In the **System Text Style** dialog that appears, go to the **Border** page
- Switch on the **Erase background** checkbox, click **OK**, then **Close**.

The ties are drawn first, then the time signature with its erased background, which "whites out" the ties, and finally the staff lines are drawn on top.

Imported graphics

By default, an imported graphic (created using **Create ▸ Graphic**) will be set to layer 1, which means that it will appear behind all other objects. This is normally desirable, since any white background around the edge of the graphic would otherwise "white out" the staff lines, notes, and so on. However, you can move an imported graphic to any layer, which can have a variety of interesting (and perhaps occasionally useful) effects.

5.15 Preferences

Preferences are options that affect the Sibelius program as a whole, and which remain permanently set until you change them again, rather than being saved in individual scores. They include things like display settings, keyboard shortcuts and word menus for speeding up text entry.

If Sibelius is used on the same computer at different times by different users, then Sibelius automatically remembers a different set of preferences for each person if they log on to the computer as a different user.

The File ▸ Preferences dialog (in the Sibelius menu on Mac; shortcut Ctrl+, *or* ⌘,) contains various miscellaneous preferences categorized into 16 pages.

Display

The Display page allows you to adjust various aspects of how things are displayed:

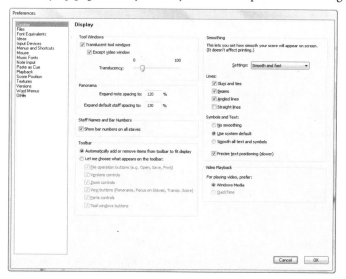

- The options in Tool windows are discussed in **Translucent windows** on page 390.
- Panorama settings are discussed in **Note spacing in Panorama** and **Staff spacing in Panorama** on page 424.
- Show bar numbers on all staves is described in **Staff Names and Bar Numbers** on page 460.
- The Toolbar options are covered in **Toolbar** on page 463.
- The Windows-only Smoothing options are discussed on **Smoothing** on page 389.
- Video Playback, which is also for Windows only, is discussed in **Windows Media and QuickTime** on page 315.

Files

The **Files** page allows you to set how Sibelius should behave when opening, saving and printing files:

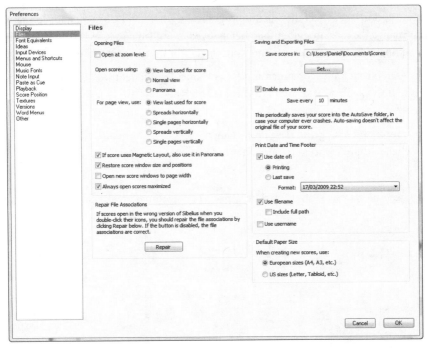

- **Open at zoom level** allows you to determine whether Sibelius opens scores at the zoom level specified here, or at the zoom level you were using when you last saved the score

- **Open scores using** allows you to choose whether Sibelius should open scores in Panorama (□ **5.13 Panorama**), normal view, or the view last used in the score (the default)

- **For page view, use** allows you to choose the default page arrangement Sibelius should use when opening a score – see **Pages** on page 460.

- **If score uses Magnetic Layout, also use it in Panorama** determines whether or not Sibelius should use Magnetic Layout in Panorama – see **Magnetic Layout in Panorama** on page 568.

- When **Restore score window size and positions** is switched on, Sibelius will remember the size and position of each score (and dynamic part) window you open, and restore each window to that position when you reopen the score (or part). On Windows, **Always open scores maximized** must be switched off for Sibelius to restore your window positions.

- **Open new score windows to page width** tells Sibelius to create new score (and dynamic part) windows to the width of the page. This is useful if, for example, you have a widescreen display: when you create a new score, Sibelius will only make the window as wide as the first page of the score, rather than as wide as your whole display. Again, on Windows, **Always open scores maximized** must be switched off for this option to have an effect.

- **Always open scores maximized** is a Windows-only option, switched on by default, which tells Sibelius whether or not all score windows should open maximized (i.e. as large as the Sibelius application window itself). When you switch this option off, Sibelius will open scores to their previously saved size, or a suitable default size.

- **Repair File Associations** is a Windows-only option. If you have multiple versions of Sibelius installed on your computer, and find that scores open in the wrong version when you double-click them, or indeed that another program altogether runs and attempts to open them, click **Repair** to restore the default file association for Sibelius files.

- **Enable Auto-saving** controls Sibelius's auto-save feature – see **Auto-save** on page 641.

- **Print Date and Time Footer** specifies the contents of the optional footer that may contain a combination of the current date or the date the score was last saved, its filename and the user's name on each page. You can choose from a variety of date and time formats and choose whether Sibelius should print just the filename or include its entire path – see **Date and time footer** on page 436.

- **Default Page Size** allows you to choose whether Sibelius should use European sizes (A4, A3, etc.) or US sizes (Letter, Tabloid, etc.) when creating new scores. Sibelius defaults this option according to the regional settings on your computer, but you can change it here if you wish.

Font Equivalents

For details on the Font Equivalents page, ⌐ **3.11 Font equivalents**.

Ideas

For details on the Ideas page, ⌐ **5.11 Ideas**.

Input Devices

For details on the Input Devices page, ⌐ **1.10 Input Devices**.

Menus and Shortcuts

For details on the Menus and Shortcuts page, ⌐ **5.12 Menus and shortcuts**.

Mouse

The Mouse page determines how Sibelius should behave when inputting music with the mouse:

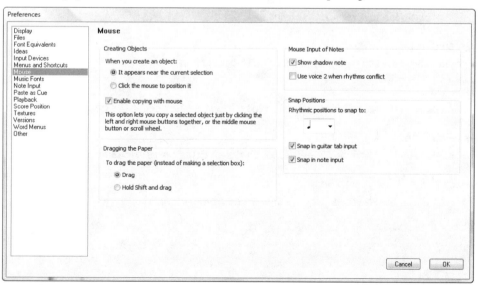

- When you create an object determines whether It appears near the current selection (the recommended setting) or whether you should Click the mouse to position it. This option is included for those users familiar with Sibelius 1.4 or earlier in which objects were always placed with the mouse; however, this Reference assumes throughout that this option is set to the default (It appears near the current selection).
- Enable copying with the mouse (Windows only) controls whether clicking the middle mouse button, left and right mouse buttons together, or the scroll wheel does the same as Alt+click
- To drag the paper (instead of making a selection box) defaults to Drag, but if you prefer you can set this to Hold Shift and drag (*or* Hold Command and drag on Mac).
- Show shadow note: determines whether shadow notes are shown during mouse input – 📖 **1.1 Note input**
- Use voice 2 when rhythms conflict: with this switched on, if you input a note halfway through the duration of an existing note, Sibelius will create the new note in voice 2, leaving the existing note alone; if you switch this off, Sibelius will shorten the first note instead
- Snap Positions: these options control how bars are divided up for inputting notes using mouse input or guitar tab input:
  - Rhythmic positions to snap to: this defaults to quarter notes (crotchets); this is the unit by which bars are divided
  - Snap in guitar tab input: when this option is switched on, typing ←/→ when inputting guitar tab into empty bars using the computer keyboard will advance through the bar by the unit specified in Rhythmic positions to snap to; with this option switched off, typing ←/→ moves through the bar by the note value chosen on the Keypad – see **Guitar tab input** on page 49
  - Snap in note input: when this option is switched on, you are able to create notes or rests at any of the snap positions created by the units specified in Rhythmic positions to snap to; with this option switched off, you can only create notes/rests with the mouse at the beginning of existing notes, rests, or bar rests.

Music Fonts

For details on the Music Fonts page, 📖 **8.11 Music fonts**.

Note Input

For details on the Note Input page, see **Note input options** on page 13.

Paste as Cue

For details on the Paste as Cue page, see **Paste as Cue preferences** on page 116.

Playback

For details on the Playback page, see **Playback preferences** on page 333.

Score Position

The Score Position page allows you to set how and when Sibelius should reposition your score:

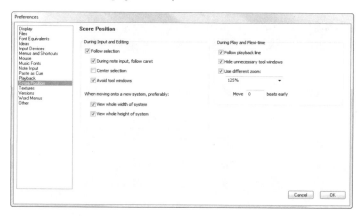

- When **Follow selection** is switched on, Sibelius will ensure that the current selection is always in view. When switched on, you will be able to switch the following options on or off:

  ○ **During note input follow caret** means that the caret will always be visible before a note is entered

  ○ **Center selection** will force the current selection to be centered in your display at all times. Some people may like to work with this option switched on, as it provides a means of working to a focal point rather than from left to right. This option is particularly recommended for users who are visually impaired.

  ○ **Avoid tool windows** ensures that Sibelius will try not to position the current selection underneath one of the tool windows

  ○ **View whole width of system** ensures that, whenever possible during note input, Sibelius will position the current view so that the entire width of the system you are working on is in view. If the system is wider than the width of your display, Sibelius retains the horizontal position of the score.

  ○ **View whole height of system** ensures that, whenever possible during note input, Sibelius will position the current view so that you can see the entire height of the system you are working on.

- If you would prefer that Sibelius never repositions your score for you automatically, switch off **Follow selection**. (You can assign a keyboard shortcut to this option if you want to – 📖 **5.12 Menus and shortcuts**.)

- Sibelius follows the score during playback with a green line that shows the current position. If you'd rather Sibelius didn't do this (e.g. to use up less processor power), switch off **Follow playback line**.

- **Hide unnecessary tool windows** is switched on by default; all except the Playback, Video, Kontakt and Navigator windows will be hidden during playback when this option is on

- **Use different zoom** allows you to set a specific zoom level for playback, independent of the zoom level used during editing. You can set the desired zoom level directly using the list in this dialog; alternatively, if you change the zoom level during playback with this option switched on, the zoom level that you end up with will be remembered the next time you play back.

Power tools

- **Move *n* beats early** allows you to choose how early Sibelius should reposition the score when the next passage of music it is going to play will be out of view. This can be useful if you're using Sibelius as an accompanist, or for when you are closely following a score during playback, as it will ensure that you are always looking at a passage of music before Sibelius actually plays it.

Textures

For details on the Textures page, see **Textures** on page 388.

Versions

The options on the Versions page are explained in 📖 **5.22 Versions**.

Word Menus

For details on the Word Menus page, see **Creating and modifying word menus** on page 207.

Others

The Others page allows you to change miscellaneous other options:

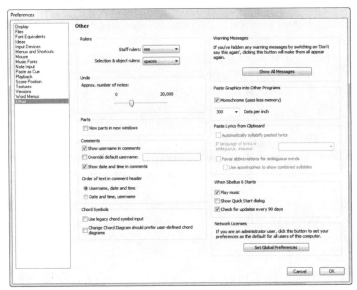

- Rulers determine the units of measurement used by the on-screen rulers – see **Rulers** on page 461
- Undo allows you to set how many changes to your score Sibelius will remember – 📖 **5.21 Undo and Redo**
- View parts in new windows allows you to choose whether Sibelius opens parts in the same window, or whether it creates a new window for each part – see **Viewing multiple parts** on page 539
- The options in the Comments group are explained in **Changing the username displayed in a comment** on page 387.
- The options in the Chord Symbols group are explained in **Legacy chord symbol input** on page 111.

- **Show all messages** resets warning messages you've suppressed – see **Warning messages** below

- **Paste Graphics into Other Programs** allows you to choose whether Sibelius should export graphics on the clipboard in **Monochrome**, and also gives you control over the image's resolution, which you can change using **Dots per inch** – 📖 **9.8 Exporting graphics**.

- The options in the **Paste Lyrics from Clipboard** group determine whether or not Sibelius should automatically split lyrics into syllables when pasting them into the score – 📖 **3.3 Lyrics**.

- The options under **When Sibelius Starts** control whether Sibelius plays a short musical excerpt when you run it, whether you want the **File ▸ Quick Start** dialog to appear automatically on start-up, and whether you want Sibelius to check for updates every 90 days.

- If you are running a network site licence copy of Sibelius on Windows, you will see a further button, **Set Global Preferences**. This allows you, or your network manager or system administrator, to set the current preferences as the global preferences for all users who log in to this computer. This is useful if your network policy prohibits limited user accounts from writing any data to the Windows Registry or other similar areas, but you still want to enforce a certain set of default preferences for users on your computer. Please refer to the Sibelius Licence Server User Guide for more information.

Warning messages

A number of the helpful messages that pop up in the course of using Sibelius can be suppressed by switching on **Don't say this again** in the message boxes if they start to get on your nerves.

If you suddenly forget how to use Sibelius and want all these messages to appear again, click **Show All Messages**. This will make all of the messages you suppressed reappear in future.

Power tools

5.16 Printing

For details of standard paper sizes and advice on what page and staff sizes to use for particular types of music, 📖 **8.6 Document Setup**.

If you want to produce quantities of high-quality printed scores, 📖 **8.18 Publishing**.

Setting the paper size

Before you print from Sibelius, you should check that your printer driver is set to use the correct paper size. On Mac, each program on your computer maintains its own default paper size, so you simply need to ensure that the correct size is set in the **File ▸ Page Setup** dialog.

On Windows, you can change the paper size via Sibelius's **File ▸ Print** dialog, but this only affects documents printed from Sibelius, and only until you quit the program. The next time you start up Sibelius, its paper size is reset to your printer driver's default again. This means that you should ensure your printer's default settings are correct. To do this:

- *On Windows XP:*
  - Choose **Start ▸ Printers and Faxes**
  - Select the default printer, then choose **File ▸ Printing Preferences**
  - In the printer driver dialog, click the **Layout** tab, then click **Advanced** (in the bottom right-hand corner of the dialog)
  - Choose the correct default paper size, then click **OK** twice to confirm the changes.
- *On Windows Vista:*
  - Choose **Start ▸ Control Panel**, then click **Printers**
  - Right-click on the printer's icon and choose **Select printing preferences**
  - In the printer driver dialog, click the **Layout** tab, then click **Advanced** (in the bottom right-hand corner of the dialog)
  - Choose the correct default paper size, then click **OK** twice to confirm the changes.

Printing

Choose **File ▸ Print** (shortcut **Ctrl+P** *or* ⌘P). A standard **Print** dialog appears, with some extra options on.

- On Windows, if you have more than one printer connected to your computer, you can choose which one you want to use from the drop-down list at the top of the dialog. You can also alter specific driver options by clicking **Properties**.
- On Mac, you should choose the **Sibelius** page of options to get the dialog containing options for booklets, spreads, etc. You can also set which pages to print on the **Copies & Pages** page.

Set the print options described below as you want them, then click **OK** (Windows) *or* **Print** (Mac) and the printing will begin.

Hint: on Windows, you can print Sibelius files without running Sibelius: right-click on the file's icon and choose **Print** from the menu that appears.

The options in the File ▸ Print dialog are as follows. Unless otherwise stated, the options are found on the main File ▸ Print dialog on Windows, or the **Sibelius** page of the File ▸ Print dialog on Mac:

Print range

If you don't want to print the whole score, you can type a list of pages to print (e.g. **1, 3, 8**), and/or a range of pages (e.g. **5-9**), which can be backwards to print in reverse order (e.g. **9-5**).

The page numbers you specify here are not necessarily the page numbers displayed in the score if your score uses page number changes. Instead they refer to the physical pages in your score: if you want to print the second, third, and fourth pages of the score, even though they may be numbered ii, iii and iv, you type **2-4** in the **Pages** control. ▢ **3.6 Page numbers**.

Copies and Collate

By default, one copy will be printed, though you can set any other quantity you want in the **Copies** box (on the **Copies & Pages** page on Mac). Multiple copies are done of each page in turn, so if you choose two copies the pages will come out in the order 1, 1, 2, 2, 3, 3, etc.

However, if you switch on **Collate**, each copy of the score is collated properly, so the pages come out in the order 1, 2, 3, 4... 1, 2, 3, 4.... This saves you having to sort the pages into order yourself, but on laser printers printing may take a little longer.

Some Windows printer drivers have bugs that prevent the **Collate** option from working correctly. If your printer driver doesn't handle collation properly, Sibelius will warn you that you should try to obtain updated drivers for your printer, and give you the option to print anyway. If Sibelius detects a problem with your printer's collation support, it will do its best to make the pages print in the right order anyway, but this is not always possible.

Border

This option prints a thin border around the page. When printing on outsize paper, this makes the pages easier to visualize, and easier to guillotine, than just using crop marks. It's also very useful to proof-read scores scaled to (say) 65%, with **Border** and **Spreads** (see below) switched on.

Crop marks

These are little cross-hairs used in professional publishing to point to the corners of the page. Crop marks are required because books are printed on oversized paper that is subsequently trimmed to the required size.

It's only sensible to use crop marks if you're printing on paper that is larger than your score's pages.

View menu options

This prints options switched on in the **View** menu, such as highlights, hidden objects and note colors – ▢ **5.23 View menu** for more details of these options.

Print in color

When switched on, Sibelius will print any objects that you have colored in your score in color (or gray if you have a black-and-white printer). Colors in any graphics you may have in your score will also be printed. When switched off, colored objects print in black.

Date and time footer

Sibelius will print date and time footers on each page of your score when this option is switched on. This is useful for keeping track of different versions of a score. For details on setting up and customizing this footer, ▢ **5.15 Preferences**.

Fit to paper

This scales the score down in size, if necessary, so that the music fits within the print margins of the paper, to avoid the edges of the music being clipped. This is particularly useful for printing Letter sized scores on A4 paper (and vice versa), and for reducing Tabloid/A3 scores onto Letter/A4 paper. **Fit to paper** does not however expand the music to fill the paper if it is larger than the page size.

Beware that US paper sizes such as Letter and Tabloid are not quite the same shape as each other, so the page margins may turn out differently than you expect. No such problem arises with European paper sizes.

This option automatically adjusts the **Scale** setting (see below), so if you have **Fit to paper** switched on, you shouldn't change the **Scale** setting yourself.

Scale

Your music is normally printed at 100% size, though you can set any other scale factor you like. To reduce the music to fit onto smaller paper, simply switch on **Fit to paper** instead of working out the scale factor yourself.

Substitute options

These options fix various printer problems and/or may improve the print speed or quality. When you have time to test them, try various combinations of these options to see if you can gain any improvements.

The options are as follows:

- **Lines**: some printer drivers do not print staff lines evenly, and may even fail to print them altogether; some drivers draw lines such as barlines and stems with rounded instead of flat ends. Some PostScript printers may give "out of memory" errors when printing many pages at once. Turning this option on may solve these problems and should increase print speed, but may make staff lines slightly uneven in thickness.

- **Braces**: some printer drivers print braces either in the wrong place or using the wrong symbol. Switch on this option if you have these problems.

- **Arpeggios, gliss., etc.**: some Windows printer drivers have a bug that makes angled text and wiggly glissando and arpeggio lines print at the wrong angle or in the wrong place; if you find this happens, switch on this option.

- **Symbols** (Windows only): this option affects how symbol fonts – used for e.g. notes, time signatures, clefs and other symbols in your score – are rendered by your printer. Symbol fonts include Opus, Reprise, Inkpen2, Opus Percussion, Opus Special, and so on, and fonts such as Symbol, Wingdings, and other dingbats fonts. If this option is set wrongly for your printer, then symbol fonts may not display or print at all. The four choices are as follows:

○ **Automatic:** Sibelius detects whether symbol fonts are in TrueType or PostScript (Type 1) format and renders them accordingly; this is the recommended setting on Windows

○ **PostScript:** Sibelius assumes all symbol fonts are in PostScript (Type 1) format

○ **TrueType:** Sibelius assumes all symbol fonts are in TrueType format.

Double-sided printing

To print your music double-sided:

- Under **Format**, select **Normal** and **Odd**. Print the score. Only odd-numbered (i.e. right-hand) pages will be printed.

- Feed the pages back into the printer, possibly face up (depending on how your printer feeds it). If the first page of your score is even-numbered – that is, if it is a left-hand page – you should feed in one extra blank sheet at the start, since the first page shouldn't end up with anything printed on the front.

- Now select **Even**. Print the score again, to print the even-numbered (i.e. left-hand) pages on the back of the odd-numbered ones.

If the pages come out of your printer face down, you may have to reverse the order of the sheets before printing the second side, or alternatively just print the second side in reverse order (by typing a backwards page range such as **8–1**). You will have to try and see, as this varies from printer to printer.

Laser printers tend to wrinkle paper slightly when printing on it. This can make printers misfeed if you put paper back in to print on the other side. This problem will be reduced if you leave the paper to settle for an hour or so after printing the first side, or if you feed the paper manually sheet by sheet for the second side (which is a bore). Some misfeed problems are also caused by residual static from the corona charge in most laser printers; it may be alleviated by "riffling" the paper before re-feeding.

Spreads

This prints two consecutive pages side by side on each sheet of paper, and odd-numbered pages are always printed at the right-hand side of the paper. This format is suitable for proofing.

Difference between spreads and 2-up on a six page document:

Spreads		2-Up	
	1	1	2
2	3	3	4
4	5	5	6
6			

With **Spreads** selected, either:

- make sure your paper is at least twice the size of your pages in Sibelius (e.g. Tabloid/A3 paper for Letter/A4 pages); or

- use the same page size as paper size but reduce the **Scale** accordingly, e.g. print Letter/A4 pages at 68% on Letter/A4 paper.

Then print as normal, using any other options such as **Border**.

2-Up

Similar to **Spreads**, except that the first page you specify is always printed on the *left*.

Booklet

A "booklet" is a small book consisting of double-sided pages stapled in the middle. Booklets are printed with two pages side-by-side on sheets of paper that are twice the size of the ultimate pages.

The pages have to be numbered strangely when printed so that it all works when the booklet is assembled. For instance, the outermost sheet of a 16-page booklet would have pages 16 and 1 on the front (in that order) and pages 2 and 15 on the back. Fortunately this complicated layout procedure, known technically as "imposition," is done automatically for you by Sibelius.

To print as a booklet, either:

* make sure your paper is twice the size of your music pages in Sibelius (e.g. A3 paper for A4 pages), or
* use the same page size as paper size but reduce the **Scale** accordingly, e.g. print two A4 pages at 70% on A4 paper.

Then:

* Click **Booklet** and **Outward pages**
* Print as normal. One side of the paper will be printed.
* Click **Inward pages**
* Feed the paper back into the printer, and print again to do the other side.

As with ordinary double-sided printing, if the pages come out of your printer face down, you may have to reverse the order of the sheets before printing the second side, or alternatively just print the second side in reverse order (by typing a backwards page range such as **8–1**). You will have to try and see, as this varies from printer to printer.

You can use all the other options when printing booklets too, e.g. **Pages**, **Crop marks**, **Odd and Even**, etc. **Collate** is particularly useful for producing a stack of copies that you only have to fold.

Sibelius assumes that the finished booklet's first page is numbered 1, even if your score's first page number is not 1. Thus if your score starts on page 2, this will appear as the inside left-hand page of the booklet, not on the front. This lets you leave the front page blank in case you want to add a special cover produced using a different program.

When printing **Outward pages** Sibelius first prints the double-page containing page 1, then 3, 5, 7 etc. Similarly, when printing **Inward pages**, Sibelius starts with the double-page containing page 2, then 4, 6 etc.

For example, the printing order of an 8-page booklet is like this:

* *Outward pages:* 1 & 8 (together, page 1 on the right), 3 & 6
* *Inward pages:* 2 & 7, 4 & 5.

Note also that two adjacent page numbers on a sheet always add up to the total number of pages (rounded up to a multiple of four), plus 1; in the above case, 9.

If you want to print a specific double-page from a booklet – e.g. pages 8 & 1 from an 8-page booklet – just specify one of the pages (e.g. page 1) and Sibelius will know to print the other next to it.

Printing multiple scores or parts at once

You can print multiple files at once (e.g. a whole folder) using the **Print Multiple Copies** plug-in; **6.1 Working with plug-ins**. To print multiple parts, use **File ▸ Print All Parts** to print all of them, or the **Print Part(s)** button on the Parts window to print the selected parts; **7.1 Working with parts**.

Choosing good paper

Investing in very good paper can make your printouts look twice as good. Good paper is bright white, is very opaque so the music doesn't show through the back, and is reasonably stiff so it doesn't flop on a music stand. Avoid ordinary thin typing paper or photocopier paper – we recommend paper of about 26 lb/ream or 100 gsm.

Problems with margins

Some printers may cut off the edges of your music, particularly the bottom edge. This is because most printers need room to grip the paper.

One solution is to move the music further away from the edge by increasing the music's page margins on the **Layout ▸ Document Setup** dialog (shortcut **Ctrl+D** *or* ⌘D).

If your music's layout is sensitive to reformatting, and you find that only (say) the bottom of the page is being cropped off, you can prevent the music reformatting by decreasing the top page margin by (say) 0.2 inches (5mm) when you increase the bottom margin by 0.2 inches (5mm), so that the music just moves up the page a little. Alternatively, use **Lock Format** before adjusting the margins (**8.1 Layout and formatting**).

Problems with double-sided printing

If your printer misfeeds, try any or all of these:

- Leave the paper to cool for a while after printing the first side
- Manual feed the second side
- Open the exit flap (if there is one) on the printer, which provides a straighter feed path.

If toner on the first side slips off when printing the second side:

- Leave the paper to cool for a while after printing the first side
- If there are settings to feed the paper faster (e.g. a lower print resolution), try these for the second side.

Power tools

5.17 Properties

For advanced users only

Almost every object in a score has properties that can be edited in various subtle ways using the **Window ▶ Properties** window (shortcut **Ctrl+Alt+P** *or* ⌥⌘P).

For instance, the font and point size of a text object can be changed from the **Text** panel of the Properties window; the horizontal offset of a particular note can be changed from the **General** panel; and so on.

In general these properties are more easily set when you create the object, but it is sometimes useful to see or edit properties subsequently. Many of the properties can also be viewed/edited from the normal menus, or edited using shortcuts.

Viewing properties

By default, the Properties window is not shown on the screen, because you won't often need to adjust settings in there. If you find yourself using the Properties window a lot, then you can congratulate yourself on being a power user!

You can show the Properties window (and subsequently hide it again) by choosing **Window ▶ Properties** (shortcut **Ctrl+Alt+P** *or* ⌥⌘P), or by clicking its button on the toolbar. You can move the Properties window anywhere on the screen by dragging its title bar.

The title of the Properties window reflects the current selection – so with nothing selected it says "No selection"; with the title or tempo marking of your piece selected it says "Edit Text"; with a single note selected it says "Edit Note"; with a passage selected it says "Edit Passage"; when the caret is visible it says "Create Note/Rest"; and rather than try to list all the types of object in a multiple selection, it will simply read "Edit Multiple Selection."

If you have a multiple selection or selected passage, only those properties that are common to *all* the selected objects will be shown. For instance, if you select two notes, only one of which has an accent, the accent button on the Keypad will *not* light up. If you click the accent button, both notes will end up with an accent, so the accent button will then light up.

To open and close each of the six panels, click the appropriate title bar. You can open each panel independently, so they can be viewed together in any combination. If you try to open more panels than will fit vertically on your screen, Sibelius will automatically close one or more panels so that the Properties window always fits on the screen.

The options on each panel are detailed below.

General panel

The General panel of the Properties window lets you change the position etc. of the selected object(s), hide it if you like, and also gives you a read-out of the current staff and bar number.

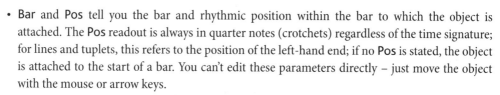

The options on this panel are as follows:

- The first line on the panel tells you the name of the staff to which the object is attached (or says "System" for system objects)

- Page *x* of *y* tells you on which page(s) of your score the selection is located

- Bar and Pos tell you the bar and rhythmic position within the bar to which the object is attached. The Pos readout is always in quarter notes (crotchets) regardless of the time signature; for lines and tuplets, this refers to the position of the left-hand end; if no Pos is stated, the object is attached to the start of a bar. You can't edit these parameters directly – just move the object with the mouse or arrow keys.

- Show and Hide etc. determine whether or not the object is hidden; ⬚ **5.9 Hiding objects**.

- X tells you the horizontal displacement of the object from the position it's attached to. (For example, the end of a hairpin can be attached to a note even if it's slightly left or right of it.)

   You can edit this value, which is particularly useful for positioning notes, rests and chords out of alignment when using two or more voices, or for displacing rehearsal marks from a barline.

- Y means different things for different objects. For notes and chords, this determines the stem length. For lines and text, it is the distance above the default vertical position.

- Scale *n*% is for scaling individual guitar chord diagrams and guitar scale diagrams; see **Changing the size of chord symbols** on page 107.

- Use magnetic layout shows whether the selected object is set to use Magnetic Layout; see **Overriding collision avoidance** on page 566.

- Custom order shows whether the selected object has a custom position in the draw order; ⬚ **5.14 Order**.

- Flip allows you to change the stem direction of selected notes, and flip certain objects above or below notes, such as slurs, tuplet brackets, articulations, and the curvature of ties. To flip an object, use this option, or choose Edit ▸ Flip (shortcut X), rather than trying to drag it with the mouse.

- Cue-sized allows you to set the selected notes, lines, symbols and staff text objects to be cue-sized, equivalent to using the cue-size button on the second (F8) Keypad layout; ⬚ **2.12 Cues**.

Text panel

The Text panel allows you to change the text style of the selected text object, and also alter its font, point size, and whether the text is bold, italic or underlined. The options are as follows:

- The first drop-down menu shows the text style of the selected text object; change the style simply by choosing another one from the menu. You can only choose compatible styles – so you cannot change a system text object (e.g. Tempo text) into a staff text object (e.g. Expression text). ⬚ **3.1 Working with text** for more details.

Power tools

- The second drop-down menu shows the font of the current text object; change the font simply by choosing another from the menu. To change the font (or size) of all text in that style in your score at once, 📖 **3.9 Edit Text Styles**.

- Size is the size of the font (in points)

- B, I and U control whether the selected text is bold, italic and/or underlined respectively. The shortcuts for these are Ctrl+B/I/U *or* ⌘B/I/U.

Playback panel

The Playback panel allows you to adjust the playback of lines, and change repeat playback settings. The options are as follows:

- **Play on pass**: these checkboxes, numbered 1–8, determine whether the selected text object, line or note should play back on a given repetition through a passage – 📖 **4.6 Repeats** for more details

- **Last time ending** determines whether or not an ending line is the last one in a repeat structure – 📖 **4.6 Repeats** for more details

- **Jump at bar end** is for making repeat jumps take effect in the middle of a bar – 📖 **4.6 Repeats** for more details

- **Live velocity**, **Live start position** and **Live duration** are the three parameters of a note that you can change using Live Playback – 📖 **4.8 Live Playback**

- **Fermata** allows you to change the duration of fermatas (pauses) – 📖 **4.2 Interpretation of your score**.

- **Gliss./Rit./Accel.** allows you to change the playback effect of these types of lines – 📖 **4.2 Interpretation of your score**.

- **Hairpin** allows you to set the final dynamic, or percentage change in dynamic, of a hairpin; the default, **Auto**, allows Sibelius to do this for you. 📖 **4.2 Interpretation of your score**.

- **Trill** allows you to choose whether or not playback should be **Diatonic**; if you want to set the interval yourself, switch off **Diatonic**, then choose the interval in **Half-steps** (semitones), **Speed** (in notes per second), and whether playback should **Start on upper note** of a selected trill. By default, Sibelius plays back trills with subtle rhythmic irregularities to make them sound more natural – if you don't like this effect, switch on **Play straight**. 📖 **4.2 Interpretation of your score**.

- **Tremolo** allows you to determine whether or not Sibelius should play a one-note tremolo or buzz roll ("z on stem"). You should only switch this off if your playback device plays tremolos via dedicated samples, and you don't want Sibelius to play multiple notes itself.

Lines panel

The Lines panel allows you to change the properties of the selected line.

End controls the horizontal (**X**) and vertical (**Y**) offset of the right-hand end of the selected line.

Slur left curve, Slur right curve and **Slur thickness** apply only to slurs – ☐ **2.28 Slurs**.

Hairpin end apertures and **Hairpin continuation apertures** apply only to hairpins – ☐ **2.17 Hairpins**.

Bars panel

To change the properties of a bar, select the bar so that it is surrounded by a light blue box (or, for some options, the barline at the end of the bar), and then change the options on the **Bars** panel, which are as follows:

- **Brackets/Initial barline/Clefs/Key signatures** determines whether these are drawn at the start of the bar when the bar is at the start of a system or occurs after the gap in a "divided" system such as a coda or prefatory staff (or incipit).

- **Split multirest** forces this barline to break a multirest – ☐ **2.24 Multirests** for more details

- **Section end** marks the barline as the end of a section for the purposes of the instrument name formats chosen in the **House Style ▸ Engraving Rules** dialog (shortcut **Ctrl+Shift+E** *or* ⇧⌘E). You should also create a system or page break at the same point.

- The first drop-down menu shows you which breaks (if any) occur at the barline – so you can add or remove a system or page break at the selected barline. This can also be done from the **Layout ▸ Breaks** submenu (or using shortcuts). Ignore **Middle of system/page**, which are used by **Lock Format, Keep Bars Together** and **Make Into System/Page**.

- **Gap before bar** alters the indent before the selected bar when it is at the start of a system, or the size of the gap just before the bar in a split system such as a coda.

Notes panel

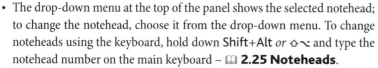

The **Notes** panel allows you to change the notehead of the selected note(s), alter the horizontal position of accidentals, and adjust the position and shape of ties. To adjust an accidental or tie from this panel, you should select its note (not the accidental/tie itself). The options are as follows:

- The drop-down menu at the top of the panel shows the selected notehead; to change the notehead, choose it from the drop-down menu. To change noteheads using the keyboard, hold down **Shift+Alt** *or* ⇧⌥ and type the notehead number on the main keyboard – ☐ **2.25 Noteheads**.

- **Accidental: X** controls the horizontal offset of the accidental attached to the selected note. Positive values move the accidental right, negative values move it left. You can also move accidentals by selecting them and typing **Alt+←/→** *or* ⌥←/→.

- **Tie shoulder:** % controls the curvature of the tie. Higher numbers will produce ties with flatter bottoms, whereas lower numbers make the shape more like a boomerang. Click **Def** (for default)

Power tools

to revert the tie's shoulder back to its original value as set on the Ties 1 page of the House Style ▸ Engraving Rules dialog, which can be useful if your boomerang didn't come back – 📖 **2.32 Ties**.

- Tie middle: Y controls the height of the tie's middle. You can also adjust this by selecting the tie and typing ↑/↓.

- Tie ends: Y controls the vertical position of the right-hand end of a tie attached to the selected note. L and R control the horizontal position of the left- and right-hand ends of the tie respectively. You can also adjust this by selecting the end of the tie and typing Shift+Alt+←/→ *or* ⇧⌥←/→.

- Tuplet allows you change the appearance of the selected tuplet, such as whether or not the bracket is displayed. 📖 **2.35 Triplets and other tuplets** for more details.

- Flip fractional beams allows you to flip a fractional secondary beam; see **Flipping fractional beams** on page 95.

5.18 SibeliusEducation.com

📖 **5.19 SibeliusMusic.com, 5.25 Worksheet Creator**.

SibeliusEducation.com is a web site for sharing and downloading teaching and learning resources and communicating with other teachers worldwide.

Who is it for?

You and your students may find it convenient to access worksheets and resources via the Internet. This will make it easier for you to organize your teaching materials, will save you having to print out or photocopy lots of copies of worksheets, and will help prevent your students losing work they have been set.

Because the music is displayed using Scorch, your students can play the music back to hear how it sounds – much more engaging than using a paper worksheet. Additionally, if they use Sibelius (at school) or Sibelius Student (at home), they can download and complete the work on computer.

Features

As SibeliusEducation.com grows we'll be adding more and more features to it over time. You can:

* Assemble worksheets and teaching materials you like to use
* Your students can then view, print and download work you have set them. They can either complete it on paper, or if they are using Sibelius (at school) or Sibelius Student (at home), they can do the work on computer and then upload their completed work to the site
* Access teaching materials produced by other teachers and schools
* Chat to other teachers worldwide to exchange information and ideas
* Get additional resources and information from Sibelius Software, such as extra worksheets and videos to compose to

Power tools

5. Power tools

- Get resources for the Sibelius Educational Suite range of products.

Full details of these are on the web site.

SibeliusEducation.com services

To sign in to SibeliusEducation.com, simply choose Help ▸ SibeliusEducation.com, or visit www.sibeliuseducation.com. By creating an account you can benefit from additional services such as posting messages on the forum and uploading worksheets to the site.

Publishing worksheets onto SibeliusEducation.com

- Once you've created your worksheet, save it to disk
- If you want students to be able to open the file with an earlier version of Sibelius or Sibelius Student, choose File ▸ Export ▸ Sibelius 2, 3 or 4 or File ▸ Export ▸ Sibelius Student to save the file
- Choose File ▸ Publish on SibeliusEducation.com, then when your web browser opens, sign in, and go to the My work section of the site. (You will need to sign in to be able do this.)
- Follow the instructions on the screen for uploading your file to the site in the worksheet area.

SibeliusMusic.com

SibeliusMusic.com has tens of thousands of scores created by composers, arrangers, teachers and students. You may want to get music from the site for teaching purposes. These are free to view and play. Many are free to print and some are for sale. 📖 **5.19 SibeliusMusic.com** for details.

5.19 SibeliusMusic.com

📖 **5.18 SibeliusEducation.com, 9.11 Exporting Scorch web pages**.

The Internet is the ideal way to reach a worldwide audience for your music. Sibelius is the only music notation program with the free web browser plug-in Scorch, which lets anyone view, play back, transpose, and print scores on the Internet.

Composers, arrangers and anyone else can publish on our self-publishing web site SibeliusMusic.com – from piano pieces to orchestral scores, from early music to avant garde and rock/pop. It's entirely free to publish scores, plus you can make money from it – if you want to sell your music (rather than provide it for free) you'll be paid a generous 50% of the price!

Scorch

Sibelius Scorch is the amazing free web browser plug-in that allows anyone to view, play back, change key and instruments, and even print scores directly from the Internet, whether or not they have Sibelius.

People visiting your site will be prompted to download Scorch automatically, and in just a couple of minutes they'll be able to see and hear the music on your own site and hundreds of others, including sites from major publishers such as **www.sheetmusicdirect.com** (rock/pop songs) and **www.boosey.com** (classical/educational music).

For details of how to install Scorch, see **Installing Sibelius** in the **Start here** section in **Handbook**. Scorch only installs automatically on Internet Explorer for Windows – but Scorch also works with other browsers, including Firefox and Opera, on both Windows and Mac.

Power tools

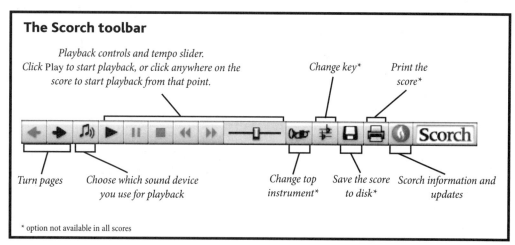

The Scorch toolbar

Playback controls and tempo slider.
Click Play *to start playback, or click anywhere on the score to start playback from that point.*

Change key*

Print the score*

Turn pages

Choose which sound device you use for playback

Change top instrument*

Save the score to disk*

Scorch information and updates

* option not available in all scores

Recommended settings

To make your score look and sound as good as possible when other people look at your music, you should standardize the following before you publish it on the Internet:

- *Fonts* – not all fonts can be assumed to be available on all computers
- *Page size* – the score must print acceptably on various kinds of paper
- *Playback* – the score must make minimal assumptions about the computer's sound capabilities.

Limit the fonts used for text in the score to common ones, such as Times, Times New Roman, Arial and Helvetica (although Scorch will substitute the nearest equivalent fonts if the person viewing your web page doesn't have the fonts you have used). Also ensure that the only music fonts you use are Sibelius's standard Opus, Helsinki, Reprise and Inkpen2 fonts, since these will be available on every computer with Scorch installed.

When preparing your scores for publishing on SibeliusMusic.com, where they can be printed, use portrait format and preferably a standard page size (e.g. Letter, Tabloid, A4 or A3). Scorch will scale the music to fit on the printer's page size.

You should also bear in mind that a score that sounds good on your own soundcard or MIDI devices may not sound good on different computers. So you should at least try listening to your score using standard General MIDI sounds, to get an idea how your score will sound when played back through Scorch.

Publishing on SibeliusMusic.com

To get started, open the Sibelius file you would like to publish online, and choose **File ▸ Publish on SibeliusMusic.com**.

- If you haven't saved the file recently, you will be prompted to do so first; save it, then choose **Publish on SibeliusMusic.com** again
- Your web browser will open and display a web page for you to specify basic information about your score, such as its title (this is automatically filled in for you if you have previously filled it in on the **File ▸ New** or **File ▸ Score Info** dialog)
- Find on your hard drive the score you wish to publish online – click **Browse** to find your score
- When you have found the score, click **Next**. Your computer will then connect to the Internet and upload your score to SibeliusMusic.com.
- You will be asked to provide further information about yourself and your score – simply follow the instructions on the screen.

SibeliusMusic.com will only publish music to which you hold the sole music copyright, i.e. original compositions or arrangements of out-of-copyright music. You are not permitted to publish transcriptions or arrangements of copyright music, verbatim transcriptions or editions of out-of-copyright music, or scores containing copyright lyrics that are used without permission. For further details about the copyright restrictions on scores you can publish, see the information provided at SibeliusMusic.com.

If you experience any problems or have any queries about self-publishing on SibeliusMusic.com, please email **info@sibeliusmusic.com**.

5.20 Transposing

For details of transposing instruments and transposing scores, 📖 **2.18 Instruments**.

To simplify key signatures and enharmonic spellings, 📖 **2.20 Key signatures**.

Transpose dialog

To transpose music:

- Select whatever you want to transpose – usually a passage or the whole score (shortcut **Ctrl+A** *or* ⌘A)
- Choose **Notes** ▸ **Transpose** (shortcut **Shift**-T)

- Choose whether you want to transpose by **Key** or by **Interval**
- If you choose to transpose by **Key**:
  - ○ Choose the key you want to transpose to from the menu
  - ○ Decide whether you want Sibelius to transpose by the smallest required interval (**Closest**), or **Up** or **Down**.
- If you choose to transpose by **Interval**:
  - ○ Click **Up** or **Down**.
  - ○ From the second box, choose the main interval.
  - ○ In the first box, **Major/Perfect** leaves the main interval unaltered, **Augmented** adds a half-step (semitone), **Minor/Diminished** subtracts a half-step.
  - ○ **Diatonic** moves the notes within the key specified by the current key signature; so transposing up a diatonic 2nd makes the third note of the key into the fourth, makes the flattened fifth into the flattened sixth, etc.
- Set the other options if you like:
  - ○ **Transpose key signatures** (available when transposing a system passage or the whole score) transposes any key changes within the selected passage. Normally leave this on. If switched off, transposed notes acquire accidentals that would otherwise be specified in the key signature.

Power tools

- ○ If **Transpose key signatures** is on, you can also switch on **Change key at start**, which will create a new key signature at the start of the transposed passage if you like.
- ○ If you don't want Sibelius to create a restorative key change at the end of the transposed passage back to the original key, switch on **Allow change of key to persist**.
- ○ **Use double sharps/flats** makes Sibelius notate remote keys using double sharps and flats rather than naturals. Switch this off for atonal music. Leave it on if you're Rachmaninov, or Alban Berg in his youth.

- Click **OK**, and Sibelius instantly transposes the music.

Shifting without accidentals

To shift notes that you don't want to end up with accidentals, simply select the music and type ↑/↓ one or more times.

Transposing by one or more octaves

The quick method is to select the music and type **Ctrl+↑/↓** *or* ⌘↑/↓.

Transposing by more than two octaves

For brevity, the **Notes ▸ Transpose** dialog (shortcut **Shift-T**) only lists intervals up to two octaves. For bigger intervals, transpose by further octaves by typing **Ctrl+↑/↓** *or* ⌘↑/↓ before or after transposing from the dialog.

Transposing by a half-step (semitone)

Although most transpositions are straightforward, this particular case merits a little explanation. If you have a score in, say, D major, and want to transpose it into D flat major, you should not transpose it down by a minor 2nd, which produces C♯ major – instead, transpose it down by an *augmented unison*.

Extreme transpositions

To do extreme transpositions for which the interval required is not listed, e.g. B to D flat (up a doubly-augmented third), split it into two less extreme transpositions: first transpose up a minor third to D, then down an augmented unison to D flat.

Chord symbols

These automatically transpose.

Moving other objects

When transposing, Sibelius will move other objects as it sees fit. For instance, ties and slurs automatically move to follow the notes. If music is transposed so far that lots of notes' stem-directions change, some slurs may need to be flipped with **Edit ▸ Flip** (shortcut **X**) so as to fit over the notes smoothly.

5.21 Undo and Redo

Undo

 Click the toolbar button shown on the left or choose **Edit ▸ Undo** (shortcut **Ctrl+Z** *or* **⌘Z**) to undo the last thing you did.

The **Edit** menu tells you what the last thing you did was, in case you have a very short memory. (Well, it tells you the last thing you did in Sibelius – it won't say **Undo Sneeze**, entertaining though that might be.)

Undo is multi-level – you can carry on undoing steps almost indefinitely far back. **Edit ▸ Undo History** (see below) jumps back to a particular earlier point.

Redo

 Redo undoes undos (or rather, Redo *redoes* undos). To redo an operation you didn't mean to undo, click the toolbar button shown on the left or choose **Edit ▸ Redo** (shortcut **Ctrl+Y** *or* **⌘Y**).

Again, the **Edit** menu tells you what it was you just undid.

Undo History

Edit ▸ Undo History (shortcut **Ctrl+Shift+Z** *or* **⇧⌘Z**) lists all the recent operations you've done, and lets you hop back to a particular earlier point in time.

The most recent operation is at the top of the list, so click the top item to undo one step, the second item to undo two steps and the bottom item to undo as far back as you can go. The antiquity of the undo history is customizable – see **Undo level** below.

Redo History

Edit ▸ Redo History (shortcut **Ctrl+Shift+Y** *or* **⇧⌘Y**) is like **Undo History**, but lists all the things you can redo after you've done a load of undoing.

The most recent operation you undid is at the top of the list, so (as with **Undo History**) click the top item to redo one step, the second item to redo two steps and the bottom item to redo everything you undid and get back to where you were. (If you see what I mean.)

Undo level

To set how far back you can undo, choose the **Other** page of **File ▸ Preferences** (in the **Sibelius** menu on Mac) and drag the slider. You can undo up to 20,000 operations, so if you set the undo level large enough you can undo right back to when you started writing the current score.

If you set it larger still, you can even undo back to before you bought Sibelius.

Power tools

5.22 Versions

When working on a particular project over an extended period of time, keeping track of progress can be problematic in most software. Typically you would have to remember to choose **File ▸ Save As** to save each draft of your work under a different filename. Fortunately, Sibelius allows you to save multiple versions of your score in the same document, so that older versions can't get lost, misplaced, or confused with the current version.

You can add comments to each version, to serve as reminders of the work you've done or have yet to do, export an older version as a separate score, and even compare two versions to get a detailed list of all the differences between versions.

Saving a new version automatically

By default, Sibelius will remind you to create a new version when you close a score after you've been editing it for a while. By default, you will see the following dialog:

You can change the provided **Version name** to anything you like: the name Sibelius provides for you includes a version number, and the date and time at which the version was started. You can also provide a **Comment**, which can be as short or as long as you like. This comment does not appear in the score like "sticky note" comments do (☐ **5.5 Comments**), and this feature is useful for writing general commentary about your progress, rather than specific things that are better suited to being attached to a particular bar.

Click **OK** to save your version, and close the score; if you click **Cancel**, you will nevertheless be offered the chance to save your score without creating a new version.

If you would prefer not to be prompted to create a version when closing your score, switch off **Create a new version when closing the score** on the **Versions** page of **File ▸ Preferences** (in the **Sibelius** menu on Mac).

Saving a new version manually

You can, of course, save a new version at any time: simply choose **File ▸ Save Version**, or click the toolbar button shown on the right. The button is only enabled once you have saved your score once and given it a filename.

When you save a new version, you will be prompted to provide a name and, by default, a comment (see above). If you would prefer not to have to provide a comment, choose **File ▸ Preferences** (in the **Sibelius** menu on Mac) and go to the **Versions** page. In the **Comments** group you can choose between three options:

- **Don't prompt for a comment**: only requires that you review the name Sibelius has chosen for your version by default; no space is provided for you to type a comment.

- **Prompt for an optional comment**: the default setting, this allows you to type a comment if you want to, but you can save a version without providing a comment if you prefer.

- **Require a comment**: requires that you type a comment of some kind before you can save a new version. This is a useful setting if you are teaching with Sibelius in the classroom and want to ensure that your students provide a comment before they finish work on their project for the day.

If you are teaching with Sibelius in the classroom, you can prompt one or more of the students in your classroom to save a new version at any time using the **Classroom Control** dialog – 📖 **5.3 Classroom Control**.

Viewing versions

You can view the versions saved in your score using the drop-down on the toolbar shown on the right. (If these controls don't appear on your toolbar, your computer's screen resolution is too low – see **Toolbar** on page 463.)

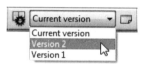

The current version of your score is always called **Current version**, and always appears at the top of the list in the menu: the oldest version is listed at the bottom, and the most recent version just underneath **Current version**.

You can also view versions by choosing **Next Version** or **Previous Version** from the **File ▸ Versions** submenu. (If you do this a lot, you may find it useful to assign keyboard shortcuts to these menu items.)

When you choose another version from the list, or choose another version from the **File ▸ Versions** submenu, Sibelius opens a new window, and gives the score a crumpled paper background, to remind you that it's an old version. (If you want to change the textures that Sibelius uses when viewing versions, see **Textures** on page 388.)

By default, Sibelius will re-use the window displaying the previously viewed version. If you would prefer Sibelius to create a separate window for each version, perhaps so you can see them tiled on a large screen, switch on **View versions in new windows** on the **Versions** page of **File ▸ Preferences** (in the **Sibelius** menu on Mac).

What you can do with versions

Only the current version of your score is editable, so once you have made a version, you can no longer make any changes to that older version. When you view a version, however, you can do lots of useful things, including play it back, print it out, or even copy music and objects to the clipboard so that you can paste them into your current version, or even another score.

To copy from an old version, simply make a selection as you would in any other score, then choose **Edit ▸ Copy** (shortcut **Ctrl+C** *or* ⌘C) to copy to the clipboard. Then switch to the current version or the other score into which you want to paste the material, and choose **Edit ▸ Paste** (shortcut **Ctrl+V** *or* ⌘V). You cannot use **Alt**+click (or chord-click) to copy from an old version.

You can also compare one version with another version – see **Comparing versions** below.

Edit Versions

You can perform a number of important file management tasks on the versions in your score using the File ▸ Versions ▸ Edit Versions dialog, which you can also open using the toolbar button shown on the right.

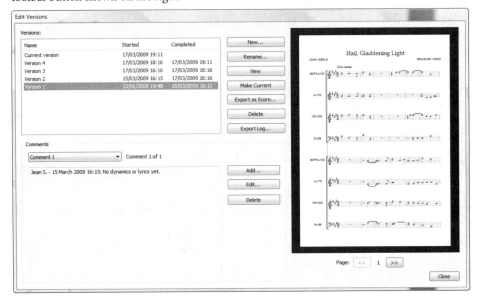

The table at the left-hand side of the dialog lists the versions in the score. You can choose to sort by the Name, the date the version was Started, or the date the version was Completed. On the right is a preview that shows the selected version. You can flip through the pages of the selected version using the buttons below the preview.

Below the table is a list of all the comments saved in the selected version, including any "sticky note" comments, and any comments provided when the version was created. You can Add, Edit and Delete comments here by clicking the appropriate button.

The buttons between the table of versions and the preview of the selected version are as follows:

- **New** creates a new version, i.e. equivalent to choosing File ▸ Save Version.
- **Rename** renames the selected version.
- **View** closes the Edit Versions dialog and opens a window to view the selected version.
- **Make Current** allows you to make a selected version into the current version. A new version is automatically created to save the state of the current version, and the selected version is then made into the new current version.
- **Export as Score** exports the selected version as a separate score, containing only that single version. You can select Current version and click Export as Score to make a copy of the current state of your score quickly without including any of the older versions.
- **Delete** deletes the selected version, after a warning.
- **Export Log** exports a Rich Text Format (RTF) file listing the differences between each version, all their associated comments, and a graphic of each page– see **Exporting a versions log** below.

Click Close to close the Edit Versions dialog.

Exporting a versions log

Sibelius can export a Rich Text Format (RTF) file that includes:

- A list of the differences between each pair of versions
- All comments saved in each version
- A thumbnail graphic of each page of each version, with the differences between them colored in.

This file can be opened in any word processor and many text editors, though the thumbnail graphics of each page may only appear in certain versions of certain word processors, e.g. Microsoft Word 2002 or later for Windows, and Microsoft Word 2008 or later for Mac OS X.

To export a versions log, choose **File ▸ Versions ▸ Edit Versions**, select any version, and click **Export Log**. The following dialog appears:

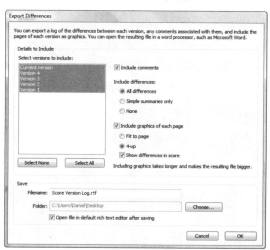

In the list at the left-hand side, you can choose which versions to include; by default, all versions are selected. The options to the right of the list are as follows:

- **Include comments** determines whether or not the comments (both "sticky notes" attached to particular bars and the comments created when saving a new version or in the **Edit Versions** dialog) should be included in the RTF file. This option is switched on by default.

- **Include differences** determines the level of detail for the lists of differences between each version: **All differences** includes both a summary of the differences (e.g. "Whole score transposed, notes added in four bars") and a table listing each difference in detail, bar by bar; **Simple summary only** excludes the table and provides only a summary of the differences; **None** excludes all information about the differences between versions altogether. This is set to **All differences** by default.

- **Include graphic of each page** determines whether the RTF file should include a graphic of each page of each version. Depending on the length of your score or the number of versions, you may wish to switch this off: generating graphics for each page can be quite time-consuming, and makes the resulting RTF file considerably larger. If you decide to include graphics, choose between **Fit to page**, which will fit a single page of each version to a single page of the RTF file, or **4-up**, which will fit four pages of each version to a single page of the RTF file. Switch on **Show**

differences in score to mark up the differences between versions by showing colors behind the objects that were added, changed and removed in the graphics of each page.

Sibelius provides a default filename, and offers to save the RTF file to the same location as the score, but you can change both of these if you wish. When you are happy with your choices, click OK to create the version log. A progress bar appears while this takes place.

By default, the **Open file in default rich text editor after saving** is switched on, and launches the default application for handling RTF files once the file has been exported; on Windows, this will be WordPad by default, and TextEdit on Mac. If you have a more fully featured word processor installed on your computer, such as Microsoft Word, consider setting it to be the default application for opening RTF files on your computer.

Comparing versions

Sibelius provides a simple way to compare two versions of the same score, and see the differences between them both as a tabulated list, and visually displayed in the scores themselves.

To compare two versions, choose **Window ▸ Compare** (shortcut **Ctrl+Alt+C** *or* ⌥⌘C), or click the toolbar button shown on the right. This window appears:

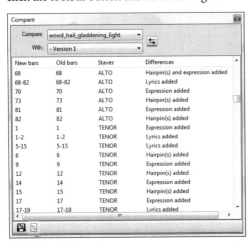

Choose the newer of the two versions from the first list, labeled **Compare**, and the older of the two versions from the second list, labeled **With**, then click the ⬆ button.

A progress bar appears as the two versions are compared; after a few seconds, the older of the two versions is shown in a window on the left, and the newer version is shown in a window on the right, tiled vertically. If you would prefer Sibelius not to tile the two windows vertically, go to the **Versions** page of **File ▸ Preferences** (in the **Sibelius** menu on Mac) and switch off **Tile windows when comparing versions**.

A window then appears titled **Summary of Differences**. This gives you a high-level overview of the changes between two versions: for example, you may see a line like "Lyrics added to 82 bars", or "Expression added to 40 bars". Click **Close** to dismiss this window. If you would prefer not to see this, switch off **Show simple summary of differences** in **Preferences**.

The Compare window shows a detailed list of all of the differences between the two versions:

- **New bars** lists the bar number or range of bar numbers in the score chosen in the **Compare** drop-down where the difference is found.

- **Old bars** lists the bar number or range of bar numbers in the score chosen in the **With** menu that corresponds to the bar numbers shown in **New bars**. (These may or may not be the same, depending on whether bars have been inserted or removed.)

- **Staves** lists the staff or staves affected by the difference. If the difference affects all staves (e.g. adding or removing bars), it will say All; otherwise it will show the name of the staff.

- **Differences** lists the nature of the difference that has been found. What this column says depends entirely on the differences found: see **What Sibelius compares** below.

By default, the table view is sorted by the **New bars** column, in ascending order, but you can change the sorting of the table by clicking on any of the column headings.

When you double-click an item in the list, Sibelius moves the view in both score windows to show the relevant bars. Sibelius takes account of whether objects have been added, changed or deleted, as follows:

- Objects that have been added in the newer version are shown with a green background in the newer version.

- Objects that have been changed in the newer version are shown with an orange background in both the older and the newer version.

- Objects that have been deleted in the newer version are shown with a red background in the older version.

If you don't want to see the differences visually in the score, either switch off **View** ▸ **Differences Between Versions**, or click the button in the toolbar at the bottom of the Compare window shown on the right.

You can also export the list of differences as shown in the Compare window as a Rich Text Format (RTF) file. Simply click the **Save Differences** button in the toolbar at the bottom of the Compare window, as shown on the left. You will be prompted to provide a filename, and an RTF file is saved that can be opened in any rich text editor, e.g. WordPad, TextEdit, or Microsoft Word.

What Sibelius compares

Sibelius does not keep track of every single edit made to your score between versions: rather, it looks at the two versions and does its best to work out the changes that were made between them. Because of this heuristic approach, there may be more than one way to characterise a particular difference between two versions.

Sibelius does not notice differences in layout, formatting, note spacing or document setup: it is concerned only with the musical content of the compared scores, and not their appearance.

The following kinds of objects are considered when comparing versions:

Power tools

- *Instruments and staves:* if the number of staves is different, Sibelius establishes which staves have been added or removed; if an instrument that was present in the older version is no longer present in the newer one, Sibelius examines the contents of each staff to establish whether the user has changed one instrument for another, or has deleted one and added another.

- *Bars:* if the number of bars is different, Sibelius establishes where bars have been added or removed.

- *Notes:* Sibelius establishes whether notes have been added or removed, and whether pitch and/or rhythm has been changed; it distinguishes between individual changes of pitch and diatonic or chromatic transposition.

- *Articulations:* if the notes in a given bar are at least 80% similar, Sibelius compares articulations on notes, and reports if any have been added, changed or removed.

- *Transposition:* if music has been transposed, Sibelius reports the affected range of bars, and the interval by which the music has been transposed.

- *Chord symbols:* Sibelius reports whether chord symbols have been added, changed or removed.

- *Dynamics:* if the notes in a given bar are at least 50% similar, Sibelius compares the Expression text and hairpins in that bar, and reports whether any dynamics have been added, changed or removed.

- *Staff text:* if text in any staff text style other than Expression or one of the lyrics text styles has been added, changed or removed from a bar, Sibelius reports it.

- *System text:* if text in any system text style other than Tempo, Metronome mark or Metric modulation has been added, changed or removed from a bar, Sibelius reports it.

- *Tempo markings:* Sibelius reports whether any tempo markings have been added, changed, moved or removed.

- *Lyrics:* if the notes in a given bar are at least 50% similar, Sibelius compares the lyrics in that bar, and reports whether they have been added, changed or removed.

- *Lines:* if the notes in a given bar are at least 80% similar, Sibelius compares the slurs, trills, pedal lines, glissando/portamento lines, arpeggio lines and octave lines in that bar, and reports whether they have been added, changed or removed.

- *Clefs:* if the notes in a given bar are at least 50% similar, Sibelius compares any clef changes in that bar.

- *Barlines:* Sibelius reports whether any special barlines (e.g. double or repeat barlines) have been added, changed or removed.

- *Key signatures:* Sibelius compares the initial key signature and subsequent changes of key, and reports if any have been added, changed or removed.

- *Instrument changes:* Sibelius reports whether any instrument changes have been added, changed or removed.

- *Symbols:* if the notes in a given bar are at least 80% similar, Sibelius compares any staff symbols in that bar; it compares system symbols (e.g. coda and segno signs) in all bars regardless of their similarity.

- *Comments:* Sibelius compares the comments in the two versions or scores, noting where they have been added, edited or deleted.

Comparing two separate scores

The Compare window can also be used to compare two separate scores. Simply open the two scores that you want to compare, choose the newer of the two scores from the Compare drop-down and the older of the two from the With drop-down, and click the ⬆ button.

There is also a plug-in that can compare two staves of the same score: see **Compare Staves** on page 485.

5.23 View menu

📖 **5.6 Display settings**, **5.24 Window menu**.

The View menu has options for controlling how scores and the Sibelius interface look on the screen.

If you want to, you can print your score with the options from the View menu included (with, for example, comments, hidden objects in gray, highlights in yellow and layout marks in blue) – 📖 **5.16 Printing**.

Pages

The View ▸ Pages submenu contains options for how Sibelius should lay out the pages of your score on the screen:

- **Spreads Horizontally** is the default, with pages laid out left-to-right, facing pages shown together.
- **Single Pages Horizontally** lays out single pages left-to-right. This is useful for music that is not normally presented in booklet or spreads form, e.g. fan-fold parts where the first page may be numbered 1 but is not the right-hand page of a spread.
- **Spreads Vertically** lays out pairs of pages vertically, e.g. pages 2 and 3 are shown next to each other, with pages 4 and 5 below them.
- **Single Pages Vertically** lays the pages of your score out in a single column, with page 2 below page 1, page 3 below page 2, and so on.

Sibelius saves the View ▸ Pages setting for each score (and each dynamic part), and will restore your setting when re-opening the score (or part). You can control this behaviour on the Files page of File ▸ Preferences (in the Sibelius menu on Mac) – 📖 **5.15 Preferences**.

Panorama

This displays your score as a single continuous system on an infinitely-wide page. 📖 **5.13 Panorama**.

Focus on Staves

This shows just the selected staves, hiding all intervening staves. It is useful for inputting and editing (particularly in conjunction with Panorama), and for hiding staves with music on for playback. 📖 **5.8 Focus on Staves**.

Staff Names and Bar Numbers

When working on scores for large-scale ensembles, or when zoomed in, it is very useful to be able to tell which staff you are working on, and which bar you are working in, without having to cast about looking for the instrument name and bar number.

This option draws bar numbers in blue above every bar of the top visible staff of each system, and draws the name of each staff at the left-hand side of the screen when the instrument names are off the left-hand side of the screen.

If you would prefer to see bar numbers above every staff, switch on **Show bar numbers on all staves** on the **Display** page of **File ▸ Preferences** (in the **Sibelius** menu on Mac).

Layout Marks

This shows system and page breaks as icons in the score, draws other icons to show where the layout has been altered, and shows where staves are hidden by drawing a dashed blue line across the page. ⌨ **8.5 Breaks**.

Because it's useful to be able to see e.g. where staves are hidden when using **View ▸ Focus on Staves**, Sibelius allows you to have **View ▸ Layout Marks** switched off when working on the full score and switched on when using Focus on Staves, and vice versa – simply switch it on or off as required, and Sibelius will remember its state for you.

Page Margins

This option draws a dashed blue rectangle to show where the margins set in **Layout ▸ Document Setup** are. ⌨ **8.6 Document Setup**.

Rulers

The options in the **View ▸ Rulers** submenu switch on and off three kinds of ruler:

- **Selection Rulers**: displays a ruler between the selected object(s) and the staff to which it is attached
- **Object Rulers** (shortcut **Shift+Alt+R** *or* ⇧⌥R): displays a ruler for all objects attached to staves, e.g. text, symbols, lines, etc., whether they are selected or not
- **Staff Rulers** (shortcut **Ctrl+Shift+Alt+R** *or* ⇧⌥⌘R): displays rulers between staves and page edges, and between adjacent staves.

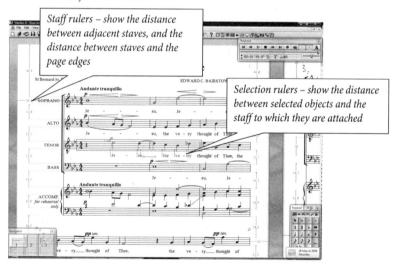

Staff rulers – show the distance between adjacent staves, and the distance between staves and the page edges

Selection rulers – show the distance between selected objects and the staff to which they are attached

Set the unit of measurement used for rulers from the **Other** page of the **File ▸ Preferences** dialog (in the **Sibelius** menu on Mac). You can choose between inches, points (1 point = 1/72 inch), millimeters and spaces.

Object and staff rulers can slow screen redrawing down significantly, so switch these off if Sibelius seems to be running slow.

In addition to rulers, Sibelius can display the music on graph paper ruled in spaces by choosing the graph paper texture; 📖 **5.6 Display settings**.

Attachment Lines

This draws a dashed gray arrow to show which staff and rhythmic position the selected object is attached to. For clarity, no attachment line appears for certain objects such as notes, rests and system objects. 📖 **8.7 Attachment**.

Handles

With this option switched on, the handles on various objects (e.g. note stems, slurs, barlines, etc.) are displayed on your score in light gray at all times. Because handles otherwise only appear when objects are selected, this is particularly useful for handles that are difficult to find, e.g. slur curve points (📖 **2.28 Slurs**) or the handle at the right-hand side of a system (📖 **2.29 Staves**).

Hidden Objects

With this option switched on, hidden objects are displayed on your score in light gray and are editable; with it switched off, they are invisible and uneditable. It's quicker to use keyboard shortcuts than menus, so memorize Ctrl+Alt+H *or* ⌥⌘H. 📖 **5.9 Hiding objects**.

Comments

Switch this off to hide any "sticky note" comments created in the score. 📖 **5.5 Comments**.

Differences In Parts

When switched on, Sibelius will show objects whose position or appearance in a part is different than the score by coloring them orange. If used in a score, Sibelius will color any objects that have a different position or appearance in one or more parts. 📖 **7.1 Working with parts**.

Differences Between Versions

Switch this off to hide the colored highlights behind objects that have been colored by comparing two versions or scores. 📖 **5.22 Versions**.

Highlights

If you have created any highlights in your score, use this option to control whether they are displayed on the screen. 📖 **5.10 Highlight**.

Magnetic Layout Collisions

Switch this off to prevent objects that collide with other objects from being displayed in red. 📖 **8.2 Magnetic Layout**.

Note Colors

The View ▸ Note Colors menu contains three options that affect the on-screen display of your score:

- Voice Colors: colors all notes in a dark shade of their voice color, so voice 1 notes are dark blue, voice 2 notes are green, voice 3 notes are orange, and voice 4 notes are pink (📖 **2.36 Voices**)

- **Notes out of Range**: the default setting; automatically reddens notes that are too high or low for an instrument to play. Notes that are uncomfortable but playable by professionals are shown in dark red. This means you can spot tricky or impossible notes at a glance and correct them before rehearsals (☐ **2.18 Instruments**).
- **None**: shows notes in black; selected notes are colored according to their voice (i.e. voice 1 is dark blue, voice 2 is green, etc.).

Live Playback Velocities

This shows colored columns above each note or chord in your score that has Live Playback data, representing their MIDI velocities. ☐ **4.8 Live Playback**.

Playback Line

Switch this off to hide the green playback line when you're not playing back.

Live Tempo

Switch this off to hide the graph display showing how the Live Tempo performance varies over time; the graph only appears in Panorama. ☐ **4.7 Live Tempo**.

Full Screen (Windows only)

Choosing this (shortcut **Ctrl+U**) makes menus and the taskbar (the bar at the bottom showing which programs you're running) disappear to save space. You can still get at the menus by moving your mouse to the very top of the screen.

Scroll Bars

This adds vertical and horizontal scroll bars to the main score editing window. It's preferable not to use these, as scrolling around your score using the Navigator is quicker and easier.

If you have a mouse with a wheel button, you can also use the wheel to scroll around the score, whether or not you have **View ▸ Scroll Bars** switched on:

- Scroll the wheel up and down to move the page up and down; hold down **Alt** *or* ⌥ to move a screen at a time
- Hold **Shift** and scroll the wheel to move the page left and right; hold down **Alt** *or* ⌥ as well to move a screen at a time (or a page at a time if the width of the page fits on the screen). If you have an Apple Mighty Mouse, scrolling the wheel horizontally moves the page left and right, with no need to hold down **Shift** (Mac only).
- You can also use the wheel to zoom by holding down **Ctrl** *or* ⌘.

On Windows, to change the scrolling speed, use the **Mouse** applet in Control Panel. The precise options available depend on the drivers installed for your particular mouse, but many mouse drivers offer the option of accelerated scrolling; increasing this allows you to scroll around the score more quickly using the wheel.

Toolbar

This makes the toolbar disappear or reappear. Switching off the toolbar can save quite a bit of space on the screen, and nearly all the toolbar buttons have simple keyboard shortcuts anyway.

If your screen resolution is not sufficiently wide to fit all of the toolbar buttons (a resolution of at least 1280 x 1024 is recommended), Sibelius will automatically hide one or more groups of buttons so that the toolbar does not run off the right-hand side of your display. You can disable this behavior on the **Display** page of **File ▸ Preferences** (in the **Sibelius** menu on Mac): select **Let me choose what appears on the toolbar** instead of **Automatically add or remove items from toolbar to fit display**. You can then choose to hide or show particular groups of buttons yourself, if you want.

Zoom

The options in the **View ▸ Zoom** menu duplicate the behavior of the **Zoom** tool on the toolbar. You can use the zoom functions of Sibelius in a variety of ways:

- Use the shortcuts **Ctrl++** *or* **⌘+** (zoom in) and **Ctrl+–** *or* **⌘–** (zoom out). You can either use the + and – keys on your numeric keypad or on the main keyboard.
- If you have a mouse with a scroll wheel, you can hold down **Ctrl** *or* **⌘** and scroll the wheel up and down to zoom in and out
- Click the zoom button on the toolbar, and click on the score to zoom in; right-click (Windows) *or* ⌥-click (Mac) to zoom out again. Hit **Esc** to stop zooming.
- Click the zoom button, and drag on the score to select the area you want to zoom into. Hit **Esc** to stop zooming.
- Use the keyboard shortcut **Ctrl+0** *or* **⌘0** to change the zoom level to **Fit page**, and **Ctrl+1** *or* **⌘1** to set the zoom level to **100%**. You can also define your own shortcuts for other zoom levels – 📖 **5.12 Menus and shortcuts**.

When the zoom button on the toolbar is switched on, it remains switched on after you click or drag on the score, so you can click again; to stop zooming, hit **Esc**, or switch the zoom button off again.

A zoom factor of 100% does not display the music at the size it will actually print; it shows it at a convenient average size for editing. The **Actual size** option (in the list on the toolbar) *does* show the music supposedly at the size it will print, though this depends on the exact size of your monitor.

The options such as **Fit page width** do what they say. However, it's best to stick to the numerical zoom factors as these have been chosen to display notes as clearly as possible, by ensuring that all the staff lines are equally spaced. You can type in your own zoom factor onto the toolbar, in which case Sibelius will round it up or down to the nearest factor that displays well.

By default, Sibelius switches the zoom level to **Fit page width** during playback, but you can change this if you like (or stop Sibelius from changing the zoom level during playback at all) in the **Score Position** page of **File ▸ Preferences** (in the **Sibelius** menu on Mac), or simply by changing the zoom level while it's playing; 📖 **4.1 Working with playback**.

The **Files** page of the **File ▸ Preferences** dialog (in the **Sibelius** menu on Mac) includes an option to set the default zoom factor used when opening scores; 📖 **5.15 Preferences**.

5.24 Window menu

📖 **5.23 View menu**.

The Window menu contains a mixture of standard options that you may be familiar with from other applications, and Sibelius-specific commands for manipulating, hiding and showing score and tool windows.

Minimize (Mac only)

Minimizes the current score window to the Dock, replete with whizzy genie effect. It does the same as clicking the yellow icon at the top left of the score's window), shortcut ⌘M.

Zoom (Mac only)

Not to be confused with Sibelius's own zoom features (see **Zoom** on page 464), this does the same thing as clicking the green "traffic signal" button on the score's title bar, i.e. zooms the window to the full size of your display.

Bring All to Front (Mac only)

If you have multiple score windows open, but one or more of them is currently behind a window belonging to another application, this brings all the score windows to the top of the pile.

New Window

New Window creates a new view of the current score. This allows you to look at different places in the same score at once, or look at the same score at different zoom factors, or look at multiple parts at once. For instance, you could have one view at 25% to keep an eye on the overall layout of the page, and another view at 200% for close-up work. This is particularly useful if your computer has multiple monitors.

Tile Horizontally, Tile Vertically

To *tile* windows is to resize the open score windows such that they can all fit on the screen, and arranged such that they do not overlap. Tile Horizontally resizes the windows to the width of the display, and arranges them one above each other. Tile Vertically, on the other hand, resizes the windows to the height of the display, and arranges them side by side.

Sibelius automatically tiles score windows when comparing two versions or two scores using the Compare window – 📖 **5.22 Versions**.

Cascade (Windows only)

Cascade resizes the open score windows such that they are smaller than the height and width of the display, and then arranges them such that the title bar of each window is visible, cascading downwards from the top left-hand corner of Sibelius's window.

Power tools

Tool windows

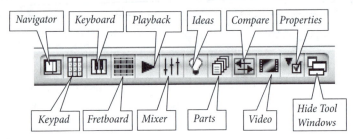

- Navigator: shows and hides the Navigator (shortcut **Ctrl+Alt+N** *or* ⌥⌘N). If you know the shortcuts for moving around the score (**Page Up** *or* ⇞, **Page Down** *or* ⇟, etc.) you should be able to survive quite happily without the Navigator. You can move the Navigator around – just drag its title bar; the same goes for the other tool windows.

- Keypad: shows and hides the Keypad (shortcut **Ctrl+Alt+K** *or* ⌥⌘K). You'd have to be quite adept at Sibelius to know what all the keys on all the Keypad layouts are without looking, but when you've used Sibelius for a bit you can try switching the Keypad off to see how much you can remember. It's a good idea to learn at least the first Keypad layout this way.

- Keyboard: shows and hides the Keyboard window (shortcut **Ctrl+Alt+B** *or* ⌥⌘B) – 📖 **1.3 Keyboard window**.

- Fretboard: shows and hides the Fretboard window (shortcut **Ctrl+Alt+E** *or* ⌥⌘E) – 📖 **1.8 Fretboard window**.

- Playback: shows and hides Playback window (shortcut **Ctrl+Alt+Y** *or* ⌥⌘Y).

- Mixer:shows and hides the Mixer (shortcut **Ctrl+Alt+M** *or* M) – 📖 **4.3 Mixer**.

- Ideas: shows and hides the Ideas window (shortcut **Ctrl+Alt+I** *or* ⌥⌘I) – 📖 **5.11 Ideas**.

- Parts: shows and hides the Parts window (shortcut **Ctrl+Alt+R** *or* ⌥⌘R) – 📖 **7.1 Working with parts**.

- Compare: shows and hides the Compare window (shortcut **Ctrl+Alt+C** *or* ⌥⌘C) – 📖 **5.22 Versions**.

- Video: shows and hides the Video window (shortcut **Ctrl+Alt+V** *or* ⌥⌘V) – 📖 **4.10 Video**.

- Properties: shows and hides the Properties window (shortcut **Ctrl+Alt+P** *or* ⌥⌘P). The Properties and Keypad windows disappear (by default) during playback, to keep the screen clear. 📖 **5.17 Properties**.

- Hide Tool Windows: if you are (say) adjusting settings on the Mixer and composing to video, the screen can become rather cluttered when lots of tool windows are open. Sibelius allows you to hide all your open tool windows simultaneously, then re-open the same set of windows later on. Use **Window ▸ Hide Tool Windows** or the keyboard shortcut **Ctrl+Alt+X** *or* ⌥⌘X.

Switch to Part/Full Score

When you are working on a score with parts, this options enables you to switch between the full score and a part. The part that will be shown depends on the selection you have made in the score prior to using **Switch to Part/Full Score**. Sibelius always tries to show the part most relevant to your selection, so if you select a note in (say) your 2nd Flute part, Sibelius will helpfully show you the 2nd Flute part. If you have not made a selection, or if the selection contains objects in more than one part, Sibelius will show the part most recently viewed instead. The menu will show **Switch to Full Score** when you are looking at a part, and **Switch to Part** when you have the full score open. You can also switch between score and parts using the shortcut **W**.

Next Part

Brings the next part in the currently open score into view, or you can use **Ctrl+Alt+Tab** *or* ⌥⌘~. If you are viewing the last part, Sibelius will show the full score.

Previous Part

Brings the previous part in the currently open score into view, or you can use **Ctrl+Shift+Alt+Tab** *or* ⇧⌥⌘~. If you are viewing the first part, Sibelius will show the full score.

For more information on working with parts, 🕮 **7.1 Working with parts**.

5.25 Worksheet Creator

🎬 **Worksheet Creator**.

Music teachers need a steady supply of teaching and learning material to support the curriculum they follow. The Worksheet Creator lets you choose from over 1700 ready-made worksheets, projects, exercises, repertoire pieces, posters, reference materials and other resources. These are carefully designed for the curricula of the USA, UK, Australia, New Zealand and Canada, and suitable for school students of all ages. Some of the materials (such as **Selected repertoire** and **Reference**) are also useful at college and university level.

You can produce both a worksheet for the student and a completed answer sheet to aid with marking. You can even generate worksheets with random questions that are different each time, so you'll never run out of materials to use. And it all takes you just a few seconds.

You can also add your own worksheets to the Worksheet Creator (in your own or your colleagues' copies of Sibelius) – 📖 **5.26 Adding your own worksheets**.

Using the Worksheet Creator

To get started, choose **File ▸ Worksheet Creator**. The following dialog appears:

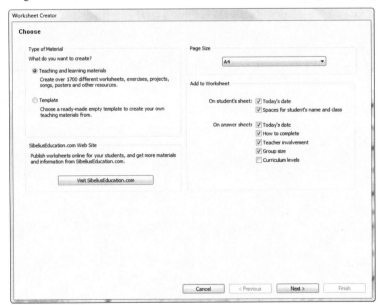

- Choose whether you want to create **Teaching and learning materials** or a **Template**. A template is a worksheet with no music in, which you can use as a basis for creating your own materials; see below.
- Extra worksheets, supplementary materials and much more are available at SibeliusEducation.com, which you can visit by clicking the **Visit SibeliusEducation Web Site** button shown in the dialog – 📖 **5.18 SibeliusEducation.com**

- Choose the page size of the worksheet you want to create: you can choose between **A4** and **Letter**
- The options under **Add to Worksheet** determine various extra things to print on the student worksheet and the teacher's answer sheet. On the student's sheet:
  - **Today's date** prints the date in the form **18 April, 2005**. (This option is available both for the student worksheet and for the teacher's answer sheet.)
  - **Spaces for student's name and class** prints lines in the top right-hand corner of the student worksheet for the student to write his or her name and class.
- On the teacher's sheet:
  - **How to complete** prints a reminder of whether a particular activity is designed to be completed on paper, at the computer, or by performing
  - **Teacher involvement** prints a reminder of whether the teacher needs to be involved in the completion of the activity, and whether the teacher needs access to Sibelius
  - **Group size** prints a reminder of whether the activity is designed to be completed by an individual, a small group, or a larger group
  - **Curriculum levels** prints details of the specific curriculum that an activity is targeted towards, where this information is available.

  If you plan to print anything from the **Resources, Reference, Selected repertoire** or **Posters, Flashcards and Games** sections, it's best to switch all of these options off.

Having chosen to create **Teaching and learning materials** and made your choices, click **Next** to narrow down the type of material you're looking for:

Because there is such a wide variety of material in the Worksheet Creator, you can choose to find only materials that meet certain criteria. For example, if you only want to find materials suitable for a group of students rather than individuals, choose **Materials for Small groups** and **Groups**

of any size, and click **Next**. If you only want to find worksheets that are to be filled in using Sibelius, choose **Can be completed At the computer** and click **Next**.

(The **Find by filename** option is useful if you have already printed out a particular worksheet and want to use it again. Each teacher's answer sheet contains the **Filename:** in the bottom right-hand corner of the first page. Type it here and click **Next** to go directly to that item so you can print it again.)

If this is the first time you have used this feature since installing Sibelius, it may take a minute or so for Sibelius to generate a list of available materials.

You're then shown the categories from which you can choose your material:

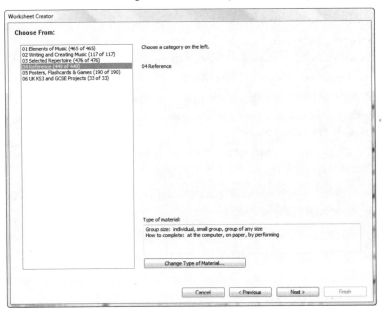

The materials are split into 6 main categories:

- **Elements of music** covers 14 core areas of music theory and musicianship, from pitch and rhythm to sight reading and ear training
- **Writing and creating music** covers notation, transposing, arranging, composing and improvising
- **Selected repertoire** has over 400 pieces for voice, piano and other instruments, including songs in 14 different languages and 50 Bach keyboard pieces, suitable for study, arranging, performance, and your own worksheet creation. There are also 45 poems for students to set to music.
- **Reference** contains a huge library of musical information, from over 80 scales and modes to ranges of different instruments
- **Posters, Flashcards & Games** has nearly 200 of these to help teach musical concepts. Topics range from notes and keys to dozens of pictures of instruments
- **UK KS3 & GCSE Projects** has UK-specific projects covering performing, listening and composing, with topics from African drumming to serialism!

For more details on the categories, see the **Categories** table below.

Each of the categories and sub-categories are numbered with a prefix, e.g. **16 Sight Reading**. This makes it easier to find your way around the large amount of supplied material, and also shows the pedagogical progression of materials within each category, moving from the simpler to the more advanced.

The numbers at the end of each category name, e.g. **(8 of 27)**, show how many of the total number of materials in the category match the selection criteria you have specified (shown near the bottom of the dialog.) The number zero, e.g. **(0 of 27)**, means there's no point choosing that category, as nothing within it matches. If you find that there are very few matching items and you require a wider choice, try changing your criteria by clicking the **Change Type of Material** button.

Choose the category you want to explore, and either double-click it in the list at the left-hand side of the dialog, or click **Next**. The same page of the dialog will appear again, this time showing you the sub-categories within your chosen category as well as the path you took to get there. If you want to return to the parent category of the sub-category you are in, just click **Previous**.

When you get to the final sub-category in a given category, you will be able to choose a specific worksheet or other material from a list:

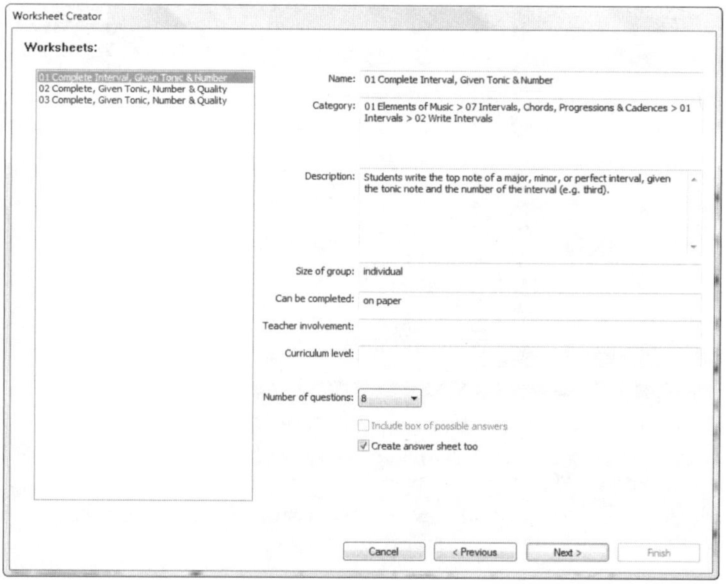

When you choose an item from the list, the right-hand side of the dialog gives information about it. The **Description** field gives details of what the students must do to complete the worksheet or activity.

There are three options at the bottom of this page that are enabled or disabled depending on the chosen material:

- **Number of questions** allows you to choose the number of questions to be included on the printed worksheet. This option is only available if the worksheet has a large number of questions available from which it will pick at random. You can re-use these worksheets, because even if you choose to include, say, 10 questions, if you come back and make this worksheet again in the future, Sibelius will choose another 10 at random (though there may be some overlap).

- **Include box of possible answers** is available if you choose a worksheet based around "matching" each question with a choice of answers

- **Create answer sheet too** creates an answer sheet for the teacher (with answers already filled in to save time when marking) together with the student sheet. This option is not available for materials such as posters, repertoire, etc. Note that many worksheets do not have single correct or incorrect answers, in which case the answer sheet will contain an example of a possible answer with the indication that answers may vary.

Having made your choices, click **Next** to see a preview:

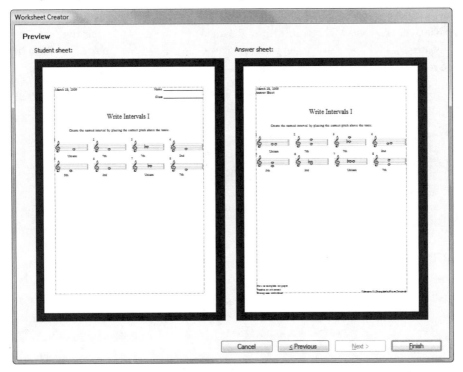

The student worksheet is shown on the left. If an answer sheet is available and you have chosen to create one, it is shown on the right.

If the worksheet isn't quite what you want, click **Previous** one or more times to go back and revise your choices. Otherwise, click **Finish** to create the worksheet.

If you chose to create both a student worksheet and an answer sheet, Sibelius will create two scores. You can now print them out, save them for later, or edit them to produce your own customized worksheet.

Rhythm levels (RL1-4) and scale levels (SL1-4)

Various worksheets are classified by rhythm level and scale level, depending on the complexity of the rhythms and scales they contain. In summary, the rhythm levels are:

- RL1: 2/4 and 3/4 time signatures, eighth notes (quavers) to dotted half note (minim), simple rests
- RL2: also 4/4, whole note (semibreve), 16th notes (semiquavers), more rests
- RL3: also 6/8, C (common time), dotted notes, simple 6/8 rhythms, syncopation, Scotch snap, more dotted rests
- RL4: all other time signatures, triplets, complex 6/8 rhythms

The scale levels are:

- SL1: major, natural (aeolian) minor, major pentatonic, minor pentatonic
- SL2: also chromatic, ionian hexatonic (i.e. pieces using just the first 6 notes of major scale)
- SL3: also harmonic minor, melodic minor, dorian, dorian hexatonic
- SL4: also all other church modes/jazz scales, Blues scale, whole tone scale

Some of the scale terminology is provided for your own pedagogical interest rather than in order to teach the terms to students. Complete details of all the levels are on www.sibeliuseducation.com (or choose Help ▸ SibeliusEducation.com).

Templates

If you want to create a blank template on which to base your own materials, then on the first page of the File ▸ Worksheet Creator dialog, choose the Template option and click Next. You are shown the available templates, with a preview of each:

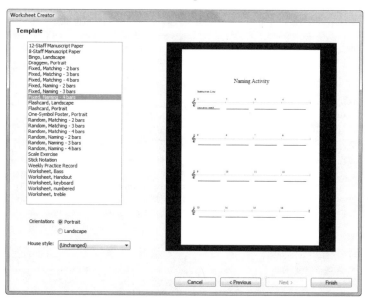

Choose the template you want to create, and click Finish. A score will be created that you can modify or add music to create your own worksheet. If you're feeling ambitious, you can add your own worksheets to the Worksheet Creator for future re-use (particularly if you want to generate random questions) – 📖 **5.26 Adding your own worksheets**.

Categories

Main category	Contains	Description
01 Elements of Music	01 Notes & Rests 02 Dynamics 03 Timbre & Tone Color 04 Meter & Tempo 05 Rhythm 06 Scales & Key Signatures 07 Intervals, Chords, Progressions & Cadences 08 Score Analysis, 09 Conducting 10 Dictation/Transcription, 11 Sight Reading 12 Ear Training 13 Auditory Discrimination 14 Aural Recall	Activities arranged in learning sequences to cover the core areas of music. Introduces the language and terminology of music, helps develop basic musicianship, introduces aspects of theory, and teaches analysis of tonality, form and structure, texture, and genre.
02 Writing and Creating Music	01 Notation 02 Adapting, Transposing & Arranging 03 Composing 04 Improvising	Activities leading to the acquisition of basic notation skills and a wide range of creative exploration, including work with sounds, rhythms, melodies, accompaniments, textures, lyrics, and orchestration.
03 Selected Repertoire	01 Bach Piano Repertoire 02 Other Piano Repertoire 03 Instrumental Repertoire 04 Songs for Teaching 05 Rounds and Canons Collection 06 Poetry for Lyrics 07 Texts for Incidental Music 08 Rhythm Collection	Nearly 500 pieces of music and poetry, many used in worksheets, and all available for extensions, other classroom use, and your own worksheet creation. Includes nearly 100 pieces of keyboard repertoire including 50 by Bach and a sampling from other masters; over 150 songs, including nearly 50 rounds and canons and works in 13 world languages; and 45 poems.
04 Reference	01 Encyclopedia of Scales & Modes 02 Chord Library 03 Instrumental & Vocal Ranges 04 US & British Music Terms Compared 05 Keyboard Handouts	A handy library of musical information, including over 80 scales and modes and nearly 150 chords with their chord symbols. To be used for research, exploration, and incorporation into creative activities.
05 Posters, Flashcards & Games	01 Posters 02 Flashcards 03 Games	Nearly 200 posters, flashcards and games to help teach and review musical concepts. Topics include notes, rests, scales, key signatures, circle of fifths, symbols, terminology, stick notation, and nearly 100 pictures of instruments that can both be used to decorate the classroom, and in preparing your own learning materials.
06 UK KS3 & GCSE Projects	01 African Drumming KS3 02 Blues (12-bar) KS3 03 Composing to Create a Specific Mood KS3/GCSE 04 Pop Songs (Reggae) KS3/GCSE 05 Pop Songs (Dance Grooves) GCSE 06 Serialism GCSE 07 Blues (Arranging) GCSE	Seven UK-specific projects supporting the three main areas of study – performing, composing and listening – for Key Stage 3 and GCSE, with comprehensive teacher's notes and ideas for extension.

5.26 Adding your own worksheets

📖 **5.25 Worksheet Creator**.

Adding your own worksheets

Sibelius allows you to create your own "intelligent" teaching materials and add them too the Worksheet Creator (in your own copy of Sibelius, of your colleagues'). You can easily create scores that contain both questions and answers, and create files that produce random questions, allowing them to be re-used over and over again.

Page size and margins

In order to produce good-looking materials, you should bear in mind a few points when laying out and formatting your score.

You could base your worksheet on a ready-made template if one is suitable (📖 **5.25 Worksheet Creator**); if so, choose A4 paper size rather than **Letter**. (Once the worksheet is added to the Worksheet Creator you will be able to create it at Letter size.) Alternatively, if you create a worksheet from scratch, then in **Layout ▸ Document Setup**:

- Use A4 as the page size
- Use top and bottom margins of 24mm and left and right margins of 15mm. These margins compensate for the differences in dimensions between A4 and Letter.
- Use 12mm as the top staff margin and 24mm as the bottom staff margin. These staff margins allow room for the text created by the Worksheet Creator at the top and bottom of the page.

Answer sheet

If you want to produce an answer sheet for your worksheet, you need to use voices consistently in the score so that Sibelius can delete one or more voice(s) to remove the answers from the student's sheet. Use different voices for items you want to appear only on the student's sheet, for items on the answer sheet, and for those on both sheets. So, for example, imagine a worksheet in which the student has to write the name of a given interval below the staff, and you want to print an answer sheet too.

- Put the each interval in (say) voice 1. The notes will be included in both the student sheet and the teacher's answer sheet. It's usually best to use voices 1 and 2 (the normal voices for writing music) for anything meant for both sheets.
- Create the answer using (say) **Lyrics line 1** text, in voice 4. You can specify later that voice 4 items will only appear on the teacher's sheet.
- You may also want to include a line under each interval for the student to write his or her answer on. Create horizontal lines (say) in voice 3. Again, you can specify later that this voice will only appear on the student's sheet.

Power tools

Random and fixed questions

There are two basic kinds of worksheet: those with *random questions* and those with *fixed questions*. Those with fixed questions are easier to produce, because you can lay them out exactly as you want them to appear when they come out of the Worksheet Creator, but for both kinds of worksheet you need to use voices carefully.

If you plan to produce a worksheet with random questions, you shouldn't add any additional text to the score, and you don't need to spend so long adjusting the layout, because the Worksheet Creator can do it all for you. So don't put a title at the top of the page, or number the questions, or add an instruction for the student.

If you plan to produce a worksheet with fixed questions, you should now add various other bits of text to your page, possibly including:

* A title – in our imagined example you may type "Name Intervals" in Title text
* Some text to give the student instructions – e.g. you might you create some Technique text above the first bar of the score that says "Write the name for the given interval in the space provided."
* Question numbers – e.g. you may want text above every bar with the question number. You can do this quickly using **Plug-ins ▸ Text ▸ Number Bars**.

You will probably want to create each of these text objects in voice 1, so that they appear in both the student and the answer worksheets.

For both fixed and random worksheets, you may also need to make some further layout adjustments. For example, you should ensure there's plenty of room above the top staff on the page so that the Worksheet Creator has enough room to add the date and the spaces for the student to write his or her name and class. You may also want to make gaps between each question, which you can do by selecting a bar and typing (say) **4** into **Gap before bar** on the **Bars** panel of the **Properties** window. You may even want to enforce a particular number of bars per system, using auto system breaks (from **Layout ▸ Auto Breaks**).

Once you've added text and adjusted the layout, you're ready to add your worksheet to the Worksheet Creator.

Using ideas in worksheets

Sibelius's Ideas feature can be a powerful tool for producing exercises and worksheets for your students – 📖 **5.11 Ideas** for an introduction.

It's possible to use ideas from Sibelius's built-in library of more than 1500 ideas, or indeed any ideas of your own creation, in any score. In particular, you can save a certain set of ideas in a score, and then prevent students from using any ideas other than those you have saved in the score. This is useful if you want your students to build a composition using ideas you have carefully chosen. For more details, see **Limiting access to the library** on page 409.

For more general information about how you might use ideas in your teaching, see **Using ideas in your teaching** on page 408.

Adding to the Worksheet Creator

Once you have created a worksheet and you want to add it to the Worksheet Creator, choose **File ▸ Add to Worksheet Creator**:

- First, choose the type of material you're adding. To add a template, simply choose **Template** and click **OK**. Otherwise, choose **Teaching and learning materials**.

- Skip over to the right-hand side of the dialog and set **Random questions** or **Fixed questions** as appropriate. This affects which fields are available in the rest of the dialog.

- **Name (in dialog)** is the name that will appear in the Worksheet Creator. You should try to keep this name as short as possible.

- **Title (in score)** is what Sibelius will create in the score as its title if you choose **Random questions**. (If you choose **Fixed questions**, you should put the title in the score yourself before adding it.)

- **Description (for teacher)** is the text that will appear in the Worksheet Creator to describe the worksheet

- **Instructions (for student)** is what Sibelius will create above the first question in the student worksheet if you choose **Random questions**. (If you choose **Fixed questions**, you should create the instructions for the student in the worksheet yourself before adding it.)

- **Curriculum level** should contain information about the specific curriculum your worksheet is targeted towards, if applicable

- Make a selection under **Can be completed** to specify the way (or ways) in which you intend the worksheet to be completed

- Choose the level of **Teacher involvement** as appropriate

- Specify the **Size of group** for which the worksheet is intended

- The **Bars per question** option is only available if you choose **Random questions**. This option tells Sibelius how many bars each question occupies: it's very important that this option is set correctly.

- The **Questions per system** option tells Sibelius how best to lay out your worksheet. If your questions are 1, 2 or 4 bars long, you can leave this option set to **Default**. Otherwise, you should set this option to tell Sibelius how many questions it should allow on a system before it inserts a system break.

- **Voices shown in student sheet** specifies which voices Sibelius should leave in the student worksheet. In our imagined example above, you would set this to **1** and **3**.
- **Answer sheet** determines whether or not you want Sibelius to offer the choice of making an answer sheet for your worksheet. If you switch it on, you also need to specify the **Voices shown in answer sheet**. In our example above, you would set this to **1** and **4**.
- Finally, you choose the place in the Worksheet Creator you want to put the worksheet. Use the **Choose** and **Back** buttons to traverse the categories. When you find the correct spot, click **OK** to add your worksheet.

Edit Worksheets

If you need to create a new category or want to modify a worksheet you have previously added, you use the **Edit Worksheets** dialog, which is accessed by clicking the **Edit** button in the **Add to Worksheet Creator** dialog, or by choosing **File ▸ Edit Worksheets**:

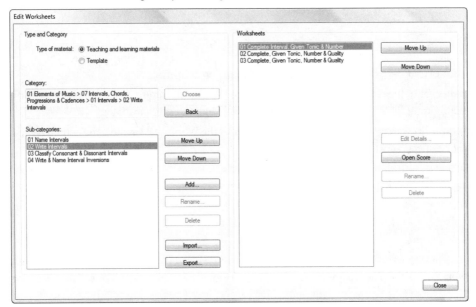

The options on the left of the dialog deal with the categories and sub-categories rather than the worksheet files themselves:

- Choose **Teaching and learning materials** or **Template** at the top of the dialog to choose between the two types of content
- **Choose** and **Back** traverse through the list of categories on the left of the dialog, as in the **Add to Worksheet Creator** dialog
- **Move Up** and **Move Down** move the selected sub-category up and down in the order within the current category
- **Add** adds a new sub-category: click the button to choose its name
- **Rename** renames the selected sub-category

- **Delete** removes the selected sub-category, and any further sub-categories and worksheets it contains, permanently. Be careful with this option!
- **Import** imports a category of material obtained from elsewhere, e.g. downloaded from SibeliusEducation.com (📖 **5.18 SibeliusEducation.com**).
- **Export** exports the selected category and its sub-categories and worksheets to a new folder inside your **Scores** folder, so that you can share it with your colleagues, who can then **Import** it.

The options on the right-hand side of the dialog are concerned with the worksheets and templates themselves. (The list will only contain items when you reach a sub-category that contains worksheets.)

- **Move Up** and **Move Down** move the selected sub-category up and down in the order within the current category
- **Edit Details** opens the **Edit Activity Details** dialog, so that you can make changes to the settings you chose when you exported the worksheet. The options in **Edit Worksheet Details** are the same as in the **Add to Worksheet Creator** dialog, except that you cannot change from a worksheet to a template, or vice versa – see **Adding to the Worksheet Creator** above.
- **Open Score** opens the chosen worksheet score so that you can make changes to the musical material in it or the answers, etc. When you've finished editing the score, simply save and close it – no need to add it to the Worksheet Creator again.
- **Rename** renames the selected worksheet, changing the **Name (in dialog)** field.
- **Delete** removes the selected worksheet permanently. Be careful with this option!

When you've finished making changes, click the **Close** button.

Power tools

6. Plug-ins

6.1 Working with plug-ins

Sibelius supports plug-ins, which are extra features created using a built-in programming language called ManuScript. A number of very useful plug-ins are provided in the **Plug-ins** menu, organized into further submenus by category, and described in the following topics. You can also assign keyboard shortcuts to plug-ins that you use frequently – 📖 **5.12 Menus and shortcuts**.

You can stop a plug-in while it's running: just click the **Stop plug-in** button that appears in the top left-hand corner of the screen. You can also undo whatever a plug-in does to your score in the usual way, by choosing **Edit ▸ Undo** (shortcut **Ctrl+Z** *or* ⌘**Z**) after running it.

Additional plug-ins

New plug-ins are constantly being developed for Sibelius. Extra free ones are added to the Sibelius web site from time to time – choose **Help ▸ Check For Updates** or go to **www.sibelius.com/download/plugins** to see what's available.

If you write a plug-in that you think would be useful to other Sibelius users, please email details to **sibhelpUK@sibelius.com** and we'll consider including it on our web site or with future versions of Sibelius. We pay good money for good plug-ins!

Alternatively, if you have an idea for a plug-in but don't feel up to writing it yourself, let us know.

Installing new plug-ins

To install a new plug-in, copy the plug-in file (with extension **.plg**) to the **Plugins** folder in your application data folder. The plug-in will automatically be loaded the next time you run Sibelius. For further help with installing plug-ins, go to **www.sibelius.com/download/plugins**.

Edit plug-ins

Plug-ins ▸ Edit Plug-ins lets you unload, reload, delete, edit and create new plug-ins.

Select a plug-in from the list and click the appropriate button:

- Unloading a plug-in removes it from Sibelius; this doesn't delete it from your hard disk, but does save memory. Unloaded plug-ins are described as such in the list.
- Reloading a plug-in gets it back again after unloading it
- Deleting a plug-in removes it from your hard disk
- New and Edit are for creating your own plug-ins.

Creating your own plug-ins

This requires a knowledge of the ManuScript language, which is straightforward enough to learn but beyond the scope of this Reference. Choose **Help ▸ Documentation ▸ ManuScript Language Reference** to read all about it.

Plug-ins ▸ Show Plug-in Trace Window shows a trace window, which is useful for debugging plug-ins you are developing yourself. See the ManuScript documentation for further details.

6.2 Accidentals plug-ins

Add Accidentals to All Notes

Forces accidentals to be placed before every note, even naturals, or sharps/flats that are already in the key signature, or even if the note is tied to the preceding note. This notation is sometimes used in atonal scores, or other scores that don't use key signatures. To use the plug-in, select the passage in which you want to add accidentals, and choose **Plug-ins ▸ Add Accidentals to All Notes**. It's a good idea to do **Layout ▸ Reset Note Spacing** afterwards to make room for all the newly-added accidentals.

Quarter-tone accidentals are not currently handled by this plug-in: these will be labeled with the text Q, which you can search for using **Edit ▸ Find** to ensure that all notes on the same line or space later in the bar are preceded with the appropriate symbol.

Plug-in written by Peter Hayter.

Add Accidentals to All Sharp and Flat Notes

This plug-in adds accidentals to all sharp and flat notes, even if they occur earlier in the same bar, but not if they already exist in the key signature.

Plug-in written by Stefan Behrisch (www.werklabor.de).

Add Ficta Above Note

In early music, accidentals are often implied but are not explicitly written in the original manuscript because of the performance practices of the day. Modern editions often show these so-called *musica ficta* by placing small editorial accidentals above the notes in question. This plug-in inserts accidental symbols above the note and also the pitch bend MIDI messages required to make the notes sharper or flatter as appropriate.

To use the plug-in, select the note(s) to which you want to add the ficta and choose **Plug-ins ▸ Accidentals ▸ Add Ficta Above Note**. A dialog appears: choose whether you want to add sharps, flats or natural signs, and then click **OK**.

The plug-in hides the note's regular accidental, then adds an appropriate symbol above the note.

Plug-in written by Chris May.

Respell Flats as Sharps/Respell Sharps as Flats

Alters the spelling of accidentals in the selected passage. Simply select a passage, choose **Plug-ins ▸ Accidentals ▸ Respell Flats as Sharps** or **Plug-ins ▸ Accidentals ▸ Respell Sharps as Flats**, and all flats/sharps in the selected passage will be respelled. Special noteheads and Live Playback data will be lost when using this plug-in.

Simplify Accidentals

This plug-in respells all accidentals in a score or selected passage according to the prevailing key signatures; it is very useful for removing stray accidentals that may be left over after certain editing operations (e.g. transposing, or adding a key signature to existing music). To use the plug-in, select a passage (or the whole score) and choose **Plug-ins ▸ Accidentals ▸ Simplify Accidentals**.

Plug-in written by Peter Hayter.

6.3 Analysis plug-ins

Add Schenkerian Scale Degrees

This plug-in analyses your score and adds Schenkerian scale degree notation above or below the staff.

To use the plug-in, select a passage in a single key (i.e. containing no key signature changes), or your whole score (if it is in a single key), and choose **Plug-ins ▸ Analysis ▸ Add Schenkerian Scale Degrees**. A simple dialog appears:

- **Stack vertically** determines whether the ^ or v symbols should be drawn above the scale degree (i.e. this option switched on), or to the left of the scale degree (i.e. switched off)
- **Voice** allows you to choose which voice on the staff to analyze
- **Text style** determines the appearance (e.g. boxed, italic, etc.) of the scale degrees and where they will be written: all text styles except Figured bass place them above the staff, Figured bass places them below
- **Add to selected passage/whole score** allows you to define the scope of the plug-in's operation; only choose the whole score option if your score does not contain any changes of key.

When you click **OK**, scale degrees are added to your score with the chosen settings.

Plug-in written by John Kennedy.

Compare Staves

Compares any two staves in the same file and highlights the differences between them. To use this plug-in, select a passage in any two staves in your score (use **Ctrl+click** *or* ⌘-click to select two non-adjacent staves if you like), then choose **Plug-ins ▸ Analysis ▸ Compare Staves**. A dialog appears:

- **Notes and rests**: looks for differences in note value, pitch, voice, cue-size, hidden, etc.
- **Lines**: looks for differences in line types, length, etc. Naturally this only works for staff lines, since system lines apply to all staves anyway.
- **Clefs**: looks for different clefs in the two staves.
- **Text**: looks for differences in text objects; it does not spot differences in font or point size between two staves, but it will spot differences in the words themselves, which makes this plug-in very useful for (say) checking lyrics on two vocal staves that share the same rhythms. As with lines, this only works for staff text, not system text.
- **Highlight differences in**: allows you to choose whether you want the highlights to be drawn in the **Top staff**, the **Bottom staff**, or both (by switching on both options).
- **Selected passage/Whole score**: choose whether to compare staves just in the selected passage, or throughout the whole score.

When you click **OK**, the plug-in will examine your score; at the end of the process, a message box will pop up, telling you how many differences were found.

If you want to remove the highlights created by this plug-in at a later stage, see **Remove All Highlights** on page 507.

Plug-in written by Neil Sands.

Find Motive

Examines your score for motives (motifs) that match either the intervallic relationships or the rhythms (or both) of a selected passage, and marks each match with a highlight (📖 **5.10 Highlight**). This is very useful for analysis, such as finding all the occurrences of a fugal subject, or examining how a particular rhythmic pattern is used in a piece.

To use this plug-in, select the motive that you want to match, and choose **Plug-ins ▸ Analysis ▸ Find Motive**. A dialog appears allowing you to set a few options:

- **Match rhythm**: switch this on if you want to find rhythmic matches; you can specify how much variation from the specified motive you will allow (a value of 0% means that you will only accept exact matches).

- **Match pitches**: switch this on if you want to find intervallic matches. Again, you can specify how much variation you will allow; if this is set to 0%, only exact transpositions of the motive are matched, but diatonic or other inexact transpositions are not; so (for example) in a fugue the plug-in would find real answers but not tonal ones. Increase the allowed variation setting from 0% to find inexact transpositions.

- **Original motive is in voice** *x*: allows you to choose in which voice the plug-in should find the original motive. (This option only determines where the example motive to be matched with is found – the plug-in will always match all voices throughout the rest of the score.)

Switch on both **Match rhythm** and **Match pitches** to find only occurrences that match both.

Click **OK** and a progress bar appears, telling you which staff the plug-in is examining. After a few moments, the plug-in will tell you how many matches it found, each of which will be highlighted in yellow.

Plug-in written by James Larcombe and Byron Hawkins.

Find Range

Calculates the range (i.e. lowest and highest notes), average pitch and the most frequently occurring pitches, all expressed in concert pitch, of a selected passage. This is useful if, for example, you are writing vocal music and want to know what kinds of demands you are placing on your singers.

To run this plug-in, select a passage (or triple-click a staff to calculate its range throughout the score) and choose **Plug-ins ▸ Analysis ▸ Find Range**.

6.4 Batch Processing plug-ins

Calculate Statistics

Creates a report listing how many bars, staves, pages and other objects are in the current score or all the scores in a given folder; this is useful for copyists to work out rates for copying jobs.

To run the plug-in on a single score, choose Plug-ins ▸ Batch Processing ▸ Calculate Statistics and then click Current Score in the dialog that appears. If you want to calculate statistics for, say, one movement of a multi-movement piece within the same score, select the bars in question before you run the plug-in, then click Current Score.

To run the plug-in on a folder, choose Plug-ins ▸ Batch Processing ▸ Calculate Statistics, then click Process Folder. Choose the folder for which you want to calculate statistics, and when you click OK, Sibelius processes each of the files in turn (no changes are made to the scores themselves).

When the current score or all the scores in the folder have been processed, Sibelius shows a dialog listing how many of each kind of object have been found. Click Write Text File to save the results as a text file in the chosen folder or the same folder as the current score.

Plug-in written by Bob Zawalich.

Convert Folder of MIDI Files

Batch converts all MIDI files in a specified folder, re-saving them with the same filenames but a .sib extension. These files should be Standard MIDI Files (with the file extension .mid on Windows) rather than in other sequencer formats – 🕮 **9.5 Opening MIDI files**.

Convert Folder of MusicXML Files

Batch converts all MusicXML files in a specified folder, re-saving them with the same filenames but a .sib extension.

To use the plug-in, choose Plug-ins ▸ Batch Processing ▸ Convert Folder of MusicXML Files, and choose the folder you want to convert. Sibelius converts each MusicXML file it finds in the specified folder, saving each one as a Sibelius score under the same filename as the original MusicXML file.

For more information about MusicXML files, 🕮 **9.6 Opening MusicXML files**.

Convert Folder of Scores to Earlier Version

Exports all scores in a specified folder as Sibelius 5, Sibelius 4, Sibelius 3 or Sibelius 2 scores – 🕮 **9.12 Exporting to previous versions**.

To use the plug-in, choose Plug-ins ▸ Batch Processing ▸ Convert Folder of Scores to Earlier Version, and choose the folder you want to convert. A simple dialog appears, in which you can specify the destination folder for the exported files, which version of Sibelius to export to, and how to alter the filenames to avoid overwriting the original files. Click OK to confirm your choices.

Plug-in written by Bob Zawalich.

Plug-ins

Convert Folder of Scores to Graphics

Converts a folder of scores into graphics files of a specified format – 📖 **9.8 Exporting graphics**.

To use the plug-in, choose Plug-ins ▸ Batch Processing ▸ Convert Folder of Scores to Graphics, and choose the folder you want to convert. You will be prompted to choose the graphics format; you can also choose whether or not to use the default settings. Generally you can leave Use default settings switched on and simply click OK to save all the files; if it is switched off, you will be prompted to choose the settings for each file in the folder.

Convert Folder of Scores to MIDI

Batch converts all scores in a folder into standard MIDI files, using the same filenames but with a .mid extension – 📖 **9.9 Exporting MIDI files**.

Convert Folder of Scores to Web Pages

Saves Scorch web pages for all the files in a folder, and also creates an index page with links to all of the individual scores, ready for uploading to your web site – 📖 **9.11 Exporting Scorch web pages**.

Choose Plug-ins ▸ Batch Processing ▸ Convert Folder of Scores to Web Pages. A dialog appears:

- Choose the source folder by clicking the Browse button under Convert all scores within; to include scores in subfolders, make sure Also convert scores in sub-folders is switched on
- Choose the destination folder by clicking the Browse button under Put web pages in, or switch on the Use same folder option to save the web pages into the same folder as the original scores
- Switch off Create index page if you don't want the plug-in to generate an index page with links to all of the other Scorch web pages; we recommend you leave this option switched on
- Choose the Style of web pages from the list provided; these templates are built in to the plug-in and cannot be changed, even by editing the templates in Sibelius's Manuscript paper folder
- Size of score in web page sets the width of the actual Scorch window in each of the web pages; the default value of 720 pixels is fine for most purposes.
- If you would like people to be able to print and save your score from your web page, choose Allow Printing and Saving.

Click OK, and Sibelius will process each file in turn. When the plug-in has finished, you will have a complete folder of files, ready for uploading to your web site or intranet!

Plug-in written by Neil Sands.

Export Each Staff as Audio

Exports each staff in the score as a separate audio file, which is useful if you want to combine them together in a Digital Audio Workstation (DAW), such as Pro Tools.

First, make sure that your copy of Sibelius is set to play back using virtual instruments, e.g. using the included Sibelius Sounds Essentials sample library – see **Setting up Sibelius Sounds Essentials** on page 276.

If you would like to export only some of the staves in your score, select those staves before running the plug-in; otherwise, to export all staves, make sure nothing is selected. Then choose Plug-ins ▸ Batch Processing ▸ Export Each Staff as Audio. A simple dialog appears, in which you can choose whether to **Export multi-staff instruments together** (which exports e.g. both the right- and left-hand staves of a piano together) or **Export each staff separately** (which exports them as separate audio files).

You can also choose the format of filename to be used, and the location where the audio files should be saved; by default they will be saved alongside the score. Click **OK**, and a progress bar appears as each audio file is exported; this can take a little while, so be patient.

Plug-in written by Bob Zawalich.

Import House Style into Folder of Scores

Applies a specified house style file to all the files in a selected folder.

To use the plug-in, choose **Plug-ins ▸ Batch Processing ▸ Import House Style into Folder of Scores**. You are prompted to select the house style library file (**.lib**) you want to apply, then you are prompted to select the folder of files to which the house style should be applied.

A number of predefined house styles are supplied in the **House Styles** folder within your Sibelius program folder – 📖 **8.8 House Style™**.

Plug-in written by Michael Kilpatrick.

Print Multiple Copies

Allows you to print multiple copies of a selection of scores in a folder (plus any subfolders that also contain scores, if desired). To print multiple copies of parts, it's easier to use the **Copies** and **Print Part(s)** features on the Parts window (📖 **7.1 Working with parts**).

To use the plug-in, close all open scores, then choose **Plug-ins ▸ Batch Processing ▸ Print Multiple Copies**. You are asked to choose a folder. Make your selection, and a dialog appears:

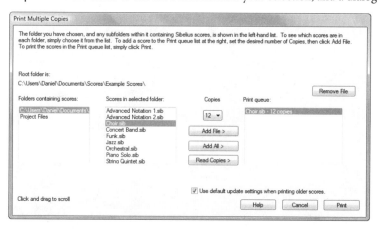

- Choose the folder from the **Folders containing scores** list at the left
- Select from the **Scores in selected folder** list, set the **Copies** drop-down to the number of copies of this file you want to print, and click **Add File**. Click **Add All** to add all of the scores in the chosen folder to the **Print queue** list, with the chosen number of copies.
- Build up the list in the **Print queue** at the right by adding more files, and when you're ready to print, click **Print**.

The plug-in will print all the scores in the queue the specified number of times with the default options (it's not possible to set options such as booklet printing etc. from the plug-in).

The **Read Copies** button opens each file in the chosen folder and looks for the text ~copies=n attached to any of the first five bars in the first five staves, where n is the number of copies that should be printed, and adds them to the **Print queue** list with the appropriate number of copies set. If a file contains more than one text object of the form ~copies=n it is assumed to be a score before part extraction and so is not added.

Plug-in written by Peter Hayter and Gunnar Hellquist.

6.5 Chord Symbols plug-ins

Add Capo Chord Symbols

Adds one or more sets of extra chord symbols, typically above the existing chord symbols, corresponding to the chords that a guitarist would need to play with a capo on a particular fret. This is useful for players who may find it difficult to play in the written key; the guitarist can instead put a capo on his guitar and then play easier chords.

To run the plug-in, select the staff that contains the existing chord symbols, and choose **Plug-ins▸ Chord Symbols▸ Add Capo Chord Symbols**. A dialog appears allowing you to choose at which fret the capo is placed, and helpfully shows you which key that corresponds to. You can choose whether or not the new chord symbols should be bold, italic or shown in parentheses, and also choose another text style if you wish (though the default of **Chord symbols** is normally appropriate).

The plug-in has its own **Help** dialog, if you need further assistance.

Plug-in written by Bob Zawalich.

Add Chord Symbols

Analyzes the harmony of your music and automatically adds appropriate chord symbols above the selected staves. You can choose to analyze any or all of the staves in your score, and choose where the chord symbols will be created.

To run the plug-in, select the staves in which the harmony occurs (e.g. the two piano staves) and then choose **Plug-ins▸ Chord Symbols▸ Add Chord Symbols**. A dialog appears:

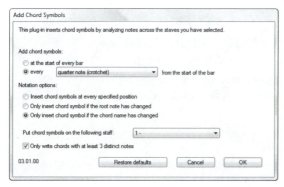

You can generally leave these settings at their defaults – simply click **OK** to add chord symbols to your score.

If you wish to change the settings, there are many options for controlling the results, as follows:

- **Add chord symbols: at the start of every bar** or **every** *note value* **from the start of the bar** (where *note value* is selected from a drop-down list): this option determines how often the plug-in will add chord symbols to the score.

- **Notation options**: these options control whether to write a chord symbol at every position specified by **Add chord symbols** (at the top of the dialog) or whether to omit redundant ones:

- ○ **Insert chord symbol at every specified position** always writes a chord symbol, regardless of whether or not the actual chord has changed.

- ○ **Only insert chord symbol if the root note has changed**: with this option selected, the plug-in will not create a new chord symbol if the root has not changed since the last chord symbol. The chord itself could change, e.g. C to C⁷, but the chord symbol would still be omitted with this option selected.

- ○ **Only insert chord symbol if the chord name has changed**: with this option selected, the plug-in will only omit a chord symbol if it would be identical to the last chord symbol created, e.g. the second of two consecutive C chords *would not* be created, but a C⁷ following a C chord *would* be written.

- ○ **Put chord symbols on the following staff**: this option determines the name of the staff in the score where the chord symbols will be created. If the plug-in seems to add no chord symbols, it may be that you have chosen to create the chord symbols onto a hidden staff.

Plug-in written by James Larcombe and Bob Zawalich.

Chord Symbols As Fractions

Converts chord symbols that have bass notes in "slash" format (e.g. Fmaj7/G) into fractional format, where the chord name, an underline, and the bass note are stacked vertically, like a fraction ($\frac{\text{Fmaj}^7}{\text{G}}$). To use this plug-in, select the music containing the chords whose format you want to change and choose **Plug-ins ▸ Chord Symbols ▸ Chord Symbols As Fractions**. You can choose whether the plug-in should split each element individually, creating three individual text objects for each chord (**Use Separate Underscore Character**), or whether it should create only two objects, the uppermost of which will be underlined (**Use Font Underlining**). To adjust the gap between the chords, click the **Engraving Rules** button. Click **OK** to start the conversion.

The plug-in modifies the existing chord symbols such that they become legacy chord symbols (see **Legacy chord symbol input** on page 111), which means that they are not taken into account when using **Layout ▸ Reset Note Spacing**, do not respond to changes made on the **Chord Symbols** page of **House Style ▸ Engraving Rules** or to the options in the **Edit ▸ Chord Symbol** submenu.

Plug-in written by Bob Zawalich.

Realize Chord Symbols

Creates simple guitar or piano accompaniments in a variety of styles, based on the chord symbols and/or chord diagrams in your score. Choose **Plug-ins ▸ Chord Symbols ▸ Realize Chord Symbols**. If you don't have a passage selected, you're asked if you want the operation to apply to the whole score. The following dialog then appears:

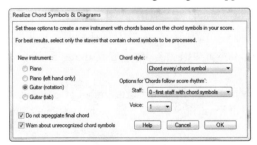

- You can choose between three different instruments to add: Piano, which adds two staves to your score and splits the chords across the two staves; Piano (left-hand only), which writes an accompaniment on a single staff, suitable for use if the melody you're realizing is in the right-hand staff; Guitar (notation), which adds a single notation staff to your score; and Guitar (tab), which adds a tab staff using standard 6-string guitar tuning (although you can change this later if you want). For other instruments, you should select one of these options and then copy the music across to your desired instrument after running the plug-in.

- The Chord style menu lets you control how the chords are realized: Chord every chord symbol creates a new chord every time the chord changes; Chord every beat creates a new chord in every beat (regardless of how often the chord changes); Chords follow score rhythm allows you to realize the chords in the same rhythm as one of the existing staves in your score; 8th note Alberti creates an Alberti-style pattern using eighth notes (quavers); 16th note Alberti creates the same kind of pattern using 16th notes (semiquavers); 8th note arpeggios creates rising arpeggio patterns in eighth notes, and 16th note arpeggios creates rising arpeggios using 16th notes.

The results you would get for each of the six options on a guitar notation staff are shown below:

- Options for 'Chords follow score rhythm' allow you to choose which staff (and which voice on that staff) to use as the basis of the rhythm for the Chords follow score rhythm chord style

- If you choose any of the Alberti or arpeggio chord styles, you may not want the final chord of the song to be arpeggiated; if so, ensure Do not arpeggiate final chord is switched on

- Warn about unrecognized chord symbols pops up a message box if the plug-in encounters a chord symbol that it doesn't know how to interpret.

Click OK, and a progress bar appears for a moment as the chords are written into your score. The plug-in creates a new instrument in which to write its realization, and you may find that it overlaps your chord symbols or chord diagrams. Use Layout ▸ Optimize Staff Spacing (see page 600) to correct this.

Plug-ins

6. Plug-ins

You can use this plug-in more than once in the same score to build up different layers of accompaniment – for example, you might want to add a piano playing block chords, and a guitar playing in fingerpicked style. To do this, just run the plug-in again, and it will create a new instrument each time you run the plug-in. If you don't like the results, you can always delete the newly-added staves using the **Create ▸ Instruments** dialog.

Plug-in written by Bob Zawalich.

6.6 Composing Tools plug-ins

12-Tone Matrix

Generates a 12-tone matrix from a specified tone row (note row) that can either be entered manually into the plug-in, or taken from a selection made in the current score. Choose **Plug-ins ▸ Composing Tools ▸ 12-Tone Matrix**. The following dialog will appear:

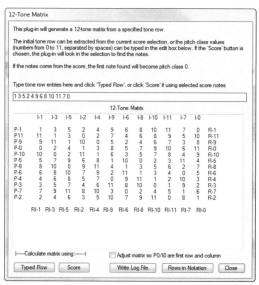

To enter the row manually, type the pitch classes using the numbers **0** to **11**, separated by spaces, into the field at the top, then click **Typed Row** (you can think of the numbers **0** to **11** representing the notes **C** to **B** respectively). To read the row from the score, just click **Score**.

When **Adjust matrix so P0/I0 are first row and column** is on, the plug-in will transpose the row so that the first note of the row is pitch class **0**. This will have no effect when reading the row from a score.

The table will be filled to show you all the possible variants of the row. The first row, when read from left to right, shows the prime tone row; reading it from right to left shows the retrograde. The first column, when read from top to bottom, shows the row's inversion; reading it from bottom to top shows the retrograde-inversion. Subsequent columns and rows show the same information using all the possible rotation permutations.

The plug-in can also notate all the rows it has generated in notation. To do this, click the **Rows in Notation** button.

Plug-in written by Bob Zawalich.

Add Drum Pattern

Creates a drum staff in your score and writes a drum pattern in one of 24 pre-defined styles. To use the plug-in, simply choose **Plug-ins ▸ Composing Tools ▸ Add Drum Patttern**. (You don't need to create a drum staff first.) The following dialog will appear:

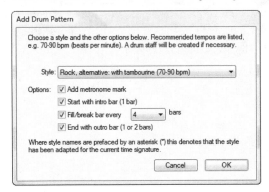

- Choose a **Style** from the drop-down list. The styles available in the list – which include blues, rock, pop, jazz, Latin and country – are appropriate for the time signature, so you'll never be offered a waltz drum pattern in 4/4, or a blues shuffle in 3/4! The patterns all indicate a recommended tempo at which they sound best, so it's a good idea to choose a pattern that is intended for the same kind of tempo as your score.

- **Add metronome mark** creates a metronome mark at the start of the score (or selected passage if you are working on part of a score), setting the playback tempo to the recommended tempo for the chosen drum pattern

- **Start with intro bar** determines whether you want the pattern to start with an introductory fill, leading into the regular pattern

- **Fill/break bar every** *n* **bars** allows you to choose whether the pattern should include a fill or break bar, and how often it should do so

- **End with outro bar** specifies whether the plug-in should end the pattern with either one or two concluding bars (depending on the pattern).

When you have set the options appropriately, click **OK**. A progress bar appears for a few moments while the plug-in creates the drum pattern, and then you're ready to play it back. If you decide that you want to change the pattern, you can simply choose **Plug-ins ▸ Composing Tools ▸ Add Drum Pattern** again; the existing drum pattern is deleted and replaced with the new one automatically.

If your score uses a variety of time signatures, when you choose **Notes ▸ Add Drum Pattern** a message will appear asking you to select a passage in a single time signature, then try again.

Plug-in written by Gunnar Hellquist.

Add Hit Point Staff

Adds a percussion staff to the bottom of the score with cross noteheads at the closest rhythmic position to the location of each hit point. To use the plug-in, simply choose **Plug-ins ▸ Composing Tools ▸ Add Hit Point Staff**.

This makes the relationship of the hit point to the music easier to see. Sibelius adds a note within one sixteenth (semiquaver) of the location of each hit point. If you change the tempo of the score or add or remove hit points, you can run the plug-in again; it will overwrite the existing notes with new ones.

Plug-in written by Bob Zawalich.

Add Simple Harmony

Adds a simple harmonization to the melodic passage selected in the current score.

- Choose your accompaniment style from **Chord style,** which can be **Block chords, arpeggios** or **Alberti bass**

- The plug-in will detect the key of the piece automatically, but can't detect relative minors, so if the key displayed is, say, G major instead of E minor, you will need to choose the correct key manually.

- Change **Melody is in voice** in the unlikely event that the melody you wish to add the harmonization to is not in voice 1

- **Change chord** allows you to set the rate of the harmonic rhythm generated by the plug-in. **Each beat group** generally works best, but if the changes of harmony are too frequent or infrequent, you may find that choosing **Each bar** or **Each beat** respectively produces better results.

- **Write harmony for** allows you to choose the instrument (piano or guitar) that the plug-in should use for the harmonization. You can of course copy or arrange the harmony onto other instruments afterwards.

- **Force mid-range accompaniment** can be useful if you're asking the plug-in to harmonize a melody that spans a particularly large range, or if you are harmonizing a melody on an instrument that is very low or high. This is because, without this option switched on, the generated harmonization will be written at a similar tessitura to that of the melody being harmonized. So if you're harmonizing a melody for the piccolo, you'll probably benefit from switching this on, unless you want the next door neighbor's dog to come running.

Plug-in written by Bob Zawalich, Andrew Davis and Daniel Spreadbury.

Explode

"Explodes" (i.e. separates) music from one staff onto a larger number of staves. To use this plug-in:

- Either select a passage from a single staff, copy it to the clipboard with **Ctrl+C** *or* ⌘**C**, then select the staves you want to explode onto, and choose **Plug-ins ▸ Composing Tools ▸ Explode.** Sibelius explodes the music onto the destination staves, using the current default settings;

- Or select the passage on a single staff you want to explode and choose **Plug-ins ▸ Composing Tools ▸ Explode,** which will show a dialog asking how many staves you wish to explode to, followed by a dialog asking which staves to explode the music onto. There are options to create new staves, or to use existing ones (see below).

You can also run the plug-in with no selection, which shows a dialog allowing you to set up how the music should be exploded:

- When **Overwrite existing material** is switched on, the plug-in will overwrite any existing music in the destination staves.

Plug-ins

- When **Put notes in all parts unless specified (by a1, 1, etc.)** is switched on, the plug-in assumes that single notes should go into all parts (and where there is more than one part or voice it puts notes into all of the parts, doubling the specified note). When this option is switched off, single notes only go into one part.

  When a single note passage is marked with specific directions in Technique text (such as 1., 2., 3., 4., a1., a2., a3., a4.), the plug-in interprets these and takes them into consideration when exploding. This continues until another direction is found, or a chord. After a chord, the plug-in reverts to its default setting for single notes (as specified by the **Put notes in all parts...** option) unless another direction is encountered.

- **Double part *n* if necessary** allows you to choose which of the notes should be doubled if there are fewer notes at any point.

- **Extra notes go into part *n*** allows you to specify which part gets the extra notes if there is a greater number of notes at any given point. The plug-in automatically distributes notes when there are twice the number of parts or more (e.g. in an eight-note chord, four parts each get two notes).

- When **Copy text, lines and symbols from all voices** is switched on, the plug-in copies objects in any voice on the source staff to the destination staves. When switched off, the plug-in adds only objects from the voice that contain the notes it is copying (or objects in all voices).

- **Cue solos in other parts** will create cue passages, and you can choose whether the cue should be labeled with the full or short instrument names, or with no instrument name at all. If **Only whole bars** is switched on, the plug-in only creates a cue in a bar if it would otherwise have been left empty. Otherwise, **Create bar rest in voice 2** will add a full size bar rest in bars that only contain cues. If you want the text "Play" to be created at the end of the cue, switch on **Add 'Play' text**.

If you need to explode music from more than one staff onto a greater number of staves, or if you need to explode music into more than four parts, you should use Sibelius's Arrange feature instead – see **Explode** on page 370.

Plug-in written by Dave Foster.

Fit Selection to Time

Changes the tempo of the selected passage in order to make it either finish at a specific timecode, or last for a specific duration.

To run the plug-in, select the music whose duration you want to change, and choose **Plug-ins ▸ Composing Tools ▸ Fit Selection to Time**. A simple dialog appears, allowing you to choose whether you want to specify a **New end time** or a **New duration**. The plug-in will insert a tempo change at the start of the selection to ensure that it matches your specified end time or duration.

You can alternatively choose an existing hit point from the **Time of selected hit point** list; the plug-in will insert a tempo change to move the hit point to the end of the selection.

The plug-in removes existing metronome marks in the selection, but if you want a gradual tempo change you can create *rit./accel.* lines as appropriate before running the plug-in, which will make use of them.

Plug-in written by Bob Zawalich.

Insert Note or Rest

Allows you to insert a note or rest before, change the duration of, or delete, an existing note, chord or rest, and shuffle the following music along by the appropriate amount.

To use the plug-in, select the note, chord or rest before which you want to insert a note or rest, or whose duration you want to change, or which you want to delete, and choose Plug-ins ▸ Composing Tools ▸ Insert Note or Rest. A dialog appears:

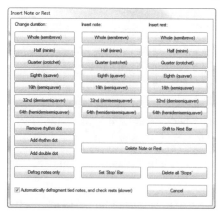

The dialog has three columns of buttons representing note values, headed **Change duration**, **Insert note**, and **Insert rest**. Simply click the note value in the column corresponding with the action you want the plug-in to take; the dialog closes, and the edit is performed in the score.

If you choose **Insert note**, the inserted note is given the pitch of the note you selected before running the plug-in (or the bottom note of the selected chord), and is left selected so that you can change its pitch immediately.

The **Change duration** column has three extra buttons: **Remove rhythm dot**, **Add rhythm dot**, and **Add double dot**. What these do is fairly obvious, except to say that if you want to insert a dotted note, it must be done in two stages: first, insert the basic duration, then run the plug-in again to add the rhythm dot.

To delete the selected note, chord or rest, click the **Delete Note or Rest** button.

Shift to Next Bar moves the select note, chord or rest and the music following it to the start of the following bar.

By default, the changes made by the plug-in will affect all bars up to the next empty bar, which the plug-in considers the natural stopping point. You can override this by setting a manual stop point: select a note, chord or rest, run the plug-in, and click **Set 'Stop' Bar**. This is useful if you know that you want to perform one or more edits on notes in one area, but definitely don't want subsequent bars to be affected. To remove your manual stop point, run the plug-in again (with any note selected) and choose **Delete all 'Stops'**.

Automatically dfragment notes and check rests (slower) attempts to keep the note and rest durations produced by the editing operations facilitated by the plug-in as simple as possible, and as such it's recommended that you leave this switched on. However, you may still find that you end up with unorthodox ways of representing durations, and you may find that using one or more of

Plug-ins

the Simplify Notation plug-ins is useful after using Insert Note or Rest – 📖 **6.11 Simplify Notation plug-ins**.

You can incorporate this plug-in into your note input and editing workflow most seamlessly by assigning a keyboard shortcut to it – 📖 **5.12 Menus and shortcuts**.

Plug-in written by Horst Kuegelgen.

Reduce

Reduces music from a greater number of staves onto a single staff. To use this plug-in: .

* Either select a passage from multiple staves, copy it to the clipboard with Ctrl+C *or* ⌘C, then select the staves you want to reduce onto, and choose **Plug-ins ▸ Composing Tools ▸ Reduce**. Sibelius reduces the music onto the destination staves, using the current default settings;

* Or select the passage from multiple staves you want to reduce and choose **Plug-ins ▸ Composing Tools ▸ Reduce**, which will show a dialog asking whether you want to reduce onto an existing staff (and if so, which one) or whether you want to create a new staff.

You can also run the plug-in with no selection, which shows a dialog allowing you to set up how the music should be reduced:

* Choose whether to **Use minimum number of voices** or to **Separate all parts into separate voices**; the default is to combine notes into the minimum possible number of voices, and to indicate solo and duplicate notes using **1.** and **a 2** (the precise appearance of which you can choose from a menu of preset choices).

* Switch on **Ignore cue passages** if you want to ensure that the plug-in will not attempt to reduce cue passages in the source staves into the destination staves

* **Ignore duplicate text, lines and symbols within** allows you to tell Sibelius to ignore identical markings on the source staves if they occur at the same or very close rhythmic positions on multiple staves. Set the distance at which Sibelius should ignore identical markings to either a **quarter (crotchet)**, **eighth (quaver)** or **16th (semiquaver)**.

* When **Overwrite existing material** is switched on, the plug-in will overwrite any existing music in the destination staff.

If you need to reduce music onto a smaller number of staves but more than a single staff, you should use Sibelius's Arrange feature instead – see **Reduction** on page 370.

Plug-in written by Dave Foster.

Show Handbells Required

This plug-in, only relevant for scores containing music for an ensemble of handbells, will add a bar to the start of your score showing all the handbells required to perform the piece. To use the plug-in, choose **Plug-ins ▸ Composing Tools ▸ Show Handbells Required**. After you have run the plug-in, you may find it necessary to delete rests or clefs in the bar that the plug-in creates.

Plug-in written by Neil Sands.

6.7 Notes and Rests plug-ins

Apply Shape Notes

Changes the noteheads according to their pitch to use either the 4-note or 7-note shape note conventions.

To use the plug-in, simply choose **Plug-ins ▸ Notes and Rests ▸ Apply Shape Notes**; choose the shape note convention you prefer, and click **OK**. If you subsequently want to return to regular notation with normal noteheads, run the plug-in again and choose **Restore normal noteheads**.

Plug-in written by Gunnar Hellquist.

Boomwhackers® Note Colors

This plug-in colors notes according to the color scheme of Boomwhackers® tuned percussion tubes (visit **www.boomwhackers.com** for details). To use the plug-in, choose **Plug-ins ▸ Notes and Rests ▸ Boomwhackers Note Colors**, select the **Apply Boomwhacker colors** radio button, and click **OK**. Sibelius will change the color of all the notes in the score.

To restore the notes' original colors, run the plug-in again, choose **Reset to default colors**, and click **OK**.

Plug-in written by Bob Zawalich.

Color Pitches

This plug-in colors notes according to their pitch, a convention occasionally used in educational music. To use this plug-in, choose the passage in which you want to change the color of notes (or leave nothing selected if you want the operation to apply to the whole score), and choose **Plug-ins ▸ Notes and Rests ▸ Color Pitches**. A simple dialog appears, in which you can choose a color for each of the twelve pitches of the chromatic scale. When you have made your choices, click **OK** and the colors are applied to the notes in the selection.

Beware that all notes in any chords in the selection will be colored according to the pitch of the highest note in the chord.

Plug-in written by Andrew Davis.

Convert Simple Time to Compound Time

Rewrites passages in 4/4, 3/4 etc. time signatures as 12/8, 9/8 etc., by doubling the length of the odd-numbered eighth notes (quavers) in each bar. (The exception to this rule is that triplet eighth notes, quarter notes and half notes are kept straight.)

To use this plug-in, select the passage you need to convert and choose **Plug-ins ▸ Notes and Rests ▸ Convert Simple Time to Compound Time**. You are given the option of running the **Straighten Written-Out Swing** plug-in (see below) before running this one, which has the effect of turning dotted note swing into compound time.

If there's no time signature in the passage you select, the plug-in will assume that it is in 4/4.

The converted notation is added to the score at the end of the selection. Where a tuplet has not been converted, a text warning is added to the score indicating the bar number that contained the

Plug-ins

original tuplet, so you can correct it. The plug-in only copies notes: articulations, lines, special barlines, lyrics, etc. will not be copied, so you will need to copy or re-create these after running the plug-in.

Plug-in written by Peter Hayter.

Copy Articulations and Slurs

This plug-in allows you to copy articulations and slurs from one musical phrase to others with the same or similar rhythm. To use this plug-in:

- First, copy the articulations and slurs you want to duplicate to the clipboard, by selecting the phrase whose articulations and slurs you wish to copy as a passage, and choose **Edit ▸ Copy** (shortcut **Ctrl+C** *or* ⌘**C**).
- If you want to paste these articulations and slurs to a specific passage in the score, select it now. You can copy articulations and slurs to multiple phrases at once by including them all in the passage you select. (You don't have to be exact about the start, end and staves enclosed in the passage, as articulations and slurs will only be copied to phrases within it that match the original rhythm.)
- Next, choose **Plug-ins ▸ Notes and Rests ▸ Copy Articulations and Slurs**.
- Make sure that the **Copy articulations** and **Copy slurs** checkboxes are set according to what you want to copy.
- If you want the plug-in to remove any existing articulations on any notes it needs to copy articulations to, choose **Replace existing articulations**
- If you want to copy articulations and slurs to passages with note values that are double or half those of the original selection, choose **Also copy to augmentations and diminutions**
- Under **Destination options**, choose the appropriate option:
  - ◦ **Copy to selection** will duplicate the copied articulations and slurs to the selected passage
  - ◦ **Copy to selection with fuzzy matching** allows the destination passage to be a less exact rhythmic match than the source passage; for example, if your source passage has articulations on four quarter notes (crotchets) in succession, and your destination passage consists of eight eighth notes (quavers) in succession, with this option selected, the plug-in will copy the articulations to the first of each pair of eighth notes in the destination, even though the match is inexact.
  - ◦ **Copy to whole score** will duplicate the copied articulations and slurs to passages that match exactly throughout the entire score.
- Click **OK**.

The plug-in will copy the articulations and slurs from the original phrase to all matching phrases in your subsequent selection.

Plug-in written by Neil Sands.

Make Pitches Constant

Sets all the notes in a selection to the same pitch, optionally changing the notehead type used, and filling the bar with notes in another voice (e.g. to fill a bar with slash notes while showing a specific rhythm that the player may wish to vamp on). For example, this plug-in can transform the bar on the left into the bar on the right in just a few clicks:

To use this plug-in, select the passage of pitches to be made constant, then choose **Plug-ins ▸ Notes and Rests ▸ Make Pitches Constant**. A dialog appears, split into two halves:

- The upper half of the dialog modifies the existing notes. Specify the voice to which the notes you want to transpose belong, and if you want to change the noteheads too, set the desired notehead type. The **Move rests with notes** option moves any rests in the passage vertically to match the pitch of the transposed notes.
- The bottom half of the dialog allows you to add new notes to another voice in the same passage; this is especially useful for creating slash notation. Choose the voice to be used for the new notes (making sure it's different from the voice of the notes you've asked it to transpose), set the pitch, notehead type, and the note value, then click **OK**.

Plug-in further developed by Stefan Behrisch (www.werklabor.de).

Paste Into Voice

Pastes a passage of music you have copied to the clipboard into the selected passage, using whichever voice you specify. This is very useful for pasting e.g. a voice 1 passage on one staff directly into voice 2 on another staff. To use this plug-in:

- Select the passage of music that contains the notes you want to paste elsewhere, and copy it to the clipboard using **Edit ▸ Copy** (shortcut **Ctrl+C** *or* **⌘C**)
- Select the destination passage, i.e. the bars where you want the music to be pasted, then choose **Plug-ins ▸ Notes and Rests ▸ Paste Into Voice**.
- A dialog appears:

- Make sure that the correct source voice is chosen in **Copy from voice**, and the correct destination voice is chosen in **Paste into voice**; if you only want some of the notes you copied to be pasted, choose **Selected notes**.
- Click **OK**, and the copied music is pasted into the specified voice in the selected passage.

Plug-ins

For more information about using voices, 📖 **2.36 Voices**.

Plug-in written by Dave Foster.

Remove Dangling Ties

Sometimes a note will continue to sound indefinitely during playback if you have inadvertently used a tie when you meant to use a slur; this plug-in checks your score for notes with ties that are left "dangling" – in other words, not tied to a subsequent note.

To use the plug-in, select the passage you want to correct and choose **Plug-ins ▸ Notes and Rests ▸ Remove Dangling Ties**.

Split Dotted Quarter Rests

In compound time signatures such as 6/8, Sibelius will notate a beat's rest as, say, a dotted quarter note (crotchet), which is the modern convention. Some musicians find it easier to read these rests if they are split into separate quarter note (crotchet) and eighth note (quaver) rests. This plug-in automatically replaces such rests, as follows:

To use the plug-in, select the passage in which you want to split the rests, and choose **Plug-ins ▸ Notes and Rests ▸ Split Dotted Quarter Rests**. The passage may of course include notes, which are left alone.

Straighten Written-Out Swing

Converts the written-out swing rhythm ♪♩ into even eighth notes (quavers).

To use the plug-in, select the passage you need to convert and choose **Plug-ins ▸ Notes and Rests ▸ Straighten Written-Out Swing**. You are given the option of whether to add the Tempo text **Swing** to the rewritten passage.

Beware that the rewritten passage will lose articulations; lyrics are not re-written and may end up in the wrong position in the bar. Other items that were lined up with the original rhythm may also need to be adjusted by hand.

Plug-in written by Peter Hayter.

6.8 Other plug-ins

Add Harp Pedaling

Automatically adds appropriate harp pedal diagrams or pedal change text instructions to harp parts, and warns when pedal changes are too close together to be played comfortably, or when the music is unplayable.

To use the plug-in, first select the passage to which you want to add pedaling (select only the harp staves), then choose **Plug-ins ▸ Other ▸ Add Harp Pedaling**. A simple dialog appears:

- **Add to** allows you to choose between processing the **Whole score** or just the **Selected passage**
- **Quarter note (crotchets) required to change pedals** allows you to adjust the time you would expect it to take to change all the pedals; for music at faster tempi, you should increase this number appropriately
- You can choose whether the pedaling added to your score will be in the form of **Diagram**s or **Boxed text**
- Finally, choose whether you want the inserted pedaling to be highlighted (this makes them easy to spot if you want to check them afterwards in a long score). **Highlight other changes** refers to pedal changes that have to be made immediately before a note is needed; the plug-in will try to avoid these if it can find a place for the change to be made in advance.

When you click **OK**, the plug-in adds the pedaling. Beware that double sharps and double flats cannot be set using harp pedals; if you have written any of these in your music, the plug-in will warn you about them when it has finished writing other changes in.

Plug-in written by Neil Sands.

Add Note Names to Noteheads

Writes the name of the note inside the notehead, using the supplied Opus Note Names font, like this:

To use this plug-in, either select the passage in which you want to write note names, or the whole score, and choose **Plug-ins ▸ Other ▸ Add Note Names to Noteheads**. A simple dialog appears, in which you can choose whether you want the note names written inside the noteheads to include accidentals. Click **OK** and the score is updated.

If you add more notes or change the pitches of the notes already in the score, you'll need to run the plug-in again to update the note names inside the noteheads.

Plug-in written by Neil Sands

Groovy Music Mark-up

Adds annotations (in the form of MIDI messages) to the current score that act as special "markers" when importing a MIDI file generated from the score into either Groovy Jungle or Groovy City. Groovy Music is a series of three programs that make teaching music to primary children easy and fun – see www.sibelius.com/products/groovy for more details.

Select a single-staff passage or one or more single notes, then choose Plug-ins ▸ Other ▸ Groovy Music Mark-up. You are asked to choose which Groovy Music product you wish to export to. In the dialog that appears, choose whether you want to mark a Melody, Bass, Rhythm, Chord, Arpeggio etc. element, then click OK. Make a new selection and run the plug-in again to mark another element, and repeat in this way until you have completed marking up your score.

Once you are satisfied that the score is fully marked up, choose File ▸ Export ▸ MIDI File and export a MIDI file (🕮 **9.9 Exporting MIDI files**), then load the resulting MIDI file into Groovy by clicking Open Song.

If you need further help, the plug-in has a Help button that provides more details.

Make Layout Uniform

Forces your score to have a specified number of bars per system and systems per page. The default of 4 and 4 is suitable for voice or solo instrument with keyboard accompaniment. Solo keyboard music typically has 4 bars per system and 6 systems per page. Music for a single-staff instrument typically has 4 bars per system and 10 systems per page.

The first page of a score often has fewer systems than subsequent pages, to make room for the title; this plug-in allows you to set the number of systems on the first page independently from the rest of the score.

Sibelius can automatically lay out your entire score with a uniform number of bars per system, and will reformat the score dynamically when it changes (🕮 **8.4 Auto Breaks**). Hence you should normally only use this plug-in if you want to make just part of a score have a layout uniform.

Select the passage to be made uniform, and choose Plug-ins ▸ Other ▸ Make Layout Uniform.

Make Piano Four Hands Layout

Takes a score written for two pianos (or indeed any two keyboard instruments), and creates a new score in the conventional format for four hands piano music, with music for the lower player (secondo) on left-hand pages, and music for the higher player (primo) on right-hand pages.

To use the plug-in, first prepare your source score. It should contain only two keyboard instruments. Next, use Create ▸ Title Page to add a title page to your score, if it doesn't already have one, or else ensure that the first page of music is a left-hand page. This helps the plug-in produce correct page turns in the created score. Finally, select the whole score and do Layout ▸ Format ▸ Lock Format, then choose Plug-ins ▸ Other ▸ Make Piano Four Hands Layout.

A simple dialog appears, in which you can choose the instrument names to use for each instrument in the newly created score. The Keep facing pages in sync option tells the plug-in to ensure that the same bars appear on each system on left-hand and right-hand pages. Click OK, and watch as progress bars whizz across the screen. Moments later, your new score is created.

Some tidying up will probably be required after running the plug-in: it helpfully creates text objects beginning "P4H" at each point where tidying up is required, which you can find with **Edit ▸ Find** in order to decide what to do in each case.

Plug-in written by Hans-Christoph Wirth.

Preferences

This plug-in is only intended for use by plug-in developers. See **Help ▸ Documentation ▸ ManuScript Language Reference** for more information.

Remove All Highlights

This plug-in simply removes all highlights from the score. To use the plug-in, just choose **Plug-ins ▸ Other ▸ Remove All Highlights**.

Scales and Arpeggios

Creates worksheets containing dozens of scales and arpeggios in just a few clicks. To use the plug-in, choose **Plug-ins ▸ Other ▸ Scales and Arpeggios**. You are guided through a series of dialogs, as follows:

- If a score is already open, you are first asked if you want to add the scales to the existing score, or create a new score. Make your choice and click **Next**.

- If you are creating a new score, you're asked whether you want to create scales for a single-staff instrument, or for a keyboard instrument. (You can also ask the plug-in to produce a single example of each type of scale and arpeggio it can create.) Make your choice, then click **Next**.

- You are asked to choose between several different types of scale or arpeggio: major scales, minor scales, modal scales, altered scales, jazz scales, and arpeggios. Again, make your choice and click **Next**.

- The next dialog allows you to set specific options about the scales or arpeggios you want to create: the type of scale, how many octaves and in which octave it should begin, the direction, the note value to be used, the clef, and so on. **Include key signature** inserts a new key signature at the start of each scale.

  If you want to create keyboard scales, you can specify whether you want to add an interval of a third or an octave above the notes in the right-hand staff.

  If you want to create a series of scales, you can choose whether each new scale should be in the key of the new starting note, or whether it should stay in the original key but simply begin on a different degree of the scale.

  When you are satisfied with the options:

  - If you are creating scales or arpeggios for a single-staff instrument, click **Finish**.
  - If you are creating scales for a keyboard instrument, click **Next**. You can make a few further choices, such as whether the scales should be created in similar or contrary motion, whether the left-hand staff should start in the same or a different octave than the right-hand staff, and so on.

- After you click **Finish**, the plug-in creates the desired scales or arpeggios within a few seconds.

Plug-in written by Gunnar Hellquist.

Plug-ins

Set Metronome Mark

Allows you to create metronome marks at specific speeds by clicking the pulse with the mouse. To use the plug-in, select the bar in which you want to create the metronome mark (or have nothing selected if you want to create it in the first bar), then choose **Plug-ins ▸ Other ▸ Set Metronome Mark**.

In the dialog that appears, click the large button at the desired tempo. After twelve clicks, the plug-in will tell you the average tempo you just clicked, and allow you to create a metronome mark either with that precise tempo, or the nearest tempo that you would find on a traditional metronome.

Plug-in written by Neil Sands and Michael Eastwood.

Split Bar

Splits a bar into two irregular bars of appropriate lengths, inserts a suitable bar number change and, if you choose to insert a system break where you split the bar, inserts an invisible barline between the two halves of the bar.

Simply choose the note before which you want the bar to be split, and choose **Plug-ins ▸ Other ▸ Split Bar**. A simple dialog appears, allowing you to choose what kind of barline to use at the end of the first half of the split bar (**Invisible** by default), and whether or not the bar numbering should count the two halves of the bar separately.

You can switch off **Show this dialog again (this session)** if you want to use the same set of options for the duration of your Sibelius session without being prompted to choose them each time; if you switch this off, the dialog will appear again when you next restart Sibelius.

Plug-in written by Bob Zawalich.

Suggest Cue Locations

Marks your score with suitable locations for cue passages, based on a minimum number of bars' rest or a minimum length of silence in seconds.

Select the passage in which you want the plug-in to suggest suitable locations for cues, e.g. triple-click a staff, then run the plug-in, or if you want to process the entire score, just choose **Plug-ins ▸ Other ▸ Suggest Cue Locations**. A dialog appears:

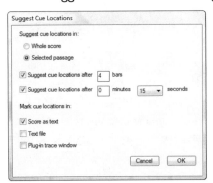

Although you can ask the plug-in to suggest locations after both a number of bars' rest and an amount of elapsed time, it is generally more useful to choose one or the other.

The three **Mark cue locations in** options present the results of running the plug-in:

- **Score as text** creates a Technique text object, colored red, above the first note following each suggested location for a cue
- **Text file** creates a text file called *filename* **cue locations.txt** in the same folder as your score file, listing the suggested cue locations
- **Plug-in Trace Window** writes each suggested cue location into the Plug-in Trace Window.

If you use the **Score as text** option, you can use **Edit ▸ Find** and **Edit ▸ Find Next** to find text beginning with "Cue:" to move to each suggested cue location.

Plug-in written by Neil Sands.

6.9 Playback plug-ins

Add Continuous Control Changes

Generates MIDI controller messages in your score, making it easier to apply the continuous controller changes required for tweaking playback, e.g. for some third-party virtual instruments or other playback devices.

To use the plug-in, first create one or more lines in the score at the position or positions where you want to apply automation data. Use the horizontal line from the **Staff lines** pane of the **Create ▸ Line** dialog, and ensure it starts and ends above the notes over which you want the MIDI controller data to be written. Then select either a line or a passage containing one or more of these lines, and choose **Plug-ins ▸ Playback ▸ Add Continuous Control Changes**.

The plug-in is supplied with a number of presets for several third-party sample libraries. Select a preset if a suitable one is available, and click **Load Preset**. If you don't need to make any further changes, click **OK**, and the plug-in will write out the appropriate MIDI controller messages in the score.

You can, of course, adjust the existing presets and create your own. Set up the options in the dialog as you want them, then click **Add Preset**. You're asked to choose a name of the preset; do so and click **OK**. If you subsequently change this preset, click **Save Preset** to make sure your changes are saved.

The plug-in allows you to write controllers that describe a number of waveforms and curves (e.g. sine, square, triangle, sawtooth, exponential, etc.), which you can choose from the **Signal Type** drop-down. Depending on your choice of **Signal Type**, different parameters need to be specified in the options on the right-hand side of the dialog. Refer to the plug-in's **Help** dialog for more information.

Plug-in written by David Budde.

Cresc./Dim. Playback

This plug-in is only necessary if your playback device does not automatically support changes of dynamic over sustained notes for appropriate instruments (e.g. wind, brass, strings and singers); most virtual instruments, including the supplied Sibelius Sounds Essentials sample library, do this automatically – see **Hairpins** on page 262.

For older MIDI devices, e.g. external MIDI modules or your computer's built-in soundcard, Sibelius can not automatically play back hairpin markings over single notes because it uses MIDI velocities to achieve gradations of dynamic on successive notes. This plug-in inserts a series of MIDI volume or expression messages in order to change dynamics during a single note.

To run this plug-in, first create hairpins where you want the volume to change, then select a bar or a passage containing the hairpin(s). If you just want to process one hairpin, the best way to do this is by selecting the hairpin.

When you have made your selection, choose Plug-ins ▸ Playback ▸ Cresc./Dim. Playback. A dialog will appear, allowing you to choose whether you wish to process every hairpin in the selected passage or just the first hairpin, and to specify the start and end dynamic of the *cresc./dim.*

You can also choose whether to use MIDI controller 7 or 11 to produce the dynamic change. By default, the plug-in uses controller 7 (volume) since this is supported on all MIDI devices, whereas controller 11 (expression) is not so widely supported. You may find that after creating the series of MIDI messages, you need to insert a further MIDI message yourself to reset the volume or expression level on that particular staff – 📖 **4.17 MIDI messages** for further information.

The plug-in requires you to put a hairpin in your score before running it, so if you don't want a hairpin to appear you can temporarily create one and then delete it after you have run the plug-in (which will not delete the MIDI messages).

The MIDI messages created by the plug-in are automatically hidden, so they will only be visible if you have View ▸ Hidden Objects switched on (shortcut Ctrl+Alt+H *or* ⌥⌘H).

Harmonics Playback

This plug-in enables playback of harmonics, e.g. on string staves, using Sibelius's Live Playback and MIDI messages features. To use the plug-in, select the passage in which you want the harmonics to be played back, and choose Plug-ins ▸ Playback ▸ Harmonics Playback. A simple dialog appears, in which you can choose what kind of harmonics you want the plug-in to process; generally you can just accept the defaults and click OK. You will be warned to save your score, and then the plug-in will process the selected passage.

Make sure Play ▸ Live Playback is switched on when you play back your score to hear the harmonics. Beware that if you transpose the music or otherwise change the pitches of the notes with harmonics after running this plug-in, you should delete the MIDI message text above the notes and run the plug-in again to ensure correct playback.

Plug-in written by Michael Eastwood.

Ornament Playback

Inserts the necessary MIDI messages to make mordents and turns play back. To use the plug-in, select the note (or notes) to which you want to add an ornament, and then choose Plug-ins ▸ Playback ▸ Ornament Playback. A simple dialog will appear, with the following options:

- **Mordent** or **Turn**: allows you to choose the type of ornament you wish to add
- If you choose **Mordent**, **Lower** and **Upper** control whether the mordent should play the note below the written note, or the note above the written note.
- If you choose **Turn**, **Inverted** controls whether or not the turn should be inverted.
- **Chromatic**: produces a chromatic ornament; when this option is switched off, the ornament produced is diatonic
- **At end of note**: intended for turns only, this option makes Sibelius insert the turn at the end of the selected note (i.e. just before the following note)
- **Add symbol**: this option adds the appropriate symbol for the ornament above the selected note (or notes).

Plug-ins

When you have chosen the desired options, click **OK**, and appropriate MIDI messages are added to your score (switch on **View ▸ Hidden Objects** to see them).

Quarter-tone Playback

Inserts MIDI messages to make quarter-tones play back. To use this plug-in, either select a passage or the whole score (using **Ctrl+A** *or* ⌘**A**), then choose **Plug-ins ▸ Playback ▸ Quarter-tone Playback**.

A dialog appears, allowing you to choose the amount of pitch bend required to produce a quarter-tone. Usually you should leave this at the default – so just click **OK**.

The MIDI messages created by this plug-in are automatically hidden, so you will not be able to see them unless you have **View ▸ Hidden Objects** switched on (shortcut **Ctrl+Alt+H** *or* ⌥⌘**H**).

This plug-in has a built-in **Help** dialog that describes its operation and limitations in more detail.

Strummer

Changes the Live Playback properties of notes in chords to provide a realistic strumming effect. The plug-in is designed with guitar in mind, but can be applied to other instruments too (you might like to experiment by using it on harp, harpsichord or pizzicato string parts).

To run the plug-in, select a passage then choose **Plug-ins ▸ Playback ▸ Strummer**. A dialog appears with options for choosing which chords to strum (chords with four or more notes are best), how to alternate down and up strums (in guitar terminology, where a down strum spreads a chord from the lowest notated pitch to the highest), by how much to spread the chord, 256 ticks being equivalent to a quarter note (crotchet), and how to annotate the strumming pattern (with a choice of no annotation, adding text **d** or **u** for down or up respectively, or using articulations, in which case the down bow and up bow symbols are used).

The half note (minim), quarter note (crotchet) and eighth note (quaver) options place down-strums on every specified beat, with up-strums on the chords found on every other beat. Strictly alternating, all down and all up options are self-explanatory.

The "use pattern" option is the most flexible, and can be used to produce impressive flamenco-style strumming patterns. Input the pattern as a string (with "d" for down-strum, "u" for up): this pattern will be applied sequentially to all chords selected, repeating as often as necessary (so if you enter the three-letter pattern **dud** and have selected eight chords, the result will be a pattern **dud-duddu**).

Plug-in written by David Harvey.

6.10 Proof-reading plug-ins

Proof-read

This plug-in allows the user to run any combination of six other proof-reading plug-ins that are in the same menu:

- **Check clefs** writes warnings in the score where a clef is repeated unnecessarily, e.g. an alto clef would be repeated if you omitted a change to treble clef in a Viola part
- **Check cues** – see below
- **Check for Parallel 5ths/8ves** – see below
- **Check harp pedaling** writes warnings in the score if any notes in the selected passage are unplayable on a harp with the pedal configuration specified in the dialog. For best results, you should select just the harp staves before running this particular plug-in, and specify a passage that contains no pedal changes. The plug-in can also optionally add a harp pedal diagram to your score corresponding to the pedal combination you specify in its dialog.
- **Check multiple stops** – see below
- **Check pizzicatos** writes warnings in the score where an "arco" or "pizz." seems to be surplus or missing
- **Check repeat barlines** writes warnings in the score where a start or end repeat seems to be surplus or missing (i.e. the repeat barlines don't match up).

If your score is very long, you could use Sibelius's **Edit ▸ Find** feature (📖 **5.7 Filters and Find**) to step through the warnings the plug-ins put in your score.

If you wish, you can run any of these plug-ins individually by choosing them from the **Plug-ins ▸ Proof-reading** submenu.

Check Attachments

This plug-in is very useful for locating those instances where you may have, say, incorrectly placed an expression marking so that it is erroneously attached to the staff above or below the one intended. To use the plug-in, choose **Plug-ins ▸ Proof Reading ▸ Check Attachments**. The plug-in can either check the current score, or look at a batch of files in a specified folder at the same time. Select the appropriate option from the first dialog shown by the plug-in, then click **Next**. The following dialog appears:

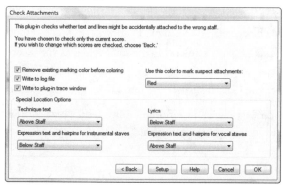

- **Removing existing marking color before coloring** is for when you have already run the plug-in before and want to confirm that the changes you have made to fix previous problems have been rectified. This option ensures that all objects that are currently colored in the score are set back to black before the plug-in makes its checks.
- **Write to log file** logs any potential problems in a text file called **Sibelius Attachment Log.txt** which is located your **Scores** folder
- **Write to plug-in trace window** logs any potential problems in Sibelius's **Plug-in Trace** window
- **Use this color to mark suspect attachments** allows you to choose the color the plug-in should use to make problems visually apparent in the score
- The **Special location options** settings allow you to set where the most common text styles are positioned in your score by default, so that the plug-in is able to ascertain attachment problems effectively.

When you have set the above options as appropriate, click the **OK** button and the plug-in will scan your score(s) and bring any potential attachment problems to your attention.

Plug-in written by Bob Zawalich.

Check Cues

Checks that cue passages in the score match the notes in the staves from which they have been copied. This is useful if you have continued to make edits to the score since adding cues to the parts, and now want to check that those edits are also reflected in the relevant cues.

Select the passage in which you want to check your cues, e.g. triple-click a staff, then run the plug-in, or if you want to process the entire score, just choose **Plug-ins ▸ Proof-reading ▸ Check Cues**. A dialog appears:

The three **Mark suspect cues in** options present the results of running the plug-in:

- **Score as text** creates a Technique text object, colored red, above the first note of each suspect cue
- **Text file** creates a text file called *filename* **suspect cues.txt** in the same folder as your score file, listing the location of each suspect cue
- **Plug-in Trace Window** writes the location of each suspect cue into the Plug-in Trace Window.

If you use the **Score as text** option, you can use **Edit ▸ Find** and **Edit ▸ Find Next** to find text beginning with "Suspect cue:" to move to each suspect cue in turn.

Plug-in written by Neil Sands.

Check First Species Counterpoint

Checks for errors in first species counterpoint, as defined in Johann Fux's 18th century treatise *Gradus ad Parnassum*.

The plug-in requires that the cantus and the counterpoint are each in separate staves, so make a passage selection that contains the staves you want to check, then choose **Plug-ins ▸ Proof-reading ▸ Check First Species Counterpoint**. The following dialog appears:

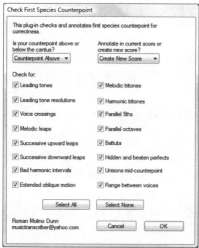

Choose whether the cantus or the counterpoint is in the upper or lower staff, and whether you would prefer the plug-in to annotate the existing score or create a new score. The various checks that the plug-in can perform are as follows:

- **Leading tones** checks for the presence of the leading tone, determined by the current key signature.
- **Leading tone resolutions** checks that any leading tones are properly resolved to the tonic.
- **Voice crossings** checks whether the cantus and the counterpoint overlap each other.
- **Melodic leaps** checks for poor or questionable melodic leaps, as determined by Fux's principles. This option also marks more advanced melodic conventions if they are resolved properly, e.g. if the leap of a minor 6th is resolved stepwise in the opposite direction, the score will be annotated at that point with the text "proper after-leap."
- **Successive upward leaps** checks for more than one successive upward melodic leap.
- **Successive downward leaps** checks for more than one successive downward melodic leap.
- **Bad harmonic intervals** checks for dissonances between the cantus and the counterpoint.
- **Extended oblique motion** checks for more than two successive oblique motions (where one voice remains on the same pitch while the other ascends or descends).
- **Melodic tritones** checks for the presence of any melodic tritone leaps.
- **Harmonic tritones** checks for the interval of a tritone between the cantus and the counterpoint.
- **Parallel 5ths** checks for parallel or consecutive fifths.
- **Parallel octaves** checks for parallel or consecutive octaves.

- Battuta (Italian for "beaten") checks for a tenth moving by stepwise contrary motion into an octave. This is forbidden in strict counterpoint, but Fux permits that there is little reason for it to be prohibited.

- **Hidden and beaten perfects** checks for hidden perfects, where two voices approach a perfect interval in similar motion, and beaten perfects, when both voices move in contrary motion and by melodic leap arrive at a perfect interval; both of these are prohibited in strict counterpoint. ("Beaten perfects" are so called by Fux because, he says, to the old masters of counterpoint it would sound as if the perfect intervals were being beaten into their heads.) Beaten fifths are marked in the score as "quinta battuta" and beaten octaves as "ottava battuta."

- **Unisons mid-counterpoint** checks for unisons that occur anywhere other than at the first and last notes of the counterpoint. In first species counterpoint this is forbidden, because it creates the illusion that there is only one voice present.

- **Range between voices** checks that the range between the cantus and the counterpoint is never greater than a perfect 12th.

Once you have chosen the things you want to check for, click **OK** and the plug-in will process the score, either annotating your existing score or creating a new score, copying your passage across, and annotating that.

Plug-in written by Roman Molino Dunn.

Check for Parallel 5ths/8ves

Checks for fifths and octaves between notes in any voice on any staves. The plug-in even checks for "hidden" fifths and octaves (i.e. where they occur in contrary motion).

If you want to check the entire score, choose **Edit ▸ Select ▸ Select All** (shortcut **Ctrl+A** *or* ⌘A), then choose **Plug-ins ▸ Proof-reading ▸ Check for Parallel 5ths/8ves**; otherwise, just select the passage you want to check before running the plug-in. In the dialog, choose whether you want to check for fifths or octaves, or both. Click **OK** – and after a few moments of busy activity, Sibelius tells you how many errors it found, which are marked in the score as text. (The warning text starts just over the first offending note of the parallel 5th/8ve.)

If your score is very long, you could use Sibelius's **Edit ▸ Find** feature to find all the annotations the plug-in has put in your score.

Check Lyrics Hyphenation

Checks the lyrics in your score for incorrect hyphenation, using Sibelius's built-in lyric syllabifier.

To use the plug-in, select a specific passage of your score if you like, then choose **Plug-ins ▸ Proof-reading ▸ Check Lyrics Hyphenation**.

You can choose whether to check the whole score or a selected passage, and choose the language that your lyrics are in (from English, French, German, Italian, Spanish and Latin).

Choose whether you want the plug-in to **Color incorrect hyphenations red**, and whether you also want it to **Correct lyrics in score** (which will overwrite the incorrectly hyphenated lyrics with correctly hyphenated ones). The **List corrections** options will save a text file listing the incorrectly hyphenated lyrics into the same folder as the score, or list them to the Plug-in Trace Window.

Plug-in written by Neil Sands.

Check Multiple Stops

Checks your score for chords that require unplayable multiple stopping. Each chord (which may either be in a single voice or as part of a contrapuntal passage) is either easy, difficult or impossible: easy chords are passed over, and difficult or impossible chords are marked as such in the score.

To use the plug-in, select a specific passage of your score if you like, then choose **Plug-ins ▸ Proof-reading ▸ Check Multiple Stops**. A dialog appears, in which you can choose whether to check the selected passage or the whole score, and whether you want to check staves belonging to stringed instruments (the recommended setting) or all staves. Click **OK**, and a progress bar appears as the plug-in examines each staff in turn.

Each difficult or impossible chord is labeled appropriately with Technique text; use Sibelius's **Edit ▸ Find** and **Edit ▸ Find Next** features (**5.7 Filters and Find**) to find each chord the plug-in has identified.

The plug-in assesses each possible arrangement of each note of the chord on each string of the instrument, played by each finger, and determines the easiest arrangement for the chord; this is the label that is then applied to the chord in the score. In order to do this, some assumptions have had to be made about how far players can stretch on each instrument; you will find that some players (with long fingers!) would be able to play some of the chords labeled impossible by this plug-in.

Chords with more than four noteheads are automatically deemed impossible, since all string instruments only have four strings.

Because bows are straight and the fingerboards of string instruments are curved, in fact only two notes can ever sound simultaneously when played on a real instrument; the plug-in allows for this, but stipulates that the upper two notes of any chord must be on adjacent strings, otherwise they can't both be held. Any chord that has its top two notes on non-adjacent strings is labeled as impossible.

Chords labeled as difficult generally involve an uncomfortable (but not impossible) stretch, or an awkward hand position (the ideal hand position is for the first finger to go on the lowest used string, the second finger on the next lowest used string, etc.; so two-string chords are generally playable, but three- and four-string chords must be fingered in the right order to be easy).

The plug-in operates regardless of musical context, e.g. a passage consisting of 24 "easy" double-stopped chords in a row will be processed without comment. Similarly it does not take into account issues such as tempo.

Plug-in written by Neil Sands.

Check Redundancies

This plug-in is able to locate redundant time signatures, clefs, key signatures, instrument changes, and rehearsal marks, e.g. two identical clef changes in succession. Unlike **Check Clefs** (see above), **Check Redundancies** allows you to select, hide or delete the redundant items in a single operation.

To use the plug-in, simply choose **Plug-ins ▸ Proof-reading ▸ Check Redunancies**. The following dialog appears:

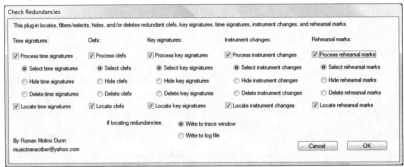

For each type of object, choose whether you want to **Select**, **Hide** or **Delete** redundant objects using the appropriate radio button. If you don't want the plug-in to check, say, instrument changes, switch off the **Process instrument changes** checkbox. Choose whether you would like the plug-in to output the results to a log file or to the Plug-in Trace Window, and click **OK**.

Plug-in written by Roman Molino Dunn.

What Is Where?

This plug-in creates a set of statistics showing which objects exist within the selection made in the current score. You can choose which objects should be included in the statistics, and also choose whether the plug-in should color the objects it has included in its analysis. When **Write to Log File** is on, the analysis is saved to a text file named **where.txt**, that you will find in the same folder as the score under analysis. You can also view the plug-in's output in the Plug-in Trace Window by switching on **Write to plug-in trace window**.

Use **Remove existing marking color before coloring** when you have previously used the plug-in and want to clear its previous colorings before the next analysis.

Plug-in written by Bob Zawalich.

6.11 Simplify Notation plug-ins

Change Split Point

Changes the split point of notes between the right-hand and left-hand staves of a piano or other instrument that uses two staves. This is useful for cleaning up keyboard music inputted via Flexitime or MIDI import.

To use the plug-in, select the passage in which you want to change the split point, and choose Plug-ins ▸ Simplify Notation ▸ Change Split Point. In the dialog that appears, specify the new split point, and whether you want notes above the split point to be on the right-hand or left-hand staff, then click OK. The plug-in moves notes between the staves as appropriate.

Plug-in written by Bob Zawalich.

Combine Tied Notes and Rests

Consolidates tied notes and groups of rests into longer note values. This is useful for cleaning up heavily-edited scores, or scores inputted via Flexi-time or MIDI import.

To use the plug-in, choose Plug-ins ▸ Simplify Notation ▸ Combined Tied Notes and Rests. If nothing is selected, you will be asked if you want the operation to apply to the whole score; otherwise, the plug-in will operate on the selected passage.

You can choose whether you want to combine either tied notes or rests, or both, and because this plug-in can dramatically alter the appearance of your score, you also have the option of creating a text file log that lists all the changes it made (you can even create a log file that lists all the changes the plug-in will make without actually making those changes).

This sophisticated plug-in has extensive built-in documentation: click Help in the initial dialog for further information about the rules it uses for combining tied notes and rests, and about its limitations.

Plug-in written by Bob Zawalich.

Duplicates In Staves

Operates on a selection containing two staves, coloring any similar notes that occur at the same time in both staves. You can choose the color used to mark duplicated notes, and the plug-in will inform you of the duplicates it finds in the Plug-in Trace window. A message telling you the number of duplicates the plug-in has found is shown when it completes.

This can be useful to (say) easily identify any instruments in a score that may be doubling each other at a given point.

Plug-in written by Bob Zawalich.

Move to Other Staff

Moves a single selected note or chord on a keyboard or other grand staff instrument to the staff above or below. This is useful for correcting split point errors on a note-by-note basis – if you want to change the split point for a longer passage of music, see **Change Split Point** above. To use the plug-in, simply select the note or chord you want to move from its current staff to the staff above or below and choose **Plug-ins ▸ Simplify Notation ▸ Move to Other Staff**.

Plug-in written by Geoff Haynes.

Remove Overlapping Notes

This plug-in removes overlapping notes in a staff, and is intended for cleaning up music that was inputted via Flexi-time (especially from a MIDI guitar) or by importing a MIDI file. It works by cutting off notes that are already sounding when the next note starts to sound, and it also checks for and removes "dangling" ties (i.e. ties that do not tie to a following note).

To use the plug-in, select the staff or staves on which you want the plug-in to be operated (or leave nothing selected to apply the plug-in to the whole score), then choose **Plug-ins ▸ Simplify Notation ▸ Remove Overlapping Notes**. You will be warned to save your score, and when you click OK, the plug-in will process the selected passage or the whole score. When the plug-in has finished, you will be told how many overlapping notes were removed.

Plug-in written by Bob Zawalich.

Remove Rests

Removes rests in the selected passage of music. If you find that you end up with unwanted rests after Flexi-time input or importing a MIDI file, you can use this plug-in to "clean up" the music.

For example, this plug-in rewrites the following music:

as:

To use the plug-in, simply select the passage from which you want to remove rests, and choose **Plug-ins ▸ Simplify Notation ▸ Remove Rests**. A dialog appears, reminding you of the plug-in's limitations; when you click OK a new score is created, containing the cleaned-up music, which you can copy back over the original.

The plug-in's limitations are as follows:

- Tuplets are omitted, but the rest of the bars in which they appear are copied correctly
- Grace notes are not copied
- Custom beamings appear using default beam groups
- User-flipped stems are not copied
- Special noteheads, articulation marks and special barlines are not copied
- Bars of irregular length, such as pick-up (upbeat) bars may not be copied correctly.

Plug-in improved by Geoff Haynes

Remove Unison Notes

Removes unison notes (two noteheads of the same pitch on the same stem, or of the same pitch in different voices), which sometimes appear after importing a MIDI file or using Arrange to produce reductions of existing music.

To use the plug-in, choose **Plug-ins ▸ Simplify Notation ▸ Remove Unison Notes**. If there is no selection, you are asked if you want the operation to apply to the whole score; otherwise, it will apply only to the selected passage. A dialog appears, in which you can set some options:

- Choose whether to remove unisons **Only within each voice** (i.e. two notes of the same pitch at the same rhythmic position but in separate voices would be left intact) or **Within and between all voices** (i.e. if two notes of the same pitch in separate voices occur at the same rhythmic position, one of them would be removed)
- Choose whether or not you want to create a text log file, detailing all of the changes the plug-in has made so that you can check them later (you can even ask the plug-in to create a log file of the changes it would make, without actually changing the score). You can choose whether to use American or British note names in the log file.

Click **OK**, and the plug-in processes the score.

Plug-in written by Bob Zawalich.

Renotate Performance

Rewrites the notation produced by a Flexi-time performance or imported from a MIDI file to make it more legible. This plug-in indirectly does the same jobs as both **Remove Overlapping Notes** and **Remove Rests**, so you won't need to run those plug-ins as well as this one. The plug-in is most useful with a pair of keyboard staves, but you can use it with any other instrument if you wish. The plug-in can fix the following kinds of problems:

- Notes are written on the wrong staff, giving them too many leger lines
- Chord voicings are unplayable, because the stretches are too wide
- Inconsistent voicing due to the **Use multiple voices** option for Flexi-time input
- Short notes being notated as chords because the Flexi-time **Minimum duration** option was set too high
- Notes are notated with shorter values than ideal, because they were played too staccato.

The plug-in aims to produce notation that is rhythmically and visually simpler than the original, while still notating every note that was part of the original performance, by revoicing and requantizing the music. As the plug-in revoices your performance, it reduces the notes to a single voice on each staff; inner voices are suggested by adding the notes where they best fit, without using ties to notate their duration. The music is requantized using the same **Minimum duration** unit as was used for the original Flexi-time input or MIDI import, but this unit is automatically decreased where necessary, e.g. where you played sixteenths (semiquavers) but where the **Minimum duration** unit was set to eighths (quavers), or where you played a spread chord, grace note, or other ornament.

To use the plug-in, simply select a passage in the staff or staves you want to renotate, then choose **Plug-ins ▸ Simplify Notation ▸ Renotate Performance**. A simple dialog appears, allowing you to override the plug-in's choice of quantization unit, and specify whether or not to **Overwrite selected passage**. If this option is switched on, the selected music is overwritten; if it is switched off, Sibelius will add a new instrument and write the renotated music on that staff, useful for the purposes of comparing the original and renotated passage.

Plug-in written by Geoff Haynes.

6.12 Text plug-ins

Add Brackets to Reprise Script

In some handwritten scores, text is marked with brackets that show whether the text applies to the staff above or the staff below, like this:

Sibelius's Reprise Script font includes special characters that can produce these kinds of brackets, and the simplest way of achieving them is to select the passage containing the text to which you want to add brackets, then choose **Plug-ins ▸ Text ▸ Add Brackets to Reprise Script**. A simple dialog appears, allowing you to choose whether you want to add or remove brackets: make your choice and click **OK**. The plug-in determines whether the text is above or below the staff and creates the right kind of bracket automatically.

If you subsequently change the font of the text that has brackets, you will find that the brackets no longer look correct: run the plug-in again and choose **Remove brackets** to correct the score's appearance.

Plug-in written by Dave Foster.

Add Brass Fingering

Adds appropriate fingering for a number of common brass instruments, including trumpets in B♭, C, D and E♭, horns using F and B♭ fingerings, and 3- and 4-valve euphoniums.

To use the plug-in, select the passage for which you want to add fingering (e.g. triple-click the staff of the brass instrument in question) and choose **Plug-ins ▸ Text ▸ Add Brass Fingering**. Choose the instrument from the dialog and click **OK** to add the fingering to your score in the Fingering text style; if you find that it collides with notes or other markings, use the **Reposition Text** plug-in to adjust it (see below).

Add Dynamics From Live Playback

Adds dynamics, in Expression text, to the selected passage or the whole score, based on the Live Playback velocities of the notes. This is useful for adding dynamics to music that was input via Flexi-time, or by importing a MIDI file.

To run the plug-in, simply select a passage and choose **Plug-ins ▸ Text ▸ Add Dynamics From Live Playback**. A dialog appears, allowing you to change various settings:

- **Change dynamic if note velocity out of range by at least** *n* determines the plug-in's sensitivity for changes in dynamic; a larger number here will produce fewer dynamics in the score, while a smaller one will produce more.
- **Insert dynamics** allows you to choose whether any new dynamics created by the plug-in should appear when the dynamic level changes (the default setting), or snap them to the next beat, or the start of the next bar.

Plug-ins

- **Restate dynamics after this many bars of rests** allows you to automatically restate the last dynamic after a passage of rests.
- The values in **Dynamic Levels** allow you to specify the maximum MIDI velocity that corresponds to each possible dynamic. These values default to the default values set in Sibelius's manuscript papers, but you can change them if you wish.
- **Delete existing Expression text** clears any existing dynamics in the selected passage before adding any new dynamics.
- **Each voice has separate dynamics** allows the plug-in to add dynamics in multiple voices, if the source passage contains notes in multiple voices.
- **Combine dynamics for multi-staff instruments** tells the plug-in to examine all staves of grand staff instruments (e.g. piano) to create a single set of dynamics for all staves.
- **Music text font for bold Expression text** allows you to specify which font should be used for the dynamics: normally you can leave this set to Opus Text.

Once you are satisfied with your choices, click **OK**. A progress bar will appear and the dynamics will be added to your score.

Plug-in written by Bob Zawalich.

Add Note Names

Writes A, C♯, etc. above every note in the score.

To run the plug-in, simply select a passage (or make sure nothing is selected if you wish to add note names to all staves throughout your score) and choose **Plug-ins ▸ Text ▸ Add Note Names**. A simple dialog appears, allowing you to specify whether the note names are added in upper or lower case, which text style is used, whether it should use sounding or written pitch (for transposing instruments), whether it should include the octave number as well as the note name, and whether note names should be added to the selected passage or the whole score. You can also choose the language that should be used to write the note names.

If you find that the added text collides with notes or other markings, select one text object and choose **Edit ▸ Select ▸ Select More** (shortcut **Ctrl+Shift+A** *or* ⇧⌘A), and move the whole row together using the ↑/↓ keys.

Add Slurs to Lyrics

It is customary for words sung over more than one note to be slurred, which makes it easier for the singer to see when the word next changes. This plug-in adds slurs to staves with lyrics, following this convention.

To use the plug-in, select the passage on which you want the plug-in to operate (though it will only look at staves with lyrics, so if you want to run the plug-in on the whole score, you don't need to select anything), then choose **Plug-ins ▸ Text ▸ Add Slurs to Lyrics**. A dialog appears, allowing you to choose whether you want to add normal slurs or dotted or dashed ones, and giving you the option of highlighting existing slurs if they're in the wrong place, or highlighting suspect lyric melismas (e.g. without hyphens or lyric lines). Click **OK**, and slurs are added to your score.

Plug-in written by Michael Kilpatrick.

Add String Fingering

This plug-in adds appropriate fingering to music for violin, viola, cello and double bass.

To use the plug-in, select the passage for which you want to add fingering (typically, triple-click the staff of the instrument in question) and choose **Plug-ins ▸ Text ▸ Add String Fingering**. Choose the desired instrument from the dialog; you can also choose the fingering position(s) to be used (the default setting is **1 and 3**, which will add the fingerings for first position and then go back and attempt to fill the gaps with fingerings from third position). Click **OK** to add the fingering to your score in the Fingering text style; if you find that it collides with notes or other markings, use the Reposition Text plug-in to adjust it (see below).

Add Tonic Sol-Fa

Adds tonic sol-fa notation to a selected passage or the entire score. Tonic sol-fa is both a form of musical notation used in vocal music and a system of teaching sight-singing that depends on it.

Pioneered by John Curwen in 1840s England, and since modified by Kodály in the twentieth century, tonic sol-fa notation is based on the moveable *doh* system of solmization. The notes of the major scale are named (in ascending order) doh, ray, me, fah, soh, lah, te, where doh is the tonic, other notes being thus related to the tonic of the moment, which changes if the piece modulates. Minor keys are treated as modes of the relative major, the minor scale being solmized as lah, te, doh, ray, etc. In notation, the notes are abbreviated as d, r, m, f, s, l, t. Sharps and flats are indicated by change of vowel, sharps to e, flats to a (pronounced aw); e.g. doh sharpened is de; me flattened is ma. Colons (:) separate one beat from the next, single dots (.) are used when a beat is divided into two half-beats, and commas divide half-beats into quarter-beats. Horizontal lines show that notes are to be held over a beat (or sub-beat) boundary; blanks indicate rests.

The following example, taken from John Curwen's snappily titled *The Standard Course of Lessons on the Tonic Sol-fa Method of Teaching to Sing*, shows how the notation looks in practice:

To use this plug-in, select a passage and then choose **Plug-ins ▸ Text ▸ Add Tonic Sol-Fa**. A dialog appears, in which you should specify the key of the selected passage. You can also specify which voice to solmize, and various options concerning the way the tonic sol-fa notation will look. When you are ready to proceed, click **OK**, and the sol-fa notation will be added to your score.

If your score includes changes in key signature, the plug-in cannot read these automatically, so you should run the plug-in for each section of your score in different keys. Note also that, by default, the tonic sol-fa notation is added in the **Lyrics line 1** text style, so you should either add the real lyrics to your music using the **Lyrics line 2** text style, or manually move any existing lyrics before running the plug-in, to prevent the sol-fa notation appearing on top of the lyrics.

This plug-in has the following limitations:

- The spacing of barlines may not be correct (these can easily be adjusted by hand afterwards)
- Empty pick-up (anacrusis) bars may not be notated correctly

- The plug-in uses non-standard 'bridge note' notation for modulation; it is usual to use subscript and superscript characters, but these cannot be created, so the plug-in instead writes [old note] new note
- The plug-in also uses non-standard tuplet markings (> instead of an inverted comma)
- Some of the rhythmic markings may be spaced too close (again, this can easily be adjusted by hand afterwards).

Add Verse Numbers

Adds verse numbers at the start of verses of lyrics, aligned in a column and using the appropriate **Lyrics line** *n* text style.

To use the plug-in, select the bar containing the start of the lyric verses, and choose **Plug-ins ▸ Text ▸ Add Verse Numbers**. There are no options; the plug-in goes ahead and adds the numbers automatically.

If you wish subsequently to select the verse of lyrics, including the verse number, select the verse number and choose **Edit ▸ Select ▸ Select More** (shortcut **Ctrl+Shift+A** *or* ⇧⌘A). If you click on a syllable instead, the verse number will not be selected. **Edit ▸ Filter ▸ Lyrics** will likewise not select the verse numbers.

Plug-in written by Peter Hayter.

Align Lyrics

Adjusts the vertical spacing of multiple verses of lyrics such that:

- the first verse lyrics are vertically aligned with the lowest placed syllable in that verse;
- the last verse lyrics are vertically aligned with the highest placed syllable in that verse; and
- there is an equal amount of space between each verse of lyrics.

The plug-in is designed to help when you have moved lyrics up or down to avoid colliding with notes. If this is done carelessly, or if the system reformats afterwards, you can end up with mis-aligned lyrics or unevenly spaced verses.

To use the plug-in, select the bar containing the start of the lyrics, and choose **Plug-ins ▸ Text ▸ Align Lyrics**. There are no options; the plug-in goes ahead and aligns the lyrics automatically.

If there is only one verse then the lyrics are aligned in a row and positioned at the mean of the highest and lowest positioned syllable in the selected passage. In general, you would apply this plug-in to a score on a system-by-system basis, since lyrics are usually positioned independently on different systems.

Plug-in written by Peter Hayter.

Change Dynamics

Adjusts all dynamics in a selection or the entire score up or down by a step – e.g. all *mp* dynamics to *p*, or all *mf* to *f* – or you can define a custom mapping of existing dynamics to new dynamics.

To use the plug-in, select the passage on which you want it to operate (or don't make a selection if you want to apply it to the whole score), and choose **Plug-ins ▸ Text ▸ Change Dynamics**. A dialog appears, in which you can choose the music text font for your dynamics (typically Opus Text or

Helsinki Text for "engraved" scores and Inkpen2 Text or Reprise Text for "handwritten" scores), and whether you want the dynamics to get one step louder, one step softer, or use a custom mapping; when you click **OK**, if you chose to set up a custom mapping, you then specify the new dynamics to which you want existing dynamics to be mapped.

This plug-in has an informative **Help** window, to which you can refer for more assistance.

Plug-in written by Michael Kilpatrick.

Export Lyrics

Exports the lyrics from your score as a plain text file. To use the plug-in, choose **Plug-ins ▸ Text ▸ Export Lyrics**. A simple dialog appears, allowing you to choose whether the plug-in should try to **Separate lines** (i.e. add line breaks after punctuation that is followed by a capital letter or number), and whether the plug-in should **Save as Unicode** text (which you should switch on if you are using lyrics which don't use the Roman alphabet, such as Japanese). When you click **OK**, a text file is created in the same folder as the Sibelius file.

If you want to copy lyrics from a particular passage or staff, select it before running the plug-in; otherwise, the plug-in will save lyrics only from the topmost staff in the score that contains lyrics.

Consistent use of text styles in your score will lead to the best results when using this plug-in, as it will enable it to separate out each verse. Use **Lyrics line 1** for verse 1 lyrics, **Lyrics line 2** for verse 2 lyrics, etc.; use **Lyrics (chorus)** for choruses; use the **Block lyrics** text style for blocks of lyrics at the end of the score, etc.

If the score contains repeats, 1st- and 2nd-ending bars, etc., the text file created will probably require editing. The plug-in is also not designed to cater for scores containing multiple songs: for each song in turn, select just that song as a passage and run the plug-in.

If you run the plug-in more than once on the same score (e.g. to export lyrics from different staves or songs), be sure to rename the saved text file, or it will overwrite any file created by running the plug-in previously.

Plug-in written by Lydia Machell.

Find and Replace Text

Searches for specific text in your score and replaces it with other text. To use the plug-in, choose **Plug-ins ▸ Text ▸ Find and Replace Text**. A dialog appears: enter the text you want to find, and the text with which you want it to be replaced; specify whether the plug-in should match the text only if it is found on its own as a text object, as a whole word within a text object, or as any part of a word within a text object. You can choose to color the processed text to make it easier to find, if you like. Click **OK**, and the plug-in finds and replaces the specified text throughout the score.

The plug-in will preserve line breaks in multi-line text objects in which it replaces text, but formatting such as bold, italic or underline will be lost.

Plug-in written by Stefan Behrisch (www.werklabor.de) and updated by Bob Zawalich.

Plug-ins

Number Bars

Adds numbers above bars; this is useful for numbering repeated bars, or bars rest. Select the bars you want to number, then choose **Plug-ins ▸ Text ▸ Number Bars**. A dialog appears:

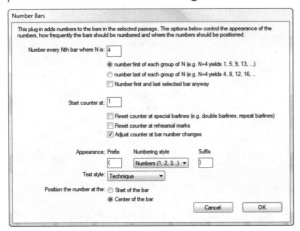

Number every Nth bar where N is allows you to specify the frequency of the numbers, and whether the plug-in should number the first bar of the group, or the last bar. Switch on **Number first and last selected bar anyway** if you want the plug-in to show a number on the first and last selected bar, even if they don't fit the pattern specified.

Start counter at determines where the plug-in should start counting from, and you can choose to restart the numbering at special barlines or rehearsal marks. **Adjust counter at bar number changes** tells the plug-in to take bar number changes into account.

The **Appearance** options allow you to choose between numbers, lower-case letters or upper-case letters, and to specify a prefix and suffix (such as parentheses) if desired. By default, the plug-in uses Technique text, but a handful of other text styles are also provided as options. Finally, you can choose whether the text should be positioned at the left-hand side of the bar or in the center of the bar.

When you click **OK**, the plug-in numbers all the bars in the selection according to the options chosen in the dialog.

Plug-in written by Hans-Christoph Wirth.

Number Beats

This plug-in numbers the beats in a bar for a selected passage; for example:

To use the plug-in, select the desired passage, and choose **Plug-ins ▸ Text ▸ Number Beats**. The beat length is taken from the time signature, e.g. 6/8 has dotted quarter note (crotchet) beats. The text is added in the Technique text style; if you find that it collides with notes or other markings, select one text object and choose **Edit ▸ Select ▸ Select More** (shortcut **Ctrl+Shift+A** *or* **⇧⌘A**), and move the whole row together using the **↑/↓** keys.

Reposition Text

General-purpose plug-in that can adjust the position of staff text, e.g. to position keyboard fingering text precisely. To use this plug-in:

- To reposition a single text object (e.g. a dynamic), select it, then choose **Plug-ins ▸ Text ▸ Reposition Text**. The plug-in will automatically adjust the position of the selected text object, moving it above or below the note.

- To reposition lots of text, either make sure nothing is selected (to process the whole score), or filter the specific text you want to reposition (📖 **5.7 Filters and Find**), or select a passage; then choose **Plug-ins ▸ Text ▸ Reposition Text**.

If you choose to reposition lots of text, a dialog appears, allowing you to choose whether you want to place the text always above the note, always below the note, above *or* below the note (useful for e.g. Fingering text), or whether you want the text to only be moved horizontally.

Either click **OK** to process the text, or click **Advanced Options** to give the plug-in further instruction: you can specify a single text style to reposition in the selected passage, and adjust the size and vertical/horizontal offset of the text, which affects the distance the plug-in will move the text to avoid collisions with notes.

The plug-in has two useful **Help** windows, to which you can turn for further assistance.

Plug-in written by Marc Nijdam.

Smarten Quotes

Replaces quotes and apostrophes of text objects in the current score, or in a set of files in a specific directory, so they appear "curly" with a more pleasing shape. The first dialog of the plug-in allows you to choose whether the operation should apply to the current score or a set of files. Clicking **Next** shows the following dialog:

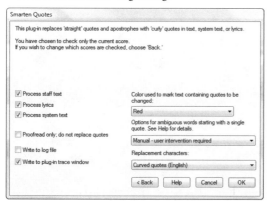

Here you can choose which text styles should be "smartened," whether the plug-in should run in proofreading mode only (in which only a log will be generated with no changes will be made to the score), set logging options and choose how any quote or apostrophe characters found in the score should be changed. If you switch on **Write to log file**, a log of all changes made to the score will be saved in a file called **Sibelius Quotes Log.txt**, which you find in your **Scores** folder.

Plug-ins

Unlike many programs, this plug-in also deals with complex cases like *'Twas,* as well as nested quote marks.

Plug-in written by Bob Zawalich.

Traditional Lyrics Beaming

Beams notes according to the underlay of the lyrics, i.e. beams are broken at every new word or syllable. To use this plug-in, select the staves on which you want it to operate (or leave nothing selected if you want to process the whole score; it will only change notes with lyrics attached, so staves for non-vocal instruments will not be affected), and choose **Plug-ins ▸ Text ▸ Traditional Lyrics Beaming**.

A dialog appears, allowing you to choose whether to process just the selected passage or the whole score, and whether or not to break the beams of notes with no lyrics (in which case you can highlight any such changes to check them). Click **OK**, and the beaming in your score is changed.

Plug-in written by Michael Kilpatrick.

6.13 Transformations plug-ins

The plug-ins in the Plug-ins ▸ Transformations subfolder provide a variety of tools that are useful for quickly generating new musical material from an existing melody or rhythm, and for learning about (or teaching) the principles behind common manipulations of pitch and rhythm. Most of the plug-ins are designed to be run on a selected passage, which they transform in place. Many have no options, and hence show no dialog; several of those that do show dialogs allow you to suppress the dialog after running the plug-in for the first time, in order to run the plug-in repeatedly with the same options chosen.

For those plug-ins where rhythms can be changed, tuplets are always moved as a complete unit, and grace notes are always moved along with the regular notes to which they belong. Tied notes present some complexities in many of these transformations, so you should check the results when transforming passages containing tied notes.

You may find it useful to assign keyboard shortcuts to some of these plug-ins in order to assimilate them seamlessly into your workflow – 📖 **5.12 Menus and shortcuts**.

All transformations plug-ins written by Bob Zawalich, except where otherwise stated.

Augment/Diminish Intervals

Increases (augments) or decreases (diminishes) the intervals between successive notes in the selection by a specified amount.

Select a passage and choose Augment Intervals or Diminish Intervals from the Plug-ins ▸ Transformations submenu. A dialog appears in which you can choose the amount by which the intervals should be augmented or diminished. Keep double accidentals determines whether Sibelius should prefer to respell any double accidentals as their simpler enharmonic equivalents. Click OK, and the selected passage is transformed.

If you want to run the plug-in repeatedly with the same options, switch on Do not show dialog again (until I restart Sibelius) in the plug-in's dialog; the dialog will then not appear again until you restart Sibelius.

Double/Halve Note Values

It is sometimes useful to halve or double all the note values in your score, e.g. if you are transcribing early music in which note values are twice as long as they would be notated in modern editions.

To run these plug-ins, select a passage of music and choose Double Note Values or Halve Note Values from the Plug-ins ▸ Transformations submenu. A dialog appears, warning you of the plug-in's limitations.

When you click OK, a new score will be created with the selected passage copied into it in its new form. The plug-in also copies time signatures (doubling or halving them as appropriate), and creates ties as appropriate.

Invert

Performs an inversion on the selected passage around a specified pitch. This plug-in overwrites the original music.

Plug-ins

To run the plug-in, select the music you want to invert, and choose **Plug-ins ▸ Transformations ▸ Invert**. A dialog appears, where you can set the pitch around which to invert the material, and whether to invert **Chromatically** or **Diatonically**.

Plug-in written by James Larcombe and Jürgen Zimmermann.

Pitch Mapping

Sometimes you may want to generate variations on an existing passage, transposing it into, say, the minor mode. This plug-in allows you to specify new pitches for each degree of the chromatic scale, and changes ("maps") the pitches in the selected passage accordingly.

To use the plug-in, select the passage you want to map, then choose **Plug-ins ▸ Transformations ▸ Pitch Mapping**. Choose the desired pitches from the drop-down menus in the plug-in dialog, and click **OK**.

By default, the plug-in treats all notes of the same pitch identically (so G♭ and F♯ are the same), but if you need to map equivalent enharmonic pitches differently, click the **More Choices** button, which allows you to do so.

You can also choose whether Sibelius should map existing notes to higher or lower notes by clicking **New Pitch Higher?**. This shows another dialog allowing you to choose whether or not Sibelius should map all notes higher or lower, or if not how large the interval between the old and new pitches should be before the notes are transposed up or down.

The plug-in examines all the notes in the selection, and calculates the pitch of each note relative to C (so 0 for C, 1 for C♯/D♭, and so on). It then alters the pitch of each note according to the settings from the plug-in's dialog. Suppose you set D to map to A♯ in the dialog: any D in the selection will be replaced by A♯ *in the same octave* as the original (octaves go from C up to B).

So if you set, say, G to map to D, it will map to the D below the original note. This isn't always what's required, hence the **Move everything above the following note up to the next octave** control. With this option switched on, if a note is higher than the pitch set here, it will be mapped to the new pitch, and then transposed up an octave.

Randomize Pitches

Replaces the existing pitches in the selection with new, randomly generated pitches.

Select a passage and choose **Plug-ins ▸ Transformations ▸ Randomize Pitches**. The rhythms of the notes in the selected passage are left unchanged, but the pitches are all changed randomly.

Retrograde

Creates a retrograde version of the selected passage – in other words, it turns the music backwards. For example, this plug-in rewrites the following passage:

as:

To use this plug-in, select the passage you want to retrograde, and choose **Plug-ins ▸ Transformations ▸ Retrograde**. A dialog appears, advising you of the limitations of the plug-in. When you click OK, a new score will be created containing the resulting music.

Retrograde Pitches

Rewrites the selection so that the order of pitches is reversed (so the last pitch becomes the first, the penultimate pitch becomes the second, and so on) without changing the durations of the notes.

Select a passage and choose **Plug-ins ▸ Transformations ▸ Retrograde Pitches**. The passage is rewritten in place.

Retrograde Rhythms

Rewrites the selection so that the order of rhythms is reversed (so the duration of the last note becomes the duration of the first, and so on) without changing the pitches of the notes.

Select a passage and choose **Plug-ins ▸ Transformations ▸ Retrograde Rhythms**. The passage is rewritten in place.

Retrograde Rhythms and Pitches

Rewrites the selection so that both the order of pitches and rhythms is reversed.

Select a passage and choose **Plug-ins ▸ Transformations ▸ Retrograde Rhythms and Pitches**. The passage is rewritten in place.

Rotate Rhythms

Rewrites the selection so that the durations of the notes are shifted to the right by one note (so the duration of the last note becomes the duration of the first, the duration of the first note becomes the duration of the second, and so on), without changing the pitches of the notes.

Select a passage and choose **Plug-ins ▸ Transformations ▸ Rotate Rhythms**. The passage is rewritten in place.

Rotate Rhythms and Pitches

Rewrites the selection so that both the durations and pitches of notes in the selection are shifted to the right by one note (so the last note of the selection becomes the first note, the first note becomes the second note, and so on).

Select a passage and choose **Plug-ins ▸ Transformations ▸ Rotate Rhythms and Pitches**. The passage is rewritten in place.

Shuffle Pitches

Rewrites the selection so that the existing pitches of the notes are randomly redistributed, changing the melodic contour in random ways but without introducing new pitches.

Select a passage and choose **Plug-ins ▸ Transformations ▸ Shuffle Pitches**. The passage is rewritten in place.

Plug-ins

Transform Scale

Changes pitches in the current score from their current scale to a new scale, e.g. to change the modality of a melody from major to minor, or change a pentatonic melody to use the whole-tone scale, and so on.

To use the plug-in, select the passage you want to transform, and choose **Plug-ins ▸ Transformations ▸ Transform Scale**. A dialog appears in which you specify the current scale of the music and the new scale into which you want to transform it. **Snap non-scale tones to scale tones** determines whether the plug-in should "snap" a note that is not in the scale to the nearest note that is in the scale (e.g. E♭ is not in the scale of G major, so you can choose whether the plug-in should leave this pitch unchanged, or "snap" it to the nearest note that is in the scale, e.g. D). Make your choice, and click **OK**.

The plug-in has many further options, which you can see by clicking **Show Options** in the dialog that appears:

- Define additional types of scales by clicking **Add/Edit Scales**
- Save and retrieve transformations you use often by clicking **Save/Restore Map**
- Determine the direction in which Sibelius should transpose the notes when transforming the scale by clicking **New Pitch Higher?**

Each of these dialogs contain detailed information on its use, and the plug-in also has a **Help** button that displays further details.

6.14 Tuplets plug-ins

All the plug-ins in the **Plug-ins ▸ Tuplets** submenu can operate on music using any number of voices. When you invoke the plug-ins with a passage selection, they will only affect notes in voice 1. If you want to manipulate notes in voices 2, 3 or 4, make a multiple selection instead, e.g. select the first note of the tuplet in voice 2, then **Ctrl**+click *or* ⌘-click the last note of the tuplet before running the plug-in.

Tuplets plug-ins written by Hans-Christoph Wirth.

Add Notes to Tuplet

Adds notes to the current tuplet, leaving it at the same overall duration (i.e. increasing its ratio). To use the plug-in, select as many notes in an existing tuplet as you wish to add (e.g. if you have a septuplet and want to make it into a nontuplet, select two of the notes in the septuplet), then choose **Plug-ins ▸ Tuplets ▸ Add Notes to Tuplet**.

Change Tuplet Ratio

Changes the ratio of the current tuplet, leaving it at the same overall duration. You can double or halve either side of the ratio (e.g. make a 3:2 tuplet 3:4, 6:4 or 6:8, and so on). To use the plug-in, either make a passage selection enclosing all the notes of the tuplet or select the tuplet number, and choose **Plug-ins ▸ Tuplets ▸ Change Tuplet Ratio**. A simple dialog appears; choose the desired ratio and click OK. The dialog has an Options button; clicking this shows the **Tuplet Preferences** dialog (see below).

Lengthen Tuplet

Lengthens a tuplet by combining the tuplet with notes either side of it. To use the plug-in, select all the notes of the existing tuplet and the notes (either before or after the tuplet) you want to add to the tuplet, and choose **Plug-ins ▸ Tuplets ▸ Lengthen Tuplet**. If you select all the notes of two or more adjacent tuplets, they will all be joined into a single tuplet.

Make Into Tuplet

Turns a selection of notes into a tuplet. To use the plug-in, select the notes you want to make into a tuplet, then choose **Plug-ins ▸ Tuplets ▸ Make Into Tuplet**. A simple dialog appears, allowing you to choose the ratio of the resulting tuplet, and whether to pad the tuplet with rests at the left-hand or right-hand side. The dialog also has an Options button; clicking this shows the **Tuplet Preferences** dialog (see below).

Remove Notes from Tuplet

Removes notes from the current tuplet, leaving it at the same overall duration (i.e. decreasing its ratio). To use the plug-in, select as many notes in an existing tuplet as you wish to remove (e.g. if you have a quintuplet and want to make it into a triplet, select two of the notes in the quintuplet), then choose **Plug-ins ▸ Tuplets ▸ Remove Notes from Tuplet**.

Shorten Tuplet

Shortens a tuplet by taking notes out of the tuplet and rewriting them outside the tuplet bracket. To use the plug-in, select as many notes in an existing tuplet you want to remain in the tuplet, then choose **Plug-ins ▸ Tuplets ▸ Shorten Tuplet**. The notes in the tuplet that were not selected are written as "normal" notes either before or after the shortened tuplet. If you select only one or two notes, running the plug-in will remove the enclosing tuplet altogether and replace it with regular notes.

Split or Join Tuplets

Either splits a single tuplet into two shorter tuplets, or joins two or more adjacent tuplets into one longer one.

To split a tuplet, select the note you want to become the first note of the second tuplet, then choose **Plug-ins ▸ Tuplets ▸ Split or Join Tuplets**.

To join tuplets together, make a passage selection containing two or more adjacent tuplets, then choose **Plug-ins ▸ Tuplets ▸ Split or Join Tuplets**. When joining tuplets, the plug-in avoids altering the precise playback timing of the notes in the new, joined tuplet, so in some cases the resulting tuplet may be more pleasing to a mathematician than a sight-reading performer. If you don't like the result, do **Edit ▸ Undo**, select both tuplets, then try **Plug-ins ▸ Tuplets ▸ Lengthen Tuplet** (see above).

Tuplet Preferences

Specifies preferences that are used by all of the other plug-ins in the **Plug-ins ▸ Tuplets** submenu. You can also access this plug-in by clicking **Options** in the dialogs shown by **Make Into Tuplet** and **Change Tuplet Ratio**.

The options are fairly self-explanatory. The first two affect the ratios of the tuplets created by the plug-ins, as there are always two alternative ways to describe the ratio of the same tuplet. For example, five notes in the time of three will be notated as 5:3 or 5:6 when you set **Keep tuplet ratio in interval** to 1:1 ... 2:1 or 1:2 ... 2:2 respectively. To change the ratio of a single tuplet, use **Plug-ins ▸ Tuplets ▸ Change Tuplet Ratio** (see above).

7. Parts

7. Dynamic parts

7.1 Working with parts

Music for several instruments is normally produced both in a full score and in separate "parts" that each contain the music of just one instrument (or sometimes several). Parts are rather different than full scores: they only contain notation relevant to the instrument; parts for transposing instruments can be in a different key; and the music is laid out differently, often on paper of a different size.

Fortunately, Sibelius takes care of all of this for you, automatically formatting, transposing and laying out parts.

What are dynamic parts?

Other notation programs require you to "extract" parts for each instrument as separate files, which means that if you need to make changes to the full score (after a first rehearsal, for example), you either have to make the same changes in the parts, or even extract them again, wasting hours.

However, Sibelius uses a revolutionary approach by which any change made in the score is automatically made in the part, and vice versa: allow us to introduce *dynamic parts*™.

You can edit dynamic parts in exactly the same way as you would a score. You can move, add and delete notes, add slurs, expression markings etc. just as you would normally. But whenever you change something in the score, the parts are instantly updated, and vice versa.

You don't need to extract dynamic parts, and in fact, they're all kept in the same file as the full score – so they're easier to organize, too.

Viewing dynamic parts

After creating or opening a Sibelius file, the full score will be displayed. Switching to and from parts is most simply done using the drop-down list marked **Full score** on the toolbar. When clicked, a list will appear, starting with the full score followed by the names of all the parts. Click the name of the part you wish to view and Sibelius will open it in a new window.

You can also switch quickly between the score and the most recently viewed part by clicking the **Switch Between Full Score and Part** button on the toolbar ▣ (shortcut **W**). If you select a note or other staff object before using **Switch Between Full Score and Part**, Sibelius will show you the part containing it. If there is nothing selected, Sibelius will show you the most recently viewed part. You can also switch to a part by double-clicking it on the Parts window (see below).

It is also possible to cycle through the parts using **Window ▸ Next Part** and **Previous Part** (shortcuts **Ctrl+Alt+Tab** *or* ⌥⌘~ and **Shift+Ctrl+Alt+Tab** *or* ⇧⌥⌘~). Once you get to the last part and advance to the next, Sibelius will show the full score.

Viewing multiple parts

By default, Sibelius will only create two windows per score: one for the full score, and the other for the parts. When switching between parts, Sibelius will always re-use the window displaying the previously viewed part. If you would prefer Sibelius to create a separate window for each part, perhaps so you can see them tiled on a large screen, switch on **View parts in new windows** on the **Other** page of **File ▸ Preferences** (in the **Sibelius** menu on Mac), shortcut **Ctrl+,** *or* ⌘,.

Parts

Distinguishing the score from a part

Sibelius uses different desk and paper textures for scores and parts so that you can instantly differentiate between the two. By default, Sibelius shows parts with a cream-colored paper and the score with white paper. To change the appearance of these textures, use the **Textures** page of **File ▸ Preferences** (in the **Sibelius** menu on Mac) – 📖 **5.6 Display settings**.

The Parts window

The Parts window allows you to print, create, modify, delete and extract parts. You shouldn't need to use this window often (since, for example, you can print parts just using **File ▸ Print** or **File ▸ Print All Parts**), so you should generally leave it switched off. But to show the Parts window, choose **Window ▸ Parts** (shortcut **Ctrl+Alt+R** *or* ⌥⌘R), or click the relevant toolbar button.

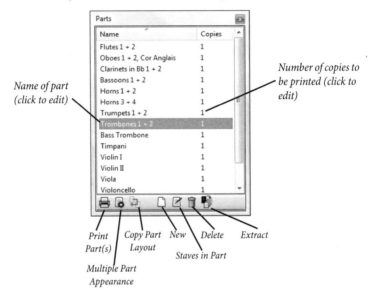

Similar to the drop-down list on the toolbar, this contains a list of all the existing parts in the score. You can switch to a part from the Parts window by double-clicking on the name of the part you wish to view.

You can apply some changes to multiple parts at the same time. To select a single part, click its name. If you wish to select more parts, use **Ctrl+click** *or* ⌘-click to add a part to the selection, or **Shift**-click to extend the selection.

Once you have one or more parts selected, you can click any of the six buttons at the bottom of the window:

- **Print Part(s)**: prints the currently selected parts; the **Copies** column allows you to specify how many copies of each part you wish to print – see **Printing multiple parts** below
- **Multiple Part Appearance**: Sibelius will ask whether you want to make changes to all parts in the score or just those currently selected, after which it will allow you to change the appearance of all the chosen parts in a single operation – 📖 **7.3 Multiple Part Appearance**
- **Copy Part Layout**: copies the layout of the currently viewed part to the part(s) selected in the Parts window – see **Copying part layout** on page 547

- **New Part**: allows you to create a new part manually, containing any number of staves from the full score
- **Staves in Part**: use this option to add or remove staves from a part. (This will only work with a single selection.)
- **Delete Part(s)**: removes the currently selected part or parts
- **Extract Parts**: extracts parts into separate Sibelius files – 📖 **7.4 Extracting parts**.

Printing multiple parts

When printing an orchestral score, you typically need one copy of the first flute part, but many more copies of the first violin part to hand out to all the players. Sibelius allows you to set the number of copies you wish to print for each part. Select the appropriate part in the Parts window and click once in the **Copies** column. A cursor will appear; type the number of copies, which can be any number between 0 and 99.

As Sibelius allows you to specify a number of copies for each part, printing a complete set of parts can literally be done with only two mouse clicks. You can print any combination of parts in one print job.

To print all the parts, choose **File ▸ Print All Parts**. To print just some parts, select the part(s) in the Part window and click the **Print Part(s)** button (🖨). You can alternatively print a single part in the normal way using **File ▸ Print**. If you are printing more than one part, you will not be able to adjust the page range or number of copies settings in the **Print** dialog.

You can print your parts directly to PDF files, which is handy if you need to send them via email. On Windows, you need to install a PDF printer driver to use this feature (see **Creating PDF files** on page 667). On Mac, simply click **Save As PDF** in the **Print** dialog. On both Windows and Mac, Sibelius will automatically save each part to a separate PDF file, choosing an appropriate filename each one.

Creating new parts

Sibelius automatically creates a part for each instrument in the score. When you open a score created in Sibelius 3 or earlier, you will be given the option whether or not to create a set of parts (📖 **9.7 Opening files from previous versions**).

If you need to manually add a further part to your score for some reason, click the **New Part** button (🗋) on the Parts window. You will see a dialog where you can choose which of the available staves in the score you wish to be visible in your new part. This is identical to the **Staves in Part** dialog (see below).

Adding or removing staves from parts

Sibelius allows you to include any number or combination of staves from your full score in a part. For example, you might make a vocal score of an opera by creating a part containing all the singers plus keyboard accompaniment.

To achieve this, make sure your full score contains all the instruments that you will need, including the keyboard staves. However, keyboard reduction staves are not usually printed in the conductor's score, so as well as the part for the vocal score, you should also create a part for the conductor's score, which contains all of the instruments *except* the keyboard accompaniment. When you come to print your scores, print the "conductor's score" part and the "vocal score" part instead of the full score.

To change the staves in an existing part, select the part and click the **Staves in Part** button (📝) on the Parts window. The following dialog appears:

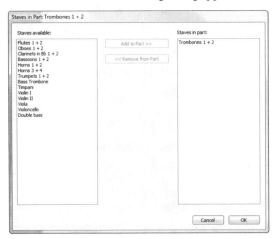

The **Staves available** list on the left shows the staves available in the full score which are not contained in the part. When a staff has been added to a part, it appears in the **Staves in part** list on the right. To add staves to a part, select the relevant staves in the list on the left and click the **Add to Part** button. Similarly, to remove staves from a part, select them in the list on the right and click the **Remove from Part** button (this does not remove the instrument from the score).

When you add or remove a staff or staves from a part, the note spacing of the entire part is reset, to ensure that the spacing is correct throughout.

Deleting parts

To delete a part, select it in the **Parts** window and click the **Delete** button (🗑). Sibelius will ask you for confirmation before going ahead. If you wish to delete more than one part at a time, simply click the **Delete** button with a multiple selection. Deleting a part does not delete the instrument from the score.

However, it is harmless to have parts listed even if you don't intend to use them, so don't feel any compunction to delete unwanted parts.

Appearance of parts and score

The following things are always the same in the score and all parts – so it doesn't matter whether you're viewing the score or a part, changing any of these will change it everywhere:

- Text styles: you can, though, set different point sizes for the full score and for all parts in **Edit Text Styles**
- Default positions: though similarly, you can set these to be different in the full score and parts in the **Default Positions** dialog

- Many rules in **House Style ▸ Engraving Rules** (e.g. positioning of accidentals, rhythm dots, articulations, brackets, clefs, key signatures, tuplets; appearance of barlines, chord diagrams, hairpins, rehearsal marks, slurs, ties; beam positions; sizes of notes; text borders and lyrics options).

However, the following things may be set in each part quite independently of the other parts and of the score, so changing them only affects the part (or score) you're viewing:

- Page and staff size etc. (in **Layout ▸ Document Setup**)
- Layout, including breaks and **Layout ▸ Auto Breaks**
- Note spacing (including **House Style ▸ Note Spacing Rule**)
- Text sizes (see **Text styles in parts** on page 546)
- Some rules in **House Style ▸ Engraving Rules** (e.g. format of bar numbers, multirests, instrument names, time signatures; appearance of system separators; first page number; staff and system spacing)
- Appearance of timecode and hit points (**Play ▸ Video and Time ▸ Timecode and Duration** and **Hit Points**).

It's useful to be able to change things in different parts independently of each other like this. However, it's also often useful to make the same changes in all parts or a group of parts at once, rather than having to do so to each part in turn. This is what the **Multiple Part Appearance** dialog is for – 📖 **7.3 Multiple Part Appearance**.

Parts

7.2 Editing parts

Editing a part works in exactly the same way as editing a score; in fact, almost anything you can do in a score will work in the same way in a part. Creating and deleting objects in a part automatically does the same to the score, and vice versa.

Moving objects in parts

However, moving objects (other than changing the pitch of notes) is another matter. You can position things slightly differently in the score and part, for layout reasons and to avoid collisions that may arise in one but not the other. The way it works is this:

- If you move an object in the score, it also moves in the relevant part(s) (as you'd expect)
- But if you move an object in a part, it *doesn't* move in the score. The same applies to changing the design of an object – if you drag the middle of a slur to change its shape in the part, it won't change in the score. This is so you can make final adjustments to parts without affecting the score. The object goes orange in the part to show that it's different than the score (see **Differences in parts** below).
- Having moved an object in a part like this, moving it in the score won't subsequently move it in the part again (because that would mess up the part when you'd just got it looking right) – unless, that is, you move it so far in the score that it attaches to a different note (otherwise the score and part wouldn't match at all), or unless you reset the object to be the same in the part and score again (see **Resetting objects in parts** below).
- You shouldn't move an object very far in a part (e.g. to a different note), because it won't move in the score and so won't match the score. If you try to, the gray attachment line will go red, to warn you that the object is too far away from where it is in the score.

So in general, the way you should work is to input music into the score, rather than the parts; and then tweak the position and design of things in the parts in the course of making final adjustments.

Note though, that you can make layout changes such as moving staves, adjusting system and page breaks and changing note spacing quite freely in parts – this doesn't count as moving objects around, because it doesn't matter that the score and part end up with a quite different layout.

Differences in parts

When you edit or move an object in a part, Sibelius helpfully shows you that it is now different than the score by coloring it orange. (If this bothers you, switch off View ▸ Differences in Parts.)

For example:

- Staff objects (e.g. Expression text, hairpins, accidentals, etc.) appear orange if they have been moved in parts
- Notes that have been flipped or made cue-sized in parts appear orange
- Objects that are shown in the part but hidden (or absent) in the score, or vice versa, appear orange.

You can also switch on **View ▸ Differences in Parts** in the full score and Sibelius will color any object that has been moved or edited in one or more of the parts. This makes it easy, for example, to see which objects you may want to use **Layout ▸ Reset to Score Position** on (see below).

Resetting objects in parts

If you need to reset the position of an object in a part, you can either reset it to its default position, or to the same position as in the score.

- To reset to the default position (i.e. the values defined in **House Style ▸ Default Positions**), choose **Layout ▸ Reset Position** (shortcut **Ctrl+Shift+P** *or* ⇧⌘P).
- To restore an object's position back to the score, choose **Layout ▸ Reset to Score Position** (shortcut **Ctrl+Shift+Alt+P** *or* ⇧⌥⌘P). If **View ▸ Differences in Parts** is switched on, the object will no longer be drawn in orange.

When editing the full score, you can use **Layout ▸ Reset to Score Position** to reset an object to the score's position in *all the parts* in which it appears.

You can also reset the appearance of an object in a part (such as a slur) either to its default design, or to the design of the same object in the score:

- To restore one or more objects back to using its default design, choose **Layout ▸ Reset Design** (shortcut **Ctrl+Shift+D** *or* ⇧⌘D)
- To reset back to the design of the same object in the score, choose **Layout ▸ Reset to Score Design** (shortcut **Ctrl+Shift+Alt+D** *or* ⇧⌥⌘D). Again, the object will no longer be orange (unless you had also changed its position).

As with restoring the score's position, choose **Layout ▸ Reset to Score Design** while editing the full score will reset the design of the selected object back to the score's appearance in *all the parts* in which it appears.

Hide and show in parts and score

Apart from in a few cases (such as clef changes and cue passages), every object in your score will, by default, be visible in both the score and any parts which should contain it. If you wish to hide an object in a score so that it only appears in a part, select the appropriate object (in the score or part) and choose **Edit ▸ Hide or Show ▸ Show in Parts**. Similarly, if you want an object to appear only in the full score and not in the parts, choose **Edit ▸ Hide or Show ▸ Show in Score**.

When viewing the full score, choosing **Edit ▸ Hide or Show ▸ Hide** hides the object in the score and *all* the parts. When viewing a part, choosing **Edit ▸ Hide or Show ▸ Hide** hides the object in that part only, leaving the score unaffected. (And you can hide/show objects in individual parts if necessary from the **General** tab of **Properties**.)

Editing part names

Part names can be edited directly from the Parts window by editing the **Name** field, or in the **File ▸ Score Info** dialog when viewing a part. To edit from the Parts window, choose the part you wish to rename and click once in the **Name** column. A cursor appears, allowing you to type the new name for the part. Editing the part name also updates the name on the first and subsequent pages of the part.

Parts

If you need to add line breaks to a part name in order to list multiple instruments on separate lines in the page header, use \n\. You can also tell Sibelius to use the music text font for individual characters by prefixing the character whose font you wish to change with a ^ (e.g. **Clarinet in B^b** would appear as "Clarinet in B♭") – see **Adding formatting changes to Score Info** on page 255 for details of other special characters you can type.

For further information about part names, see **Part name and Instrument changes** on page 253. For more general information about instrument names, 📖 **3.8 Instrument names**.

Text styles in parts

Each text style in Sibelius has two sizes: one for the score and the other for all the parts. To change the size of text in your parts independently from the score, click **Edit Text Styles**, either in the **House Style** menu or on the **House Style** page of **Multiple Part Appearance**. The **Edit Text Styles** dialog will appear. Select the name of the text style you wish to edit, and click **Edit**. The following dialog appears:

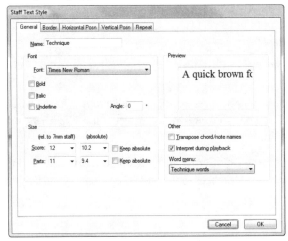

To adjust the size of the text style in parts, enter a new point size, either relative to a 7mm staff or as an **absolute** value. If you do not want the text to scale according to the size of the staff, switch on **Keep absolute**. For more information on editing text styles, 📖 **3.9 Edit Text Styles**.

If you need text to appear at a different size in the score and parts, as you would for (say) Title text – which is typically larger in the score than it is in the parts – you should never adjust its size using the **Text** panel of Properties. Any change you make to the size of a text object in this way will affect *both* the score *and* the part. Therefore, you should instead change the default sizes for your text style using **House Style ▸ Edit Text Styles**.

If you encounter text that is far too big or small in your score or part, you probably changed the size using Properties, so select it and choose **Layout ▸ Reset Design** (shortcut **Ctrl+Shift+D** *or* ⌥⌘D), then go to **House Style ▸ Edit Text Styles** and set up suitable sizes for the score and the parts.

Clef changes in parts

Sibelius allows you to create clef changes in parts that do not appear in the full score; such clefs appear colored orange (if View ▶ Differences in Parts is switched on). Beware, however, that if the initial clef in the part is different from the initial clef for that instrument in the full score, the Omit clef changes option on the House Style page of Multiple Part Appearance (⌨ **7.3 Multiple Part Appearance**) may prevent any new clef changes you create in the part from appearing, in which case Sibelius will warn you.

Also beware that if a clef change exists in the full score and is visible in the part, if you drag the clef in the part, it will also move in the score too. If you need to move the clef in the part without moving the clef in the score, create a new clef in the part directly on top of the existing clef; this new clef will be independent for that specific part, and can then be moved independently of the clef in the full score.

Codas in parts

Sibelius allows you to set whether the split in the system that customarily appears before a coda should also appear in parts. A coda is marked as such by a barline that has Split multirest switched on with a Gap before bar of greater than 0. (When you choose Layout ▶ Break ▶ Split System, Sibelius will do this for you automatically – ⌨ **4.6 Repeats**.) If you would like the system to split automatically at the same place in parts, switch on Keep gaps before codas (that have split multirests) on the Layout page of Multiple Part Appearance. To suppress the split in parts, switch it off – ⌨ **7.3 Multiple Part Appearance**.

Copying part layout

In some kinds of music – especially music for film, TV and stage shows – it's common for the layout of all the instrumental parts to be very similar, with system breaks and page turns in the same place in all the parts. Sibelius makes it easy to copy the layout from one part to any or all of the others:

* First, adjust the layout of one of the parts, including the vertical positioning of system objects such as rehearsal marks, tempo markings, and so on, until it's how you want it for the other parts too
* While viewing the part whose layout you want to copy:
  * To copy the layout to all the other parts, click the Copy Part Layout button (🔁) with all (or no) parts selected in the window
  * To copy the layout to one or more parts, select the parts you want to update, and click the Copy Part Layout button
* You're asked if you want to proceed: click Yes.

Instantly, the layout of the current part is copied to the selected parts. Page and staff size, orientation, page and staff margins, system, page and special page breaks, Layout ▶ Auto Breaks settings, and the positions of system objects are all updated to match the chosen part.

Parts

Exporting house styles from parts

Having set up the appearance of a part via the Multiple Part Appearance, Auto Breaks and Engraving Rules dialogs, you can then export its house style, either to import into other parts in the same score or to import into parts in another score in future.

To export a house style from a part, make sure you're viewing that part, and choose House Style ▸ Export House Style.

To import the house style into other parts in the same (or a different) score, select those parts in the Parts window, click the Multiple Part Appearance button, then click Import House Style on the House Style page of the dialog.

When you export a house style from a part, it includes things like the Auto Breaks and Document Setup settings that make it look like a part. Therefore the house style is only suitable for importing into other parts, not into a full score. Likewise, if you export a house style from a full score, it is not suitable for importing into parts. So you should export different house styles for full scores and for parts.

Parts in different transpositions

You may need to have the same part in several different transpositions (e.g. wind bands may require some brass parts in both B♭ and E♭, depending on the instruments available), which Sibelius makes easy:

- First, create a new part containing the instrument for which you need to create a part in a different transposition – see **Creating new parts** on page 541
- Change the name of the part so that you can tell it apart, e.g. 1st Horn (E♭) – see **Editing part names** above
- Now view the part, by double-clicking its name in the Parts window, or by choosing it from the menu on the toolbar
- To change the transposition of the part, make sure nothing is selected in the part (hit Esc), then choose Create ▸ Other ▸ Instrument Change. Choose the variant of the instrument that has the desired transposition and click OK, then click at the very start of the first staff of the part to create it. This instrument change exists only in this part, and does not affect the full score, or any of the other parts.
- You may also need to change the key signature used by your newly-transposed part. Again first making sure that nothing is selected (hit Esc), choose Create ▸ Key Signature (shortcut K), select the desired key signature, and click OK, then click at the very start of the part. Like the instrument change, this key signature exists only in this part.
- Finally, for particularly extreme transpositions, you may need to adjust the clef. With nothing selected, choose Create ▸ Clef (shortcut Q), select the desired clef, and click OK, then click at the start of the part. You may also need further clef changes – see **Clef changes in parts** above.

Though it is required less often, you can also create instrument changes, clef changes and key signature changes at any point in a dynamic part without affecting the full score or any other parts based on the same instrument in the score. Beware, therefore, that if you add a key signature to a part, it will affect only the part you are working on, and will not be created in the full score. If you want to add a key change to the full score and all parts, create it in the full score.

7.3 Multiple Part Appearance

The **Multiple Part Appearance** dialog can be used to change the appearance of any number of parts in a single operation. First select the part(s) you want to change in the Parts window, then click ▣ .

If you are changing the appearance of multiple parts, there may be instances under which some settings are different in different parts, in which case they will appear blank. If no changes are made to the settings in this state, then the individual values for each of the parts in the selection will be left unchanged.

The dialog consists of three tabbed pages:

Document Setup page

The **Document Setup** page allows you to set the page size, orientation and staff size of your parts:

* Setting the page size to **Same as score** will set both the page size and orientation of the parts to be identical to the score. If you wish to use different settings, then choose the desired size from the drop-down list and click either **Portrait** or **Landscape**.

* Setting the staff size to **Same as score** will ensure that all staves in your parts are identical in size to the staves in the score. However, parts generally have larger staves, so to set a different value choose from either **mm** or **inches** and enter the desired staff size.

* Clicking **Margins** allows you to change the page and staff margins for the parts independently of the score – see **Page margins** and **Staff margins** on page 585. This is especially useful for increasing the top staff margin on the first page to make room for the title text, etc.

* On Mac, you can click **Page Setup** (and extra button not shown here) to set up the printing defaults for your parts, e.g. setting them to require a particular paper size for printing – 📖 **5.16 Printing**.

Parts

Layout page

The **Layout** page has the following options; if in doubt, leave them at the default settings (which are sensible ones):

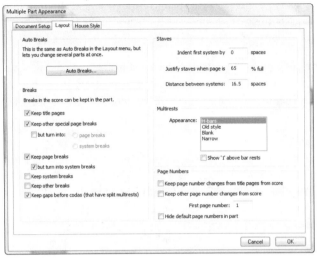

* To change your **Auto Breaks** settings, click **Auto Breaks**. This dialog allows you to choose how Sibelius should lay out systems, pages and multirests (□ **8.4 Auto Breaks**).
* System breaks, page breaks and special page breaks that have been manually added to the score can be suppressed, retained or modified in parts (if in doubt, just leave these options alone):
  ○ If you want blank pages at the start of the score (i.e. before the first bar of music) to appear in your parts, switch on **Keep title pages**
  ○ If you want other blank pages (i.e. those that occur after the first bar of music) to appear in your parts exactly in the same way as they do in the score, switch on **Keep other special page breaks**
  ○ If you would prefer they were changed into other kinds of breaks, switch on the **but turn into** checkbox, and choose whether they should be changed into **page breaks** or **system breaks**
  ○ If you want page breaks to appear in parts in exactly the same way as they do in the score, switch on **Keep page breaks**
  ○ If you would prefer they were changed into system breaks, switch on **but turn into system breaks**
  ○ If you want system breaks in the score also to appear in parts, switch on **Keep system breaks**
  ○ Other formatting (e.g. locked systems, "bars kept together") in the score can also appear in the parts if you switch on **Keep other breaks**
  ○ **Keep gaps before codas (that have split multirests)** – see **Codas in parts** on page 547 for more information.
* It is fairly common for the start of the first staff in a part to be indented rightwards. Sibelius allows you to indent all your parts automatically by setting **Indent first system by** to (say) 4 spaces. When set to zero, the stave will appear in its usual position.

- To set how staves should be justified in your parts, set **Justify staves when page is** *n***% full.** (See **Vertical justification** on page 599.)

- Adjusting the **Distance between systems** controls the standard distance between systems in the select part or parts. Decreasing the number saves space in parts. On pages where the music is vertically justified, the distance between staves can be larger than the numbers specified.

- To change the appearance of multirests in your parts, choose the appropriate style from the **Appearance** list. If you would like Sibelius to include the number 1 above single bar rests, switch on **Show '1' above bar rests** (□ **2.24 Multirests**).

- By default your parts will all have their pages numbered from 1. If you want a different first page number, specify it by changing **First page number.** If, more unusually, you want your parts to use the same page numbers as the score:

    ○ **Keep page number changes from title pages from score,** which is only available if **Keep title pages** is switched on (because page number changes are always attached to page breaks), makes the page number change attached to the title page in the score (if present) appear in the parts.

    ○ **Keep other page number changes from the score,** which is only available if **Keep other special page breaks** is switched on, makes page number changes that occur after the start of the full score appear in the parts.

    If you want to hide all page numbers in your parts, switch on **Hide default page numbers in parts.** For more information about page numbers, □ **3.6 Page numbers.**

House Style page

The **House Style** page has the following options:.

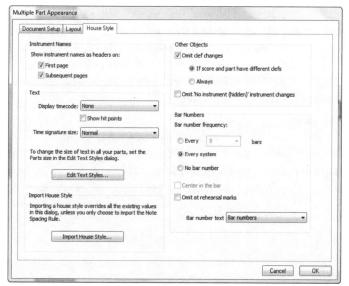

- Sibelius can add instrument names to each of your parts. By default, these will appear at the top left of the **First Page**, and at the top of **Subsequent pages**. If you don't want instrument names, switch off either or both of these options.

(Instrument name headers are automatically generated from each part's name using text wild-cards – 📖 **3.10 Wildcards** – and will always exist in every part. If you switch the headers off here, Sibelius will hide the relevant text objects in the parts, not delete them, so you can switch them back on again later.)

- By default, timecode and hit points are not displayed in parts. If you wish to make timecode visible, then choose from either **Above every bar** or **At start of every system** in Display time-code. If you want hit points to show, then switch on **Show hit points** (📖 **4.11 Timecode and hit points**).

- Time signatures will appear as normal, snuggled between the top and bottom staff lines, by default. If you wish to use **Large** or **Huge** time signatures in parts, then choose the relevant option from **Time signature size** (see **Big time signatures etc.** on page 188).

- Clicking the **Edit Text Styles** button will take you directly to the **Edit Text Styles** dialog (see **Text styles in parts** on page 546)

- You can import a house style into all the selected parts by clicking **Import House Style** – see **Exporting house styles from parts** on page 548. Only the Engraving rules and Document setup and **Note spacing rule** options are enabled when importing into a part.

- Switching off **Omit clef changes** will ensure that all clef changes in the score will appear in the parts. To suppress all clef changes in every instrument in parts, switch on **Omit clef changes** and choose **Always**. Some transposing instruments (such as bass clarinet) may use a different clef in parts to the score, so clef changes that are necessary in the score may not make any sense in the part. Sibelius gives you the option to omit such clef changes by choosing **Omit clef changes** and clicking **If score and part have different clefs**. You can manually add any necessary clef changes to a part, and they will *not* appear in the score – see **Clef changes in parts** on page 547.

- It is the style of some composers to hide segments of a stave where an instrument is not playing (this is known as a "cut-away" or "scrapbook" look – see **Staves with gaps in** on page 175). This convention, however, does not usually apply to parts, so Sibelius gives you the option to suppress all instrument changes to hidden (no lines) instruments in parts; to do this, switch on **Omit 'No instrument (hidden)' instrument changes**.

- To set the frequency of bar numbers in your parts, choose from **Every *n* bars**, **Every system** or **No bar numbers**. You can also center the numbers by choosing **Center in the bar**. If you do not want bar numbers to appear on the same bars as rehearsal marks, switch on **Omit at rehearsal marks**. If you wish to make bar numbers look different in the parts than in the score, choose the text style you want to use from the **Bar number text** style drop-down list. (The **Bar numbers (parts)** text style is intended for this purpose.) But normally, this should just be left set to **Bar numbers**.

7.4 Extracting parts

Extracting parts simply means that any dynamic parts chosen for extraction will be exported as individual files, retaining their music, formatting and layout precisely. The original dynamic parts themselves remain unaffected.

Why extract parts?

In practice, you should rarely need to extract parts from your score, and should not bother doing so unless you have to; however, there are some situations in which you may find it necessary:

- *Parts that have variable numbers of staves in the score or staves containing music for multiple players*: if a score has a staff for "Horns 1+3" and also *separate* staves for "Horn 1" and "Horn 3" that are used at different points in the score for the sake of clarity, you will not be able to create a part for "Horn 1" or "Horn 3" automatically, though you can create a combined Horn 1 and Horn 3 dynamic part.

  If a single staff in the score contains music for two players, such as "Flutes 1.2.," you will not be able to create individual parts from "Flute 1" and "Flute 2" automatically. You may need to extract the "Flutes 1.2." part as two separate files, then edit each of them to remove the unwanted player – but see **Multiple players on the same staff** below before you go ahead and extract parts.

- *If you want the parts to be opened by Sibelius Student or an earlier version of Sibelius*: You will need to extract the parts from the score and subsequently export them as version 2, 3, 4 or Student files as appropriate.

- *If you want to publish the parts on SibeliusMusic.com*: Because Scorch cannot currently view dynamic parts, you will need to extract the parts from the score and upload them separately to SibeliusMusic.com.

You should always aim to extract parts as late as possible. If you need to revise a score at a later date, this will keep any corresponding changes you need to make to the parts to a minimum.

If you make quite a few revisions to the score later, it may be quicker to re-extract some or all of the parts than to revise them.

Parts

Extract Parts dialog

To extract parts, click the **Extract Parts** button () on the Parts window. The dialog shown below appears:

At the left of the dialog you can select the parts to extract. You can select one part to extract just that one, add individual parts to the selection with **Ctrl**+click *or* ⌘-click, add consecutive parts with **Shift**-click, or click and drag down the list to add consecutive parts with the mouse.

Ignoring the remaining options (which we'll deal with in a minute), click **OK**, and in just seconds the part(s) will be saved and re-opened in Sibelius as separate files.

The other options in the dialog are as follows:

- Sibelius saves the extracted parts into the path entered in **Save to folder**. You can enter a path manually or click **Browse** to locate the directory.

  Sibelius allows you to create useful filenames for each of the parts being saved using codes. Sibelius lists its recognized codes on the dialog. By way of example, if your score were called **Opus 1** and you were extracting the 2nd oboe part, entering a filename of **%f - %p (part %n of %o).sib** would evaluate to **Opus 1 - 2nd Oboe (part 4 of 29).sib**.

  By default, Sibelius names the parts in a sensible format including the score's filename, the part name and the date and time the parts were saved.

- If you switch **View parts now** off, you can extract and save a set of parts without having them appear on the screen. If you leave this option switched on, you will have to close all of the parts (using e.g. **File ▸ Close All**) after they have been extracted.

Multiple players on the same staff

Though dynamic parts aren't always suitable for situations where multiple players (e.g. Horn 1+2) share the same staff, they can provide some efficiency gains if you keep both the Horn 1+2 staff and two separate Horn 1 and Horn 2 staves in the score, so that you can easily make edits to all three staves while being able to see them all at once. To do this:

- In the full score, write the music on a combined Horn 1+2 staff (or alternating this with separate staves)

- When you've finished the music, add separate Horn 1 and 2 staves and copy/filter the music across to them from the combined Horn 1+2 staff, as described in **Extracting individual players** below.

- Create a dynamic "part" (called, say, "Conductor's score") consisting of all the instruments *except* the new separate Horn 1 and 2 staves (see **Adding or removing staves from parts** on page 541). Print this for the conductor. Print the separate Horn 1 and 2 staves (rather than the combined staff) as the horns' parts.

- If you need to revise anything in the horns in future, just make the same revisions (in the full score) to the combined Horn 1+2 staff and the separate Horn 1 and 2 staves.

Extracting individual players

As described in 📖 **2.18 Instruments**, sometimes you will have separately numbered players in the score for which you need to extract individual parts – e.g. Trumpets 1, 2 and 3. How this is done depends on the case:

- If the players jump from staff to staff, you'll need to extract more than one staff into the same part. For instance, if your score has instruments called "Trumpets 1.2.3," "Trumpets 1.2" and "Trumpet 3," and you want to get the Trumpet 3 part, you should extract Trumpets 1.2.3 and Trumpet 3 into the same part, then delete any notes not played by Trumpet 3. You can use filters to help with this last stage (📖 **5.7 Filters and Find**). As in the score, you may need to put system breaks in the part where a player jumps from one staff to another, so that you can hide the unused staves on either side of the changeover point.

- If there are just two players (e.g. Flutes 1 and 2) that sometimes or always share the same staff, you can extract both players into the same part and then remove the unwanted notes using filters – read on.

The most common of the above cases is the last one, where two players share the same staff, as in the example below for two flutes:

In this example, the music is sometimes in two-note chords, sometimes in unison (*a 2*) and sometimes in two voices.

Sibelius has built-in filters to make extracting individual players as simple as a few mouse clicks. The Edit ▸ Filter ▸ Player 1 (For Deletion) and Player 2 (For Deletion) filters are specifically designed for this purpose.

- View the Flute 1 & 2 staff or staves as a single dynamic part. You should at this point make any changes that you know you will need to make to both players, such as removing collisions between objects, or adding cues.

- Extract the part

- Make a copy of the extracted part using File ▸ Save As, calling it, say, Flute 2

Parts

- To make the Flute 1 part, select in turn each section that is for both flutes as a passage, choose **Edit ▸ Filter ▸ Player 2 (For Deletion)**, then hit **Delete** twice to delete the Flute 2 music – the first **Delete** turns unwanted notes in extra voices into rests, and the second **Delete** hides these rests. If your music contained sections of chords in one voice, as in the example above, you will need to filter for the rests specifically, as simply hitting **Delete** again will also delete some of the Flute 1 notes, which remain selected after you hit **Delete** for the first time.

- Leave any sections of music where only Flute 1 is playing, as indicated by e.g. '1.' above the staff. But any sections where one flute plays and the other has explicit rests (using two voices) can be handled by the **Player 2 (For Deletion)** filter.

- You'll be left with the Flute 1 part, all dynamics, text and so on intact. Edit the instrument name to read "Flute 1":

- To make the Flute 2 part, open the copy of the extracted part and follow the same procedure, using **Edit ▸ Filter ▸ Player 1 (For Deletion)**. After adjusting the instrument name, checking articulations and so on, you should have:

One case that these filters cannot automatically deal with is where a mixture of two-note chords and multiple voices occur *in the same bar*, such as:

In this instance, filtering, say, **Player 2 (For Deletion)** would leave the two eighth notes (quavers) at the end of the bar unselected. Sibelius always assumes that, within a single bar, if there are multiple voices then each voice constitutes a player; so to get the correct results, you should ensure that voices are used consistently within the same bar. In this particular case, simply selecting the lower pair of eighth notes and swapping them into voice 2 (shortcut **Alt+2** *or* ⌥2) would do the trick.

These **Player** filters can only cope with separating two players, not three (such as our three trumpets described above).

Don't try to use the **Player** filters to select a particular player and then copy it – this may well not copy all the music you intended. For further details about filters, 📖 **5.7 Filters and Find**.

8. Layout & engraving

8.1 Layout and formatting

📖 **2.29 Staves**, **7.1 Working with parts**, **5.23 View menu**, **8.3 Music engraving**, **8.4 Auto Breaks**, **8.5 Breaks**, **8.6 Document Setup**, **8.7 Attachment**, **8.9 Note spacing**, **8.10 Staff spacing**.

Layout means how music looks on the page. *Formatting* is the process of creating a good layout. Sibelius knows so much about music engraving that it automatically formats music to produce an instant, excellent layout. In most other music notation programs, formatting is largely left up to the user, which can waste hours of time.

But Sibelius also lets you adjust the layout manually. Described below is the armory of methods at your disposal; most of these options are on the **Layout** menu. For instance, you can put your own page-turns into parts, or force a score to fit into a convenient number of pages.

Because Sibelius reformats the score in a fraction of a second, you can instantly adjust the layout at any stage, even when the music is finished, which eliminates the need to plan layout in advance.

The three main weapons in your formatting armory are to adjust the page and staff size, the vertical spacing, and the horizontal spacing. There are also options to force a passage of music to fit into a system or page, and to lock the music so that it can't reformat.

Page and staff size

The bluntest tools are changing the staff, margin and/or page sizes in the **Layout ▸ Document Setup** dialog (shortcut **Ctrl+D** *or* ⌘D). Altering these is one way to increase or reduce the number of pages in a score, or to free up some space between the staves.

Adjusting the staff size (the distance between the top and bottom staff lines of a 5-line staff) is generally the most effective. You will find that a tiny adjustment often has a dramatic effect on the amount of music that can fit on a page, without affecting the legibility of the notes. For instance, in an orchestral score this might tip the balance between fitting one system per page and fitting two, thus halving the length of the score.

Equally, a small adjustment to the margins or even the page size can have a large effect on the layout. Of course, for practical reasons altering these may not be options open to you.

For detailed instructions on these options, 📖 **8.6 Document Setup**.

Vertical spacing

Changing the vertical spacing means, in effect, moving the staves. This should be done with care, and it's worth understanding the concepts behind vertical spacing so you can set Sibelius up to do what you want it to do automatically. For detailed instructions, 📖 **8.10 Staff spacing**.

In addition to changing the distance between staves, you can save space by hiding empty staves (📖 **2.29 Staves**). Another easy way to reduce the number of staves on a page, particularly in parts, is to create a page break: the remaining staves will be spaced out proportionally without you having to drag them (📖 **8.5 Breaks**).

Layout

Horizontal spacing

Changing horizontal spacing means changing the distance between notes, rests and barlines – 📖 **8.9 Note spacing**.

System and page breaks

If you need to change Sibelius's default formatting, you can insert manual system and page breaks at any barline – 📖 **8.5 Breaks**.

Make Into System/Page

You can force any passage to fit into a system or a page. Simply select the passage, then from the Layout ▸ Format submenu choose Make Into System (shortcut Shift+Alt+M *or* ⇧⌥M) or Make Into Page (shortcut Ctrl+Shift+Alt+M *or* ⇧⌥⌘M). It will remain locked as a system or page thereafter, even if you reformat the score.

To undo this, unlock the format (see below).

As with other formatting overrides, you should not routinely make passages into systems/pages. Doing so can produce undesirable formatting elsewhere if you don't know what you're doing – it is intended for special circumstances only.

Keep Bars Together

It is sometimes desirable to ensure that two or three bars should always appear on the same system. To achieve this, select the bars you want to keep together, and choose Layout ▸ Format ▸ Keep Bars Together.

Make Layout Uniform

If you want to set a constant number of bars per system, and/or systems per page, choose Plug-ins ▸ Other ▸ Make Layout Uniform – see **Make Layout Uniform** on page 506.

Lock Format

If you have input a passage of music that requires very special formatting that you don't want to mess up, you can *lock* it. This stops the bars from reflowing onto other systems (though it doesn't prevent spacing changes within a system, e.g. moving a note left or right). To lock the format, simply select the passage in question and choose Layout ▸ Format ▸ Lock Format (shortcut Ctrl+Shift+L *or* ⇧⌘L).

When you lock the format or use Layout ▸ Format ▸ Make Into System/Page, invisible elves and pixies place little layout symbols on each barline to stop the bars moving around. These icons are visible when View ▸ Layout Marks is switched on.

Unlock Format

To undo Lock Format, re-select the bars and choose Layout ▸ Format ▸ Unlock Format (shortcut Ctrl+Shift+U *or* ⇧⌘U). This makes the blue icons disappear, and the bars are free to flow from system to system once more.

Unlock Format also removes page breaks, system breaks, and undoes Make Into System/Page, Keep Bars Together and the effects of the Make Layout Uniform plug-in.

Auto Breaks

The Auto Breaks dialog lets you specify various sensible places for Sibelius to put system and page breaks for you, particularly in parts – 📖 **8.4 Auto Breaks**.

Indenting staves

You can drag the left-hand and right-hand ends of systems to indent them – 📖 **2.29 Staves**.

Reset Position

You can move objects to their default position by making a selection and choosing Layout ▸ Reset Position (shortcut Ctrl+Shift+P *or* ⇧⌘P).

The specific effects this has for some particular objects are:

- *Text and rehearsal marks:* aligns with notes, and realigns rows of lyrics and chord symbols
- *Symbols:* aligns with notes – e.g. for putting an ornament over a note
- *Lines:* snaps the ends to notes, and makes any non-magnetic slurs go magnetic. The House Style ▸ Default Positions dialog lets you set the exact default position relative to the note.
- *Tuplets:* makes any non-magnetic tuplets (such as any created with Sibelius 1.4 or earlier) go magnetic
- *Accidentals:* resets the horizontal position of accidentals
- *Beam angles and stem lengths:* resets these to the default settings (as with Notes ▸ Reset Stems and Beam Positions).

You can also use the mouse to move objects to sensible positions: when copying text objects with Alt+click *or* ⌥-click, you can hold down Shift, which automatically puts the copied objects directly in their default positions.

Reset to Score Position

Acts in the same way as Reset Position, except that objects in the part are set to use the same position as they appear in the full score. If this feature is used in a full score, Sibelius will reset the position in *all* the parts in which the object appears.

Reset Design

If you make changes to the appearance (rather than the position) of an object, you can reset an item's design to its default using Layout ▸ Reset Design (shortcut Ctrl+Shift+D *or* ⇧⌘D).

The specific effects on particular objects are as follows:

- Unhides hidden beams, flags or hooks
- Unhides deleted instances of system text (e.g. Tempo text or rehearsal marks)
- Resets the scale factor of imported graphics
- Resets the curvature and symmetry of slurs and ties
- Resets text objects to their default formatting.

Layout

Reset to Score Design

Acts in the same way as **Reset Design**, except that objects in the part revert to the same appearance as they have in the full score. If this feature is used in a full score, Sibelius will reset the design in *all* the parts in which the object appears.

For more information on **Reset to Score Position** and **Reset to Score Design**, ⌨ **8.4 Auto Breaks** and **Resetting objects in parts** on page 545.

Align objects

To align several selected objects in a row/column, choose **Layout ▸ Align in a Row** (shortcut **Ctrl+Shift+R** *or* ⌂⌘R) or **Layout ▸ Align in a Column** (shortcut **Ctrl+Shift+C** *or* ⌂⌘C). The line the objects end up in is the average of their original horizontal/vertical positions.

This is particularly useful for aligning lyrics, chord symbols, chord diagrams, etc. along a staff. Usefully, if you select a number of objects attached to different staves (e.g. with **Ctrl+click** *or* ⌘-click), **Layout ▸ Align in a Row** aligns them to the same distance above or below the staff to which they are attached.

Layout ▸ Align in a Row also works on system text styles: you can use it to align e.g. tempo and metronome marks. However, it can't be used to align system objects with staff objects, and nor can you use it to align text styles with different default vertical positions with each other (e.g. you can't align Composer text with Subtitle text, etc.).

Hint: to select all similar text objects (e.g. all lyrics, or all rehearsal marks) in a staff or system before aligning, select one object and choose **Edit ▸ Select ▸ Select More** (shortcut **Ctrl+Shift+A** *or* ⌂⌘A).

Rulers and graph paper

Sibelius can draw rulers on the screen to help you align objects and make precise adjustments to the layout of your score – ⌨ **5.23 View menu**.

You can also choose the **Paper, graph** texture in the **Textures** page of **File ▸ Preferences** (in the **Sibelius** menu on Mac), which draws a grid on your score. The grid lines are 1 space apart when viewed at 100%.

8.2 Magnetic Layout

Magnetic Layout is Sibelius's unique automatic collision avoidance feature, designed to position objects like dynamics, rehearsal marks, bar numbers, lyrics, chord symbols and so on correctly without requiring you to reposition them by hand. Sibelius understands the rules of how particular objects should be aligned, both across the width of a system and across multiple staves vertically, with the result that, for most kinds of scores, you will rarely if ever need to adjust the positions of any objects.

What Magnetic Layout does

In conventional music notation there exists, roughly speaking, a natural order of precedence for the proximity to the staff of different types of objects. For example, notes are always positioned on or closest to the staff, along with things that must stay with notes (e.g. accidentals, articulations, ties, rhythm dots, slurs), and related things like key signatures, time signatures and so on. Other kinds of objects then radiate outwards from the staff, with important instructions like lyrics, dynamics and playing techniques next closest to the staff, either above or below as appropriate. Above these objects come things like chord symbols, which should be aligned along the width of the system and close enough that they can be read comfortably along with the notes. Above chord symbols come system markings like tempo markings, 1st and 2nd ending lines and other repeat instructions, and rehearsal marks. Meanwhile, below the staff, text that runs across the width of the system such as figured bass and Roman numerals should sit close enough to the staff to be read comfortably, and finally pedal lines for keyboard instruments sit below that.

Magnetic Layout works by enforcing this natural order of precedence to the objects in your score. It examines all the objects attached to a staff in a given system and repositions them in the available space according to these rules in an effort to resolve all collisions, intelligently grouping together objects that should be aligned together across or down the system. It does all of this dynamically, in real time: as you input music and edit your score, Sibelius instantly moves objects to avoid collisions, and maintains legibility and clarity at all times.

For objects that have been moved by Magnetic Layout, their original position (i.e. where they would be if Magnetic Layout were switched off) is shown in gray when you select them:

As you drag objects around, you will see them snap to positions that do not collide, rather than following the mouse pointer exactly. If you want the object to follow the mouse pointer exactly, hold down **Ctrl** *or* ⌘ after starting to drag the item, which disables Magnetic Layout temporarily.

Layout

What Magnetic Layout doesn't do

Magnetic Layout does not change the note spacing, which determines the amount of horizontal space available, or the staff spacing, which determines the amount of vertical space between staves. This means that Sibelius can only resolve collisions between objects using the space available: it cannot itself create more space.

This means that you may occasionally encounter situations in which Sibelius is unable to resolve all collisions satisfactorily, with the result that one or more objects may appear in an unsuitable position, and will be colored red (see **Finding collisions** below). More often than not, all you need to do to help Sibelius resolve this collision is select the affected staff and the staff above or below, then choose Layout▸ Optimize Staff Spacing, which will adjust the staff spacing sufficiently to resolve the collision – 📖 **8.10 Staff spacing**.

More rarely, you may find that the best way to resolve a collision is to give Sibelius a little more horizontal space by expanding the note spacing: select the affected bars, and type **Shift+Alt+→** *or* ⇧⌥→ (hold **Ctrl** *or* ⌘ for larger steps) – 📖 **8.9 Note spacing**.

Finding collisions

When Sibelius is unable to resolve a collision on its own, the colliding object is colored red. To find objects that collide, choose Edit▸ Collisions▸ Find Next or Find Previous. The next or previous colliding object will be selected and brought into view, so that you can decide how to resolve the collision (see **What Magnetic Layout doesn't do** above).

Colliding objects will only be colored red if View▸ Magnetic Layout Collisions is switched on.

Grouping similar objects

Sibelius intelligently groups objects together both across the width of a system and, where appropriate, across multiple staves of the system vertically.

When you select an object that is part of a group, a light blue dashed line appears behind the object, showing you the extent of the group:

If you, say, change the pitch of a note on a vocal staff such that it would collide with the lyrics below, Sibelius will move all of the lyrics attached to that staff out of the way, subject to there being sufficient space above the staff below. It moves all the lyrics across the system together, because lyrics should always be aligned along the width of the system.

Similarly, if you add a slur below a passage of notes that would collide with a dynamic below the staff, Sibelius will move the dynamic out of the way to avoid a collision with the slur. If there are several dynamics (including both Expression text and hairpins) in close proximity, Sibelius will move the dynamics together, so that they remain correctly aligned together as a group. Sibelius does not, however, automatically group all dynamics across the width of the entire system together: instead, it only groups nearby dynamics together, meaning that if dynamics are forced to be especially far from the staff at the start of the system (e.g. because of an unusually low note), dynamics further along the system are not necessarily positioned so far from the staff, allowing them to be positioned closer to the notes above, and making better use of the available space.

Furthermore, dynamics at the same rhythmic position on adjacent staves will also be grouped together, so if Sibelius has to move one of the dynamics left or right in order to avoid a collision, all dynamics on adjacent staves at that rhythmic position will move together. This makes it easier to spot at a glance which instruments have dynamic changes at the same position when reading the score.

The following kinds of objects will be grouped together along the width of a system:

• Bar numbers

• Lyrics

• Dynamics (Expression text and hairpins)

• Chord symbols

• 1st and 2nd ending lines

• Rehearsal marks

• Tempo marks (Tempo text, Metronome mark text, Metric modulation text, and *rit./accel.* lines)

• Figured bass

• Roman numerals

• Function symbols

• Pedal lines

The following kinds of objects are also grouped together vertically if they are found at the same rhythmic positions:

• Dynamics on adjacent staves

• Rehearsal marks

• Tempo marks

To remove an object from a group, you can either:

• Move the object so that it is no longer positioned within a space horizontally or vertically aligned with the other objects in the group; when the object leaves the group, the dashed light blue line disappears; or

• Disable collision avoidance for that specific object, which will leave the other objects in the group unaffected – see **Overriding collision avoidance** below.

In rare circumstances, you may decide that in fact you would prefer a particular kind of object not to be grouped together at all, in which case you can use Layout ▸ Magnetic Layout Options to change this – see **Magnetic Layout Options** below.

Layout

Overriding collision avoidance

You may sometimes want to override an object's Magnetic Layout position. You can still move objects that have been moved by Magnetic Layout by selecting them and dragging them with the mouse, or using the arrow keys (with **Ctrl** *or* ⌘ for big steps), but you may notice that the object does not go exactly where you drag or nudge it: that's because Magnetic Layout is still doing its best to move the object to a position where it doesn't collide.

You may therefore find that you want to disable Magnetic Layout for that specific object, which is done by selecting the object and choosing **Edit ▸ Magnetic Layout ▸ Off**. You can also find this menu item in the context menu that appears when you right-click (Windows) *or* **Control**-click (Mac) a selected object.

You can see whether Magnetic Layout is enabled or disabled for an object by looking in the **General** panel of Properties when it is selected: the **Magnetic Layout** menu will show **Default** for objects that have not been explicitly overridden (which normally means that Magnetic Layout is enabled, because only a few kinds of objects have Magnetic Layout disabled by default), **Off** for objects for which you have disabled Magnetic Layout, and **On** for objects for which you have explicitly enabled Magnetic Layout.

When you disable Magnetic Layout for an object, it is effectively ignored by Magnetic Layout thereafter, which means that other objects may collide with it.

To re-enable Magnetic Layout, select the object again and choose **Edit ▸ Magnetic Layout ▸ Default**, which removes your override. (This is preferable to choosing **On** explicitly, as it means that any changes you make to the default behavior for that type of object in **Layout ▸ Magnetic Layout Options** will apply automatically.)

Freezing Magnetic Layout positions

When Magnetic Layout is switched on, the position of each object in your score is dynamic and will change as you edit the score. You may from time to time want to tell Sibelius to fix the position of an object such that the position Magnetic Layout has chosen for them becomes its actual position.

For larger scores, this will provide an increase in editing speed, because Sibelius doesn't have to continually recalculate the Magnetic Layout positions of all objects.

To freeze positions, select an object, a passage, or even the whole score, and choose **Layout ▸ Freeze Magnetic Layout Positions**. This sets the position of the objects in the selection to their current Magnetic Layout position, then disables Magnetic Layout for those objects, so that they will not be moved again by Magnetic Layout.

If you subsequently decide you would like Magnetic Layout to take effect again, make the same selection again, then choose **Edit ▸ Magnetic Layout ▸ Default**. You may also want to choose **Layout ▸ Reset Position**, to allow Sibelius free rein over the position of the objects.

Disabling Magnetic Layout altogether

If you want to disable Magnetic Layout altogether, switch off **Layout ▸ Magnetic Layout**. All objects will return to their original positions, which will introduce collisions throughout your score. For that reason, you are recommended to freeze the positions of items in your score (see above) before you switch off Magnetic Layout.

Magnetic Layout Options

For advanced users only.

Although you should rarely need to adjust the default Magnetic Layout options, should you find that you want to make some changes, choose Layout ▸ Magnetic Layout Options. This dialog appears:

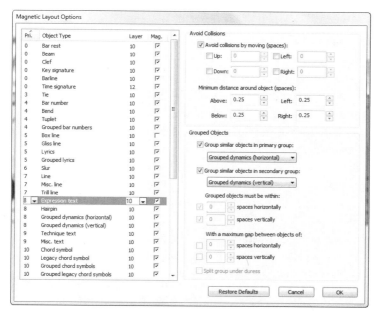

The list of types of objects at the left-hand side has four columns:

- Pri.: short for "priority," this shows the order of precedence of this type of object; the lower the number, the higher the precedence, and the closer to the staff the object is typically positioned.
- Object Type: the name of the object or group of objects.
- Order: the default position in the draw order for this type of object. Objects ordered 0 draw behind all other objects, and objects ordered 31 draw in front of all other objects (🕮 **5.14 Order**).
- Mag.: short for "Magnetic", this shows whether or not this type of object should avoid collisions with other objects by default.

The options on the right-hand side of the dialog show the current values for the selected type of object:

- If Mag. is switched on for an object type, the Avoid collisions by moving (spaces) checkbox is available. When switched on, you can specify whether this type of object should be allowed to move Up, Down, Left, or Right, and by how many spaces in each allowed direction.
- Minimum distance around object (spaces) allows you to specify how much white space Sibelius should maintain around an object. For Expression text, this also provides the amount of white space either side of the dynamic when it truncates a hairpin.
- Group similar objects in primary group and Group similar objects in secondary group allow you to specify whether or not this type of object should be grouped together across the system. You cannot create entirely new groups, but you can add objects to existing groups.

More usefully, you may find that an object is grouped together and you would prefer it not to be, e.g. bar numbers are grouped across the width of the system by default, and if you would prefer them to be able to move individually, you can switch off **Group similar objects in primary group** for the **Bar number** object type.

Only a handful of object types are set to belong to both a primary and a secondary group, most notably Expression text, which is in both **Grouped dynamics (horizontal)** and **Grouped dynamics (vertical)**.

If you add an object to a group, to determine the directions in which the object is allowed to move to avoid collisions, you should specify the **Avoid collisions by moving (spaces)** value for the *group* to which it belongs rather than the object type itself.

* **Grouped objects must be within** n **spaces horizontally** / n **spaces vertically** specifies how closely horizontally or vertically aligned an object must be to be considered part of the group.
* **With a maximum gap between objects of** n **spaces horizontally** / n **spaces vertically** specifies how close together objects must be to be considered part of the group. Notice that for e.g. **Grouped lyrics** there is no maximum gap specified, because lyrics should always be grouped across the entire width of the system, whereas for **Grouped dynamics (vertical)**, a maximum gap of 16 spaces is specified, because only dynamics on adjacent staves should be grouped together.
* **Split group under duress** determines whether Sibelius is allowed to break up the group in the event that it is impossible to keep all of the objects in the group aligned and still avoid collisions. This option is only available if you specify a maximum gap between objects in the group.

The **Restore Defaults** button, as its name suggests, resets all of the settings in the score to Sibelius's defaults.

Changes you make in **Magnetic Layout Options** are saved in the score, and can be transferred to other scores by way of house styles – 📖 **8.8 House Style™**.

Magnetic Layout in Panorama

Many of the rules for the positioning and alignment of objects when Magnetic Layout is switched on are dependent on working one system at a time. For example, lyrics are aligned across the width of the system, and dynamics at the same rhythmic position on multiple staves may be aligned down the system.

When **View ▸ Panorama** is switched on, the score is drawn as a single, infinitely wide system, so any positioning of objects that relies on knowing which bars are on which system will not produce the same results in Panorama. Do not take the position of an object in Panorama to be its actual position in normal view.

If you would prefer not to use Magnetic Layout at all in Panorama (which will make Panorama a bit faster, but will show all objects in their original, colliding positions), switch off **If score uses Magnetic Layout, also use it in Panorama** on the **Files** page of **File ▸ Preferences** (in the **Sibelius** menu on Mac).

8.3 Music engraving

📖 **8.1 Layout and formatting**, **8.8 House Style™**, **8.9 Note spacing**, **8.10 Staff spacing**.

This topic summarizes the key principles of music engraving, the subtle art that underlies most of what Sibelius does. Although this is only a very brief introduction to this huge subject, learning a little about it will improve the appearance of your scores and help you to acquire an eye for good music engraving.

Brief history

Sibelius represents the latest stage of a tradition that is many centuries old. Music notation dates from the 12th century, and music printing from the 15th century. Various methods that have been used to reproduce ("engrave") music include:

• Hand copying

• Plate engraving: cutting or stamping music directly onto printing plates using special tools. This high quality but extraordinarily laborious technique was the leading technology for centuries.

• Moveable type: also widely used since the 15th century

• Music typewriters, brushing ink through stencils, and "Not-a-set" (dry transfer symbols on a translucent sheet, like Letraset®) were also in use during the 20th century.

Music engraving technologies changed little in centuries; a hand-copyist writing out music for publication in 1990 would have been easily recognizable to a monk performing the same task in 1190.

But during the 1990s, computerization brought about a sudden and total revolution in music engraving, with Sibelius playing a major part. In just a decade, the old technologies were almost entirely abandoned (with the exception of the oldest technology of all – writing out music by hand).

Even printing on paper is no longer an essential end result of music engraving, thanks to electronic publishing via the Internet (📖 **5.19 SibeliusMusic.com**). History is in the making.

What music engraving is

Music engraving is the art of reproducing music notation clearly. It is rather like typography – just as typography is about the design and positioning of letters and the layout of text on the page, music engraving governs the design and positioning of musical symbols and the layout of music on the page.

Music engraving is *not* the same as music notation – anyone who can read music knows about music notation, but few musicians know about music engraving. Continuing the analogy with text, music notation is like spelling and grammar – it says in general how to write music down, but not the specifics of precisely how and where to draw the symbols; those crucial details are the domain of music engraving.

Layout

It takes considerable experience to be able to recognize and gauge the subtleties of music engraving. The trained eye can easily tell which publisher a score is from, or which computer program or other method was used to produce it – whereas to most musicians, the engraving of all scores looks much the same. (This is because good engraving should be invisible to the untrained eye; engraving only sticks out when it's badly done.)

This also means that music engraving is a highly refined art, concerned with subtleties many of which may seem pedantic (and a few of which are). Fortunately Sibelius handles most of these subtleties automatically, so you don't need to know about them.

Engraving rules

Few books are available on music engraving – it is a tradition that for centuries has been handed down mainly by word of mouth, from master to apprentice. It is governed by hundreds of so-called *engraving rules*, many originating in the 19th century when music publishing attained a really high level of quality.

A set of engraving rules, together with things like music symbol designs, constitute a music publisher's *house style*. Though called engraving "rules," most are actually just conventions, as few are used universally and even the most respected publishers differ in the rules they adhere to. Nonetheless, engravers and publishers can become very attached to the particular rules they use themselves, and protest bitterly that theirs are the best or even the only "correct" ones.

Sibelius automatically applies hundreds of engraving rules to your score, some of which have never been formulated before. It uses the most standard rules by default, and advanced users can adjust these to their taste from the **House Style ▸ Engraving Rules** dialog. Sibelius reformats your entire score using these rules in a tenth of a second whenever you change it in any way – even if you make a drastic alteration such as changing the page size.

Even so, Sibelius is *not* a perfect music engraver.

This is simply because engraving rules themselves are imperfect: some are too vague to computerize, and many don't deal with all cases, sometimes requiring adjustment by eye (i.e. to look right). Sometimes rules conflict, making it necessary to break one rule in order to avoid breaking a more important one. These situations are best left to human engravers to resolve; Sibelius can be no better than the engraving rules themselves. We can put this as an Aristotelian syllogism:

* Music engraving rules are imperfect (and sometimes need adjustment by eye)
* Sibelius uses music engraving rules
* Therefore Sibelius's music engraving is imperfect (and sometimes needs adjustment by eye).

There are however a few universal rules, and one absolutely fundamental one:

Rule 1: Clarity

The music should look as clear as possible.

No other engraving rule can override this one; if something looks unclear, it is incorrect. Because of this, adjustments to the dictates of engraving rules are often made "by eye"; and in the various situations for which no specific rule has been formulated, the fallback is also to go "by eye."

When you are more experienced at music engraving, you should expect to make quite a few adjustments to your score by eye. But for now it's sufficient to rely on Sibelius to follow the rules.

Why is clarity the fundamental rule? The purpose of music engraving is to enable you to read a score without conscious thought, such as having to consider what a particular rhythm or chord is, which note a particular lyric, dynamic or articulation applies to, and so on. By contrast, a poorly engraved (unclear) score can easily trip you up and cause mistakes, particularly in sight-reading, without your quite knowing why. We have all come across scores like this – even published ones.

Rule 2: Avoid collisions

When objects in music notation overlap they become hard to read, and unclear. So to avoid breaching Rule 1, you should follow this second rule:

Avoid collisions between different objects.

Many engraving rules are effectively ways of avoiding collisions, and fortunately Sibelius incorporates most of these. For example, when two voices cross, Sibelius displaces one to the left or right to avoid colliding with the other; when writing long syllables in lyrics, Sibelius allows extra room for them by increasing the gap between the notes.

Even though Sibelius incorporates these rules, it cannot always avoid collisions, because there are not strict rules for how to resolve all collisions – in tight situations the engraving may have to be reorganized by eye to fit an object in. For example, if a dynamic collides with the stem of a note, you may want to move the dynamic left or right or possibly into the staff, depending on how clear these would look; or in a very tight situation you may even decide to leave the dynamic where it is, and shorten the stem instead.

Such high-level decisions cannot be formulated into rules, and so they are your responsibility to resolve, not Sibelius's. Even though you may not be an experienced music engraver, you should nonetheless remove any collisions that occur.

A few types of collision are permitted as they are almost unavoidable and aren't particularly unclear. The main ones are ties, slurs and hairpins crossing a barline that joins two staves. Slurs are also permitted to go into staves, though text and most lines and symbols are not (except in very tight situations).

Units

The main unit of music engraving is the *space*, which is the distance between adjacent staff lines. This unit is relative rather than absolute because everything in music is in proportion to the staff size; the absolute size of notes, text etc. is less important. (Sibelius even uses a relative rather than absolute point size for text.) Almost all engraving rules use spaces as their unit; inches and millimeters are only really relevant when deciding page and margin sizes.

Horizontal layout: note spacing

The horizontal layout of music is basically about note spacing. There are lots of objects other than notes, but they are mostly positioned relative to notes; e.g. articulations, slurs, lyrics and dynamics go above/below the notes they apply to.

Notes and rests are spaced depending on their note values. The spacings Sibelius uses are in its **House Style ▸ Note Spacing Rule** dialog. For example, a quarter note (crotchet) has 3.5 spaces after it, a half note (minim) has 5.94 spaces, and a whole note (semibreve) has 8.19 spaces. Different publishers use slightly different spacings.

A quick mental calculation will prove to you that the space after a note or rest is *not* proportional to its note value: if it were, a whole note (semibreve) would have 4 x 3.5 spaces (for a quarter note) = 14 spaces after it, rather than 8.19. The reason note spacing is not proportional is that, if it were, very short notes would have to be crammed illegibly close together, and long notes would waste huge amounts of space.

If several simultaneous staves or voices have different rhythms at the same time, which one's notes are used to set the note spacing? The answer is that the *shortest note or rest* at any point determines the spacing: so if a piano right hand is playing quarter notes (crotchets) while the left hand is playing whole notes (semibreves), it's the quarter notes that determine the spacing, and the whole notes are just positioned in alignment with them. However, it gets much harder to keep the spacing looking good when there are lots of staves (e.g. orchestral/band scores) and complicated cross-rhythms such as tuplets.

Because note spacing is not proportional, bars are not of equal width – bars with shorter notes are wider (perhaps paradoxically):

This means that there is not normally a constant number of bars per system. (Jazz and commercial music is often written out with e.g. four bars per system, but this is an exception.)

One adjustment made to the basic note spacing is justification: notes need to be spread out somewhat to ensure that a whole number of bars fills the width of the page. The way this is done is that as many bars as possible are fitted into the width of the page (using the note spacings above), and then any leftover space is added evenly between all the notes, spreading them out until they reach the right margin. This is exactly like the justification of words to fill a line in a word processor.

Various other spacing adjustments are also made: extra room needs to be allowed for things like accidentals, rhythm dots, leger lines, tails on up-pointing stems (as they stick out), barlines, grace notes, "back-notes" (noteheads on the wrong side of the stem in clustery chords), crossing voices, lyrics, and changes of clef, key and time signature.

Again, Sibelius automates all of this using a complex algorithm called the Optical spacing rule – though that's not to say that you shouldn't sometimes adjust it by eye. In particular, you should consider adjusting the note spacing if it gets particularly uneven due to widely varying note values or complicated lyrics; ▤ **8.9 Note spacing** for advice on this.

Vertical layout: staff spacing

Vertical layout is rather less precise than horizontal layout. But just as horizontal layout is basically about where notes go (other objects being positioned relative to them), vertical layout is basically about staff spacing. The vertical positions of other objects such as notes, rests, clefs, time signatures, instrument names, titles, bar numbers and rehearsal marks are determined relative to the staves they belong to.

Broadly speaking, staves should have the same distance between them, with a slightly wider gap between systems, and often a wider gap between instrumental families in large scores (e.g. for orchestra or band). As it happens, Sibelius does not automatically add this latter gap, but you can do it easily enough yourself (by selecting the top staff of a family throughout the score and moving it down).

Scores are often justified vertically to spread staves down to the bottom margin, in a similar fashion to the horizontal justification of notes. Sibelius does this automatically if the page is more than half full (and, as usual, you can adjust the specifics from the **Engraving Rules** dialog).

However, it's sometimes necessary to allow extra space between staves or to reposition other objects to avoid collisions between (say) high or low notes on one staff and objects on an adjacent one. This is a classic case of adjustment by eye, which you should do yourself.

Another reason to move staves around is to align corresponding staves on facing pages. This is useful for orchestral/band scores, to make it easier for the conductor to read a particular instrument's music across from one page to another. Sibelius's **Layout ▸ Align Staves** dialog automates this for you (**8.10 Staff spacing**).

Further information

In particular, **8.9 Note spacing** and **8.1 Layout and formatting** for various ways to improve your score's appearance in Sibelius.

There are numerous other engraving rules, too many to bore you with here; though many of them are summarized in other topics in this Reference, either in boxes (particularly for non-automatic rules) or under the **Engraving Rules options** heading at the end of the topic. Most rules are automatically handled by Sibelius, so you don't need to know much about them.

Should you be slavering for further information on music engraving, a good book on the basics for those new to the subject is the small, inexpensive but very readable *Essential Dictionary of Music Notation* (Alfred Publishing). There are various large, expensive and not-so-readable books for the more advanced engraver.

If you leave this topic with just two morsels of information, please apply Rules 1 and 2 given above: avoid collisions, and above all else, make your score look clear.

Layout

8.4 Auto Breaks

📖 **2.24 Multirests, 7.1 Working with parts, 8.1 Layout and formatting, 8.5 Breaks**.

Sibelius can create system and page breaks for you automatically at a musically convenient place using Layout ▸ Auto Breaks, which saves a lot of time when formatting parts. You can also use these options in scores if you wish.

Laying out parts

In parts, it's helpful to put page breaks where there are one or more bars' rest on the right-hand page, so that the player has time to turn the page. Sibelius's Layout ▸ Auto Breaks feature takes care of all this for you, and updates the layout whenever necessary, so if you insert bars, put notes in empty bars etc., the layout may change to put a page break at a different convenient point.

It's also useful to put system breaks at particular points in the music, such as at changes of tempo, key, rehearsal marks or multirests, to make these objects easier to see at a glance.

By default, auto layout is switched off in scores, but Sibelius switches it on in parts. To change how Sibelius lays out the page, choose Layout ▸ Auto Breaks, or you can change one or more parts simultaneously by clicking Auto Breaks on the Layout page of Multiple Part Appearance (📖 **7.3 Multiple Part Appearance**). In either case you will see this dialog:

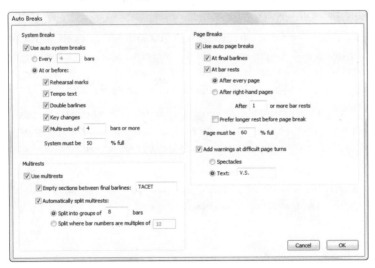

Auto system breaks

- **Use auto system breaks** allows the user to choose whether or not to use auto system breaks. Sibelius can either create system breaks regularly after a specified number of bars, or otherwise add system breaks at points in the part where a separation of the material either side of the break is likely to assist in visually representing a musical change
- If you wish Sibelius to add system breaks at regular intervals, choose **Every** *n* **bars** and enter the number of bars you want per system. If you want regular system breaks for only a section of

music rather than the whole score, use the **Make Layout Uniform** plug-in instead (📖 **6.1 Working with plug-ins**).

- Using **At or before**, Sibelius will add system breaks where specific objects appear:

  ○ **Rehearsal marks**: when switched on, Sibelius makes rehearsal marks go at the start of a system

  ○ **Tempo text**: Sibelius will make tempo text appear at the start of a system

  ○ **Double barlines** generally indicate the end of a section, so if you wish to make the musical division more obvious, switch on this option to add a system break where a double barline appears

  ○ **Key changes**: when switched on, Sibelius will add a system break *before* a change of key, so that the new key signature is displayed at the start of a system. (This only applies to key or instrument changes at the end of a bar, not in the middle of a bar.)

  ○ **Multirests of** *n* **bars of more**: to add system breaks after multirests of a given length, switch on this option

  ○ **System must be** *n*% **full**: to prevent Sibelius from spacing the music too widely, use this option to set a minimum threshold for an auto break to appear.

Auto system breaks appear as a dotted system break mark, like this: ⌣ They are orange because they appear in the part but not the score (if **View ▸ Differences in Parts** is on).

Auto page breaks

- **Use auto page breaks** allows you to choose whether Sibelius should create automatic page breaks at convenient places. All the other **Page Break** options will be disabled if **Use auto page breaks** is switched off.

- **At final barlines**: when switched on, Sibelius will add a page break after a final barline. This is useful when working on scores that contain more than one movement, piece or song.

- **At bar rests**: makes Sibelius add a page break after rests to enable easier page turns, with these options:

  ○ Choose whether you want Sibelius to look for auto page breaks **After every page** or **After right-hand pages** (i.e. odd-numbered pages). If the players will be reading off single sheets, you should choose **After every page**; if they will use two-page spreads, choose **After right-hand pages**.

  ○ **After** *n* **or more bar rests** determines the minimum number of bar rests before an auto page break (and hence the time needed to turn the page)

  ○ **Prefer longer rest before page break** makes Sibelius break the page after a longer multirest rather than a shorter one (given the choice) to allow more time for turning, even if this means fitting less music on the page.

- **Page must be** *n*% **full** prevents Sibelius from putting auto page turns very early in the page because the page wouldn't have enough music on and would look odd

- **Add warnings at difficult page turns** puts a printed warning in the margin after the final bar of the page if there isn't a suitable place for an auto page break. The default warning is "V.S." (which stands for *verso subito*, Italian for "turn quickly"), but you can also use your own text or the **Spectacles** symbol if you wish.

Layout

(If you want to use a different symbol, edit the spectacles symbol in the **Layout Marks** row of the **House Style ▸ Edit Symbols** dialog – ▢ **8.17 Edit Symbols**.)

If you want to remove a warning from the end of a particular page, just put a manual page break there (see below), to show that the break is intentional.

If you switch on **View ▸ Layout Marks**, a symbol showing whether Sibelius has found a good (⌣) or a bad (╱) page break will appear on the screen (but won't print) at the end of right-hand pages (or every page).

Suppressing auto page and system breaks

There may be some circumstances under which you want to suppress an automatic system or page break. To do this:

- Select the barline whose auto break you wish to suppress
- In the **Layout ▸ Break** submenu, choose **System Break** (shortcut **Return**, on the main keyboard) or **Page Break** (shortcut **Ctrl+Return** *or* **⌘-Return**). The auto break symbol will appear with a cross through it to indicate it has been suppressed.

Because Sibelius obeys normal page breaks, system breaks and other formatting when deciding where to put an auto break, you can override auto breaks by selecting the bars you want to be on the page or system and using **Layout ▸ Format ▸ Make Into Page** or (less likely) **Layout ▸ Format ▸ Make Into System**.

If you select the barline on which there is an auto system or page break and change its break type, the break will go through three states: auto, suppressed and manual.

Multirests

Layout ▸ Auto Breaks also contains options for determining the appearance of multirests in your parts (or even the score if you wish):

- **Use multirests**: as already mentioned, when switched on, Sibelius will notate multiple consecutive bars rest as multirests. This is switched on by default in parts. When switched off, the other settings regarding the appearance of multirests are disabled.

- **Empty sections between final barlines**: if a passage of music between the start of a score and the final barline or between subsequent final barlines is empty, Sibelius can prevent multirests from being broken at time signature changes, Tempo text and the like, and simply display a single "tacet" multirest spanning a system's width. You can use this option in both scores and parts that contain no music. You can also manually set the text that appears above the multirest.

- **Automatically split multirests**: by default, Sibelius will only split multirests at points in the score or part where this is absolutely necessary (e.g. at changes of time signature or at double barlines). However, if your piece follows a regular phrasing pattern, you may find it useful to switch on this setting, choosing one of these two options:
  - **Split into groups of *n* bars**: when switched on, Sibelius will divide multirests up into groups of *n* bars. For example, if a part has 14 bars rest and this option is set to **8**, Sibelius will write two multirests, the first of eight bars' length and the second, six.

○ **Split where bar numbers are multiples of** *n* breaks a multirest at multiples of *n* bars from bar one, taking any bar number changes into account. For example, if you type **8** here, and a 12-bar multirest begins at bar 3, the multirest will split into two multirests of 6 bars each, the division between the two falling at bar 9; this means multirests will always split at the end of regular 8-bar phrases, such as in much jazz, pop and show music.

For more information about multirests, ▭ **2.24 Multirests**.

8.5 Breaks

📖 **3.6 Page numbers**, **8.1 Layout and formatting**, **8.4 Auto Breaks**, **8.6 Document Setup**.

Breaks are points in the music where you force a system or a page to end, such as at the end of a section. Think of them like starting a new paragraph or a new page in a word processor: generally, a word processor takes care of flowing the words and sentences in paragraphs automatically, and you only need to hit Return when you want to start a new paragraph; more rarely, you need to hit Ctrl+Return *or* ⌘-Return to insert a page break and start a new page.

It's much the same in Sibelius: it takes care of flowing bars and systems into pages for you automatically, and you only need to insert a break when you need a particular bar to occur at the start of a new system or page, except in special cases like for title pages or other pages with no music on (e.g. to facilitate a page turn in an instrumental part). To emphasize the analogy with word processors, Sibelius even uses the same shortcuts for breaks as most word processors.

Sibelius can even insert explicit system and page breaks for you automatically, which can be a huge time-saver, particularly for parts – 📖 **8.4 Auto Breaks**.

For general advice on the layout of your score, 📖 **8.1 Layout and formatting**.

Adding or removing manual system or page breaks

To add a manual system or page break at any point in the score or part:

- Select the barline at which you want to break
- In the Layout ▸ Break submenu, choose System Break (shortcut Return, on the main keyboard) or Page Break (shortcut Ctrl+Return *or* ⌘-Return).

The music will spread out so it ends at the specified point – more specifically, Sibelius spreads out the two systems leading up to the break. Thereafter, the bar ending with the break will always go at the end of a system or page.

To remove a break that you previously created, just do exactly the same as above, or select the layout mark symbol that appears above the barline (see **Viewing breaks** below) and hit Delete.

Where to put system breaks

Though Sibelius's Auto Breaks feature can do most of this for you, you may wish to force system breaks:

- at the end of sections of music (e.g. at a repeat barline)
- at the end of sections in parts, especially when the next section has a new title at the start. In parts, it's usually better to use system breaks instead of page breaks so you don't get huge gaps in the part.
- where instruments divide onto two staves or rejoin onto one, so you don't get sequences of bar rests that aren't performed by anyone.

Do not routinely put system breaks at the end of normal systems as this will cause formatting problems if you change the music. If in doubt, don't use a system break.

Where to put page breaks

Though Sibelius's **Auto Breaks** feature can do this for you, you may wish to force page breaks:

- at a convenient point on right-hand pages in parts, so that the performer doesn't have to turn the page while playing
- at the end of sections, especially when the next section has a new title at the start.

Do not routinely put manual page breaks at the end of every page, as this will be likely to impair the formatting if you change the music in any way. If you really must use a break, normally you can use a system break (because a system break on the last system on a page is effectively the same as a page break, but will have less impact on layout if you reformat the score); if in doubt, don't use a page break.

Special page breaks

Sometimes it's necessary to have pages without music on in your score; for example, you may want one or more title pages at the front of your score, or perhaps a page for performance directions between movements, or even a blank page to facilitate a page turn later on in an instrumental part. You may also need to change the margins on different pages of the score, e.g. to leave more room for titles and other text at the top of the first page.

Sibelius makes it easy to create all of these using a special kind of page break, called (funnily enough) a special page break, which allows you to create one or more blank pages, as well as change the page and staff margins of subsequent pages (you don't have to create a blank page to change the margins).

To create a special page break:

- Select the barline at which you want the break to occur; if you want to create blank pages at the start of your score, select the initial barline of the first bar (i.e. the barline to the left of the initial clef and key signature), or use **Create ▸ Title Page** instead – see below
- Choose **Layout ▸ Break ▸ Special Page Break** (shortcut **Ctrl+Shift+Return** *or* ⇧⌘-**Return**). A simple dialog appears:

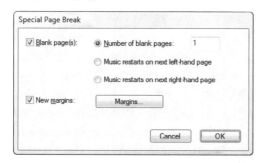

- If you want to create one or more blank pages, switch on the **Blank page(s)** checkbox, then choose from the three kinds of blank page you can create:
  - ○ **Number of blank pages** *n* inserts a fixed number of blank pages

- ○ **Music restarts on next left-hand page** will only insert a blank page if the barline to which the special page break is attached is at the end of a left-hand (i.e. even-numbered) page. This option is useful when preparing instrumental parts and you want to ensure a certain pair of pages will appear together as a spread without needing a page turn between them. As the lay-out of the score changes (e.g. you add or remove bars before the bar where the special page break occurs), the blank page will appear and disappear as appropriate.

- ○ **Music restarts on next right-hand page** will only insert a blank page if the special page break comes at the end of a right-hand (i.e. odd-numbered) page. As above, this is useful in some situations when preparing instrumental parts.

- If you want to change the margins on the pages following the special page break, switch on **New margins**, then click **Margins**, which shows another dialog – see **Changing page and staff margins with special page breaks** below. (Notice that you can choose **Blank pages** and **New margins** independently of each other, allowing you to change the page and staff margins without inserting a blank page, and vice versa.)

- Click **OK** and the special page break is created. As with other kinds of breaks, Sibelius shows a helpful light blue symbol above the barline where the special page break occurs.

Alternatively, if you simply want to create a single blank page, you can select the barline after which you want the blank page to appear (or choose the initial barline at the start of bar 1 to create a title page before the first page of music), then choose **Special Page Break** from the menu in the **Bars** panel of Properties (📖 **5.17 Properties**).

Creating a title page

You can create a title page when you first create your score by switching on the **Create title page** option on the final page of the **File ▸ New** dialog. If you want to create a title page later, simply choose **Create ▸ Title Page**. You can choose how many blank pages to add at the start of the score, and Sibelius will also add title and composer text for you on the first blank page.

When adding title pages for parts, you may also want to print the name of the instrument the part is for on the title page, in which case switch on the **Include part name** option.

Creating text and graphics on blank pages

Having created a page with no music on, chances are you won't want it to stay blank for long.

Note that you can't create normal staff text, lyrics or system text on a blank page because all those kinds of text attach to bars or notes, which don't exist on blank pages. (As a consequence, it's also impossible to copy and paste staff or system text from a page with music on to a blank page.)

But instead, you can add text to blank pages using the text styles listed in the **Create ▸ Text ▸ Blank Page Text** submenu – 📖 **3.1 Working with text**. Running headers and footers (e.g. page numbers, or **Header (after first page)** text) will appear on blank pages, the same way they appear on pages with music on.

You can also add graphics to blank pages using **Create ▸ Graphic**. Unlike text, you can copy and paste graphics between pages of music and blank pages if you want to. For more information on importing graphics, 📖 **9.4 Importing graphics**.

Editing special page breaks

If you want to edit an existing special page break (e.g. to change the number of blank pages, or to adjust the margins), simply select the barline at which the break occurs, or the layout mark above the barline, and choose Layout ▸ Break ▸ Special Page Break.

The Special Page Break dialog will appear, showing you the current options for that special page break. Make the required changes, then click OK. If you reduce the number of blank pages, Sibelius will warn you that any text or graphics on those blank pages will be deleted. When deleting blank pages, Sibelius trims from the right, i.e. it deletes the rightmost blank page.

Deleting special page breaks

To delete a special page break, either select the layout mark above the barline at which the break occurs and hit Delete. Alternatively, you can replace the special page break with another kind of break (e.g. a system or page break) in the usual way.

When you delete a special page break that produces one or more blank pages, any text or graphics on those blank pages is deleted too.

Changing page and staff margins with special page breaks

You can change the either or both the page and staff margins on the pages following a special page break. In the Special Page Break dialog, switch on New margins, then click the Margins button.

The dialog that appears is based on Layout ▸ Document Setup, but with the page and staff size options disabled. For help with using this dialog, ☐ **8.6 Document Setup**.

Breaks and dynamic parts

Breaks that you create in the full score will affect the dynamic parts differently, depending on the options you have chosen in Multiple Part Appearance (☐ **7.3 Multiple Part Appearance**). By default, though:

* Special page breaks in the full score are not shown in the parts, because you probably don't want title pages and other front matter to be printed in every part
* Page breaks in the full score are turned into system breaks in the parts, because page breaks are normally used to mark the start of a section or movement in the full score, which are normally indicated just with system breaks in parts to save space
* System breaks in the full score are not shown in the parts, because system breaks are normally used to tidy up the formatting in the full score and are irrelevant to the layout of the parts.

You can also create any break in a dynamic part without it affecting the full score. So if you need (say) a blank page to facilitate a page turn, simply create it in the normal way in the part in question.

Notice that the layout marks that appear above barlines to show you which breaks are present can appear in different colors in parts – see **Viewing breaks** below.

Removing lots of breaks

To remove page and system breaks in the score or in a passage of bars:

* Select the bars in question (or type Ctrl+A *or* ⌘A to select the whole score)
* Choose Layout ▸ Format ▸ Unlock Format (shortcut Ctrl+Shift+U *or* ⇧⌘U).

Layout

The music will reformat back to how it was originally, including removing formatting produced by the Layout ▸ Format options. However, special page breaks are not removed by Unlock Format.

Viewing breaks

The View ▸ Layout Marks option (on by default) shows system and page breaks and other formatting in the score like this:

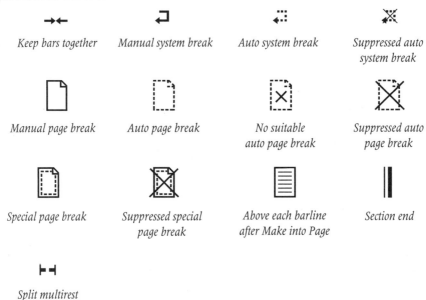

Keep bars together	*Manual system break*	*Auto system break*	*Suppressed auto system break*
Manual page break	*Auto page break*	*No suitable auto page break*	*Suppressed auto page break*
Special page break	*Suppressed special page break*	*Above each barline after Make into Page*	*Section end*

Split multirest

It is possible to suppress auto system and page breaks, simply by toggling the break (e.g. to suppress a system break, select the barline and hit Return to suppress it). Sibelius shows that a break has been suppressed by drawing a cross through it.

Layout marks can appear in different colors:

- Blue marks means breaks that are in the score, or showing through to the parts.
- Orange marks only appear in parts and mean breaks that exist only in the parts (when View ▸ Differences in Parts is switched on) – 📖 **7.1 Working with parts**.
- Red break marks only appear when using auto page breaks, and mean a "bad" auto page break, i.e. an unsuitable location – 📖 **8.1 Layout and formatting**.

Notice that layout marks appear at both sides of a break: a system break, for example, shows a symbol above the barline at the end of the system, and above the initial barline at the start of the next system; a special page break shows a symbol above the barline at the end of the page, and above the initial barline at the start of the next page with music on. You can select any layout mark symbol and hit Delete to delete the break.

8.6 Document Setup

📖 **5.16 Printing**, **8.1 Layout and formatting**, **8.5 Breaks**.

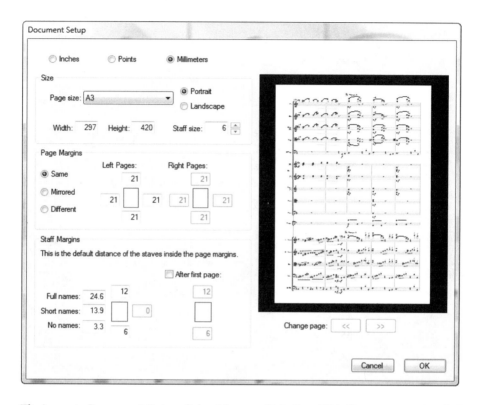

The **Layout ▸ Document Setup** dialog (shortcut **Ctrl+D** *or* ⌘D) allows you to set up the page size, staff size and margins of your score. Sibelius will reformat your score instantly for the new settings, so you can try out different sizes or shapes of paper, or different staff sizes, to see what looks best.

Since this affects the amount of music per page and the number of pages in the score, you can use **Layout ▸ Document Setup** to fit your score onto any number of pages you want. 📖 **8.1 Layout and formatting** for general advice on layout.

Changing the page settings

Choose **Layout ▸ Document Setup** (shortcut **Ctrl+D** *or* ⌘D). You can then adjust the page size, page shape and staff size, as detailed below.

The preview shows how the first page will look with the settings you've chosen; click the arrows to look through subsequent pages.

When you click **OK**, the score will be instantly reformatted using the new measurements. (If you don't like how it ends up, just choose **Edit ▸ Undo!**)

Paper sizes

The **Paper size** list includes the following US and European paper sizes (although you can specify any width or height you like):

Letter	8.5 x 11"	216 x 279mm
Tabloid	11 x 17"	279 x 432mm (sometimes known as "B" size)
A5	5.9 x 8.3"	149 x 210mm (A4 folded in half)
B5	6.9 x 9.8"	177 x 250mm
A4	8.3 x 11.7"	210 x 297mm
B4	9.8 x 13.9"	250 x 354mm
A3	11.7 x 16.5"	297 x 420mm (twice as big as A4)
Band	5 x 7"	127 x 178mm (usually landscape format)
Statement	5.5 x 8.5"	140 x 216mm
Hymn	5.75" x 8.25"	146 x 205mm
Octavo	6.75 x 10.5"	171 x 267mm
Executive	7.25 x 10.5"	184 x 266mm
Quarto	8.5 x 10.8"	215 x 275mm
Concert	9 x 12"	229 x 305mm
Folio	8.5 x 13"	216 x 330mm
Legal	8.5 x 14"	216 x 356mm
Part	9.5 x 12.5"	241 x 317mm
Part	10 x 13"	254 x 330mm

(The terms "Octavo" and "Quarto" refer to various other paper sizes too.)

You can switch between inches, millimeters and points using the buttons provided. 1 inch = 25.4mm (absolutely exactly), 1mm = 0.0397 inches (almost exactly), and 1 point = exactly 1/72 inch = 0.353mm (approximately).

Here are some recommended paper and staff sizes:

- *Keyboard, songs, solo instrument*: Letter/A4, 0.25–0.3"/6–7mm staves
- *Orchestral/band scores*: Letter/Tabloid/A4/A3, 0.1–0.2"/3–5mm staves
- *Parts*: Letter/Concert/A4/B4, 0.25–0.3"/6–7mm staves
- *Choral music*: Letter/A4 or smaller, 0.2"/5mm staves
- *Books for beginners*: Letter/A4, 0.3–0.4"/8–10mm staves

All these page sizes are portrait format; landscape format is seldom used, except for organ, marching band and brass band music. You'll find that published music often doesn't correspond exactly to any standard paper size.

Staff size

The staff size is the distance from the center of the top staff line to the center of the bottom staff line. Everything in a score is scaled to be in proportion to the staff size – notes, clefs, text, etc.

You can either type in a staff size or click the little arrows to change it in small steps. Click and hold the little arrows and watch the preview to see the effect of the staves growing and shrinking.

Although staff sizes vary considerably, you should take care to set one appropriate to the kind of music you are writing. In general, if you set the staff size too small the performers will feel uncomfortable without necessarily knowing quite why. See above for recommended paper and staff sizes.

Sibelius won't change the staff size without your permission, so with lots of instruments on a small page the staves may have to squash very close together (or even overlap!). To alleviate this, simply pick a smaller staff size (or a larger page size).

Page margins

You can also set the page margins on the **Layout ▸ Document Setup** dialog. Music can go right up to the page margins, but not outside.

To make these margins visible in the score (as dashed blue lines), choose **View ▸ Page Margins**.

Your score can have the **Same** margins on left- and right-facing pages (recommended for single-sided printing), **Mirrored** margins (sometimes called "inside" and "outside" margins), or **Different** margins on left- and right-facing pages. The top and bottom margins are always identical on left- and right-facing pages.

Specifically, the margins are defined as follows (if **Same** is chosen):

- *Top margin*: where the top of the page number normally goes, if it's at the top of the page
- *Bottom margin*: where the bottom of the page number normally goes, if it's at the bottom of the page
- *Left margin*: the left-hand side of the leftmost instrument name
- *Right margin*: the right-hand end of the staves.

Staff margins

Staff margins control the distance between the top and bottom staves on a page and the top and bottom page margins, and also the distance between the left-hand page margin and the left-hand side of the system. This allows you to set the default position of the staves on the page.

It is common to require different top and bottom staff margins on the first page of a score, to accommodate things like the title and the name of the composer at the top, and copyright or publisher details at the bottom. Fortunately this is easily done:

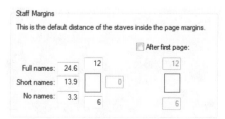

Type the staff margins you want to use for the first page of music in the score into the boxes on the left, then switch on **After first page** and type the values you want to use for subsequent pages into the boxes underneath the checkbox.

For the left-hand margin there are three different values, depending on whether the staves have full instrument names, short instrument names (e.g. after the first page) or no instrument names. (Settings for instrument names may be found on the **Instruments** page of the **House Style ▸ Engraving Rules** dialog – ▢ **2.18 Instruments**.)

These values update automatically if you change the staff size or change the length of the instrument names themselves (e.g. by editing an existing name, adding new instruments, or creating an instrument change). You can't specify these separately for different pages in the score, as they update based on the width of the longest instrument name used in the entire score.

Changing Document Setup partway through a score

You cannot change the page size, orientation or staff size partway through a score, but you can change the page and staff margins at any point using special page breaks – see **Changing page and staff margins with special page breaks** on page 581.

8.7 Attachment

In Sibelius, every object in a score, including notes, lines, text and so on, is *attached* both horizontally and vertically to the music so that it moves correctly when the format of the score changes.

This makes the music immune to any layout changes that may occur in future, which means you don't have to go around cleaning everything up after making a major change to a score, such as adding a new instrument.

Viewing attachment

When an object is selected, you can see what it's attached to as a dashed gray arrow. This indicates the staff the object is attached to and the rhythmic point on the staff. If you find the dashed arrow irritating, switch off View ▸ **Attachment Lines**. On the other hand, if you want to see all attachments in your score, type **Ctrl+A** *or* ⌘A to select all the objects in the score. Likewise, if you want to see all the objects attached to a single staff, simply triple-click it.

Sibelius can also draw rulers to show the precise distances between staves and attached objects – 📖 **5.23 View menu**.

Viewing attachment in parts

Viewing attachment in parts works in exactly the same way as it does in a full score. However, attachment lines may be colored red with increasing intensity as the object is moved further away from the place to which it is attached, to warn that you shouldn't be moving it that far – 📖 **7.1 Working with parts**.

Horizontal attachment

All objects are attached horizontally to a rhythmic position in the music. If you move a note left or right, all notes at the same rhythmic position will move with it.

If an object is attached to a note, its attachment arrow will point to the note (or to the note's horizontal position). Anything you put directly over or near a note will remain attached to that note, so if (say) a slur starts or ends at a note, the whole slur will stretch or contract in the future if necessary to follow the note around.

If an object is in between two notes, it will attach to an in-between rhythmic position. This means that an object halfway between two notes will always stay halfway in between, even if the size of the gap changes. Here's a classic case, where the ends of the hairpins and the f stay proportionally positioned between the notes even when the spacing changes:

Because Sibelius copes with this itself, it saves you a large amount of cleaning up when making major changes to the layout, such as creating bars or adding system or page breaks.

Layout

Vertical attachment

Most objects apply to a particular staff and are vertically positioned relative to it. For instance, a trumpet trill applies only to the trumpet's staff, and should stay above the trumpet staff if that staff moves. Objects that belong to a particular staff are called "staff objects."

If you move a staff up or down, all the attached objects follow it. Most importantly, all the objects attached to the appropriate staves appear in the relevant part or parts. So it's important that every staff object is attached to the correct staff.

To ensure this, keep an eye on the dashed attachment arrow – particularly when text is in an ambiguous position between two staves and could be attached to either.

Attaching to another staff

If an object between two staves is attached to the wrong staff, drag it to touch the other staff and it will re-attach itself to that one instead – the dashed arrow jumps to show this. Then move the object back to its original position.

Sibelius comes with a plug-in called **Check Attachments** that cleverly detects where you may have unintentionally dragged it too far away from the intended staff – 📖 **6.1 Working with plug-ins**.

A word of warning: don't put objects between two separate instruments meaning them to apply to both. This is a convention sometimes used in manuscript but never in publishing, as it is incorrect notation. Any staff object will only attach to one staff, so it will not appear in any parts containing the instrument's stave that the object has failed to attach to.

But it's fine to write an object applying to both staves of the same instrument, such as dynamics between keyboard staves, because they will end up in the same part.

Adjusting attachment in parts

It is impossible to change the attachment of any object in a part. If you drag an object away from its default position in a part, its attachment point will remain fixed; only its horizontal and vertical offsets will be affected. If you wish to change the attachment of an object, move it to its new position in the full score, and it will also move in the part.

System objects

Some objects apply to all the staves in a system, not any particular staff, and are called "system objects." System objects are colored purple when you select them. Typical examples of system objects are titles, tempo marks, rehearsal marks and 1st and 2nd endings (1st-/2nd-time bars). Although these objects appear at the top of a system (and are sometimes duplicated lower down as well), they really refer to every staff in the system. For instance, they should go into every instrumental part, not just the instrument at the top of the score.

Some menus and dialogs distinguish between staff and system objects. For instance, on the Create ▸ Text menu, the text styles that are system objects are listed below the staff objects.

To adjust which staves system objects appear above, see **System Object Positions** in 📖 **8.12 Default Positions**.

Putting objects in weird places

Occasionally you may want to put a piece of text or other object somewhere far from the music, such as off into a margin. It is fine to do this so long as you bear in mind that all objects are attached to the music, rather than being fixed to a particular point on the paper. For example, staff objects in the margin are usually attached to the nearest bar in the nearest staff, and will stay a fixed distance from that bar.

If the music reformats, the bar will move somewhere else and so the object could end up in an even weirder place than you anticipated. So you may want to lock the format of the system or page to stop it from reformatting; 🕮 **8.1 Layout and formatting**.

Layout

8.8 House Style™

📖 **2.23 Manuscript paper**, **3.9 Edit Text Styles**, **4.11 Timecode and hit points**, **8.3 Music engraving**, **8.1 Layout and formatting**, **8.12 Default Positions**, **8.18 Publishing**.

Exactly how a printed score looks is defined by its house style; different publishers have their own house styles, and Sibelius allows you to modify the house style of your scores to an almost unlimited degree.

Aspects of a house style include:

* Engraving Rules options – see below
* Text styles – 📖 **3.9 Edit Text Styles**
* Symbol fonts and designs – 📖 **2.31 Symbols**, **8.11 Music fonts**, **8.17 Edit Symbols**
* Notehead designs – 📖 **2.25 Noteheads**, **8.16 Edit Noteheads**
* Instrument definitions and ensembles – 📖 **8.14 Edit Instruments**
* Line designs – 📖 **2.21 Lines**, **8.15 Edit Lines**
* Object positions – 📖 **8.12 Default Positions**
* Note spacing rule – 📖 **8.9 Note spacing**
* Document setup (e.g. page and staff size) – 📖 **8.6 Document Setup**
* Playback dictionary words – 📖 **4.9 Playback dictionary**
* Default Multiple Part Appearance settings – 📖 **7.1 Working with parts**

Most of these may be edited from the House Style menu.

Predefined house styles

When creating a new score or importing a house style (see below), you can choose from a list of ready-made house styles depending on the type of music and the overall look you want for the score.

Each house style name says the type of music it's for (e.g. jazz), the music font used (Opus, Helsinki, Reprise or Inkpen2) and optionally the text font (Times, Georgia or Arial). Opus is a standard-looking music font, Helsinki is more traditional, and Reprise and Inkpen2 are handwritten.

Times is a very standard text font, Georgia is a less common (and perhaps more traditional-looking) serif font, and Arial (based on the famous Helvetica) is a modern sans serif font, for a much more contemporary (and perhaps less elegant) look. The Reprise house styles all use Reprise for the text as well as the music; similarly, Inkpen2 house styles all use Inkpen2 for the text too.

The types of music are as follows:

* **Standard** – the style used by the **Blank** manuscript paper; suitable for most kinds of music
* **Jazz** – as **Standard** but with winged repeat barlines and all articulations above the staff, as used in jazz music
* **Keyboard** – for solo keyboard music. Same as **Standard** but with dynamics exactly between the hands, no instruments names, no staff justification.

- **Larger notes** – as **Standard** but with an alternative notehead shape that follows the design recommendations of the US Music Publishers Association
- **Lead sheet** – same as **Jazz** but with initial barlines drawn on single-line systems.

We recommend you make a note of the **Layout ▸ Document Setup** (page size, staff size and margins) settings of your score before importing them into existing scores. Then import the house style *including* the **Engraving Rules and Document Setup** settings; this will set your score to use A4 paper and 6mm staves, so after importing, change the **Layout ▸ Document Setup** settings back to how they were previously.

Reprise and Inkpen2 house styles

The Reprise house styles have a lot of special settings. For example, rehearsal marks appear boxed with a drop shadow, titles use a special rubber stamp font called Reprise Title (in which all the characters are capitals, but typing lower and upper case produces the same letter form with different imperfections), while the instrument names at the top left-hand corner of the first page of dynamic parts use another rubber stamp font called Reprise Stamp. You can also add special curved brackets to text instructions above or below the staff – see **Add Brackets to Reprise Script** on page 523.

The Inkpen2 house styles aren't quite as dramatic as Reprise, but you may prefer the slightly thicker characters in Inkpen2 over the characters of Reprise, which look like they were drawn with a thinner nib. Other lines, such as staff lines, barlines, slurs and so on, are also thicker in general in the Inkpen2 house styles than in the Reprise house styles.

For keyboard music, try printing with **Substitute Braces** switched off in the **File ▸ Print** dialog (shortcut **Ctrl+P** *or* ⌘P), to make braces look hand-drawn (as they do on the screen). However, this won't work with some printers.

Similarly, for parts, try switching on **Draw H-bar using a symbol** on the **Bar Rests** page of **House Style ▸ Engraving Rules** (shortcut **Ctrl+Shift+E** *or* ⌂⌘E) to make multirests look hand-drawn, though some printer drivers have bugs in which may prevent this printing correctly (and in extreme cases may even cause a crash).

Engraving Rules

Sibelius incorporates numerous music engraving rules that you can customize as part of designing your own house style, or to make different house styles for different kinds of music. These rules are all defined in the **House Style ▸ Engraving Rules** dialog (shortcut **Ctrl+Shift+E** *or* ⌂⌘E).

Engraving rules options include preferred positions for articulations, distances between notes and other objects, staff justification, and so on.

Details of the options are scattered among relevant sections throughout this **Reference**. For instance, the options on the **Bar numbers** page are detailed in 🕮 **3.5 Bar numbers**. Check the **Index** under "Engraving Rules" for a list of page references.

Setting house styles for all your scores

The house style settings apply only to the score you are working on, so if you want to use the same settings for all your files, you have two options:

Layout

- Set up manuscript papers for the instrumentations you most often use, containing your pre-ferred house style (📖 **2.23 Manuscript paper**), or

- Export your preferred house styles using House Style ▸ Export House Style (see below) and import them into other files. You can import a house style into multiple files at once (see **Import House Style** below).

Export House Style

You can export a house style file from a score or part to disk so it can be imported into other scores:

- Choose House Style ▸ Export House Style

- Enter a name for your house style and click OK.

Sibelius will save the new house style in the user application data folder (see **User-editable files in** 📖 **9.1 Working with files**). Unless you want to share the house style with somebody else, you do not need to worry about the location of the file as Sibelius will detect it as an available house style each time the program is run.

If you are a music publisher, you can send house style files to all of your composers, arrangers and copyists to base their scores on, or you can import your house style into any scores you receive from them to ensure a consistent appearance.

For more details about exporting house styles from dynamic parts, see **Exporting house styles from parts** on page 548.

Import House Style

To import a house style into the current score:

- If the score has parts, ensure you are viewing the full score rather than a part (so as to import the house style into the score and all parts). You can also import a house style into parts – see page 552.

- Choose House Style ▸ Import House Style:

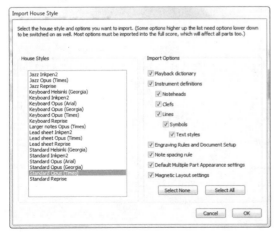

- Select the house style you want to import from the list

- Notice how the checkboxes on the right are indented, to show that some of the options are required by others, and so cannot be independently switched off. You can, for example, transfer only the **Text styles** from a house style file into your score without importing any other settings, but if you want to import, say, **Noteheads**, you have to import **Symbols** and **Text styles** too.

* Switch off any options you don't want to import, so that they don't override the existing settings; it may be quickest to click **Select None** and then switch on only the options you want to import.

* Click **OK**

* The music text font (which is used for dynamics, metronome marks, etc.) won't automatically be updated, so you should choose **House Style ▸ Edit All Fonts** and choose the correct one from the **Music Text Font** list (Opus Text, Helsinki Text, Reprise Text or Inkpen2 Text, depending on the music font you choose).

Several predefined house styles are supplied with Sibelius – see **Predefined house styles** above. Sibelius also includes a plug-in that allows you to import a particular house style file into a folder full of files at once – see **Import House Style into Folder of Scores** on page 489.

If you import a new note spacing rule into a score, the existing spacings are unaffected. The new rule is only used when you create more notes or use **Layout ▸ Reset Note Spacing**. This means that you can use different spacings for different sections of a score.

When you import a house style that alters the default position of objects, most objects will not be repositioned unless you select them (e.g. using a filter) and choose **Layout ▸ Reset Position**.

Layout

8.9 Note spacing

📖 **8.3 Music engraving**, **8.1 Layout and formatting**, **8.10 Staff spacing**.

Changing the note spacing means, in effect, adjusting the spacing between notes, chords, rests and barlines. You can do this in various ways:

- Move individual notes and rests left or right with the mouse or by typing **Shift+Alt+←/→** *or* ⇧⌥←/→, with **Ctrl** *or* ⌘ for big steps
- To squash a passage of music closer together or spread it out, select the passage and type **Shift+Alt+←/→** *or* ⇧⌥←/→ a few times. Again, hold down **Ctrl** *or* ⌘ at the same time to move in bigger steps.
- Use **Layout ▸ Format ▸ Make Into System/Page** to condense or expand the selected passage to fill a system or page – 📖 **8.1 Layout and formatting**
- To alter the note spacing rule, see below
- If you've messed up some note spacing and want to reset it to default, select a passage, and choose **Layout ▸ Reset Note Spacing** (shortcut **Ctrl+Shift+N** *or* ⇧⌘N). This also takes account of the space required by clefs, accidentals, lyrics, etc.

Note spacing rule

Sibelius uses a sophisticated note spacing algorithm called Optical™ spacing. This is rather more complex than just a series of spacings for different note values; however, you can specify these basic spacings in the **House Style ▸ Note Spacing Rule** dialog:

- For each note value you can specify the unjustified space after it. ("Unjustified" because horizontal justification increases the space after notes/rests by an amount that depends on the context.)

- Spacings are measured from the left-hand side of one note to the left-hand side of the next (i.e. they include notehead width).

- You can specify the gap before the first note/rest in a bar, and the width of an empty bar, which by default is the same as the space allocated to a note that would fill a bar of the current time signature, e.g. a whole note (semibreve) in 4/4, or a dotted half (dotted minim) in 6/8.

- **Allow extra space for colliding voices** is for the specific case where a note in an opposing voice at the interval of a second has to be displaced to the right; with this option switched on, Sibelius adds extra space to accommodate for the displacement, which might otherwise cause the spacing to appear tighter than it actually is.

- The **Grace Notes** options control the default space around grace notes and the space after the last grace note, before the next regular note.

- The **Chord Symbols** options allow you to choose whether Sibelius should consider chord symbols when spacing notes (which, by default, it does), and if so, the minimum gap between chord symbols.

- The settings under **Minimum Space** define the smallest gap that Sibelius will leave around notes, accidentals, leger lines, arpeggio lines, tails (flags on unbeamed notes), and at the start and end of bars in the case of extremely tight spacing – these are typically much smaller than the "ideal" spacing values at the left of the dialog. Sibelius will include these defined minimum spacings in its spacing calculations, with the result that collisions between solid objects will be rare, even in very tight situations. Only if Sibelius cannot fit the total minimum spacings for all objects on the system will it have to squash them even closer together, at which point collisions may begin to occur.

- The **Ties** options control the minimum length of ties to prevent them becoming "squashed" or invisible when spacing is tight. You can set different minimum lengths for ties positioned above or below notes and ties between notes.

- The **Lyrics** options determine whether the width of lyrics should be taken into account when spacing the music, together with options for the default gap between lyrics, leaving extra room for lyric hyphens, and whether long syllables at the start of the bar should be allowed to overhang the previous barline – 📖 **3.3 Lyrics**.

For more details on how these settings control the spacing, 📖 **8.3 Music engraving**.

House Style ▸ Engraving Rules includes settings for the gap between objects other than notes and rests. Additionally, the **Notes and Tremolos** page lets you allow Sibelius to contract the note spacing slightly in order to fit bars more neatly onto a staff.

Beware that values you enter in the **Note Spacing Rule** dialog may appear to have changed slightly when you re-open the dialog; this is because Sibelius measures spacings in 1/32nds of a space, but decimal divisions of a space are easier for mortals to understand than 1/32 fractions, so whatever value you type in the dialog will be rounded to the nearest 1/32nd of a space.

Notes out of alignment

Sibelius handles the alignment of notes automatically, even in complex cases involving multiple voices. However, sometimes you might wish to change the horizontal position of an individual note within a bar. To do this, select the note, open the **General** panel of the Properties window,

Layout

and alter the X parameter, which adjusts its horizontal offset. Negative numbers move the note left, positive numbers move it right. The units are spaces. 📖 **5.17 Properties**.

Optimizing note spacing

Like so much else in music engraving, note spacing is an esoteric art for which the rules are not hard and fast (📖 **8.3 Music engraving**).

Notes are not and should not be spaced proportionally to their note values (📖 **8.3 Music engraving**), so it's normal for bars to get wider and narrower as the music changes. However, if there is wide variation in note values, particularly involving cross-rhythms between different staves, the spacing can get fairly uneven – e.g. these boxed notes:

Default spacing

This requires a compromise between using this uneven default spacing, and using proportional spacing throughout to make the second half of bar 1 like the first, which would make bar 2 too narrow by comparison.

A good strategy is to make the note spacing look even on a beat-by-beat or bar-by-bar basis. Here we can make the first bar roughly even and the second bar even but not too much narrower than the first, like this:

Better: after manual adjustment

Uneven spacing due to flat

In fact we have made the second half of bar 1 slightly narrower than the first half, to produce a smoother transition into the still narrower spacing of bar 2. There is extra space between the G and Bb sixteenth notes (semiquavers) in the lower staff to allow for the accidental; this is quite acceptable in tight spacing.

Optimizing lyric spacing

Music with lyrics presents special note spacing problems, especially if the note values are short and the lyrics are wide. If you were to space the music just according to the notes, you might get results like this:

Spaced according to notes only

the   cat scratched and stretched un - til   it   got   in through the mouse hole

Fortunately, Sibelius automatically allows extra space between notes for extra-wide syllables, to ensure that they don't collide. However, if some syllables are wide and others aren't, this could make the note spacing very uneven, like this:

Sibelius default: wider spacing for wide lyrics (to avoid collisions)

Notice how the lyrics are nicely spaced, but as a result the notes aren't and in fact vary wildly in spacing, particularly the ones in the box. Of course, this is a particularly awkward example. In fact, "scratched" and "stretched" are, at nine letters each, among the widest syllables in English (an accolade they share with "squelched"), but "through" is almost as troublesome, and occurs often.

Making both the lyric spacing and the note spacing acceptable requires something of a compromise. As when evening up note spacing (above), a good strategy is to make the note spacing look even on a beat-by-beat or bar-by-bar basis; so if you have a beat or a bar with an extra-wide syllable in it, adjust the spacing of all notes in that beat or bar to match.

In very tight situations, it can also help to move some syllables horizontally a little, in order to take advantage of free space around earlier or later syllables. Perhaps the best result you can get with the above example is this:

Better: note and lyric spacing evened up

8.10 Staff spacing

This topic explains how to alter the vertical position of staves in your score. For general information about the layout tools in Sibelius, ☐ **8.1 Layout and formatting**. For information about hiding empty staves, or indenting the left- or right-hand side of the system, ☐ **2.29 Staves**. For information about creating system and page breaks to put fewer bars on a system or page, see ☐ **8.5 Breaks** (and see ☐ **8.4 Auto Breaks** for information about how Sibelius does this automatically in instrumental parts). To find out about making the staves larger or smaller, or changing the page size of your score, ☐ **8.6 Document Setup**.

Default staff spacing

The staves in your score are spaced according to a set of default values on the **Staves** page of **House Style ▸ Engraving Rules**, and Sibelius uses vertical justification to ensure that the staves and systems are spread out to fill the page.

If you imagine a page with a single system, by default the top line of the top staff is positioned at the top staff margin, and the bottom line of the bottom staff is positioned at the bottom staff margin, with the other staves spaced at equal distances between them. Typically the first page will have a larger top and bottom staff margin, to allow room for the text that normally appears there (e.g. title and composer at the top of the page, and copyright or publisher information at the bottom), and Sibelius does this automatically too. (Staff margins are set in **Layout ▸ Document Setup**, and are explained on page 585.)

The default distance between staves within a system is specified by the *n* **spaces between staves** value. However, because vertical justification spreads staves out to fill the height of the page, typically this value is the minimum value that Sibelius will use. One notable exception is for instruments that have two staves braced together by default, such as piano and harp: by default, Sibelius does not justify (spread out) the distance between these instruments' two staves, so the *n* **spaces between staves** value will always be used literally. (If, however, you want Sibelius to justify the distance between braced staves, switch on **Justify both staves of grand staff instruments**.)

Now imagine that our score contains instruments from different families, e.g. wind, brass and strings. Each family of instruments is typically bracketed or braced together in the score (☐ **2.9 Brackets and braces**), and to improve the clarity of the page, Sibelius automatically adds a little extra space between the bottom staff enclosed in one bracket or brace and the next staff beneath it, controlled by the *n* **extra spaces between groups of staves** value. As before, this value is effectively a minimum gap, because it is scaled in the same way as other gaps between systems by vertical justification.

Next, let's imagine that our score also contains vocal staves for singers. You typically need some extra space below vocal staves to allow room for lyrics, and Sibelius automatically does this for you, controlled by the *n* **extra spaces below vocal staves (for lyrics)** value. This value is also scaled by vertical justification.

Our imaginary score has enough instruments that only one system fits on a page, so it's likely that system objects like rehearsal marks, tempo instructions and bar numbers will appear not only above the top staff in the system, but also above one or two other staves further down the system –

perhaps above the strings, or above the vocal staves. Sibelius automatically allows a little extra room above staves on which system objects are set to appear, controlled by the *n* **extra spaces above for System Object Positions** value. (System object positions are set in **House Style ▸ System Object Positions**, and are explained on page 610.)

Finally, imagine for a moment that our score has fewer staves, such that two or perhaps three systems can comfortably fit on the page. The distance between the bottom staff of one system and the top staff of the next is defined by the *n* **spaces between systems** value. As with the other default values, this value is scaled by vertical justification.

Sibelius will only allow staves to be closer together than the distances specified above if you use e.g. **Layout ▸ Format ▸ Make Into Page** to force an extra system onto a page, or if you set **System spacings may be contracted to** *n*% to a value smaller than 100% on the **Staves** page of **Engraving Rules** (by default, it's set to 97%, which allows a tiny amount of leeway to make staves closer together than the default values specified). However, the staves will more often than not be further apart than the distances specified above, because of vertical justification.

Vertical justification

Although the distances between individual staves and systems may vary between pages – to account for things like very low or high notes in particular places in the score – the distance between the top of the page and the top staff line of the first staff, and the distance between the bottom of the page and the bottom staff line of the last staff is normally consistent across all pages of the score, except for the first page, which has to make room for extra text at the top and bottom.

Vertical justification spreads staves and systems out such that they fill the height of the page, providing the consistency across pages described above, proportionally increasing the distance between staves and systems where possible to improve clarity and legibility, without affecting your ability to adjust the distance between staves and systems as required on an individual basis.

By default, vertical justification takes effect if the total height of the staves and systems (including the gaps between them) is more than 65% the height of the distance between the top and bottom staff margin. This is controlled by the **Justify staves when page is at least** *n*% full value on the **Staves** page of **House Style ▸ Engraving Rules**.

Vertical justification only kicks in over this threshold because if a page is less than two-thirds full (as it may be in e.g. hymn layouts with block lyrics below two or three systems of music, or on the final page of a score for a small ensemble), it would look worse to spread the staves and systems out than it would to leave a larger gap at the bottom of the page.

If you want to disable vertical justification, effectively producing a "ragged bottom" (if you'll pardon the expression!), set **Justify staves when page is at least** *n*% full to 100%. However, this would very rarely be recommended: only perhaps when producing documents that are not scores in the true sense of the word (for example, when preparing music examples for exporting as graphics to another application, or when creating text-heavy worksheets).

Once you understand what vertical justification does and how it interacts with the distances between staves and systems on the **Staves** page of **Engraving Rules**, you will find that it is a tremendously useful tool for producing a clear, consistent layout completely automatically.

Layout

Adjusting the distances between staves and systems

If a page looks a little crowded vertically, before you adjust the staff spacing at all, the first and best course of action is often to reduce the staff size slightly in **Layout ▸ Document Setup**. Even a small change in staff size can have a dramatic effect on the layout of your score. Don't assume that you should always reduce the staff size, however: sometimes, a small *increase* in the staff size results in one system fewer per page, which will add to the total number of pages, but may result in a much clearer score that will be considerably easier for the performers or conductor to read. See page 584 for guidance on good combinations of page and staff size for different kinds of music.

If you find that staves are still too close or too far apart after adjusting the staff size, you should adjust the distances between staves and systems using the **Staves** page of **House Style ▸ Engraving Rules**: this changes the default staff and system spacing, and is by far the quickest way to experiment and make changes.

Using these two tools, you will normally be able to produce a consistent and clear layout that will leave you with very little manual editing to do. However, in many scores, the texture and density of the music changes over time, which may cause collisions between notes on adjacent staves, or more commonly between objects attached to adjacent staves (e.g. a dynamic below one staff colliding with a slur above the notes on the staff below), on particular systems.

Sibelius can normally resolve these kinds of collisions automatically for you, using **Layout ▸ Optimize Staff Spacing**. This examines each staff, works out the ideal amount of space that should be allocated for it across the width of the system (by considering that staff and all objects attached to it in isolation, as if no other staves were present), then interlocks the staves as closely as it can, adjusting them only the smallest distance necessary to resolve the collisions between them. For example, if one staff has low notes at the left-hand end of the system, and the staff below has high notes at the right-hand end of the system, Sibelius knows that it doesn't need to leave room for low notes on the first staff at the right-hand end of the system, and is therefore able to move the staff below closer to the staff above without causing any collisions.

You can control the amount of horizontal and vertical distance **Optimize Staff Spacing** should try to leave between objects on each staff on the **Staves** page of **House Style ▸ Engraving Rules**.

For best effect, you should select at least an entire system or, preferably, an entire page before choosing **Layout ▸ Optimize Staff Spacing**: the more context Sibelius has, the better the result. You can, of course, select the whole score before using **Optimize Staff Spacing**.

In some particularly tight situations, Sibelius may not be able to resolve all the collisions, in which case you may need to adjust the results manually. To find collisions, see **Finding collisions** on page 564. Once you've found a collision, you may decide that the best way to resolve the collision is to move one or more objects, or you may want to adjust the staff spacing manually.

Moving staves manually

Most staff operations, including moving them, require that you first select which staff or staves you want to work with:

- Click on a blank part of a bar to select that bar (double-clicking selects the staff, but selecting a bar is sufficient for moving staves etc.)
- Triple-click on a blank part of a bar to select a staff throughout the score

• Select a passage to work on several staves.

For more information on selections, ⎙ **1.9 Selections and passages**.

The basic ways of moving staves are:

• *Normal move* – select a staff or staves and drag with the mouse (shortcut Alt+↑/↓ or ⌥↑/↓, with Ctrl *or* ⌘ for larger steps): changes the distance between the selected staff/staves and the staff above (or the top staff margin if the top staff is selected) and retains the spacing between all other staves. Sibelius may have to squash up other staves to allow room if the page is full.

• *Independent move* – select a staff or staves, first hold down **Shift**, then click and drag (shortcut Shift+Alt+↑/↓ or ⇧⌥↑/↓, with Ctrl *or* ⌘ for larger steps): moves only the selected staff/ staves, leaving all other staves in the same place on the page. Although you can use this to move staves almost on top of one another, you cannot move one staff beyond another staff and thus change the order of the staves in your score (to do this, ⎙ **2.18 Instruments**).

You might find it useful to switch on View ▸ Rulers ▸ Staff Rulers (shortcut Ctrl+Shift+Alt+R *or* ⇧⌥⌘R) before moving staves – ⎙ **5.23 View menu**.

Precisely which staves and systems move is determined by the extent of your initial selection. This means that you can alter staff spacing between staves on the same system, the same page, or any number of pages, simply by selecting the passage for which you want to change the spacing. (You can even select a passage containing multiple staves and move it up and down independently, which changes the gap above the top selected staff and/or below the bottom selected staff.)

However, you are recommended to make the smallest adjustment possible (e.g. a single staff on a single system), since adjusting the staff spacing manually prevents changes to the default staff spacing from taking effect until you reset the position of the staves.

Restoring default staff spacing

To restore the default staff spacing (i.e. the settings on the Staves page of the House Style ▸ Engraving Rules dialog) to a staff or staves, select the desired passage and choose Layout ▸ Reset Space Above Staff or Layout ▸ Reset Space Below Staff.

Align Staves

To apply the staff and system spacing on one page in your score to other pages, select a passage extending across the pages you want to alter and choose Layout ▸ Align Staves.

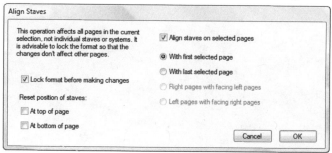

Any changes made from this dialog apply to all pages that the selected passage appears on, so you can select from any bar on any staff of the first page you want to alter to any bar on any staff of the last page. The options are as follows:

- **Lock format before making changes**: locks the format of all bars in the selected pages, thus ensuring bars stay on the same pages after staves have been aligned
- **Reset position of staves**: these options restore the default gap above the top or bottom staff on a page to the staff margin positions (as specified in **Layout ▸ Document Setup**)
- **Align staves on selected pages**: when switched on, you can choose between any one of the four available options:
  - **With first selected page**: aligns all subsequent pages with the first page of the selection
  - **With last selected page**: aligns all preceding pages with the last page of the selection
  - **Right pages with facing left pages**: aligns each right-hand page with the left page it is facing
  - **Left pages with facing right pages**: aligns each left-hand page with the right page it is facing.

To use these options, you must select more than one page.

Aligning staves via this dialog is only possible if the pages being aligned with each other have the same number of systems and the same number of staves on each system. If not, then only the top and bottom staves are aligned. If one or both of the pages have only one system, then only the top staff is aligned.

8.11 Music fonts

📖 **3.9 Edit Text Styles**, **8.8 House Style™**, **8.17 Edit Symbols**.

Noteheads, clefs, accidentals and most other objects that appear in Sibelius scores are drawn using a symbol, which itself is a character or combination of characters from a music font.

Music fonts have proliferated rather messily over the years; different fonts often have a semi-random selection of musical symbols present (or often woefully absent). Different people have different preferences as to which music fonts they like; moreover, each font has its strong and weak points, so none is ideal.

Because of this, we've taken extreme care to make Sibelius's music fonts include just about every symbol that you're likely to want or that is available in other fonts, and moreover to have symbol designs suitable for the highest quality publishing.

However, as music font tastes differ wildly (and sometimes violently), we've also sorted out the complex confusion inherent in other music fonts, and designed Sibelius so that it's compatible with any other music font you're likely to have – including Petrucci™, Chaconne™, Sonata™, Susato™, Jazz™, Franck™, Maestro™, November™, Partita™, Swing™, Tamburo™, Piu™ and Ghent™. You can even mix all of these fonts together in the same score.

Changing music font

The simplest way to change the music font used by your score is to choose **House Style ▸ Edit All Fonts**, choose a new music font from the **Main Music Font** list provided, and click **OK**.

The following fonts will appear as options in the **Edit All Fonts** dialog, if they are installed on your system: Opus, Helsinki, Reprise, Inkpen2, Maestro, Petrucci, Sonata, Partita, Franck, Virtuoso, Chaconne, November, Jazz, Swing, LeeMusic, RussMusic, and AshMusic.

To enable further music fonts to appear in this list, see **Using fonts not supplied with Sibelius** below.

Most Sibelius scores use the Opus font. If you want to change to the handwritten appearance of Reprise or Inkpen2, it's best to import one of the **Reprise** or **Inkpen2** house styles, as this will also change the appearance of other objects, such as staff and barlines, slurs, hairpins, and so on – 📖 **8.8 House Style™**.

You can also use Sibelius's Helsinki music font, which has a more traditional and elegant appearance. As with the Reprise and Inkpen2 fonts, you should import a **Helsinki** house style to benefit from the many subtleties the house style makes to other aspects of your score's appearance – 📖 **8.8 House Style™**.

Changing font of a subset of symbols

If you want to change music font to a different one, you don't have to change all of Sibelius's symbols. You can change just the clefs, or the percussion symbols, or even just a single symbol.

Each symbol in Sibelius is drawn using the font specified by a particular text style. By changing the text style settings you can change the appearance of whole sets of symbols at once:

Layout

- **Common symbols**: this covers pretty much all the symbols normally used – standard notes, accidentals, clefs, articulations, etc.

  You may want to change **Common symbols** to Reprise, Inkpen2, Helsinki, Petrucci, Susato or Sonata. Sonata has clefs in non-standard places, but you can easily move them.

- **Special noteheads etc.**: this includes unusual noteheads and microtones. You may want to substitute Reprise Special, Inkpen2 Special, Helsinki Special, Tamburo or Piu.

- **Percussion instruments**: weird pictures of mallets, brushes, coins and anything else you can hit things with. You may want to substitute Ghent.

- **Special symbols**: this contains symbols not found in any other font except Opus Special, Reprise Special, Helsinki Special and Inkpen2 Special, so you won't want to substitute any other font (unless you design your own).

- **Note flags**: you can change between Opus, Helsinki, Reprise, Inkpen2, and Petrucci – Susato, Sonata, etc. are unsuitable as they have incompatible flags.

To change the font of one of these sets of symbols:

- In the **House Style ▸ Edit Symbols** dialog, click **Music fonts**
- Click the symbol set you want to modify, and click **Edit**
- Change the font and possibly also size, then click **OK** and **OK** again to close the **Edit Symbols** dialog.

If you intend to change the size, the standard size for all symbols is 19.8pt (relative) – if you increase or decrease this, the symbols get bigger or smaller. You can use this (say) to make noteheads extra-big in beginners' books, or to scale a symbol (by creating its own symbol text style) – see **Creating a new symbol text style** in 📖 **8.17 Edit Symbols**.

(For the curious: changing the music font and size takes place in the **House Style ▸ Edit Text Styles** dialog. This is because the above symbol sets are in fact treated by Sibelius as text styles, even though the font and size are the only options you can usefully change. Don't think too hard about it.)

For more information about customizing Sibelius's symbols, 📖 **8.17 Edit Symbols**.

Music text font

Various musical symbols such as $\boldsymbol{f}$, $\boldsymbol{p}$ and ♩ can be typed into text such as Expression text and metronome marks. These so-called *music text* characters are by default drawn using the Opus Text font, as are the numerals 0–9 and : (colon) used in tuplets.

You can change the font used for music text in the **House Style ▸ Edit All Fonts** dialog. We recommend you only change it to an italic or bold italic text font, and only change it to a normal text font if you are not using metronome marks, as text fonts do not contain little pictures of notes.

(However, if you really want to change the music text font and also really want to use metronome marks, you can manually change the font of metronome marks back to Opus Text, Helsinki Text, Reprise Text or Inkpen2 Text as you type them in.)

When you change the music text font, there's an option for whether or not you want to apply the change to existing text in your score. This allows you, for example, to change the font used for dynamics already in the score. (You can't do this by editing the Expression text style as text styles only define the font used for normal text such as *cresc.*, not music text characters such as *mf*.)

Using fonts not supplied with Sibelius

Sibelius allows you to use any compatible music font to render notation in your score if you so wish. Because – as far as your computer is concerned – a font is just a font, you need to tell Sibelius which of the fonts on your system are valid music fonts before it is able to use them.

Supported music fonts are listed in the **House Style ▸ Edit All Fonts** dialog; when you tell Sibelius about a new music font, it will appear in the **Main Music Font** list.

Choose the **Music Fonts** page of the **File ▸ Preferences** dialog (in the **Sibelius** menu on Mac). The following dialog appears:

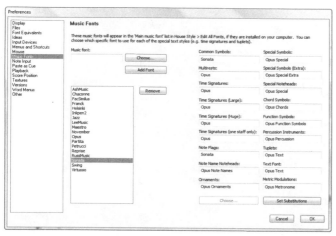

The list of fonts on the left shows those that Sibelius recognizes as music fonts. If you wish to add a new font to the list:

- Type the name of the new music font into the **Music font** font field on the left, or click the **Choose** button to select from a list of the fonts installed on your computer. When you have entered the name of the font, click the **Add Font** button. The font will be added to the list.
- With the new font selected in the list on the left, enter the name of the font you want to use for each aspect of the notation into the various fields on the right, or click the **Choose** button to select the font from a list. When you have filled all the fields, click the **Set Substitutions** button.

Very few available music fonts have separate fonts suitable for all of Sibelius's symbol text styles, so it is normally only necessary to substitute your chosen font in **Common Symbols**.

Installing Type 1 music fonts

The Opus, Helsinki, Reprise and Inkpen2 music fonts are supplied in both TrueType and Adobe Type 1 (PostScript) format, and TrueType fonts are installed by default. You can print to PostScript printers and create EPS files using *either* of these font formats.

However, for some publishing purposes, Adobe Type 1 fonts are preferable to TrueType fonts, though you typically need to install extra software to use them. On Windows, Type 1 versions of Opus, Helsinki, Reprise and Inkpen2 are included in the **PostScript Fonts** folder (in the **Extras**

Layout

folder within your **Sibelius** program folder). On Mac, Type 1 fonts are located in the **Other Appli-cations** folder on your Sibelius 6 DVD-ROM.

Designing your own music font

For designing fonts of any kind we recommend the FontLab program (www.fontlab.com); however, font design is a sophisticated art, so this is not recommended for the faint-hearted.

The Opus, Helsinki, Reprise and Inkpen2 font families are copyright, so you are not permitted to include symbols from them in any new font you design.

8.12 Default Positions

For advanced users only

The **House Style ▸ Default Positions** dialog allows you to change the positioning behavior of text, lines, and various other objects, when creating and moving them and resetting their positions. Sibelius's default settings are sensible, and you won't usually need to change them, but should you be overcome by the urge to do so, this topic will tell you how.

The dialog looks like this:

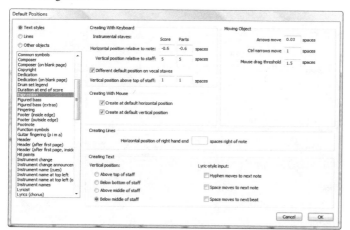

To change the default position of an object, choose the category in the top-left corner (either **Text styles**, **Lines** or **Other objects**), and then select the desired text style or object from the list. You can even select multiple styles or objects to modify their common properties at the same time.

Options that are not applicable to the selected text style or object are disabled, as you might expect (so for text styles, you won't be able to set the **Creating Lines** options, and vice versa). Likewise, if you select multiple lines (say), then values that all the selected objects have in common are shown on the dialog, and values that are not in common are shown blank.

The options on the dialog are as follows:

Creating Object

There are separate options for creating objects with the mouse and keyboard. When you create objects with the mouse, you can click precisely where you intend them to go; when you create objects with the keyboard, you can't indicate precisely where you want the object to be created, so they appear at a sensible position near to the caret (if inputting notes) or selected object.

Objects can be set to appear in a different place by default in parts than they do in the score. Usually this isn't necessary, but objects such as rehearsal marks generally look better if they are positioned closer to the top of a staff in parts than they are in the score. Sibelius allows you to, say, position rehearsal marks five spaces away from staves in the score and only two spaces away from staves in parts.

The **Creating With Keyboard** options control the rules for positioning of the object when it is created via the keyboard, or when you select it and choose **Layout ▸ Reset Position** (shortcut **Ctrl+Shift+P** *or* ⇧⌘P):

- **Horizontal position relative to note** sets the default horizontal position for both a score and parts; enter negative numbers if you want to position objects to the left of the note to which they are attached (for, say, dynamics)
- **Vertical position relative to staff** automatically positions the object vertically for you, relative to the option chosen at the bottom of the dialog under **Vertical Position** (**Above top of staff**, **Below bottom of staff**, **Above middle of staff** and **Below middle of staff**). You can enter different values for the score and its parts, if you wish.
- **Different default position on vocal staves** allows you to specify that the object should be positioned differently on vocal staves and instrumental staves; if you switch this on, you can then specify a separate **Vertical position above top of staff** for the selected object. This is done by default for Expression text and the various hairpin lines, such that they appear above vocal staves, but below instrumental staves.

The **Creating With Mouse** options simply determine whether, when created with the mouse, the object should be positioned at its default horizontal and/or vertical position (as determined in the **Creating With Keyboard** settings above) instead of at the mouse position, for example:

- Text such as chord symbols, figured bass, fingering, and lyrics, are all most usefully created at their default horizontal and vertical positions;
- System text such as title, composer, copyright, footnote and so on are all most usefully created at their default vertical positions;
- Some other text styles, such as tempo and metronome mark text, are best created at the position you click with your mouse – to obtain this behavior, simply switch off both of the **With mouse** options.

Moving Object

Although all objects can be dragged using the mouse in a score, a finer degree of control is possible by moving objects with the arrow keys and their modifiers (e.g. ←/→ for small steps and **Ctrl+←/→** *or* ⌘←/→ for large steps). The **Moving Object** options allow you control over the behavior of these operations:

- **Arrows move** is the distance an object moves when moved with the arrow keys
- **Ctrl+arrows/Command-arrows move** is the distance an object moves when moved with the arrow keys in conjunction with the **Ctrl** *or* ⌘ key
- **Mouse drag threshold** is how far you have to drag an object with the mouse before it moves from its present position; set this to a large number if you want to make objects "stickier" and less likely to be dragged by mistake.

You can adjust these options for text styles and lines separately, but not for individual text styles or line styles; so any change you make to these settings will affect *all* similar objects (e.g. change the drag threshold for Technique text and you also change it for all other text styles). The **Moving Object** options (unlike the others on this dialog) are global preferences and are thus not associated with any particular score – they apply to every score you work on in Sibelius.

Creating Lines

Horizontal position of right hand end does what the name suggests: it determines how many spaces to the right of the end of the line the right-hand end will appear by default.

Creating Text

Above/Below top/middle/bottom of staff specifies the position of the baseline (i.e. bottom of the capital letters), relative to the specified staff line. The distance from the staff-line is specified under **Creating With Keyboard** at the top of the dialog.

Some text styles, such as lyrics, figured bass and fingering, are created by jumping from note to note using the **space bar** (☐ **3.3 Lyrics**, **3.1 Working with text**). The options under **Lyric-style input** control this behavior:

- **Space / Hyphen moves to next note** do what they say
- **Space moves to next beat** is used by chord symbols, so that you can write different chord symbols on each beat of the bar, even if the note is several beats long.

If both of the bottom two options are switched on, hitting **space** while creating text will move to either the next note *or* the next beat, whichever occurs sooner.

Special cases

There are a few special considerations to bear in mind when using the **House Style ▸ Default Positions** dialog, as follows:

- The **Creating Object** options have no effect on clefs, key signatures, special barlines, time signatures or transpositions. To reset the position of any of these, make a system selection around the object and choose **Layout ▸ Reset Note Spacing** (shortcut **Ctrl+Shift+N** *or* ⇧⌘N).
- For *system* objects (e.g. text styles such as Title, Tempo, *rit./accel.* lines, etc.), the default vertical position and **Above/Below top/bottom/middle of staff** settings are retroactive – in other words, any change you make to these settings will automatically change all system text objects in your score
- However, for *staff* objects (e.g. Chord Symbols, **Lyrics line 1** text, or bracket lines) the changes affect only newly-created objects – if you have, say, some Expression text in your score and then change the Expression text style's default position, the existing Expression text in your score will not automatically change position.

  So if you want to change the position of some or all existing objects as well as new ones, use filters to select them (☐ **5.7 Filters and Find**), then choose **Layout ▸ Reset Position** (shortcut **Ctrl+Shift+P** *or* ⇧⌘P).
- The settings in the **House Style ▸ Edit Text Style** dialog for aligning text relative to the page take precedence over the settings in the **House Style ▸ Default Positions** dialog
- For slurs, if neither of the **Create at default horizontal/vertical position** options are switched on, creating slurs with the mouse produces non-magnetic slurs. If you switch on either or both of these options, the mouse creates magnetic slurs. Creating magnetic slurs with the mouse can be a little confusing – for example, if you want to input an up-arching slur (shortcut S) and try to put it over some notes whose stems point upwards using the mouse, the slur will

Layout

appear below the noteheads instead. However, if you're married to your mouse, this could be a useful feature for you!

- For rehearsal marks, their horizontal position is determined by the settings in the **Other objects** section, and their vertical position is determined by the settings in the **Text styles** section
- The positions of some other objects with complex positioning rules (such as magnetic slurs and tuplets) can only be modified via the **House Style ▸ Engraving Rules** dialog, rather than the **House Style ▸ Default Positions** dialog.

System Object Positions

In large scores, some system objects such as rehearsal marks and tempo text can appear in several positions down a system simultaneously, e.g. at the top and above the strings in orchestral music. To edit the positions where these objects go:

- Choose **House Style ▸ System Object Positions**
- Click the staves you want system objects to appear above – up to five in total. The top staff is compulsory. System objects can also go below the bottom staff.

System objects don't all have to appear at all of these positions. The **Vertical posn** tab of **House Style ▸ Edit Text Styles** (shortcut **Ctrl+Shift+Alt+T** *or* ⇧⌥⌘T) lets you specify which of these positions a particular text style will actually appear at. This allows you (for instance) to have rehearsal marks at the top, above the strings and below the bottom staff, but tempo text at the top only. 📖 **3.9 Edit Text Styles**.

You can also delete individual instances of system objects, so, for example, if a Tempo text marking appears three times down your score, you could **Delete** the bottom two instances individually – deleting the top instance deletes all other instances. To restore instances of system objects that you have deleted, select the top instance and choose **Layout ▸ Reset Design** (**Ctrl+Shift+D** *or* ⇧⌘D).

8.13 Edit Chord Symbols

📖 **2.10 Chord symbols**.

Sibelius provides a tremendous amount of control over the appearance of chord symbols. To make global changes to the default appearance of chord symbols, use the Chord Symbols page of House Style ▸ Engraving Rules (explained in full on page 109). If you want to adjust the chord text or chord diagram used by a specific chord type, use House Style ▸ Edit Chord Symbols.

Changes you make in Engraving Rules apply only to the score in which they are made, and can be transferred between scores by way of exporting its house style and importing it into other scores (📖 **8.8 House Style™**). By contrast, any changes you make in House Style ▸ Edit Chord Symbols are saved in a library that is independent of any particular score file, and the settings in your library file are used whenever you create a chord symbol in any score.

Choosing a chord symbol to edit

House Style ▸ Edit Chord Symbols looks like this:

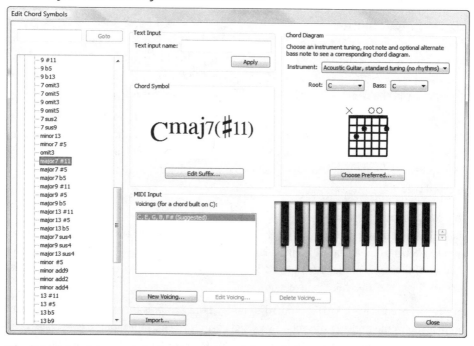

The list of chord types at the left-hand side of the dialog is split into five categories: Common Chords, More Major Chords, More Minor Chords, More Dominant Chords, and Other Chords. The Common Chords category contains just over 100 of the most common chord types, with the more remaining, more esoteric 500 or so split between the other four categories. To change the settings for a particular chord type, simply select it in the left-hand list.

Layout

At the top left-hand corner is a box into which you can type a particular chord type to go to it quickly in the list below. To find a chord, type its extension in plain text, omitting the root note (e.g. "maj13#11"), and click Go To; Sibelius will then immediately select that chord type in the list.

Once you have selected a chord type, you will see the settings that you can change, which are arranged into groups:

* Text Input allows you to define an alternative plain text string to input a chord symbol quickly – see **Editing text input names** below.
* Chord Text is for altering the appearance of each of the suffix elements that makes up the chord text component of the chord symbol – see **Editing chord symbol suffixes** below.
* Chord Diagram is for choosing the default chord diagram that should appear for a chord type, allowing you to specify a different chord diagram for each different guitar tuning if you like – see **Editing guitar chord diagrams** below.
* MIDI input allows you to define the combination of notes on your MIDI keyboard that you play to input a chord type – see **Editing MIDI input voicings** below.

The Import button is for importing chord symbol libraries created by other Sibelius users, or created in earlier versions of Sibelius – see **Importing chord symbol libraries** below.

Editing text input names

By default, you input a chord symbol by typing a simple, plain text version of the chord you want, which is easy enough (and is explained in full on page 104), but you may find that you end up using chord symbols that require a lot of typing, e.g. "13#11b9omit3." By defining a custom text input name, you could instead type in, say, "bob" to obtain this chord symbol.

To define a custom text input name, simply type it into the Text input name box, and click Apply. Remember that you shouldn't type the root note of the chord here. If the text input name you define is already in use by another chord type, Sibelius will warn you, and give you the choice of either applying your custom text input name to the new chord type, or leaving it assigned to the old chord type.

Editing MIDI input voicings

Inputting chord symbols using a MIDI keyboard is really efficient (and is explained in full on page 105). Sibelius understands a particular voicing for each chord type by default, which is normally all of the notes of the chord played in root position (and Sibelius will interpret inversions correctly if you play the chord in inversion).

Once you've been using a MIDI keyboard to input chord symbols for a while, however, you may find that you would prefer to use your own set of custom voicings for input to gain an extra speed boost. For example, you may want all inversions of the major triad to produce a chord symbol in root position, so you can shift between different chords in close position without moving your hand too far. To achieve this, you would define voicings in root position, first inversion and second inversion for the major triad chord type. (If you then subsequently wanted to input a major chord with an altered bass note, you would do so by playing the chord in any inversion with one hand, and playing the desired root note an octave below the other notes of the chord with the other.)

You may also find that you can input chord symbols more quickly if you invent a kind of shorthand: for example, a dyad of a major third could input a major triad, a dyad of a minor third a minor triad, a major second an ^add9^ chord, a diminished fifth a diminished chord, and so on.

Similarly, there are many chord types that are made up of the same notes – e.g. $C^{\varnothing 7}$ and $Cm^{7(\flat 5)}$ – and you may find that Sibelius by default produces a different chord symbol than you would expect when you play a particular chord on your MIDI keyboard. To overcome this, find the chord type that you want to appear by default, and set your own custom voicing: this can be the same as the existing voicing if you like.

To create a custom MIDI input voicing, click **New Voicing**, and this dialog appears:

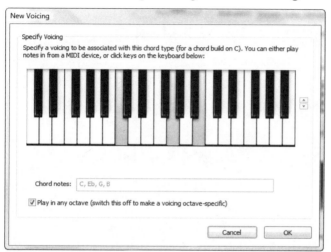

Simply play the notes you want to use to input the chord symbol, as if you were playing the chord on a root note of C; alternatively, you can click the notes on the keyboard in the dialog. By default, the **Play in any octave** option is switched on; if you want to be able to define the same pattern of intervals in separate octaves to input different chord symbols, switch this option off, in which case Sibelius will show the octave number for each note in the **Chord notes** read-out. You can hop the keyboard display up and down by octaves by clicking the arrows at the right-hand side.

When recording a custom voicing for a particular chord type, make your voicing as unique and specific as possible, and in particular try not to play the same pitch in different octaves. This will help Sibelius to pick the best results when you input chord symbols from a MIDI device: the more ambiguous the voicing, the less likely Sibelius will choose the chord you intend.

Once you're happy with your custom voicing, click **OK**. Sibelius will warn you if this voicing is already assigned to another chord type, giving you the choice of either applying your voicing to the new chord type, or leaving it assigned to the old chord type.

To edit an existing voicing, click **Edit Voicing**, which shows the dialog above; to delete an existing voicing, simply click **Delete Voicing**.

Editing chord symbol suffixes

If you want to change the appearance of the chord text component of the chord symbol, you should first check to see whether a global adjustment can be made on the **Chord Symbols** page of House

Layout

Style ▸ Engraving Rules that will save you from having to adjust lots of chord types individually. For example, if you always want the "minor" element of chord symbols to be represented by, say, mi rather than m, you should change this in Engraving Rules – see **Engraving Rules options** on page 109.

If you want to adjust the appearance of an individual chord symbol, click Edit Suffix:

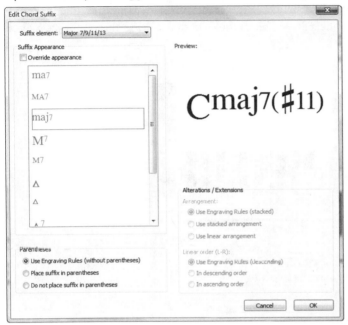

The **Suffix element** menu at the top of the dialog allows you to choose between the suffix elements that make up the chord symbol in question. In the example above, you can choose between **Major 7/9/11/13**, which corresponds to the ^{maj7} bit, and **Sharp alterations**, which corresponds to the ($\sharp$11) bit. Depending on the **Suffix element** choice, the choices elsewhere in the dialog are updated.

The **Suffix Appearance** list shows all of the different appearances Sibelius knows about for that particular suffix element. To change the appearance used, switch on **Override appearance**, then choose the desired appearance from the list. The preview on the right updates to show you how the chord symbol will eventually appear.

The options under **Parentheses** allow you to see what the current default appearance is for this suffix element by appending it to the **Use Engraving Rules** radio button; it will say either **(with parentheses)** or **(without parentheses)**. If you want to override the appearance, choose either **Place suffix in parentheses** or **Do not place suffix in parentheses**. Sibelius will automatically choose small or large parentheses as appropriate.

The **Alterations / Extensions** options only apply to chord symbols with two or more extensions or alterations, and allow you to specify whether they should be stacked vertically (e.g. $\binom{\flat13}{\sharp11}$) or drawn linearly (e.g. $(\flat13\sharp11)$). As with the **Parentheses** options, Sibelius tells you whether alterations are stacked vertically or drawn linearly by default, and you can override this by choosing either **Use stacked arrangement** or **Use linear arrangement**. If linear arrangement is used, you can also specify whether they should be shown ascending or descending from left to right.

Any change you make in the **Edit Chord Suffix** dialog will prevent any changes you subsequently make in **Engraving Rules** from having any effect on any chord symbol of this type in your score.

Editing guitar chord diagrams

When you create a chord symbol, a chord diagram will appear by default if you are creating the chord symbol on a notation staff belonging to a guitar or another fretted instrument, although you can naturally change this if you wish – see **Choosing when chord diagrams should appear** on page 106.

The chord diagram that appears by default when you create a chord symbol is known as the *preferred* chord diagram, and there can be a preferred chord diagram for every different guitar tuning or fretted instrument Sibelius knows about, and for every combination of root note and bass note. You can see these preferred diagrams by changing the **Instrument**, **Root** and **Bass** menus in the **Chord Diagram** group in **Edit Chord Symbols**.

To change a preferred chord diagram, choose the appropriate guitar tuning or other fretted instrument, root note and bass note, then click **Choose Preferred**, which shows this dialog:

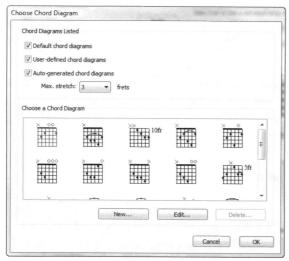

At the top of the dialog, you can choose which chord diagrams should be displayed:

- **Default chord diagrams** is a set of specially chosen chord diagrams for 6-string guitar in the standard tuning, for most of the common chord types. There are typically three chord diagrams for each chord type: one close to the nut, one around the fifth fret, and another around the ninth fret.
- **User-defined chord diagrams** shows any chord diagram created or edited by you – read on.
- **Auto-generated chord diagrams** shows a (typically large) number of chord diagrams that Sibelius has generated automatically for this type. The **Max. stretch** *n* **frets** option determines the maximum distance between fingered frets in the generated chord diagrams; this defaults to **3**, but if you want to generate a larger number of chords, you can increase this number at the expense of making the chords more difficult to play.

The preview control below these checkboxes shows the available chord diagrams. Once you find the chord diagram you want to make the preferred chord diagram for this chord type, simply select it and click OK. If, however, you don't find the chord diagram you're looking for, you can edit an existing one or create a new one to suit your purposes: select the chord diagram closest to the one you have in mind, then click **New** or **Edit**.

In either case, you'll see this dialog:

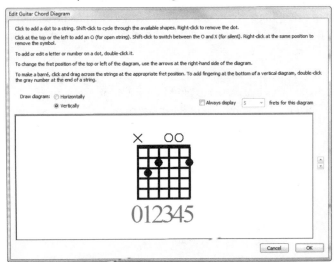

You can choose whether the diagram should be drawn **Horizontally** (with the nut at the left-hand side) or **Vertically** (as shown above, with the nut at the top). You can override the default number of frets shown in the diagram (as specified on the **Guitar** page of **House Style ▸ Engraving Rules**) by switching on the **Always display** *n* **frets per diagram** option, and choosing the number of frets (between 3 and 15).

To add a dot to a string, simply click at the desired position; **Shift**-click will cycle through the available dot shapes (black circle, white circle, black square, white square, black diamond, white diamond). To remove a dot, right-click the dot you want to remove. To add an open string marker at the nut, simply click at the left or the top, as appropriate; click again to turn that into an X (denoting that the string should not be played). To remove an O or an X, simply right-click it.

You can also add a fingering number or note name to a dot by double-clicking it: a flashing cursor will appear. Type the number or letter you want to appear in the dot, and right-click (Windows) *or* **Control**-click (Mac) to see a word menu, from which you can choose accidentals.

Alternatively, you can add fingering numbers above or below the chord diagram by double-clicking the gray numbers at the bottom of the window, and typing the desired number: hit **space** to advance to the next string without typing a number, and hit **Backspace** to skip back to the previous string.

Once you're happy with your diagram, click OK. The diagram is automatically added to your user library, and will appear when the **User-defined chord diagrams** checkbox is switched on in the **Choose Chord Diagram** dialog.

If you want to quickly edit the chord diagram belonging to an existing chord symbol in your score, select it and choose **Edit ▸ Chord Symbol ▸ Edit Chord Diagram**, which makes the dialog shown above appear. Any changes you make to the chord diagram are then instantly updated in the score when you click OK.

Engraving Rules options

The **Guitar** page of **House Style ▸ Engraving Rules** contains some options related to guitar tab, explained on page 127, and some options for controlling the appearance of the chord diagram components of chord symbols (and guitar scale diagrams – 🕮 **2.16 Guitar scale diagrams**):

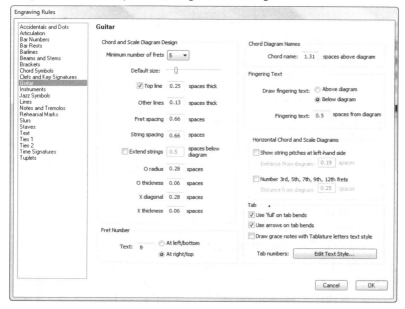

- The options in the **Chord and Scale Diagram Design** group allow you to change the default size of chord diagrams. The simplest way is to adjust the **Default size** slider, which changes all of the other values below appropriately. Some publishers like to indicate that the guitar's fretboard continues beyond the last fret of the diagram by having the strings protrude a bit beyond the last fret line; if you want to emulate this, switch on **Extend strings** *n* **spaces below diagram**, and adjust to taste.

- The **Fret Number** options allow you to choose whether you want the text that labels the first fret of a chord or scale diagram if it begins partway down the fretboard (e.g. "5fr") to appear **At left/ bottom** or **At right/top** (the default).

- **Chord text** *n* **spaces above diagram** allows you to specify the gap between the top of the chord diagram and the bottom of the chord text above it.

- **Draw fingering text** determines whether the fingering text should be drawn **Below diagram** (the default) or **Above diagram**. When fingering text is drawn above the diagram, it is drawn in line with the O and X symbols. Fingering text takes precedence over the O and X symbols, so if both a fingering and an O or X should appear over the same string, the fingering text will be displayed.

- **Fingering text** *n* **spaces from diagram** determines the distance from the bottom or top of the chord diagram that the fingering text will be drawn (the default is 0.5 spaces). If fingering text is set to display above the diagram, this parameter also changes the distance of the O and X symbols from the frame, to ensure that the fingering text appears in line with the symbols.

- **Show string pitches at left-hand side** (switched off by default) is useful for horizontal chord and scale diagrams, and labels the left-hand end of each string with its note name.

Layout

- **Number 3rd, 5th, 7th, 9th, 12th frets** (switched on by default) displays fret numbers below horizontal chord and scale diagrams.

Editing the fonts used by chord diagrams

You can further change the appearance of chord diagrams in subtle ways by adjusting the font, style (e.g. bold, italic) and point size of the various bits of text used in them. Choose **House Style ▸ Edit Text Styles** and edit the following text styles:

- **Chord diagram fingering** is for the fingering numbers above or below a chord diagram.
- **Chord diagram fret** is for the "5fr" text that appears to the right of a chord diagram.
- **Chord diagram fret numbers** is for the fret numbers below a horizontal diagram.
- **Chord diagram string names** is for the string names to the left of a horizontal diagram.

Be conservative in the choices that you make for these text styles, particularly in terms of point size: Sibelius will not automatically, say, make the entire chord diagram larger if you double the size of the fingering numbers.

Importing chord symbol libraries

You can import chord symbol libraries created in Sibelius 6, or chord diagram libraries created in Sibelius 3, Sibelius 4 or Sibelius 5. The contents of any libraries you import are merged into your existing chord symbol library. Importing a chord symbol library doesn't add or remove any chord types: it merely allows you to change the appearance of individual chord types, change the available chord diagrams for each chord type, and change the text input names and MIDI input voicings.

To begin, choose **House Style ▸ Edit Chord Symbols** and click **Import** to open the **Import Chord Library** dialog.

To import a Sibelius 6 chord symbol library, choose **Specify the location of a Sibelius 6 chord symbol library (.xml)** and click **Browse** to choose the file. Check the options in the **Sibelius 6 Chord Symbol Libraries** group on the right-hand side; they are reasonably self-explanatory, and allow you to choose whether to import various kinds of data contained in the library, and whether any existing conflicting data in your own library should take precedence over or be overwritten by the data in the imported library. Once you are happy with your choices, click **OK** to finish the import.

If you have an earlier version of Sibelius installed on your computer, Sibelius 6 will automatically locate any chord diagram libraries that you created in that version and add it to the list under **Choose a chord diagram library from a previous version**. If your library is not listed there, choose **Specify the location of a chord diagram library from a previous version (.scl)** and click **Browse** to choose the file. In the **Sibelius 3, 4 and 5 Chord Diagram Libraries** group on the right-hand side, you are recommended to choose **Identify chords by name or pitches** to ensure that the chord diagrams are imported as accurately as possible. Click **OK** to finish the import.

8.14 Edit Instruments

📖 **2.18 Instruments**, **2.29 Staves**, **3.8 Instrument names**.

Even though Sibelius has an exhaustive list of more than 600 built-in instruments, you may sometimes need to edit an instrument type that is used in your score (for example, if you need a particular combination of percussion instruments on a single staff not accommodated by Sibelius's built-in instruments), or, more rarely, create an instrument type that isn't listed in **Create ▶ Instruments** at all.

Sibelius makes this easy, using **House Style ▶ Edit Instruments**. Any changes to the existing instruments or new instruments you create are then saved in the score you are working on, and can be used in other scores by exporting a house style or saving them in a manuscript paper.

Edit Instruments dialog

House Style ▶ Edit Instruments allows you to create, edit and delete instrument types, and organize them into *ensembles*, which is just a fancy word for the groups of instruments that appear in the **Choose from** list in **Create ▶ Instruments**. Each ensemble contains one or more *families* (which are normally arranged according to instrument families, such as **Brass**, **Woodwind**, **Strings**, etc.) and each family then contains one or more instruments.

With a score open, choose **House Style ▶ Edit Instruments**. A handy tip: if you select a bar in a staff before you choose **Edit Instruments**, Sibelius will automatically select the appropriate instrument type in the dialog:

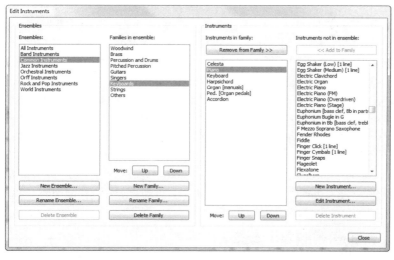

Read the dialog from left to right:

- The **Ensembles** list at the left-hand side of the dialog lists all the ensembles available in the current score; the **Families in ensemble** list to the right lists the families in the selected ensemble;
- **Instruments in family** lists the available instruments in the selected family;
- Finally, **Instruments not in ensemble** lists all the instruments that are defined in the score but are not currently in any of the families in the selected ensemble. This is useful, as it means you

Layout

can set up your own ensembles containing just the instruments you use. (Note that the **All instruments** ensemble must always contain all the instruments defined in the score.)

All Sibelius scores contain several pre-defined ensembles (see **Creating instruments** on page 133 for a list), and you cannot rename or delete these; however, you can change the families and instruments contained within them.

Creating and deleting an ensemble

You don't need to create an ensemble in order to create a new instrument or edit an existing one, but if there is a particular set of instruments you use often, or you have strong feelings about the order in which instruments should appear vertically in the score, it can be convenient to create your own ensemble containing any number of instruments, in an order of your choosing.

To create a new ensemble:

*   Select an existing ensemble in the **Ensembles** list to base your new ensemble upon
*   Click **New Ensemble**; Sibelius will ask you if you want to create a new ensemble based upon this one; click **Yes**
*   A simple dialog will appear in which you can give your ensemble a name; type a name and click **OK**.

To delete an ensemble you created, simply select it in the **Ensembles** list and click **Delete Ensemble**; Sibelius will ask you if you're sure, and if you click **Yes**, the ensemble will be deleted.

Creating and deleting a family

To create a new family in an ensemble:

*   Choose the ensemble in the **Ensembles** list, then click **New Family**
*   A simple dialog will appear for you to type the name of your new family; do so and click **OK**
*   The new family will be empty by default
*   Move the family up and down in the list of existing families with the **Up** and **Down** buttons below the **Families in ensemble** list. The order of families is significant because it determines the default vertical order when instruments are created in the score; if the **Brass** family is above the **Strings** family, then any instrument added to the score from the **Brass** family will be positioned above any instrument added from the **Strings** family.

To rename a family, simply select it and click **Rename Family**, type the new name into the dialog that appears, and click **OK**. To delete a family, select it and click **Delete Family**; after a warning the family will be deleted.

Adding and removing existing instruments

To add instruments (that have already been defined) to a family:

*   Find the instrument or instruments you want to add in the **Instruments not in ensemble** list and select them. Note that you cannot add the same instrument to more than one family in the same ensemble, so if the instrument is already in another family, it won't appear in the **Instruments not in ensemble** list. (You can, however, create a new instrument based on an existing instrument if you want similar instruments to appear in different families.)

- Click **Add to Family** to move the selected instrument(s) from **Instruments not in ensemble** to the **Instruments in family** list.
- Move the instrument(s) up and down in the list with the **Up** and **Down** buttons below the **Instruments in family** list. Just as with the order of families, the order of instruments here determines the vertical order when instruments are created in the score.

To remove instruments from a family, simply select the instruments in the **Instruments in family** list and click **Remove from Family** (or to remove all instruments from a family, you can simply delete the family itself).

Creating, editing and deleting instruments

You can only delete an instrument altogether if it is not used in the score and if it is not one of the predefined instrument types included in all scores – Sibelius will only enable the **Delete Instrument** button if the selected instruments can be deleted.

You can edit an existing instrument by selecting it in either the **Instruments in family** or **Instruments not in ensemble** list, then clicking **Edit Instrument**. If the instrument is used in your score, you will be warned that editing the instrument may change the appearance of your score; click **Yes** to proceed.

To create an entirely new instrument type, select the instrument your new instrument most closely resembles, then click **New Instrument**. You're asked if you want to continue; click **Yes** to proceed.

Whether you are editing an existing instrument or creating a new one, you see the same dialog:

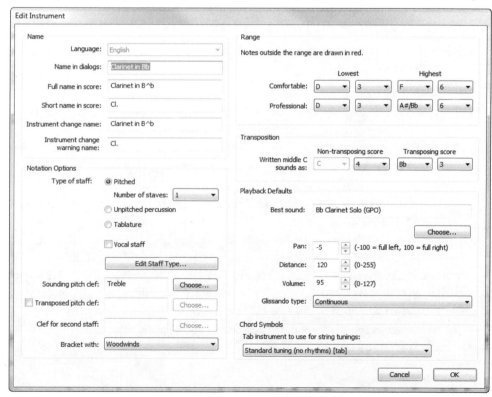

Layout

The **Name** options allow you to set up the three forms of instrument name used in Sibelius:

* **Language** cannot be changed unless you are using a localized (non-English-language) version of Sibelius. In localized versions, you can choose between displaying instrument names in your score in English or in the language of your copy of Sibelius, but in English versions, **Language** is always set to **English**.

* **Name in dialogs** is the name that appears in House Style ▸ Edit Instruments and Create ▸ Instruments. These names can be more descriptive than the ones that appear in the score itself, perhaps describing an unusual transposition or the fact that this instrument doesn't display a key signature.

* **Full name in score** is the default name that appears to the left of the staff, normally on the first system and then at the start of new sections – 📖 **3.8 Instrument names**

* **Short name in score** is the default name that typically appears to the left of the staff after the first system of the score.

* **Instrument change name** is the name that appears above the staff at the point you create an instrument change; by default, this is the same as the **Full name in score**.

* **Instrument change warning name** is the name that appears above the staff if you choose to create a warning before an instrument change; by default, this is the same as the **Short name in score**.

If you want to use music text font characters in the instrument names in your score, e.g. for the flat symbol in a name like "Clarinet in B♭", then type a caret (^) before the characters that correspond to flat (letter b) and sharp (hash symbol #) – indeed, you can use any of the formatting codes listed under **Adding formatting changes to Score Info** on page 255.

The options in the **Notation Options** group determine how the instrument's staff or staves will behave in the score:

* Choose the appropriate **Type of staff**:
    * **Pitched** instruments can have either one staff (e.g. flute, clarinet, violin) or two staves (e.g. piano, harp, celesta, marimba); set **Number of staves** appropriately
    * **Unpitched percussion** instruments (e.g. drum kit, woodblock) can only have one staff, and you can't set **Transposed pitch clef**, **Range** or **Transposition** options for them
    * **Tablature** instruments (e.g. guitar, lute, dulcimer) can only have one staff, and, like unpitched instruments, you can't set **Transposed pitch clef**, **Range** or **Transposition** options for them.

* Switch on **Vocal staff** if the instrument normally requires lyrics; this option determines several special behaviors, such as ensuring dynamics appear above the staff (as defined in House Style ▸ Default Positions – 📖 **8.12 Default Positions**), tuplets likewise (📖 **2.35 Triplets and other tuplets**), and allowing extra space between staves to make room for lyrics (📖 **8.10 Staff spacing**).

* To edit the detailed properties of the staff to be used by the instrument, click **Edit Staff Type** – see **Edit Staff Type** below

- **Sounding pitch clef** determines the normal clef to be used. For a two-staff pitched instrument such as piano, this is the clef used on the top staff. Click **Choose** to pick the clef – □ **2.11 Clefs** if you need help working out which is which.

- **Transposed pitch clef** determines the clef to be used by a single-staff pitched instrument, if it is a transposing instrument, and if it transposes by a sufficiently large interval that it is helpful to use a different clef in sounding pitch than at transposed pitch (e.g. for low brass and wind instruments). To use this option, switch on **Transposed pitch clef**, then click **Choose** to pick the clef; the clef you use here will be used when **Notes ▸ Transposing Score** is switched on. This option is not available for two-staff pitched instruments or for any unpitched or tablature instrument.

- **Clef for second staff** determines the clef to be used by the lower staff of a two-staff pitched instrument, e.g. bass clef for piano left hand. Click **Choose** to pick the clef.

- **Bracket with** determines how Sibelius should bracket the instrument when it is created in the score. Sibelius follows the usual conventions for how instruments should be bracketed together by instrument family. The list here doesn't reflect the families in a particular ensemble (because they can be different in every ensemble in your score) but rather it is a list of the standard instrumental families. So if you want, say, your instrument to be bracketed with other string instruments, choose **Strings**.

  Be aware, though, that the **Bracket with** option does not determine the order in which your instruments will be created in the score, which is instead determined by the order of the instruments within families and, in turn, families within the ensemble. All it does is tell Sibelius that when your instrument is created, if it's created next to another instrument with the same **Bracket with** setting, they should be bracketed together. One further little detail: two-staff pitched instruments (e.g. piano) are always given a brace and hence aren't bracketed with any other instruments.

The options under **Range** are used by Sibelius to show notes in red when **View ▸ Note Colors ▸ Notes Out of Range** is switched on (see **Note Colors** on page 462). You can only set the range for pitched instruments; for tablature instruments, the range is described by the pitches of the strings defined in the instrument's staff type.

The options under **Transposition** allow you to set how transposing instruments transpose:

- Instruments that are sometimes referred to as being in a particular key, e.g. Clarinet in A/B♭, or families of instruments that are identical other than in size and hence produce different pitches, e.g. Tenor/Alto Sax, or (if you live in the nineteenth century) Horn with crooks, transpose when **Notes ▸ Transposing Score** is switched on. For these kinds of instruments, set the **Transposing score** drop-downs appropriately; e.g. for a Clarinet in A, set this to **A** in octave **3**, because written middle C on Clarinet in A sounds as the A below middle C. Middle C = **C4**.

- The **Non-transposing score** option is required only for instruments such as piccolo, double bass and tenor voice, which are customarily notated an octave higher or lower than they sound, even in non-transposing scores. The option lets you specify which octave such an instrument sounds in. As all such instruments are pre-defined for you, you needn't use or even think about this option under any normal circumstances.

  However (takes big breath): if you do use this option, and if you want to give that instrument a clef with a little 8 or 15 on, bear in mind that Sibelius deliberately ignores the little 8 or 15 because it is *optional*, and instead takes its information about which octave the instrument plays in from this setting instead. This is because the octave transposition is a property of the instrument (e.g. the piccolo), not of the clef.

The options under **Playback Defaults** tell Sibelius how to play back music written for this instrument:

*   **Best sound** is the sound ID that describes, as specifically as possible, the sound that this instrument produces. Think of this in terms of the actual sound produced by the real instrument, rather than a specific sound on a playback device. For more information about sound IDs, 📖 **4.18 SoundWorld™**.

*   **Pan** is the default pan position of the instrument when you add it to your score; -100 is full left and 100 is full right

*   **Distance** is the distance of the instrument from the listener, and determines the relative amount of reverb the instrument should get by default

*   **Volume** specifies the default volume level for the instrument when you add it to your score

*   **Glissando type** determines whether the instrument should play glissandi using **Continuous** pitch bend, using discrete notes (**Black notes**, **White notes**, **Chromatic**), or not at all (**None**).

The single option in the **Chord Symbols** group, **Tab instrument to use for string tunings**, allows you to specify the closest tablature instrument to the instrument you're defining. This is used to determine the tuning for guitar chord diagrams as part of chord symbols (see **Choosing when chord diagrams should appear** on page 106) and how to display notes in the Fretboard window (📖 **1.8 Fretboard window**).

When you've finished, click **OK** to confirm your changes.

If you were creating a new instrument, it is automatically added to the **All instruments** ensemble, in the same family as the instrument upon which you based your new one.

Edit Staff Type

When you click **Edit Staff Type** in the **New/Edit Instrument** dialog, you will see a dialog with either two or three pages. The pages are:

*   **General** applies to all kinds of instruments; allows you to set up the number of staff lines, etc.

*   **Notes and Rests** also applies to all kinds of instruments; allows you to determine stem directions and stem lengths, etc.

*   **Percussion** is only available for unpitched instruments, and allows you to specify a mapping between noteheads on the staff and unpitched percussion sounds

*   **Tab** is only available for tablature instruments, and allows you to specify the pitch of each string, etc.

The options on each page are described below.

General page

- **Number of staff lines** allows you to choose any number of staff lines (or strings on a tab staff)

- **Gap between staff lines** allows you to change the distance between staff lines, and thus the height of the staff. Note, however, that changing this parameter *does not* make other objects larger or smaller to match the new staff height, so there's no reason to change this unless you're after a particularly strange effect. (For the proper ways to change a staff's size, ☐ **2.29 Staves**.)

- **Bracket** controls whether brackets and/or braces are drawn at the beginning of the staff

- **Initial clef** refers to the clef at the start of each system, not just the initial clef at the very start of the score. Lead sheets and marching brass band parts often omit clefs from most systems.

- **Key signatures/Tuning** determines whether key signatures and guitar string tunings are shown on the staff. Again, these are often omitted in lead sheets and marching brass band parts.

- **Extend above center of staff by** n **staff line gaps** determines how far above the center staff line of the staff the barline should extend. For a 5-line staff, you would set this to **2** to make the barline extend as far as the top staff line.

- **Extend below center of staff by** n **staff line gaps** determines how far below the center line of the staff the lower half of the barline should extend. You can use negative numbers here to shorten the lower half of the barline such that it does not reach the middle line of the staff.

- **Initial barline** determines whether the initial barline is drawn at the start of each system. (This option doesn't determine the presence of an initial barline on a system consisting of a single staff; you control this from the **Barlines** page of the **House Style ▸ Engraving Rules** dialog.)

- **Barlines** controls whether or not barlines are drawn on that staff.

Notes and Rests page

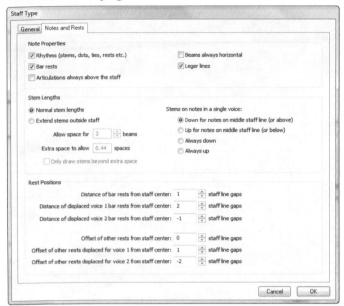

- **Rhythms (stems, beams, ties etc.)** controls stems, flags, and rhythm dots. It's generally only switched off for tab staff types where rhythms are not indicated (i.e. where there's usually an accompanying notation staff to show the rhythms).
- **Bar rests** can be switched off if you don't want bar rests to appear in a particular staff. This option should usually be switched off if **Rhythms** is also switched off.
- **Articulations always above the staff** is useful for vocal and single-line percussion staves; positioning articulations above the staff avoids collisions with e.g. lyrics
- **Beams always horizontal** forces all beams to be level. This is especially useful in percussion music, and is also often used in some styles of tab that show rhythms using stems and beams outside the staff.
- **Leger lines** determines whether leger lines will appear when notes go above or below the staff. This is usually switched off for percussion staves.
- The **Stem Lengths** options allow you to choose whether stems should have normal stem lengths (the default setting for most staff types), or whether they should extend outside the staff (which is useful for tab staff types where rhythms are shown).
- If **Extend stems outside staff** is switched on, you can choose whether stems should be drawn entirely outside the staff (i.e. not extending to the fret number/letter or notehead) by switching on **Only draw stems beyond extra space**; this look is commonly used in lute tablature and in some rhythmic guitar tab.
- **Allow space for** *n* **beams** determines how far outside the staff stems should be extended; by default, enough space is allowed for three beams, i.e. a 32nd note (or demisemiquaver). The **Extra space to allow** option is most useful for determining the distance between the outermost staff line and the innermost point of the stem above or below the staff if **Only draw stems beyond extra space** is switched on.

- The **Stems on notes in a single voice** options determine whether stems in a single voice should point down for notes on the mid-line (the conventional behavior for most staff types), point up for notes on the mid-line (conventional for single-line percussion staves), whether all stems in a single voice should point down (conventional for banjo tab), or up (conventional for most guitar and lute tab, and for bagpipe music). Where two or more voices are used, these settings are ignored and stems will point up or down according to the voice in the normal way.

- The options under **Rest Positions** allow you to determine how rests should be positioned on this staff.

  Normally, bar rests sit hang from the second staff line of a 5-line staff, though you can adjust this by setting **Distance of bar rests from staff center** *n* **staff line gaps** to something other than 1; values greater than 0 mean staff positions above the middle staff line, while negative values mean positions below the middle staff line.

  Other rests are (roughly speaking) centered on the middle staff line, though you can also adjust this, by setting **Offset of other rests from staff center** *n* **staff line gaps** to something other than 0.

  You can also adjust the positions of *displaced* rests, meaning rests that have been moved from their natural position by the presence of notes or rests in another voice. Sibelius will only automatically displace notes and rests in voices 1 and 2. Notice that, for example, displaced voice 1 bar rests normally hang from the top staff line, and displaced voice 2 bar rests normally hang from the fourth staff line.

Percussion page

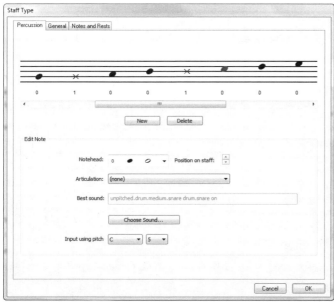

- The graphical representation of the staff shows the drum mapping (see **Unpitched percussion instruments** on page 160) – notice how you can set different noteheads, or even the same notehead with different articulations, to produce different sounds on the same line or space

- To remove an existing notehead, select it (by clicking it) and click **Delete**
- To change a notehead, select the notehead you want to change, then use the drop-down **Note-head** menu to choose the desired design
- To add an articulation to the selected notehead, use the drop-down **Articulation** menu
- The sound used by the selected notehead is displayed either as a sound ID (e.g. unpitched.wood.high.woodblock) or as a drum sound name from a specific device (e.g. **High Woodblock**), depending on whether you have the **Display** option on the **Playback** page of **File ▸ Preferences** (in the **Sibelius** menu on Mac) set to **Sound IDs** or **Program names** (see **Playback preferences** on page 333).

  To change the sound used by the selected notehead, click the **Choose Sound** button. If you are working with sound IDs, you will see a hierarchical menu of unpitched sound IDs, from which you should choose the sound ID that most closely matches the sound you want to hear. Thanks to Sibelius's SoundWorld system, Sibelius will choose the best available matching sound during playback (⊞ **4.18 SoundWorld™**).

  If, on the other hand, you are working with program names, you will see a hierarchical menu in which each of the sound sets in your active playback configuration are listed in the first level, then the drum programs from each sound set in the second level, and finally the names of the individual drum sounds in the third level. Note that you should not choose sounds from different programs within the same staff type, as Sibelius can only use a single drum program to play back all the sounds required by a given instrument.

- To add a new notehead, choose the notehead and sound you want from the **Notehead**, **Articulation** and **Sound** lists, then click **New**. The mouse pointer changes color; now click on the staff to place the new notehead.
- If you create drum set notation using step-time or Flexi-time input, you should check that the setting for each notehead in the **Input using pitch** menus corresponds with the key you press on your MIDI keyboard to produce the same sound (see **Note input for unpitched percussion** on page 161)
- When you add a new notehead to the drum map, the **Input using pitch** settings default to the pitch as if notated on a treble clef staff. If a notehead is already present on the line or space, Sibelius adds a sharp to the pitch.

Tab page

- To change the tuning of a string, click the string in the large window at the top of the dialog, then choose the new pitch from the drop-down **Pitch** menu underneath
- You can specify whether the note should be spelled as a sharp or a flat (occasionally required in unusual tunings) by selecting the appropriate radio button
- If you need to change the number of strings, click the **General** tab and change the number of strings, then switch back to the **Tab** page to adjust their tunings
- The **Tab Notes** options determine whether the tab staff should **Use numbers** (conventional for guitar tab) or **Use letters** (conventional for most lute tablature styles); **Draw notes between staff lines** or not (on the lines is conventional for guitar tab, between the lines is conventional for lute tablature); whether the numbers or letters should have a white background behind them (useful for tab staff types which depict rhythm); and whether stems should be drawn between notes in chords (by default, stems extend through all the notes of a chord, but in some rhythmic tab styles the stem is only drawn as far as the first note it reaches).

Layout

8.15 Edit Lines

📖 **2.21 Lines, 2.28 Slurs, 8.8 House Style™.**

For advanced users only

Sibelius lets you edit the design of lines and create your own new ones. If you edit an existing line, any change you make to the design of the line will affect all existing instances of that line in your score, and all instances you subsequently create.

Editing a line

To edit a line, choose **House Style ▸ Edit Lines**. Once you've selected a line from the list, you can **Edit** it, **Delete** it (if it's one you've defined yourself), or click **New** to create a new line based on it.

When creating a new line, base it on one with similar playback and positioning characteristics; for instance, to create a line that you want to play back like a trill, base it on a trill.

Clicking **Edit** brings up a dialog where you can change a line's characteristics.:

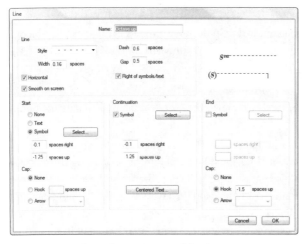

In all its generality, a line consists of five bits:

- An optional start – either a symbol (such as "Ped") or item of text (such as "1.2."), plus an optional arrowhead or a short line at right angles called a "hook," such as on a 1st ending (1st-time bar)
- The actual line itself – this can be continuous, dotted, dashed or wiggly, of various possible widths, and can be horizontal or diagonal
- Some optional text running along the line, e.g. *gliss.*
- An optional continuation symbol – this is what appears at the start of the system when a line continues on from an earlier system, such as (8) for an 8va line
- An optional end bit – like the start, this can be a symbol, a hook or an arrowhead.

It's reasonably self-explanatory how you modify these five bits from the dialog., but let's spell it out anyway:

- Line options control the appearance of the line itself:
  - ◦ **Style:** specifies whether the line is continuous, dotted, dashed or wiggly
  - ◦ **Dash:** the length of the dashes for dashed lines
  - ◦ **Gap:** the size of the gap between dashes/dots in dashed/dotted lines
  - ◦ **Horizontal:** forces the line to be horizontal (e.g. a trill)
  - ◦ **Smooth on screen:** anti-aliases (smoothes) the line as it appears on the screen (depending on your overall smoothing settings), but doesn't affect how it prints (Sibelius always prints smoothly!) – you should leave this option switched on
  - ◦ **Right of symbols/text:** puts the left-hand end of the line after the start bit.
- **Start** options define whether the line begins with a cap, symbol or text object:
  - ◦ **None/Text/Symbol:** it's obvious what these do. Clicking the **Text** radio button brings up a dialog from which you can choose the text that should appear, the text style to use, and the position of the text relative to the line.

    To position the text so the line appears mid-way up, change the **x spaces up** parameter; using the **Small text** style, a value of **0.5** spaces is ideal.
  - ◦ **spaces right/up:** used to adjust the position of the symbol, text or hook
  - ◦ **Cap** allows you to choose a hook (and define its offset from the line) or an arrowhead from a defined list.
- **Continuation** options determine what the line does if it continues over a system or page break:
  - ◦ **Symbol:** allows you to start the continuation with a symbol
  - ◦ **spaces right/up:** used to adjust the position of the optional symbol
  - ◦ The **Text** button sets any text running along the line
- **End** options are similar to the **Start** options, except that you can't end a line with text.

The preview shows the line as it would appear when split over two systems, so you can see the continuation bit as well as the start, middle and end.

As an example of using this dialog, to change the symbol at the beginning of a standard *8va* line (as in the picture above) to, say, just *8*, click **Select** in the **Start** section of the **Edit Line** dialog to choose a new symbol. You can change the **Continuation** symbol in the same way.

Layout

8.16 Edit Noteheads

📖 **2.25 Noteheads, 2.30 Stems and leger lines**.

For advanced users only

To modify a notehead design or define a new one:

- Choose **House Style ▸ Edit Noteheads**
- On the dialog that appears, click **New** to create a new type of notehead, or click one of the listed types and click **Edit** to change it. (You can also click and **Delete** notehead types you've defined.)

The **Notehead** dialog that then appears allows you to configure every aspect of the notehead:

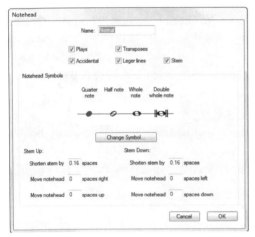

- **Name:** this is the name of the notehead type (although you don't really need to know what it's called)
- **Plays:** determines whether the notehead type plays back. Some noteheads (e.g. slashes) don't play back by default
- **Accidental:** switch this off if you want the notehead not to have accidentals (e.g. for slashes)
- **Transposes:** determines whether the notehead transposes (e.g. if you alter **Notes ▸ Transposing Score**, if you transpose your music, or in parts). Some noteheads (e.g. slashes) don't transpose by default.
- **Leger lines:** determines whether the notehead should ever appear with leger lines
- **Stem:** determines whether the notehead should appear on a stem
- To change the symbol used for the notehead, select one of the note values, click **Change Symbol** and select the symbol to use for it from the **Symbols** dialog that appears (📖 **2.31 Symbols**). The quarter note (crotchet) notehead is also used for eighths (quavers) and shorter note values.

Below the notehead symbols there are separate options for the positioning of stems and noteheads when stems are pointing up and down:

- **Shorten stem by**: lets you make a neater join between the stem and certain noteheads such as crosses (this option is only available if **Stem** is switched on above)
- **Move notehead** *x* **spaces right/left**: moves the notehead the specified number of spaces right or left from the stem, again to make a neater join
- **Move notehead** *x* **spaces up/down**: moves the notehead the specified number of spaces up or down from the stem.

When you're done, click **OK** followed by **OK** again to close the **Edit Noteheads** dialog.

One subtlety is that the **Leger lines** and **Stem** options take effect based on the notehead type of the *top* note of a chord; so if you have, say, a chord with two notes that would normally be written on leger lines, but you set the top notehead to use a notehead that doesn't use leger lines, neither note will have leger lines. Conversely, if, in the same situation, you set the lower of the two notes on leger lines to use a notehead that doesn't use leger lines, both notes *will* be printed with leger lines (because the notehead at the top of the chord *does* use leger lines).

If you created a new notehead type, it will appear at the bottom of the **House Style ▸ Edit Note-heads** dialog and the notehead list in the **Notes** panel of the Properties window, and can be typed as a numerical shortcut like other noteheads.

Layout

8.17 Edit Symbols

📖 **2.31 Symbols**, **8.11 Music fonts**.

For advanced users only

The symbols that Sibelius uses for standard objects such as noteheads, clefs and articulations can all be found in the Create ▸ Symbol dialog (shortcut Z), and you can edit them in the House Style ▸ Edit Symbols dialog.

Changing existing symbols

Not surprisingly, the symbols in the House Style ▸ Edit Symbols dialog for standard objects have particular meanings. If you change the sharp symbol to a dollar sign, Sibelius will still treat it as a sharp (e.g. when playing back or transposing).

It will even treat it as a sharp if you change the symbol design to look like a flat (because it interprets the symbols based on where they are in the grid, not what they look like). This causes Sibelius no conceptual difficulties, but it may cause you some, so to avoid confusion only change existing symbols to designs that look like they mean the same thing as the previous design.

One use for this might be to change the symbols used for microtonal accidentals. The first nine symbols on the Accidentals row of the Create ▸ Symbol dialog correspond to the symbols on the sixth Keypad layout (shortcut F12). See the table of notable symbols in the **2.31 Symbols** topic for a list of the various alternative symbols. If you change a symbol used on the Keypad in the House Style ▸ Edit Symbols dialog, the Keypad will still show the original symbol but will input your new one.

New symbols

If, however, you want a new symbol that isn't just a different design of an existing one, there are various convenient gaps in the House Style ▸ Edit Symbols table you can put the new symbol into. Use a gap in an appropriately-named row, or in the User-defined row at the bottom.

If you use up all the gaps in the User-defined row, click New on the House Style ▸ Edit Symbols dialog to create a new symbol on a new row.

Composite symbols

Some symbols include one or more other symbols. This has two benefits:

- It means you can create a new symbol even if it is not available in a music font, by piecing together other symbols. For instance, the symbol for a tenor voice clef (treble clef with an *8* below) is made up from a treble clef plus an *8*.

- It means that if you change the font, size or design of a symbol (such as a treble clef), then all symbols based on this will also change, to ensure a consistent appearance and to avoid your having to change lots of other symbols at the same time.

Editing and creating new symbols

- Choose House Style ▸ Edit Symbols
- Select a symbol to edit and click Edit; to create a new symbol, select an empty slot in the dialog and click Edit, or click New to create a new symbol in a new row

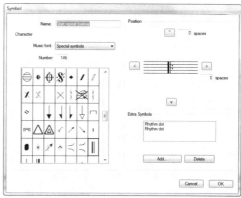

- To change the symbol to a different character, click on a new symbol in the table at the left of the dialog or type a character number into Number. (If you are using a mixture of music fonts you can also choose which font to use from the Music font list, explained below.)
- To make the symbol blank, or to make it just a composite of existing symbols (without also having a character chosen directly from a music font), set Number to 0
- You can also change the Name of the symbol; this name is useful for identification when including this symbol in a composite symbol
- To move the symbol with respect to its origin, click the arrow buttons to the right of the dialog
- To add another symbol to make a composite, click Add, then click another symbol and click Add Symbol. You can move these extra symbols independently using the arrow buttons.

Creating a new symbol text style

This important but rather abstract concept is best described by example. Let's suppose you want all of your clefs to use a special music font of their own that you've obtained from somewhere, called TrebleFont. (For more information on music fonts and how they relate to symbols, 📖 **8.11 Music fonts**.)

To make this happen, you can't just change the font of the Common symbols text style, as that would change notes, accidentals and so on, too. Instead, you should create a new text style called (say) Clefs, set this to TrebleFont, and set all clef symbols to use the Clefs text style so that they all use this font. To do this:

- In the House Style ▸ Edit Symbols dialog, click Music Fonts
- In the Music fonts dialog, select an existing text style (say, Common Symbols) to base your new one on, click New, then click Yes
- In the dialog that appears, type Clefs as the name for your new text style, and change the font to TrebleFont
- Click OK, then OK again to close the Music fonts dialog
- Then, for each clef in the House Style ▸ Edit Symbols dialog, select the clef, click Edit, change Music Font (meaning the text style that specifies the symbol's font and size) to Clefs, and click OK.

You should follow the same procedure even if you just want a single symbol in a special font or size.

Layout

8.18 Publishing

📖 **5.19 SibeliusMusic.com, 9.11 Exporting Scorch web pages**.

This tells you how to produce high-quality printed scores in small or large print runs, so that you can do your own music publishing from start to finish.

Being your own publisher

Most music is never published. Even well-known composers belonging to leading music publishers sometimes find that much of their music exists only in photocopies of their original manuscript, which only see the light of day if someone hires it out for a performance. Certainly a lot of the classical music of the last 50 years or so that gets published is done as a loss-making promotional exercise, in the hope that its presence on a bookshelf might bring it to the attention of potential performers. This is also sometimes true of more commercial scores such as musicals. So the situation for lesser-known composers and arrangers can be very frustrating.

Fortunately Sibelius changes all this. If you want to distribute your music quickly and easily, you can publish it via the Internet – 📖 **5.19 SibeliusMusic.com** for details. But Sibelius can also help you to bring a score right from its gestation in your head to a warehouse-full of scores and parts, printed and bound, as well as any publisher can do it. This is because even large publishers often have no more equipment than you do. What they do have is a famous name, a logo and the attendant mystique. All you need is a little know-how and a friendly local printer's.

Music engraving and house style

Good publishers all have high standards of music engraving. It takes time and experience to acquire the expertise to produce high-quality engraving; however, for a start, try reading 📖 **8.3 Music engraving** and **8.1 Layout and formatting**.

Additionally, publishers often establish their own house style. 📖 **8.8 House Style™** will give you some pointers on doing this. Simply choosing tasteful and distinctive text fonts will help considerably; 📖 **Tasteful fonts** on page 250.

Short print runs

If you only want to produce, say, 100 copies of a score it is probably uneconomic to have it printed on a press. You can either print out copies on your own printer, or produce a master copy and get it photocopied and bound.

Nowadays short print runs are normally done using digital printing techniques, not dissimilar from a laser printer you might use yourself at home, but typically of a higher quality. Unlike litho printing (see below), which requires a set of plates to be made before anything can be printed, digital printing uses your digital file (typically a PDF) directly, and it costs the same whether you are printing one copy or 100 copies.

Provided you have a good quality laser printer, you can achieve similar results at home, though you may find the "finishing" – normally folding and stapling or saddle-stitching – sufficiently laborious that it is worth asking a printing company to do this for you.

Longer print runs

To publish music in quantity (say hundreds of copies or more) it should be printed by a printing company using a digital printing process. This used to be done by giving them a high quality print-out that they would photograph; these days, the norm is to provide the artwork as a PDF file (□ **9.8 Exporting graphics**) on CD-R or sent via email.

Litho printing

For very large runs (say thousands of copies), the printing company may use an imagesetter (a special high-resolution printer – 2540 dpi or more) to output your music onto transparent film, which is then made into printing plates. But many companies can produce plates straight from your disk, without producing film first.

The plates then go into the printing press. Litho printing is done onto large sheets of paper that are then trimmed to size. Hence printing companies will much prefer your artwork to have 'crop marks', which are cross-hairs at the corners of the page showing where the paper should be cut. You can switch on crop marks when you save your score as EPS files or produce a PDF file.

The printing company should be able to print, collate and bind as many copies as you want. The cost per copy tends to drop rapidly as the number of copies increases, because there is quite a significant initial setting-up cost.

Factors affecting print quality

- *Resolution:* when you get above 600 dpi, the resolutions of printouts are hard to distinguish on large staff sizes, but with smaller staves the difference is perceptible. For instance, there is a just perceptible difference between 1200 dpi and 2540 dpi.
- *Paper:* most books and music are printed on "white bond"– plain white uncoated (non-glossy) paper. "lb/ream" (North America) and "g/m²" or "gsm" (Europe, meaning grams per square meter) indicate the weight and hence the thickness of the paper. About 21 lb/ream or 80 gsm is used for typing paper, photocopy paper and fairly thick books. Around 26 lb/ream or 100 gsm is preferable for music because it's less translucent and single sheets are less likely to flop over on music stands.
- *Plates:* litho printing plates are made out of various materials. Generally your printer will decide which is best. Metal plates produce the highest quality, polyester plates are cheaper but nearly as good, and paper plates are of lesser quality and only suitable for posters and other undetailed documents.

Summary

To recap, if you want publication-quality artwork suitable for mass-printing you must either:

- Invest in a laser printer of 600 dpi or higher quality and print it yourself; or
- Create a PDF file of your music and give it to a printing company on CD-R (or send it via email) for them to print digitally or using litho printing. If possible, also give them a paper printout of the score as a proof. In general, litho printing is more expensive (except for large quantities) than digital printing, but will give very high quality results.

Layout

9. Files

9.1 Working with files

This topic explains saving scores in Sibelius format, and (for more advanced users) how to access files containing custom Sibelius settings (e.g. house styles). The other topics in this chapter will tell you how to share files with other people, whether or not they have Sibelius, and how to import and export files in various formats.

Creating a score

For details of how to start a new score in Sibelius, see the Handbook.

File size

Sibelius files typically occupy around 20K plus 1K per page (excluding any imported graphics), even for band or orchestral music. This means you can fit literally millions of pages on your hard disk, and even huge scores can easily be sent by email. So even if your name is J.S. Bach, disk space is unlikely ever to present a problem when using Sibelius.

Saving

Saving works just like in any other program, using **File ▸ Save As** (shortcut **Ctrl+Shift+S** *or* ⇧⌘S) and **File ▸ Save** (shortcut **Ctrl+S** *or* ⌘S). In addition to being able to save Sibelius scores, you can also export other formats, such as MIDI, audio, and graphics; for more details, see the relevant topics in this Reference. To save lyrics, see **Export Lyrics** on page 527.

A convenient place to save is the **Scores** folder that Sibelius has helpfully created for you. On Windows, the **Scores** folder is created inside your **My Documents** folder; on Mac, it is inside your user **Documents** folder.

You can change which folder is the default for saving scores on the **Files** page of **File ▸ Preferences** (in the **Sibelius** menu on Mac).

When you next open the score after saving, it will open at the point at which you were working on it when you saved, even at the same zoom factor. If you'd prefer Sibelius to open scores at a default zoom level rather than the last zoom level you were working at, switch on **Open at default zoom level** on the **Files** page of the **File ▸ Preferences** dialog (in the **Sibelius** menu on Mac).

Auto-save

Sibelius can automatically save your score at timed intervals so that, should your computer crash, the most work you can lose is a few minutes' worth. Rather than saving your actual file, Sibelius makes a copy of your score and saves it into a folder called **AutoSave** within the **Backup Scores** folder (see below).

If Sibelius doesn't shut down correctly (for example, if your computer crashes or there is an interruption in power), the next time you start the program, it checks the **AutoSave** folder, and if it finds any scores in that folder, you will be asked if you want to restore them.

When you close Sibelius normally, it deletes all the files in the **AutoSave** folder – so it's essential that you don't save any files in there yourself!

Files

Auto-save is switched on by default, but if for some reason you want to switch it off, do so from the Files page of the File ▸ Preferences dialog (in the Sibelius menu on Mac). You can also specify in this dialog how often Sibelius automatically saves your score; the default is 10 minutes.

Backups

Each time you save, the score (with a version number added to the name) is also saved in Backup Scores in your Scores folder. If you ever accidentally delete or mess up a score, look in this backup folder to get the latest version you saved, or earlier versions too. This folder stores the last 40 scores you saved; older copies are progressively deleted to stop your disk from filling up, so don't use this folder to store your own backups!

Backup scores are created when you save manually, not each time Sibelius auto-saves; but unlike auto-saved scores, backup scores are not deleted when you close Sibelius.

Score Info

The File ▸ Score Info dialog can be used to enter information about your score, such as its title, composer, arranger, copyright, and so on, which is automatically used when you publish your score on the Internet (📖 **9.11 Exporting Scorch web pages**). You can also enter this information on the final page of the File ▸ New dialog when creating a score. The File tab of File ▸ Score Info shows you useful details about your score, such as the date it was created, when it was last saved, how many pages, staves and bars it contains, and so on. This tab only appears after you have saved your score at least once.

The values you enter into the fields on the Score Info dialog can also be used as *wildcards* in text objects throughout your score. For details on wildcards and how to use them in Sibelius, 📖 **3.10 Wildcards**.

User-editable files

Sibelius allows you to create your own:

- Ideas (📖 **5.11 Ideas**)
- House styles (📖 **8.8 House Style™**)
- Plug-ins (📖 **6.1 Working with plug-ins**)
- Worksheets (📖 **5.25 Worksheet Creator**)
- Arrange styles (📖 **5.2 Edit Arrange Styles**)
- Chord symbol libraries (📖 **2.10 Chord symbols**)
- Guitar scale diagram libraries (📖 **2.16 Guitar scale diagrams**)
- Text and music font equivalents (📖 **3.1 Working with text**, **8.11 Music fonts**)
- Manuscript papers (📖 **2.23 Manuscript paper**)
- Feature sets (📖 **5.12 Menus and shortcuts**)
- Word menus (📖 **3.1 Working with text**)

As Sibelius comes with its own sets of each of these kinds of files, any additional ones you create are saved in a location separately from those supplied with the program. The standard files included with Sibelius are non-deletable; you should *not* change anything inside the application folder itself (or the application package – sometimes known as a "bundle" – on Mac), which is where they are stored.

Your own (user-editable) files are stored in specific folders inside your user account's application data folder of your computer, the location of which will differ depending on the operating system you are using:

- *Windows Vista:* C:\Users*username*\Application Data\Sibelius Software\Sibelius 6\
- *Windows XP*: C:\Documents and Settings*username*\Application Data\ Sibelius Software\Sibelius 6
- *Mac*: /Users/*username*/Library/Application Support/Sibelius Software/Sibelius 6

Note that on Windows, the application data folder is hidden by default and will not be visible in Windows Explorer. If you wish to access this folder, choose Tools ▸ Folder Options from any open Explorer window. Click the View tab and from the Files and Folders list choose Show hidden files and folders.

Inside the Sibelius application data folder you will find various folders whose names indicate the content they contain. (It is possible for there to be no folders at all, as they are only created when you create or edit a file that is saved in that location.)

You can copy any appropriate file to the user area directories and Sibelius will use it when you next start the program. Files you have added or created can also be deleted with no ill side-effects.

Scorch templates and textures

You can create your own Scorch templates and paper/desk textures. Place them inside the relevant folder in the application data folder, and Sibelius will detect them. Scorch templates go in the folder called Scorch templates, and textures in the folder called Textures.

Files

9.2 Sharing files

It's easy to share music you have written in Sibelius with other people.

Sharing files with other users of Sibelius

If the person you are working with also has Sibelius, then simply send the file by email (see below), or on removable media such as a CD-R.

Find out what version of Sibelius the person you're sending files to is using. If they have the same or a later version of Sibelius as you, you can simply save your file as normal and send it to them. If, however, they have an earlier version of Sibelius, or are using Sibelius Student or G7, you will need to export your score in an earlier file format – 📖 **9.12 Exporting to previous versions**.

Sharing files with people who don't use Sibelius

If the recipient doesn't have Sibelius, there are a number of other means of sharing files with them:

- Ask them to download and install the free Sibelius demo from **www.sibelius.com**, then send the file to them. Beware that the demo version can only print a single, watermarked page, so if you want them to be able to print your score, this isn't the best way.
- Publish the music on SibeliusMusic.com, SibeliusEducation.com or on your own web site – 📖 **5.19 SibeliusMusic.com**, **5.18 SibeliusEducation.com** and **9.11 Exporting Scorch web pages**.
- Create a PDF of your score and send it to them – see **Creating PDF files** on page 667
- Export the music as a graphics file from Sibelius and send it to them – 📖 **9.8 Exporting graphics**
- Save the music as a Scorch web page and attach both files to an email (see below)
- If the recipient has another music program and wants to listen to and perhaps edit your music, send them a MIDI file – 📖 **9.9 Exporting MIDI files**
- If you want to send your music to somebody else so they can hear it, but you don't need them to see the score, you could also export an audio file from Sibelius and then either burn it to an audio CD or compress it into an MP3 file and send it via email – 📖 **9.10 Exporting audio files**.

Sending files via email

Sending files by email is very simple, but the exact procedure differs according to the email program you use:

- *Windows Mail, Outlook Express or Mozilla Thunderbird*: start a new message, then click the **Attach** button (with a paperclip icon), find the file and click **Attach** to attach it to the message. Then send it as normal.
- *Apple Mail*: start a new message, then simply drag and drop the file you want to attach to the message into the message window, and send it as normal.
- *Netscape Messenger*: start a new message, then click the **Attach** button and choose **File** from the drop down list. Find the file you want to attach, and double-click its name to attach it to the message, which you can then send as normal.

- *Eudora*: start a new message, right-click (Windows) *or* **Control**-click (Mac) on the message body, and choose **Attach file**. Find the file you want to attach, and double-click its name to attach it to the message, which you can then send as normal.

If you don't use any of the above programs, consult the documentation for your particular email client for details on sending file attachments.

If you want to send a Sibelius file as a Scorch web page to somebody via email:

- First, export it (📖 **9.11 Exporting Scorch web pages**)
- Remember to attach both the .sib and .htm files to your email message
- Tell the recipient that they will need to have Scorch installed on their computer; tell them to save *both* files to a folder on their computer (e.g. the Desktop), and then to double-click the saved .htm file to view the score in their web browser.

Files on Windows or Mac

Sibelius for Windows and Sibelius for Mac use exactly the same file format. You can move a Sibelius score between Mac and Windows without any conversion at all – see below.

Both file formats use Unicode, a standard international character set, which means that special characters (like accented letters) are automatically translated between Mac and Windows. Music and text fonts are also substituted intelligently – 📖 **3.11 Font equivalents**.

Sibelius files have a .sib extension. On Mac, Sibelius files are also of kind "Sibelius document" (internally the Creator is "SIBE" and the Type is "SIBL").

Opening Mac scores on Windows

If you are trying to open a score created on the Mac given to you on a CD-R or another disk, make sure the disk is formatted for Windows – although the Mac can read Windows disks, Windows cannot read Mac disks.

To open the file in Sibelius for Windows, you may have to add the file extension **.sib**. Although Sibelius adds this file extension by default on both Windows and Mac, some Mac users prefer not to use file extensions; this causes a problem on Windows, because the file extension tells Windows this is a Sibelius file.

You can add the file extension in Windows by right-clicking on the file icon (in My Computer or Windows Explorer) and selecting **Rename**. Change the extension, and then hit **Return** (on the main keyboard). You may be prompted that changing file types can render them unusable, because Windows assumes that you don't know what you're doing. If asked whether you are sure you wish to proceed, click **Yes**.

Once you have renamed the file, you can open it in the usual way by double-clicking.

Opening Windows scores on Mac

To open a file created using Sibelius for Windows, simply choose **File ▸ Open** and double-click the name of the file in the dialog.

9.3 Splitting and joining scores

You can write several movements, songs or pieces inside the same score file, or write them in separate scores and combine them later. You can also split a score containing several pieces into individual scores.

Several movements, songs or pieces

It's preferable to put several sections (e.g. movements, songs or pieces of music) into one score instead of having a separate score for each. Moreover, if you want any new sections to be on the same page as each other, in the score *or* in parts, you *must* input them in the same file.

If you have different sections in two or more files that you want to join together, see **Append Score** below.

To write, say, a couple of two-system exercises on the same page:

- Input the first exercise as normal
- Select the barline at the end of the first exercise and hit **Return** (on the main keyboard) to create a system break
- If you also need full instrument names and an indented staff, select the bar at the end of the previous system, open the **Bars** panel of the Properties window, and switch on **Section end**
- Create a double or final barline at the end of the first exercise if desired (**Create ▸ Barline ▸ Final** or **Double**)
- If the key signature is different at the beginning of the second exercise, create a new one in the usual way, making sure to switch on **Hide** in the **Create ▸ Key Signature** dialog; this will hide the key change at the end of the previous system
- Similarly, if you require a different time signature in the next exercise, create it in the usual way, making sure to switch off **Allow cautionary** in the **Time Signature** dialog; this prevents a cautionary time signature from being drawn at the end of the previous system
- Reset the bar number at the beginning of the second exercise if desired (**Create ▸ Other ▸ Bar Number Change**).

Inputting a score in several files

If you want to input a single score in several separate files – perhaps if several people are copying or orchestrating it simultaneously – you will probably want to adjust the first bar number, first page number and first rehearsal mark of each file so that the bars, pages and rehearsal marks follow on from the previous one.

Beware that if you plan to use parts, each section into which the full score was divided will start on a new page in every part, which may produce inconvenient page-turns. So once the score is finished, it's best to join the files together using the **File ▸ Append Score** feature – see below.

Append Score

You may want to join two scores together if, for example, you are creating songbooks out of separate song files. Sibelius has a feature to append a score to the end of an existing score, automatically checking that the two scores have matching staves, and ensuring that the appended score starts on a new page.

To use this feature, open the first score and choose **File ▸ Append Score**. A dialog appears from which you can choose another score to append (the file you choose to append will not itself be changed).

If it doesn't have the same number of staves, Sibelius will tell you (it won't append a score unless the staves match exactly). If the number of staves is the same but some of the instrument names are different, Sibelius will warn you but let you continue if you like.

Text styles, symbols, noteheads etc. are merged between the two files; if two text styles have the same name but are set up differently, the one in the first score is used. Sibelius does several things to make sure the join between the scores is neat: changes of time signature, key signature, clef and instrument are created at the join if necessary. The final barline in the first score is set to be a page break and a "section end," so that the appended score starts on a new page with (typically) full instrument names. Thus the appended score's layout will normally be just the same as it was.

You may want to hide the cautionary clef and time signature changes, as well as key changes, where the two scores join, particularly if it's at a break between two movements or pieces – 📖 **5.9 Hiding objects**.

9.4 Importing graphics

This topic explains how you can add graphics to your scores by importing bitmap images in TIFF format into Sibelius.

If you want to turn a graphics file (e.g. a scanned image or PDF file) of printed music into a score, 📖 **1.5 Scanning**.

If you want to turn a score into a graphics file (e.g. an EPS file) for publishing or to add music extracts to a document, 📖 **9.8 Exporting graphics**.

File formats

Sibelius can import graphics files in TIFF format, at any color depth (in other words, it can be black and white, grayscale, or full color using any number of colors).

If your graphic is not in TIFF format, you can convert it into a TIFF file. There are many suitable graphics programs available for download free of charge from the Internet. On Windows, for example, try IrfanView (**www.irfanview.com**). On Mac, the built-in Preview application can convert most graphics to TIFF: simply open the graphic you want to convert, choose **File ▸ Save As**, and choose **TIFF** from the **Format** drop-down.

Importing a graphic

To import a TIFF file:

* Select a note, rest, bar or other object in your score where you want the graphic to appear
* Choose **Create ▸ Graphic**. A dialog appears prompting you to find the TIFF file you want to import. Once you've found the file, click **Open**.
* The graphic is created in the score and you can move it, copy it, and so on
* If you want to place the graphic with the mouse or put a graphic on a blank page (📖 **8.5 Breaks**) instead, ensure nothing is selected in your score before you choose **Create ▸ Graphic**; the mouse pointer will then change color to show that it is "loaded" with an object: click in the score to place the graphic.

Imported graphics often look best on the screen with the paper texture set to plain white, so that the white background around non-rectangular shapes blends in (📖 **5.6 Display settings**). However, graphics will print fine whatever the screen texture is.

Copying, editing and deleting graphics

Once the graphic appears in your score, you can manipulate it in much the same way as any other object:

* copy it with **Alt**+click *or* ⌥-click
* move it by clicking on the graphic so that it is shaded blue, then drag it with the mouse or use the arrow keys (with **Ctrl** *or* ⌘ for larger steps)
* scale it, while keeping its proportions, by clicking on the small handle at the bottom right-hand corner, so that it is surrounded by a light blue box, then drag the mouse or use ↑/↓ (with **Ctrl** *or* ⌘ for larger steps)

- scale it, while altering its proportions, by holding **Ctrl** *or* ⌘ before clicking on the bottom right-hand corner of the graphic (where the handle appears); release **Ctrl** *or* ⌘, then drag the mouse or use ↑/↓ (with **Ctrl** *or* ⌘ for larger steps)

- delete it with **Delete**.

To reset a graphic after manipulating it, choose **Layout ▸ Reset Design** (shortcut **Ctrl+Shift+D** *or* ⇧⌘D), which puts the graphic back to its original size and proportions.

Changing the draw order of imported graphics

By default, imported graphics draw behind all other objects. You can change this if you like, using the controls in the **Edit ▸ Order** submenu – 📖 **5.14 Order**.

File size

Importing a graphic into your score will increase its file size considerably. To keep the file size as small as possible, Sibelius compresses the TIFF file when it imports it, and if you use the same graphic multiple times in your score, you can and should just copy it instead of importing it again.

Files

9.5 Opening MIDI files

If you don't know much about MIDI, 📖 **4.13 MIDI for beginners**, which explains what MIDI files are. If you're wondering where you can get MIDI files from, see **Downloading MIDI files** below.

Importing a MIDI file

Open a MIDI file just like a normal Sibelius file: simply choose **File ▸ Open** (shortcut **Ctrl+O** *or* ⌘O), locate the file (on Windows, MIDI files usually have the file extension .mid), and click **Open**.

A dialog appears with importing options you can set (detailed below). Normally, you should just click **OK**, and then wait a few seconds for the MIDI file to open.

Some MIDI files contain no program changes (even though they contain instrument names), which means that the instruments have to be guessed. If so, Sibelius warns you that the instrument names, sounds, clefs, and other details may be wrong. You should either adjust the instrument's clef etc. by hand, or (preferably) make or obtain a copy of the MIDI file that does contain the necessary program change information, and import that MIDI file instead.

If you find that the imported MIDI file doesn't look as good as you had hoped, try changing some of the import settings – see **Import options** below.

Once the MIDI file is imported you can play back, edit, save, print and create parts from it just as if you'd inputted the music yourself. Imported MIDI files play back with every nuance of the original sequence – the exact velocity and timing of each note – thanks to Sibelius's Live Playback feature (📖 **4.8 Live Playback**).

Import options

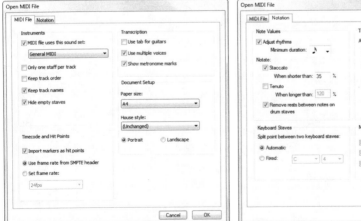 

The options on the **MIDI File** tab of the **Open MIDI File** dialog are as follows:

- **MIDI file uses this sound set** allows you to specify whether the program and bank numbers use General MIDI or another sound set. This helps Sibelius guess what the instruments are.

Normally you can leave this option at General MIDI, or switch it off altogether if you simply want to import the MIDI file "as is."

- **Only one staff per track** is useful if you open a MIDI file which notates a piano (say) as two separate piano tracks, one for the left hand and another for the right hand. Switch on this option and each hand will be written as one staff, not two; you can then clean it up by creating a new piano and copying the two hands into it. Finally, delete the original two pianos.

- **Keep track order** is switched off by default; this makes Sibelius choose the order of the instruments. Switch it on to keep the instruments in the same order as the tracks in the MIDI file.

- **Keep track names** makes Sibelius use the name of each track as the instrument name; switch it off to use the default instrument names for the instruments Sibelius guesses

- **Hide empty staves** is switched on by default; this makes Sibelius hide empty staves throughout the resulting score, which is often useful because many MIDI files have tracks that are empty except for short passages; as a result, hiding empty staves can make the score easier to read

- **Import markers as hit points** makes Sibelius convert all markers in the MIDI file into hit points in the score it creates. When switched off, Sibelius will import the markers as standard text objects.

- **Use frame rate from SMPTE header** tells Sibelius to set the frame rate settings in **Play ▸ Video** and **Time ▸ Timecode and Duration** according to the settings in the MIDI file – see **SMPTE offset** below.

- **Use tab for guitars** specifies whether Sibelius should import any guitar tracks in the MIDI file onto tab staves; if the option is switched off, guitars will be imported onto notation staves

- **Use multiple voices** determines whether Sibelius should use two voices where appropriate to produce cleaner notation; normally this option should be switched on

- **Show metronome marks** makes all metronome marks visible. If there are lots of changes of tempo (e.g. *rits.* and *accels.*) then you may want to switch this option off, which will hide the metronome marks in the score, making it look cleaner but still playing back the same.

- The **Document Setup** options allow you to choose the **Page size**, **House style** and orientation (**Portrait** or **Landscape**) of the resulting score.

For details of the options on the **Notation** tab, see **Flexi-time options** on page 23.

Recommended import options

The precise combination of options you should choose in the **Open MIDI file** dialog will depend on a number of different factors, for example:

- If you are importing a MIDI file to create clean notation, you should switch off the **Notation** tab options to notate staccatos and tenutos, and try a number of different **Minimum note value** settings until you get the cleanest result

- If you are importing a MIDI file for playback only, it doesn't matter which options you choose, as Sibelius will always play back the MIDI file exactly as it sounds, using Live Playback

- If you are importing a file created by someone else, probably on a different device (e.g. a MIDI file you have downloaded from the Internet), you should set **MIDI file uses this sound set** to the device it was created for

Files

- If you are importing a file that you know uses the General MIDI sound set, make sure you have chosen **General MIDI** under **MIDI file uses this sound set**.

The default **Notation** tab settings work well in most cases, as follows: **Adjust rhythms** on, **Minimum note value** sixteenth note (semiquaver), **Staccato** and **Tenuto** on. If you are reading a MIDI file in which the rhythms are completely exact (if it's already quantized, say), switch **Adjust rhythms** off.

If you set **Minimum note value** unrealistically long – e.g. if it's set to eighth notes (quavers) when the MIDI file contains long runs of sixteenth notes (semiquavers) – Sibelius obviously can't render the runs properly using eighth notes and may be forced to produce junk. (Sibelius will have to approximate the runs of sixteenth notes using tuplets of eighth notes or by joining some pairs of sixteenth notes together to form eighth note chords.)

The tuplet options are up to you:

- **Simple** means tuplets are notated only if they contain equal note values
- **Moderate** and **Complex** for more irregular rhythms.

Remember that if a particular tuplet (say a triplet) is used in a MIDI file, you must set this option to at least **Simple**, or it won't be read correctly! Beware however that if, say, you set all the tuplets to **Complex**, Sibelius may discover elaborate tuplet rhythms where you weren't expecting them, so be cautious.

Batch conversion

Sibelius includes a plug-in to convert a complete folder full of MIDI files at once. To use it, choose **Plug-ins ▸ Batch Processing ▸ Convert Folder of MIDI Files**. You are asked to find the folder to convert; find it and click **OK**. All MIDI files in the folder will be converted to Sibelius files.

Cleaning up MIDI files

Because MIDI files don't contain any notation data, they can end up looking a little messy after opening them in Sibelius. Here are some hints for getting better results, both before and after conversion:

- If the MIDI file uses non-standard program numbers (e.g. if it is set up to play on an unusual MIDI device), Sibelius will not be able to identify the instruments correctly and they may appear with unexpected characteristics, such as with the wrong clefs or in the wrong order. Similarly, if the MIDI file uses channel 10 for pitched instruments, these may be imported by Sibelius as percussion instruments. This depends on whether or not you selected an appropriate MIDI device when opening the MIDI file.
- If this happens, try importing the file again, changing the **MIDI file uses this sound set** setting
- If the MIDI file is not fully or properly quantized, you may find that the rhythms are not notated as cleanly as you might expect. If you have access to a sequencer, you could try re-quantizing the file and opening it in Sibelius again. Alternatively, try using **Plug-ins ▸ Simplify Notation ▸ Renotate Performance**, which can both revoice and requantize the music intelligently (see **Renotate Performance** on page 521 for more details).

The kind of cleaning up that is most commonly required after opening a MIDI file is making unpitched percussion staves more legible – 📖 **2.26 Percussion** for more details.

When Sibelius imports unpitched percussion in a MIDI file, each drum sound is converted to the notehead and staff position (i.e. line or space) defined in the **5 lines (drum set)** instrument. If a drum sound is used where the notation isn't defined in this instrument type, Sibelius makes up a notation using normal, cross and diamond noteheads in empty positions on the staff.

Sometimes you may find that you end up with unwanted rests between notes, or with unwanted unisons (two noteheads sharing the same pitch). Use the **Plug-ins ▸ Simplify Notation ▸ Remove Rests** and **Plug-ins ▸ Simplify Notation ▸ Remove Unison Notes** plug-ins to correct this – 📖 **6.1 Working with plug-ins**.

SMPTE offset

The MIDI SMPTE offset event is imported (if present) and sets **Start Time** in the **Play ▸ Video and Time ▸ Timecode and Duration** dialog. It can also be used to set the frame rate to be used for timecode in the score; however, because the MIDI SMPTE offset event doesn't describe all of the frame rate formats used by all sequencer programs, if you know the frame rate you actually want to use, choose **Set frame rate** on the **MIDI File** page of the **Open MIDI File** dialog, and select the desired frame rate from the menu instead. (If you have no idea what any of this means, don't worry – just leave these options as they are.)

Technical details

Sibelius imports MIDI files of types 0 and 1. When importing, Sibelius intelligently works out which instruments to use (using track names if they are present, otherwise using the sounds), and is able to distinguish between, say, Violin and Viola, Clarinet and Bass Clarinet, or Soprano and Alto by the range of the music in each track. Sibelius cleans up the rhythm using the Flexi-time algorithm, and retains as much or as little MIDI message data as you specify (e.g. metronome marks, program changes and so on). Sibelius also automatically reduces the staff size if there are too many instruments for the page size.

Downloading MIDI files

There are many online resources for MIDI files. If you are looking for a particular piece, you can try a search using www.google.com, e.g. typing the name of the piece followed by the words "MIDI file." Or you could try visiting one of the following sites:

• www.prs.net: more than 16,000 or so classical music files, all public domain

• www.musicrobot.com: a search engine for locating pop music MIDI files on the web

• www.cpdl.org: an excellent choral music public domain site with thousands of files

• www.cyberhymnal.org: every major hymn tune, with downloadable lyrics too.

Not all the files on these sites are in MIDI format – some may be in Finale, PDF or another format. Some may even be in an audio format, like MP3, which cannot be opened by Sibelius. So look carefully to see what the actual format of the file is, before you try and download it. (Sibelius can, however, open files in various formats – check the other topics in this chapter for details.)

Files

Once you've found the MIDI file you're looking for in your web browser, identify the link to download it; links are normally underlined. Do *not* click on the link directly, as that will simply make the MIDI file play inside your web browser: we want to download it, not play it. Instead:

* Right-click (Windows) *or* **Control**-click (Mac) the link, and a menu will appear.
* Choose **Save Link As, Save Target As** or **Download Link** (the exact wording depends on which web browser you are using)
* Depending on your web browser, you may be prompted to choose where to save the file, in which case choose somewhere easy to remember, like your Desktop
* Now the file will be downloaded. MIDI files are normally very small, so this will probably take only a second or two.

Congratulations! You've now downloaded a MIDI file – and in fact the above steps can be used to download any type of file from the web.

Make sure you know what the MIDI file is called and where you saved it (normally to your Desktop), then open Sibelius, and follow the steps in **Importing a MIDI file** at the start of this topic.

You should be aware that if you download or publish MIDI files of someone else's music without permission you are likely to infringe copyright. Copyright infringement is illegal, and in any case is forbidden by the Sibelius license agreement.

Most music states if it is copyright and who the copyright owner is. If you have are unsure of the copyright status of a MIDI file you have downloaded, please contact the music's publisher, composer or arranger.

9.6 Opening MusicXML files

Sibelius's built-in MusicXML 2.0 file convertor allows you to open MusicXML files created in a number of music applications, including Finale version 2003 and later and SharpEye.

The purpose of the file convertor is to save you time, not to convert every score so that it is identical to the original.

What is MusicXML?

MusicXML is an interchange file format for music notation applications. It provides a better way to transfer notation between different programs than other formats such as MIDI files.

Creating MusicXML files in Finale

How you create MusicXML files in Finale depends on the version of Finale you are using:

* *Finale 2006 or later:* choose **File ▸ MusicXML ▸ Export**
* *Finale 2003, 2004 or 2005 (Windows only):* choose **Plug-ins ▸ MusicXML Export**

If you are using Finale 2004 or Finale 2005 on Mac OS X, or are using a version earlier than Finale 2003 on Windows, you will require the Dolet plug-in to export MusicXML files. If you are using Dolet, you can export a MusicXML file by choosing **Plug-ins ▸ MusicXML ▸ Export MusicXML**.

The full Dolet plug-in also allows you to benefit from additional Finale file format support, greater accuracy in translations from MusicXML files saved using Dolet for Sibelius, and support for exporting percussion notation, tablature, staff styles, custom lines and brackets. For more details, see **www.recordare.com**.

Opening a MusicXML file

MusicXML files typically have one of two file extensions: uncompressed MusicXML files have the extension **.xml**, and compressed MusicXML 2.0 or later files have the extension **.mxl**. Sibelius can open MusicXML files with either extension.

Open a MusicXML file just like a normal Sibelius file: simply choose **File ▸ Open** (shortcut **Ctrl+O** *or* **⌘O**), locate the file, and click **Open**. Sibelius will show a dialog, shown on the right, with the following options:

* **Use page and staff size from MusicXML file** is switched on by default if the MusicXML file you are opening is version 1.1 or later; this tells Sibelius to try and preserve the page and staff size of the MusicXML file. If you switch this off, you can set the paper size and orientation for the imported MusicXML file, and Sibelius will use the default staff size as determined by the house style chosen below in the dialog.
* **Use layout and formatting from MusicXML file** is also switched on by default if the MusicXML file is version 1.1 or later; when switched on, Sibelius will try to preserve the layout and formatting (e.g. distances between staves, system and page breaks, etc.) of the original

Files

MusicXML file. If you switch this off, Sibelius will effectively unlock the format of the resulting score, using its default layout and formatting.

* **House style** allows you to import a specific house style into the resulting score; if you leave this set to **Unchanged**, Sibelius will use its default house style. If you choose another house style, note that the page size and staff size specified in the house style will not be used in the resulting score unless you switch off **Use page and staff size from MusicXML file.**

* **Let Sibelius choose instruments** tells Sibelius to attempt to automatically identify the instruments in the MusicXML file. If you find that Sibelius creates the wrong instruments, import the file again, and switch this option off, which will prompt Sibelius to show you the following dialog after you click **OK**:

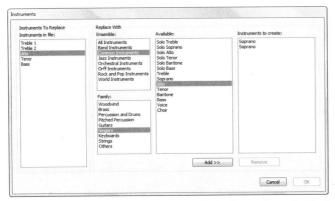

  ○ **Instruments in file** at the left-hand side shows the individual parts in the MusicXML file

  ○ In the order that the staves are displayed in the **Instruments in file** list, use the **Ensemble**, **Family** and **Available** lists to choose the Sibelius instruments you want to use for each part (rather like in the **Instruments** dialog); either double-click the instrument or click **Add** to add it to the **Instruments to create** list at the right-hand side of the dialog.

  ○ When all of the parts have been mapped onto Sibelius instruments, the **OK** button becomes enabled; click this to finish opening the file.

* **Use instrument names from MusicXML file** tells Sibelius to set the instrument names at the start of systems to the names specified in the MusicXML file. If you want Sibelius to use its own default instrument names instead, switch this option off.

When you have set the options as you wish, click **OK**, and the MusicXML file will be imported. You can then check and edit the file as necessary.

Warning messages

Some MusicXML files may contain errors, which will be displayed in a dialog listing each error and the location at which it occurred in the file you are opening. Each error may be one of three kinds:

* *Fatal errors*: if the file is not valid XML, this is a fatal error, and it cannot be opened at all

* *Validation errors*: if the file is valid XML, but the specific syntax of the MusicXML elements contains errors or inconsistencies, then Sibelius will attempt to open the file, but the resulting score may have unexpected problems in it, and you should proceed with caution

• *Warnings*: the XML validator sometimes reports warnings about the XML files when they are opened. These should not normally prevent the file from opening correctly.

Importing MusicXML files saved in a sequencer

Sibelius's MusicXML importer is optimized to give the best results when opening MusicXML files saved directly from Finale or using Finale's Dolet plug-in. In extreme circumstances, some MusicXML files, especially those created in sequencers with no notation capabilities, may fail to produce any legible notation at all.

Supported versions

Sibelius's MusicXML converter is based around MusicXML 2.0. Files created in earlier MusicXML formats open correctly, provided they are valid. Files created with future versions of MusicXML should also open, though the majority of the new features will not be imported.

Sibelius can only open MusicXML files that use the **partwise.dtd** top-level DTD (Document Type Definition). If your file uses the **timewise.dtd** DTD, you will need to use XSLT to convert your timewise MusicXML file into a partwise MusicXML file. One such convertor is available online at: www2.freeweb.hu/mozartmusic/pttp/converter.html.

Batch conversion

Sibelius includes a plug-in to convert a complete folder full of MusicXML files at once. To use it, choose **Plug-ins ▶ Batch Processing ▶ Convert Folder of MusicXML Files** – see **Convert Folder of MusicXML Files** on page 487.

Limitations

The limitations of Sibelius's MusicXML import feature are summarized below:

Feature	Limitation
Articulations	Breath-marks, caesuras, scoops, plops, doits and falloffs are not imported. Some articulations may be positioned on the wrong side of a note or chord. The **technical** and **ornaments** elements are not imported.
Barlines	If different staves have different barline types simultaneously, Sibelius will use the barline type of the uppermost part. Heavy, **heavy-light** and **heavy-heavy** barlines are not imported.
Beams	Sub-beams do not import. The repeater attribute is not imported (for tremolos).
Chord symbols	The Dolet plug-in for Finale only exports chord symbols when chord playback is correctly defined. Some chord symbols may not be imported (when they are using a **function** element). MusicXML specifies that all chord symbols go above the top staff in a part only. The **kind** instances **Neapolitan, Italian, French, German, pedal (pedal-point bass)** and **Tristan** are all imported as major chords. If the **function** element is not present in the **harmony** element, the chord symbol is not imported. If a chord has its inversion specified, this will be ignored.
Clefs	Special percussion and tab clefs available in MusicXML will be replaced with the closest matching clef available in Sibelius. MusicXML is not capable of differentiating between clefs at the start or end of a bar.
Color	The **color** attribute is not imported, so colored objects are imported as black.
Cross-stave notes	MusicXML files that use a number of voices across staves may import some notes on the wrong staff. Files containing chords with notes in different staves are not imported correctly.

Files

Feature	Limitation
End repeat lines	Sibelius may import complex end repeat lines incorrectly. Only end repeat lines existing in the uppermost part of the XML file will be imported. The positioning of end repeat lines may need manual adjustment after they have been imported.
Guitar tab	Hammer-ons, pull-offs and bends are not imported. Almost all the child elements of the technical element are not imported.
Key signatures	Only major and minor modes are recognized for the mode element. If the fifths element is missing, the key signature will be imported as an atonal key signature. Other key child elements (e.g. key-step and key-alter) are ignored. If a part has more than one staff, key signatures may be omitted from one or more of those staves. Key signatures that fall after the barline in some other music notation programs may fall behind the barline in Sibelius.
Layout	Sibelius can only use one page size for the entire score being imported. Objects that are only graphically offset in the file may have an impact on playback in Sibelius.
Lyrics	The laughing, humming, end-line, end-paragraph and editorial elements are ignored.
Metronome marks	Metronome marks containing 256th, 128th, 64th and long (breve) notes are not imported by Sibelius. All metronome marks adopt Sibelius's default positions. Only metronome marks in the top staff of the uppermost part are read by the XML importer. Metronome marks may be duplicated if the uppermost part in the file has more than one staff.
Ornaments	Some ornaments will not be imported. Mordents, trills and turns are imported.
Rests	Extra rests resulting from multiple voices on the same staff are automatically removed, but some extra rests may still occur, e.g. in cross-staff passages.
Slur	The continue attribute is not imported. The entity attributes position and bezier are not imported. Dashed and dotted slurs are not imported. placement and orientation are not imported.
Symbols	Symbols are not imported.
Staves	Changes of staff type are not imported.
Stems	The stem values none and double are not imported.
Text	Some text items are imported via the dynamics element, but none of the dynamics attributes are imported. Specific figured bass elements such as parentheses, elision and extend are not imported. The directive element is not imported.
Ties	The tie element is ignored completely; only ties specified by the tied element are imported. The number attribute is ignored. All ties are imported as solid ties. The position, placement, orientation, bezier-offset, bezier-x and bezier-y attributes are not imported.
Time signatures	Sibelius will not import compound time signatures (e.g. 2/4 + 6/8), but beat divisions that occur only in the numerator (e.g. 2+3 / 4) will be imported. Senza-misura elements are not imported. The single-number attribute value for symbol is not imported (if present it is imported as normal) If different time signatures occur in different staves simultaneously, Sibelius will use the time signature from the uppermost staff.
Tuplets	Some versions of the Dolet plug-in for Finale don't place the start and stop elements of tuplets in the right place, which may cause tuplets to import incorrectly. The tuplet attributes placement, position, show-type, show-number, bracket and line-shape are not imported.

9.7 Opening files from previous versions

Sibelius is fully backwards compatible. Sibelius 6 can open files from all previous versions of Sibelius for Windows and Mac, including files saved in Sibelius Student, Sibelius First and G7. Simply choose File ▸ Open and open the score as normal.

Update Score dialog

As each new version of Sibelius comes with a new set of features, when opening an existing score you will be presented with the Update Score dialog so you can choose which aspects, if any, of your score you wish to update. (You will only be able to choose options that were not available in the version of Sibelius that your score was saved in.)

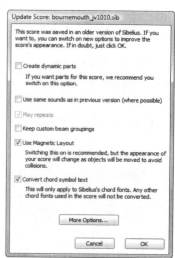

The options on the main Update Score dialog are the most important, and do the following:

- **Create dynamic parts** will create a default set of dynamic parts if is switched on (□ **7.1 Working with parts**).

- **Use same sounds as previous version (where possible)** allows you to choose whether Sibelius should attempt to retain the same sound for each staff in your score as was used to play it back in Sibelius 4 or earlier. This option will only take effect if you have compatible sound sets installed for the devices you were using when you were working on the score in your previous version.

- **Play repeats** determines whether Sibelius should pay attention to any repeat barlines in the score. Normally this checkbox will be disabled, since the option has been switched on by default in all but the earliest versions of Sibelius, but if it is enabled, you should switch it on to ensure correct playback and display of bar numbers in the score.

- **Keep custom beam groupings** determines whether Sibelius should retain any individual edits made to beam groups in the score. Normally this checkbox should be left on to ensure that beam groups are not changed when you open the score: if you subsequently want to reset the beam groups to their new defaults, use Notes ▸ Reset Beam Groups (□ **2.6 Beam groups**).

- **Use Magnetic Layout** allows you to enable automatic collision avoidance for your score. You should leave this option switched on: if you subsequently want to disable Magnetic Layout in your score, simply switch off Layout ▸ Magnetic Layout (□ **8.2 Magnetic Layout**).

- **Convert chord symbol text** updates text-based chord symbols from Sibelius 5 and earlier into newer, more intelligent chord symbol objects. Their original appearance will be retained until you select them and choose Layout ▸ Reset Design. Sibelius is only able to update chord symbols that use one of Sibelius's own chord symbol fonts; if you used a chord symbol font not supplied with Sibelius, it will be unable to convert them (□ **2.10 Chord symbols**).

Clicking the More Options button allows you to use new options that may improve the appearance of your score:

Files

- **Magnetic slurs on normal notes** makes slurs above or below normal notes magnetic, so that either end of each slur is attached to the closest note or chord (□ **2.28 Slurs**)

- **Magnetic slurs on cross-staff notes** works similarly, but applies only to slurs on cross-staff notes (e.g. in keyboard music) (□ **2.28 Slurs**)

- **Version 1.3 stem length rule** makes the stems of notes on or either side of the middle line 0.25 spaces longer than with the option off, which many engravers and publishers prefer

- Sibelius's voice positioning rule was improved in Sibelius 2, so to apply the new rule to older scores, switch on **Version 2 voice positioning rule** (□ **2.36 Voices**)

- **Magnetic tuplets** ensures that the numbers and brackets of tuplets are positioned correctly above or below the notes of the tuplet according to their position on the staff (□ **2.35 Triplets and other tuplets**)

- **Adjust note spelling in transposing instruments in remote keys** makes sure that the spelling of notes in transposing instruments will be enharmonically correct (□ **2.18 Instruments**)

- **Allow note and staff spacings to be contracted** takes advantage of the improvements in Sibelius's spacing algorithms to tighten the horizontal and vertical spacing of older scores (□ **8.9 Note spacing**)

- **Optical beam positions** applies Optical beam positions (□ **2.7 Beam positions**)

- **Optical ties** applies Optical tie positions (□ **2.32 Ties**)

- **Optical note spacing** overrides any manual adjustments made to note spacing in your score and applies Sibelius's Optical rule (□ **8.9 Note spacing**)

- **Hidden notes and rests don't affect stem directions and rests** should be switched on, unless you know you have flipped stems and changed the vertical position of rests in the score and want those changes to be retained.

- **Version 5 vertical text positioning rule** should be switched on, unless you know you have adjusted the vertical position of text objects (such as bar numbers) to compensate for the text appearing too close to the staff following instrument changes along a staff that change the number of staff lines.

- **Adjust stem lengths to avoid beamed rests** applies an improved rule for the position of beams, moving them such that they don't collide with rests (□ **2.7 Beam positions**).

- **Draw automatic cautionary accidentals** enables Sibelius's automatic cautionary accidentals feature, which shows a cautionary accidental for a note in the preceding bar with an accidental (□ **2.1 Accidentals**).

- **Position slurs on mixed stem notes above the notes** applies an improved rule for the direction of slurs: if all of the notes under the compass of the slur have stems pointing upwards, the slur will curve below the notes; if any of the notes have stems pointing downwards, the slur will curve above the notes (□ **2.28 Slurs**).

Other settings to consider

There are a number of more subtle settings that you may want to consider after opening a score created in a previous version of Sibelius:

- For articulations, switching on **New articulation positioning rule** on the **Articulations** page of **House Style ▸ Engraving Rules** is recommended. This option will change the position of articulations that appear outside the staff on stem-down notes above the middle line of the staff, and will also change the position of articulations (e.g. staccato, tenuto) inside the staff on stem-up notes above the middle line of the staff (e.g. flipped notes). If you have previously dragged any articulations in order to achieve correct positioning, you should select those notes and use **Layout ▸ Reset Position** to see the effect of the **New articulation positioning rule**. Also, if you prefer to follow the convention whereby accents should be positioned inside slurs, switch on the appropriate Inside slur checkbox for that articulation.

* For accidentals, in addition to switching on the automatic cautionary accidentals options on the **Accidentals** page of **House Style ▸ Engraving Rules**, you may also want to switch off **Reset accidentals to current key signature on clef change** on the **Clefs and Key Signatures** page, which ensures that notes following mid-bar clef changes follow the normal conventions regarding accidentals prior to the clef change in the same bar.

* For staff spacing, consider switching off **Justify both staves of grand staff instruments** and setting up values for the new *n* **extra spaces...** options on the **Staves** page of **House Style ▸ Engraving Rules**.

* For dynamics on vocal staves, switch on the new **Vocal staff** option in the **Edit Instrument** dialog for the vocal instruments in your score, then switch on the new **Different default position on vocal staves** checkbox in **House Style ▸ Default Positions** for Expression text and the various hairpin line styles and set suitable values to position them above the staff by default.

* For Magnetic Layout, you may find that selecting objects and choose **Layout ▸ Reset Position** substantially improves the appearance of your score.

The majority of the above options can be set quickly to their recommended settings by importing one of the supplied house styles – 📖 **8.8 House Style™**.

Files

9.8 Exporting graphics

Sibelius can export (save) a passage or page of music as a picture in various standard graphics file formats, and you can even just copy and paste graphics from Sibelius directly into another application such as Microsoft Word. This means you can easily include music in other documents, e.g. articles, worksheets, essays, music books, cover designs, posters and program notes.

All music examples in this Reference were exported directly from Sibelius into Adobe FrameMaker – no scissors and glue were required!

If your final document will consist mostly of music, you can alternatively use Sibelius itself as the program in which to assemble music and graphics, e.g. to create worksheets or scores with a graphical cover page – 📖 **9.4 Importing graphics**.

Copying graphics to the clipboard

Sibelius allows you to copy an area of a score to the clipboard, which you can then paste directly into another application as a graphic.

- If you want to export a specific bar or passage, select it first
- Choose **Edit ▸ Select ▸ Select Graphic** (shortcut **Alt+G** *or* ⌥G)
- If you made a selection, a dashed box appears around the selection. If you didn't make a selection, the cursor will turn into a crosshair and you can click and drag around the area of the score you wish to export.
- Adjust the size of the marquee (see below) so that it encloses exactly what you want to copy
- Choose **Edit ▸ Copy** (shortcut **Ctrl+C** *or* ⌘C)
- Switch to the destination application, and choose **Edit ▸ Paste** (shortcut normally **Ctrl+V** *or* ⌘V) or **Edit ▸ Paste Special**.

You can set the resolution of the graphic and choose whether Sibelius should export in monochrome or color from the **Other** page of **File ▸ Preferences** (in the **Sibelius** menu on Mac) – 📖 **5.15 Preferences**.

When you use copy and paste graphics export, Sibelius produces a bitmap graphic. If you want to use a vector graphic, use the **Export Graphics** dialog instead – see **Export Graphics** below.

Adjusting the marquee

To adjust the marquee, you can:

- Click and drag a handle to extend the marquee in that direction
- Hold down **Ctrl** *or* ⌘ and drag either left- or right-hand handles to snap the ends of the marquee to barlines
- Hold down **Shift** and drag any handles to enlarge the marquee proportionally in both directions, e.g. to make the marquee taller both above and below the staff, grab one of the top handles and hold down **Shift** as you drag to extend the marquee both upwards and downwards.

If you have a passage or system selection in the score prior to carrying out the above steps, Sibelius will automatically draw a box around that area when you choose **Edit ▸ Select ▸ Select Graphic**.

The box will snap to the top and bottom of staves and so you will probably find it necessary to extend the selection both up and down. To do this, hold down **Shift** and drag the top handle of the box up.

Inserting graphics into Microsoft Word

To place a graphic created in Sibelius that you have copied to the clipboard using the steps above into a Word document:

* Position the caret in your Word document where you want the graphic to go
* Choose **Edit ▸ Paste**, shortcut **Ctrl+V** *or* ⌘V. The graphic will appear in your document.
* Now, increase or decrease the size of the music by dragging any corner of the box. Do not drag an edge, otherwise the music will stretch and lose the correct aspect ratio. (Type **Ctrl+Z** *or* ⌘Z to undo if you do this by accident.)

In some versions of Microsoft Word, you may find that attempting to paste a graphic from another application does not work correctly. If you find this to be the case, choose **Edit ▸ Paste Special** and, from the list of available formats, choose **Bitmap**.

Beware of editing the graphic within Word – its graphics editor does not handle music well and might produce unexpected results. Use a dedicated graphics program instead.

Export Graphics

Instead of using the clipboard, you can export a graphics file to disk.

Because most of us prefer not to think about technicalities, Sibelius takes the strain out of exporting graphics files – you generally don't even need to know which kind of graphics file you need to export; just which program you want to use it in.

Sibelius allows you to export the whole score, a single page, one or more systems or a specific area of the score just as easily:

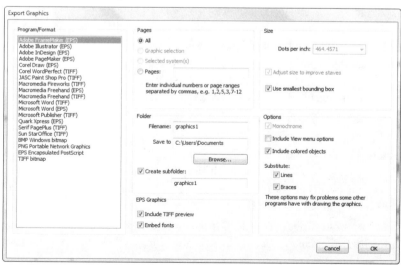

* If you want to export one or more systems, first select the desired systems as a passage, then choose **File ▸ Export ▸ Graphic**. On the **Export Graphics** dialog, click **Selected systems**.

- If you want to export one or more whole pages, or the whole score, just choose **File ▸ Export ▸ Graphic**. On the **Export Graphics** dialog, click **All** or **Pages** and enter the page numbers you wish to export as appropriate.

- If you want to export a specific area of the score, make a passage selection around the area you wish to export, then choose **Edit ▸ Select ▸ Graphic** (shortcut **Alt+G** *or* ⌥G). The cursor will change into a cross, at which point you can fine-tune the selected area by dragging any of the marquee's handles (see above). Now choose **File ▸ Export ▸ Graphic** and click **Graphic selection**.

The **Export Graphics** dialog has the following options:

- **Program/Format**: lists the programs Sibelius directly supports, together with the various graphics file formats that it can save, so if your chosen program isn't listed, you can choose the most appropriate format for your software

- **Filename**: determines the name of the file given to the exported graphics file; if you save multiple pages, the name entered here forms the basis of the name of each file (which will be followed by the page number of the score), and optionally also the name of the folder

- **Save to folder**: allows you to choose where the exported graphics file(s) will be saved; click **Browse** and choose the desired folder

- **Create subfolder**: if you choose to export a range of pages or the whole score and you switch this on, Sibelius will create a folder to put all the graphics files in, by default taking its name from the **Filename** specified above and appending the name of the format; so if you specify a filename of, say, **Concerto 1st movt** and export EPS files, the folder will be called **Concerto 1st movt EPS** (although you can change this if you like)

- **EPS Graphics**: these options are (as the name would suggest) for exporting EPS files:
  - **Include TIFF preview**: allows you to include a monochrome TIFF preview (compressed using the CCITT modified Huffman RLE scheme) in the EPS file, which will enable most graphics programs to show you a low-resolution preview of the EPS file before printing
  - **Embed fonts**: with this option switched on, Sibelius will embed all the fonts used in the document in the EPS file. Although embedding fonts increases the size of each EPS file you create, it ensures that the publisher or printer who wants to use your EPS files can print them correctly without requiring separate copies of the fonts themselves. It is recommended that you switch on this option, unless you have a good reason not to.

- **Size**: these options control the size of the saved graphics file; different options are available for different formats:
  - **Dots per inch** (TIFF, PNG, BMP only): allows you to control the resolution of exported bitmap images. The higher the dpi setting, the higher the resolution of the exported file. The value here gives the quality of the bitmap as compared with a laser printer; so choosing **300** will look the same quality as a 300dpi laser print.
  - **Adjust size to improve staves** (TIFF, PNG, BMP only): this option allows Sibelius to make slight adjustments to the chosen **Dots per inch/Scale** settings in order to ensure that the distance between all the staff lines in the exported file will be an even number of pixels, which improves their appearance

○ **Use smallest bounding box**: defines the dimensions of the resulting graphics file. If this option is switched off, the graphics file will use the page dimensions of the score (including the margins) as the bounding box. With the option switched on, the file will be cropped to the smallest size possible, i.e. just to the edges of the music.

• **Options**: further options, some of which are only available for certain formats:

○ **Monochrome** (TIFF, PNG, BMP only): unless you need to export a score that contains colored objects (or imported graphics that use color), it's a good idea to leave this switched on. Saving monochrome graphics files keeps the size of the resulting file down to the minimum, but doesn't compromise any quality (provided you don't need color).

○ **Include View menu options**: this option specifies whether the current options from the **View** menu (such as hidden objects, highlights, note colors and so on) should be included visibly in the graphics file(s). By default this option is switched off.

○ **Include colored objects**: if you have this option switched off (or if **Monochrome** is switched on), any colored objects in your score will be colored black in the exported graphics file

○ **Substitute**: these options do the same as for printing (🕮 **5.16 Printing**), namely fix bugs in certain graphics programs that can make lines and braces draw incorrectly.

When you've chosen your options, click **OK** to export the graphics file(s).

Batch conversion

Sibelius includes a plug-in that can automatically save graphics files for all the scores in a folder – see **Convert Folder of Scores to Graphics** on page 488.

Graphics formats

Graphics file formats fall into two kinds: *vector* graphics and *bitmap* graphics.

Vector graphics are scalable – in other words, you can make them larger or smaller without any degradation in quality – and the files also tend to use less memory than bitmap graphics.

Bitmap graphics are lower quality than vector graphics (unless you use a very high resolution) and usually occupy more memory, but are supported by a wider variety of programs.

The specific formats available in Sibelius are as follows:

• *Vector:* EPS (Windows and Mac)
• *Bitmap:* TIFF, PNG, BMP (Windows and Mac).

Each of these formats is detailed below. You can also create PDF files from Sibelius – see **Creating PDF files** below.

Encapsulated PostScript (EPS) files

Most publishers and printers prefer to receive music in EPS or PDF format for publication, and Sibelius allows you to export your music directly as an EPS file.

EPS files *will not print* on non-PostScript printers from most programs. Printing an EPS file to a non-PostScript printer may result either in a blank page, a message informing you that you cannot

Files

print EPS files on a non-PostScript printer, or a low-resolution printout of the TIFF preview image embedded in the EPS file.

We recommend that you embed fonts in your EPS files; you are licensed by Sibelius to supply the Opus, Helsinki, Reprise and Inkpen2 fonts to your publisher or printer in order to print your EPS files, but you *must* ensure that you have permission to distribute fonts from other companies.

You can create EPS files in Sibelius whether you are using TrueType or Type 1 fonts; the TrueType fonts are installed by default (you cannot have both TrueType and PostScript Type 1 fonts installed simultaneously) – see **Installing Type 1 music fonts** in ☐ **8.11 Music fonts**. There are, however, some limitations on the fonts that may be embedded in EPS files from Sibelius:

* Type 42 fonts are not supported. The Type 42 font format is PostScript's version of the TrueType standard. All PostScript Level 3 interpreters (such as printers) can display TrueType fonts as long as they are packaged inside the PS Type 42 font format.
* TrueType font outlines have a different representation to PS font outlines so when they are converted from TrueType to Type 3 in order to embed them in the EPS file, some information might get lost. There might be very slight differences in appearance between the embedded font in the EPS file and the original TrueType font, although in almost all cases these differences will be undetectable.
* Only fonts with Latin character sets can be embedded
* OpenType fonts with TrueType outlines can be embedded; OpenType fonts with PostScript outlines cannot be embedded
* Multiple Master fonts can be embedded, but the embedded font won't look exactly the same as the multiple master instance used
* Macintosh PostScript Type 1 enabled font suitcases (SFNT) and Macintosh PostScript Type 1 CID enabled font suitcases (SFNT/CID) cannot be embedded.

Some graphics programs on the Mac (e.g. Corel Draw 8) may give errors when opening EPS files from Sibelius; if you get an error message, try saving the EPS file from Sibelius again with the **TIFF preview** option switched off.

If you import EPS files into Adobe Illustrator version 9.0 or later, we recommend that you switch off **Type ▸ Smart Punctuation**, as this changes certain font characters, causing some of the music symbols to disappear.

If you import EPS files into Adobe PageMaker, you may see a message when you print the document containing the EPS file warning you that the fonts in the EPS file could not be found. Provided your EPS file has fonts embedded, this doesn't matter, and the document will still print correctly despite this warning.

TIFF files

TIFF (Tagged Image File Format) is a widely-supported bitmap format particularly suitable for music because it can be compressed efficiently. If you can't use EPS graphics (e.g. because you don't have a PostScript printer), then we recommend using TIFF instead.

TIFF export can use quite a lot of memory as files are exported; however, it should be possible to export whole pages at up to 1200dpi without problems. Unless you need color in your TIFF files, keep the **Monochrome** option switched on, as this minimizes the size of the saved file.

PNG files

PNG (Portable Network Graphics) is another widely-supported bitmap format with excellent compression. PNG is not as widely supported as TIFF in desktop publishing applications, but it is the ideal format for putting images of your music on the Internet.

BMP files

BMP format is similar to TIFF and PNG, though less widely supported. The color depth of the saved BMP file will be the same as the color depth of your current display settings, unless you switch on the **Monochrome** option in the **File ▸ Export ▸ Graphics** dialog, which will make the file much smaller. In general, it is recommended to use PNG instead of BMP format, because the resulting files will always be smaller, even with color.

Creating PDF files

Portable Document Format (PDF) files allow documents generated by programs such as word processors and desktop publishers to be published electronically, preserving their original appearance, for viewing and printing on any system.

On Mac, no additional software is required. To save a PDF of your score, choose **File ▸ Print**, and click the **Save as PDF** button.

On Windows, Sibelius supports the creation of PDF files provided you have a suitable PDF creator installed on your computer. The official PDF creator is Adobe Acrobat, which is a commercial product available from **www.adobe.com** for both Mac and Windows, but there are several free alternatives available, including PDFCreator, which you can download from:

http://pdfcreator.sourceforge.net

PDF files are generated by software that installs and behaves like a printer driver. This means that creating a PDF is as simple as printing a file from Sibelius, choosing the PDF "printer" as you do so. For further instructions, consult the documentation that accompanies your PDF creation software.

To view PDF files, you need to have the free Adobe Reader installed on your computer (on Mac you can use the built-in Preview application instead). You can download the latest version of Adobe Reader from:

http://www.acrobat.com

Files

9.9 Exporting MIDI files

You can export a score as a MIDI file, so you can easily transfer music into virtually any other music program. You do not need a MIDI interface or any MIDI devices in order to export a MIDI file.

Exporting a MIDI file

- Choose File ▸ Export ▸ MIDI File. A simple dialog appears, as shown on the right.

- You can choose whether you want to export the MIDI file for The current playback device or A different playback device. By default, Sibelius will choose to export a MIDI file suitable for playback on a General MIDI device, which is appropriate for e.g. sending a MIDI file to somebody else for them to listen to. However, if you're using a virtual instrument and want to export a MIDI file to open in, say, a sequencer like Pro Tools in order to continue working on the MIDI performance, then choose the appropriate sound set from the A different playback device list. Sibelius will export the MIDI file with all the appropriate MIDI controller changes, keyswitches and so on.

- You can also choose whether you want to export a Type 0 or Type 1 MIDI file. For nearly every purpose, a Type 1 MIDI file is recommended. However, there are certain devices, such as some electronic pianos and keyboards, that can only play Type 0 MIDI files. Refer to your device's documentation to find out whether it requires Type 0 or Type 1 MIDI files; if in doubt, choose Type 1.

- Tick resolution is a comfortingly obscure option. The default of 256 PPQN ("Pulses Per Quarter Note") matches Sibelius's internal resolution and is recommended. Again, however, there are certain devices that can only play MIDI files with specific PPQN settings. Refer to your device's documentation to find out whether it requires a specific value; if in doubt, leave this set to 256. (Choosing a higher PPQN value doesn't make the exported MIDI file any more "accurate", since Sibelius's internal resolution is fixed at 256.)

- If you have muted any of the instruments in your score, Sibelius will not by default include these instruments in an exported MIDI file (on the grounds that the MIDI file should play back the same as the score plays back in Sibelius). You may, however, want to include all instruments in your MIDI file so that you can work with them in your sequencer, in which case switch off Omit muted instruments.

- Once you have chosen the right options, click OK. Then type in the File name you want to use – make it different than your original Sibelius file to avoid confusion! Find a suitable place to save, then click Save.

When exporting MIDI files, Sibelius includes all of the playback options such as Espressivo, Rubato and Rhythmic feel. So you can even use Sibelius as an ingenious "MIDI file improver" – just open a MIDI file, switch on some interesting playback settings and save an improved version as a MIDI file in a moment!

Batch conversion

Sibelius includes a plug-in to save MIDI files of all the Sibelius scores in a folder – see **Convert Folder of Scores to MIDI** on page 488.

Rubato

If Rubato is switched on in the Play ▸ Performance dialog, and the score is saved as a MIDI file, the timing changes made by Rubato will appear in the file, and consequently the notes will be "out of alignment" when the file is opened in a MIDI sequencer.

This is because Rubato manipulates note start times directly, rather than creating tempo changes. So if you want to save a MIDI file for use in other programs, and you want it to be correctly quantized, set Rubato to Meccanico before you save the MIDI file.

Repeats

By default, MIDI files saved from Sibelius will include any repeats present in the original score. If, for some reason, you would prefer repeats not to be included, switch off Play repeats in the Play ▸ Performance dialog before saving the MIDI file.

Scores with more than 15 staves

For advanced users only!

Because Sibelius uses the same code to export MIDI files as for playing back your scores, it is able to incorporate effects like Espressivo into MIDI files. However, a major difference comes into play only for scores with more than 15 staves.

A standard MIDI file may only contain 16 channels (but a much larger number of tracks), which means that, theoretically, only 16 different sounds can be playing at once. Sibelius allows more than one instrument to share the same MIDI channel thanks to a complex system that inserts appropriate program change messages before notes in order to make them play back with the correct sound.

However, when exporting MIDI files, each staff corresponds to a different MIDI track in a type 1 MIDI file; in other words, two staves sharing the same channel in Sibelius occupy two different tracks in the MIDI file, both assigned to the same channel. This means that if you play back a MIDI file containing more than 15 staves, one or more of the staves may play back with the wrong sound.

The only way to avoid this would be to insert program changes before every note in the score, which is undesirable since some MIDI devices (e.g. the Roland JV series) respond very slowly to program changes, and the MIDI file would not play back smoothly. Inserting program changes before every note would also make the MIDI file very difficult to edit in a sequencer program; so instead, Sibelius simply exports the file with shared channels. You can open the MIDI file in a sequencer and reallocate some of the channels that are shared to use other playback devices (since it is fairly normal for MIDI devices to offer 32 channels rather than 16 nowadays).

There is no ideal solution to this problem – since MIDI simply wasn't designed to play back large-scale scores, any solution is a compromise and an attempt to fit a quart into a pint pot. Sibelius's method, however, is the most useful for users who need to edit their music in a sequencer, and provides the best playback possible within the limitations of MIDI.

Files

9.10 Exporting audio files

□ **4.4 Sibelius Sounds Essentials**.

Sibelius can save a digital audio file of your score, ready to burn straight onto CD or turn into an MP3 file to post on the Internet. You must be using a playback configuration that uses one or more virtual instruments in order to save audio files from Sibelius, such as the supplied Sibelius Sounds Essentials sound library (□ **4.4 Sibelius Sounds Essentials**).

Export Audio

To create a digital audio file of your score in WAV (on Windows) or AIFF (Mac) format:

- If you are using virtual instruments simultaneously with other MIDI devices for playback, only the staves that are played back through virtual instruments can be exported as audio. Therefore, you should preferably ensure that your current playback configuration only uses virtual instruments before you start (□ **4.12 Playback Devices**).

- Choose File ▸ Export ▸ Audio or click the toolbar button shown.

- A simple dialog appears, allowing you to set where the audio file should be saved and what it should be called. Sibelius tells you how long the audio file will be, and approximately how much hard disk space it will occupy.

- When you are happy with these settings, click **Save** and export will begin. Sibelius exports the audio file *off-line*, meaning that it does not play the score back audibly while it works; instead, it streams the audio data direct to your hard disk. Depending on the complexity of the score and the speed of your computer, export may be faster or slower than real time. This has the advantage that if the score is too complex for your computer to be able to play back in real time without glitching or stuttering, you will still be able to export a glitch-free audio track: it will just take longer to export than it would take to play the score back directly.

- If you want to stop the recording at any point, click **Cancel** in the progress window that appears. The partial audio file will be saved in the specified location. You can use this to record e.g. the opening of a larger score.

Burning audio files to CD

If you have a CD-R/RW drive (or "CD burner" as they are often known) in your computer, it should have come supplied with some software for creating data and audio CDs. The exact process for burning audio files saved from Sibelius onto an audio CD will vary according to the program supplied with your CD burner; see its manual for details.

Creating MP3 files

MP3 (or MPEG Audio Layer 3 to give it its full name) is the most widely-used format for sharing music on the Internet or via email, as it is much smaller than a WAV or AIFF file. Once you have saved an audio file from Sibelius, you can easily convert it into an MP3 file using freely-available software. For example:

- *Mac:* mAC3dec (http://sourceforge.net/projects/mac3dec/) converts between AIFF and MP3 with a simple, drag-and-drop interface
- *Windows:* dbPowerAmp Music Converter (http://www.dbpoweramp.com/dmc.htm) converts between many different audio formats, simply by right-clicking on the file in Windows Explorer.

Many other programs can convert to and from MP3, including the audio editor Audacity (http://audacity.sourceforge.net/), and QuickTime Pro (http://www.apple.com/quicktime/pro/).

Files

9.11 Exporting Scorch web pages

📖 **5.18 SibeliusEducation.com, 5.19 SibeliusMusic.com**.

The Internet is the ideal way to reach a worldwide audience for your music. Sibelius lets anyone view, play back, transpose, and print scores from your own web site, using the free Scorch plug-in (📖 **5.19 SibeliusMusic.com**).

Recommended settings

📖 **5.19 SibeliusMusic.com** for various settings you should make to your scores to ensure other people can view, play and print them whatever equipment they may have.

When preparing scores for publishing on your own web site, you might also consider changing the page and staff size of your score to ensure it is as legible as possible on the screen. For portrait format scores for small ensembles, try setting your page size so that only one system fits on each page; this means that visitors to your web site won't have to scroll up and down the page to see each system of your music. There are web templates provided which are set to show just one system at a time – see **Web page templates** below.

Exporting

- First, choose **File ▸ Score Info**, click the **Composer/Title** tab, and enter some information about your piece (if you didn't do so on the **New Score** dialog when you created the score originally) – the web page you are about to generate assumes you've filled in the **Title** and **Composer** fields so that it can include them in the web page

- Choose **File ▸ Export ▸ Scorch web page**

- Enter a filename. Sibelius removes any spaces from the filenames of both the Sibelius (**.sib**) and HTML (**.htm**) files and shortens the name to 27 characters plus a 3 character extension to make them safe for all web servers.

- If you haven't entered anything in the **File ▸ Score Info** dialog, you will be warned, for example, that the **Title** and **Composer** fields are blank

- You are asked to choose a template web page to insert the score into – see **Web page templates** below. You can also adjust the width and height of the score as it will appear within the web page. If you don't feel ambitious, just choose the **Classic** web template, leaving the other settings alone, and click **OK**.

Setting a larger **Width** makes the page and hence the music bigger; there's no need to enter a **Height** value if you want the page to be the same shape, which is advisable.

The Snap Zoom Level option (switched on by default) automatically adjusts the size of the score to ensure that the staff lines always appear equidistant. Leave this option switched on.

Allow printing and saving, as the name suggests, allows you to choose whether visitors to your web site can print and save your music, or simply play it back – see **Printing and saving from Scorch** below.

* Sibelius then saves two files in the chosen location: an HTML file (with the file extension .htm), and a Sibelius score (with the extension .sib).

You're now ready to upload these two files to your web site. Depending on how your web site is hosted, you may need to use an FTP client or upload them via your web browser.

You must include *both* the actual Sibelius score file and the web page *in the same folder* on your web site, and don't rename the Sibelius file – the HTML in the web page refers to the Sibelius file.

Batch conversion

Sibelius includes a plug-in to save Scorch web pages for all the scores in a folder, as well as to generate an index page with links to all the individual scores – see **Convert Folder of Scores to Web Pages** on page 488.

Printing and saving from Scorch

If you switch on the Allow printing and saving option when saving your score as a Scorch web page, visitors to your site will be allowed to print your score to their computer's printer, and also save the score as a Sibelius file to their hard disk so that they can open it in Sibelius themselves.

This makes it easy to share your music with others: teachers can put worksheets on their school web site, and students can print them out directly from their web browser, or, if they have Sibelius themselves, download the music to their computer and complete the worksheet in Sibelius.

The Allow printing and saving option does not have some of the benefits of publishing your music on SibeliusMusic.com:

* You are not permitted to put Scorch to commercial use on your own web site without a special license from us – i.e. you may not charge money for allowing visitors to your site to print and save your music

* Music on your own web site is not securely encrypted, so any visitors who use Sibelius themselves can download your music to their computers simply by clicking the Save button in Scorch, and they will then be able to edit it in Sibelius.

Beware that even if you don't allow printing and saving, your scores are still downloaded to the visitor's computer in unencrypted form. Whenever you view something in your web browser – whether it is text, an image, or even a Sibelius score using the Scorch plug-in – it has been downloaded to the temporary Internet files folder on your computer's hard disk. This means that anybody who views your music on your personal web page will potentially be able to edit the original file (if they have Sibelius).

In other words, if you publish your music on your own web site, you will be doing so in an insecure way. However, if you publish your music on SibeliusMusic.com, your music is secure.

Files

SibeliusMusic.com uses an encrypted file format understood only by the Scorch plug-in – this means that even if somebody were to find the file on their hard disk, they couldn't open it with any program apart from Scorch (not even Sibelius). This also ensures that even if somebody looks at an encrypted Sibelius file in Scorch, they can't print it out, because printing these files relies on communication between Scorch and the SibeliusMusic.com server.

If you want to publish securely on your own web site, contact Sibelius Software about licensing Sibelius Internet Edition, a special version of Sibelius for commercial Internet publishing.

Score information

You can include catalog information such as the composer, title and so on in your web site. All you have to do is type the details into the **File ▸ New** dialog when creating your score, or subsequently into the **File ▸ Score Info** dialog; then when you save a web page, Sibelius can include this information automatically as HTML tags, as well as putting the main information as text in the web page.

First you have to design a template web page that displays the kind of catalog information you want to include (see **Customizing your web site** below).

If you have a knack for programming, you can write a program to create an on-line catalog (or even a search engine) of the scores on your web site automatically from these tags, with links to the scores.

Web page templates

A number of web page templates are provided for you, in a variety of styles and color combinations. Some templates use one of Scorch's most useful features: *split playback*. Split playback is designed to allow you to play along with Scorch without having to worry about turning pages – it's like having an intelligent page turner at your beck and call.

As Scorch reaches the end of one system during playback, it automatically replaces the system it's just played back with a system from further down the page. Your eye naturally follows the music down the page, and when you reach the bottom of the page, you'll find that the next few systems are already visible at the top of the Scorch window.

Split playback works best with music for solo instruments, or small ensembles (such as solo instrument and keyboard). Choose from the **2 system split playback**, **3 system split playback** or **4 system split playback** templates to try out this feature.

The **1 system playback** and **1 system view** templates only keep one system in view: this is useful if you want visitors to your web site to be able to follow your music without having to scroll their web browser window up and down. (**1 system playback** shows a full page when Scorch isn't playing back, but just one system during playback.)

If you have enabled printing and saving from Scorch, your scores will save and print exactly the way they appear in Sibelius – in other words, split playback has no effect on the actual scores themselves; it is simply an alternative way of viewing the scores in Scorch.

Customizing your web site

If you don't want to use Sibelius's provided web page templates, or would like to improve them, you will need a very basic knowledge of HTML (or an HTML-speaking friend).

The web page produced by Sibelius is very straightforward, and you can make any changes you like to it – you may want to add your own background or graphics, further information, links, or whatever.

You can design your own template web pages and save them with a .htm extension in the Scorch Templates folder inside your application data folder (see **User-editable files** on page 642). They will then appear in the list of web page templates.

A web page template is a standard HTML file with some special tags where the filename and image size are inserted when you save as a Scorch web page. There are also optional tags that are replaced by the Title, Composer etc. fields from the File ▸ Score Info dialog. The full list of tags (not all used in the sample templates) is:

$FILENAME$	Filename + extension of the Sibelius file
$PATHNAME$	Path of the Sibelius file
$WIDTH$, $HEIGHT$	From Export Scorch Web Page dialog
$TITLE$, $COMPOSER$, $ARRANGER$, $LYRICIST$, $ARTIST$, $MOREINFO$	From File ▸ New and File ▸ Score Info dialog

See the web page templates provided for examples of how to use these tags.

The only required elements are the nested **<object>** and **<embed>** tags, which should look something like this:

```
<object id="ScorchPlugin"
    classid="clsid:A8F2B9BD-A6A0-486A-9744-18920D898429"
    width="x"
    height="y"
    codebase="http://www.sibelius.com/download/software/win/ActiveXPlugin.cab">
<param name="src" value="filename.sib">
<embed src="filename.sib"
    width="x"
    height="y"
    type="application/x-sibelius-score"
    pluginspage="http://www.sibelius.com/cgi/plugin.pl">
</object>
```

where *filename.sib* is the path to the Sibelius file, *x* is the width of the Scorch window in pixels, and *y* is the height of the Scorch window in pixels. You can get these filled in automatically when you use File ▸ Export ▸ Scorch web page in Sibelius if you set them in your web page template to $FILENAME$, $WIDTH$ and $HEIGHT$ respectively.

Don't change the **classid**, **codebase**, **type** or **pluginspage** attributes, as these tell the browser about Scorch and where to get it if it hasn't been installed yet.

Problems and solutions

Some web servers may not display Scorch web pages, in which case you may be warned by your browser that a suitable plug-in could not be found. This is because the server doesn't recognize Sibelius's **.sib** file extension.

If this happens on your web site, contact your ISP or the system administrator of your web server and ask them to add the Sibelius MIME-type to the server's configuration, which will fix the problem.

Files

Using email and CD-ROM

If you want to send someone a Sibelius file via email to view in Scorch, 📖 **9.2 Sharing files**.

You can equally well use Sibelius's Internet publishing facility to promote your music via CD-ROM. Simply save your web site to a CD – other people can then access it from the CD in exactly the same way as over the Internet.

Note, however, that people will still need to download Scorch from the Internet, which they can do just by following the link in any Scorch web page on the disk. You are not allowed to distribute Scorch yourself (see **Legal notice** below).

Legal notice

It is illegal to place copyright music on the Internet without permission from the copyright owner. This is the case even if you have made your own arrangement of a copyright piece of music.

Sibelius's Internet publishing facility is licensed to you for non-commercial use only. (See the Sibelius license agreement for details.)

You are not allowed to distribute Scorch, e.g. to put it on your own web site – people visiting your site must follow the link supplied in order to download Scorch. Licensing conditions for the plug-in are shown when you install it.

9.12 Exporting to previous versions

Sibelius is fully backwards compatible. Sibelius 6 can open files from all previous versions of Sibelius, including files saved in Sibelius Student, Sibelius First and G7.

Older versions cannot open files saved in the present version, but you can use File ▸ Export ▸ Sibelius 2, 3, 4 or 5 to save files that can be opened by Sibelius 2, Sibelius 3, Sibelius 4 or Sibelius 5. (The guitar program G7 also uses the same format as Sibelius 3 and Sibelius 3 Student.) Note, however, that these earlier versions don't have all the features of Sibelius 6, so scores may not look precisely the same when opened in them as they look in Sibelius 6. In particular, the elements listed below are omitted or changed (i.e. not exported in the file).

To export files that can be opened by Sibelius 3 Student or Sibelius 5 Student, choose File ▸ Export ▸ Sibelius Student. Note that Sibelius 3 Student can only open scores with a maximum of eight staves, and Sibelius 5 Student a maximum of 12 staves.

Differences in all previous and cut-down versions of Sibelius

The following are omitted or changed when exporting files to all other versions of Sibelius:

- *Arpeggio lines* attached to notes, as created from the Keypad, will be converted into regular arpeggio lines.
- *Articulations:*
  - Articulations below the note that have been independently dragged will be shown at their default position, unless the articulations above the note have not been dragged (in which case the bottom position will be used)
  - Articulations in the staff may move to less ideal positions
  - Bowing markings that are positioned outside slurs above the staff when other articulations are inside the slur will appear inside the slur.
- *Bar rests:* double whole note (breve) bar rests in 4/2 will appear as normal whole note (semibreve) bar rests.
- *Beams:*
  - The state of the Beam over rests and Beam to and from rests options in Engraving Rules are set in each time signature in the score, which will produce near-identical beaming results in earlier versions but are not guaranteed to be the same.
  - Beams may collide with rests, because earlier versions of Sibelius do not have the Adjust stem lengths to avoid beamed rests option.
  - Automatic secondary beam breaks for beamed rests will not appear, because earlier versions of Sibelius do not have the Break secondary beams option.
  - Stemlets will not appear.
- *Cautionary accidentals* will be omitted.
- *Chord symbols:*
  - Horizontal guitar chord diagrams will appear as vertical chord diagrams.
  - Fingering shown in dots on guitar chord diagrams will not appear.

Files

- All fingering dots will appear as black dots, regardless of the design used in Sibelius 6.
- Chord diagrams that are set to show a different number of frets than the default setting on the **Guitar** page of **House Style ▸ Engraving Rules** will appear using the default number of frets.
- Chord diagrams that do not have a dot on a specific string but also do not show an O or an X above the frame will show an O above the string.
- Chord diagrams that are set to a non-default size using the **Scale** control in the **General** panel of Properties will appear at their default size.
- *Comments* will be omitted.
- *Guitar scale diagrams* will be omitted.
- *Jazz symbols* (plop, scoop, fall, doit) will be converted into regular symbols.
- *Live Tempo* data will be omitted.
- *Magnetic Layout* positions will be frozen, and not all objects will appear in the same positions in earlier versions, e.g. continuation segments of lines after system or page breaks.
- *Slash noteheads* may appear in different positions on the staff for transposing instruments.
- *Slurs* will appear at their default thickness, shape and design; they may also curve in the opposite direction (i.e. slurs that are below the staff in Sibelius 6 may appear above in earlier versions)
- *Staff spacing* will be different, because earlier versions of Sibelius always justify the distance between staves of multi-staff instruments. (Extra space provided for lyrics, system object positions, and between groups of bracketed/braced instruments will be retained until the staff spacing is reset in the earlier version.)
- *Ties* will appear at the same thickness as slurs.
- Two-bar and four-bar repeat bars will not look correct, and any automatic formatting produced by such repeat bars will not be retained in earlier versions, so bars may appear on different systems.
- Objects that are drawn at custom layers (e.g. behind the staff) will all be drawn on the same layer.
- The vertical positions of system objects such as rehearsal marks at system object positions other than above the top staff may be different.
- Any fermatas whose playback settings have been individually adjusted will play back using the default settings in earlier versions.
- Repeat bars will not play back in earlier versions.

Differences in Sibelius 2, 3, 4, G7 and Sibelius 3 Student

The following are retained in Sibelius 5, but omitted or changed in earlier versions:

- *Bar numbers:*
  - If bar numbers are set to appear every *n* bars, *n* will be turned into one of the existing options in earlier versions, so bar numbers may appear on different bars.
  - Bar number changes that include new bar number formats will be turned into normal bar number changes.
  - Bar number changes that include text before or after the number will be turned into normal bar number changes.
  - Bar numbers automatically hidden at the same locations as rehearsal marks will not be hidden.
  - Bar numbering will not take repeats into account.

○ Bar numbers will appear on the staves set in Layout ▸ System Object Positions, not the staves set in House Style ▸ Engraving Rules.

• *Cue-sized objects* other than notes will appear at "normal" size.

• *Ideas* saved in the score will be omitted.

• *Instrument changes* will be converted into appropriate staff type and transposition changes. Note, however, that the playback sound will not change at the point of the instrument change when the score is played back in the earlier version of Sibelius.

• *Margin changes* (including those produced by the After first page option in Layout ▸ Document Setup, and by special page breaks) are omitted; all pages in the score will use the margins defined on the first page of the score.

• *Multirests* in parts may split differently in Sibelius 4 and earlier, due to page-attached system text not splitting multirests in Sibelius 5 and later.

• *Page number changes* are omitted; when opened in earlier versions, the pages will simply be numbered from the first page.

• *Special page breaks* are converted into regular page breaks, and any text items, symbols or graphics set to appear on the blank pages are deleted from the score, together with blank page text styles

• *Stem directions and rest placement* may change, if Hidden notes and rests don't affect stem directions and rests is switched on (on the Notes and Tremolos page of House Style ▸ Engraving Rules)

• *Technique text* such as "pizz." and "arco" will not play back correctly in the earlier version.

• All new instrument definitions, staff types, and ensemble data are omitted (⌨ **8.14 Edit Instruments**).

Differences in Sibelius 2, 3, G7 and Sibelius 3 Student

The following are retained in Sibelius 4, but omitted or changed in earlier versions:

• *Dynamic parts:* any parts that exist in your score are omitted (⌨ **7.1 Working with parts**), though you could extract parts in Sibelius 5 and then export those in the same way as the score.

• *Auto Breaks options:* all Auto Breaks options are omitted. This includes auto system breaks, splitting of multirests and tacet multirests, and advanced page break settings.

• *Optical beam positions:* beams will slightly change position when opened in earlier versions (⌨ **2.7 Beam positions**).

• *Optical ties:* ties will slightly change position when opened in earlier versions (⌨ **2.32 Ties**).

• *Justification:* the horizontal and vertical justification of notes and systems may change when opened in earlier versions (⌨ **8.10 Staff spacing**).

• Text styles whose sizes are set to Keep absolute will not scale correctly on small staves (⌨ **3.9 Edit Text Styles**).

Further differences in Sibelius 2

The following are retained in Sibelius 4, Sibelius 3, G7 and Sibelius 3 Student, but omitted or changed in Sibelius 2:

Files

- *Note spacing:* some note spacing options (e.g. minimum space around notes, flags, etc.) are omitted; note spacing may adjust slightly when the file is opened, especially when the spacing is particularly tight or loose, but the overall layout (number of bars per system and page) will not change.
- *Playback:* all Live Playback data will be omitted (📖 **4.8 Live Playback**); Play on pass options (📖 **4.6 Repeats**); Play ▸ Dictionary terms that use repeat behaviors or regular expressions (📖 **4.9 Playback dictionary**); gaps between movements in the same score (📖 **4.5 Performance**).
- *Layout:* Focus on Staves state will be omitted (📖 **5.8 Focus on Staves**).
- *Engraving rules:* Allow beams after rests option is omitted (📖 **2.8 Beamed rests and stemlets**), Center staccatos on stem is converted to Half-center staccatos on stem (📖 **2.3 Articulations**).
- *Colored objects* (including the color of highlights) will not appear colored when you open the score in Sibelius 2, *but* will be preserved and reappear in color if you open the file in Sibelius 3 or 4 (provided you haven't resaved it in Sibelius 2 since).

Sibelius 1.4 users

If you know people who use Sibelius 1.4 and you want to share files with them, they must update to the current version, as you cannot export a Sibelius 5 file in version 1.4 format.

Glossary

This explains musical and computer terms used in this Reference that are uncommon, technical or have a special meaning in Sibelius. Cross-references are in **bold**.

acciaccatura a short grace note normally played before the beat, drawn with a line through its stem.

accidental a symbol (e.g. flat, sharp) indicating that a pitch is to be adjusted up or down by a small interval – usually by a half-step (semitone), but occasionally by a whole-step (tone) or a **microtone**.

aftertouch in MIDI, the degree of pressure exerted on a key after you press it, normally used to control modulation (vibrato).

alphabetic input creating music with the computer keyboard, mainly using the letters A–G and the numeric keypad. See **step-time input**, **mouse input**, **Flexi-time™**.

appoggiatura a long grace note normally played on the beat; unlike an acciaccatura, it is drawn without a line through its stem.

articulation a symbol appearing above or below a note or chord that indicates how it should be played – e.g. staccato, tenuto, up-bow, accent, fermata (pause).

ASIO stands for Audio Stream Input/Output, a standard invented by Steinberg that provides low-**latency** audio input and output.

attachment notes, text, lines, symbols, etc. are said to be "attached" to particular staves and rhythmic positions in the music. This means that they belong to that staff/position and move with it when the music is reformatted. When you select most objects, a dashed gray arrow shows what the object is attached to.

Audio Unit (or **AU**) the name of a format for virtual instruments and effects invented by Apple. Audio Units are only compatible with Mac computers.

bank a set of up to 128 **program numbers**. MIDI devices that have more than 128 sounds group them into banks.

bar (or *measure*) is a segment of time defined as a given number of beats of a given duration.

beams the thick lines connecting groups of eighth notes (quavers) and shorter note values. A *fractional beam* is another term for a **flag**.

BMP file a standard Windows bitmap graphics format.

brace the { to the left of keyboard instruments and other instruments that use a grand staff (also used in place of a sub-bracket in older orchestral scores, particularly to group horns).

bracket (a) the thick vertical [that groups together the staves of instruments in the same family. The thin vertical [that groups divided instruments is a *sub-bracket*.

(b) The horizontal [that sometimes groups notes in tuplets.

break see **page break**, **system break**.

caret the vertical line that shows where you are when you're creating notes or typing text; sometimes called a *cursor* or *insertion point*.

channel the MIDI equivalent of a staff, usually specified by a number from 1 to 16. Most MIDI devices only allow 16 channels. Each channel can only be set to one specific **program number**, **pan position**, etc. at a time.

chord in this Reference, *chord* means specifically two or more noteheads on a single **stem** (or, in the case of double whole notes (breves) and whole-notes (semibreves), in the same **voice**). Noteheads in different voices or staves count as being in different chords.

chord symbol text above a staff specifying a chord for the performer to play or improvise around, e.g. Bbm (meaning B flat minor).

clipboard an (invisible) place where cut or copied music is temporarily stored before being pasted to another location in the score.

codec acronym for *compressor/decompressor* or *coder/decoder*, a software component that translates video or audio data between its uncompressed and compressed forms.

configuration (for playback) a collection of playback device settings that determines which devices are available to Sibelius and how they should be used for playback.

control change a **MIDI message** that controls effects such as reverb, pan position and sustain.

controller a MIDI input device, such as a keyboard, sustain pedal, modulation or **pitch bend** wheel, etc.

convert to change the format of a file.

crop marks ("crops") thin cross-hairs used in litho printing to pinpoint the corners of a page appearing on a larger sheet of paper. The paper is then trimmed along the lines indicated by the crop marks.

cue note a small (*cue-size*) note, so named because it is most often used for writing cues in instrumental parts. Unlike **grace notes**, cue notes have a real duration – that is, they take up rhythmic space in the bar. Any note, rest or bar rest can be made cue-size – whether it's a normal note, special **notehead** or grace note. You can even write cue notes on a small staff, which makes them go smaller still.

DAW (Digital Audio Workstation) a computer-based or hard-drive equipped audio recording and editing system. Typically refers to applications like Pro Tools, Cubase, Logic, and so on.

default whatever an option is provisionally set to until you change it. Sibelius is designed to have intelligent defaults, so you don't often need to change things it does automatically.

dialog (or **dialog box**) a window asking you for information, with buttons (such as OK or Cancel) to press when you've finished.

diatonic a diatonic scale is a major or minor scale. To transpose diatonically means to shift notes up or down the scale, so in the scale of C major, transposing a G major triad up a diatonic 2nd produces A minor, or up a diatonic 3rd produces a B diminished triad.

dpi (dots per inch) the unit of printing and scanning **resolution**. The more dpi you print or scan at, the higher the resolution is, and the more detailed the resulting printout or **scan**.

When printing, 1200 dpi or higher produces publishing quality print in which the dots are invisible. 600dpi (the standard resolution of most laser printers) is almost as good and is often good enough for publishing music.

For scanning music, 200 dpi to 400 dpi is a normal range of resolutions. Higher resolutions such as 600 dpi are used for scanning photos and graphics at high quality.

dynamic part see **part**

dynamics text (e.g. *mf*) or **hairpins** specifying loudness or changes of loudness.

element part of a **Sound ID** between two periods (full stops), e.g. the elements of the sound ID strings.violin.ensemble are "strings", "violin" and "ensemble."

effect a computer program that processes an audio signal in order to change one or more characteristics of a sound, e.g. to produce **reverb**.

EMF (Enhanced MetaFile) a standard Windows vector graphics format.

engraving rules rules used for **music engraving**. Sibelius incorporates all of the standard engraving rules, which you can choose between using the many options provided in the House Style ▸ Engraving Rules dialog and elsewhere.

ensemble a set of instruments, grouped into one or more **families**, and each family then contains one or more instruments. Several ensembles appear in Create ▸ Instruments.

EPS (Encapsulated PostScript) a standard vector graphics file format very similar to the **PostScript** file format. But unlike a PostScript file, an EPS file is used to place a single page of text or graphics as an illustration into a page layout program such as Quark XPress. EPS files are mainly used in professional publishing.

explode to split the notes of a chord or passage of chords from one or two staves onto a larger number of staves. Opposite of **reduce**.

export to save in a file format used by a different program. Opposite of **import**.

extract to create a separate file of a **part**.

fader a sliding knob used in audio equipment such as mixers, which controls (e.g.) the volume of a particular audio channel. Sibelius's Mixer window has faders for controlling the volume and pan position of individual staves.

family instruments of a similar kind that appear together in a score, such as woodwind, brass, percussion and strings. Also called an instrumental "section."

filter a feature in Sibelius that selects objects of a particular kind (e.g. hairpins, text) or that have particular characteristics (e.g. three-note chords).

flag the short bit of beam that appears in dotted rhythms; also called a *fractional beam*.

footer text that appears at the bottom of every page of a document; sometimes called a "running footer." See also **header**.

Flexi-time™ Sibelius's intelligent real-time input feature. 📖 **step-time input**, **alphabetic input**, **mouse input**.

formatting spreading out music to fill systems and pages. Sibelius instantly reformats the whole score whenever you make any change, so you always see it as it will be when finally printed.

full score a **score** that contains every instrument playing a piece of music, as opposed to a **part**.

General MIDI (GM) the name of the most widely-used **sound set**.

grace note a small note that (unlike a **cue note**) does not subtract from the duration of a bar – in performance it is "crushed" into the previous or following note. Grace notes with a diagonal line through the stem are called acciaccaturas; ones without lines are **appoggiaturas**.

grayscale (scanning) shades of gray, as opposed to color or plain black and white.

group a list of instruments into which Sibelius will copy similar **lines of notes** as part of its Arrange feature.

H-bar the thick horizontal line, normally used for **multirests**.

hairpin a crescendo or diminuendo written as a hairpin-shaped double-line.

header text that appears at the top of every page of a document when it is printed; often called a "running header." See also **footer**.

hit point an event in a film (e.g. a gun firing) that is to be synchronized with a musical event in the score (e.g. a loud chord or climax of a phrase). Hit points are indicated by special boxed text in the score.

house style the overall "look" of a score, as defined by a publisher; in Sibelius, the house style is mostly determined by the items in the House Style menu, including **engraving rules**, **text styles**, line and notehead types, etc.

imagesetter a high-resolution (typically 2540 dpi or higher) printer used to produce litho printing plates. Imagesetters use **PostScript**, usually go by the brand name Linotronic, and can output very large pages.

import to open or incorporate a file that is in a format used by a different program. Opposite of **export**.

initial barline the barline at the very left-hand end of each system that joins all the staves together; Sibelius automatically adds these. The initial barline is normally omitted in single-staff systems.

instrument as far as Sibelius is concerned, anything that has its own name at the left of a system, so the term includes singers, electronic tape, etc. Instruments can have more than one staff (e.g. keyboards), and can also have more than one **player** (e.g. wind instruments in orchestral/band music).

justified spread out horizontally or vertically to fill a page up to the margins. E.g. most of the text in this Reference is justified horizontally so that it reaches the right margin; bars of music are almost always justified horizontally in the same way. Staves are often justified vertically so they spread down to the bottom margin of the page instead of leaving a gap at the bottom.

Keypad the window from which you can pick notes, articulations, accidentals, etc. using the mouse or numeric keys. By clicking the five little buttons at the top underneath the numbers (or typing + on the keypad, or F7–F12) you can choose between six different Keypad layouts, called the *first Keypad layout, second Keypad layout*, etc.

keyswitch a technique used by many **virtual instruments**, normally meaning a very low note that produces no sound when played, which instead tells the virtual instrument to use a different sound for subsequent notes played in the normal range.

latency the delay between Sibelius sending a message to a sound device to trigger a note and the sounding of that note; latency is generally higher (i.e. a longer delay) with software devices, such as virtual instruments, than hardware devices, such as sound modules.

layer used by some notation programs to mean **voice**; can also mean different sounds within the same **program** in a **virtual instrument**, accessed by way of techniques such as **keyswitches** and **control changes**; can also mean graphical layers, i.e. the order in which objects are drawn.

line spacing (technical term *leading*, rhymes with "wedding" and not with "weeding") the distance between successive lines of text. A standard line spacing in books is 120%, meaning that the separation between lines of text is 1.2 times the **point size**; in music, 100% is often preferable.

line a hairpin, slur, *8va*, glissando or any other object in the Create ▸ Line dialog.

line of notes a succession of single notes and rests taken from the source passage as part of the Arrange feature's processing, e.g. a series of three-note chords is turned into three separate lines of notes.

Live a special kind of playback that captures every nuance of your original performance, right down to the velocity and timing of each note.

lyric line the horizontal line that follows any word whose final syllable is sung to more than one note.

magnetic describes the intelligent behavior of slurs, tuplets, accidentals, articulations, ties, slides, bends, etc., which stick to notes and reposition themselves if the notes change pitch.

manuscript paper whenever you create a score it is written on a particular type of "manuscript paper" that you choose at the start. Manuscript paper specifies the instruments, plus other options such as house style settings.

microtone a fraction of a half-step (semitone), used in some avant garde and ethnic music. The most common microtone is the *quarter-tone*, which is half of a half-step (semitone). Microtones are indicated by a wide range of odd-looking accidentals, generally made from sharps, flats and naturals cut up or with extra bits stuck on. In order to produce microtones, some instruments need to be cut up or have extra bits stuck on.

MIDI (rhymes with "giddy") *Musical Instrument Digital Interface* – the worldwide standard for electronic musical instruments and computer soundcards. 📖 **MIDI file** (below).

Glossary

MIDI file a file in Standard MIDI File format, which is understood by virtually every music program. MIDI files are designed specifically for playback, and so are not ideal for transferring music notation between programs.

MIDI messages commands sent to MIDI devices used to achieve particular playback effects such as **program number** changes and **pitch bend**; Sibelius generates these automatically during playback and you can also add explicit ones to your score using slightly arcane text objects.

Mixer the window in Sibelius that lets you adjust the **volume**, **pan position** and muting of staves.

mouse input creating music with the mouse. This is generally the slowest way of inputting. ⌨ **alphabetic input**, **step-time input**, **Flexi-time™**.

multirest the marking for several bar rests, used in parts; longer multirests are usually drawn as a number above an **H-bar**.

music engraving the art of drawing music notation, covering topics such as the design of music symbols, the positioning and spacing of notes and other objects, the layout of pages, and the use of particular text fonts and sizes. Much (but not all) of music engraving has been formulated into **engraving rules**.

music text font a special font (such as Opus Text) containing musical symbols that occur in text, such as *mf* or ♩ = 60.

MusicXML a file format for transferring music notation between different programs. It is the recommended way of moving music from Finale 2004 or later to Sibelius.

Navigator the miniature view of the score in the bottom left-hand corner. You can drag the white rectangle with the mouse to move through the score.

note a single **notehead** with a **stem** (unless the note is a whole note (semibreve) or double whole note (breve)). Notes can also have accidentals, articulations, rhythm dots, beams, leger lines and tremolos. Individual pitches on a chord are properly called *noteheads*, not "notes."

note value the length of a single note, chord or rest, e.g. eighth note (quaver), half note (minim).

notehead a blob or other shape (e.g. cross or diamond) in a note or chord that specifies the pitch, **note value** and sometimes the playing technique.

NoteOn / NoteOff the **MIDI messages** that start or end a note.

object anything you can put in a score – a note, accidental, clef, piece of text, slur, etc. ⌨ **staff object**, **system object**.

OCR (scanning) optical character recognition; usually applied to scanning text, but also to music.

Optical™ describes several special **engraving rules** unique to Sibelius that produce very high-quality engraved results, such as for the positioning of notes, ties and beams.

original (scanning) the page or score you are scanning from.

ossia a small bar or so of music above a normal-sized staff to show an alternative way of playing something.

output (scanning) music that has been **read** from **scans**.

page (a) one side of a sheet of music as it appears when finally published. The page size is not necessarily the same as the *paper* size, as you can print a small page on a large sheet of paper.

(b) a complete set of options within a dialog (e.g. House Style ▸ Engraving Rules) accessible either by clicking a **tab** or an item in a list.

page break the forced termination of a page at a particular barline, often made at the end of a **section**, or to avoid inconvenient page-turns in **parts**. 📖 **system break**.

pan position (or **pan**) the left-to-right direction of a sound, specified for the purposes of stereo playback.

part the music of one or more instruments extracted from a full score, sometimes called an *instrumental, orchestral* or *band* part. Performers read off parts so that they only have to see the music they play. A *dynamic part* is a part that is stored in the same file as the full score and is automatically updated whenever you edit the score. An *extracted part* is a part in a separate file from the score that is not automatically updated.

passage a continuous stretch of music along one staff or along several simultaneous staves, which may or may not be adjacent vertically (e.g. Flute and Cello in an orchestral score). In its simplest form, you can think of it as a "rectangle" of music. A passage can extend over several systems, or even an entire score. Usually passages are enclosed by a light blue box; there is also a special kind of passage called a **system passage** that contains all instruments and is drawn with a purple double-box.

PDF (Portable Document Format) a common file format that allows documents generated by programs such as word processors and desktop publishers to be published electronically, preserving their original appearance, for viewing and printing on any computer. Most often used by Adobe Acrobat and Adobe Reader.

PhotoScore the program for scanning printed music into Sibelius. There are two version – PhotoScore Lite is included with Sibelius; PhotoScore Ultimate has additional features and can be bought separately.

PICT a standard Mac vector graphics file format.

pitch bend in MIDI, the effect of "bending" a pitch up and down, achieved by operating a lever or wheel, or by sending a pitch bend **MIDI message**.

playback line the green vertical line that shows where in the score Sibelius is playing back or will play back. This line is also used when recording with Flexi-time, when it is red.

players several performers sharing the same staves but distinguished usually by a number. For instance, horn players usually share one or two staves and are often numbered 1, 2, 3 and 4.

plug-in a piece of software that can operate inside another software environment. In Sibelius, a plug-in is a small program which adds an extra Sibelius feature, written in a scripting language called ManuScript. The word "plug-in" is also often used to describe **virtual instruments** that can be loaded into host applications like Sibelius.

PNG (Portable Network Graphics) a standard bitmap graphics file format.

point size the height of a font, measured from the top of the capital letters to the bottom of the lower-case descender letters (such as p). This height is specified in *points* (1 point or *pt* = 1/72 inch = about 0.353mm).

PostScript a vector graphics file format used by some laser printers and most **imagesetters**. See also **EPS**.

program a sound (or collection of sounds in different **layers**) accessed by a single **program number**.

program change a **MIDI message** that changes a **MIDI channel's program number**.

program number (or *patch number*, or *voice number*) a number specifying an instrument sound on a MIDI device. Program numbers go from 0 to 127 or from 1 to 128. If more than 128 program numbers are available, these are grouped into extra **banks**.

properties the characteristics of objects in your score – such as position, playback behavior, font and size, and so on – accessible from the Properties window.

read (scanning) to work out what all the notes and other objects in the **scan** are.

real-time input inputting music on a MIDI keyboard in time to a click in order to specify rhythms as well as pitches. Sibelius's real-time input method is **Flexi-time™**.

reduce (or *implode*) to put the notes of several instruments onto one or two staves, e.g. to create a keyboard accompaniment or *reduction*. Opposite of **explode**.

reformat ▭ **formatting**.

rehearsal mark a big letter and/or number, normally in a box, used in long scores to aid rehearsing.

resolution the level of detail at which a page is printed or scanned, measured in **dpi**; or the number of pixels displayed on a computer screen, e.g. 1024 x 768.

reverb (pronounced "ree-verb") an effect like a blurred echo within a room. Bigger rooms produce more reverb. The amount of reverb is sometimes specified by the *reverb time*, which is the time it takes a sound to die away (by 60 decibels).

ReWire a software protocol for the transfer of audio and MIDI data between **DAW**s.

roman font (or "Roman font") any medium-weight non-italic **serif** font.

sample a digital recording of a sound, typically a short fragment such as a drum loop or a single note.

sans serif font (or "sanserif" font. Pronounced *san-serif*, but without a French accent) a font without **serifs**, generally considered suitable for short pieces of text such as titles.

scan (a) to get a page of music, text or graphics into a computer program using a scanner.

(b) the image produced when a page has been scanned. In PhotoScore Lite, scans are always displayed with a buff background to distinguish them from music that has been **read**, and from music in Sibelius.

scanner driver the program that tells the computer what type of scanner you have; analogous to a printer driver.

score any music notation document; sometimes used loosely to mean a **full score**. See **full score**, **part**, **transposing score**.

section a subdivision of a score, such as a song from an album or a movement from a symphony. New sections often start with a new title and with full instrument names, and sometimes bar numbers restart at 1 and rehearsal marks restart at A or 1.

select to click an object (or objects or **passage**) you want to edit, copy, move or delete, and thereby turn it colored. The color indicates which **voice** the object is in, or whether it's a **system object**.

selection anything that is **select**ed. A *single selection* consists of one selected object; a *multiple selection* consists of two or more selected objects. See **passage**

sequencer a computer program designed primarily for recording, editing and playing back music using MIDI. Most sequencers can also print notation to some extent, but as they are designed around MIDI rather than notation, they are quite distinct from music notation programs. Many sequencers also record and edit audio (such as singing) in addition to MIDI.

serif the spike on corners and tips of letters in certain fonts, known as serif fonts. Serif fonts are considered more legible than sans serif fonts for large quantities of text, such as books.

shortcut menu slightly confusing term for the menu you get when you right-click (Windows) *or* Control-click (Mac). (Nothing to do with keyboard shortcuts.) Sometimes called a "context-sensitive menu," because the menu contents depend on what you click on.

sound ID a structured name that describes a particular sound timbre; examples might be woodwind.flutes.flute, woodwind.flutes.piccolo.flutter-tongue or strings.violin.ensemble.pizzicato. A collection of sound IDs is called a **SoundWorld**.

sound set the complete set of sounds available on a MIDI device or **virtual instrument**. Thus Sibelius lets you choose between a General MIDI sound set, a sound set for Garritan Personal Orchestra, and so on.

soundfont a collection of sampled sounds, usually in one of two formats (SF2 and DLS). Initially intended to provide a way of changing the sounds available on soundcards from some manufacturers, it is now possible to use soundfonts without the need for a specific soundcard, normally by loading them into a **virtual instrument**.

SoundWorld a standard designed by Sibelius Software to replace the messy patchwork of program names and **program numbers** used by **MIDI** devices and **virtual instruments**. A SoundWorld is a collection of **sound IDs**, organized into a tree structure.

space the distance between two staff lines, used as the main unit of measurement in **music engraving**. For instance, beams are normally 0.5 spaces thick, and a **staff size** is four spaces by definition.

spelling the way in which a pitch is written as a note-name with an accidental. Most pitches have three spellings, e.g. C natural can also be "spelled" as B♯ or as D♭♭.

spreads the printing format in which pairs of consecutive pages are printed side-by-side on the same sheet of paper to show how the finished score will look when opened flat.

staff the British word for this is "stave."

staff objects objects that are attached to (and refer to) a particular staff. These include notes, chords, rests and clef changes, and most lines, text styles, and symbols. 📖 **system objects**.

staff size the height of a five-line staff, measured between the middle of the top and bottom lines. The size of everything in a score – notes, lines, most text and all other objects – is proportional to the staff size. The staff size equals 4 **spaces** by definition.

stem the vertical line, sometimes inaccurately called a "tail," on notes and chords. 📖 **tail**.

step-time input inputting notes and chords by specifying pitches on a MIDI keyboard and note values etc. on the **keypad**. 📖 **Flexi-time™**, **alphabetic input**, **mouse input**.

sub-bracket 📖 **bracket**.

symbol an object of fixed shape that you can put anywhere in the score; used for miscellaneous objects such as ornaments and percussion symbols. Symbols are customizable: they can be any character from any font, or a composite of any number of existing symbols.

synthesis producing sound by mathematical means.

system a group of staves that are played simultaneously and usually joined at the left-hand side by an **initial barline**. Music for a solo instrument is often written on one staff, in which case the words "system" and "staff" refer to the same thing.

system break the forced termination of a system at a particular barline, often at the end of a musical section. 📖 **page break**.

system objects objects that apply to all instruments rather than to just one staff, such as time signatures, key signatures, tempo and title text, rehearsal marks and some lines and symbols. Most system objects are drawn just above the system, and sometimes in the middle as well. System objects are not attached to any particular staff, and appear in all **parts**. 📖 **staff objects**.

system passage a selected **passage** spanning all staves in the score, surrounded by a purple double-box. The main differences between a system passage and a normal passage are: copying a system passage *inserts* into the score rather than *overwriting* existing music; copying a system passage copies **system objects** in addition to **staff objects**; and deleting a system passage deletes the bars themselves, rather than turning them into bar rests.

system separators thick double diagonal lines drawn between systems in large scores to emphasize where there is more than one system per page.

tab (a) *guitar tab* (short for "tablature") is a notation in which staff lines represent the guitar strings, and fret numbers indicate where to position the fingers.

(b) One of several buttons along the top of a dialog that flick between different **pages** of options. The **Keypad** also has six tabs that choose different Keypad layouts.

tail the curved hook of an unbeamed eighth note (quaver) or shorter note. (Sometimes used inaccurately to mean a **stem**.)

text style the text style of each piece of text in a score specifies the font, size, positioning, etc. Different uses of text have different styles; for instance, dynamics (e.g. *mp*) are in the Expression style.

tick A tick is the smallest unit of time in Sibelius. There are 256 ticks per quarter note (crotchet).

TIFF (Tagged Image File Format) a standard bitmap graphics format.

timecode numbers that indicate the time position in a score or video; timecode typically shows hours, minutes, seconds and either tenths of a second or frames.

timeline slider a slider on the Playback window that lets you move the playback line (and video) to any point in the score.

track the **MIDI file** equivalent of a staff. (MIDI **channels** served this purpose in older (type 0) MIDI files but had the drawback of being limited to 16, whereas the number of tracks is unlimited in type 1 MIDI files.)

transposing instrument an instrument that sounds at a different pitch from how its music is written, such as a clarinet, horn or piccolo. The transposition (or "key") of the instrument is specified by the pitch produced when the performer reads a C; for instance, when a trumpet "in B♭" reads a C, it produces a B♭.

transposing score a score in which the music of **transposing instruments** is not written at the pitch at which it sounds. A non-transposing score is said to be a *score in C*, or written at *sounding pitch* or *concert pitch*.

tuplet (most people rhyme it with "duplet," some with "couplet") a rhythm that is played at a fraction of its normal speed, such as a triplet. It is drawn as a single number or a ratio above or below the notes, often with a **bracket** to show which notes it applies to, occasionally with a little note to indicate the rhythmic unit referred to by the number(s).

"Tuplet" is actually music software jargon – in the real world of music, tuplets are usually called *irrational rhythms* or occasionally *polyrhythms* or *countermetric rhythms*.

TWAIN the communications standard used between programs and scanners; analogous to MIDI.

USB (Universal Serial Bus) most modern computers have two or more USB sockets, allowing the connection of a wide range of peripheral hardware, including printers and MIDI devices.

velocity in MIDI, the speed (and hence force) with which you press a key on a MIDI keyboard, which determines the loudness of that note. (The word is also occasionally used for the speed with which you lift a key, which controls how quickly the note dies away.)

virtual instrument a program that emulates the sound of a real instrument, whether it is a synthesizer or analog instrument, generally using either **samples** or **synthesis** to produce sound.

voice a series of notes, chords and rests in rhythmic succession on a staff (sometimes known as a "layer," or more loosely as a "part" or "line"). Normally there is just one voice on a staff, in which case the stems can point up or down depending on the pitch of the notes.

Two voices are written on the same staff when two independent rhythms need to be shown simultaneously. The voices are distinguished by stem direction – *voice 1's* notes and chords have stems up, and *voice 2* has stems down.

In guitar and (occasionally) keyboard music, third and fourth voices can be used. These also have stems up and down.

When you select a note or other object, the selection color tells you which voices it's in.

volume in MIDI, the general loudness of a MIDI **channel**, as opposed to **velocity**, which determines the loudness of individual notes.

VST (**Virtual Studio Technology**) the name of a format, invented by Steinberg, for **virtual instruments** and **effects**. VST virtual instruments and effects can run on both Windows and Mac computers.

wildcard a code used in a text object that inserts a special bit of text from elsewhere (e.g. the date, instrument name, page number).

worksheet a sheet of paper with an exercise on it for a student to do in class or for homework. In Sibelius the term is used more generally for anything produced by the Worksheet Creator, which can also include reference materials, posters etc.

zither a jangly stringed instrument shaped like a box, popular in Hungary, unpopular outside Hungary. (Not actually referred to in this Reference, but it does begin with a Z.)

Visual index

Basic notation

Advanced notation

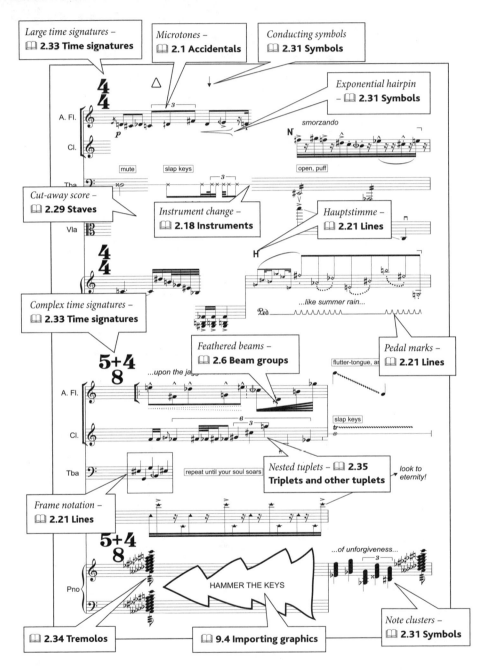

Choral

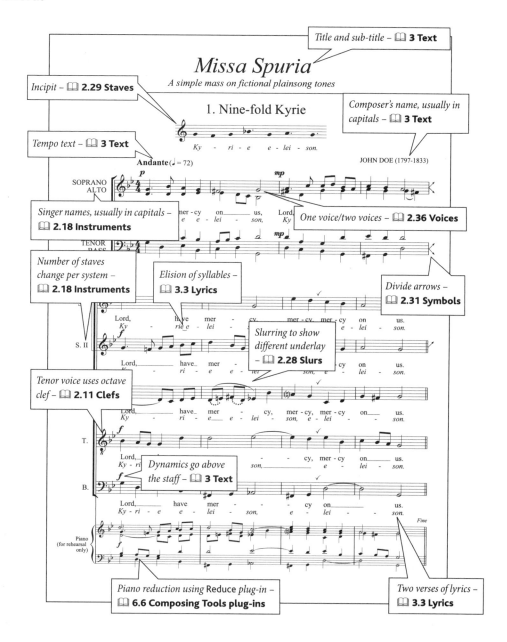

Piano

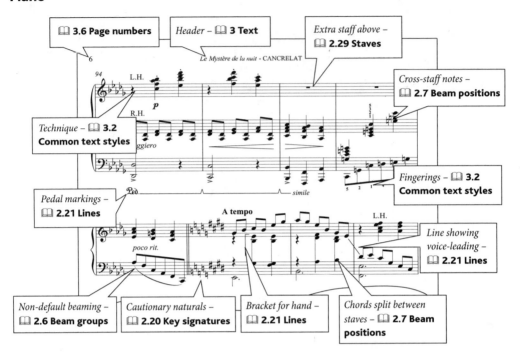

Organ

Registration in Technique text –
📖 **3.2 Common text styles**

Automatic cautionary –
📖 **2.33 Time signatures**

Pedal markings –
📖 **2.31 Symbols**

Octave line –
📖 **2.21 Lines**

Dynamics between staves – 📖 **3 Text**

Alternating time signatures –
📖 **2.33 Time signatures**

Automatic continuation

Registration –
📖 **3 Text**

Hidden tuplets – 📖 **2.35**
Triplets and other tuplets

Clef changes –
📖 **2.11 Clefs**

Double barline –
📖 **2.4 Barlines**

Cross-staff beaming –
📖 **2.7 Beam positions**

Lead sheets

Jazz

Guitar notation

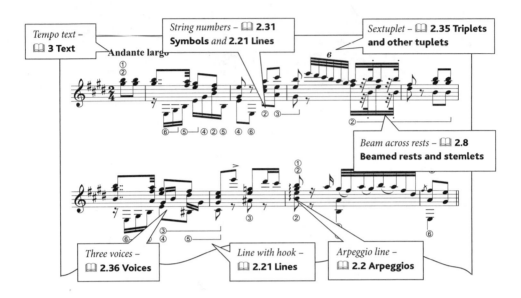

Tempo text – 📖 3 Text

String numbers – 📖 2.31 *Symbols* and 2.21 Lines

Sextuplet – 📖 2.35 Triplets and other tuplets

Beam across rests – 📖 2.8 Beamed rests and stemlets

Three voices – 📖 2.36 Voices

Line with hook – 📖 2.21 Lines

Arpeggio line – 📖 2.2 Arpeggios

Guitar tab

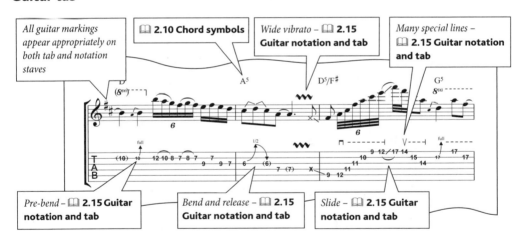

All guitar markings appear appropriately on both tab and notation staves

📖 2.10 Chord symbols

Wide vibrato – 📖 2.15 Guitar notation and tab

Many special lines – 📖 2.15 Guitar notation and tab

Pre-bend – 📖 2.15 Guitar notation and tab

Bend and release – 📖 2.15 Guitar notation and tab

Slide – 📖 2.15 Guitar notation and tab

Percussion

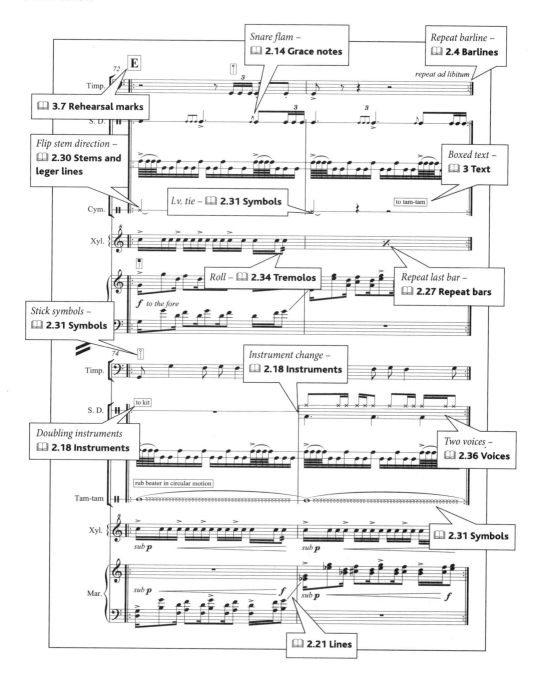

Early music

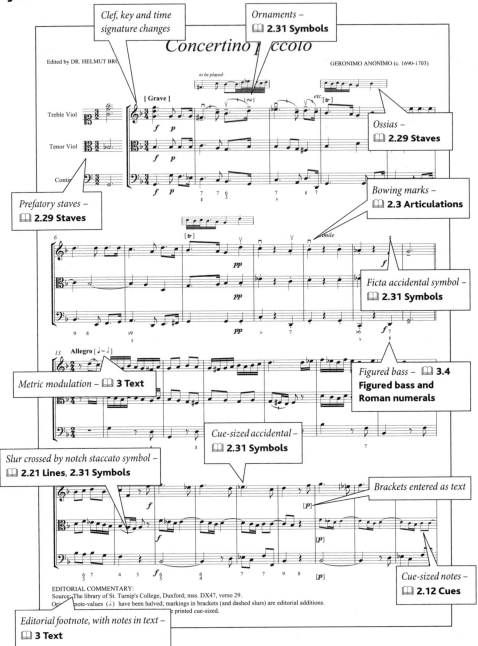

Clef, key and time signature changes

Ornaments –
📖 **2.31 Symbols**

Concertino Piccolo

Edited by DR. HELMUT BR…

GERONIMO ANONIMO (c. 1690–1703)

Ossias –
📖 **2.29 Staves**

Prefatory staves –
📖 **2.29 Staves**

Bowing marks –
📖 **2.3 Articulations**

Ficta accidental symbol –
📖 **2.31 Symbols**

Metric modulation – 📖 **3 Text**

Figured bass – 📖 **3.4**
Figured bass and Roman numerals

Slur crossed by notch staccato symbol –
📖 **2.21 Lines**, **2.31 Symbols**

Cue-sized accidental –
📖 **2.31 Symbols**

Brackets entered as text

Cue-sized notes –
📖 **2.12 Cues**

EDITORIAL COMMENTARY:
Source: The library of St. Turnip's College, Duxford; mss. DX47, verso 29.
Ori… note-values (♩) have been halved; markings in brackets (and dashed slurs) are editorial additions. … printed cue-sized.

Editorial footnote, with notes in text –
📖 **3 Text**

Index

N

T

U

V

W

License Agreement

By installing or using any component of the Software, or by registering the Product, you (an individual or legal entity) agree with the Licensor to be bound by the terms of this License which will govern your use of the Product. If you do not accept these terms you may within 14 days of purchase return the Product, its packaging and documentation unused and intact to your supplier together with dated proof of purchase for a full refund.

The Product is copyright © Avid Technology, Inc., and its licensors 1987–2009.

This license agreement does not apply to Sibelius Internet Edition.

1. DEFINITIONS

In this License the following words and expressions have the following meanings:

"Documentation": the Sibelius Handbook, Sibelius Reference, Latest Information & Technical Help leaflet, tutorial videos and any other documentation relating to the Software supplied to you in any form by the Licensor or with the Software.

"License": this agreement between you and the Licensor and, if permitted by the context, the conditional license granted to you in this agreement.

"Licensor": Sibelius Software Limited, an English company (registered no. 3338819) of The Old Toy Factory, 20-22 City North, Fonthill Road, London N4 3HF, UK.

"Network Copy": a Product provided for use on multiple computer terminals on a network.

"Product": the Software and the Documentation.

"Single Copy": a Product provided for use on a single computer terminal.

"Software": Sibelius for Windows/Mac, Sibelius Scorch, Opus, Helsinki, Reprise and Inkpen2 font families, example music files & videos, PhotoScore Lite, Kontakt Player Silver, installers, demonstrations of other software, and any other programs or files supplied to you on or with the Sibelius DVD-ROM or download.

"Stand-Alone Site License": a Product provided for use on multiple non-networked computer terminals.

2. License

2.1 (1) The Licensor grants to you a non-exclusive non-transferable license to use the Software in accordance with the Documentation, subject to the terms of any educational or other discount, offer or scheme which the Product may have been obtained under. Additionally, educational discount copies are not for commercial use. Some components of the Software may be subject to separate license agreements which you will need to agree to in order to use them.

(2) If the Product is a Single Copy, you may install the Software on a single computer. You may also install the Software on one additional computer, provided that you ensure that you are the only person who uses the Software on either computer, and that the Software is never used on both computers simultaneously.

(3) If the Product is a Stand-Alone Site License, you may use the Software only as a non-networked application and only on the licensed number of computer terminals located on a single geographical site.

(4) If the Product is a Network Copy, you may only install the Software on computers on a single network and located on a single geographical site (unless otherwise authorized in writing by the Licensor), and may use it on no more than the licensed number of computer terminals simultaneously. Any further use is prohibited.

(5) Title to the Product is not transferred to you. Ownership of the Product remains vested in the Licensor and its licensors, subject to the rights granted to you under this License. All other rights are reserved.

(6) If the Software was supplied as an upgrade or update from an earlier version, you retain the license to use that earlier version. Usage of the earlier version is subject to its original license agreements. As set forth in Section 6.2, earlier and current versions of the Software are non-transferable.

2.2 You may make one printout for your own use of any part of the Documentation provided in electronic form. You shall not make or permit any third party to make any further copies of any part of the Product whether in eye or machine-readable form.

2.3 You shall not, and shall not cause or permit any third party to, translate, enhance, modify, alter, adapt or create derivative works based on the Product or any part of it for any purpose (including without limitation for the purpose of error correction), or cause the whole or any part of the Product to be combined with or incorporated into any other program, file or product for any purpose, except as expressly permitted by the Documentation.

2.4 You shall not, and shall not cause or permit any third party to, decompile, decode, disassemble or reverse engineer the Software in whole or in part for any purpose.

2.5 You shall not, and shall not cause any third party to, translate, convert, decode or reverse engineer any file in any version of the Sibelius or Sibelius Scorch formats (whether created by your copy of the Software or not), or modify any such file (except by using the Software in accordance with the Documentation), in whole or in part for any purpose.

2.6 In accordance with the Documentation and subject to compliance with Section 2.1, the Software's "Save as Scorch Web Page" feature and Sibelius Scorch web browser plug-in may be used to publish music scores on the Internet or by means of DVD-ROM, CD-ROM, floppy disk or by other similar means; provided, however, that you shall not and shall not permit any third party to, directly or indirectly, charge or receive any fee, payment or other consideration for the viewing, playing, printing or other use via Sibelius Scorch or via the Internet of any file which is created by (or based on any file created by) the Software, unless expressly permitted by the Licensor in writing.

2.7 The Product or any part of it must not be used to infringe any right of copyright or right of privacy, publicity or personality or any other right whatsoever of any other person or entity, including without limitation infringement of any such right by use of the Product in conjunction with any of the scanning programs PhotoScore Lite, PhotoScore MIDI or PhotoScore Ultimate, or by use of the Product's Internet publishing capability.

2.8 Teaching materials, Ideas content, music files and videos provided in the Product are solely for private use by you and/or your students or educational institution. You shall not publish or make commercial use of them in whole or in part.

3. Copyright

3.1 You acknowledge that copyright in the Product as a whole and in the components of the Product as between you and the Licensor belongs to the Licensor or its licensors and is protected by copyright laws, national and international, and all other applicable laws. Further details of the ownership of all copyright in the components of the Product are set out in the Product.

4. Liability of the Licensor

4.1 The Licensor warrants that the Product will be free from defects in materials and workmanship and perform substantially in accordance with the Documentation under normal use for a period of 90 days after the date of original purchase (the "Warranty Period"). If a defect in the Product shall occur during the Warranty Period, the Product may be returned with dated proof of purchase to the Licensor who will at its sole discretion either return the price paid or repair or replace it free of charge.

4.2 The Licensor shall not be liable for any claim arising from:

(1) any failure or malfunction resulting wholly or to any material extent from your negligence, operator error, use other than in accordance with the Documentation or any other misuse or abuse of the Product;

(2) any loss of or corruption to any data, however caused, where such loss or corruption could have been avoided or corrected or substantially reduced if you had taken and retained in a secure place appropriate backup copies;

(3) the decompilation or modification of the Software or its merger with any other program or any maintenance repair adjustment alteration or enhancement of the Software by any person other than the Licensor or its authorized agent;

(4) the failure by you to implement recommendations previously advised by the Licensor in respect of, or solutions for faults in, the Product;

(5) any loss or damage whatsoever resulting from any omissions or inaccuracies in any information or data contained in the Product.

(6) Except as otherwise expressly provided in Section 4.1, all conditions, warranties, terms representations and undertakings express or implied, statutory or otherwise in respect of the Product are hereby expressly excluded.

(7) Except as expressly provided in Section 4.1, the Licensor shall have no liability to you for loss of profits, revenue or goodwill or any type of special, indirect or consequential loss (including loss or damages suffered by you as a result of an action brought by a third party) whether such loss is caused by the Licensor's breach of its contractual obligations hereunder or any negligence or other tortious act or omission.

(8) The Licensor's entire liability for breach of its covenants and warranties in this License and for any defect or errors in the Product shall (except as expressly provided in Section 4.1) be limited to the price paid by you for the Product.

5. Termination

5.1 This License shall terminate automatically upon your destruction of the Product. In addition, the Licensor may elect to terminate this License in the event of a material breach by you of any condition of this License or of any of your representations, warranties, covenants or obligations hereunder. Upon notification of such termination by the Licensor, you will immediately delete all copies of the Software from your computer(s), destroy any other copies of the Product or any part thereof, and return the Product to the Licensor.

6. Miscellaneous

6.1 No failure to exercise and no delay in exercising on the part of the Licensor of any right, power or privilege arising hereunder shall operate as a waiver thereof, nor shall any single or partial exercise of any right, power or privilege preclude any other or further exercise thereof or the exercise of any other right, power or privilege. The rights and remedies of the Licensor in connection herewith are not exclusive of any rights or remedies provided by law.

6.2 You may not distribute, loan, sub-license, rent, lease (including without limitation renting or leasing a computer on which the Product is installed) or otherwise transfer the Product to any third party without the Licensor's prior written consent, which the Licensor may grant, condition or withhold in the Licensor's sole discretion.

6.3 You agree to provide accurate personal data when registering the Product and to the use of this data in accordance with the Licensor's privacy policy (available from the Licensor or on www.sibelius.com) which may change from time to time.

6.4 This License is intended by the parties hereto to be a final expression of their agreement with respect to the subject matter hereof and a complete and exclusive statement of the terms of such agreement. This License supersedes any and all prior understandings, whether written or oral, between you and the Licensor relating to the subject matter hereof.

6.5 (This section only applies if you are resident in the European Union:) This License shall be construed and governed by the laws of England, and both parties agree to submit to the exclusive jurisdiction of the English courts.

6.6 (This section only applies if you are not resident in the European Union:) This License shall be construed and enforced in accordance with and governed by the laws of the State of California. Any suit, action or proceeding arising out of or in any way related or connected to this License shall be brought and maintained only in the United States District Court for the Northern District of California, sitting in the City of San Francisco. Each party irrevocably submits to the jurisdiction of such federal court over any such suit, action or proceeding. Each party knowingly, voluntarily and irrevocably waives trial by jury in any suit, action or proceeding (including any counterclaim), whether at law or in equity, arising out of or in any way related or connected to this License or the subject matter hereof.

(License v6, 24 February 2009)